PENGUIN

CW00385656

JOURNALS A

FRANCES BURNEY (1752–1840), the daughter of musicologist Dr Charles Burney, spent her youth in the midst of the London society which included Dr Johnson, Edmund Burke, Sir Joshua Reynolds, David Garrick, the Bluestocking Circle and many members of the aristocracy. When she published her first novel, *Evelina*, anonymously in 1778, the revelation of its authorship brought her immediate fame. Her later novels are *Cecilia* (1782), *Camilla* (1796) and *The Wanderer* (1814). She also wrote four comic dramas and four tragedies. None of these was published and only one was produced during her lifetime. From 1786 to 1791 she endured an unhappy existence at Court as Second Keeper of the Robes to Queen Charlotte. In 1793 she married Alexandre d'Arblay, an aristocratic but penniless French refugee in England; their only child, Alexander, was born in 1795. She and her husband were interned by Napoleon and lived in France from 1802 to 1812. She was also in France 1814–15, recording in her journals the final stages of the Napoleonic wars. Widowed in 1818, she lived in London for the remainder of her life, publishing the *Memoirs of Doctor Burney* in 1832. Burney's journals and letters, written over a seventy-year period from 1768 to 1839, are distinguished by their remarkable range and variety, and by her ability to bring the world around her to life.

PETER SABOR is Professor of English at Laval University, Quebec. His other edition for Penguin Classics is Richardson's *Pamela*. He has also edited Burney's *Cecilia* (with Margaret Anne Doody), *The Wanderer* (with Doody and Robert Mack) and her *Complete Plays* (with Stewart Cooke and Geoffrey Sill), as well as Carlyle's *Sartor Resartus* (with Kerry McSweeney), Cleland's *Memoirs of a Woman of Pleasure* and Sarah Fielding's *David Simple*. He has published two books on Horace Walpole, *Horace Walpole: A Reference Guide* and *Horace Walpole: The Critical Heritage*.

LARS E. TROIDE is Professor of English and Director of the Burney Papers Project at McGill University, Montreal. He was formerly a Research Associate on the Horace Walpole Project at Yale University, where he co-edited *Horace Walpole's Correspondence with Henry Seymour Conway*. He is also editor of *Horace Walpole's Miscellany* and *The Early Journals and Letters of Fanny Burney*. He has twice been a Research Fellow of the National Endowment for the Humanities, Washington, DC.

FRANCES BURNEY

Journals and Letters

Selected with an introduction by
PETER SABOR *and* LARS E. TROIDE
with the assistance of STEWART COOKE
and VICTORIA KORTES-PAPP

PENGUIN BOOKS

PENGUIN BOOKS

Published by the Penguin Group
Penguin Books Ltd, 80 Strand, London WC2R 0RL, England
Penguin Putnam Inc., 375 Hudson Street, New York, New York 10014, USA
Penguin Books Australia Ltd, 250 Camberwell Road, Camberwell, Victoria 3124, Australia
Penguin Books Canada Ltd, 10 Alcorn Avenue, Toronto, Ontario, Canada M4V 3B2
Penguin Books India (P) Ltd, 11 Community Centre, Panchsheel Park, New Delhi – 110 017, India
Penguin Books (NZ) Ltd, Cnr Rosedale and Airborne Roads, Albany, Auckland, New Zealand
Penguin Books (South Africa) (Pty) Ltd, 24 Sturdee Avenue, Rosebank 2196, South Africa

Penguin Books Ltd, Registered Offices: 80 Strand, London WC2R 0RL, England

www.penguin.com

This selection published 2001

5

Set in 9.25/11.75 pt PostScript Monotype Bembo
Typeset by Rowland Phototypesetting Ltd, Bury St Edmunds, Suffolk
Printed in England by Clays Ltd, St Ives plc

www.greenpenguin.co.uk

Penguin Books is committed to a sustainable future
for our business, our readers and our planet.
The book in your hands is made from paper
certified by the Forest Stewardship Council.

Contents

Journals and Letters

Acknowledgements

For permission to publish the manuscripts in their custody we are indebted to the Henry W. and Albert A. Berg Collection, New York Public Library, Curator Rodney Phillips; the Manuscripts Department, British Library (Barrett Collection of Burney Papers, Egerton 3690–3708); the James Marshall and Marie-Louise Osborn Collection, Yale University Library, Curator Stephen Parks; the Yale Editions of the Private Papers of James Boswell, Chairman Claude Rawson; and the Pierpont Morgan Library, New York, MA 35. For manuscripts in private collections we are grateful to John R. G. Comyn and Michael Burney-Cumming.

The Bogle miniature of Frances Burney on the cover is used by courtesy of Paula F. Peyraud. The illustration of the first page of Burney's journals is by permission of the Berg Collection.

We have profited from the editorial expertise, at Penguin Books, of Tim Bates, Robert Mighall and Lindeth Vasey. For help with specific problems we are indebted to Hester Davenport, Margaret Anne Doody, Isobel Grundy, Eva Kortes-Papp, Alvaro Ribeiro, SJ, and Lisa Saroli. We also thank Rodney Clark, Oscar Grossman, Marie Legroulx, Emmi Sabor, and Maia, Nathan and Teresa Troide for their love and constant support.

Abbreviations

Chronology

1752   *13 June* Frances ('Fanny') Burney, the third of six children of Charles Burney, musicologist, and Esther Sleepe, born in King's Lynn, Norfolk. (Siblings are James and Esther ('Hetty').)

1755   *4 January* Sister Susanna born.

1757   *4 December* Brother Charles born.

1760   *c. April* Burney family moves to Poland Street, Westminster, London, where CB becomes a fashionable music master.

1761   *4 November* Sister Charlotte Ann born.

1762   *27 September* Death of mother.

1763   Samuel Crisp becomes a close friend of the Burney family.

1767   *13 June* Destroys juvenilia in bonfire on her birthday.

      2 October On second marriage of CB, to Elizabeth Allen, acquires three siblings (Stephen, Maria and Elizabeth ('Bessy')).

1768   *27 March* Begins journal, addressed to 'Nobody'.

      20 November Half-brother Richard born.

1769   *23 June* CB receives degree of Doctor of Music, Oxford; FB writes commemorative verses 'To Doctor Last'.

1770   *20 September* Esther marries her cousin Charles Rousseau Burney.

      November Burney family moves to Queen Square, Bloomsbury.

1771   *30 June* Plays Lady Easy and Lady Graveairs in family performance of scenes from Colley Cibber's comedy *The Careless Husband*.

      29 September Plays Lady Truman in family performance of Addison's comedy *The Drummer*.

1772   *16 May* Maria Allen secretly marries Martin Rishton in Ypres.

      29 August Half-sister Sarah Harriet born.

1774   *8 October* Burney family moves to St Martin's Street, Leicester Square.

1777   *7 April* Plays Mrs Lovemore in elaborate family performance of Arthur Murphy's *The Way to Keep Him*, including an additional scene probably written by herself, and Huncamunca in Henry Fielding's *Tom Thumb*.

12 October Bessy Allen secretly marries Samuel Meeke in Ypres.

Late October Brother Charles expelled from Caius College, Cambridge, for stealing library books.

1778   *29 January* Publishes first novel, *Evelina; or, a Young Lady's Entrance into the World*.

Begins writing first comedy, *The Witlings*.

August Begins friendships with Samuel Johnson, members of the Johnson circle and Hester Lynch Thrale.

1779   *4 May* Completes first draft of *The Witlings*. After reading a revised draft, CB and Crisp urge her to suppress it (*2 August*).

1780   *January* Revises Act IV of *The Witlings* with a view to showing the whole play to Richard Brinsley Sheridan, but is persuaded by CB and Crisp to abandon it.

March–June Visits Bath with Hester and Henry Thrale.

10 June When Gordon Riots reach Bath, FB and the Thrales flee to Brighton.

1781   *February* Work on *Cecilia* retarded by FB's 'vile & irksome fever'.

1782   *10 January* Susanna marries Molesworth Phillips.

12 July Publishes second novel, *Cecilia, or Memoirs of an Heiress*.

1783   *24 April* Death of Crisp.

1784   *23 July* Rupture of friendship with Hester Thrale over marriage to Gabriel Piozzi.

13 December Death of Johnson.

1786   *17 July* Becomes Second Keeper of the Robes to Queen Charlotte.

1788   *October* Begins writing first tragedy, *Edwy and Elgiva*, during a period of madness of King George III.

1790   *4 April* Returns to *Edwy and Elgiva*.

August Completes first draft of *Edwy and Elgiva*; begins writing two more tragedies *Hubert De Vere* and *The Siege of Pevensey*.

1791   *June* Completes first draft of *Hubert De Vere*; begins writing fourth tragedy, *Elberta*, which will remain incomplete.

7 July Ill health compels FB to leave service of the Queen; granted annual pension.

August–September Tour of western England with Anna Ord.

1793   *January* Visits the Lockes of Norbury Park, Surrey, where she meets Alexandre d'Arblay; secret courtship follows.

5 July Hubert De Vere accepted by John Philip Kemble for production at Drury Lane Theatre; later withdrawn in favour of *Edwy and Elgiva*.

28 July Marries AA in Protestant ceremony, followed by Catholic rite (*30 July*).

19 November Publishes pamphlet, *Brief Reflections Relative to the Emigrant French Clergy*.

1794   *December* Revised version of *Edwy and Elgiva* accepted for production.

18 December FB's only child, Alexander, born.

1795   *21 March Edwy and Elgiva* produced at Drury Lane, with prologue by brother Charles; withdrawn after only one performance.

1796   *12 July* Publishes by subscription third novel, *Camilla: or, A Picture of Youth*.

20 October Death of stepmother.

1798   Writes second comedy, *Love and Fashion*.

1799   *30 October Love and Fashion* accepted for March 1800 production by Thomas Harris at Covent Garden Theatre.

1800   *6 January* Death of Susanna.

2 February At the urging of CB, *Love and Fashion* withdrawn from production.

Begins writing two more comedies, *The Woman-Hater*, intended for Drury Lane, and *A Busy Day*, intended for Covent Garden; neither produced.

1802   *15 April* FB and Alexander follow AA to France, arriving in Paris on 20 April.

1803   *12 May* Outbreak of war between France and England.

1811   *30 September* Undergoes mastectomy for breast cancer, at home in Paris.

1812   *14 August* Returns surreptitiously to England, with Alexander, on an American ship that is seized by the English; disembarks at Deal.

1814   *28 March* Publishes fourth novel, *The Wanderer; or, Female Difficulties*.

12 April Death of CB.

November Returns to France, leaving Alexander at Cambridge.

1815   *19 March* Flees from France to Belgium while AA fights in army opposing Napoleon.

17 October Returns to England with wounded AA.

2 November Takes lodgings with AA in Bath.

16 December Partial reconciliation with Hester Piozzi at Bath.

1817   *24 September* Narrowly escapes drowning when trapped by the tide at Ilfracombe.

28 December Death of brother Charles.

1818   *3 May* Death of AA at home in Bath.

30 September Moves from Bath to London, settling in Bolton Street, Piccadilly.

1819   *11 April* Alexander ordained priest in Church of England.

1821   *19 July* James appointed Rear-Admiral.

  17 November Death of James.

1824   *June* Alexander presented as Perpetual Curate to a new Chapel in Camden Town.

1832   *17 February* Death of Esther.

  6 November Death of FB's closest friend, Frederica Locke.

  24 November Publishes final work, *Memoirs of Doctor Burney*.

1836   *November* Alexander presented as Perpetual Curate to the Chapel of Ely in High Holborn.

1837   *19 January* Death of Alexander. His fiancée, Mary Ann Smith, settles with FB.

1838   *12 September* Death of Charlotte.

1840   *6 January* Death of FB in London, aged 87. Buried in Wolcot Churchyard, Bath.

Introduction

On 13 June 1767, her fifteenth birthday, Frances Burney lit a bonfire in the courtyard of her father's house in Poland Street, London. The conflagration consisted of a great heap of manuscript 'Elegies, Odes, Plays, Songs, Stories, Farces', 'Tragedies and Epic Poems', and a novel, 'The History of Caroline Evelyn' – virtually all that she had written up to that time.[1]

The only witness to this conflagration was her younger and favourite sister, Susanna, who wept at the mass destruction. Frances (or 'Fanny' to her family and closest friends) was impelled to this species of self-immolation by a powerful sense of guilt. Contemporary society frowned upon any female who 'wasted' her time writing anything other than familiar letters or household memoranda. Private letters were regarded as an extension of conversation and therefore tolerated as practical or one of the social graces. Household notes helped women in their ideal capacity as homemakers. Any other form of composition – especially novels, which were morally suspect – consumed hours that were better spent on useful household chores, such as needlework, or in reading morally improving works, such as sermons, or in learning French or music, decorative accomplishments allowed to the female sex.

Burney's nod to feminine literary propriety lasted only nine months. In March 1768 she began a private journal, giving her reason in the opening sentence: 'To have some account of my thoughts, manners, acquaintance and actions, when the Hour arrives at which time is more nimble than memory, is the reason which induces me to keep a Journal: a Journal in which I must confess my *every* thought, must open my whole Heart!' (selection 1). It is the confessional nature of her journal that was paramount; the need to commit to paper her innermost thoughts overrode the fear of accidental discovery, which was realized one evening when her father, the music historian Dr Charles Burney, picked up a page which she had absent-mindedly left on the piano (selection 5). Luckily for her it contained nothing that was objectionable, and Dr Burney, a liberal man by the standards of the day, gave her his tacit approval to continue the journal, provided she be more careful in the future.

Frances Burney *would* continue her private journal for the next ten years, to be replaced increasingly by journal letters to Susanna. Outside her immediate family her most important epistolary confidant would be Samuel Crisp, a friend of her father who lived in retirement at Chessington, Surrey, and who became a second 'Daddy' to the Burney children. After Crisp's death in 1783 and Susanna's in 1800, she would reveal herself most in letters to other members of her family, including her brother Charles and sister Esther, and various nephews and nieces, most notably her niece Charlotte Barrett, whom she made her literary executrix.

Besides voluminous journals and letters, Burney's compulsion to write would result in four novels and eight plays over the course of her long life. But her literary talent had not always been apparent. She was born in King's Lynn, Norfolk, on 13 June 1752, the third child and second daughter of Charles Burney, a rising musician who had been forced to flee the coal smoke of London because of a lung ailment. When the Burney family returned to London in 1760, the eight-year-old Frances had not yet learned her letters, and was even thought somewhat 'slow'. By the age of ten, however, she had not only learned to read but had already begun writing, and the following year she produced her earliest surviving composition, a brief 'Ode to Content', remarkable for its precocity.[2]

In 1762 Burney's mother died, a loss which devastated the sensitive young girl. Her father also felt the loss keenly, but five years later he remarried. His second wife was Elizabeth Allen, widow of a wealthy King's Lynn grain merchant. This union swelled the Burney household, adding Elizabeth's three children to Charles Burney's six, and the couple would have two more children.

In 1769 Charles Burney was awarded a doctorate in music by Oxford University. During the years that followed Frances served as her father's amanuensis for a monumental *General History of Music*, which would establish his reputation as the foremost music historian in England. She also found the time secretly to write a sequel to the destroyed 'History of Caroline Evelyn', about Caroline Evelyn's daughter. *Evelina; or, a Young Lady's Entrance into the World*, was published anonymously in January 1778. The novel took the London literary world by storm. Revealed as its author, the hypersensitive and extremely shy young writer found herself the focus of intense interest and curiosity. She became a frequent guest at the Streatham

This strange medley of Thoughts & Facts
was written at the age of 15. for my Genuine &
most private Amusement.

Fanny Burney.

Note 1.

Poland Street, London, March 2 7

To have some account of my thoughts,
manners, acquaintance & actions, when the Hour arrives
in which time is more nimble than memory, is the
reason which induces me to keep a Journal: a
Journal in which I must confess my every thought,
must open my whole Heart! But a thing of this
kind ought to be addressed to somebody—I must imagine
myself to be talking—talking to the most intimate of friends—to one in whom I should take
delight in confiding, & remorse in concealing: but who
must this friend be?—to make choice of one in
whom I can but half rely, would be to frustrate all
the intention of my plan. The only one I should wholly,
totally confide in, lives in the same House with me,
& not only never has, but never will, leave me one Secret
to tell her. To whom, then, must I dedicate my wonderful, surprising & interesting Adventures?—to whom dare
I reveal my private opinion of my nearest Relations?
the secret thoughts of my dearest friends? my own hopes,

First page of Frances Burney's journals

seat of Henry Thrale, a wealthy brewer and Member of Parliament, and his wife Hester Lynch Thrale. The most famous member of the Thrales' circle was Samuel Johnson, who took a strong avuncular liking to Fanny.

Encouraged by Johnson, Hester Thrale, Joshua Reynolds, the dramatists Richard Brinsley Sheridan and Arthur Murphy, and others, Frances undertook the writing of a comedy, *The Witlings*. She was forced to suppress it at the urging of her father and Crisp, who feared that the subject would offend prominent bluestockings, in particular Elizabeth Montagu. In 1782 Frances published a second novel, *Cecilia*, also a great success. In 1783 she was introduced to Mary Delany, a revered friend of King George III and Queen Charlotte, who would be instrumental in procuring Burney's appointment to the Court as Second Keeper of the Robes to Queen Charlotte, a position she took up in July 1786.

The removal from her family and friends, the suffocating etiquette and the bad-tempered tyranny of her immediate superior, Elizabeth Schwellenberg, made Burney's years at Court extremely unhappy ones. During the period of the King's 'madness', October 1788 to March 1789, she began writing a tragedy, *Edwy and Elgiva*. In 1791 she received the Queen's permission to retire from her position for reasons of ill health.

Freed from the Court with a pension of £100 a year (half her Court salary), Burney went on a tour of western England with her friend, Anna Ord, and then settled with her father at his lodgings in Chelsea College. In 1793 she met Alexandre d'Arblay – a French officer who had fled Revolutionary France – while on a visit to William and Frederica Locke, neighbours in Surrey and friends of Susanna and her husband Molesworth Phillips. They married, after a six-month courtship, in July 1793, having gained the reluctant consent of Dr Burney, and in December 1794 their only child, Alexander, was born. The marriage was, by all accounts, an exceptionally happy one, and Alexandre proved to be a devoted husband, despite disagreements between the couple over the upbringing of their son.

When liberated from Court service, Burney could return more fully to literary activities. In 1793 she published a pamphlet, *Brief Reflections Relative to the Emigrant French Clergy*, written on behalf of the Catholic clergy who had fled to England from Revolutionary France. In March 1795, her first tragedy, *Edwy and Elgiva*, with a prologue by her brother Charles, was performed at the Drury Lane Theatre, but withdrawn after a single, spectacularly unsuccessful performance. And in 1796 Burney published by subscription a third novel, *Camilla*. With the proceeds from this book her husband designed and built 'Camilla Cottage' on a piece of property given them by the Lockes.

In 1802 Burney and her son followed d'Arblay to France, where the renewal of hostilities with England forced them all to remain for ten years. During her years in France Burney worked steadily on a novel, *The Wanderer*.

Back in England she published this novel, which was to be her last, in 1814. In 1815 her husband was wounded fighting in the army opposing Napoleon. Later that year they took lodgings in Bath, where d'Arblay died in 1818. Four months later Burney moved to London. She spent a good part of the next twenty years going over the family papers, her own and those of her father, which she had inherited upon his death in 1814. In 1832 she published her final work, *Memoirs of Doctor Burney*, and in 1840 she died, aged eighty-seven, on 6 January, exactly forty years to the day after the death of her beloved Susanna. She was buried in Wolcot Churchyard, Bath, beside her husband and her son (who had predeceased her by three years).

Famous in her lifetime as a novelist, Burney also became celebrated as a diarist with the posthumous publication of a seven-volume selection of *The Diary and Letters of Madame d'Arblay* (1842–6), edited by Charlotte Barrett. These were later supplemented by the two-volume *Early Diary of Frances Burney* (1889), edited by Annie Raine Ellis. These editions have been supplanted by the modern complete editions of Joyce Hemlow and Lars E. Troide, which will eventually total twenty-four volumes (see Further Reading). For this Penguin Classics edition the volume editors have gone back to the original manuscripts, mostly in the Barrett Collection of the British Library and the Berg Collection of the New York Public Library. We have aimed to select representative passages which reflect the great range and variety of Burney's journals and letters, giving the reader a sense both of Burney – her life and thought – and of the world – the events and personalities – that she presents to us.

Burney's earliest journals and letters are very much those of a precocious young girl – humorous, playful, self-centred and irreverent. She dreams about falling in love, chafes at social customs which require visits to people one doesn't like and lampoons the marriage of two family servants. When her beloved father receives his doctorate from Oxford University, she sends him a comic verse letter comparing him to a fictional shoemaker who receives a physician's licence.

Her exuberance in her letters and with her family and friends is balanced by the gravity she assumes in the presence of strangers. A friend of her sister Esther dubs her '*the silent observant Miss Fanny*',[3] and observant she is, filling her journals with memorable sketches of many of the famous and interesting people who visit her father in Poland Street, Queen Square and St Martin's Street.

As Burney gets older she begins to travel. In 1774 she sends Susanna journal letters of her visit to the seaside resort of Teignmouth in Devon, where she experiences a frightening ride in a storm-tossed boat with a fat clergyman who is more worried about missing his supper than losing his life. In 1777 she visits her cousins in Worcester, and suffers excruciating stage fright while taking part in an amateur domestic performance of a popular play. Two years later she visits Brighton with her friends the Thrales, and the following year she accompanies them to Bath, whence they are forced to flee by the spread of the Gordon Riots from London.

Whether at home or away Burney never loses her eye for the comic or grotesque. At Teignmouth she witnesses a 'barbarous' wrestling match between working-class opponents and is reduced to helpless laughter by an anthem set by a weaver and sung in church by a 'trilling and squalling' choir (selection 17). In Worcester she meets an ineffably silly young woman, Miss Waldron, who is persuaded to sing a song in a croaking and squeaking voice, and continues even after a local baronet has dropped a large spoon down her dress. At Streatham she encounters Mr Blakeney, an old Irishman who misquotes the classics, condescends to Johnson as 'a clever fellow', calls a Reynolds picture '2 or 3 Dabs of Paint', and tells the same story '3 or 4 Times a Day' about the swollen feet and shrunken calves he suffered from the physicians (selections 62–3).

Of course Burney's journals and letters are full of references to the composition, publication and reception of her novels. Despite her public shyness she takes keen delight in the success of *Evelina* and *Cecilia*. She also records the encouragement given her to write a play, and her severe disappointment upon being forced to suppress *The Witlings*.

Disappointment is also her early lot in 'affairs of the heart'. At first she expresses no aversion to remaining single. When a well-to-do and well-educated young man, Thomas Barlow, tries to court her she resists family pressure and rebuffs him because he does not touch her heart. But in 1782 she meets George Owen Cambridge, a young clergyman whose charm, sincerity and intelligence penetrate her defences. His failure ultimately to propose causes her great emotional anguish. A similar, though less painful, disappointment happens at Court when she is 'led on' by Colonel Stephen Digby, Vice-Chamberlain to the Queen, who instead marries a wealthy Maid of Honour.

Disappointment of another sort is caused by the marriage of Hester

Thrale to Gabriel Piozzi in 1784. Virtually adopted by Hester and Henry Thrale after the success of *Evelina*, Burney in her journals mostly shows us the surface of the Thrales' marriage, which is that of a dutiful and respectful wife to a masterful husband; indeed, Hester Thrale, Burney and even Samuel Johnson call Thrale 'Master'. But the Thrales' marriage was an arranged one (the custom among the gentry), Thrale is a philanderer and after his premature death in 1781 the emotionally starved Hester falls in love with Piozzi, her children's Italian music master. Burney's letter to Hester just before the wedding expresses the contemporary and conventional prejudices against such a match: '*Children – Religion, Friends, Country, Character,* – – What on Earth can compensate the loss of all these?' (selection 95). Piozzi is unacceptable to Burney and most of London society as an Italian (country), a Catholic (religion) and a musician (class). Hester never forgives Burney's refusal to accept her new husband, though they will have a partial reconciliation years later.

Samuel Johnson, who has virtually lived with the Thrales for twenty years, also sees the marriage as Hester's abandonment of religion, class, morality and (not least) himself. When Burney first comes to Streatham she is charmed by a Johnson who, contrary to his portentous public image, is playful and affectionate; he likes to call her his 'little Burney', and hugs and 'salutes' (kisses) her with ponderous warmth. But she also records the least attractive side of his personality, which is a compulsion to bully mercilessly in the heat of argument (see, for example, his attack on William Weller Pepys, selection 79). In his last years, after Henry Thrale's death, Johnson's increasingly indifferent health deteriorates rapidly, and he reacts bitterly to Hester Thrale's 'defection'. On one of her last visits before his death, when Burney mentions Hester, Johnson exclaims: 'I drive her quite from my mind. She has disgraced herself, disgraced her friends and connections, disgraced her sex, and disgraced all the expectations of mankind! . . . I never speak of her, and I desire never to hear of her more' (selection 96).

In 1785 Burney meets the King and Queen at the house of Mary Delany in Windsor, and the following year she is invited to become a member of the Queen's household. She describes in her journals her grave misgivings over this appointment, her reverence and affection for George III and Charlotte, and her mistreatment by Mrs Schwellenberg, who repeatedly forces her to endure a biting wind in carriage rides which causes her severe eye problems. She records the King's composure and the Queen's shock after his attempted assassination by a deranged woman, and gives lengthy accounts of George's behaviour and treatment during his attack of 'madness'. She attends and describes the opening and some later sessions of the trial of Warren Hastings in Westminster Hall, which will last seven years. Stephen Digby having failed to rescue her from Court by marrying her, she finally prevails upon her father and the Queen to obtain her resignation, which she thankfully records in her journal as occurring 'After having lived in the service of Her Majesty Five Years within Ten Days' (selection 142).

Alexandre d'Arblay makes his first appearance in Burney's letters and journals in January 1793 at the same time as another fascinating exile from France, Mme de Staël. Despite her admiration for de Staël's writings, Burney gives in to her father's 'absolute resolution . . . to crush this acquaintance' because of de Staël's immorality (selection 155), but in the case of d'Arblay, happily, she follows her heart. In a moving letter of July 1793, she tells her brother Charles that Dr Burney 'from prudential scruples is coldly averse to this transaction' (selection 157), yet a few days later she and d'Arblay are married. Burney's letters and journals reveal the depth of her love for her husband, and their mutual devotion to their only child, Alexander, although he never lives up to his parents' high expectations.

Burney's ambition to succeed as a playwright as well as a novelist is manifested in a letter of April 1795 to Georgiana Waddington and, five years later, in a letter to her father of February 1800. In the first we see her conviction that the failure of the performance of *Edwy and Elgiva* was due not to her incapacity as a tragic dramatist but to her lack of time to revise and correct the piece (she had given birth to Alexander only three months earlier) and to the disgraceful weakness of the cast. Writing to Dr Burney less than a month after the death of her sister Susanna, she acknowledges that the expected production of *Love and Fashion* must now be postponed, but insists on her lifelong desire to write a successful comic drama: 'I thought the field more than open – inviting to me. The chance held out golden dreams' (selection 174).

During her residence in France, from 1802 to 1812, Burney could write few letters to her family and friends in England: war between the two countries made any communications increasingly difficult and even dangerous. Before Britain's declaration of war in May 1803, however, she does send her father a fine account of Napoleon's reviewing his troops, and later, in Spring 1812, she describes at length two paintings of Napoleon that she has seen in David's studio: one depicting him on horseback and the other in his study, where he 'appears to have been solitarily occupied in Nocturnal studies, and ruminations all Night' (selection 194). At about the same time

Burney writes the most powerful of all her journals: an appallingly vivid account of the mastectomy, without anaesthetic, that she had endured in September 1811. Like many of her finest set-pieces, this was written well after the events that it records. (Her Waterloo Journal, similarly, reporting the climax of the Napoleonic wars from February to July 1815, was composed only in 1823, while a vivid account of her flight from France to England in July–August 1812 was written still later, in *c.* 1825.)

By 1815, when she returned to England for good, Burney was sixty-three. In the journals and letters of her later years she describes some meetings with former friends, most notably Hester Piozzi in letters of December 1815 and November 1816, and the Duke of Clarence (later William IV) in a letter of November 1817. There are many anxious letters to her beloved son Alex, who becomes a clergyman but much prefers playing chess to his clerical duties and whose unwillingness to keep his mother informed of his where-abouts and well-being drives her to distraction. Engaged to be married and apparently settling down at last, he dies of influenza in 1837. This is one of many deaths that Burney is compelled to record, including her husband, two brothers and two sisters. The 'Narrative of the Last Illness and Death of General d'Arblay', written in 1820, is another of Burney's retrospective journals, as is the story of her narrow escape from drowning at Ifracombe, describing events of September 1817. She composed this superbly dramatic account in French in 1823 at the behest of her late husband for the benefit of two of their closest friends, before she produced an English version.

In some of the later letters, Burney describes the problems posed by her stewardship of her father's papers: a letter to Esther of November 1820 provides a detailed account of her disappointment as she discovers that his memoirs and correspondence are (she thinks) far less significant than she had supposed them to be. In her final years Burney's own papers, her 'myriads of hoards of MSS.', cause her similar distress: half laughing, half crying she writes a letter in 1838 to her sister Charlotte and her niece Charlotte Barrett asking 'what I had best do with the killing mass . . . My Eyes will work at them no more!' (selection 242). Fifteen months later, in July 1839, she writes her last surviving letter, again to her niece Charlotte. As she had been fifty years earlier, Burney is preoccupied with events at Court. She has outlived George III and Queen Charlotte, as well as George IV and William IV, and is now concerned with a scandal casting a shadow over the recently crowned Queen Victoria, whom she defends from common gossip: 'There is some mystery in the terrible calumny, to which the poor young innocent and inexperienced Queen is doubtless a Dupe' (selection 243). A few lines later, Burney is quoting Ecclesiastes and Pope: her style remains strong, clear and engaging to the end.

NOTES

1. *EJL*, i. xv and n. 2.
2. See *EJL*, i. 328.
3. *JL*, xi. 286.

Further Reading

EDITIONS

Brief Reflections Relative to the Emigrant French Clergy, ed. Claudia L. Johnson (Los Angeles, 1990).

Camilla: or, A Picture of Youth, ed. Edward A. Bloom and Lillian D. Bloom (Oxford, 1972).

Cecilia, or Memoirs of an Heiress, ed. Peter Sabor and Margaret Anne Doody (Oxford, 1988).

The Complete Plays of Frances Burney, ed. Peter Sabor, Stewart Cooke and Geoffrey Sill, 2 vols. (London, 1995).

The Diary and Letters of Madame d'Arblay, ed. Charlotte Barrett, 7 vols. (London, 1842–6); rev. Austin Dobson, 6 vols. (London, 1904–5).

The Early Journals and Letters of Fanny Burney, ed. Lars E. Troide et al. (Oxford, 1988–).

Evelina, or the History of a Young Lady's Entrance into the World, ed. Margaret Anne Doody (London, 1993).

Evelina, or the History of a Young Lady's Entrance into the World, ed. Stewart J. Cooke (New York, 1998).

The Journals and Letters of Fanny Burney (Madame d'Arblay), ed. Joyce Hemlow et al., 12 vols. (Oxford, 1972–84).

Selected Letters and Journals, ed. Joyce Hemlow (Oxford, 1986).

The Wanderer, ed. Margaret Anne Doody, Robert L. Mack and Peter Sabor (Oxford, 1991).

BIOGRAPHICAL AND CRITICAL STUDIES

Michael E. Adelstein, *Fanny Burney* (New York, 1968).
Kate Chisholm, *Fanny Burney: Her Life* (London, 1998).

Hester Davenport, *Faithful Handmaid: Fanny Burney at the Court of King George III* (London, 2000).

D. D. Devlin, *The Novels and Journals of Fanny Burney* (London, 1987).

Margaret Anne Doody, *Frances Burney: The Life in the Works* (New Brunswick, N.J., 1988).

——, 'Missing *Les Muses*: Madame de Staël and Frances Burney', *Colloquium Helveticum* 25 (1997), 81–117.

Julia L. Epstein, *The Iron Pen: Frances Burney and the Politics of Women's Writing* (Madison, Wis., 1989).

Evelyn Farr, *The World of Fanny Burney* (London, 1993).

John Glendening, 'Young Fanny Burney and the Mentor', *The Age of Johnson* 4 (1991), 281–312.

Joseph A. Grau, *Fanny Burney: An Annotated Bibliography* (New York, 1981).

Claire Harman, *Fanny Burney: A Biography* (London, 2000).

Joyce Hemlow, *A Catalogue of the Burney Family Correspondence 1749–1878* (Oxford, 1968).

——, 'Fanny Burney and the Courtesy Books', *PMLA* 65 (1950), 732–61.

——, *The History of Fanny Burney* (Oxford, 1958).

——, 'Letters and Journals of Fanny Burney: Establishing the Text', in *Editing Eighteenth-Century Texts*, ed. D. I. B. Smith (Toronto, 1968), 25–43.

Beth Kowaleski-Wallace, 'A Night at the Opera: The Body, Class, and Art in *Evelina* and Frances Burney's Early Diaries', in *History, Gender and Eighteenth-Century Literature*, ed. Beth Fowkes Tobin (Athens, Ga., 1994), 141–58.

Betty Rizzo, 'How (and How Not) to Explore the Burneys: Questions of Decorum', *Review* 11 (1989), 197–218.

Katharine M. Rogers, 'Fanny Burney: the Private Self and the Public Self', *International Journal of Women's Studies* 7 (1984), 110–17.

——, *Frances Burney: The World of Female Difficulties* (London, 1990).

Peter Sabor, 'Annie Raine Ellis, Austin Dobson, and the Rise of Burney Studies', *Burney Journal* 1 (1998), 25–45.

Judy Simons, *Fanny Burney* (London, 1987).

——, 'Miss Somebody: The Diary of Fanny Burney or A Star is Born', *Burney Journal* 1 (1998), 3–17.

Patricia M. Spacks, 'Dynamics of Fear: Fanny Burney', in *Imagining a Self: Autobiography and Novel in Eighteenth-Century England* (Cambridge, Mass., 1976), 158–92.

Kristina Straub, *Divided Fictions: Fanny Burney and Feminine Strategy* (Lexington, Ky., 1987).

Janice Thaddeus, *Frances Burney: A Literary Life* (London, 2000).

——, 'Hoards of Sorrow: Hester Lynch Piozzi, Frances Burney d'Arblay, and Intimate Death', *Eighteenth-Century Life* 14 (1990), 108–29.

Lars E. Troide, 'The McGill Burney Project', *Burney Journal* 2 (1999), 40–52.

J. N. Waddell, 'Fanny Burney's Contribution to English Vocabulary', *Neuphilologische Mitteilungen* 81 (1980), 260–63.

——, 'Additions to *O.E.D.* from the Writings of Fanny Burney', *Notes and Queries* 225 (1980), 27–32.

John Wiltshire, 'Early Nineteenth-Century Pathography: The Case of Frances Burney', *Literature and History* 2 (1993), 9–23.

——, 'Fanny Burney's Face, Madame d'Arblay's Veil', in *Literature and Medicine during the Eighteenth Century*, ed. Marie Mulvey Roberts and Roy Porter (London, 1993), 245–65.

——, 'Love unto Death: Fanny Burney's "Narrative of the Last Illness and Death of General d'Arblay" (1820)', *Literature and Medicine* 12 (1993), 215–34.

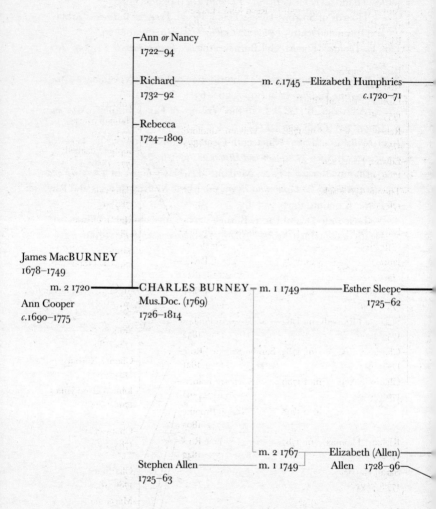

Ann *or* Nancy
1722–94

Richard —————————— m. *c.*1745 —Elizabeth Humphries——
1732–92   *c.*1720–71

Rebecca
1724–1809

James MacBURNEY
1678–1749

m. 2 1720 —— CHARLES BURNEY — m. 1 1749 ——— Esther Sleepe——
                        Mus.Doc. (1769)   1725–62
Ann Cooper   1726–1814
*c.*1690–1775

                                              m. 2 1767 —— Elizabeth (Allen)——
                        Stephen Allen —— m. 1 1749 —— Allen   1728–96—
                        1725–63

- Charles Rousseau —— m. 1770 —— Esther Burney
  1747–1819   (see below)
- Ann *or* Nancy —— m. 1781 —— Revd John Hawkins
  1749–1819   *post* 1735–1804
- Richard Gustavus
  1751–90
- James Adolphus
  1753–98
- Elizabeth Warren ('Blue')
  1755–1832
- Rebecca —— m. 1788 —— William Sandford
  1758–1835   1759–1823
- Edward Francesco
  1760–1848
- Thomas Frederick
  1765–85

- 5 others
- Hannah Maria
  1772–1856
- Sophia Elizabeth
  1777–1856

- Catherine
  1786–93
- Martin Charles
  1788–1852
- Sarah
  1796–*post* 1868

- Esther (Hetty) —— m. 1770 —— Charles R. Burney
  1749–1832   (see above)
- James —— m. 1785 —— Sarah Payne
  1750–1821   1758–1832
- **FRANCES** —— m. 1793 —— Alexandre d'Arblay
  1752–1840   1754–1818
- Susanna Elizabeth —— m. 1782 —— Molesworth Phillips
  1755–1800   1755–1832
- Charles —— m. 1783 —— Sarah ('Rosette') Rose
  1757–1817   1759–1821
- Charlotte Ann —— m. 1 1786 —— Clement Francis
  1761–1838   *c.*1744–92
  —— m. 2 1798 —— Ralph Broome
                  1742–1805

- Alexander Charles Louis
  1794–1837

- Frances
  1782–1860
- Charles Norbury
  1785–1814
- John William James
  1791–1833

- Charles Parr
  1785–1864

- Charlotte
  1786–1870
- Marianne
  1790–1832
- Clement Robert
  1792–1829

- Richard Thomas —— m. 1787 —— Jane Ross
  1768–1808   1772–1842
- Sarah Harriet
  1772–1844

- Maria Allen —— m. 1772 —— Martin Folkes Rishton
  1751–1820   *c.*1747–1820
- Stephen Allen —— m. 1772 —— Susanna Sharpin
  1755–1847   1755–1816
- Elizabeth Allen —— m. 1 1777 —— Samuel Meeke
  1761–*c.*1826   d. *c.*1796
  —— m. 2 (by 1797) —— ___ Bruce

- Ralph (Dolph)
  1801–17

- ?11 children

- 12 children

Manuscript Sources

Note on the Text

The texts for this edition are based on the manuscripts or, on the few occasions when these are missing or inaccessible, on printed sources. FB spent the last twenty years of her life editing her papers, and we present them in their final form.

We have retained her distinctive spelling, punctuation, capitalization, underlining (represented by italics), and paragraphing. Obvious slips of the pen, however (unlike eccentric spellings) have been silently corrected. Raised letters have been lowered; abbreviations (such as the ampersand, 'yr', etc.) have been expanded and 'its' and 'hers' as possessives have the apostrophe removed. Names and titles, which FB frequently represents by initials and shortened forms, have likewise been expanded: 'Gnl. d'A.' thus becomes 'General d'Arblay'. Capitals are supplied, when required, for proper names and for the beginnings of sentences. Final periods are supplied when required at the end of sentences, and quotation marks added when missing from dialogue. Standard forms are used for 'Mr', 'Mme', 'Mlle', etc., as well as for numerals. Full stops in titles (Mr, Mrs, Dr) have been omitted. Ellipses (on a separate line) indicate omissions within a selection.

Our headings to each selection indicate whether the selection is a journal, a journal letter or a letter (or in one case a verse letter). 'Journal' alone means an entry FB addressed to herself (or 'Miss Nobody', her fanciful alter ego); a 'journal letter' is a substantial effort written to a correspondent over a period of at least several days; a 'letter' is typically written in one day. In the case of journal letters our dates indicate the specific day of an entry, rather than the inclusive dates of the whole. An extract from a selection on a given date is indicated by 'From', as in 'From Journal *17 July 1768*'. Selections given substantially in their entirety are designated, for example, 'Letter to Esther Burney *8 January 1781*'.

Our annotations provide essential context. Full names, titles (as appropriate) and dates of birth and death are given in the index. We have translated foreign words and phrases (usually French), explained obscure terms and expressions, identified unattributed quotations, elucidated historical and personal events, and so on. Information is taken from the standard editions of *EJL* and *JL*, supplemented by the editors' additional research.

1768–1777

The Apprentice Years

1. Journal *27 March 1768*

Poland Street,[1] London

To have some account of my thoughts, manners, acquaintance and actions, when the Hour arrives at which time is more nimble than memory, is the reason which induces me to keep a Journal: a Journal in which I must confess my *every* thought, must open my whole Heart! But a thing of this kind ought to be addressed to somebody – I must imagine myself to be talking – talking to the most intimate of friends – to one in whom I should take delight in confiding, and feel remorse in concealment: but who must this friend be? – to make choice of one to whom I can but *half* rely, would be to frustrate entirely the intention of my plan. The only one I could wholly, totally confide in, lives in the same House with me, and not only never *has*, but never *will*, leave me one secret *to* tell her.[2] To whom, then, *must* I dedicate my wonderful, surprising and interesting adventures? – to *whom* dare I reveal my private opinion of my nearest Relations? the secret thoughts of my dearest friends? my own hopes, fears, reflections and dislikes – Nobody!

To Nobody, then, will I write my Journal! since To Nobody can I be wholly unreserved – to Nobody can I reveal every thought, every wish of my Heart, with the most unlimited confidence, the most unremitting sincerity to the end of my Life! For what chance, what accident can end my connections with

---

1. In 1760 eight-year-old FB had moved with her family to Poland Street from King's Lynn, Norfolk, where her father, CB, had been the organist of St Margaret's Church. Poland Street was then part of a fashionable neighbourhood where CB gave lessons to 'pupils of rank, wealth, and talents' (*Memoirs of Doctor Burney . . . by his daughter, Madame d'Arblay* (1832), i. 135). FB begins her diary eleven weeks and a day before her sixteenth birthday (13 June).

2. FB's younger sister Susanna ('Susan'), thirteen years old; the two were especially close. See also p. 180 note 1.

Nobody? No secret *can* I conceal from No – body, and to No – body can I be *ever* unreserved. Disagreement cannot stop our affection, Time itself has no power to end our friendship. The love, the esteem I entertain for Nobody, No-body's self has not power to destroy. From Nobody I have nothing to fear, the secrets sacred to friendship, Nobody will not reveal, when the affair is doubtful, Nobody will not look towards the side least favourable. –

I will suppose you, then, to be my best friend; tho' God forbid' you ever should! my dearest companion – and a romantick Girl, for mere oddity may perhaps be more sincere – more *tender* – than if you were a friend in propria personae[3] – in as much as imagination often exceeds reality. In your Breast my errors may create pity without exciting contempt; may raise your compassion, without eradicating your love.

From this moment, then, my dear Girl – but why, permit me to ask, must a *female* be made Nobody? Ah! my dear, what were this world good for, *were* Nobody a female? And now I have done with *preambulation*.

2. From Journal *July 1768*

I am going to tell you something concerning myself, which, if I have not chanced to mention it before will I believe a little surprise you – it is, that I scarse wish for any thing so truly, really and greatly, as to be *in love* – upon my word I am serious – and very *gravely* and *sedately*, assure you it is a real and *true* wish. I cannot help thinking it is a great happiness to have a strong and particular attachment to some *one* person, independent of duty, interest, relationship or pleasure: but I carry not my wish so far as for a *mutual tendresse* – No, I should be contented to love *sola* – and let *Duets* be reserved for those who have a proper sense of their superiourity. For my own part I vow and declare that the mere pleasure of having a great affection for some one person to which I was neither guided by fear, hope of profit, gratitude, respect – or any motive but mere *fancy* would sufficiently satisfy me, and I should not at all wish a return. Lord Bless me – how I run in! foolish and ill-Judged! – how despicable a picture have I drawn of an object of Love! – mere giddiness, not inclination, I am sure, penn'd it – Love without respect or gratitude! – that could only be felt for a person wholly undeserving – but indeed I write so much at random that it is much more a chance if I know what I am saying, than if I do not.

3. Properly 'persona': in person, a *real* friend (Latin).

3. Journal *13 July 1768*

Cabin[1] – Wednesday afternoon.
I always spend the Evening, sometimes all the afternoon, in this sweet Cabin
– except sometimes, when unusually thoughtful, I prefer the Garden. – I
cannot express the pleasure I have in writing down my thoughts, at the very
moment – my opinion of people when I first see them, and *how* I alter, or
how confirm myself in it – and I am much deceived in my *fore sight*, if I shall
not have very great delight in reading this *living proof* of my manner of
passing my time, my sentiments, my thoughts of people I know, and a
thousand other things in future. – There is something to me very Unsatisfac-
tory in passing year after year without even a memorandum of what you
did, etc. And then, all the happy Hours I spend with particular Friends and
Favourites, would fade from my recollection. –

4. From Journal *17 July 1768*

I have lately Read the Prince of Abyssinia[1] – I am almost equally charm'd
and shock'd at it – the style, the sentiments are inimitable – but the subject
is dreadful – and, handled as it is by Dr Johnson, might make *any* young,
perhaps old, person tremble – O, how dreadful, how terrible is it to be told
by a man of his genius and knowledge, in so affectingly probable a manner,
that true, real happiness is ever unattainable in this world! – Thro' all the
scenes, publick or private, domestick or solitary, that Nekaya or Rasselas
pass, real felicity eludes their pursuit and mocks their solicitude. In high
Life, superiority, envy and haughtiness battle the power of preferment,
favour and greatness – and with or without them, all is Animosity, suspicion,
apprehension, and misery – in Private familys, disagreement, Jealousy and
partiality, destroy all domestick felicity and all social chearfulness, and all is
peevishness, contradiction, ill will and wretchedness! – And in solitude,
Imagination paints the World in a new light, every bliss which was wanting

---

1. CB's first wife, Esther Sleepe, FB's mother, had died in 1762. In 1767 he married Elizabeth
Allen, the widow of a wealthy King's Lynn merchant. The 'Cabin' was a little building that
overlooked the river behind her dower house in King's Lynn.

1. Samuel Johnson's *The History of Rasselas, Prince of Abissinia*, had appeared in 1759. FB would
first meet Dr Johnson in 1777 (see selection 38), and became a great favourite of his after the
publication of her first novel, *Evelina* (1778).

when in it, appears easily attained when away from it, but the loneliness of retirement seems unsocial, dreary, savouring of misanthropy and melancholy – and all is anxiety, doubt, fear and anguish! In this manner does Dr Johnson proceed in his melancholy conviction of the instability of all human enjoyments, and the impossibility of all earthly happiness. One thing during the Course of the successless enquiry struck me, which gave me much comfort, which is, that those who wander in the world avowedly and purposely in search of happiness, who view every scene of present Joy with an Eye to what may succeed, certainly are more liable to disappointment, misfortune and sorrow, than those who give up their fate to chance and take the goods and evils of fortune as they come, without making happiness their study, or misery their foresight.

5. From Journal *August 1768*[1]

I have been having a long conversation with Miss Young[2] on journals. She has very seriously and earnestly advised me to give mine up – heigho-ho! Do you think I can bring myself to oblige her? What she says has great weight with me; but, indeed, I should be very loath to *quite* give my poor friend up. She says that it is the most dangerous employment young persons can have – it makes them often record things which ought *not* to be recorded, but instantly forgot. I told her, that as *my* Journal was *solely* for my own perusal, nobody could in justice, or even in sense, be angry or displeased at my writing any thing.

'But how can you answer,' said she, 'that it *is* only for your perusal? That very circumstance of your papa's finding it, shows you are not so very careful as is necessary for such a work. And if you drop it, and any improper person finds it, you know not the uneasiness it may cost you.'

'Well but, dear ma'am, this is an "if" that may not happen once in a century.'

'I beg your pardon; I know not how often it may happen; and even *once* might prove enough to give you more pain than you are aware of.'

'Why, dear ma'am, papa never prohibited my writing, and he knows that I *do* write, and *what* I do write.'

---

1. The manuscript of this passage is not extant. It is reprinted from *The Early Diary of Frances Burney, 1768–1778*, ed. A. R. Ellis (1913), i. 19–21.
2. Dorothy ('Dolly') Young of King's Lynn was the closest friend of FB's mother.

'I question that. However, 'tis impossible for you to answer for the curiosity of others. And suppose any body finds a part in which they are extremely censured.'

'Why then, they must take it for their pains. It was not wrote for *them*, but *me*, and I cannot see any harm in writing to *myself*.'

'It was very well whilst there were only your sisters with you to do anything of this kind; but, depend upon it, when your connections are enlarged, your family increased, your acquaintance multiplied, young and old *so* apt to be curious – depend upon it, Fanny, 'tis the most dangerous employment you can have. Suppose now, for example, your favourite wish were granted, and you were *to fall in love*, and then the object of your passion were to get sight of some part which related to himself?'

'Why then, Miss Young, I must make a little trip to Rosamond's Pond.'[3]

'Why, ay, I doubt it would be all you would have left.'

'Dear Miss Young! – But I'm sure, by your earnestness, that you think worse of my poor Journal than it deserves.'

'I know very well the nature of these things. I know that in journals, thoughts, actions, looks, conversations – *all* go down; do they not?'

The conclusion of our debate was, that if I would show her some part of what I had wrote she should be a better judge, and would then give me her best advice whether to proceed or not. I believe I shall accept her condition; though I own I shall show it with shame and fear, for such nonsense is *so* unworthy her perusal.

I'm sure, besides, I know not what part to choose. Shall I take at random?

6. From Journal *September 1768*

[Poland Street]

Mr Smart[1] the poet was here yesterday. He is the Author of the 'Old Woman's Magazine' and of several poetical productions, some of which are sweetly elegant and pretty – for example – 'Harriet's Birth Day' – 'Care

3. To drown herself. Rosamond's Pond, in St James's Park, was filled in in 1770 because it had become the scene of so many lovers' suicides.

1. CB had been a friend of Christopher Smart since 1744. Smart had directed *The Midwife, or The Old Women's Magazine*, a threepenny journal, from 1750 to 1753. 'Care and Generosity' first appeared in it in 1751. By 'Harriet's Birth Day' FB presumably means his 'Ode on the Fifth of December, Being the Birth-Day of a Very Beautiful Young Lady' (1750). Smart was confined in St Luke's Hospital, 1757–8, and in Potter's madhouse, Bethnal Green, 1759–63.

and Generosity' – and many more. This ingenius Writer is one of the most unfortunate of men – he has been twice confined in a mad House – and but last year sent a most affecting Epistle to papa, to entreat him to lend him ½ a Guinea! – How great a pity so clever, so ingenius a man should be reduced to such shocking circumstances. He is extremely grave, and has still great wildness in his manner, looks and voice – but 'tis impossible to *see* him and to *think* of his works, without feeling the utmost pity and concern for him.

7. From Journal *14–15 May 1769*

O! I am to go to a Wedding to-morrow – the partys – one Mr John Hutton, Glass polisher,[1] and Mrs Betty Langely spinster, our old Cook – perhaps I may give you, Miss Nobody, an account of this affair tomorrow. I never had the honour of being at a Wedding in my life – but tho' this will be the first, I fancy it will not be the last too.

Monday Eve. May 15th

Well, the wedding is over, the good folks are Join'd for better for worse – – A shocking Clause that! – 'tis preparing one to lead a long Journey, and to know the path is not altogether strew'd with Roses – This same marriage Ceremony is so short, I really should have doubted its validity had *I* been the Bride; though perhaps she may not find the Road it leads her to be very short; be that as it may, she must now trudge on, she can only return with her wishes, be she ever so wearied.

We have spent an exceeding agreeable Day. I speak for myself and a few more at least, I will not answer for the Bride and the Groom's feelings, at least not for the latter – tho' they niether of them appeared miserable; but had I been that *latter*, I fear I could not have said so much for myself. – As to the Bride, she is blythe as the month; if one can compare in any degree a weed of December, with the fragrance of May; for a weed in truth it is, and a weed not in its first prime. But I must give some account of the *wedding*; – To begin with the Company, first,

The Bride. A maiden of about fifty, short, thick, clumsy, vulgar; her complection the finest saffron, and her Features suited to it: she was Dress'd

---

1. I.e. the Burneys' manservant.

in a white Linnen Gown, and with all the elegance which *marks* her character and station, having the honour to be Cook to Mr Burney.

The Bridegroom. A young man who had the appearance of being her son. A good, modest, sober and decent youth. Every body must allow this Couple to be exceedingly well and very properly match'd. He was in Blue, trim'd with Red: N:B: the choice of these Colours are suited to the choice of the partys.[2]

The Father – (of the Day) Mr Charles Burney Junior.[3] It must be acknowledged that this accomplish'd virgin was determin'd to have every thing in Character; as not meerly her Husband, but her Father too was young enough to own her for a mother. It is generally allow'd Originality displays genius.

The Bride's maids. Miss Anne Burney, a Virgin who may count years with the Bride herself, though I fear she would not pretend to equal her in accomplishments: Miss Esther Burney,[4] who, more modest still, pretends not to equal her in *any* thing; – not even in her wishes, except it be for this last step she has taken: and Miss Frances Burney, who in *nothing* can equal the Bride.

The rest of the Company – a Mrs Ritson and a Mr Somebody, no matter what, – Betty's friends –

And thus the Train closed.

We went in Papa's Coach, as many as it would hold, – the *Gentlemen* were obliged to walk – which condescendsion is not inconsiderable, for the Mr *Somebody*, and the Bridegroom too, have the honour of being Footman to very *topping* people! The Bride supported her spirits amazingly.

8. From Journal *15 June 1769*

Miss Crawford[1] call'd here lately – she is very earnest for us to visit her – but *we* a.e not very earnest about the matter: – however, the laws of custom make our spending one Evening with her necessary. O how I hate this vile custom which obliges us to make slaves of ourselves! to sell the most

---

2. White represents virginity, of course, while blue and red may stand for hope and martyrdom.
3. Charles Rousseau Burney, FB's Worcester cousin and future brother-in-law.
4. Ann Burney was FB's aunt and Esther ('Hetty') Burney was FB's elder sister, who would marry Charles Rousseau Burney in 1770.

1. Sister of one of Esther Burney's admirers.

precious property we boast, our Time; – and to sacrifice it to every prattling impertinent who chuses to demand it! – yet those who shall pretend to defy this irksome confinement of our happiness, must stand accused of incivility, – breach of manners – love of originality, – and what not – nevertheless, they who will nobly dare to be above submitting to Chains their reason disapproves, they shall I always honour – if that will be of any service to them!

For why should we not be permitted to be masters of our Time? – why may we not venture to love, and to dislike – and why, if we do, may we not give to those we love the richest Jewel we own, our Time? what is it can stimulate us to bestow *that* on all alike? – 'tis not affection – 'tis not a desire of pleasing – or if it is, 'tis a very weak one; – no! 'tis indolence – 'tis Custom – Custom – which is so woven around us – which so universally commands us – which we all blame – and all obey, without knowing why or wherefore – which keeps our better Reason, that sometimes dares to shew its folly, in subjection –

And which, in short, is a very ridiculous affair, more particularly as it hath kept me writing on it till I have forgot what introduced it – – I feel myself in no excellent mood – I will walk out and give my spirits another *turn*, and then resume my Pen.

9. Verse Letter to Dr Charles Burney *23 June 1769* [1]

Poland Street
Friday

To Doctor Last [2]
O aid me, ye muses of ev'ry Degree,
O give me the standish of Mulberry Tree
　　Which was cut for the Author of Ferney; [3]
O give me a Quil to the stump worn by Gray, [4]
And Paper which cut was on Milton's Birth Day
　　To write to the great Doctor Burney!

1. FB sent these verses to CB on his being awarded a doctorate in music by Oxford University.
2. Character in several contemporary comic plays: a shoemaker who gets a physician's licence.
3. George Keate, minor author, had written *Ferney*, a poem praising both Voltaire and Shakespeare. For the latter the town fathers of Stratford had given him a standish, an inkstand, cut from a mulberry tree traditionally supposed to have been planted by the Bard.
4. The poet Thomas Gray.

O Doctor! of Doctor's the Last and the Best
By Fortune most honour'd, distinguish'd and blest
   And may you for ever be her nigh!
O smile (if a Doctor's permitted to smile)
And your natural gravity lessen a while
   To Read this, O dread Doctor Burney!

For the Letter most kind we to Day did receive
With grateful affection our Bosoms do heave
   And to see you, O grave sir! how yern I!
'Tis true the Time's short since you last was in Town
Yet both fatter and Taller you doubtless are grown
   Or you'll make but a poor Doctor Burney.

For I never can think of a Doctor, not big
As a Falstaf, or without a full bottom'd wig
   And the slyness Fame gives an Attorney;
Not more at the Bag did the Citizen's stare
Of Harley, when Harley was made a Lord Mayor[5]
   Than I shall at thin Doctor Burney.

May Wisdom, which still to good humour gives Birth
May fatness with dignity, goodness with mirth
   Still attend you, and speed your Town Journey;
And O till the Hour when Death us shall part
May Fanny a Corner possess of the Heart
   Of the owner of hers, Doctor Burney!

10. From Journal *August 1769*

               [King's Lynn, Norfolk]
We have nothing but visiting here, and this perpetual Round of constrained
Civilities to Persons quite indifferent to us, is the most provoking and
tiresome thing in the World, but it is unavoidable in a Country Town,

---

5. Thomas Harley, Lord Mayor of London, 1767–8, had scandalized some onlookers at his
installation ceremony when he wore an informal bag-wig instead of the customary full-bottomed
wig.

where every body is known, as here. 'Tis a most shocking and unworthy way of spending our precious irrecoverable Time, to devote it to those who know not its value – why are we not permitted to *decline* as well as *accept* visits and acquaintance? It is not that we are ignorant of means to better employ ourselves, but that we dare not persue them. However, restraint of this kind is much much less practiced or necessary in London than else where – excuses there are no sooner made than admitted – acquaintance as easily drop'd as courted – and Company chose or rejected at pleasure – undoubtedly the same plan *might* be persued here but how? with breaking the customs of the place, disobliging the Inhabitants, and incurring the censure of the Town in general as unsociable, proud, or impertinant Innovators. Seeing therefore what must be submitted to, 'tis best to assume a good grace – only its hard hard!

11. From Journal *10 January 1770*

I observed a Nun, Dressed in Black, who was speaking with great earnestness, and who discovered by her Voice to be a Miss Milne, a pretty Scotch Nymph I have met at Mrs Stranges.[1] I stopt to listen to her. She turn'd about and took my Hand and led me into a Corner of the Room – 'Beautiful Creature!' cried she, in a plaintive Voice, 'with what pain do I see you here, beset by this Crowd of folly and deceit! O could I prevail on you to quit this wicked world, and all its vices, and to follow my footsteps!'

'But how am I to account,' said I, 'for the reason that one who so much despises the world, should chuse to mix with the gayest part of it? What do you do here?'

'I come but,' said she, 'to see and to save such innocent, beautiful, young Creatures as you from the snares of the Wicked. Listen to me, I was once such as you are, I mixed with the World; I was caressed by it, I loved it – I was deceived! – surrounded by an artful set of flattering, designing men, I fell but too easily into the net they spread for me; I am now convinced of the vanity of Life, and in this peaceful, tranquil state shall I pass the remainder of my Days.'

1. From FB's description of a masquerade she attended at the home of Charles Lalauze, a French dancing master in London. Miss Milne was perhaps Anne Mylne, who married (1775) Sir John Gordon, fourth Baronet. Isabella and Robert Strange were old friends of the Burneys; their children were taught by Lalauze. Participants in masquerades were expected to act completely 'in character' until the unmasking later on.

'It is so impossible,' said I, 'to listen to you without being benefitted by your Conversation, that I shall to the utmost of my power *imitate you*, and always chuse to despise the World, and hold it in contempt. – At a *masquerade*! –.'

'Alas,' said she, 'I am here meerly to contemplate on the strange follies and vices of mankind – this scene affords me only a subject of joy to think I have quitted it.'

We were here interrupted, and parted.

. . .

I siezed the first opportunity that offered of again joining my sage monitor the fair Nun – who did not seem averse to honouring me with her Conversation. She renewed her former subject, expatiated on the wickedness and degeneracy of the World, dwelt with great energy and warmth on the deceit and craft of man, and pressed me to join her holy Order with the zeal of an Enthusiast. A pink Domino advanced, and charged her not to instill her preposterous sentiments into my mind; she answered him with so much contempt that he immediately quitted us. – We were then accosted by the shepherd, who would fain have appeared of some consequence, and aimed at being gallant and agreeable – Poor man! wofully was he the contrary. The Nun did not spare him. 'Hence,' cried she, 'thou gaudy Animal, with thy trifling and ridiculous trappings away – Let not this fair Creature be corrupted by this Company. O fly the pernicious impertinance of these shadows which surround thee! –' 'The – the Lady –' stammered the poor swain – 'the Lady will be – will be more likely – to be hurt – by – – by you than – than –' 'Yes, yes,' cried she, 'she would be safe enough were she followed only by such as thee!' Hetty just then bid me observe a very droll old Dutch man, who soon after joined us – He accosted us in High Dutch – – not that I would Quarrel with any one who told me it was *Low* Dutch! – it might be Arabick for ought I could tell! He was very completely Dressed, and had on an exceeding droll old man's mask, and was smoaking a Pipe – He presented me with a Quid of Tobaco, I accepted it very cordially: – the Nun was not disposed to be pleased – she attacked poor Mynheer with much haughtiness – 'Thou savage! – hence to thy native Land of Brutes and Barbarians, smoak thy Pipe there, but pollute not us with thy dull and coarse attempts at Wit and pleasantry –'

The Dutch man however heeded her not, he amused himself with talking and making signs of devotion to me, while the Nun railed, and I Laughed. – At last she took my Hand, and led me to another part of the Room, where

11

we renewed our former Conversation. 'You see,' she cried, 'what a Herd of Danglers flutter around you; thus it once was with me; your form is elegant; your Face I doubt not is beautiful; your sentiments are superior to both: regard these Vipers then with a proper disdain; they will follow you, will admire, Court, caress and flatter you – they will engage your affections – – and then they will desert you! it is not that you are less amiable, or that they cease to esteem you; but they are weary of you; novelty must attone in another for every loss they may regret in you: – it is not merit they seek, but variety. *I* speak from experience!'

' 'Tis rather surprising,' said I, 'that one who speaks with such vigour of the World, – and professes having quitted it from *knowing* its degeneracy, and who talks of experience in the style of Age; should have a Voice which is a perpetual reminder of her own Youth; and should in all visible respects, be so formed to grace and adorn the World she holds in such contempt.'

'Hold,' cried she, 'remember my sacred order, and remember that we Nuns can never admit to our Conferences that baleful Enemy of innocence, Flattery! Alas, you learn this from men! Would you but renounce them! what happiness would such a Convert give me!'

The Dutchman and the shepherd soon joined us again – the former was very liberal of his tobaco, and supported his Character with much drollery, speaking no English, but a few Dutch words, and making signs. The shepherd seemed formed for all the stupidity of a Dutch man more than the man who assumed that Dress; but *he* aimed at something superior. – The Nun, looking on her Veil and Habit as a sanction to the utmost liberty of speech, spoke to them both without the least ceremony. – All she said to *me* did honour to the Name she assumed – it was sensible and delicate, it was *probably* very true; it was *certainly* very well adapted to her apparent character: but when we were joined by men, her exhortation degenerated into railing; which though she might intend the better to support her part, by displaying her indignation against the sex, nevertheless seemed rather suited to the virulency and bitterness of a revengeful woman of the World, than the gentleness and dignity which were expected from the piety, patience and forbearance of a Cloister. 'And what,' said she to the Dutch man, 'what can have induced such a savage to venture himself here? Go, seek thy fellow Brutes! the vulgar, bestial society thou art used to, is such alone as thou ought to mix with.'

He *jabbered* something in his defence, and seemed inclined to make his Court to me. 'Perhaps,' said she, 'it may be in the power of this fair Creature to reform thee; she may civilise thy gross and barbarous manners.' The Dutch man bowed, said *yaw*, and put his Hand on his Heart in token of approbation. 'Ay,' said the poor shepherd, whose Eyes had the most marked expression of stupidity (if stupidity can be said to have *any* expression) that I ever saw, and his words and manner so exactly coincided with his appearance, that he was meerly an object for Laughter – he served only for such to *me* at least; for indeed my spirits were not very low.

12. From Journal *May 1770*

Friday

I am just returned from making a visit to 5 sisters, 2 married and 3 single, who all Live together – and rejoiced am I that I *am* returned. There is with them a child, not 3 years old, Grandson to one of them, who is the Idol of them All: the poor Boy, by their ill judged and ruinous indulgence, is rendered an object of dislike to all others: they have taught him to speak, like a Parrot, only such words as they dictate; they make him affect the Language of a man, and then boast that *no child ever talked like him*, and what is the effect of this singularity, but making him appear affected, troublesome and unnatural? How infinitely more amiable is the native simplicity and artlessness with which children are born! Then they permit him to amuse himself at pleasure with all Insects – Flys, Butterflys – poor little Animals – the torture he gave to one of the last really turned me so sick that I could not recover myself the whole evening – Is not humanity disgraced by this barbarity to the dumb creation? – the poor child belongs to a sex sufficiently prone to cruelty: is it for *women* thus early to encourage it? Another, to my thoughts, worse than absurd way they have chose to make him *shine*, – which is, to bid him say the Lords Prayer and Belief in order to display his fine memory – why won't they make him get Ballads by Heart? To sport thus with our religious duties is to me exceedingly shocking, and had I been old enough to dare speak my sentiments unasked, I would have told them so.

13. From Journal *16 November 1770*

Queen's Square, –
I have now changed my abode, and quitted dear Poland Street forever.
How well satisfied shall I be if after having Lived as long in Queen's Square
I can look back to equally happy Days.

We have a charming House here. It is situated at the upper End of the
square, and has a delightful prospect of Hamstead and Hygate, we have
more than room for our Family, large as it is, and all the rooms are well
fitted up, convenient, and handsome.

14. From Journal *March 1772*

[Mr Poggenpohl] then began a comic mock flirtation with little Bessy.[1] – I
could gather by what he said – though all *in badinage*, with what ridicule –
perhaps contempt – he had remarked the prejudiced opinions our Nation
in general entertain of the Russians – the droll absurd account he gave her
of his Country, could have no other meaning.

'Will you not go to Russia with me?' said he – 'O – you will admire it
beyond expression! –' 'No,' cried Bessy, 'I should not, I am sure I should
not like your Country –'

'No! – why?'

'Oh – I don't know! – but I should not like it.'

'O yes, you would; – very much – if you will go with me – you will find
it charming. – You should live in the Woods, with wild Beasts. O yes – you
would like it vastly! – you should always be with a Tyger, or a Lyon, or a
Wolfe – or some such fine Beast –'

'No, no – I won't go –'

'O yes – very agreeable! – and you should live on high mountains, covered
with snow – and sit upon ice. – And you should Eat Trees – and sometimes
Hay; – and you should have Grass and briers for sauce –'

'O no – I should not like it at all –'

'O yes! – very good! – very excellent! – and you should have the sea

---

1. William Henry Poggenpohl was a Russian army officer and diplomat detailed to the Russian
Embassy in London. Bessy was FB's ten-year-old stepsister Elizabeth ('Bessie') Allen.

always before you; and the Waves should dash against you – and you should Dress in Tyger's skins –'

'O no, indeed Sir, I won't go! –'

'O very agreeable! – you will much like my Country.'

'Aren't you a French man? –'

'A French man? – for why do you think me a French man?'

'I don't know, Sir; – because you are one –'

'I a French man! – look at me another Time! – do I look like a French man?'

'Yes, Sir.'

'In what? tell me? –'

'Why I don't know, Sir. – – Because you don't look like an English man –'

'No? – look at me another Time! – why don't I look like an English man? –'

'Why – because an English man don't wear such a thing as this.' Taking hold of his shoulder knot –

'O yes, they do – the English Officer wear all the same – only they have silver, and mine are Gold. And don't you like that?'

'Yes – I like it very well – but an English man does not wear such a Coat as this.'

'O yes – it is only a Uniform – all Officer wear their Uniform. – And now what have I like a French man?'

'Why – this thing here –' taking hold of a Gold tassel hanging to his sword.

'O yes – very common. Nothing in that. And now – look at me another Time –'

'Why *this* is not like an English man –' pointing to the scarf round his Arm.

'O – every Officer wear it – it is only for mourning, for the Princess of Hesse – and it will be soon for the Princess of Wales. –'[2]

Bessy, quite at a loss, broke from him, and ran to Dr King.[3]

'Ah, Mlle,' cried he, 'vous aimez le Docteur mieux que moi, – mais c'est faute de votre bon Gout!'[4]

---

2. Princess Mary, daughter of George II and wife of Friedrich II, Landgrave of Hesse-Cassel, had died on 14 January at Hanau; Augusta, Princess Dowager of Wales, mother of George III and widow of Frederick Lewis, Prince of Wales, had died on 8 February.

3. Revd Dr John Glen King, friend of the Burney family.

4. 'Ah, Miss, . . . you like the Doctor better than me, – but that's because of your good taste!' (French – as are all translations, unless otherwise indicated).

15. From Journal *30 May 1772*

Maria, Susan and myself had the happiness to see Garrick,[1] last Night, in Richard the Third. We had always longed to see him in all his great characters, though least in this which is *so* shocking, though not the least, of the praise of his acting.

Garrick was sublimely horrible! – how he made me shudder whenever he appeared! it is inconceivable, how terribly great he is in this Character. I will never see him so disfigured again – he seemed so truly the monster he performed, that I felt myself glow with indignation every time I saw him. The Applause he met with exceeds all belief of the Absent. I thought, at the End, they would have torn the House down: Our seats shook under us.

16. From Journal *13 February 1773*

We stayed very late, to avoid the Crowd.[1] When we went down, we got with difficulty to our Coach; but, after the usual perils and dangers, we were driven out of the Haymarket, and into Suffolk Street. Here we concluded we were safe, – but, as we afterwards found, there had been left a load of Gravel in the street, which the shade (being moonlight) hid from the Coach man. We found ourselves suddenly mounting on one side – Mama, who is soon alarmed, cried out 'We are going! we are going!' I sat quite quiet, thinking it a false alarm: but presently the Coach was entirely overturned, and we came side ways on the Ground. Stupefied between surprise and fright, I fell without moving a finger, and laid quite silent – the Glass at my side was fortunately down, and the Blind up, which saved my Temples from the Pavement, but the Glass above me broke, and the Pieces fell on me – Mama and Susan both imagined me to be most in danger, from being undermost, and my tender Susan called out to me, repeatedly, 'Fanny, are you hurt? are you *very* much hurt, Fanny? my dear Fanny? – '

It was some time, from an unaccountable effect of fear, before I could

1. The actor David Garrick, in a performance of Shakespeare's play at the Drury Lane Theatre. He was a close friend of the Burneys. FB attended the play with her stepsister Maria Allen and Susanna.

1. FB, with her stepmother and Susanna, had attended a Saturday evening performance at the King's Opera House in Haymarket.

answer; – but the falling of the Glass roused me. – Some People immediately gathered about the Cariage, and, I believe, opened the Door, which was now at the Top of the Coach. Mama called out 'Here's Nobody hurt! – ' but desired them to assist me, – with some difficulty, I made shift to stand up – and a Gentleman lifted me out of the Carriage. He had no Hat on, being come out of a Neighbouring House. He beg'd me to go with him to his sisters, who were close by, that I might get out of the mob, and promised to take care of me: – but I was now terified for Mama and Susan, and could not leave the Place, as, though we were all separated by different Assistants, I heard the former call out that her arm was broken! I quite wrung my Hands with horror – This Gentleman took hold of me, and almost used violence to make me come away – I remember I called out to him, as he forced me on, that he would drive me distracted! – he assured me that the other ladies would be safe; – but as if he had not had trouble enough with me, I answered all his civilities to me, with 'But, go!, why can't you go and help Them?' However he would not leave me, for which I believe I am very much obliged to him, as I was surrounded by a mob, and as there were Assistants enough about the Coach. When Mama and Susan were taken out, we accepted this Gentleman's offer, and went into his House, where we were very hospitably received, by some ladies – my poor mother had her Arm dreadfully hurt. Susan had only sprained two Fingers in supporting herself from falling on us. – My Face was very bloody, from two small Cuts I had received on my Nose. We stayed here near a quarter of an Hour, and met with the utmost kindness and civility.

17. From Journal Letters to Susanna Burney
(Teignmouth Journal) *August–September 1773*[1]

Monday and Tuesday [26–27 July], Mrs R[ishton] and myself spent in the most comfortable manner possible, – but for Wednesday – I must be more particular.

Mr Hurrel[2] has an exceeding pretty Boat of his own here, with which he makes frequent excursions on the River Ting, and sometimes on the sea.

1. In late July 1773 FB journeyed to Teignmouth ('Tingmouth'), Devonshire, to visit Maria and Maria's husband Martin Rishton; they had married in 1772. Teignmouth, at the mouth of the River Teign ('Ting'), was one of the first of the English seaside resort towns. The Rishtons had a cottage near the sea.
2. The Revd Thomas Hurrel, Rector of Drewsteignton, Devonshire.

His Wife called here on Tuesday Evening, to invite us to be of their Party on Wednesday, when they intended sailing to Torbay, to see a Fleet under Admiral Spry, which was just come from Portsmouth. We very gladly accepted the offer, and set off the next morning, about 7 O'clock, our Company consisting of Mr and Mrs Hurrel, Mr Phips,[3] a Boatswain, another sailor, Mr Hurrel's servant and ourselves.

Mr Hurrel is quite a Poet's Priest. He is fat as Falstaff, unable to use exercise and Eke unwilling; his love of ease is surpassed by nothing – but his love of good living, which equals whatever *detraction* has hitherto devised for a Parson's Gluttony.

Mrs Hurrel is an obliging, civil, tiresome Woman.

Our Plan was, to see the Fleet, and if possible, a man of War's *inside*, – and then to land on one of the safest and pleasantest Rocks, to Dine, as Mr Hurrel had taken special care of this particular.

But when we came near the ships, the sea grew rough, and having no invitation, we were obliged to give up the thought of entering any of them. There were 7 men of War in the Bay, and we sailed round them. – They are most noble Vessels. I had reason to think myself very fortunate that I was not sea sick, though I never before was on the ocean. We *put in* at Brixham, a most excellent fishing Town, but very dirty and disagreeable. We made but a short stay, and set sail again. Brixham is about 10 miles from Ting Mouth by sea.

The Wind was against us – and we were hardly out of the Harbour, before we found the sea terribly rough – I own I was not very easy, as our Boat, though a large one for the Thames, was very small for the sea: but still, I considered myself as the Person of the least Consequence, whatever our danger.

However, it was no sport to me to be Danced up and down, and to find the Waves higher and rougher every instant: especially when I saw Mr Hurrel, who had hitherto guided us, quit the Helm to the Boatswain, and exclaim 'We shall run foul of these Rocks!' –

The Waves foamed in little white mountains, rising above the Green surface of the sea – they dashed against the Rocks off the Coast of Brixham with monstrous fury – and really to own the truth, I felt no inclination to be Boat Wrecked, however pathetic and moving a Tale our Adventure might have made.

Mrs Hurrel grasped my hand, and looked very much frightened: her

3. Rear-Admiral Richard Spry; Constantine Phipps, gentleman of Exeter.

agreeable Husband repeated several Times his most comfortable Exclammation of 'We shall run foul of the Rocks! – ' There followed a most terrible
confusion – I don't remember, or understand, sea phrases, but the hurrying,
loud, violent manner in which they gave orders to one another was really
frightful. 'Is there any danger, cried Mrs Hurrel, pray Boatswain, tell me, is
there any danger?' 'No – I don't think there is, Ma'am.'

This was the most alarming sound I had heard yet – *I don't think there is*! –
however, I found we were all in equal danger, for the two sailors assured us
their swimming would be totally useless, as the fury of the Waves would
presently swallow them up.

Mrs Hurrel grasped my Hand harder than ever – her Husband forgot
his *Cloth*, and began to swear, but always adding '*God forgive me*!' – at length,
after being tost up and down in a most terrible manner for about a ¼ of an
Hour, the Boatswain said we should not reach Ting Mouth before mid
night. – And just then, the Waves seemed to redouble their violence, and
the Boat scooped one fairly over us.

I gave up the Ghost: – Mrs Hurrel burst into Tears – and cried vehemently, 'for mercy's sake – Mr Hurrel, pray let us go back to Brixham –
pray do – we shall be all Drowned! O pray don't let me be Drowned! – Set
me down! Set me down!'

'But where are we to *Dine*?' cried he.

'O, any where, Mr Hurrel, – any where, so as we do but get a shore! – I
don't mind, I assure *ee*.'

'O, that's pretty talking – answered he, but that won't serve for a meal. – '

However, I believe he also had no objection to prolong his Days for when
the Boatswain said that it blew *fresher* higher up, he immediately ordered
that we should *tack about*: – and so we returned to Brixham! When we
Landed, I was so very giddy, that I could hardly stand – and was obliged to
go into the first House, for a Glass of Water: but I am only amazed that I
was not dreadfully sea sick.

Saturday morning [31 July], Mrs Rishton and I walked out early to avoid
a very disagreeable scene at Home: for the Day before, Mr Rishton came
Home in a great haste, and perturbation; and, calling his Wife, told her that
he had broke Romeo's Leg! – this was occasioned by the poor Dog's running
after sheep, for which he has often been, in vain, very severely beat: but
now, he and one of the spaniels got a poor sheep quite down, and began to
tear her to Pieces: Mr R. rode up to them, and catching Romeo first, by the
Leg, to prevent his biting, began to flog him violently, till he found that by

the Twist, he had broke his Leg short off. – He was beyond measure concerned, and gave a man a Crown to carry him Home gently in his Arms: and the next morning he had a surgeon to set the poor animal's Leg,

[Friday, 6 August]

The Cricket match was hardly over, before the *Ting Mouth Games* began. All that was to be done this second Day, was Wrestling, a most barbarous Diversion, and which I could not look on, and would not have gone to, if I had not feared being thought affected.

A Ring was formed for the Combattants by a Rope railing from which we stood to see the sport. The Wrestler was to Conquer twice, one opponent immediately after another, to entitle himself to the Prize.

A strong labouring man came off Victorious in the first Battle: but, while his shins were yet bleeding, he was obliged to attack another; the Hat (their Gauntlet) was thrown by a servant of Mr Colbourn's.[4] He was reckoned by the Judges an admirable Wrestler; and he very fairly beat his Adversary: A sailor directly flung his Hat: he was sworn friend of the defeated Labourer: he Entered the Lists in a Passion, and attacked the servant, as all the Gentlemen said, very unfairly: and, while a short Truce was declared for the man to have his shoe unbuckled, he very dishonourably hit him a Violent Blow: upon this, they both prepared for a *Boxing* match – and were upon the Point of Engaging, (though the whole Ring cried out shame upon the sailor) when Mr Rishton, inflamed with a generous rage at this foul Play, rushed precipitately into the Ring, and getting between the Combattants, Collored the sailor, declaring he should be turned out of the Lists.

I am really amazed that he Escaped being ill treated, – but at the same Instant, two of the young Mills[5] ran into the Ring, and catching hold of Mr Rishton, insisted on his not venturing himself against the brutality of the enraged sailor: however, he would not retire, till the sailor was Voted out of the Lists, as a foul Player. Mr Rishton then returned to us, between the Mr Mills. Every body seemed in admiration of the spirit which he exerted on this occasion.

*

4. Benjamin Colborne, formerly an apothecary at Bath, had retired after inheriting an immense fortune and was now on holiday at Teignmouth with his family.
5. Sons of the Revd Dr Jeremiah Milles, Dean of Exeter. He had three sons, Jeremiah, Thomas and Richard, who were all currently students at Oxford University.

We all went on Monday Evening [16 August] to the sea shore, to see the *scene* Drawn: this is a most curious Work: and all done by Women.[6] They have a very long Net, so considerable as to Cost them 13 or 16 pounds – this they first draw into a Boat, which they go off the shore in, and Row in a kind of semi Circle, till they Land at some distance: all the way, they spread this Net, one side of which is kept above Water by Corks. Then they Land, and divide Forces; half of them return to the beginning of the Net, and half remain at the End: and then, with amazing strength, they both *divisions*, at the same Time, pull the Net in, by the two Ends: whatever Fish they catch, are always encircled in the middle of the Net, which comes out of the Water the last; and, as they draw towards each other, they all join in getting their prey: when once they perceive that there is Fish in their Nets, they set up a loud shout, and make an almost unintelligible Noise, in expressing their joy, and in disputing at the same Time upon their shares, and on what Fish Escaped them. They are all robust and well made, and have remarkably beautiful Teeth: and some of them are really very fine Women: their Dress is barbarous: they have stays half Laced, and some thing by way of Handkerchiefs about their Necks, they wear a single colored Flannel, or stuff petticoat; – no shoes or stockings; notwithstanding the hard Pebbles and stones all along the Beach: – and their Coat is Pin'd up in the shape of a pair of trousers, leaving them wholly Naked to the knee.

Mr Western[7] declares he could not have imagined such a Race of Females existed in a Civilized Country – and had he come hither by sea, he should have almost fancied he had been Cast on a new discovered Coast. They caught, this Evening, at one Time 9 large salmon, a John Dory, and a Gurnet: on Tuesday Evening, we went again, and saw them Catch 4 dozen of mackeral at a Haul.

Sunday, [29] August

This morning *all the World* was at Church, as the Dean of Exeter Preached. He gave us an excellent Discourse, which he delivered extremely well. We met all the Family as we came out, and Mr T. Mills joined our party: the morning was lovely, and we took a very pleasant Walk. Mr Rishton proposes

---

6. By *scene* FB means 'seine'. Teignmouth was also an important port in the Newfoundland trade and fisheries, and the women's husbands were now away fishing off Newfoundland.

7. Maximilian Western of Cokethorpe, Oxfordshire, whose wife was a cousin of Martin Rishton.

going to Ivy Bridge or Staverton in a short Time, for a few Days, in order
to Fish: Mr T. Mills invited himself to be of our Party.

We had again the pleasure to hear the Dean in the Afternoon, who gave
us a most admirable sermon on moral Duties. The singing here is the most
extraordinary I ever heard, – there is no Instrument, but the People attempt
to sing in Parts – with such Voices! such expression and such Composition!
They to Day, in honour, I presume, of the Dean, performed an Anthem. It
was really too much to be borne decently – it was set by a Weaver, – and
so very unlike any thing that was ever before imagined, so truly barbarous,
that, with the addition of the singers trilling and squalling, – no Comedy
could have afforded more Diversion: Mrs Rishton and I Laughed ourselves
sick – though we very much endeavoured to be grave – Mr Rishton was
quite offended, and told his Wife that the Eyes of the whole Congregation
were on her – but nothing could restrain us, till the Dean began his prayer
– and there is a something *commanding* in his Voice, that immediately gained
all our Attention.

Sunday, [5] September

This morning we heard Mr Onslow[8] preach. He says he always Travels
with a Brace of sermons, that he may be ready to give occasional assistance
to his Brother Clergymen, when requested. I did not at all admire him, as
he seems to be conceited; and, indeed, the Dean has at present made me
difficult.

After service, the two youngest Mills, and Mr Onslow Called in, to settle
their next shooting party with Mr Rishton. It is amazing what a laborious
business this shooting is: they go out before Breakfast, – after two or 3 Hours
shooting, they get what they can at any Farm House – then toil till 3 or 4
o'Clock, when sometimes they return Home, but if they have any prospect
of more sport, they take *pot luck* at some Cottage, and stay out till 8 or 9
o'Clock. The Weather makes no alteration in their pursuits, – a sportsman
defies Wind, Rain, and all inclemencies of either heat or Cold. As to Mr
Rishton, he seems bent on being proof against every thing; he seeks all kinds
of manly Exercise and grows sun Burnt, strong and hardy.

8. The Revd Arthur Onslow.

18. From Journal *24 November 1773*

[Queen Square]

Since I wrote last, I have myself been ill with a sore Throat, which I believe was the effect of overrating my strength. Dr Fothergill[1] has been my very good friend, and that whether I would or not; he immediately perceived when I was taken ill, and, after seeing Mama, said to me 'I am afraid Thee art not well thyself?' On Examining my Throat, he advised me to be very careful for that it was Catching, the sort which I had, which was the putrid, though in a slight degree. He told me what to take etc., and was most exceeding Attentive to me the whole Time and really, for him, has been amazingly civil and polite to me. But yesterday, after complaining of his fatigue and great business, he turned suddenly to me, and taking my Hand, cried 'My dear, never marry a Physician! If he has but little to do, he may be distressed; if he has much – it is a very uncomfortable life for his Companion.'

He came here several Times before he saw my Father, who, when at Home, is always shut up in his study; but one Evening, when Mama was very ill, being anxious to hear the Doctor's opinion, he came up stairs. He addressed himself, like a man of the World, to the Doctor, – who rose, and with great solemnity said 'I suppose it is Dr Burney that I see?' My Father Bowed, and said he was happy in being known to him – 'I never,' answered he, 'had the satisfaction of seeing Dr Burney before!' 'No, Sir,' said my Father, 'I have always been so unfortunate as to be out when you have been here.' '*Most commonly*,' answered the old Quaker, with a dryness that seemed not to give implicit faith to the assertion. But since this, they have had many Conversations, and are very good friends. And really, with all his stiffness and solemnity, he appears to be as humane as he is skillful.

19. From Letter to Samuel Crisp[1] *December 1773*

The Death of poor Dr Hawkesworth[2] is most sincerely lamented by us all, the more so, as we do really attribute it to the Abuse he has of late met with

---

1. Dr John Fothergill was a celebrated Quaker physician, one of the most forward-looking of his profession.

1. For Crisp, see Introduction, p. xiv.

2. John Hawkesworth, LL.D., miscellaneous writer, another family friend, had died on 17 November. He had published in June *An Account of the Voyages* of the explorers Commodore

from the news papers: his book was dearly purchased, at the price of his Character and peace – and those envious and malignant Witlings who persecuted him, from his gaining money, are now satisfied and silent. You may perhaps doubt of this – but indeed if you had known him more, you would not. He Dined with us about a month before he died – and we all agreed that we never saw a man more Altered – thin, livid – harrassed! He conversed very freely upon the affair of his Book and abuse: my Father told him that there was hardly a man in the kingdom who had never had a Pen in his Hand, who did not think that he could have done it with more propriety – and that his Enemies were all occasioned by his success, for that if he had failed, every one would have said 'Poor man! 'tis an ingenious, well written Book – he deserved more encouragement.' Dr Hawkesworth said that he had not *yet* made any answer to the torrent poured upon him – except to Dalrymple, who had attacked him by Name[3] – he told my Father, that he had earned every thing he possessed by dint of labour and industry, except the last £6000 – that he had had no Education or advantage but what he had given himself: but that he had preserved an unblemished Character and reputation till his last year. – Since when, I believe, he has had reason to detest the Fortune, which only preceded detraction and defamation. He Died of a lingering Fever – which had begun to prey upon him when we last saw him.

20. From Letter to Samuel Crisp *9 February 1774*

Coquetry, I must acknowledge is almost universal – and I know fewer Girls exempt from *that* passion, than from any other. It seems irresistable – I was going to add something of Vanity and love of pleasure – but there is no sort of occasion to make concessions to *you*, who are so little inclined to over rate our merits – I will therefore only say, that though I readily allow you a *general*

Byron, Captain Wallis, Captain Byron and Captain Cook, drawn up from their journals and from the papers of Joseph Banks, who had accompanied Cook. Hawkesworth was excoriated in the newspapers for the huge sum (£6,000) he had received from the publishers, for alleged factual and textual exaggerations and inaccuracies, for religious impiety and for indecently frank descriptions of the sexual habits of the South Sea islanders. Though he was certainly ill, it was even rumoured that mental distress had caused him to take an overdose of opium.

3. Alexander Dalrymple, hydrographer to the Admiralty, had published an open *Letter . . . to Dr Hawkesworth, Occasioned by Some Groundless and Illiberal Imputations in his Account of the Late Voyages to the South* (1773).

superiority over us in most other particulars, yet in constancy, Gratitude and Virtue, I regard you as unworthy all competition or comparison. The flights and failings of Women are oftener from some defect in the *Head* than the *Heart*, which is just reversed by you – so that where we are *Weak*, you are *Wicked* – Now which is least justifiable?

21. From Journal *May 1774*

We had a good deal of Conversation upon Lord Chesterfield's Letters, which I have just read.[1] I had the satisfaction to find that our opinions exactly coincided – that they were extremely well written, contained some excellent *hints* for Education – but were written with a tendency to make his son a man wholly unprincipled; inculcating immorality; countenancing all *Gentlemanlike* vices; *advising* deceit; and *exhorting* to Inconstancy.[2]

'It pleased me much,' said Mr Hutton, 'in speaking to the King[3] about these Letters, to hear him say – "*For my part, I like more streight forward work.*" '

22. From Journal *July 1774*

But now let me come to a matter of more importance, and at the same Time more pleasure. My Brother[1] is returned; – in Health, spirits and Credit. He has made what he calls a very fine Voyage; – but it must have been very dangerous: indeed he has had several *personal* Dangers – and in these Voyages of hazard and Enterprise so I imagine, must every Individual of the ship.

Captain Cooke was parted from in bad weather accidentally[2] – in the

---

1. The famous letters of Philip Dormer Stanhope, Earl of Chesterfield, to his natural son Philip Stanhope, had been recently published by Philip's widow following the death of the Earl in 1773. FB's conversation was with James Hutton, founder of the Moravian Church in England, whom she had recently met.

2. Cf. Samuel Johnson's oft-quoted judgement that Chesterfield's letters taught 'the morals of a whore, and the manners of a dancing master' (*Life of Johnson*, i. 266).

3. George III.

1. FB's elder brother, James ('Jem') Burney, second lieutenant in the Royal Navy, had accompanied Captain Cook on his second voyage of discovery (see p. 23 note 2).

2. Cook's ship, *Resolution*, and the accompanying ship, *Adventure*, commanded by Tobias Furneaux, had become separated. James had started the voyage on board *Resolution* but had been transferred to *Adventure*.

passage from the Society Isles to New Zealand, in the second and so fatal Visit which they made to that Barbarous Country, where they lost 10 men in the most inhuman manner.

My Brother, unfortunately for himself, was the witness and Informer of that horrid massacre.

Mr Rowe, the acting Lieutenant, a midshipman, and 8 men, were sent from the ship, in a Boat to shore, to get some vegetables. The whole ship's Company had Lived so long upon good terms with the New Zealanders, that there was no suspicion of treachery or ill usage. They were ordered to return at 3 o'clock; but upon their failure, Capt. Furneaux sent a Launch, with Jem to Command it, in search of them. They Landed at 2 places without seeing any thing of them – they went among the people and bought Fish – and Jem says he imagined they were gone further up the Country, but never supposed how *very* long a way they were gone. At the 3d place – it is almost too terrible to mention – they found –[3]

23. From Journal Letter to Susanna Burney *28 September 1774*

[Chessington]

I have almost, though very undesignedly, occasioned a *grand fracas* in the House, by a ridiculous conceit which I *sported* for the amusement of Miss Simmons and Kitty.[1] We had been laughing at some of poor Mrs Moone's queer phrases, and then I mentioned some of Kitty's own, – her Cousin joined in laughing violently, and as I proceeded from one absurd thing to another, I took Miss Simmons herself to task upon some speeches she had made; and in conclusion, I told them that I intended to write *a Treatise upon politeness* for their Edification. All this was taken as it was said, *in sport*, and

3. There follows a blank half page in the journal; FB probably intended to supply details of what James and his party found, but was rather squeamish. Upon landing in Grass Cove they came upon the partial remains of Rowe and his crew, who had been massacred and eaten by the Maoris. Despite James's disclaimer of tension between the ship's company and the natives, the attack was the culmination of increasing hostility, the immediate spark probably being a quarrel over the Maoris' theft of food.

1. FB and CB were on a visit to Crisp at Chessington Hall in Chessington, Surrey. Chessington Hall was a boarding house kept by Papilian Catherine ('Kitty') Cooke and her aunt Sarah Hamilton. Other boarders besides Crisp included Kitty Cooke's cousin Mrs Moone and Mlle Rosat. Other visitors present included 'cousins' Mrs Elizabeth Symons ('Simmons') and her daughter 'Miss Simmons' (Mrs Moone's sister and niece), and Mlle Courvoisyois, Swiss friend of Mlle Rosat.

we had much diversion in consequence of my scheme, which I accompanied by a thousand flighty speaches and *capricios*.

After this, upon all indecorums, real or fanciful, I referred Miss Simmons and Kitty to my Book for Instruction – and it became a sort of standard among us, to which we made every thing that passed applicable, and Miss Simmons, who enjoyed hearing me *run on*, as she called it, introduced the subject perpetually. Indeed the chief amusement I have made myself when with the two Cousins, has been in indulging liberally in that kind of Rhodomantide[2] Discourse, that it will be easy to you to recollect some Instances of.

All this did very well among ourselves; – but the Day after the Simmons left us, while we were at Dinner, Kitty blundered out 'Good people I tell you what; – *she's* going to write something about politeness, *and that*, and it's to be for all of you, here at *chiss* [Chessington], to mind your manners.'

'I'm sure,' cried Mlle Courvoisyois, 'we shall be very much *obligé* to the lady.'

'I'll subscribe to the Book with all my Heart,' cried Mlle Rosat. 'I beg leave to bespeak the first Copy. I am sure it will be a very useful Work.'

'She's to tell you all what you're to do,' resumed Kitty, 'and how you're to do this – and all that.'

'Exceedingly well defined, Kate.' said Mr Crisp, 'but pray, Fannikin, what shall you *particularly* treat of?'

'O Sir,' cried I, 'all parts of life! it will be a very comprehensive work. – And I hope you'll all have a copy.'

'Pray what will it cost?' demanded Mrs Moone, seriously.

'A Guinea a Volume,' answered I, 'and I hope to comprize it in 9 Volumes.'

'O lord!' exclaimed she, 'I shan't give *no such money* for it.'

'*I* will have 2 Copies,' said Mlle Rosat, 'let it Cost what it will. I am sure it will be exceeding well Executed.'

'I don't doubt *in least*,' cried Mlle Courvoisyois, 'of politeness of Miss Burney – but I should like to see the Book, to see if I should *sought* the same.'

'Will it be like Swift's Polite Conversation?'[3] said Mr Crisp.

'I intend to Dedicate it to Miss Notable,' answered I. 'It will contain all *the newest fashioned* regulations. In the first place, you are never again to Cough.'

---

2. Properly 'rodomontade', boastful or bragging talk.
3. Three dialogues published by Jonathan Swift in 1738. 'Miss Notable' is one of the participants.

'Not to *Cough?*' exclaimed every one at once, 'but how are you to help it?'

'As to *that*,' answered I, 'I am not very clear about it myself, as I own I am guilty sometimes of doing it. But it is as much a mark of ill breeding as it is to *Laugh*, which is a thing that Lord Chesterfield has stigmatized.'[4]

'Indeed! – well, for my part,' said Mrs Moone, 'I think there's no fun without it.'

'Not for to *Laugh!*' exclaimed Courvoisyois, with Hands uplifted – 'well, I declare I *did* not *sought* of such a *sing!*'

'And pray,' said Mr Crisp, making a fine affected Face, 'may you *simper?*'

'You may *smile*, Sir,' answered I. 'But to *laugh* is quite abominable. Though not quite so bad as *sneezing*, or *blowing the Nose.*'

'Why, if you don't blow it,' cried Kitty, taking me literally, 'what *are* you to do with it, don't you think it nastier *not* to?'

I pretended to be too much shocked to answer her.

'But pray, is it permitted,' said Mr Crisp, very drily, 'to *Breathe?*'

'*That* is not yet, I believe, quite exploded.' answered I, 'but I shall be more exact about it in my Book, of which I shall send *you* six Copies. I shall only tell you in general, that whatever is Natural, plain or easy, *is* entirely banished from polite Circles.'

'And all is sentiment and *Delicacy*, hay Fannikin?'

'No, Sir, not so,' replied I, with due gravity, '*sentiments* and *sensations* were the *last* fashion; they are now done with – they were *laughed* out of use, just before laughing was abolished. The *present Ton*[5] is *refinement*; – nothing *is to be*, that *has been*; all things are to be *new polished*, and *highly finished*. I shall explain this fully in my Book.'

'Well, for my part,' cried Mrs Moone, who took every word I said seriously, 'I don't desire to read *no* such *tiddling* Books. I'm very well as I am.'

It's well you think so. thought I.

'Pray ma'am,' said Mlle Rosat, 'is it within the Rules of politeness to *pick the Teeth?*'

'Provided you have a little *Glass* to look in before you.' answered I, and rose to go up stairs to my Father. –

'And pray, Ma'am,' cried she again, 'is it polite, when a person talks, if you don't understand them, to look at another as if you said "what Nonsence she says!"'

---

4. Chesterfield asserted in his letters (see selection 21 and note) that a gentleman never laughed, though he might occasionally smile.
5. *Fashion.*

'I should imagine not.' answered I, moving off, alarmed, as I found these Questions were *pointed* against poor Kitty.

'Pray is it polite, Ma'am,' cried Mlle Rosat again, 'to make *signs* and to *whisper?*'

'I suppose not.' cried I, opening the Door.

'And *pray*,' cried Kitty colouring, 'is it *pelite* to be *touchy*? And *has* people any business to suspect, and to be suspicious?'

'O,' cried I, 'these are things that don't come into my Cognisance –' and away I ran.

My Father, however, sent me down again to ask Mr Crisp up stairs to play at Back Gammon. I found them all silent. Mr Crisp went up immediately, and presently every body went out but Kitty, Courvoisyois, and me.

I told Kitty, who I saw was swelling with anger, that I began to be sorry she had mentioned the Book – 'O, – it does not signify,' – cried she, bursting into a violent fit of Tears – 'I don't mind – if people will be cross – it's nothing to *me* – I'm sure I'm as obliging as I can – and if people don't like me, they must let it alone.' –

We tried to pacify her. Courvoisyois gave her a Glass of wine, and insisted on her Drinking it – 'I did not *sought*,' said she, 'that Miss Rosat did mean you – I am sure she always says you are very good –'

'You're very obliging, Miss *Crewe*,' cried Kitty, sobbing, 'but I can *see*, as well as other people – and I know what Miss *Rossiter* meant –' (N.B. She calls her *Rossiter*, no one knows why, not even herself) 'because the thing was, that one Day my Cousin and I were together, and so *Rossiter* came in – and I'm sure I did not more than I do at this moment – my Cousin can witness for me – but she went out of the Room in a huff, Nobody knows for what, – and then afterwards, she goes and tells my aunt that when she came into the Room, I said *Humph*! – now I *purtest* I never said *no* such a thing, – and so my Cousin would say, if she was here – for I should scorn it – and though I a'n't so *pelite* as Miss *Rossiter*, I'm sure I always try to be as obliging as I can, and if ever she wants any thing, at any Time, I'm always ready to go for her.'

'I'm sure I always *hear* her say so, Miss Cooke,' cried Courvoisyois, 'I *sink* you are certainly *of* a mistake.'

I was very glad *she* spoke, as *I* could not, for the account of the cause of the disagreement was told so very ridiculously, that it required a painful effort to forbear laughing out – it was all I could do: however, after some Time, we consoled her, and made her dry her Tears, which she did, all the

while protesting *that she 'would not say such a thing as Humph* for the World,' –
and that 'Nobody was *further from it.'*

They are now upon very good terms again. Poor Kitty has as honest and
worthy a Heart as any human Being, and cannot bear to be thought ill of.
Yet I can never cease to be astonished that she can have Lived so many
years under the same Roof with such a man as Mr Crisp, and yet be so *very*
unformed.

24. From Letter to Samuel Crisp *1 December 1774*

St. Martin's Street[1]
Thursday Night

My Brother [James] went last Monday to the play of Isabella[2] at Drury
Lane, – he sat in one of the Upper Boxes, from whence he spied Omai and
Mr Banks[3] – Upon which, he crossed over to speak to his friend. Omai
received him with a hearty shake of the Hand, and made room for him by
his side.

On Tuesday night, very late, there came a note which I will write down.
It was directed to my Brother. – Omai presents his Compts to Mr Burney.
And if it is agreeable and convenient to him, he will do himself the Honour
of Dining with Mr Burney to morrow. But if it is not so, Omai will wait
upon Mr Burney some other Time that shall suit him better. Omai begs to
have an answer, and that if he is to come, begs Mr Burney will fetch him.

Early on Wednesday morning, Jem called at Mr Banks, with my Father's
Compts to him and to Dr Solander,[4] and begging their company also. But
they were Engaged at the Royal Society.

Mr Strange and Mr Hayes,[5] at their own motion, came to Dinner to

1. Because of difficulties with the title to their Queen Square house, the Burney family moved in
October 1774 to a house in St Martin's Street, just off Leicester Square; it had once belonged to
Sir Isaac Newton. CB and his wife would remain there until 1789.
2. *Isabella, or the Fatal Marriage* by David Garrick (from Thomas Southerne's play), first performed
in 1758.
3. Omai was a native of Raiatea near Tahiti, who had been brought to England on board the
Adventure. He was introduced to the King and fêted by London society as the seeming incarnation
of the 'Noble Savage'. He and James Burney had become friends on the voyage home. Joseph
(later Sir Joseph) Banks was the famous naturalist and future President of the Royal Society who
had accompanied Captain Cook on his first circumnavigation of the globe (1768–71).
4. Dr Daniel Carl Solander, Swedish botanist who had gone on Cook's first voyage as Banks's
companion.
5. Robert Strange and John Hayes, friends of CB.

meet our Guest. We did not Dine till 4, but Omai came at 2, and Mr Banks and Dr Solander brought him, in order to make a short visit to my Father. They were all just come from the House of Lords, where they had taken Omai to hear the King make his speech from the Throne.[6]

For my part, I had been confined Up stairs for 3 Days – however, I was much better, and obtained leave to come down, though very much wrapt up, and *quite a figure*. But I did not chuse to appear till Mr Banks and Dr Solander were gone. I found Omai seated on the Great Chair, and my Brother next to him, and talking Otaheite as fast as possible. You cannot suppose how fluently and easily Jem speaks it. Mama and Susy were opposite. As soon as there was a *cessation* of talk, Jem Introduced me, and told him I was another sister. He rose, and made a very fine Bow. And then seated himself again. But when Jem went on, and told him that I was not well, he again directly rose, and muttering something of the *Fire*, in a very polite *manner*, without *speech* insisted upon my taking his seat, – and he *would* not be refused. He then drew his chair next to mine, and looking at me with an expression of pity, said 'very well to *morrow-morrow*?' – I imagine he meant *I hope* you will be very well in *two or 3 morrows*. – And when I shook my Head, he said '*No*? *O very bad*!' –

When Mr Strange and Mr Hayes were Introduced to him, he paid his Compliments with great politeness to them, which he has found a method of doing without *words*.

As he had been to Court, he was very fine. He had on a suit of Manchester velvet, Lined with white satten, a *Bag*, lace Ruffles, and a very handsome sword which the King had given to him. He is tall and very well made. Much Darker than I expected to see him, but had a pleasing Countenance.

He makes *remarkably* good Bows – not for *him*, but for *any body*, however long under a Dancing Master's care. Indeed he seems to shame Education, for his manners are so extremely graceful, and he is so polite, attentive, and easy, that you would have thought he came from some foreign Court. You will think that I speak in a *high* style; but I assure you there was but one opinion about him.

At Dinner I had the pleasure of sitting next to him, as my Cold kept me near the Fire. The moment he was helped, he presented his plate to me, which, when I declined, he had not the *over shot* politeness to offer *all around*, as I have seen some people do, but took it quietly Again. He Eat heartily, and committed not the slightest blunder at Table, niether did he do any

6. To open the new session of Parliament.

thing *awkwardly* or *ungainly*. He found by the turn of the Conversation, and some wry faces, that a Joint of Beef was not roasted enough, and therefore when he was helped, he took great pains to assure mama that he liked it, and said two or three Times '*very dood* – very *dood.*' It is very odd, but true, that he can pronounce the *th*, as in *Thank you*, and the *W*, as in *well*, and yet cannot say *G*, which he uses a *d* for.

He took a good deal of Notice of Dick, yet was not quite so well pleased with him as I had expected him to be.[7]

During Dinner, he called for some Drink. The man, not understanding what he would have, brought the Porter. We saw that he was wrong. However, Omai was too well bred to send it back. He took it in his Hand, and the man then brought him the small Beer; – he laughed, and said 'Two!' – however, he sent off the *small* Beer, as the *worse* of the *two*. Another Time, he called for *port wine*. And when the Bread was Handed, he took two Bits and laughed and said '*one – two.*' –

He even observed *my abstinence*, which I think you would have laughed at, for he turned to me with some surprise, when Dinner was almost over, and said '*No wine?*'

Mr Hayes asked him, through Jem, how he liked the King and his speech. He had the politeness to try to answer in English, and *to* Mr Hayes – and said '*very well, King George!*'

After Dinner, mama gave the King for a Toast. He made a Bow, and said '*Thank you, Madam,*' and then *tost off King George!*

He told Jem that he had an Engagement at 6 o'clock, to go with Dr Solander to see no less than 12 Ladies. – Jem translated this to us – he understands enough of English to find out when he is talked of, in general, and so he did now, and he laughed heartily, and began to Count, with his Fingers, in order to be understood – '1. 2. 3. 4. 5. 6. 7. 8. 9. 10. – *twelve – Woman!*' said he.

When Mr Banks and Dr Solander went away, he said to them *good bye – good bye.*

He never looked at his Dress, though it was on for the first Time. Indeed he appears to be a perfectly rational and intelligent man, with an understanding far superiour to the common race of *us cultivated gentry*: he could not else have borne so well the way of Life into which he is thrown.

---

7. Richard Thomas ('Dick') Burney, FB's six-year-old half-brother, was the spoiled darling of the family. He was a very pretty child by English standards, but may not have seemed so appealing to a South Sea islander. (See also selection 236 and note 2.)

When the man brought him the *two* Beers, I forgot to mention that in returning them, one hit against the other, and occasioned a little sprinkling. He was *shocked* extremely – indeed I was afraid for his fine Cloaths, and would have pin'd up the wet Table Cloth, to prevent its hurting them – but he would not permit me; and, by his *manner* seemed to *intreat* me not to trouble myself! – however, he had thought enough to spread his Napkin wider over his knee.

Before 6, the Coach came. Our man said 'Mr Omai's servant.' He heard it at once, and answered *'very well.'* He kept his seat about 5 minutes after, and then rose and got his Hat and sword. My Father happening to be talking to Mr Strange, Omai stood still, niether chusing to interrupt him, nor to make his Compliments to any body else first. When he was disengaged, Omai went up to him, and made an exceeding fine Bow, – the same to mama – then seperately to every one in the company, and then went out with Jem to his Coach.

He must certainly possess an uncommon share of observation and attention. I assure you every body was delighted with him. I only wished I could have spoken his Language. His *Hands* are very much *tattooed*, but his Face is not at all. He is *by no means* handsome, though I like his *Countenance*.

The Conversation of our House has turned ever since upon Mr *Stanhope* and *Omai* – the 1st with all the advantage of Lord Chesterfield's Instructions, brought up at a great school, Introduced at 15 to a court,[8] taught all possible accomplishments from an Infant, and having all the care, expence, labour and benefit of the best Education that any man can receive, – proved after it all a meer *pedantic Booby*: – the 2d with no Tutor but Nature, changes after he is grown up, his Dress, his way of Life, his Diet, his Country and his friends; – and appears in a *new world* like a man who had all his life studied *the Graces*, and attended with unremitting application and diligence to form his manners, to render his appearance and behaviour *politely easy*, and *thoroughly well bred*: I think this shews how much more *Nature* can do without *art*, than *art* with all her refinement, unassisted by *Nature*.

---

8. Philip Stanhope was educated at Westminster School and presented at the Court of Dresden in 1748.

25. From Journal *28 February 1775*

Yesterday morning, my mother, Susan and self, accompanied by Mr Twining, went to Sir Joshua Reynolds' to see his Pictures.[1] We were very much delighted; the ease and elegance of this Painter seem unrivalled among English Artists.

But what most delighted me, was the beautiful Mrs Sheridan, who is taken seated at a Harp, a whole Figure, in Character of Saint Cecelia, a denomination she greatly merits.[2] My Father is to supply Sir Joshua with some Greek music to place before her.

We then went to Miss Reid,[3] to see her paintings, which, in Crayons, seem nearly to reach perfection; their not standing appears to me the only inferiority they have to Oil Colours: while they are new, nothing can be so soft, so delicate, so blooming.

26. From Letter to Samuel Crisp *2 March 1775* and *Journal* 1775

Signora Agujari, detta Bastardini, sent very particular Compliments to my Father by Dr Matty, of the [British] Museum, regretting that she had not seen him when he was Abroad, and very much desiring to be Introduced to his Acquaintance.[1] It was somewhat remarkable, that this is the second Capital Female singer who has sent to *solicit* my Father's Acquaintance.

An Evening was accordingly appointed, and Mr Burney and Hetty came

---

1. The Revd Thomas Twining, Curate of Fordham, Essex, one of the most learned men of his day, assisted CB in the preparation of his *General History of Music* (4 vols., 1776–89). Sir Joshua Reynolds, President of the Royal Academy, was the pre-eminent portrait painter of his day. He lived near the Burneys in Leicester Square.
2. Elizabeth Linley was a famous beauty and talented singer who gave up her career upon marrying the playwright Richard Brinsley Sheridan. St Cecilia is the patron saint of music. FB had originally written 'Harpsichord', which she later emended to 'Harp', but Mrs Sheridan is actually seated at an organ (which St Cecilia was supposed to have invented). The painting is in the collection of Waddesdon Manor, Buckinghamshire.
3. Catherine Read, fashionable painter in crayons and oils.

1. Lucrezia Aguiari (Agujari) was a celebrated Italian soprano, praised by Mozart, who was beginning a two-year visit to London. She was called 'La Bastardina' or 'La Bastardella' because of her alleged illegitimate birth. Dr Matthew Maty was principal librarian of the British Museum. CB had been in Italy in 1770.

here to meet this *silver side* lady, who is reckoned, next to Gabriella the greatest singer in the world.[2]

Dr Matty, who is a little, formal man, very civil, and very affected, Handed the Bastardini into the Room, she is of middle stature, and a little Lame; she has a very good Complection, and was *well*, not *absurdly*, Painted; she has fine, expressive, languishing Eyes, and all together is a handsome Woman, and appears about 4 or 5 and Twenty.

She was Accompanied by Signor Colla, who is maître de musique à la Cour at Parma,[3] and who attends her in her Travels, and is, like her, pensioned by the Duke. He is a Tall, thin, spirited Italian, full of fire, and not wanting in Grimace.

We were all of us excessively eager to hear her sing, but as it was not convenient to offer her her Pantheon-price of 50 Guineas a song,[4] we were rather fearful of asking that favour: however, my Father ventured to hint at it to Signor Colla; who told us that she certainly *would* sing – *but* that she had a bad cold, and slight sore Throat!

As to Signor Colla, he was *so* Civil to my Father! talked so much of his *Fame* Abroad, and of the *ardent* Desire which he had of the *Honour* of knowing so *celebrated* a person! It seems he Composes for Agujari, who he suffers not to sing any music but his own. He talked of *her* as of the greatest Wonder of the World, – '*c'est une prodige!*'[5] He said that Nature had been so very lavish of its gifts to her, that he had had hardly any trouble in teaching her – every thing was ready done!

One very ridiculous circumstance I cannot forebear mentioning: Susette had, I know not how, understood by Dr Maty, that Signora Agujari was married to Signor Colla: This she told to Hetty and me, and we therefore concluded that it was only a *foreign* custom, that she still kept her name; as it is the case with many other singers. Well, when my sister was asked to play, she pleaded want of Practice, and said to Agujari that she had other Things to mind than Harpsichords. –[6]

2. Agujari was alleged to have a silver plate in her side, as a result of having been mauled as an infant by a hog or a dog. Caterina Gabrielli, another eminent Italian soprano, made her London debut later this year.

3. Giuseppe Colla, Italian composer, 'master of music at the Court' of Parma.

4. Agujari was contracted to sing in the rotunda of the Pantheon, a new and elegant building in Oxford Street, where concerts, masquerades and other large assemblies were held.

5. '*She's a prodigy!*'

6. Esther Burney had been a child prodigy on the harpsichord, but played only occasionally at private gatherings after her marriage. Her husband was a professional musician and keyboard virtuoso.

'Et qu'avez vous donc, Mlle?' demanded the Bastardini. 'Des Enfans!'[7] answered Hetty. 'Ah Diable!' exclaimed she, (for that is her favourite Exclammation) 'et vous etes si juine encore! and combien en avez vous?'

'J'en ai trois.' answered Hetty –

'Ah Diable! C'est bien extraordinaire!'

'Avez *vous* une Enfant?' asked Hetty, –

She stared – and after some Gestures of surprise, said 'Moi! – je ne suis pas mariée, moi!'

Hetty was quite confounded, – she begged her pardon, and said 'mais en verité j'ai toujours cru que ce monsieur étoit votre epoux!'

'Non, Mlle' answered the Bastardini, 'c'est mon maître.'[8] And looked very dignified.

This was a very ridiculous mistake, however, she took it good naturedly, and without being offended, as it was evident that it was not designed.

Dr Maty has assured us that she bears an unexceptionable character,[9] and that she is therefore visited by his Wife and Daughters. She has been strongly recommended to him from abroad.

Her Behaviour was very *proper*, and she displayed none of her airs, though it was not difficult to see that she *could* behave otherwise; for she betrayed, perhaps involuntarily, a consciousness of her greatness, superiority and consequence by a thousand little speeches and looks. I believe that she allows *Gabriella* to be a *Rival*; all the rest of the world she holds in Contempt. She has not even the curiosity to *hear* any singing but her own. She said she had not been once to the opera; and when we asked her if she had ever heard Rausini,[10] she answered 'No! mais on dit qu'il Chante joliment.'![11] My Father asked her how she liked *Galluci*, a new woman who sings at the Pantheon, as well as Agujari. She answered that she had never heard her! that she went into her own Room the moment she had done singing herself. How conceitedly incurious!

'Mais vous, monsieur,' said she, 'vous avez entendu la Gabriella? n'est-ce pas?'

My Father told her that Gabriella was in Sicily when he was in Italy,

7. Hannah Maria ('Marianne'), three years old; Richard Allen, two; and Charles Crisp, one.
8. 'And so what do you have, Miss?' . . . 'Children!' . . . 'The Devil! . . . and you are still so young! and how many do you have?' 'I have three.' . . . 'The Devil! That's extraordinary!' 'Do *you* have a child?' . . . 'Me! – but I'm not married!' . . . 'but in truth I thought that this gentleman [Colla] was your husband!' 'No, Miss . . . he's my [music] master.'
9. The irony of this scene is that Colla was Agujari's secret lover. They married in 1780.
10. Venanzio Rauzzini, prominent singer and composer.
11. 'No! but they say he's a pretty singer.'

and therefore he could not hear her. 'No?' said she, 'mais vraiment c'est dommage!'[12]

My Father then asked if *she* had heard her?

'O no,' she said, and Signor Colla added that they two could never be in the same place together.

'Two suns,' said Dr Maty, 'never appear at once.'

'O, ce n'est pas possible!'[13] cried Agujari, composedly.

———

This singer is really a *slave* to her Voice; she fears the least Breath of air – she is equally apprehensive of Any heat – she seems to have a perpetual anxiety lest she should take Cold; and I do believe she niether Eats, Drinks, sleeps or Talks, without considering in what manner she may perform those vulgar duties of Life so as to be most beneficial to her Voice. However, there are so few who are gifted with eminent Talents, that it is better to cultivate them even labouriously, than to let them suffer Injury from Carelessness or Neglect.[14]

27. Journal *4 March 1775*

I had Yesterday the Honour of Drinking Tea in Company with his *Abyssinian majesty*, for so Mrs Strange Calls Mr Bruce.[1]

My mother and I went to Mr Stranges, by Appointment to meet Mr and Mrs Turner of Lynn,[2] who are lately become acquainted in that Family, and who are in Town for the Winter. And this majestic Personage Chanced to be there.

He has been Acquainted intimately with Mrs Strange all his Life, and is very much attached to her and her Family. He seldom passes a Day without Visiting her; but Miss Strange,[3] who has told me of many of his singularities,

---

12. 'But you, Sir, . . . you have heard the Gabriella? haven't you?' . . . 'No? . . . but truly that's a shame!'

13. 'Oh, that's not possible!'

14. This paragraph is taken from a parallel account of Agujari's visit in FB's journal for 1775.

1. James Bruce, African explorer, was called 'Abyssinian' Bruce because of his pioneer travels in that country from 1769 to 1772.

2. Catherine Turner, born Allen, was a sister or sister-in-law of Elizabeth Burney. Her husband, Charles Turner, had been Mayor of Lynn and became Collector of Customs there.

3. Mary Bruce Strange, the Stranges' elder daughter.

says that he is generally put into a *pet* when they have any Company, as his excessive haughtiness prevents his being sociable with them, and makes him think them impertinant if they take the liberty to speak to him.

Indeed, she also told me, he has been really very ill used from the effects of curiosity, for many people gathered anecdotes and observations from him, and then printed them. This, as he intends to publish his Travels himself, was most abominably provoking.[4]

But it is not enough to say that this has put him *upon his Gaurd*, it has really made him shy of being asked how he does? or what's o'clock? – Haughty by Nature, his extraordinary Travels, and perhaps his long Residence among savages, have contributed to render him one of the most imperious of men. He is, indeed, far the most so of any that *I* ever saw.

He is more than six foot high, is extremely well proportioned in shape, and has a handsome and expressive Face. If his *vanity* were half as great as his *pride*, he would certainly become more courteous if he knew how much smiles become him, for when he *is* pleased to soften the severity of his Countenance, and to suffer his Features to relax into smiling, he is quite another Creature.

Mr Bruce, as my Father did not accompany us, I doubt not wished himself alone with the Stranges, for he looked so important, that he awed almost into total silence Mr and Mrs Turner, who secretly wished the same for themselves. Mr Turner, who is a very *Jocular* man, could not bear to be deprived of his Laugh, and yet had not courage sufficient to venture at Joking before so terrible a personage, who looks as if Born to command the World! Besides, he had heard so much of his Character before they met, that he was *prepared* to fear him. And Mrs Turner is too little used to the Company of strangers, to be at her Ease when in it.

As to my little self, I sat next to Miss Strange, and was comfortable enough in Conversing with her: till my mother, finding herself little Noticed by the Great Man, quitted her seat, and went and placed herself next to Mrs Turner, saying 'Well, I shall come and sit by you, and leave Mr Bruce to the young lassies.'

I do heartily hate these sort of speeches, which *oblige* one to be remarked; nothing can be more provoking. Mr Bruce, accordingly, turning towards

---

4. Bruce did not publish his *Travels* until 1790. His veracity about certain native customs was questioned by a public made sceptical by the extravagant claims of earlier travel writers who invented details to make their books sell better (or who simply wished to hoax their readers). Bruce, whose account was substantially truthful, took offence and delayed the publication.

me, said 'Well, Miss Burney, I think you can do no less than take the seat your Mama has left.'

I did not half like it, but thought he would suppose me *afraid* of him, if I refused, so I changed Chairs; but made Miss Strange move next to me, and then renewed our Conversation, lest he should think himself obliged to take further Notice of me.

An Advertisement had been put in the Papers the Evening before, which said that Mr Bruce was *Dying* or *Dead*; my Father, who knew he was well, wafered the paragraph upon a sheet of paper, and sent to his Lodgings. My mother asked him if he had seen it? 'I thought,' answered he, 'it had come from *Brucey*' (for Miss Strange, who was Christianed *Bruce*, he always calls *Brucey*). 'Yes, I saw it, and Read my Death with great Composure.' Then turning himself to me, he added 'Was not you sorry, Miss Burney, to Read of my Death?'

These immense sized men speak to young Women as if they were Children; I answered that as my Father had seen him the Day before, I was not much *alarmed*. Mr Turner, then, gathering Courage, said 'Well, Sir, I think as Times go, it is very well that when they killed you, they said no ill of you.'

'I know of no reason they had to do otherwise,' answered Mr Bruce, so haughtily, that Mr Turner, failing in his first attempt, never afterwards spoke to him. – Or indeed again dared to open his mouth.

Soon after, a servant came in with General Melville's[5] Compliments, and a desire to know if it was true that Mr Bruce was Dangerously ill? Mr Bruce answered drily, 'Yes, – tell him I am Dead.'

'Ah poor soul!' cried Mrs Strange, 'I dare say he has been vexed enough! Honest man! I don't think that man ever wronged or deceived a human Being!'

'Don't you, faith?' cried Mr Bruce: 'that's saying more than I would! Can you really suppose he has risen to the Rank of General with so little trouble?'

'O, you know, it's only the *Women* that are ever deceived; and for my part, I never allowed that the best among you could deceive *me*, for whenever you say pretty Things to me, I make it a Rule to *believe* them to be true!'

Bell Strange[6] then carried him his Tea; she is about 12 years old. Mr Bruce turning to me, said 'Do you know, Miss Burney, that I intend to run

5. Major-General Robert Melville of the British Army.
6. Isabella Katherina Strange, the younger daughter.

away with Bell? We are to go to Scotland together. She won't let me rest till I take her.'

'How can you say so, Sir?' cried Bell, 'pray, Ma'am, don't believe it,' colouring, and much fidgetted.

'Why, how now, Bell,' returned he, 'what! won't you go?'

'No, Sir.'

'This is the first lady,' said Mr Bruce, rising, 'who ever refused me!' Then addressing Mrs Strange, he asked her if she had heard of Lord Rosemary lately? They then joined in drawing a most odious character of him, especially for avarice; after which, Mr Bruce walking up to me, said 'And yet *this man is my Rival*!' 'Really?' cried I, 'I am sure I wonder that he should venture –' (I *meant* upon account of his prodigious Figure) 'O,' answered he, thinking I meant a compliment, 'it's really true! Mrs Strange, is it not that he is my Rival?' 'O yes, they say so.' said she.[7]

'I am surprised that he *dares*,' said my mother, 'be Rival to Mr Bruce, for I wonder he does not apprehend that his long residence in Egypt made him so acquainted with magic, that –'

'O!' cried Mr Bruce, 'I shall not poison him! – but I believe that I shall Bribe his servant to fasten a string across his stair Case, by which, as I dare say the miser never uses a Candle to Light him, he may fall down and Break his Neck.'[8]

He then asked Miss Strange how she could let her Harpsichord be so much out of order? 'I went down,' said he, 'to try it, but upon my Word it is too bad to be touched: However, while I was at it, in comes Bell, and seats herself quietly behind me; but no sooner did I rise, then away she flew down a flight of stairs, quite to the Cellar, I suppose; expecting, no doubt, that I should follow! but,' added he drily, 'I did not. Well, Bell, what do you *Glowr* at? (I don't know if I spell the word right) do you understand Scotch, Miss Burney?'

'I Believe I can go so far as that word, Sir.'

'But, *Brucey*, why are you so negligent of your music? – you play, Miss Burney?'

'Very little, Sir.'

'O I hope I shall hear you; I am to come to your House some Day, with Mrs Strange, and then –'

---

7. 'Lord Rosemary' was Bruce's derisive name for Lord Rosebery. Bruce and Rosebery, widowers in search of a second wife, were rivals for the hand of Lady Anne Lindsay, who rejected them both.

8. Ironically, Bruce would die accidentally by falling down a staircase in 1794.

'When we have the Honour of seeing you, Sir,' cried I, 'I hope you will hear a much better player than me.'

'O as to that,' answered he, 'I would not give a *fig* to hear a *man* play, comparatively.'

'Well,' said Mrs Strange, 'I knew a young lady who was at a Concert for the first Time, and she sat and sighed, and groaned, and groaned and sighed, and at last she said Well, I can't help it! and burst into Tears!'

'There's a Woman,' cried Mr Bruce with some emotion, 'who could never make a man unhappy! Her soul must be all Harmony!'

We then joined in recommending it to Miss Strange to Practice; and Mr Bruce took it into his Head to affect to speak to me in a Whisper, bending his Head, not without difficulty, to a level with mine; what he said I have forgot, though I know it was something of no manner of consequence; but every body's Eyes, struck with his attitude, were fixed upon us in total silence, so that I really wished him safe back to the mouth of the Nile.

Except what I have Written, every Word that he said was either addressed *en badinage* to plague Bell, or in diverting himself with Miss Strange's Parrot. He seemed determined not to Enter into Conversation with the Company in general, nor to speak upon any but trifling Topics.

It is pity that a man who seems to have some generous feelings, that break out by starts, and who certainly is a man of both Learning and Humour, should be thus run away with by Pride and self-conceit.

28. From Journal *10 March 1775*

The Conversation during supper turned upon madness, a subject which the Stranges are very full of, as a lady of their intimate acquaintance left their House but on Friday in that terrible disorder. We asked how she happened to *be* with them? They answered that she had seemed recovered. Mr Bruce, who had seen her, was very inquisitive about her. Mrs Strange said that the beginning of her *Wandering* that Evening, was, by coming up to her, and asking her if she could *make Faces*?

'I wish,' said Mr Bruce, 'she had asked *me*! – I believe I could have satisfied her that way!'

'O,' said Miss Strange, 'she had a great desire to speak to you, Sir; she said that she had much to say to you.'

'If,' said Mr Bruce, 'without any preface, she had Entered the Room, and come up to me making Faces; I confess I should have been rather surprised!'

'I am sure,' cried I, '*I* should have made a Face without much difficulty! I am amazed at Miss Strange's Courage in staying in the room with her!'

'I have been a great deal with her,' answered Miss Strange, 'and she particularly minds whatever I say.'

'But how are you to answer for your life a moment,' added Mr Bruce, 'in Company with a mad Woman? When she seems most quiet, may she not snatch up a pair of scissars, or whatever is near her, and destroy you,? or at least run them into your Eyes, and blind or maim you for life?'

'While I tried to hold her from going into the street,' said Mrs Strange, 'she scratched my arm, as you see. – '

'Did she fetch Blood?' cried Mr Bruce; 'if she did you will surely go mad too: you may depend upon that! Nay, I would Advise you to go directly to the sea, and be dipt! I assure you I would not be in your situation!'

He said this so drily, that I stared at him, and could not forbear beginning to Expostulate, when turning round to me, I saw he was Laughing.

'If you are bit by a mad *Cat*,' continued he, 'will you not go mad? and how much more by a mad *Woman*?'

'But I was *not* bit,' answered Mrs Strange, 'I only felt her Nail, and where there Enters no *slaver*, there is no Danger.'

'I hope,' said my mother, 'that her friends will not place her in a private mad House; there is so much iniquity practiced at those places, that in order to keep them captives they will not let their friends know when they are really recovered.'

'Ay, indeed?' cried Mr Bruce, 'why this is very bad Encouragement to go mad!'

And now I must have done with this Evening, unless I were to Write horrid Tales of madness; for that shocking subject being started, every body had something terrible to say upon it.

29. Journal *26 March 1775*

Early in the morning, the most entertaining of mortals, Mr Garrick, came.

He marched up stairs immediately into the study where my Father was having his Hair Dressed, surrounded by Books and Papers innumerable;

Charlotte[1] was Reading the News paper, and I was making Breakfast. The rest of the Family had not quitted their Downy Pillows.

My Father was beginning a laughing sort of Apology for his letters and so forth, – but Mr Garrick interrupted him with – 'Ay, now, do be in a little Confusion, – it will make things comfortable!'

He then began to look very gravely at the Hair Dresser; He was himself in a most odious scratch Wig, which Nobody but himself could dare be seen in: He put on a look, in the Abel Drugger style,[2] of *envy* and sadness as he examined the Hair Dresser's progress; – and when he had done, he turned to him with a dejected Face, and said ' – pray Sir, – could you touch up *This* a little?' taking hold of his frightful scratch.

The man only Grinned, and left the Room.

He shook Hands with me, and told my Father that he had *almost* run away with me a Day or two before.

He then Enquired after some Books which he had lent my Father, and how many he had?

'I have 10 of the Memoirs of the French academy.' said my Father.

'And what others?' Cried Mr Garrick.

'I don't know. Do you, Fanny?'

'O – what – ' cried Mr Garrick, archly, 'I suppose you don't chuse to know of any others? – O very well! – pray Sir make free with me! – pray keep them, if you chuse it. But pray, Doctor, when shall we have the History out?[3] Do let me know in Time, that I may prepare to Blow the Trumpet of Fame' –

He then put his stick to his mouth, and in a *raree* show man's Voice, cried – 'Here is the only true History – Gentlemen, please to Buy – Sir, I shall Blow it in the very Ear of yon scurvy magistrate (meaning Sir John Hawkins, who is writing the same History).'[4]

He then ran on with great humour upon twenty subjects, but so much of his drollery belongs to his Voice, looks and manner, that *Writing* loses it almost all.

My Father asked him to Breakfast; but he said he was Engaged at Home

1. Charlotte Ann Burney, FB's sister, aged thirteen at this time. She would marry (1786) Clement Francis, surgeon, and secondly (1798) Ralph Broome, Captain in the Bengal Army.
2. A famous role for Garrick, in Ben Jonson's *The Alchemist*.
3. See selection 25 note 1.
4. All five volumes of Sir John Hawkins's rival *General History of the Science and Practice of Music* appeared in November 1776. The two works actually complemented each other. Hawkins is especially strong on the baroque and music before 1700, while CB's sympathies lie with the contemporary Italian school.

with Mr Boswell and Mr Twiss. He then took the latter off, as he did also Dr Arne,[5] very comically; and afterwards Dr Johnson, in a little Conversation concerning his borrowing a Book of him; – 'David – will you lend me Petraca?'[6] 'Yes, Sir.' 'David, – you sigh?' – 'Sir, you shall have it!' Accordingly, the Book – finely bound! – was sent; but scarse had he received it, when uttering a Latin Ejaculation, (which Mr G. repeated) in a fit of Enthusiasm – over his Head goes poor Petraca, – Russian Leather and all!

He soon after started up, and said he must run – 'Not yet!' cried I. – He turned to me, and in mock Heroics cried – 'ah! I will make *your* Heart ache! – *you* shall sigh –'

He then went out of the study, followed by my Father, and he took a survey of the Books in the Library. – Charlotte and I soon joined them – he called Charlotte his little Dimpling Queen – 'See, how she follows me with her blushes! – and here comes another with her smiles – (to me) ay – I see how it is! all the House in Love with me! – here is one (to Charlotte) whose love is in the *Bud* – and here (to me) here it is in *blow*: – and now, (to my Father) I must go to one whose is full *blown – full blown*, egad!'

He would not be prevailed with to lengthen his visit – we all followed him instinctively down stairs – though he *assured* us he would not pilfer any thing! 'Here is a certain maid here,'[7] said he, 'whom I love to speak to, because she is *Cross*; – Egad, Sir, she does not know the great Roscius![8] – but I frightened her this morning a little: – Child, said I, – you don't know who you have the happiness to speak to! – do you know I am one of the first Genius's of the Age? – Why, Child, you would *faint away* if you knew who I am!'

In this sportive manner he continued till the Door was shut. He is sensible that we all doat on him – but I believe it is the same thing where ever he goes, except where he has had a personal Quarrel, which I am sorry to hear is frequently the case with those who have been his best friends.

He promised he would often Call in the same sort of way, *to plague us*; we assured him we would freely forgive him if he did. In truth, I desire no better Entertainment than his Company affords.

---

5. James Boswell, biographer of Johnson, and Richard Twiss, wealthy young traveller and author who had scandalized the Burney family one evening by recommending John Cleland's *Dictionary of Love*. Dr Thomas Augustine Arne, composer and CB's former music master; his most famous work is *Rule Britannia*.
6. An edition of Petrarch.
7. A young house servant.
8. Garrick was nicknamed Roscius after a famous actor of classical Rome.

30. From Journal *May–June 1775*

May 8th

This month is Called a *tender* one – It has proved so *to* me – – but not *in* me – I have not breathed one sigh, – felt one sensation, – or uttered one folly the more for the softness of the season. – However – I have met with a youth whose Heart, if he is to be Credited, has been less guarded – indeed it has yielded itself so suddenly, that had it been in any other month – I should not have known how to have accounted for so easy a Conquest.

The First Day of this month I Drank Tea and spent the Evening at Mr Burney's, at the request of my sister [Esther], to meet a very stupid Family, which she told me it would be Charity to herself to give my Time to.

This Family consisted of Mrs O'Connor, and her Daughter, by a first marriage, Miss Dickenson, who, poor Creature, has the misfortune to be both Deaf and Dumb. They are very old acquaintances of my Grandmother Burney, to oblige whom my sister Invited them. My Grandmother and 2 aunts[1] therefore were of the Party: – as was, also, Mr Barlow,[2] a young man who has lived and Boarded with Mrs O'Connor for about 2 years.

Mr Barlow is short but rather handsome, he is a very well bred, good tempered and sensible young man, and he is highly spoken of, both for Disposition and morals. He has Read more than he has Conversed, and seems to know but little of the World; his Language therefore is stiff and uncommon, and seems laboured, if not affected – he has a great desire to please, but no elegance of manners; niether, though he may be very worthy, is he at all agreeable.

Unfortunately, however, he happened to be prodigiously Civil to me, and though I have met with much more gallantry occasionally, yet I could not but observe a *seriousness* of attention much more expressive than Complimenting.

As my sister knew not well how to *wile away the Time*, somebody proposed, after supper, a round of Cross Questions. This was agreed to. Mr Barlow,

---

1. FB's paternal grandmother Ann Cooper Burney and her maiden aunts Ann Burney and Rebecca Burney.

2. Thomas Barlow lives for posterity only in FB's portrait of him as the rejected suitor. We know from Esther Burney that he was twenty-four years old, well-to-do and well educated. Other than that, we can only surmise that he came from a family of merchants. (He did not attend Oxford or Cambridge or any of the well-known public schools.)

who sat next to me, took near half an Hour to settle what he should ask me, – and at last his question was – 'what I thought most necessary in Love?' I answered, *Constancy*, I hope, for his own sake, he will not remember this answer long, though he readily subscribed to it at the Time.

The Coach came for me about Eleven. I rose to go. He earnestly entreated me to stay only 2 minutes. I did not, however, think such compliance at all requisite, and therefore only begged to set my Grandmother down in my way. The Party then broke up. Mrs O'Connor began an urgent Invitation to all present to return the visit the next Week. Mr Barlow, who followed me, repeated it very pressingly, to *me*, hoping I would make one. I promised that I would.

When we had all taken leave of our Host and Hostess, – my Grandmother, according to custom, gave me a kiss and her blessing. I would fain have eluded my aunts, as Nothing can be so disagreeable as kissing before young men; however, they chose it should go round; and after them, Mrs O'Connor also saluted me, as did her Daughter, desiring to be better Acquainted with me. This disagreeable Ceremony over, Mr Barlow, came up to me, and making an apology which, not suspecting his intention, I did not understand, – he gave me a most ardent salute! I have seldom been more surprised. I had no idea of his taking such a freedom. However, I have told my friends that for the future I will not chuse to lead, or have led, so contagious an Example. I wonder *so modest a man* could dare to be so bold.

He came down stairs with us, and waited at the Door, I believe, till the Coach was out of sight.

Four Days after this meeting, my mother and Mrs Young[3] happened to be in the Parlour, when I received a Letter which from the strong resemblance of the Hand writing in the direction to that of Mr Crisp, I immediately opened and thought came from Chesington. But what was my surprise, to see Madam, at the beginning, and at the Conclusion

your sincere Admirer and

very humble servant Thomas Barlow

I Read it 3 or 4 Times before I could credit my Eyes. An Acquaintance so short, and a procedure so hasty astonished me. It is a most tender Epistle and contains a passionate Declaration of Attachment, hinting at hopes of a *return*, and so forth.

I took not a moment to deliberate. – I felt that my Heart was totally

---

3. Martha Allen Young was Elizabeth Burney's sister and wife of the noted agricultural writer Arthur Young.

insensible – and felt that I could never Consent to unite myself to a man who I did not *very* highly value.

However, as I do not consider myself as an independant member of society, and as I knew I could depend upon my Father's kindness, I thought it incumbent upon me to act with his Concurrence. I therefore, at Night, before I sent an answer, shewed him the Letter. He asked me a great many Questions – I assured him that forming a Connection without attachment – (and that I was totally indifferent to the Youth in Question) was what I could never think of. My Father was all indulgence and goodness; he at first proposed that I should write him Word that our acquaintance had been too short to authorise so high an opinion as he expressed for me; but I objected to that, as seeming to infer that a *longer* acquaintance might be Acceptable. He therefore concluded upon the whole, that I should send no answer at all.

I was not very easy at this determination, as it seemed to treat Mr Barlow with a degree of Contempt, which his partiality to me by no means merited from myself; and as I apprehended it to be possible for him to put, perhaps, *another* and more favourable interpretation upon my silence. I shewed Hetty the Letter next Day. She most vehemently took the young man's part: urged me to think differently, and above all advised me to certainly Write an answer, and to be of their party, according to my promise, when they went to Mrs O Connor's.

I told her I would speak to my Father again in regard to writing an Answer, which I wished much to do, but could not now without his consent: but as to the Party, I could not make one, as it would be a kind of tacit approbation and assent of his further attentions.

I went afterwards to call on my Grandmother; my sister followed me, and directly told her and my aunts of the affair. They all of them became most zealous Advocates for Mr Barlow; they spoke most highly of the Character they had heard of him, and my aunt Anne humourously bid me beware of her and Beckey's fate!

I assured them I was not intimidated, and that I had rather a thousand Times Die an old maid than be married, except from affection.

When I came Home, I wrote the following Answer which I proposed sending, with my Father's leave.

Miss Burney presents her Compliments to Mr Barlow; she is much obliged for, though greatly surprised at the good opinion with which on so short an Acquaintance he is pleased to Honour her; she wishes Mr Barlow all happiness, but must beg leave to recommend to him to Transfer to some person better known to him a partiality which she so little merits.

My Father, however, did not approve of my Writing. I could not imagine why, but have since heard from my sister that he was unwilling I should give a No without some further knowledge of the young man.

Further knowledge will little avail. In Connections of this sort, the *Heart* ought to be heard, and mine will never speak a word I am sure, for any one I do not truly enough honour to cheerfully, in all things serious, obey. How hard must be the duty of a wife practised without high esteem! And I am too spoilt by such men as my father and Mr Crisp to content myself with a character merely inoffensive. I should expire of fatigue with him.

My sister was not contented with giving her own advice; she Wrote about the affair to Mr Crisp, representing in the strongest light the utility of my listening to Mr Barlow. He has written me such a Letter! God knows how I shall have Courage to answer it. Every body is against me but my beloved Father.

They all of them are kindly interested in my welfare; but they know not so well as myself what may make me happy or miserable. To unite myself for Life to a man who is not *infinitely* dear to me, is what I can never, never Consent to. Unless, indeed, I was strongly urged by my Father. I thank God most gratefully he has not interfered.

They tell me they do not desire me to *marry*, but not to give up the *power* of it, without seeing more of the proposer: but this reasoning I cannot give into. – It is foreign to all my Notions: how can I see more of Mr Barlow without encourageing him to believe I am willing to think of him? I detest all trifling. If ever I marry, my consent shall be prompt and unaffected.

Sunday, May 14th

The Visit to Mrs O Connor was made yesterday. I Commissioned my Aunts – – though they would hardly hear me – to say that I was prevented from Waiting on her by a bad Cold. How the message was taken, and what passed, I know not; but this morning, while we were all at Breakfast, except my Father, who was in the study; John came into the Parlour, and said that a Gentleman enquired for me.

I guessed who it was – and was inexpressibly Confused. Mama stared, but desired he might walk in – the Door opened – and Mr Barlow appeared. – He had Dressed himself elegantly – but could hardly speak. – He Bowed two or three Times – I coloured like scarlet, and I believe he was the only person in the Room who did not see it.

'Mrs O Connor – he called – my Cold – he understood – he was very sorry – '

He could not get on. – My voice too, failed me terribly – for his silence at his first Entrance made me fear he was going to reproach me for not answering his Letter. – I told him my Cold had been too bad to allow me to go out – but I was so terribly frightened lest my mother should say *what Cold – I did not know you had one*! – that I had great difficulty to get out the Words: and he himself took Notice that my *Voice* spoke how bad my Cold was! – though in fact I have no Cold at all, but grew *husky* from embarrassment: my mother then asked him to sit down – and Sukey [Susanna], very good naturedly, entered into Conversation with him, to our mutual relief, – particularly to his, as he seemed so confounded he scarse knew where he was. I sat upon Thorns from the fear he would desire to speak to me alone – I looked another way, and hardly opened my mouth. In about ½ an Hour, he rose to go.

Whether he was induced to make this visit from expecting he might speak to me, or whether in order to see if I had any Cold or not, I cannot tell: but it proved cruelly distressing to him, and confusing to me.

Had I sent an answer, this would not have happened: but it is now too late. I am very sorry to find this young man seems so serious; – however, an attachment so precipitately formed, so totally discouraged, and *so* placed – cannot be difficult to Cure.

June 6th

On Saturday morning [27 May], while we were at Breakfast, I had a Letter brought me in a Hand which I immediately knew to be Barlow's.

Notwithstanding I was at once sorry and provoked at perceiving how sanguine this youth chose to be, I was not absolutely concerned at receiving this 2d Letter, because I regarded it as a fortunate opportunity of putting an unalterable Conclusion to the whole Affair. However, I thought it my duty to speak to my Father before I sent an Answer, never doubting his immediate concurrence.

My mother, Sukey and I went to the opera that Evening; it was therefore too late when I returned to send a Letter to Hoxton[4] – but I went up stairs

4. Where Barlow boarded with Mrs O'Connor.

into the study, and told my Father I had received another Epistle from Mr Barlow which I could only attribute to my not answering, as I had wished, his first; I added that I proposed, with his leave, to Write to Mr Barlow the next morning.

My Father looked grave, asked me for the Letter, put it in his Pocket unread, and wished me good Night.

I was siezed with a kind of pannic – I trembled at the idea of his Espousing, however mildly, the Cause of this young man: – I passed a restless Night, and in the morning dared not Write without his permission, which I was now half afraid to ask.

About 2 O'clock, while I was dawdling in the study, and Waiting for an opportunity to speak, John came in, and said 'A Gentleman is below, who asks for Miss Burney, – Mr Barlow.'

I think I was never more distressed in my life – to have taken pains to avoid a private Conversation so highly disagreeable to me, and at last to be forced into it at so unfavourable a Juncture, – for I had now 2 Letters from him, both Unanswered and consequently open to his Conjectures. I exclaimed 'Lord! – how provoking! what shall I do?'

My Father looked uneasy and perplexed: – he said something about not being hasty, which I did not desire him to explain. Terrified lest he should hint at the advantage of an early establishment – like Mr Crisp – quick from the study – but slow enough afterwards – I went down stairs. – I saw my mother pass from the front into the Back Parlour; which did not add to the *Graciousness* of my Reception of poor Mr Barlow, who I found alone in the front Parlour. I was not sorry that none of the Family were there, as I now began to seriously dread any protraction of this affair.

He came up to me, and with an Air of *tenderness* and satisfaction, began some anxious Enquiries about my Health, but I interrupted him with saying 'I fancy, Sir, You have not received a Letter I – I –'

I stopt, for I could not say which I had *sent*!

'A Letter? – no, Ma'am!'

'You will have it, then, to-morrow, Sir.'

We were both silent for a minute or two, when he said 'In consequence, I presume, Ma'am, of the one I –'

'Yes, Sir!' Cried I.

'And pray – Ma'am – Miss Burney! – may I – beg to ask the contents? that is – the – the –' he could not go on.

'Sir – I – it was only – it was merely – in short, you will see it to-morrow.'

'But if you would favour me with the Contents now, I could perhaps Answer it at once?'

'Sir, it requires no Answer!'

A second silence ensued. I was really distressed myself to see *his* distress, which was very apparent. After some time, he stammered out something of *hoping* – and *beseeching*, – which, gathering more firmness, I announced – 'I am much obliged to You, Sir, for the too good opinion You are pleased to have of me – but I should be sorry you should lose any more Time upon my account – as I have no thoughts at all of changing my situation and abode.'

He seemed to be quite overset: having, therefore so freely explained myself, I then asked him to sit down, and began to talk of the Weather. When he had a little recovered himself, he drew a Chair close to me, and began making most ardent professions of respect and regard, and so forth. I interrupted him, as soon as I could, and begged him to rest satisfied with my Answer.

'*Satisfied?*' repeated he – 'my dear Ma'am – is that possible?'

'Perhaps, Sir,' said I, 'I ought to make some apologies for not answering your first Letter – but really, I was so much surprised – upon so short an Acquaintance.'

He then began making Excuses for having written but as to *short acquaintance*, he owned it was a reason for *me* – but for *him* – fifty Years could not have more convinced him of my etc. etc.

'You have taken a sudden, and far too partial idea of me,' answered I. 'If you look round among your older Acquaintance, I doubt not but you will very soon be able to make a better choice.'

He shook his Head: 'I have seen, Madam, a great many Ladies, it is true – but never –'

'You do me much honour'; cried I, 'but I must desire you would take no further trouble about me – for I have not, at present, the slightest thoughts of ever leaving this House.'

'*At present?*' repeated he, eagerly, – 'no, I would not expect it – I would not *wish* to precipitate – but in future –'

'Niether now or ever, Sir,' returned I, 'have I any view of any change.'

'But surely – surely this can never be! so severe a resolution – you cannot mean it – it would be wronging all the World!'

'I am extremely sorry, Sir, that you have not received my answer – because it might have saved you this trouble.'

He looked very much mortified, and said, in a dejected voice – 'If there is any thing in me – in my connections – or in my situation in Life – which you wholly think unworthy of You – and beneath you – – or if my Character or Disposition meet with your disapprobation – I will immediately forgo all – I will not – I would not –'

'No, indeed, Sir,' cried I, 'I have niether seen or heard any thing of you that was to your disadvantage – and I have no doubts of your worthiness –'

He thanked me, and seemed reassured; and renewed his solicitation in the most urgent manner. He repeatedly begged my permission to acquaint my Family of the state of his affairs, and to abide by their decision – but I would not let him say two words following upon that subject. I told him that my Answer was a final one, and begged him to take it as such.

He remonstrated very earnestly. 'This is the severest decision! – Surely you must allow that the *social state* is what we were all meant for? – that we were created for one another? – that to form such a resolution is contrary to the design of our Being? –'

'All this may be true, –' said I; – 'I have nothing to say in contradiction to it – but you know there are many odd Characters in the World – and perhaps I am one of them.'

'O no, no, no, – that can never be! – but is it possible you can have so bad an opinion of the married state? It seems to me the *only* state for happiness! –'

'Well, Sir, *You* are attached to the married Life – *I* am to the single – therefore, *every man in his humour*[5] – do *you* follow *your* opinion, – and let *me* follow *mine*.'

'But surely – is not this – *singular?* –'

'I give you leave, Sir,' cried I, laughing, 'to think me singular – odd – Queer – nay, even whimsical, if you please.'

'But, my *dear* Miss Burney, only –'

'I entreat you, Sir, to take my Answer – You really pain me by being so urgent. –'

'That would not I do for the World! – I only beg You to suffer me – perhaps in future –'

'No, indeed; I shall never change – I do assure you you will find me very obstinate!'

He began to lament his own Destiny. I grew extremely tired of saying so often the same thing; – but I could not absolutely turn him out of the House, and indeed he seemed so dejected and unhappy, that I made it my study to

5. Title of Ben Jonson's play.

soften my refusal as much as I could without leaving room for future expectation.

About this Time, my mother came in. We both rose. – I was horridly provoked at my situation –

'I am only come in for a Letter,' cried she, – 'pray don't let me disturb you. –' And away she went.

This could not but be encouraging to him, for she was no sooner gone, than he began again the same story, and seemed determined not to give up his Cause. He hoped, at least, that I would allow him to enquire after my Health? –

'I must beg you, Sir, to send me no more Letters.'

He seemed much hurt.

'You had better, Sir, think of me no more – if you study your own happiness –'

'I *do* study my own happiness – more than I have ever had Any probability of doing before –!'

'You have made an unfortunate Choice, Sir; but you will find it easier to forget it than you imagine. You have only to suppose I was not at Mr Burney's on May Day – and it was a mere chance my being there – and then you will be –'

'But if I *could* – could I also forget seeing you at old Mrs Burney's?[6] – and if I did – can I forget that I see you now? –'

'O yes! – in 3 months Time you may forget you ever knew me. You will not find it so difficult as you suppose.'

'You have heard, Ma'am, of an Old man being Growed young? – perhaps you believe *that*? – But you will not deny me leave to sometimes see you? –'

'My Father, Sir, is seldom, – hardly ever, indeed, at Home –'

'I have never seen the Doctor – but I hope he would not refuse me permission to enquire after your Health? I have no wish without his Consent.'

'Though I acknowledge myself to be *singular* I would not have you think me either *affected* or *trifling*, – and therefore I must assure you that I am *fixed* in the Answer I have given You; *Unalterably* fixed.'

His entreaties grew now extremely distressing to me: – he besought me to take more Time, said it should be the study of his life to make me happy. 'Allow me – my *dear* Miss Burney – only to hope that my future Conduct –'

---

6. FB had visited her grandmother and aunts in York Street where she unexpectedly met Barlow again. She suspected that her aunt Rebecca had planned this surprise meeting.

'I shall always think myself obliged, nay honoured by your good opinion – and you are entitled to my best wishes for your Health and Happiness – but indeed, the less we meet the better.'

'What – what can I do?' cried he, very sorrowfully.

'Why – go and ponder upon this affair for about half an Hour – then say, what an odd, queer, strange Creature she is! and then – think of something else.'

'O no; no! – you cannot suppose all that? – I shall think of nothing else; *your* refusal is more pleasing than any other Lady's acceptance –'

He said this very simply, but too seriously for me to Laugh at it. Just then, Sukey came in – but did not stay two minutes. It would have been shocking to be thus left purposely as if with a declared Lover, and then I was not sorry to have an opportunity of preventing future doubts or expectations.

I rose and Walked to the Window, thinking it high Time to End a Conversation already much too long; and when he again began to entreat me not to be so *very severe*, I told him that I was *sure* I should never alter the Answer I made at first; that I was very happy at Home, and not at all inclined to try my fate elsewhere; I then desired my Compliments to Mrs O'Connor, and Miss Dickenson, and made a *reverence* by way of leave taking.

'I am extremely sorry to detain you so long, Ma'am, –' said he, in a melancholy Voice. I made no answer. He Walked about the Room; and then again besought my leave to ask me how I did some other Time – I absolutely, though Civilly, refused it; and told him frankly that, fixed as I was, it was better that we should not meet.

He then took his leave: – returned back – took leave – and returned again: – I now made a more formal reverence of the head, at the same time expressing my good wishes for his Welfare, in a sort of way that implied I expected never to see him again – he would fain have taken a more *tender* leave of me, – but I repulsed him with great surprise and displeasure. I did not, however, as he was so terribly sorrowful, refuse him my Hand, which he had made sundry vain attempts to take in the course of our Conversation; but when I withdrew it, as I did presently, I rang the Bell, to prevent him again returning from the Door.

Though I was really sorry for the unfortunate and misplaced attachment which this Young man professes for me, yet I could almost have *Jumped* for Joy when he was gone, to think that the affair was thus finally over.

Indeed I think it hardly possible for a Woman to be in a more irksome situation, than when rejecting a worthy man who is all humility, Respect and submission, and who throws himself and his Fortune at her Feet.

I had no opportunity of speaking to my Father all that Day. In the Evening Mr Burney and Hetty came. Hetty told me, that the Day before, Mrs O Connor had Called on her, and acquainted her that Mr Barlow had owned his Attachment to me, and requested to know, first, whether I had any pre-engagement, and secondly, whether I had ever expressed any *Antipathy* to him. She answered both these in the Negative, and then Mrs O'Connor, in Mr Barlow's Name, entreated her to be his Advocate; which she readily promised.

After his Conversation with me, he Called on her himself. She says he was all dejection and sadness. He expressed the greatest *Respect* for me, feared I thought him wanting in it; – apologised for his early Declaration, which, he said, resulted from his sincerity, and his having no Experience either in the arts, or the ways of men.

My Father sent for Hetty up stairs, and made a thousand Enquiries concerning Mr Barlow.

The next Day [29 May] – a Day the remembrance of which will be never erased from my memory – my Father first spoke to me *in favour* of Mr Barlow! and desired me not to be *peremtory* in the Answer I had still to Write, though it was to appear written previously.

I scarce made any answer – I was terrified to Death – I felt the utter impossibility of resisting not merely my Father's *persuasion*, but even his *Advice*. – I felt, too, that I had no *argumentative* objections to make to Mr Barlow, his Character – Disposition – situation – I knew nothing against – but O! – I felt he was no Companion for my Heart! – I wept like an Infant when alone – Eat nothing – seemed as if already married – and passed the whole Day in more misery than, merely on my own account, I ever passed one before in my life, – except when a child, upon the loss of my own beloved mother – and ever revered and most dear Grandmother!

After supper, I went into the study, while my dear Father was alone, to wish him Good Night, which I did as chearfully as I could, though pretty evidently in dreadful uneasiness. When I had got to the Door, he called me back, and asked some questions concerning a new Court mourning, kindly saying he would assist Susette [Susanna] and me in our fitting-out, which he accordingly did, and affectionately embraced me, saying 'I wish I could do more for Thee, Fanny!' 'O Sir! –' cried I – '*I* wish for Nothing! – only let me Live with you! –' – 'My life!' cried he, kissing me kindly, 'Thee shalt live with me for ever, if Thee wilt! Thou canst not think I meant to get rid of thee?'

'I could not, Sir! I could not!' cried I, 'I could not out-live such a thought – ' and, as I kissed him – O! how gratefully and thankfully! with what a relief to my heart! I saw his dear Eyes full of Tears! a mark of his tenderness which I shall never forget!

'God knows' – continued he – 'I wish not to part with my Girls! – they are my greatest Comfort! – only – do not be too hasty! – '

Thus relieved, restored to future hopes, I went to Bed as light, happy and thankful as if Escaped from Destruction.

From that Day to this, my Father, I thank Heaven, has never again mentioned Mr Barlow.[7]

31. From Letter to Samuel Crisp *May 1775*

Our Concert proved to be very much *the Thing*: The Company consisted of
The Baron Deiden, the Danish Ambassadour.

The Baronness, his Lady. She is young, pretty, well made, polite and amiable. We were all charmed with her.

Miss Phipps, sister of the famous Capt. Phipps,[1] and Daughter of Lord Mulgrave. She is a very sweet Girl. Her Face is not handsome, but full of *Expression* and *intelligence*. She is arch, clever, and Engaging.

Sir James and Lady Lake.

Miss Lake, sister of Sir James.[2] A very agreeable *old maid*. I *respect* and *admire* – and wish to *imitate* her.

Sir Thomas Clarges. He is just returned from Italy, whither he was sent by his Relations, upon account of a violent passion which he had for Miss Linley, now Mrs Sheridan; he is a very Tall youth, and has not by his Travels lost his native bashfulness and shyness.

Mr Harris of Salisbury,[3] author of 3 Treatises, on Happiness, music, etc. and of some other Books, particularly one just published, called Philosophical arrangements. He is a charming old man, – well bred even to humility, gentle in his manners, and communicative and agreeable in his Conversation.

---

7. From an objective standpoint Barlow would have been an excellent 'catch' for FB, who at twenty-three was already rather old to be unmarried. CB must have been strongly tempted to settle her in this marriage, but he relented in the face of FB's obvious misery.

1. Constantine John Phipps was a naval captain who had led an expedition to find the north-west passage. He succeeded his father as second Baron Mulgrave.
2. Sir James Winter Lake, his wife Joyce, Lady Lake, and his sister Mary who married (1782) Major William Webb.
3. James Harris, philosophical writer.

Mrs Harris, his wife. A so, so, sort of woman.

Miss Louisa Harris, his Daughter. She has a bad figure, and is not handsome. She is reserved, modest and sensible. She has Acquired a *name* as a lady singer, and is a scholar of Sacchini's.[4]

Mr Earl. A very musical man.

Mrs Ord, a very musical woman.[5]

Miss Ord, a fine Girl, but totally inanimate and insipid.

Mr Merlin,[6] the very ingenious mechanic, who is also a very entertaining character. There is a *simplicity* so unaffected and so uncommon, in his manners and Conversation, that his Company always gives me amusement. He utters his opinion upon all subjects, and about all persons without the least disguise; he is humbly grateful for all civility that he receives, but at the same Time, he shews an honest and warm resentment if he meets with any slight. He pronounces English very comically, for though he is never at a loss for a word, he almost always puts the *emphasis* on the wrong syllable.

Mr Jones, a Welch Harper. A silly young man.

Miss Harrison. Daughter of the late Commodore Harrison. She is rather pretty, very young, proud, I believe, and uninteresting.

Mr Burney, Hetty, and our Noble Selves bring up the Rear.

The Company in general came early, and there was a great deal of Conversation before any music; but as the party was too large for a *general Chatterment*, we were obliged to make parties with our next Neighbours. I had the satisfaction of having Mr Harris for mine till the Concert began.

As we had no violins, we were obliged to be contented without any overture; and the Concert was opened by Mr Burney at the desire of the Baroness Deiden. He Fired away, with his usual successful velocity, to the amazement and delight of all present, particularly of the Baroness, who is a very celebrated lady performer; – it was to her that Boccherini and Eichner,[7] whose Lessons you have so very much admired, Dedicated their music, as have many other Composers of less merit.

Mr Burney played a Concerto of Schobert,[8] and one of my Father's, and a great deal of Extemporary Preluding.

When he rose, my Father petitioned the Baroness to take his seat – o no!

---

4. Antonio Sacchini was a prominent Italian composer working in London.

5. Anna Dillingham Ord was a noted bluestocking hostess. She later became a close friend of FB but ostracized her after FB's marriage.

6. John Joseph Merlin was a well-known instrument maker and inventor.

7. Luigi Boccherini and Ernst Eichner, composers.

8. Johann Schobert was a much admired composer in his day.

she would not hear of it – she said it would be like a Figurante's Dancing after Mlle Heinel![9] – Miss Phipps joined violently in intreating her, and the Baron seemed to wish her to comply – and she was at length prevailed with. She played a Lesson of Schobert. I think her the best lady player I ever heard. She is a good musician, – does not blunder or make false steps, – has a remarkable strong left Hand – and plays with much *meaning*, as well as Execution. She is, at the same Time, so modest and unassuming, and so pretty, that she was the general object of admiration. When my Father went to Thank her, she said she had never been so frightened before in her life.

My Father begged her to favour us with some thing else. She was going to play again – but the Baron, looking at my sister Hetty, said – 'après, ma chere.' 'Eh bien,'[10] cried Miss Phipps, who is her intimate friend, 'après Madame Burney.'

She immediately, and very gracefully rose, and gave her place to Hetty, who, to avoid the appearance of *emulation*, with great propriety chose to begin with a slow movement, as the Baroness had been Exerting all her Execution.

She played *your bit* of Echard.[11] And I may safely say that I never heard her play it better, if so well; Merlin's Harpsichord made it divine – and the Expression, feeling and Taste with which she performed it raised a general murmur of applause and satisfaction from all. Mr Harris enquired eagerly whose it was? Every body seemed to feel and to be enchanted with it. If a Pin had dropt, it would have made a Universal start! Every one was silent, attentive, and pleased.

After this, she played a very difficult Lesson of my Father's; but she was flurried, and niether did that or herself Justice.

At my Father's request, Miss Harris then consented to sing.

Her Father accompanied her on the Piano Forte. She sung a most beautiful slow song of Sacchini's, which has never been printed, but which we remembered having formerly heard him sing. She has very little voice, scarce any, indeed, – having niether power, compass, or sweetness, *and yet* – which is wonderful – her singing gave us all pleasure! She is extremely well taught, and makes up for the deficiencies of Nature by the acquirements of Art; for she sings with great Taste and feeling, and in an excellent style.

She protested she was more frightened at singing to *such an audience*, than

9. Anne Frédérique Heinel, French, was considered the finest dancer in Europe. A 'Figurante' is an extra, i.e. a supernumerary dancer.
10. 'Afterwards, my dear.' 'Good'.
11. Johann Gottfried Eckard.

she should have been in a Theatre. She consented, however, to sing another Air, when somewhat recovered: and she gave us a new and favourite Rondeau of Rauzzini's, which he sings in the New opera of Piramo and Tisbé.[12]

After this, followed the *great Gun* of the Concert, namely a Harpsichord Duet between Mr Burney and my sister.

It is the Noblest Composition that was ever made.

They came off with flying Colours – Nothing could exceed the general applause. Mr Harris was in *extacy*; Sr James Lake who is silent and shy, broke forth into the warmest expressions of delight – Lady Lake, more prone to be pleased, was quite in raptures – the charming Baroness repeatedly declared she had never been at so agreeable a Concert before; and many said They had never *heard music* till then.

What would I give that you could hear it? It is not possible for Instrumental music to be more *finished*.

The Baroness was then again Called upon – but she excused herself from playing any more – and, with the Baron and Miss Phipps, soon after took her leave.

I quite forgot to speak of Mr Jones, who played upon a Harp with new pedals constructed by Mr Merlin: it is a sweet Instrument. He plays very well, he is precisely neat, and has a good deal of Execution: but the poor young man has no *soul* to spare for his playing.[13]

The Concert concluded by another song from Miss Harris, it was a Bravura, a MS. of Sacchini's. A fine song, and very well sung.

The Company went away to all appearances extremely well pleased; and we who remained at Home were in all reality the same.

So much for our Concert.

32. From Letter to Samuel Crisp *10 June 1775*

At length – – we have heard Agujari! – We wished for you! – I cannot tell you how *much* we wished for you! the great singers of former years, whom I have heard you so emphatically describe seem to have all their Talents revived in this wonderful singer. I could compare her to nothing *I* ever *heard*

12. Rauzzini's best-loved opera, *Piramo e Tisbe*, first performed at Munich in 1769, had received its London premiere on 16 March 1775.
13. Edward Jones would later have a distinguished career as a historian and recorder of Welsh music.

but only to what *you* have heard – Your Carestino – Farinelli – – Senesino[1] – alone are worthy to be ranked with the Bastardini. Such a powerful voice! – so astonishing a Compass – reaching from C in the middle of the Harpsichord, to *2* notes *above* the Harpsichord! Every tone so clear, so full – so charming! Then her *shake* – so *plump* – so true, so open! – it is as strong and distinct as Mr Burney's upon the Harpsichord. –

Besides its great power, her voice is all sweetness, – and, when she pleases, all softness and delicacy. She sings in the highest style of Taste, and with an *Expression* so pathetic, it is impossible to hear it unmoved. She executes the greatest difficulties that are possible to be given to her, with all the ease and facility that I could say 'my dear Daddy!'

She came before 7 – and stayed till 12, and was singing almost all the Time! She permitted us to encore almost every song. She sung in 20 different styles. The greatest was son Regina e sono amante from Didone.[2] Good Heaven! what a song! and how sung! Then she gave us 2 or 3 *Cantabiles*, sung divinely, then she *chaunted* some *Church Music*, in a style so nobly simple and unadorned, that it stole into one's very soul! Then she gave us a Bravura, with difficulties which seemed only possible for an Instrument in the Hands of a great master – Then she spoke some Recitative – so nobly. –

In short – whether she most astonished, or most delighted us, I cannot say – but she is really a *sublime* singer.

We had not a soul here but our own Family, which was her particular desire. She gave us some hopes of coming once more before she quits England – if she does – and if we know it in Time – could you resist coming to Town for one Night? Besides her musical Talents she has really a great deal of singularity and would entertain you by her conversation.

She also has great ideas of action – and grew so animated in singing an *Arria* Parlante from Didone, that she acted it through out, with great spirit and feeling.

I could not help regretting to her that she should sing at the *Pantheon*, when she was so much formed for the *Theatre*. She made Faces and shrugs, in the Italian way, and said 'oui – j'y suis *comme une* statue! – *comme une petite Ecoliere*!'[3] – and then she took up a Book, to take herself off when singing at the Pantheon.

We all hoped that, After the Gabriella was gone, she would return to

---

1. Giovanni Carestini, Carlo Broschi (called Farinelli) and Francesco Bernardi (called Senesino) were famous Italian castrato singers whom Crisp had heard as a young man.
2. Libretto by Metastasio, set by Colla (1773).
3. 'Yes – I am like a *statue*! – like a little schoolgirl!'

England, and to the Opera House. She said that if ever she did – it should be through the means of Dr *Burney* – into whose Hands she would put her Engagements – and to *no one else*!

She professes great contempt for the managers. – Her Talents are so very superior that she cannot chuse but hold all other performers cheap. The Gabriella, her only Rival, she never heard, and consequently she has never met with any singer equal to herself.

She is a wonderful Creature! –

33. From Letters to Samuel Crisp *13 November–11 December 1775*

I will say no more, but change the subject, and *come* to *Yesterday*, to give you an Account of a *little Concert* we had, at which *Assisted* a most superb party of company. It was occasioned by the desire of Dr King[1] to have Prince Orloff of Russia hear Mr Burney and my sister in a Duet before he left England.

Prince Orloff is the identical man who was the Reigning favourite with the Empress of Russia at the Time the Czar was murdered. He is *said* to have seized the Emperor, but he is *known* to have immediately succeeded to the *good will* of the Czarina. This Prince was sent to negotiate peace at Constantinople, some little Time since, but in his absence, he was unfortunately supplanted in the favour of the Empress, by some other *Adonis*, and, though loaded with Honours, preferments and all sort of orders, he chose to *Travel* a little while, when, upon his return to Russia, he found the Empress had received another friend into her good graces.[2]

He is now, therefore in England, where he Lives in great splendour, is perpetually at Court, and has had Entertainments made for him by all the ministers of state. etc.

We had no performers but Mr Burney and Hetty, but a good deal of Company.

*

1. He had been chaplain to the English factory at St Petersburg.
2. Count Aleksei Grigor'evich Orlov, Prince of the Roman Empire, was the third of five Orlov brothers who helped Catherine II (the Great) usurp the Russian throne in 1762. He was the leader of the group of officers who assassinated Tsar Peter III, Catherine's husband, but he was never her lover. FB confuses him with his brother Count Grigorii Grigor'evich Orlov, who had been Catherine's emissary to a peace conference with the Turks, where he learned that he had been replaced by a new favourite, a new Adonis (the handsome lover of Venus in classical myth).

So now, Enter his Highness, attended by a Russian Nobleman, and followed by General Bawr.[3]

The Prince is another Mr Bruce, being immensely Tall, and stout in proportion. He is a handsome and magnificent Figure. His Dress was very superb. Besides a Blue Garter, he had a star of Diamonds, of prodigious brilliancy; he had likewise a *shoulder knot* of the same *precious Jewels*, and a Picture of the Empress Hung from his Neck, which was set round with Diamonds of such magnitude and lustre that, when near the Candle, they were too dazzling for the Eye. His Jewels, Dr King says, are Valued at above £100,000.

He was extremely gracious and polite, and appeared to be *addicted to pleasantry*. He speaks very little English, but knows French perfectly. He was received by my Father in the Drawing Room. The Library, where the music was, was so Crowded he only shewed himself at the Door, where he Bowed to Mr Chamier,[4] who had met with him elsewhere.

I felt myself so *Dwarfish* by his *high* Highness, that I could not forbear whispering Mr Chamier 'How I hate those enormous Tall men!'

'He has been less unfortunate,' answered he, archly, elsewhere! – 'that objection has not been made to him by *all* Ladies.' I knew he meant the Empress, but by no means desired a Conversation on the subject, and told him, I only *hated* them, because they made *me*, and such *as* me look so very insignificant. You may be sure his gallantry would by no means subscribe to this speech, which was followed by the usual style of *small talk*.

Lord Bruce rose and bowed very respectfully to the Prince, and quitting his seat to make way for him, went to the further End of the Room. 'Ah!' cried Prince Orloff, '*milord me fuit!*'[5]

Mr Brudenal then offered *his* seat to his Highness, but he would not accept it, and declared that if he disturbed any body, he would immediately retire: – he desired him, therefore, to re-seat himself, and when Mr Brudenal *demurred*, he said, with a Laugh (in answer to Mr B.'s pressing him to take his seat) 'Non, non, Monsieur, je ne *veux* pas, *absolument*, je suis *opiniatre*, moi! je ne le *veux* pas! – Je suis un peu comme messieurs les Anglois!'[6]

He gained his point, and the Prince at last *squatted* himself on the corner

---

3. Friedrich Wilhelm von Bauer was a German general in the service of Catherine the Great.
4. Anthony Chamier was a wealthy financier, a member of Dr Johnson's club and a friend of the Burneys.
5. '*My lord flees from me!*'
6. 'No, no, Sir, I don't *want* to, *absolutely*, I am stubborn! I don't *want* to! – I'm a little like the English gentlemen!' Hon. James Brudenell, later fifth Earl of Cardigan.

of a Form, just by Suzette, who as he seemed to shut her in, he called his *petite prisonniere.*[7]

Mr Chamier, in a whisper, said that 'I wish Dr Burney would have had *Omiah* [Omai] here, instead of Prince Orloff!'

The Grand Duet, of Müthel,[8] was then played.

Added to the applause given to the *music*, every body had something to say, upon the singularity of the performers being man and Wife.

Mr Boone said, to me, 'See what a man and his Wife can do together, when they Live in *Harmony*!'

'O Dr Burney,' cried Lady Edgecumbe, 'You have set me *a madding*. I shall never bear any other music!'

Lord Bruce, turning to Prince Orloff, told him that the performers of the Duet were *mari et femme.*[9]

The Prince seemed surprised, and Walking up to Hetty, made her many Compliments; and expressed his wonder that two such Performers should chance to be United: and added 'Mais, *qu'a produit tant d'Harmonie?*'

'*Rien, mon seigneur,*' answered Hetty; laughing, '*que trois Enfans.*'[10]

She vows she was *irresistably* led to make this queer answer at the moment, but was sorry afterwards, for the Prince laughed immoderately; and went immediately to Lord Bruce, and repeated *ce que Madame avoit dit*[11] – with many droll comments and observations, such as, that such an *harmonious* secret should be communicated to the foreign academies; that it was of consequence to Natural philosophy – etc. etc.

Mr Harris said he rejoiced, in *these degenerate Days*, to see such *Harmony* in married People.

Lady Edgecumbe was Introduced to Prince Orloff, whom she had never met with before. She Entered into a flirtation with him; and was so Courteous, and made so many reverences, that the Dean of Winchester, (who is very satirical) observed afterwards,[12] that his *Diamonds*, and his *Highness* together, had quite penetrated her Ladyship.

Lady Edgecumbe, being obliged to *shew herself* at Lady Harrington's, *retired* soon after the last Duet.

When the Room was a good deal *Thinned*, Mr Harris told me he wished

---

7. *Little prisoner.*
8. Johann Gottfried Müthel.
9. *Husband and wife.*
10. '*What has produced such harmony?*' '*Nothing, my lord, . . . but three children.*'
11. *What Madam had said.*
12. Dr Newton Ogle.

some of *the ladies* would express a desire of seeing the *Empress's Picture* nearer; 'I, you know,' said he, 'as a *man*, cannot, but my Old Eyes can't see it at a distance.'

I went up to Dr King, and made the request to him. He hesitated some time, but afterwards assented the demand to General Bawr who boldly made it to the Prince. His Highness laughed, and with great good humour, desired the General to untie the picture from his Neck, and present it to us; and he was very facetious upon the occasion, desiring to know if we wanted any thing *else*? and saying that, if they pleased, *the ladies* might *strip him entirely*! Not very elegant, methinks, his pleasantry!

When we got it, there was hardly any looking at the *Empress* for the glare of the Diamonds. Their size is almost incredible. One of them, I am sure, was as big as a *Nutmeg* at *least*.

When we were all satisfied, it was returned, and the Prince most graciously made a Bow to, and received a Curtsie from, every one who looked at it.

34. From Journal *14 December 1775*

To our great surprise, who, late in the Evening, should Enter, but Omiah!

How he found out the House, I cannot tell, as it is a Year since he was here before. But he now Walks every where quite alone, and has Lodgings in Warwick Street, where he lives by himself. The King allows him a Pension.

He has learnt a great deal of English since his last Visit, and can, with the assistance of signs, and Action, make himself tolerably well understood. He pronounces English in a manner quite different from other Foreigners, and sometimes unintelligibly. However, he has really made a great proficiency, considering the disadvantages he labours under, which render his studying the Language so much more difficult to him, than to other strangers; for he knows nothing of *Letters*, and there are so very few Persons who are acquainted with his Language, that it must have been extremely difficult to have Instructed him at all.

He is lively and intelligent, and seems so open and Frank Hearted that he looks *every* one in the Face as his Friend and well wisher. Indeed, *to me*, he seems to have shewn no small share of real greatness of mind, in having thus thrown himself into the power of a Nation of strangers, and placing such entire confidence in their Honour and Benevolence.

As we are totally unacquainted with his Country, Connections, and affairs, our Conversation was necessarily very much confined, indeed it wholly consisted in Questions of what he had seen here, which he answered, when he understood, very *entertainingly*.

He began immediately to talk of my Brother.

'Lord Sandwich[1] write, one, two, three,' (counting on his Fingers) '*monts* ago – Mr Burney, – come Home.'

'He will be very happy,' said I, 'to see *you*.'

He Bowed, and said 'Mr Burney very *dood* man!'

We asked if he had seen the King lately.

'Yes. King George *bid me*, – Omy, you go Home. O very *dood* man King George.'

He then, with our assisting him, made us understand that he was extremely rejoiced at the thought of seeing again his Native Land, but at the same Time, that he should much regret leaving his friends in England.

'Lord Sandwich,' he added, '*bid me*, Mr Omy, you two ships – you go Home – I say,' (making a fine Bow) 'very much *oblige*, my Lord.'

We asked if he had been to the Opera?

He immediately began a *squeak*, by way of *imitation*, which was very ridiculous; however, he told us he thought the music was *very fine*; which, when he *first* heard it, he thought *detestable*.

We then enquired how he liked the Theatres, but could not make him understand us; though, with a most astonishing politeness, he always endeavoured, by his Bows and smiles, to save us the trouble of knowing that he was not able to comprehend whatever we said.

When we spoke of Riding, an idea entered his Head, which much diverted him, and which he endeavoured to explain, of riding double, which I suppose he has seen upon the Roads.

'First goes man, so!' (making a motion of whipping a Horse) 'then *here*' (pointing behind him) '*here* goes Woman! Ha, Ha, Ha!'

Miss Lidderdale, of Lynn,[2] who was with us, and was in a riding Habit, told him that *she* was prepared to go on Horseback.

He made her a very civil Bow, and said 'O you, – you *dood* woman, you *no man*; – dirty woman, – Beggar woman; – ride so; – not you.'

We mentioned Dick to him, who is now at Harrow School, as we told him. He recollected and enquired after him. When we said he was gone to school, He cried 'O! to learn his Book? so!' (putting his two Hands up to his

---

1. John Montagu, fourth Earl of Sandwich, First Lord of the Admiralty.
2. Maria Georgina ('Liddy') Lidderdale, daughter of a Lynn physician.

Eyes in Imitation of holding a Book.) He then attempted to describe to us a school to which he had been taken to see its *humours*.

'Boys here, – Boys there, – Boys all over! – one Boy come up – do so,' (again imitating Reading) '*not well*; – *man* not like – man do so!' Then he shewed us how the master had hit the Boy a violent Blow with the Book on his shoulder.

Miss Lidderdale asked him if he had seen Lady Townshend lately? 'Very pretty Woman, lady Townshend!' cried he, – 'I drink Tea with lady Townshend in 1: 2: *tree* Days. – Lord Townshend, my friend: Lady Townshend, my friend: very pretty Woman, Lady Townshend! – very pretty Woman, Mrs Crewe! – very pretty Woman Mrs Bouverie! – very pretty Woman Lady Craven! – '[3]

We all approved his Taste, and he told us that when any of his acquaintance wished to see him, they 'write, and *bid me*, Mr Omy, you come, – Dinner – Tea – or supper. – Then I go.'

My Father, who fortunately, came in during his visit, asked him very much to favour us with a song of his own Country, which he had heard him sing at Hinchinbrooke.[4] He seemed to be quite ashamed, – but we all joined, and made the request so earnestly, that he could not refuse us: but he was either so modest that he blushed for his own performance, or his Residence here had made him so conscious of the *barbarity* of the South Sea Islands' Music, that he could hardly prevail with himself to comply with our request. And when he did, he began two or three Times before he could acquire Voice or firmness to go on.

Nothing can be more *curious*, or less *pleasing*, than his singing Voice, he seems to have none, and *Tune*, or *air*, hardly seem to be *aimed* at; so queer, wild, strange a *rumbling of sounds* never did I before hear; and very contentedly can I go to the Grave if I never do again. His *song* is the only thing that is *savage* belonging to him.

The *story* that the Words told was laughable enough; for he took great pains to explain to us the *English* of the song. It appeared to be a sort of *Trio*, between an old Woman, a young Woman, and a young man. The two latter are entertaining each other with praises of their merits, and protestations of their passions, when the old woman enters, and endeavours to *faire l'aimable*[5] to the Youth; but, as she cannot boast of her *Charms*, she is very earnest in

3. All were noted beauties.
4. Lord Sandwich's seat.
5. *Endear herself.*

displaying her *Dress*, and making him observe and admire her taste and fancy; Omiah, who stood up to *Act* the Tune, was extremely droll and diverting by the Grimace, *minauderies*[6] and affectation he assumed for this Character, examining and regarding himself and his Dress with the most conceited self-complacence. The Youth then avows his passion for the Nymph; the old Woman sends her away, and, to use Omiah's own words, coming forward to offer *herself,* says 'Come! *Marry* me!' The young man starts as if he had seen a Viper, then makes her a Bow, begs to be excused, and runs off.

Though the singing of Omy is so barbarous, his Actions and the expression he gives to each Character, are so original and so diverting, that they did not fail to afford us very great entertainment, of the *risible* kind.

35. From Letter to Samuel Crisp *April 1776*

Mr Burney, Hetty and I took a walk in the Park on Sunday morning, where, among others, we saw the young and handsome Duchess of Devonshire, walking in such an undressed and slaternly manner as, in former Times, Mrs Rishton might have done in Chesington Garden. Two of her Curls came quite Unpinned, and fell lank on One of her shoulders; one shoe was down at Heel, the Trimming of her Jacket and coat was in some places unsewn; her Cap was awry, and her cloak, which was rusty and powdered, was flung half on and half off. Had she not had a servant in superb Livery behind her, she would certainly have been affronted.[1] Every creature turned back to stare at her. Indeed I think her very handsome; and she has a look of innocence and artlessness that made me quite sorry she should be so foolishly negligent of her Person. She had hold of the Duke's arm, who is the very reverse of herself, for he is ugly, tidy, and grave. He looks like a very mean shop keeper's Journey man.

Omai, who was in the Park, called here this morning, and says that he went to her Grace, and asked her why she let her Hair go in that manner? Ha, Ha, Ha, – don't you Laugh at her having a Lesson of Attention from an Otaheitan?

---

6. *Simpering manner.*

1. As a loose woman, or prostitute. Georgiana Spencer had at seventeen married the fifth Duke of Devonshire. Now two years later, she was a famous beauty whose charm and ebullience made her a leading figure in London society. For a woman of her social stature she was unusually

36. Letters to Thomas Lowndes[1] *25 and 26 December 1776*

Sir,   As Business, with those who understand it, makes its own apology, I will not take up your Time with reading Excuses for this address, but proceed immediately to the motives which have induced me to give you this trouble.

I have in my possession a M:S. novel, which has never yet been seen but by myself; I am desirous of having the 2 first volumes printed immediately, – and the publication of the rest, shall depend wholly on their success.

But, sir, such is my situation in Life, that I have objections unconquerable to being known in this transaction; – I, therefore, must solicit the favour of you to answer me the following queries, which I hope you will not think impertinent.

1st whether you will give a candid and impartial Reading, to a Book that has no *recommendation* to previously prejudice you in its favour?

Secondly, whether, if, upon perusal, the work should meet with your approbation, you will Buy the Copy, of a Friend whom I shall commission to wait upon you, without ever seeing or knowing the Editor?

I shall be obliged to you to direct your answer to Mr King, to be left at the Orange Coffee House till called for, in the Haymarket.[2]

Sir,

The frankness, with which you favoured me with an answer to my Letter, induces me to send you the M:S. with the firmest reliance upon your candour.

The plan of the first Volume, is the Introduction of a well educated, but inexperienced young woman into public company, and a round of the most fashionable Spring Diversions of·London. I believe it has not before been executed, though it seems a fair field open for the Novelist, as it offers a fund inexhaustible for Conversation, observations, and probable Incidents.

---

informal and unaffected, which, coupled with her youth, probably accounts for her unkempt dress on this occasion.

1. These letters inaugurate FB's correspondence, anonymous on her side, with Thomas Lowndes, a bookseller in Fleet Street, which would lead to his publishing *Evelina* in January 1778.

2. Only FB's sisters Susanna and Charlotte and her brother Charles were in the secret of her authorship. Charles acted as her intermediary with Lowndes, meeting him (or his emissary) at the Orange Coffee House while preposterously disguised as 'Mr King'. Later Edward Francesco Burney fulfilled this function, meeting the publisher at Gregg's Coffee House in York Street. (See selection 43.) FB wished anonymity because of the stigma attached to female authorship.

The characters of the Sea Captain, and *would be* French woman,[3] are intended to draw out each the other; and the ignorance of the former, in regard to modern customs, and fashionable modes, assists in marking their absurdity and extravagance.

I shall send you the second volume with all the expedition in my power, if that which is now under your examination, makes you desirous of seeing it,[4]

I am,

Sr

Your most obdt servant

37. From Letter to Susanna Burney *15 March 1777*

[Chessington]

We pass our Time here very serenely, and, distant as you may think us from the Great World, I some times, find myself in the midst of it, – though nobody suspects the brilliancy of the Company I occasionally keep.[1] We Walk, Talk, Write, Read, Eat, Drink, Thrum,[2] and sleep. These are our recreations, which, for your better conception, I will some what enlarge upon.

Imprimis;[3] – *We Walk*: The brightness of the sun, invites us abroad, – the tranquility of the scene, promises all the pleasures of philosophic contemplation, which, *ever studious of rural amusement*, I eagerly pursue, mais, helas![4] scarse have I wandered over half a meadow, ere the *bleak Winds whistle round my Head*, off flies my faithless Hat, – my perfidious Cloak endeavours to follow, – even though it clings, with well acted fondness, to my Neck; – my Apron, my Gown, – all my habiliments, with rebellious emotion, wage a Civil War with the *mother Country*![5] – though there is not an Individual among them but has been indebted to me for the very existence by which they so treacherously betray me! My shoes, too, though they cannot, like the rest, brave me to my Teeth, are equally false and worthless; for, far from aiding

---

3. Captain Mirvan, brutal sea captain, and Madame Duval, Evelina's vulgar English-born grandmother who married a Frenchman and seeks to pass herself off as a Frenchwoman.
4. Not knowing FB's circumstances, Lowndes wanted her to complete the third volume immediately and publish the whole novel at once, but she could not comply.

1. FB refers to her secret writing of *Evelina*.
2. Strum (the harpsichord or fortepiano).
3. In the first place (Latin).
4. But alas!
5. FB alludes to the war with the British colonies in what would become the United States.

me by springing forward, with the generous zeal they owe me, for having rescued them from the dark and dusty Warehouse in which they were pent, – they fail me in the very moment I require their assistance, – sink me in Bogs, – pop me into the mud, – and, attaching themselves rather to the mire, than to the Feet which guide them, threaten me perpetually with desertion: and I shall not be much surprised, if, some Day when I least think of it, they should give me the slip, and settle themselves by the way.

Secondly: *We Talk*: *That*, you can do yourself, so shall not enter into a minute discussion of this point.

Thirdly: *We Write*: *That is thus*; Mr Crisp, writes to Miss Simmons; Mrs Hamilton, to the Butcher; and Miss Cooke, a list of Cloaths for the Washerwoman: and as to *me*, – do you know I write to *you* every Evening, while the family play at Cards? The folks here often marvel at your ingratitude in sending me so few returns in kind.[6]

Fourthly: *We Read*: Mr Crisp pores over Critical Reviews to Sir John Hawkins;[7] Mrs Hamilton, the Tradesmen's Bills; Miss Cook, her own pocket Book, or *Ladies Memorandum*,[8] and I, – am studying, against I return to Town, Le Diable Boiteux,[9] which contains no few moral sentences, proper for those who dwell in a great *Methropolis*.

Fifthly, *We Eat*. There is something, in this part of our Daily occupation, too singular and uncommon to be passed over without some particular Notice and observation. Our method is as follows; We have certain substances, of various sorts, consisting *chiefly* of Beasts, Birds, and vegetables, which, being first Roasted, Boiled or Baked, (N.B. We shall not Eat Raw flesh, till Mr Bruce publishes his Travels,)[10] are put upon Dishes, either of Pewter, or Earthern ware, or China; – and then, being cut into small Divisions, every plate receives a part: after this, with the aid of a knife and fork, the Divisions are made still smaller; they are then (care being taken not to maim the mouth by the above offensive Weapons) put between the Lips, where, by the aid of the Teeth, the Divisions are made yet more delicate, till, diminishing almost insensibly they form a general *mash*, or *wad*, and are then swallowed.[11]

6. FB was pretending to write to Susanna while she was writing *Evelina*.

7. See p. 43 note 4. The *Critical Review* and *Monthly Review* were influential monthly periodicals, and Crisp was interested in their reception of Hawkins's history (as a rival to CB's).

8. *The Ladies' Own Memorandum Book, or Daily Pocket Journal* was published annually.

9. *The Lame Devil* (1707), novel by Alain René Le Sage.

10. Bruce had claimed that certain natives of Abyssinia ate raw flesh. See p. 38 note 4.

11. Besides making fun of the banality of life in the country, FB perhaps reveals a fastidious aversion to food. All her life she was an abstemious and finicky eater.

38. From Letter to Samuel Crisp *27–28 March 1777*

Mrs and Miss Thrale, Miss Owen and Mr Seward came long before *Lexaphanes*;[1] – Mrs Thrale is a very pretty woman still, – she is extremely lively and chatty, – has no supercilious or pedantic airs, and is really gay and agreeable. Her Daughter is about 12 years old, stiff and proud, I believe, or else shy and reserved: I don't yet know which. Miss Owen, who is a Relation, is good humoured and sensible *enough*; she is a sort of *Butt*, and as such, a general favourite: for those sort of characters are prodigiously useful in drawing out the Wit and pleasantry of others: Mr Seward is a very polite, agreeable young man:

My sister [Esther] was invited to meet them.

The Conversation was supported with a good deal of vivacity – (N.B. my Father being at Home) for about half an Hour, and then Hetty, and *Suzette*, for the first Time *in public*, played a Duet, and, in the midst of this performance, Dr Johnson was announced.

He is, indeed, very ill favoured, – he is tall and stout, but stoops terribly, – he is almost bent double. His mouth is almost constantly opening and shutting, as if he was chewing; – he has a strange method of frequently twirling his Fingers, and twisting his Hands; – his Body is in continual agitation, *see sawing* up and down; his Feet are never a moment quiet, – and, in short, his whole person is in perpetual motion:[2]

His Dress, too, considering the Times, and that he had meant to put on his best becomes,[3] being engaged to Dine in a large Company, was as much out of the common Road as his Figure: he had a large Wig, snuff colour coat, and Gold Buttons; but no Ruffles to his shirt, doughty fists, and black worsted stockings.

He is shockingly near sighted, and did not, till she held out her Hand to him, even know Mrs Thrale. He *poked his Nose* over the keys of the Harpsichord, till the Duet was finished, and then, my Father introduced Hetty to

1. Hester Lynch Thrale, writer and hostess, her daughter Hester Maria ('Queeney') Thrale, Margaret Owen, cousin and friend of Mrs Thrale, and William Seward, future author and member of the Thrales' circle. *Lexaphanes*, a name given to Dr Johnson by a critic who attacked the style of his *Rambler* essays. FB here records her first sight of Johnson, at a morning party in St Martin's Street.

2. It is now suggested that Johnson suffered from La Tourette's Syndrome, a disorder of the central nervous system.

3. FB's coinage for his most becoming attire.

him, as an old acquaintance, and he cordially kissed her. When she was a little girl, he had made her a present of *The Idler.*[4]

His attention, however, was not to be diverted five minutes from the Books, as we were in the Library; he poured over them, shelf by shelf, almost brushing the Backs of them, with his Eye lashes, as he read their Titles; at last, having fixed upon one, he began, without further ceremony, to Read to himself, all the Time standing at a distance from the Company. We were all very much provoked, as we perfectly languished to hear him talk; but, it seems, he is the most silent creature, when not particularly drawn out, in the World.

My sister then played another Duet, with my Father: but Dr Johnson was so deep in the Encyclopedie,[5] that, as he is very deaf, I question if he even knew what was going forward. When this was over, Mrs Thrale, in a laughing manner, said 'Pray, Dr Burney, can you tell me what that song was, and whose, which Savoi sung last night at Bach's[6] Concert, and which you did not hear?' My Father confessed himself by no means so good a Diviner, not having had Time to consult the stars, though in the House of Sir Isaac Newton. However, wishing to draw Dr Johnson into some Conversation, he told him the Question. The Doctor, seeing his drift, good naturedly put away his Book, and said very drolly 'And pray, Sir – *Who is Bach*? – is he a Piper?'[7] – Many exclamations of surprise, you will believe, followed this Question. 'Why you have Read his name often in the papers,' said Mrs Thrale; and then she gave him some account of his Concert, and the number of fine performances she had heard at it.

'Pray,' said he, gravely, 'Madam, what is the Expence?'

'O,' answered she, 'much trouble and solicitation to get a subscriber's Ticket; – or else half a Guinea.'

'Trouble and solicitation,' said he, 'I will have nothing to do with; – but I would be willing to give Eighteen Pence.'

Ha! ha!

Chocolate being then brought, we adjourned to the Dining Room. And here, Dr Johnson, being taken from the Books, entered freely and most cleverly into conversation: though it is remarkable, that he never speaks at

---

4. Collection of periodical essays which Johnson wrote from 1758 to 1760.
5. The famous *Encyclopédie* (35 vols., 1751–80) of Denis Diderot.
6. Johann (John) Christian Bach, the so-called 'London Bach', one of the composer sons of Johann Sebastian Bach. The singer was Gasparo Savoi.
7. Johnson's ignorance of Bach was probably feigned, but his indifference to music was not.

all, but when spoken to; nor does he ever *start*, though he so admirably *supports* any subject.

The whole party was engaged to Dine at Mrs Montague's:[8] Dr Johnson said he had received the most flattering note he had ever read, or that any body else had ever Read, by way of invitation. 'Well, so have I, too,' cried Mrs Thrale, 'so if a note from Mrs Montague is to be boasted of, I beg mine may not be forgot.'

'*Your* note,' cried Dr Johnson, 'can bear no comparison with *mine*; – I am *at the Head of Philosophers*; she says.'

'And I,' cried Mrs Thrale, '*have all the muses in my Train!*'

'A fair Battle,' said my Father; 'come, Compliment for Compliment, and see who will hold out longest.'

'O, I am afraid for Mrs Thrale!' cried Mr Seward, 'for I know Mrs Montague exerts all her forces when she attacks Dr Johnson.'

'O yes,' said Mrs Thrale, 'she has often, I know, flattered *him* till he has been ready to Faint.'

'Well, Ladies,' said my Father, 'You must get him between you to Day, and see which can lay on the paint thickest, Mrs Thrale or Mrs Montague.'

'I had rather,' cried the Doctor, drily, 'go to Bach's Concert!'

After this, they talked of Mr Garrick, and his late Exhibition before the King, to whom, and to the Queen[9] and Royal Family, he read Lethe, *in character, c'est à dire*, in different Voices, and Theatrically.[10] Mr Seward gave us an account of a Fable, which Mr Garrick had written, by way of Prologue, or Introduction, upon the occasion: In this, he says, that a Black Bird, grown old and feeble, droops his Wings, etc., etc., and gives up singing; but, being called upon by the Eagle, his Voice recovers its powers, his spirits revive, he sets age at defiance, and sings better than ever. The application is obvious.

'There is not,' said Dr Johnson, 'much of the spirit of *Fabulosity* in this Fable; for the call of an *Eagle* never yet had much tendency to restore the voice of a *Black Bird*! 'Tis true, the Fabulists frequently make the *Wolves* converse with the *Lambs*, – but, when the conversation is over, the *Lambs* are sure to be Eaten! – and so, the *Eagle* may entertain the *Black Bird*, – but the Entertainment always ends in a *Feast* for the Eagles!'

'They say,' cried Mrs Thrale, 'that Garrick was extremely hurt at the

8. Elizabeth Montagu, noted bluestocking, 'Queen of the Blues'.

9. Queen Charlotte, consort of George III. She was German and came from Mecklenburg-Strelitz.

10. Garrick's adaptation of *Lethe, or, Aesop in the Shades* (1740), a farce which was the very first of his plays.

coolness of the King's applause, and did not find his reception such as he expected.'

'He has been so long accustomed,' said Mr Seward, 'to the Thundering approbation of the Theatre, that a mere *very well*, must necessarily and naturally disappoint him.'

'Sir,' said Dr Johnson, 'he should not, in a Royal apartment, expect the hallowing and clamour of the one shilling gallery. The King, I doubt not, gave him as much applause as was rationally his due: and, indeed, great and uncommon as is the merit of Mr Garrick, no man will be bold enough to assert that he has not had his just proportion both of Fame and Profit: he has long reigned the unequaled favourite of the public, – and therefore, nobody will mourn his hard fate, if the King, and the Royal Family, were not transported into rapture, upon hearing him Read Lethe. Yet, Mr Garrick will complain to his Friends, and his Friends will lament the King's want of feeling and taste; – and then, Mr Garrick will kindly *excuse* the King! he will say that His Majesty might be thinking of something else; – that the affairs of America might occur to him, – or some subject of more importance than Lethe; – but though he will say this himself, he will not forgive his Friends, if they do not contradict him!'

But now, that I have written this *satire*, it is but just both to Mr Garrick, and to Dr Johnson, to tell you what he said of him afterwards, when he discriminated his character with equal candour and humour.

'Garrick,' said he, 'is accused of vanity; – but few men would have borne such unremitting prosperity with greater, if with equal moderation: he is accused, too, of avarice, – but, were he not, he would be accused of just the contrary, for he now Lives rather as a *prince*, than as an Actor: but the frugality he practiced when he first appeared in the World, and which, even then, was perhaps beyond his necessity, has marked his character ever since; and now, though his Table, his Equipage, and manner of Living, are all the most expensive, and equal to those of a Nobleman, yet the original stain still blots his name, – yet, had he not fixed upon himself the charge of Avarice, he would, long since, have been reproached with that of *luxury*, and with living beyond his station in magnificence and splendour.'

Another Time, he said of him 'Garrick never enters a Room, but he regards himself as the object of general attention, from whom the Entertainment of the Company is expected, – and true it is, that he seldom disappoints them; for he has infinite humour, a very just proportion of Wit, and more convivial pleasantry than almost any other man living. But then, off, as well as *on* the stage, he is always an Actor! for he thinks it so incumbent upon him to be sportive, that his gaity becomes mechanical from being habitual, and he can exert his spirits at all Times alike, without consulting his real Disposition to hilarity.'

39. From Journal *April 1777*[1]

The Band was now got into order for the Overture, and the Company going to be summoned up stairs, – when another Chaise arrived, – and it proved from Gloucester, with the Doctor and the Captain![2]

I assure you this frightened me so much, that I most heartily wished myself 20 miles off; – I was quite sick, and, if I had dared, should have given up the part.

When I came to be Painted, my Cheeks were already of so high a Colour, that I could hardly bear to have any added: but, before I went on, I seemed siezed with an Ague fit, and was so extremely Cold, that my Uncle, upon taking my Hand, said he thought he had touched ice or marble.

At length, they all came up stairs: a Green Curtain was drawn before them, and the overture was played. Miss Humphries did all the Honours, for Nancy was engaged as Prompter,[3] and my Uncle one of the Band.

The Theatre looked extremely well, and was fitted up in a very Dramatic manner: with side scenes, – and 2 figures, of Tragedy and Comedy at each end, and a Head of Shakespear in the middle. We had 4 Change of scenes. The play we acted was 'The Way to Keep Him.'

As soon as the Overture was played, – which, you must know, was performed in the *passage*, for we had no Room for an Orchestra in the Theatre, – Edward and Tom were seated at Cards, and the Curtain Drawn. Tom's part was very soon over, and then Betsy entered; she was much

1. FB describes an amateur performance of Arthur Murphy's comedy *The Way to Keep Him* at Barborne Lodge, the home of the Worcester branch of the Burney family. Richard Burney, brother of CB, was head of the Worcester Burneys. The actors were FB herself (as Mrs Lovemore) and her cousins Edward Francesco (William, a servant to Lovemore), Thomas Frederick (another servant), Elizabeth ('Betsy') Warren (Muslin, waiting-woman to Mrs Lovemore, and Mignonet, Widow Belmour's maid), James Adolphus (Sir Brilliant Fashion), Richard Gustavus (Lovemore) and Rebecca ('Becky') (Widow Belmour). The audience consisted of family and friends from as far away as Gloucester. Murphy was a friend of the Thrales.

2. John Wall, wealthy physician of Tewkesbury Park, Gloucester, and George Kien Hayward Coussmaker, army officer and brother of Catherine Coussmaker, a particular friend of Susanna Burney.

3. Hannah Humphries, sister-in-law of Richard Burney, who se wife had died in 1771, and Ann ('Nancy'), another cousin of FB.

flurried, and yet in very great spirits, and acquitted herself *greatly* beyond my expectations: Edward was, I believe, very little frightened, yet not quite so easy or so excellent as I had imagined he would have been. Indeed the part is extremely unworthy of him, and I fancy he was determined to let it take its chance, without troubling himself with much exertion.

Take notice, that, from the beginning to the End, no *applause* was given to the play. The Company judged that it would be inelegant, and therefore, as they all said, *forbore*; – but indeed a little clapping would have been very encouraging, and I heartily wish they had not practiced such *self denial*!

At length came *my* scene; I was discovered Drinking Tea; – to tell you how *infinitely*, how *beyond measure* I was terrified at my situation, I really cannot, – but my fright was nearly such as I should have suffered had I made my appearance upon a public Theatre, since Miss Humphries and Captain Coussmaker were the only two of the Audience I had ever before seen.

The few Words I had to speak before Muslin came to me, I know not whether I spoke or not, – niether does any body else: – so you need not enquire of others, for the matter is, to this moment, unknown.

Fortunately for me, all the next scene gave me hardly 3 words in a speech, for Muslin has it almost to herself: so I had little else to do than to lean on the Table, and twirl my Thumbs, and, sometimes, bite my fingers: – which, indeed, I once or twice did very severely, without knowing why, or yet being able to help it.

I am sure, *without flattery*, I looked like a most egregious fool; – for I made no use of the Tea things, – I never tasted a drop, – once, indeed, I made an attempt, by way of passing the Time better, to drink a little, but my Hand shook so violently, I was fain to put down the Cup instantly, in order to save my Gown.

By the way, I have forgot to mention Dresses.

Edward had a Coat Trim'd to have the effect of a rich Lace Livery; – He had a Capital Bag,[4] long Ruffles and so forth.

Tom much the same.

Betsy, as Muslin, had a very showy striped pink and white Manchester, pink shoes, red Ribbons in abundance and a short Apron. The Paint upon her very pale Cheeks set her off to the greatest advantage, and I never saw her look nearly so well.

Mrs Lovemore wore her Green and Grey, which I have trimed with Gause, white Ribbons, Gause Apron, Cuffs, Robings, etc.

4. A bag-wig.

The next who made his appearance, was Cousin James, – he was most superbly Dressed, but, as you saw his Cloaths at the music meeting, I will not describe them. His Hair, however, I must not pass unnoticed; for you never saw the most foppish stage Character better Dressed in the *macaroni* style.[5] Indeed, all our Hairs were done to the astonishment of all the Company.

He entered with an air so immensely conceited and affected, and, at the same Time, so uncommonly bold, that I could scarse stand his *Abord*:[6] and, through out the scene that followed, he acted with such a satisfied, nay, *insolent* assurance of success, that, I declare, had I been entirely myself, and free from fear, he would have wholly disconcerted me: as it was, my flurry hardly admitted of encrease: yet I felt myself glow most violently.

I must assure you, notwithstanding my embarrassment, I found he did the part *admirably*, – not merely *very much* beyond my expectations, but, I think, as well as it *could* be done. He looked very fashionable, very assured, very affected, and very *every way the thing*. Not one part in the piece was better or more properly done: nor did any give *more* entertainment.

We were, next, joined by Richard: whose *non chalence*, indifference, half vacancy and half absence, excellently marked the careless, unfeeling husband which he represented. Between his extreme unconcern, and Sir Brilliant's extreme assurance, I had not much trouble in appearing the only languid and discontented person in the Company.

Richard was in a very genteel morning Dress.

A short scene next followed, between Betsy and me, which I made as little of as any body might desire – indeed, I would Challenge all my Acquaintance around, to go through an act more thoroughly to their own dissatisfaction. So, that is saying more than every body can, however.

The Act finished by a *solo* of Betsy, which I did not hear, for I ran into a Corner to recover Breath against next act.

My Uncle was very good natured, and spoke very comfortable things to me – which I did by no means expect, as at first, he seemed not delighted that Betsy had given me her part. He said I wanted *nothing but exertion*, and charged me to speak louder, and take courage.

'O!' cried Edward, 'that this had but been Lady Betty Modish!'[7]

---

5. Based on continental fashions, affected by young exquisite men who had travelled abroad and banded together in what they called the Macaroni Club (after the pasta).
6. *Approach.*
7. In Colly Cibber's *The Careless Husband.*

However, since I was so terribly Cowardly, I now rejoice that I had a part so serious and solemn, sad and sorrowful.

Cousin James was prodigiously gallant in comforting me, taking my Hand, and supporting his *tendresse* yet more strongly off than on the stage. The truth is, he is so very good natured, that the least idea of pity really softens him into down right tenderness.

Richard was entirely occupied in changing his Dress for Lord Etheridge.[8]

In the next Act, the widow Belmour made her appearance. Beckey's elegant Figure and Face were charmingly set off, for her Dress was fashionable and becoming: she had on a lilac Negligee, Gause Cuffs trimmed richly, with Flowers and spangles, spangled shoes, Bows of Gause and Flowers, and a Cap! – *quite the thing*, I assure you! – full of flowers, frivolete, spangles, Gause, and long Feathers; – immensely high, and her Hair delightfully well Dressed. She was in great spirits, and not at all frightened. Her Entrance, I am sure, must be striking, and I was surprised the folks could forbear giving her applause. She was throughout lively, easy and elegant; and her whole appearance was so charming, there was no looking at any thing else.

Betsy changed her Dress entirely for Mignonet,[9] and did the Character very well; though the worse for having another in the same play, as she saved herself very much for Muslin, which she did admirably.

During my reprieve from Business, I thought I had entirely banished my fears, and assumed sufficient Courage to go through the rest of my part to the best of my capacity; – but far otherwise I found it, for, the moment I entered, I was again gone! – knew not where I stood, nor what I said, – a mist was before my Eyes, so strong that it almost blinded me, and my Voice faltered so cruelly, that, had they not all been particularly silent whenever I aimed at speaking, not a word the better would they have been for my presence! –

And all this for pleasure! – but indeed it was too much, – and I have not yet recovered from the really painful sensations I experienced that night, – sensations which will always make my recollection of the Way to keep him disagreeable to me.

Fortunately for me, my part and my spirits, in this Act, had great simpathy; – for Mrs Lovemore is almost unhappy enough for a Tragedy Heroine: – and, I assure you, she lost none of her *pathos* by any giddiness of

8. Lovemore's disguise which he assumes for his affair with the Widow Belmour.
9. The Widow Belmour's maid.

mine! – I gave her melancholy feelings very fair play, and *looked* her misfortunes with as much sadness as if I really experienced them.

In this Act, therefore, circumstances were so happily miserable for me, that I believe some of my auditors thought me a much better and more *arttificial* actress than I dreamt of being myself, and I had the satisfaction of hearing some few *buzzes* of approbation which did me no harm.

But I would never have engaged in this scheme, had I not been persuaded that my fright would have ended with the first scene: I had not any idea of being so completely overcome by it.

The grand scene between the Widow and Lord Etheridge, Richard and Beckey acquitted themselves extremely well in. If Richard had a fault, it was being *too* easy, – he would have had more spirit, had he been *rather* less *at Home*. His Dress for this part was all elegance.

This Act concluded with the scene that I prevailed with Edward and Betsy to add, – they did it vastly well, and are both, I believe, well pleased that they listened to me.[10]

Again, my Uncle said the most flattering things to encourage me, 'Only speak out, Miss Fanny,' said he, 'and you will leave nothing to wish; – it is impossible to do the part with greater propriety, or to speak with greater feeling, or more sensibly, – every, the most insignificant thing you have to say, *comes Home* to me.'

You can't imagine how much this kindness from him Cheared me. In the third act I recovered myself very decently, *compared* to the 2 first, – but indeed I was very, very far from being easy, or from doing the part according to my own ideas.

So that, in short, I am totally, wholly, and entirely – dissatisfied with myself in the whole performance. Not once could I command my voice to any steadiness, – or look about me with any ease or pleasure.

In the most Capital scene of Mrs Lovemore, with her Husband, in the third Act, when she is all *Air, alertness, pleasure and enjoyment*, I endeavoured what I could to soften off the affectation of her sudden change of Disposition; and I *gagged*[11] the Gentleman with as much ease as my very little ease would allow me to assume. Richard was really charming in this scene; so thoroughly negligent, inattentive and sleepy, that he kept a continual *titter* among the young Ladies; – but, when he was roused from his indifference by Mrs Lovemore's pretended alteration of Temper and Conduct, – he *sung small*

10. Probably written by FB herself; it does not survive.
11. Deceived or imposed upon.

indeed! – when *her* flightiness began, you can hardly suppose how *little* he looked, – how mortified! – astonished! and simple! – it was admirably in character, and yet he seemed as if he *really could not help it*, – and as if her unexpected gaity quite confounded him.

Betsy, Beckey and James were all of them very lively, and very clever in all they had to do in this Act.

I am very sorry that Edward could not have more justice done to those talents which I know only want to be called forth.

At the End of all, there was a faint something in *imitation* of applause, – but very faint, indeed: yet, though it would much have encouraged us, we have no reason to be mortified by its omission, since they all repeatedly declared they *longed* to clap, but thought it would not be approved: and since we have heard, from all quarters, nothing but praise and compliment.

Richard spoke the last speech in a very spirited manner: and he was very delicate and very comfortable to me in our reconciliation, when Mrs Belmour says 'Come, kiss and Friends!' – and *he* adds 'it is in *your* power, Madam, to make a reclaimed libertine of me indeed,' – for he excused all the embracing part, and without making any fuss, only took my Hand, which, Bowing over, (*like Sir Charles Grandison*,)[12] he most respectfully pressed to his Lips.

40. From Journal *June 1777*

James, in a Whisper, asked me where I thought Richard was? – I could not possibly guess. 'Why,' said he, 'he is in the back Lane, leading to the House, standing in the Rain, without his Great Coat, and talking to Mrs Wall,[1] who is leaning out of her Window, to answer him, with all her Hair about her Ears!' –

Mrs Wall did not make her appearance till Tea was half over; for the Doctor insisted that Nancy should make Tea, and not wait for *Mrs Brilly*, which, or *my Ladyship*, he always calls her. I think *you know* that Mrs Wall's name is *Briliana*?

12. The hero of Samuel Richardson's novel of that title. Richard kisses FB's hand rather than embracing her and kissing her cheek because of his recognition of her extreme shyness and prudishness before strangers.

1. Mary Brilliana Wall, wife of John Wall. FB and her cousins were on a side-visit to Gloucester from Worcester. Mrs Wall the coquette and cousin Richard the gallant are made for each other.

As she is in mourning, her Dress did not shew to so much advantage as to pay us for Waiting so long to see it. And now, if you would have my opinion of Mrs Wall, from what I saw of her in a visit of 3 Days, take it. I think her very plain, though very smart in Dress and appearance; she is clever, but very satirical; she makes it a rule never to look at a Woman, when she can see a man; she takes it in turn to be very natural, and very affected; she spends infinitely more than half her Time at her Toilette, to which she is an absolute slave; she is exceedingly fond of Laughing and making merry, but rather tiresome in *pointing out* that *penchant*, not leaving it to others to *discover*, and, in short, she has 3 ruling passions, each of them so strong, it would be difficult to say which predominates: and these are Dress, Admiration, and *Fun* – simple, honest, unrefined *Fun*.

I can believe any thing as to *the present* to Richard from her behaviour and looks: she is forever seeking Richard's Eyes, and, when they meet, they smile so significantly! – and look with such intelligence at each other! but, indeed, Mrs Wall does not *confine* her smiles to him, any more than *he* does his gallantry to her: were I Dr Wall, I should be infinitely miserable to have a Wife so apparently addicted to flirting, and seeking objects with whom to Coquet from morning to Night.

41. From Journal *July 1777*

But the most agreeable circumstance of my Visit remains to be told, – namely, that *Miss Waldron* was at Westwood the two first Days of my residence there.[1] Now, as you know nothing of her but from Richard's Imitation, I shall take the liberty to enlarge upon her person, Character and behaviour. She is short, thick set, fat, clumsy, clunch and heavy: but her Face is very handsome; she has pretty blue Eyes, and a most brilliant Complection, with a Colour the finest that can be seen. She is very good natured, and is not *a natural*, – that is, not an absolute Ideot, – but she is the veriest *Booby* I ever knew: she cannot speak, without making some blunder; she is so *bothered* in every speech, that she is eternally contradicting herself; she never says a word without exciting mirth, yet seldom discovering the *cause*, she always joins in the *effect*, and Laughs as simply as she makes others

---

1. FB was visiting Westwood Park, seven miles from Worcester, the seat of Sir Herbert Pakington, Baronet. His wife was Elizabeth, Lady Pakington, and his daughter, Elizabeth, married (1793) William Russell. Elizabeth Hannah Waldron, twenty-one years old, was the daughter of the Revd John Waldron, rector and schoolmaster in the patronage of Sir Herbert.

do artfully: and, at the same Time that her ignorance invites pity, her happiness renders it unnecessary.

She was, indeed, the very *quintessence* of sport during the Visit; every body Laughs at her with little or no ceremony, but Nobody affronts her: she takes all in good part, and if you do but *tell* her she is not the subject of your mirth, she is thoroughly satisfied, and Laughs on herself without further enquiry.

At Dinner Time, she was the general *Butt*, Sir Herbert piques himself upon *shewing her off*, and makes ridiculous Comments upon every thing she says; Lady Packington sneers, and exposes her to the strongest ridicule; the young Ladies titter unmercifully; – even Nancy's smiles border upon the full grin; – and, for my part, I Laughed most heartily; yet was nobody more merry than herself. I would fain give you a specimen of the Conversation, that *you* might Laugh too, – but, unless I could *paint* her, and shew you, at the same Time, the extreme vacancy of her Countenance, – and give you some idea of the *drone* of her Voice, and of her unmeaning manner, – I could hope for no success at all equal to my wishes, or to the subject.

. . .

At supper, Miss Waldron was requested to *sing*; she declined it for some Time, saying 'I don't sing at all well; – you'll only think I'm a squalling, – for I don't know any thing of the music, – so sometimes I'm *in* the Tune, and sometimes I'm out of it, – but I never know which. And so it's the same with my Brother, for he sings just as I do; we both squall, after a sort, but it isn't very well.'

We all, however, pressed her very much, and Sir Herbert in particular, 'Come, *Lillies* and *Roses*, (that is the name he gives her,) come, give us *Guardian angels*, – come, tune your pipe, – now! – quick!'

'Ay, come, Miss Waldron,' cried Lady Packington, 'give us a fine Italian air, – I suppose, Miss Fanny, you are very fond of Italian music?'

'Lord, my Lady,' cried Miss Waldron, 'I really don't know *the music* at all, – I'm sure I shall only frighten you.'

'O, we *know* you don't,' returned she, 'but never mind, you can let us hear your Voice.'

'Come, Lillies and Roses,' said Sir Herbert, 'don't be too long, – begin at once.' Chucking her under the Chin.

'Ay, do, Miss Waldron,' said Miss Packington, 'or else you'll make us expect too much.'

'Do you know no pretty new song?' said her Ladyship.

'No, my Lady, I know hardly any songs, – that is to be sure. I dare say I know above a Hundred, – but I don't know the music of 'em.'

'Well, any thing, – just what you please,' cried Lady Packington, 'only don't make us wait, – for that is not very well worth while.'

'Why then, if you please, my Lady,' said she, 'I'll sing "before the Urchin well could go," – only I can't sing it very well, – so I tell you that before Hand.'

'Is *that* by way of something new, Miss Waldron?'

Regardless of this question, the poor Girl began: – and never before did I hear any thing so ludicrous: she has not even a natural good *voice* to excuse her miserable performance: on the contrary, it is a *Croak*, a *squeak*, – Nature has been as little her Friend as Art has been her Assistant.

For some Time, I sat in an Agony, almost killing myself by restraining my Laughter; – but finding that Nobody else took the same trouble, by degrees I began to excuse it myself, and very soon after took the general liberty which example gave me, and Laughed without controul or disguise.

She could not get on *3 words* at a Time, on account of the confusion, for she caught the Laugh, and stopped to join in it; and then, like a Noodle, the moment she recovered her own Countenance, with the utmost solemnity, she again began the song.

Nothing affected her, in the manner any other person would have been affected for the merriment she excited only served, occasionally, to *interrupt* her, but she never thought of stopping it by ceasing to sing, – the *only* way in her power. Nay, *Sir Herbert*, though the *most* desirous to hear her, took such methods to render her ridiculous, as must have most cruelly *affronted* any other character in the World: he burst out a Laughing in her Face; patted her Cheeks, slapped her shoulders, chucked her under the Chin, and exclaimed '*Brava*, Lillies and Roses!' perpetually: – but, it was *all one to her*, for whenever she could conquer her own foolish tittering, she made up a Face of stupid composure, and, with the utmost indifference, began her song again.

Sir Herbert, determined to spare no pains to expose her, finding how well she took all he had hither to offered, at length took up a large spoon, and fairly *entered it* down her Bosom, where the opening of her Handkerchief left a most inviting vacancy.

I expected that this stroke would have raised some spirit; but she *continued* her song with the same gravity, only, and with the utmost deliberation, taking the spoon out, and quietly putting it into its place upon the table!

The interruptions, however, in spite of her own Tranquility, were so frequent, that, as she always *began again* upon any stop of her own, she could get no further than the two first Lines: and the case, now, appearing desperate, with regard to this song, Sir Herbert desired her to begin another.

'Come, Lillies and Roses, now try Guardian Angels.'

'Ay, do, Miss Waldron,' said Lady Packington, 'and never mind the Girls, – don't stop for their Laughing.'

'No more I would, my Lady,' said she, 'only that I can't help it, – for they make *me* Laugh too.'

Guardian Angels was then begun, – but so long was it in performing, that we all retired the moment it was sung: and really I was glad of a little *relaxation* from Laughter: though I did not obtain it immediately, for as Miss Waldron slept in the next Room to ours, she Undressed herself in company with us. And she was so entertaining the whole Time she stayed without having the least design or knowledge of being so, that when I went to Bed I was quite weak and exhausted.

Thursday morning she came to sit with me, till Lady Packington was ready for Breakfast, –

She then gave me a very circumstantial account of her Life and employments, and told me all her Affairs with as much openess and unreserve as if she had known me many years. I will recollect what I can of her Relations. And, when you read what she says, you must suppose it spoken in a very *slow* and *slovenly* Voice.

Her Father keeps a school at Hartlebury, and our Conversation began by my enquiring if they did not *make very merry* when Richard was among them?

'Why, yes, he's merry enough, sometimes; – only he mustn't be so with our young Gentlemen: but he makes fun enough with my Brother, sometimes, they two'll Laugh like any thing, – but it's mostly at my expense! but the thing is, I don't much mind 'em, for it's all one to me; for if I was to mind it, they do it as bad again.'

'Well, but, I hope *you* Laugh, too?'

'Yes, I Laugh enough, too, some times; but then when I do, my Brother says I'm just like a Jack ass in fits; – besides, I mustn't Laugh much, when my papa's at Home, because if I do, he says, "come, let's have no more Noise; it's all Levity; – "" but I talk enough, for all that, sometimes, for Mr Smith and Mr Giles say they can hear me at their House, I talk so loud, – and that's as far off as half a mile, almost, I believe; – but I've enough to do, some times, because of our young Gentlemen, for I've no Time to myself; – I'm always doing some odd Job or another, – yet you'd think I do nothing, – and no more I do, – only papa says I've a mind to make a fuss about it: but I never get up till past 9 o'clock, – Lady Packington would be finely angry if she knew it, for she'd say it was all a whim, – but I never tell her about it, but I'm tired as any thing before Night, for our young gentlemen will have their own way, and one has enough to do to content 'em all.'

'But I hope Mr Waldron will leave off his school soon, or else that you will settle some where else, – for it must be a fatiguing Life to you – '

'No, he won't leave it off, – and indeed I like it very well, – we *both* like it, because the thing is we've found the profits of it. For before my Papa kept that school, he had but 60 pounds a year; – and you know that would do nothing, to Live upon, with 8 children: it wasn't half enough. And another thing is, I never get any Dinner, – so that's bad enough for me, when I'm at Home, and so I'm glad enough to get out, sometimes: I'm sure I'm never so happy as at Westwood, for I Eat what I like.'

'But how comes it about that you have no Dinner?'

'Why as soon as ever I sit down to Dinner, I'm forced to begin helping the young Gentlemen, – and so by the Time I have helped them all round, why him as I helped first, is ready to begin again, and so then I can get none at all: for if I was to put myself a bit by, they'd think I took the best: so I only Eat a bit of Bread and Cheese.'

'Well, but that's very hard upon you: I wonder you don't make them wait a little?'

'Why there's nothing I love so well as Bread and Cheese; – I prefer it to meat a great deal. Sometimes I'm as dirty as can be, – and I hardly know how, for I do nothing: but one Day a Gentleman came to our House, he's one of my Cousins, so he said to me very gravely, says he, do pray get me a wash Hands Bason, and a Towel, and a piece of soap: so I went, and found that I could not bring them all at once, so I'd two Journeys for my pain, never suspecting all the while what he meant: so when I'd brought 'em, he gets up, and he falls to scrubbing the Towel with the soap as hard as ever he could: and then, he comes up to me, and says, "Now you've taken the trouble to bring the things, I must have the pleasure to wash your Face, for it's as black as soot." So you can't think how angry I was, for I said, says I, couldn't you as well have said to me at once, go and wash your Face; as to give me all this trouble to bring the things here for nothing?'

When we were summoned to Breakfast, 'I think,' said she, 'I may as well put away my things this morning, because may be Lady Packington may take the whim to come in my Room, for perhaps she may have a mind to shew you the House herself: so I think I had best be before Hand with her, – for she's very particular, you must know.'

1778–1781

Evelina *and Streatham Park*

42. From Journal *March 1778*

This Year was ushered in by a grand and most important Event, – for, at the latter end of January, the Literary World was favoured with the first publication of the ingenious, learned, and most profound Fanny Burney! – I doubt not but this memorable affair will, in future Times, mark the period whence chronologers will date the Zenith of the polite arts in this Island!

This admirable authoress has named her most elaborate Performance '*Evelina, or a Young Lady's Entrance into the World.*'

Perhaps this may seem a rather bold attempt and Title, for a Female whose knowledge of the World is very confined, and whose inclinations, as well as situations, incline her to a private and domestic Life. – All I can urge, is that I have only presumed to trace the accidents and adventures to which a '*young woman*' is liable, I have not pretended to shew the World what it actually *is*, but what it *appears* to a Girl of 17: – and so far as that, surely any Girl who is *past* 17, may safely do?

43. From Journal *23 June 1778*

[Chessington]

I have had a visit from my beloved, my kindest Father – and he came determined to complete my recovery by his goodness.[1] I was *almost* afraid – and *quite* ashamed to be alone with him – but he soon sent for me to his little Gallery Cabinet – and then, with a significant smile that told me what was coming, and made me glow to my very forehead with anxious

---

1. FB had been staying since early May at Chessington where she was trying to recover from a long and serious illness.

expectation, he said 'I have read your Book, Fanny – but you need not blush at it. – It is full of merit – it is really extraordinary. – ' I fell upon his Neck with heart-beating emotion, and he folded me in his arms so tenderly that I sobbed upon his shoulder – so delighted was I with his precious approbation. But I soon recovered to a gayer pleasure, more like his own: though the length of my illness, joined to severe mental suffering from a Family calamity which had occurred at that period, had really made me too weak for a joy mixt with such excess of amazement. I had written my little Book simply for my amusement; I printed it, by the means first of my Brother, Charles, next of my Cousin, Edward Burney, merely for a frolic, to see how a production of my own would figure in that Author like form: but as I had never read any thing I had written to any human being but my sisters, I had taken it for granted that They, only, could be partial enough to endure my compositions. My unlooked for success surprized, therefore, my Father as much as my self –

44. From Letter to Susanna Burney *5 July 1778*

I often think, when I am counting my Laurels, what pity it would have been had I *popt off* in my last Illness, without knowing what a *person of Consequence* I was! – and I sometimes think, that, were I *now* to have a relapse, I could never *go off* with so much *Eclat*! – I am now at the *summit* of a high Hill, – my prospects, on one side, are bright, glowing, and invitingly beautiful; – but when I turn round, I perceive, on the other side, sundry Caverns, Gulphs, pits and precipices, that to *look at*, make my Head giddy, and my Heart sick! – I see about me, indeed, many Hills of far greater height and sublimity; – but I have not the strength to attempt climbing them; – if *I* move, it must be in *descending*! I have already, I fear, reached the *pinnacle* of my Abilities, and therefore to *stand still* will be my best policy: – but there is nothing under Heaven so difficult to do! – Creatures who are formed for motion, *must* move, however great their inducements to forbear. The Wisest Course I could take, would be to bid an eternal adieu to Writing; then would the Cry be ' 'Tis pity she does not go on! – she might do something better by and by; – ' etc., etc., Evelina as a First, and a youthful publication, has been received with the utmost favour and lenity, – but would a future attempt be treated with the same mercy? – No, my dear Susy, quite the contrary, – there would not, indeed, be the same *plea* to save it, – it would no longer be a *Young Lady's first appearance* in public; – those who have met with less indulgence, would all *peck* at any new Book, – and even those who most encouraged the 1st offspring, might prove Enemies to the 2d, by receiving it with Expectations which it could not answer – and so, between either the Friends or the Foes of the *Eldest*, the *2d* would stand an equally bad chance, and a million of *flaws* which were overlooked in the former, would be ridiculed as villainous and intolerable *Blunders* in the latter. – But, though my Eyes Ache as I strain them to look forward, – the temptations before me are *almost* irresistible. –

45. From Journal *August 1778*

I have now to write an account of the most *Consequential* Day I have spent since my Birth: namely, my Streatham Visit.

Our Journey to Streatham was the least pleasant part of the Day: for the Roads were dreadfully dusty, – and I was really *in the Fidgets* from thinking what my reception might be, and from fearing they would expect a less awkward and backward kind of person than I was sure they would find.

Mr Thrale's[1] House is white, and very pleasantly situated, in a fine Paddock. Mrs Thrale was strolling about and came to us as we got out of the Chaise. 'Ah,' cried she, 'I hear Dr Burney's Voice! – and you have brought your Daughter? – well, now you *are* good!' She then received me, taking both my Hands, and with a mixt politeness and cordiality, welcoming me to Streatham.

She led us into the House, and addressed herself almost wholly, for a few minutes, to my Father, as if to give me an assurance she did not mean to regard me as *a shew*, or to distress or frighten me by *drawing me out*. Afterwards, she took me up stairs, and shewed me the House: and said she had very much wished to see me at Streatham, and should always think herself much obliged to Dr Burney for his goodness in bringing me, which she looked upon as a very great favour. But, though we were some Time together, and though she was so very civil, she did not *hint* at my Book: and I love her much more than ever for her delicacy in avoiding a subject which she could not but see would have greatly embarrassed me.

When we returned to the Music Room, we found Miss Thrale was with

---

1. Henry Thrale was a wealthy Southwark brewer and Member of Parliament. Streatham Park was his country seat in Surrey, just south of London. CB had been a regular guest for several years there, and gave music lessons to Queeney Thrale. FB's invitation is evidence of her new fame.

my Father. Miss Thrale is a very fine Girl, about 14 years of age, but cold and reserved, though full of knowledge and intelligence. She may, and I doubt not, *will* be as *learned* as her mother, but never half so amiable, *selon apparance*.[2]

Here the subject that was started was *Dick*, who played truant at Winchester, and is now under the displeasure of Dr Warton.[3] Mrs Thrale interests herself greatly for Dick, and spoke all sort of comforting things to my Father: and, when he expressed his vexation at the affair, 'Pho,' said she, 'Boys *will* be naughty, there's nothing in that; – but let him be what he will, I sha'n't suffer the man who has such Daughters as Miss Burney to complain.'

'That's aside,' said my Father, Laughing; 'Fanny must not hear that.'

In truth, I was employed in looking at Prints, and therefore affected not to attend.

'Ay, well,' said Mrs Thrale, 'she often, I doubt not, hears more praise than she believes, though not more than she deserves.'

My Father, then, enquired after Mr Thrale. 'Why,' said she, 'my master is gone out on Horseback, with Mr Seward.'

This Mr Seward is a Young man of Fortune, who is a great favourite at Streatham. He is handsome, and very sensible and intelligent: but Mrs Thrale told us, he had a very strange singularity of Disposition, for that, with real goodness of Heart, Benevolence and Generosity of Temper, he always affected the utmost sourness, bluntness and moroseness. She added, that there was, at this Time, a poor man in great distress, and that, to her certain knowledge, he had insisted on lending him 100 pounds yearly, till his affairs were retrieved: 'and,' said she, 'he can never hear the name of this man, without Tears; yet he pretends to a Character the very reverse, and aims at a kind of misanthropy.'

I have had *very* little conversation with this Gentleman, but I have seen him 3 or 4 Times. And I was much rejoiced in finding that no other Company was expected.

Soon after, Mrs Thrale took me to the Library. She talked a little while upon common topics, and then, – at last, – she mentioned Evelina, calling it '*the Book of which I alone was ashamed*.' And ashamed enough I felt, in

2. Judging by appearances.

3. FB's half-brother, now nine, had run away from the home of Joseph Warton, headmaster of Winchester School and poet and literary critic. Warton had kindly taken him into his home until a vacancy should occur in his school. Samuel Johnson had agreed to sponsor Dick at the urging of Hester Thrale, who had been persuaded to approach Johnson by CB. Needless to say, Dick's escapade ruined his chances for admission.

Conscience! and I began poring over the Books, in order to turn from her.

'Well,' said she, 'it is a sweet pretty Book indeed! and Yesterday at supper we talked it all over, and discussed all your Characters; but Mr Johnson's favourite is Mr Smith! – he is *so* smart! – he declares the *fine Gentleman manqué* was never better drawn: and he acted – him all the Evening, saying *he was 'all for the Ladies! whatever was agreeable to the Ladies,'* and so on; while *I* took up Madame Duval, and told them *I desired I might hear no more of such vulgar pieces of Fun!* – But Mr Johnson repeated whole scenes by Heart! – I declare I was astonished at him! – O you can't imagine how much he is pleased with the Book; – *he "could not get rid of the Rogue"*, he told me.'

I could only Laugh and thank her: and express, though not very *audibly*, my surprise, and assure her I hardly knew *how* to credit flatteries so unexpected and so undeserved.

'But was it not droll,' said she, 'that *I* should *recommend* it to Dr Burney? and teize him, so innocently, to read it?'

In the midst of this conversation, Mrs Thrale, from the Window, perceived Mr Thrale, and called to him; – 'Mr Thrale,' said she, 'if you will come hither, I can give you very great pleasure; I have a Young Lady to introduce to you whom you want very much to know.'

So! thought I, what, is he, too, acquainted with my frolic! – And I am sure, by her looks, and the earnest curiosity of her regards, that *Miss* Thrale was not ignorant of it. Heigh ho! how difficult is *secret keeping*!

Mr Thrale came immediately, and was extremely civil to me. He is a very Tall, well looking man, and very well bred; but shy and reserved: however, he was attentively obliging to me all the Day.

I found, by the enquiries that followed of *if* and *when* they had seen me, that I, as well as my Book, had had the Honour to supply them with conversation the preceding Evening, and they had recollected all they knew of me. 'But,' said Mr Thrale, to his Wife, who was in a white muslin Jacket, 'I think you might as well have been better equipped to receive your Guests.'

'And so I *would*, I assure You,' answered she, 'if I had imagined Miss Burney would have thought at all the better of me for *Dress*; but I had no Notion it would be any recommendation to her.'

When he left us I prevailed upon Mrs Thrale to let me amuse *myself*, and she went to obey her master's order and Dress. I then *prowled* about, to chuse some Book, and I saw, upon the Reading Table, Evelina; – I had just fixed upon a new Translation of Cicero's Laelius[4] when the Library

4. A new translation of *De Amicitia* ('On Friendship') by William Melmoth.

Door was opened, and Mr Seward Entered. I instantly put away my Book, because I dreaded being thought *studious* and affected. He offered his service to find any thing for me, and then, in the same Breath, ran on to speak of the Book with which I had, myself, *favoured the World*! The exact Words he began with I cannot recollect, for I was actually confounded by the attack: I had not any idea that he knew of the affair; and his abrupt manner of letting me know he was *au fait*[5] equally *astonished* and *provoked* me: how different from the delicacy of Mr and Mrs Thrale! – I was so much amazed, and so much displeased, that I could not speak a word, and he then went on with some general praises, and said that I had hit off the *City manners* wonderfully.

I doubt not but he expected my thanks! – but I only stammered out something of my surprise to find the affair *so spread*, and then, with the coldest gravity, I seated myself, and looked another way.

It could not be very difficult for him, now, to perceive that he had wholly mistaken *his Game*, and that my *Greediness* for praise was by no means so *gluttonous* as to make me swallow it when so ill Cooked; but I fancy he imagined I should, of course, be delighted to hear my *own* Book mentioned with Compliments, and so he concluded I should, with much eagerness, Enter upon the subject. However, when he discovered his mistake, he spared no endeavours to repair it, for he Changed his Theme, and did not again ever go back to his first topic, notwithstanding he continued with me near 2 Hours, and never once suffered the Conversation to *flag*. Indeed, I was for some Time, so totally disconcerted by his abrupt attack, that I hardly knew what I answered him, but, by degrees I *tranquillised*, as I found he forbore distressing me any further, by such *Home* strokes; And I must do him the justice to own that I believe he was sorry himself that he had started the subject, when he saw how I received it.[6]

He stayed, talking upon divers matters, till he was obliged to go and Dress for Dinner: – and then, before he left me, he offered his service to find me any Book; – I accepted his offer, as I did not know where to look, or for what. He spent no little Time ere he could satisfy himself, and, at last, he brought me a Book of Poems by Miss Aiken.

'But the doubt is, Ma'am,' said he, 'whether they are her own writing.' I asked him who *was* suspected as Author? 'Why her Brother – they Live in

---

5. *In the know.*

6. FB's excessive diffidence about *Evelina* stemmed from her extreme shyness, exacerbated by guilt over her having dared both to write and to publish a novel. (See Introduction.) But FB's panic and distress must have been inexplicable and annoying to her admirers.

the same House.'[7] Ah, thought I, how kindly willing is the World to make charitable constructions!

I then began reading, and he left the Room.

Mrs Thrale soon after joined me: I wished much to have expostulated with her upon betraying me to Mr Seward, but could not myself introduce the subject, and *she* never again led to it; I am sure she *spared* me from good nature, as she could not but observe how much more easy I was upon all other Topics.

The rest of the morning was all spent charmingly; – we went into the Music Room, and there joined Mr and Miss Thrale, Mr Seward and my Father.

When we were summoned to Dinner, Mrs Thrale made my Father and me sit each side of her: I said that I hoped I did not take Dr Johnson's place? – for he had not yet appeared. 'No,' answered Mrs Thrale, 'he will sit by you, – which I am sure will give him great pleasure.'

Soon after we were seated, this great man entered. I have so true a veneration for him, that the very sight of him inspires me with delight and reverence, notwithstanding the cruel infirmities to which he is subject; for he has almost perpetual convulsive movements, either of his Hands, lips, Feet, knees, and sometimes of all together. However, the sight of them can never excite ridicule, or, indeed, any other than melancholy reflections upon the imperfections of Human Nature; for this man, who is the acknowledged first Literary man in this kingdom, and who has the most extensive knowledge, the clearest understanding, and the greatest abilities of any Living Author, – has a Face the most ugly, a Person the most awkward, and manners the most singular, that ever were, or ever can be seen. But all that is unfortunate in his *exterior*, is so greatly compensated for in his *interior*, that I can only, like Desdemona to Othello, '*see his Visage in his mind*.'[8] His Conversation is so replete with instruction and entertainment, his Wit is so ready, and his Language at once so original and so comprehensive, that I hardly know any satisfaction I can receive, that is equal to listening to him.

Mrs Thrale introduced me to him, and he took his place. We had a Noble

---

7. Anna Laetitia Aikin published a volume of *Poems* in 1773. She married the following year and is better known by her married name, Anna Barbauld. Her brother was also a writer. The false rumour that he had ghost-written the poems reflects the low contemporary opinion of women's abilities.

8. Adaptation of Desdemona's words in Shakespeare, *Othello*, I. iii. 252: 'I saw Othello's visage in his mind'.

Dinner, and a most elegant Desert. Dr Johnson, in the middle of Dinner, asked Mrs Thrale what was in some little pies that were near him? 'Mutton,' answered she, 'so I don't ask you to Eat any, because I know you despise it.'

'No, Madam, no;' cried he, 'I despise *nothing* that is good of its sort: – but I am too proud *now* to Eat of it; – sitting by Miss Burney makes me very proud to Day!'

'Miss Burney,' said Mrs Thrale, Laughing, 'you must take great care of your Heart if Dr Johnson attacks it! – for I assure you he is not often successless.'

'What's that you say, Madam?' cried he, 'are you making mischief between the young lady and me already?'

A little while after, he Drank Miss Thrale's Health and mine; and then added – ' 'Tis a terrible thing that we cannot wish young Ladies *well*, without wishing them to become Old Women!'

'But some people,' said Mr Seward, 'are old and young at the same Time, for they wear so well that they never look old.'

'No, Sir, no;' cried the Doctor, Laughing; 'that never yet was; You might as well say they are at the same Time Tall and short! I remember an Epitaph to that purpose, which is in——'

I have quite forgot *what*, – and also the *name* it was made upon; but the *rest* I recollect exactly; –

> —— —— lies Buried here;
> So *early* wise, so *lasting* fair,
> That none, unless her Years You told,
> Thought her a Child, or thought her Old.

Mrs Thrale then repeated some Lines in French, and Dr Johnson some more in Latin; an Epilogue of Mr Garrick's to Bonduca[9] was then mentioned, and Dr Johnson said it was a miserable peformance, and every body agreed it was the worst he had ever made. 'And yet,' said Mr Seward, 'it has been very much admired; but it is in praise of English valour, and so I suppose the *subject* made it popular.'

'I don't know, Sir,' said Dr Johnson, 'any thing about the subject, for I could not read on till I came to it: I got through half a dozen Lines, but I

---

9. Garrick provided the prologue (not epilogue) to George Colman the elder's revision of Beaumont and Fletcher's tragedy *Bonduca*, which had opened at the Theatre Royal, Haymarket, on 30 July.

could observe no other subject than eternal dullness. I don't know what is the matter with David; I am afraid he is grown superannuated, for his Prologues and Epilogues used to be incomparable.'

'Nothing is so fatiguing,' said Mrs Thrale, 'as the Life of a Wit: he and Wilks[10] are the 2 oldest men of their ages I know, for they have both worn themselves out by being eternally on the rack to give entertainment to others.'

'David, Madam,' said the Doctor, '*looks* much older than he *is*;[11] for his Face has had double the Business of any other man's, – it is never at rest, – when he speaks one minute, he has quite a different Countenance to what he assumes the next; I don't believe he ever kept the same look for half an Hour to gether in the whole course of his Life; and such an eternal, restless, fatiguing play of the muscles, must certainly wear out a man's Face much before its real Time.'

'O yes,' cried Mrs Thrale, 'we must certainly make some allowance for such *wear and Tear* of a man's Face.'

The next Name that was started, was that of Sir John Hawkins: and Mrs Thrale said 'Why now, Mr Johnson, he is another of those whom you suffer nobody to abuse but yourself; why Garrick is one, too, – for if any other person speaks against him, you Brow-beat him in a minute!'

'Why, Madam,' answered he, 'they don't know *when* to abuse him, and *when* to praise him; I will allow no man to speak ill of David that he does not *deserve*; and as to Sir John: why really I believe him to be an honest man at the *bottom*, – but to be sure he is penurious; and he is mean; – and it must be owned he has a degree of brutality, and a tendency to savageness, that cannot easily be defended. – '

We all Laughed, as he *meant* we should, at this curious manner of speaking in his *favour*; and he then related an anecdote that he *knew* to be true in regard to his meanness. He said that Sir John and he once belonged to the same Club; – but that, as he *Eat no supper*, after the first night of his admission, he desired to be excused *paying his share*!

'And *was* he excused?'

'O yes, – for no man is angry at another for being inferior to himself! we all scorned him, – and admitted his plea. For my part, I was such a fool to

---

10. John Wilkes, politician and wit. Formerly a radical responsible for riots against the government, he had turned conservative and was now a friend of the establishment, and of Johnson himself.

11. He was sixty-one, and would die the following year of a stroke.

pay my share for *Wine*, though I never tasted any. But Sir John was a most *unclubable* man!'

How delighted was I to hear this *master of Languages* so unaffectedly and sociably and good naturedly *make* Words, for the promotion of sport and good humour!

'And this,' continued he, 'reminds me of a Gentleman and Lady with whom I travelled once; I suppose I *must* call them Gentleman and Lady according to form, because they travelled in their own Coach and 4 Horses: But at the first Inn where we stopt, the Lady called for – – a pint of Ale! – and when it came, quarrelled with the Waiter for not giving full measure! – Now *Madame Duval* could not have done a grosser thing!'

O how every body Laughed! – and to be sure *I* did not *glow* at all! nor *munch fast*, – nor look on my plate, – nor lose any part of my usual composure! But how grateful do I feel to this dear Dr Johnson for never naming *me* and the *Book* as belonging one to the other, and yet making an allusion that shewed his *thoughts* led to it! – and, at the same Time, that seemed to justify the Character, as being *Natural*! But, indeed, the delicacy I met with from him and from all the Thrales was yet *more* flattering to me than all the praise with which I have *heard* they have Honoured my Book. And though *I* was displeased with Mr Seward for his abruptness, which indeed most vilely disconcerted me, perhaps most others would have been *gratified* by it, and therefore –, upon further consideration, he appears less to blame in the affair than he did at first.

After Dinner, when Mrs Thrale and I left the Gentlemen, we had a Conversation that to *me*, could not but be delightful, as she was all good humour, spirits, sense and *agreeability*. Surely *I* may make words, when at a loss, if *Dr Johnson* does.[12] However, I shall not attempt to *write* any more particulars of this Day, – than which I have never known a happier, – because the Chief subject that was started and kept up, was an invitation for me to Stretham, and a desire that I might accompany my Father thither next Week, and stay with them some Time. Now, though no subject could be so highly agreeable to me, it would yet appear to no advantage upon paper, and therefore I shall *abridge* it into saying that Mrs Thrale was quite *violently* urgent, and assured my Father my *Health* might depend upon my returning again to spend some Time in the Country, for that, after such an illness, London might half kill me, – and a thousand other pleas, all uttered

---

12. 'Agreeability' is FB's coinage according to *The Oxford English Dictionary*, which frequently cites her innovative use of language.

with the most good natured cordiality; and *Mr* Thrale joined her request with great politeness; – but nothing was absolutely fixed. We left them at about 8 o'clock, and Mr Seward, who Handed me into the Chaise, added *his* interest to the rest, that my Father would not fail to bring me. In short, I was loaded with civilities from them all. And my ride Home was equally happy with the rest of the Day, for my kind and most beloved Father was so happy in *my* happiness, and congratulated me so sweetly, that he could, like myself, think on no other subject. And he told me that, after passing through such a House as that, I could have nothing to fear. Meaning for my Book, my honoured Book.

46. From Journal Letter to Susanna Burney[1] *23 August 1778*

'And yet,' continued the Doctor [Johnson], with the most comical look; 'I have known *All* the Wits, from Mrs Montagu, – down to Bet Flint!'

'Bet Flint!' cried Mrs Thrale, 'pray who is she?'

'O, a fine Character, Madam! – she was *habitually* a slut and a Drunkard, and *occasionally* a Thief and a Harlot.'

'And, for Heaven's sake, how came *you* to know her?'

'Why, Madam, she figured in the *Literary* world, too! – Bet Flint wrote her own Life, and called herself Cassandra, – and it was in Verse; – it began

> When Nature first ordained my Birth
> A Diminitive I was Born on Earth;
> And then I came from a Dark abode
> Into a gay and gaudy World.

'So Bet brought me her Verses to correct; – but I gave her half a Crown, and she liked it as well. Bet had a fine spirit; – she Advertised for a Husband, but she had no success, for she told me no man aspired to her! – Then she hired very handsome Lodgings, and a Foot Boy; – and she got a Harpsichord, but Bet could not *play*; – however, she put herself in fine attitudes, and *Drum'd*.'

Then he gave an account of another of these Geniuses, who called herself some fine Name, I have forgotten what. 'She had not quite the same stock of *virtue*,' continued he, 'nor the same stock of *Honesty* as Bet Flint, but I suppose she envied her accomplishments, for she was so little moved by the power of Harmony, that while Bet Flint thought she was Drumming very *divinely*, the other Jade had her indited for a Nuisance!'

'And pray what became of her? Sir!'

'Why, Madam, she stole a Quilt from the man of the House, and he had her taken up; – but Bet Flint had a spirit not to be subdued, – so when she found herself obliged to go to Jail, she ordered a sedan Chair, and bid her Foot boy walk before her! However, the Boy proved refractory, for *he* was ashamed, though his mistress was not.'

'And did she ever get out of Jail again, Sir?'

'Yes, Madam; when she came to her Trial, – the Judge, – who Loved a Wench at his Heart, acquitted her. So now, she said to me, the Quilt is my own! – and now I'll make a petticoat of it. – O, – I Loved Bet Flint! – '[2]

47. From Journal Letter to Susanna Burney *30 August 1778*

[Streatham]

I then escaped to look for a Book which we had been talking of, and Dr Johnson, when I returned to my seat, said he wished [Samuel] Richardson had been alive, 'And then,' he added, 'you should have been Introduced to him, – though, I don't know, niether; – Richardson would have been afraid of her!'

'O yes! – that's a likely matter!' quoth I.

'It's very true,' continued he; 'Richardson would have been really *afraid* of her; – there is merit in Evelina which he could not have borne. – No, it would not have done! – unless, indeed, she would have flattered him prodigiously. – Harry Fielding, too, would have been afraid of her, – there is nothing so delicately finished in *all* Harry Fielding's Works,[1] as in Evelina; – ' (Then, shaking his Head at me, he exclaimed) 'O, you little *Character-monger*, you!'

Mrs Thrale then returned to her charge, and again urged me about a Comedy, – and again I tried to silence her, – and we had a *fine fight* together; – till she called upon Dr Johnson to *back* her, – 'Why, Madam,' said he, Laughing, – 'she *is* Writing one! – What a rout is here, indeed! – She is

2. Bet's trial took place at the Old Bailey in September 1758. The judge was Sir John Willes, who had a reputation for lechery. Bet was accused by her landlady of stealing the quilt (and five other articles), which the landlady claimed had been given her by the former keeper of the lodgings, Captain Baldwin. But he was out of the country and could not testify, so Willes acquitted Bet.

1. Henry Fielding, author of *Tom Jones* (1749), *Amelia* (1751), etc.

writing one up stairs all the Time. – Who ever knew when she began Evelina? She is working at some drama, depend upon it.'

'True, true Oh King!' thought I.[2]

'Well, that *will* be a sly trick!' cried Mrs Thrale; – 'however, you know best, I believe, about That, as well as about every other Thing.'

. . .

I told her [Mrs Thrale] how much I dreaded being discovered, and besought her not to betray me any further. She again began Laughing, and openly declared she should not consult me about the matter. I was really uneasy, – nay, quite uncomfortable, – for the *first* Time I have been so since I came hither; – but as we were obliged soon to return, I could not then press my request with the earnestness I wished. – But she told me that, as soon as I had left the Room when Mr Lort took up Evelina, he exclaimed contemptuously 'Why it's printed for *Lowndes*! – '[3] and that Dr Johnson then told him there were things and Characters in it *more* than worthy of Fielding! 'Oho!' cried Mr Lort, 'what, is it better than *Fielding?*' 'Harry Fielding,' answered Dr Johnson, 'knew nothing but the shell of Life.' 'So *You*, Ma'am,' added the flattering Mrs Thrale, 'have found the *kernel*!'

Are they all mad? or do they want to make me so?

When we returned, to my great joy they were talking of other subjects, – yet I could not sufficiently recover myself the whole Evening to Speak one word but in *answer*; for the dread of the Criticisms which Mr Lort might, innocently, make the next Day, kept me in a most uncomfortable state of agitation.

When Mrs Thrale and I retired, she not only, as usual, accompanied me to my Room, but stayed with me at least an Hour, talking over the affair. I seized, with eagerness, this favourable opportunity of conjuring her not merely not to tell Mr *Lort* my secret, but ever after never to tell *any* body. For a great while she only *Laughed*, saying 'Poor Miss Burney! – so you thought just to have played and sported with your sisters and Cousins, and had it all your own way! – but now you are *in for* it! – – but if you *will* be an Author and a Wit, – you must take the Consequence!'

But, when she found me seriously urgent, and really frightened, – she changed her Note, and said 'O, – if I find you are in *earnest* in desiring

2. FB quotes Daniel 3: 24 (Authorized Version) and indicates that she may have already begun work on her comedy *The Witlings*.
3. The Revd Michael Lort was a well-known antiquarian scholar. Lowndes had a low reputation among booksellers and publishers.

concealment, I shall quite *scold* you! – for if such a desire does not proceed from *Affectation*, – 'tis from something *Worse*.'

'No, indeed,' cried I, 'not from *Affectation*, – for my *conduct* has been as uniform in trying to keep snug as my *words*: and I *never* have wavered: I *never* have told *any body* out of my own Family; nor half the Bodies in it. – And I have so long forborne making this request to you, for no other reason in the World but for *fear* you should think me affected.'

'Well, I *won't* suspect you of affectation,' – returned she, – 'nay, I *can't*, for you have looked, like your name sake in the Clandestine Marriage, all this Evening, of *50 Colours, I wow and purtest*;[4] – but – when I clear you of *that*, I leave something *worse*.'

'And what, – dear Madam, *what* can be worse?'

'Why an over-delicacy that may make you unhappy all your Life! – Indeed you must *check* it, – you must get the better of it: – for *why* should you *write* a Book, *Print* a Book, and have every Body *Read* and *like* your Book, – and then sneak in a Corner and disown it!'

'My *printing* it, indeed,' said I, 'tells terribly against me, to all who are unacquainted with the circumstances that belonged to it: but I had so little notion of being *discovered*, and was so well persuaded that the Book would never be *heard of*, that I really *thought* myself as safe, and *meant* to be as private, when the Book was at Mr Lowndes', as when it was in my own Bureau.'

'Well, – I don't know what we shall do with you! it is a *sweet* Book, and it *will* make its way, but indeed you must blunt a little of this delicacy, – for the Book has such success, that if *you* don't own it – somebody else will!'

I then told her that I had never, in the course of my life, been so much confounded as at Mr Seward's attack; as I had not had any idea he was *au fait*; she Laughed, and said 'Poor Seward! – I am sure *he* would be hurt, if he found he had done wrong! but I told him myself.'

Again I entreated her to rest, at least, contented with the communications she had already made, and to promise not to tell Mr Lort, nor any others.

'O,' cried she, with quickness, 'you must excuse me! – *You* did not tell it me, – *Dr Burney* did, and he made no conditions: so I have told it to all the people I have *seen*, if I have *liked* them, and thought they would have a *taste* for the Book.'

'O Mrs Thrale! – ' was all I could exclaim, – for I had not had any *idea* her communications had been so general, or that my Case was so desperate.

---

4. Hester Thrale quotes Mrs Heidelberg speaking to Fanny Sterling in Colman and Garrick's comedy (I. ii. 128).

'No, no,' continued she, 'You must *blunt* your feelings, and learn to bear, and to hear, the praises you deserve: if *I* had written the Book, I should have been proud to own it.'

'O Mrs Thrale! this is going too far indeed!'

'Not at all; *any body* would be proud of it.'

You will not wonder I should be ashamed to hear such Words at the Time, when I assure you I am ashamed of *writing* them now. – Even to my most partial dearest Susan. –

Yet notwithstanding all her advice, and all her encouragement, I was so much agitated by the certainty of being known as a scribbler, that I was really ill all night and I could not sleep, – and, at 4 in the morning, found myself so very unwell, that I was obliged to get up, and take a dose of nastiness with which Mr Devaynes[5] had furnished me, but which I had, hitherto, despised and rejected.

When Mrs Thrale came to me the next morning, she was quite concerned to find I had *really* suffered from my panics; – 'O Miss Burney,' cried she, 'what shall we do with you? – this *must* be conquered, indeed; this delicacy *must* be got over.'

'Don't call it *delicacy*,' cried I, 'when I know you only think it folly.'

'Why indeed,' said she, Laughing, 'it is not very *wise*!'

'Well,' cried I, 'if, indeed, I *am* in for it, – why I must seriously set about reconciling myself – yet I never can!'

'We all Love you,' said the sweet woman, – 'we all Love you *dearly* already, – but the Time will come when we shall all be *proud* of you; – so proud we shall not know where to place you! – you must set about a *Comedy*, – and set about it openly; it is the true style of writing for you, – but you must give up all these fears and this shyness, – you must do it without any disadvantages, – and we will have no more of such sly, sneaking, private ways!'

I told her of my fright, while at Chesington, concerning Mrs Williams, and of the Letter I wrote to beg my Father would hasten to caution her.[6]

'And did he?' said she.

'O yes, directly.'

'O fie! – I am ashamed of him! how can he think of humouring you in such maggots![7] If the Book had not been *liked*, I would have said *nothing* to it. – But it is a sweet Book, – and the great beauty of it is, that it reflects

5. An apothecary.
6. Anna Williams was a blind poet who lived in Dr Johnson's household. He had told her of FB's authorship, and FB had asked CB to caution her not to spread the word further.
7. Whimsical or perverse fancies.

back all our own ideas and observations: for every body must have met with *something* similar to almost all the incidents.'

In short, had I been the *Child* of this delightful woman; she could not have taken more pains to reconcile me to my situation: even when she *Laughed*, she continued, by her manner, still to *Assure*, or to *sooth* me.

48. From Journal Letter to Susanna Burney *September 1778*

Mrs Thrale. 'To morrow, Sir, Mrs Montagu Dines here! and then you will have Talk enough.'

Dr Johnson began to see-saw, with a Countenance strongly expressive of *inward fun*, – and, after enjoying it some Time in silence, he suddenly, and with great animation, turned to me, and cried '*Down* with her, Burney! – *down* with her! – spare her not! attack her, fight her, and *down* with her at once! – *You* are a *rising* Wit, – *she* is at the *Top*, – and when *I* was beginning the World, and was nothing and nobody, the Joy of my Life was to fire at all the established Wits! – and then, every body loved to hallow me on; – but there is no Game *now*, and *now*, every body would be glad to see me *conquered*: but *then*, when I was *new*, – to vanquish the Great ones was all the delight of my poor little dear soul! – So at her, Burney! – at her, and *down* with her!'

O how we were all amused! By the way, I must tell you that Mrs Montagu is in very great estimation here, even with Dr Johnson himself, when others do not praise her *improperly*: Mrs Thrale ranks her as the *first of Women*, in the Literary way.

49. From Letter to Susanna Burney *4 December 1778*

St Martin's Street

Well but – how will you bear to hear about Pac – *may* I finish the name? – I am almost afraid, – yet think it a miserable compliment to treat you as a Baby, and *hide* from you the play things you must not have in your *own Hand*. So I will only remind you of similar situations in which *I* have been, – and, at the same Time, reminding *myself* of your conduct upon those occasions – the *upshot* of all which will be a true account of the transaction.

Well, – last Saturday morning [28 November] mine Fader sent a present of his History to Pachierotti,[1] – by way of an incentive to the study of the English Language. At the Opera, at night, – he promised to call here on Sunday. And *so* – on Sunday morning he came, – attended by Signor Bertoni.[2]

Well but he did not sing, – *so far* be easy.

I like him of all things. He is perfectly modest, humble, well bred and unassuming. He has a very anxious desire to learn English, which he has studied Grammatically and with much application and diligence Abroad: and he promised to come hither *frequently*, to take Lessons of Conversation: By way of beginning with *vigour*, he settled to Drink Tea here the next Day [30 November].

Now, Susy, for fortitude!

They came early, – and I am more pleased with Pachierotti than ever; he seems to be perfectly amiable, gentle and *good*: his Countenance is extremely benevolent; and his manners, infinitely interesting. We are all become very good friends, and talked *English, French* and *Italian* by *commodious* starts, just as phrases occurred: – an excellent device for *appearing* a good linguist.

He had a very bad Cold, – yet *sung*, – with the utmost good humour, as soon as asked. Bertoni accompanied him. He first sung a rondeau of Artaserse,[3] –: it is a very fine one, and had it been a very execrable one, he would have made it exquisite: such taste, expression, freedom, fancy and variety never were before joined, but in Agujari. His Voice, however, was by no means *clear*, though extremely *touching*: but his Cold quite tormented him. He afterwards sung a song for a *Tenor* in the same Opera, – and admirably. Then some accompanied recitative to a song in the *Orfeo* of Bertoni: – and lastly the '*che farò senza Euridice.*'[4]

He and I were very sociable: and he said, in English, 'Miss *Borni* give me very much *encourage*: – but, is very troublesome the *difficulties*.'

---

1. Gasparo Pachierotti was a celebrated Italian castrato soprano who had made his first appearance in London at the Opera on 28 November. He became a lifelong friend of the Burney family. 'Mine Fader' is FB's humorous imitation of the speech of German musicians who visited the Burney home.
2. Ferdinando Bertoni, Italian composer who had brought Pachierotti to London with him and created roles in his operas specifically for Pachierotti to showcase his voice, talents and style.
3. Opera by Bertoni.
4. 'What will I do without Euridice' (Italian), from *Orfeo*; an aria still famous in the setting by Gluck.

50. From Journal Letter to Susanna Burney *20 December 1778*

A violent rapping bespoke, I was *sure*, Mrs Cholmondeley,[1] – and I ran from the *standers*, and, turning my back against the Door, looked over Miss Palmer's Cards: for, you may well imagine, I was really in a *tremor* at a meeting which so long has been in agitation, and with the person who, of *all* Persons, has been *most* warm and enthusiastic for my Book.

She had not, however, been in the room *half* an instant, ere my Father came up to me, and, tapping me on the shoulder, said 'Fanny, here's a lady who wishes to speak to you.'

I courtsied, in silent *reverence*, – she, too, Courtsied, and fixed her Eyes full on my Face; and then, tapping me with her Fan, she cried 'Come, come, You must not look grave upon *me!*'

Upon this, – I *te-he'd*, – she now looked at me yet more earnestly, – and, after an odd silence, said, abruptly 'But is it *true?*'

'What – ma'am?'

'It can't be! – tell me, though, *is* it true?'

I could only *simper*.

'Why don't you tell me? – but it *can't* be, – I don't believe it! – no, – you are an *Impostor!*'

Sir Joshua and Lord Palmerston[2] were both at her side; Oh how notably silly must I look! She again repeated her question of *is it true?* – and I again affected not to understand her, – and then Sir Joshua, taking hold of her arm, attempted to pull her away saying 'Come, come, Mrs Cholmondeley, I won't have her over-powered here!'

I love Sir Joshua much for this. But Mrs Cholmondeley, turning to him, said with quickness and vehemence 'Why, I a'n't going to *kill* her! – don't be afraid, – I sha'n't *compliment* her! – I *can't*, indeed! – ' Then, taking my Hand, she led me through them all, to another part of the Room, where again, she examined my *Phiz*,[3] and viewed and re-viewed my whole person! – '*Now,*' said she, '*do* tell me, – is it true? – '

'*What*, Ma'am? – I don't – I don't know *what* – '

---

1. Mrs Mary Woffington Cholmondeley, society hostess and the earliest champion of *Evelina*. FB describes their first meeting at a party at Sir Joshua Reynolds's home. Miss Palmer was Sir Joshua's elder niece Mary Palmer, later Lady Thomond.
2. Henry Temple, second Viscount Palmerston (father of the statesman).
3. *Face.*

'Pho, *what*, – why you *know* what, – in short, *can* you read? and *can* you write?'

'N – o – ma'am!'

'I thought so!' cried she; 'I have *suspected* it was a trick, some time, – and *now* I am sure of it! you are too young by half! it *can't* be! –'

I Laughed, and would have got away, – but she would not let me. 'No,' cried she, 'one thing you must, at least, tell me; – are you very conceited?'

What a question! 'Come, answer me!' continued she; – 'you won't? – Mrs Burney, – Dr Burney, – come here, – tell me if she is not *very* conceited? if she is not *Eat up* with conceit by this Time?'

They were both pleased to answer '*not half enough.*'

'Well!' exclaimed she, 'that is the most wonderful part of all! Why that is yet more extraordinary than writing the Book!'

I then got away from her, and again looked over Miss Palmer's Cards: but she was after me in a minute. 'Pray, Miss Burney,' cried she, aloud, 'do You know any thing of this Game?'

'No, ma'am.' 'No?' repeated she; '*ma foi*,[4] that's pity!' This raised *such* a Laugh! I was forced to move on, – yet every body seemed *afraid* to Laugh, too, and *studying* to be delicate, as if they had been *cautioned*: which, I have since found, was really the case, and by Sir Joshua himself.

Again, however, she was at my side. 'What Game *do* you like, Miss Burney?' cried she.

'I play at none, ma'am.'

'No? – *pardie*,[5] I wonder at that!'

Did you ever know such a Toad? Again I moved on, and got behind Mr W. Burke,[6] who, turning round to me, said 'This is not very politic in us, Miss Burney, to play at cards, and have *You* listen to our follies.'

There's for you! *I* am to pass for a censor*ess* now!

51. From Journal Letter to Susanna Burney *11 January 1779*

Your repeated call, my dear Susan, makes me once more attempt to finish my Visit to Sir Joshua; but I have very much forgotten where I left off, therefore if I am guilty of repetition or tautology, you must not much *marvel.*

---

4. '*Faith*'. Mrs Cholmondeley here and later echoes the speech of Madame Duval.
5. *By God.*
6. William Burke, close friend of Sir Joshua and of Edmund Burke (no relation), the writer and politician.

Mrs Cholmondeley hunted me quite round the Card Table, from Chair to Chair; repeating various speeches of Madame Duval; and when, at last, I got behind a sofa, out of her reach, she called out aloud 'Polly! – Polly! only think! Miss has Danced with a Lord!'

Some Time after, contriving to again get near me, she began flirting her Fan, and exclaiming 'Well, Miss, *I* have had a Beau, I assure you! ay, and a very pretty Beau, too, though I don't know if his *Lodgings* were so *prettily furnished*, and *every thing*, as Mr Smith's!'

Then, applying to Mr Cholmondeley, she said 'Pray, Sir, what is become of my Lottery Ticket?'

'I don't know.' answered he.

'*Pardi*,' cried she, 'you *don't know nothing*!'

I had now again made off, – and, after much rambling, I at last seated myself near the Card Table: – But Mrs Cholmondeley was after me in a minute, and drew a chair next mine. I now found it impossible to escape, and therefore forced myself to sit still. Lord Palmerston and Sir Joshua in a few moments seated themselves by us.

I must now write Dialogue fashion, to avoid the enormous length of Mrs C.'s Name.

Mrs Chol. I have been very ill, – monstrous ill, indeed! or else I should have been at *your* House long ago. – Sir Joshua, pray how do do? – you know, I suppose, that I don't come to see *you*?

Sir Joshua could only Laugh; though this was her first address to him.

Mrs Chol. Pray, *Miss*, what's your Name?

F:B. Frances, Ma'am.

Mrs Chol. Fanny? – Well, *all* the Fanny's are excellent! and *yet*, – my Name is Mary! – Pray, Miss Palmer, how are you? though I hardly know if I shall speak to *you* to-night! I thought I should never have got here! I have been *so* out of humour with the People for keeping me. If You but *knew*, cried I, to *whom* I am going to Night! and *who* I shall see to Night! – you would not dare keep me *muzzing*[1] here!'

During all these pointed speeches, her penetrating Eyes were fixed upon me; and what could I do? – what, indeed, could *any* body do, but colour and simper? *all* the company watching us! though all, very delicately, avoided joining the confab.

Mrs Chol. My Lord Palmerston, I was told to night that Nobody could see your Lordship for *me*, for that you supped at my House *every* Night? – –

1. Loitering, hanging about.

Dear, bless me, no! cried I, not *every* night! – and I looked as confused as I was able, – but I am *afraid* I did not blush, though I tried hard for it. (Then again turning to me.) That Mr what d'ye call him, in Fleet Street, is a mighty silly fellow; – – perhaps You don't know who I mean? – one T. Lowndes, – but may be you don't know such a person?

F:B. No, *indeed* I do not! *That* I can safely say.

Mrs Chol. I could get nothing from him: but I told him I hoped he gave a good *price*, and he answered me that he always did things *genteel*. What trouble and tagging[2] we had! Mr – (I cannot recollect the name she mentioned) laid a wager the Writer was a *man*, – *I* said I was sure it was a *Woman*, – but now we are *both* out, for it's a *Girl*!

In this comical, queer, flighty, whimsical, manner she ran on, till we were summoned to supper, – for we were not allowed to break up before; – and then, – when Sir Joshua and almost every body was gone down stairs, she changed her tone, and, with a Face and voice both grave, said 'Well, Miss Burney, You *must* give me leave to say *one* thing to you, – yet perhaps you won't, niether, – will you?'

'What is it, Ma'am?'

'Why it is – that I admire you more than any human Being! and *that* I can't help! –'

Then, suddenly rising, she hurried down stairs.

Did you ever hear the like? –

. . .

Just then, – the Door opened, – and Mr Sheridan[3] Entered.

Was I not in luck? not that I believe the meeting was *accidental*! – but I had more wished to meet him and his wife than any people I know not.

I could not endure my ridiculous situation, but re-placed myself in an orderly manner immediately. Mr Sheridan stared at them all, and Mrs Chol. said she meant it as a hint for a *Comedy*.

Mr Sheridan has a very fine figure, and a good, though I don't think a handsome Face. He is Tall and very upright, and his appearance and address are at once manly and fashionable, without the smallest tincture of foppery or modish graces. In short, I like him vastly, – and think him every way worthy his beautiful Companion. And let me tell you, what I know will give *you* as much pleasure as it gave *me*, that by all I could observe in the

---

2. Dogging his heels.

3. Sheridan was already renowned for *The Rivals* and *The School for Scandal*.

course of the Evening, – and we stayed very late, – they are *extremely* happy in each other: he evidently adores her, – and she as evidently idolises him. The World has by no means done him justice.[4]

When he had paid his Compliments to all his acquaintance, he went behind the sofa on which Mrs Sheridan and Miss Cholmondeley were seated, and entered into earnest conversation with them.

Upon Lord Harcourt's[5] again paying Mrs Cholmondeley some Compliment, she said 'Well, my Lord, after this I shall be quite sublime for some Days! – I sha'n't descend into common Life till – till – Saturday, – and then, I shall drop into the vulgar style, – I shall be in – the *ma foi* way.'

I do really believe she could not *resist* this, for she had seemed *determined* to be quiet. Every body, very provokingly, heard this silently, – not a word was spoke for at least 2 minutes, – and to be sure *I* looked very wise mean Time!

When next there was a Rat-Tat, – Mrs Cholmondeley and Lord Harcourt and my Father again, at the command of the former, moved into the middle of the Room: – And then Sir Joshua Reynolds and Dr Wharton entered. No further Company came. You may imagine there was a general *war* at the *breaking of the Circle*, – and, when they got into order, Mr Sheridan seated himself in the place Mrs Cholmondeley had left, between my Father and myself.

And now I must tell you a little conversation which I did not hear myself till I came Home, – it was between Mr Sheridan and my Father.

'Good God, Dr Burney,' cried the former, 'have you no *older* Daughters? can *this* possibly be the authoress of Evelina? – ' and then he said abundance of fine things, and begged my Father to Introduce him to me! 'Why, it will be a very formidable thing to her,' answered he, 'to be introduced to *you!*' 'Well then, – by and by, – ' returned he.

Some Time after this, my Eyes happening to meet his, he waved the Ceremony of introduction, and, in a low voice, said 'I have been telling Dr Burney that I have long expected to see in Miss Burney a lady of the gravest appearance, with the quickest parts.'

I was never much more astonished than at this unexpected address, as, among all my numerous puffers, the Name of Sheridan has never reached me, and I did really imagine he had never deigned to look at my trash.

Of course I could make no *verbal* answer: and he proceeded then to speak

4. Sheridan had a reputation for philandering.
5. George Simon, first Earl Harcourt, had been ambassador to France and viceroy to Ireland.

of Evelina in terms of the highest praise, but I was in such a *ferment* from surprise (not to say pleasure) that I have no recollection of his expressions. I only remember telling him that I was much amazed he had spared Time to read it, – and that he repeatedly called it a most *surprising Book*. And, some Time after, he added 'But I hope, Miss Burney, you don't intend to throw away your Pen?'

'You should take care, Sir,' said I, 'what you say, – for you know not what weight it may have.'

He wished it might have any, he said. – And soon after, turned again to my Father.

I protest, since the approbation of the Streathamites, I have met with none so *highly* flattering to me as this of Mr Sheridan, and so *very* unexpected.

Sir Joshua, then, came up to me, and, after some general conversation, said 'Pray do you know any thing of the Sylph?'[6] –

This is a Novel, lately advertised by Lowndes. Mr Hutton has already been with me to enquire if it was *mine*.

'No.' quoth I. 'Don't you upon your Honour?'

'Upon my Honour! did you suspect me?'

'Why a friend of mine sent for it upon suspicion. – '

'So did we,' said Miss Linley,[7] 'but I did not suspect after I had *read* it!'

'What is the reason,' said Sir Joshua, 'that Lowndes always advertises it with Evelina?'

'Indeed I know nothing about it.'

'Ma'am,' cried Mr Sheridan, turning to me abruptly, 'you should send and order him *not*, – it is a take in, and ought to be forbid; – (and, with great vehemence he added) it is a most impudent thing in that fellow!'

I assure you I took it quite *koind*[8] in him to give me this advice. By the way, Mrs Thrale has sent me a message to the same purpose.

Sir Joshua went on with the Conversation. This, by the way, was the first Time he ever spoke to *me* of this so much honoured Book, but, now the subject was once started, he scrupled not to support it. He did not, however, begin any *formal* or *formidable Eloge*,[9] but *dashed* his general Discourse with occasional civilities equally flattering and delicate.

---

6. Lowndes advertised *The Sylph*, a mildly indecent anonymous novel, together with *Evelina* to give the impression that FB was the author. He desisted after CB sent him a heated letter, but FB was still being rumoured as the author in 1782 (see selection 69 and note 1).

7. Mrs Sheridan's sister.

8. FB mimics Sheridan's Irish accent.

9. *Praise.*

Among other things, he said that 'Mr Sheridan has declared he holds it *superior* to Fielding.'

'God! – impossible, impossible!'

'Nay, he has indeed, – and he must *really* think so, for he said it publicly at our Club.[10] – But I dare say he has been telling you so himself?'

F:B. No indeed; – but if he *had*, many things are said to *me* that are not to be believed.

Sir Joshua. But what is said at our *Club, is* to be believed. It is his real opinion.

F:B. Well, – I begin to think a Proclamation has been issued that all folks are to attack and try the strength of my poor Head! – and I fear they are determined Not to leave me short of Moorfields.[11]

About this Time Mrs Cholmondeley was making much sport by wishing for an Acrostic on her Name. She said she had several Times begged for one in vain, and began to entertain thoughts of writing one herself: 'For,' said she, 'I am very famous for my *rhymes*, though I never made a line of *Poetry* in my life.'

'An Acrostic on *your* Name,' said Mr Sheridan, 'would be a formidable task; – it must be so long, that I think it should be divided into Cantos.'

'Miss Burney,' cried Sir Joshua, who was now re-seated, 'are not you a writer of Verses?'

F:B. No Sir!

Mrs Chol. O don't believe her! *I* have made a resolution not to believe any thing she says.

Mr Sheridan. I think a *lady* should not *write* verses, till she is past receiving them.

Mrs Chol. (rising and stalking majestically towards him) – Mr Sheridan! pray, Sir, what may you mean by this insinuation? Did I not say *I* writ verses?

Mr Sheridan. O – but you, –

Mrs Chol. Say no more, Sir! you have made your meaning but too plain already! – There, now, – I think that's a speech for a Tragedy!

Some Time after, Sir Joshua, returning to his *standing* place, entered into *confab.* with Miss Linley and your slave upon various matters; – during which, Mr Sheridan, joining us, said 'Sir Joshua I have been telling Miss Burney that she must not suffer her Pen to lie idle; – *ought* she?'

10. The famous Literary Club of Dr Johnson, founded by Reynolds in 1764. Johnson himself had proposed Sheridan for membership in 1777.
11. The location of Bethlehem (Bedlam) Hospital, the lunatic asylum.

Sir Joshua. No, indeed, ought she not.

Mr Sheridan. – Do *you*, then, Sir Joshua, persuade her. – But perhaps you *have* begun some thing? – may we *ask*? – Will you answer a Question candidly?

F:B. – I don't know, – but *as* candidly as *Mrs Candour*[12] I think I certainly shall!

Mr Sheridan. What, then, are you about now?

F:B. – Why – twirling my Fan, I think!

Mr Sheridan. No, no, – but what are you about *at Home*? – however, – it is not a fair Question, so I won't press it.

Yet he *looked* very inquisitive; but I was glad to get off without any *downright* answer.

Sir Joshua. *Any* thing in the *Dialogue* way, I think, she *must* succeed in, – and I am sure *invention* will not be wanting. –

Mr Sheridan. No, indeed; – I think, and say, she should write a *Comedy*.

Lord, Susy, I could not believe my own Ears! *This* from Mr *Sheridan*!

Sir Joshua. I am sure *I* think so; and I hope she *will*.

I could only answer by *incredulous* exclamations. 'Consider,' continued Sir Joshua, 'you have already had all the applause and fame you *can* have given you in the *Clozet*,[13] – but the Acclamation of a *Theatre* will be *new* to you.'

And then he put down his Trumpet,[14] and began a violent clapping of his Hands.

I actually shook from Head to foot! I felt myself already in Drury Lane, amidst the *Hub bub* of a first Night.

'O no!' cried I, 'there *may* be a *Noise*, – but it will be just the *reverse*. –' And I returned his salute with a Hissing.

Mr Sheridan joined Sir Joshua very warmly.

'O Sir!' cried I, '*you* should not run on so, – you don't know what mischief you may do!'

Mr Sheridan. I wish I *may*, – I shall be very glad to be accessory.

Sir Joshua. She has, certainly, something of a knack at Characters; – *where* she got it, I don't know, – and *how* she got it, I can't imagine, – but she certainly *has* it. And to throw it away is – –

Mr Sheridan. O she *won't*, – she will write a Comedy, – she has promised me she will!

---

12. Character in Sheridan's *School for Scandal*, who merely *affects* frankness, openness, sincerity.

13. Meaning the private rooms where *Evelina* would be read.

14. A hearing trumpet; Sir Joshua was very deaf.

F:B. O! – if you both run on in this manner, I shall – –

I was going to say *get under the Chair*, but Mr Sheridan, interrupting me with a Laugh, said 'Set about one? – very well, that's right!'

'Ay,' cried Sir Joshua, 'that's *very* right. – And *you*, (to Mr Sheridan,) would *take* any thing of *Hers*, – would you not? – *Unsight unseen?*'

What a *point blank* Question! Who but Sir Joshua would have ventured it!

'*Yes*,' answered Mr Sheridan, with quickness, – 'and make her a Bow and my best Thanks into the Bargain!'

Now, my dear Susy, tell me, did you ever hear the *fellow* to such a speech as this! – it was all I could do to sit it.

'Mr Sheridan,' I exclaimed, 'are you not mocking me?'

'No, upon my Honour! this is what I have *meditated* to say to you the first Time I should have the pleasure of seeing you.'

To be sure, as Mrs Thrale says, if folks *are* to be spoilt, – there is nothing in the World so *pleasant* as spoiling! But I *never* was so much Astonished, and *seldom* have been so much delighted as by this attack of Mr Sheridan. Afterwards he took my Father aside, and formally repeated his opinion that I should write for the stage, and his desire to see my Play, – with encomiums the most flattering of Evelina.

Consider Mr Sheridan, as an *Author* and a *manager*,[15] and really this conduct appears to me at once generous and uncommon. As an *Author*, and one so high, and *now* in his first Eclat, to be so lavish of his praise – is it not rare? As a *manager*, who must, of course, be *loaded* with Pieces and recommendations, to *urge* me to write, and to promise to *thank* me for my Writing, instead of making a favour and a difficulty of even *looking* at it, – is it not truly good-natured and liberal-minded?

And now, my dear Susy, – if I *should* attempt the stage, – I think I may be fairly acquitted of presumption, and however I may fail, – that I was strongly pressed to *try* by Mrs Thrale, – and by Mr Sheridan, – the most successful and powerful of all Dramatic living Authors, – will abundantly excuse my temerity.

In short, – this Evening seems to have been *decisive*, my many and encreasing scruples *all* give way to encouragement so warm from so experienced a Judge, who is himself *interested* in not making such a request *par pure complaisance*.[16]

15. Of Drury Lane since 1776, when Garrick had retired.
16. *Simply in order to please.*

52. From Journal Letter to Susanna Burney *c. 16 February 1779*

Streatham

The next Day Sir Philip Jennings Clerke[1] came. He is, at least, an *Elderly* man, not at all a man of *Letters*, but extremely well bred, nay *elegant* in his manners, and sensible and agreeable in his Conversation. He is a professed *minority* man, and very active and zealous in the opposition. He has almost lived here lately, as he has some affairs of consequence to settle at Tooting, which is just by. He had, when I came, a Bill in agitation, concerning *contractors*, – too long a matter to explain on Paper, – but which was levelled against Bribery and Corruption in the ministry; and which he was to make a motion for in the House of Commons the next Week.

Men of such different principles as Dr Johnson and Sir Philip, *you* may imagine, cannot have much simpathy or cordiality in their political debates; – however, the *very* superior abilities of the former, and the remarkable good breeding of the latter, have kept both upon good terms, though they have had several arguments, in which each has exerted his utmost force for conquest.

The *Heads* of *one* of their debates, I must try to remember, because I should be sorry to forget. Sir Philip explained his *Bill*, – Dr Johnson, at first, scoffed it; – Mr Thrale, (who was just come Home) Betted a Guinea the motion would not pass; – and Sir Philip that he should divide *150* upon it.

Sir Philip, addressing himself to *Mrs* Thrale, hoped she would not suffer the *Tories* to warp *her* Judgement: – and told *me* he hoped my Father had not tainted *my* principles: – and then he further explained his Bill, and, indeed, made it appear so equitable, that Mrs Thrale gave into it, and *wished* her Husband to vote for it; – he still hung back; – but, to our general surprise, Dr Johnson, having made more particular enquiries into its merits, first *softened* towards it, and then declared it a very rational and fair Bill, and joined with Mrs Thrale in soliciting Mr Thrale's vote.

Sir Philip was, and with very good reason, quite delighted. He opened upon politics more amply and freely declared his opinions, – which were so strongly against the Government, and so much bordering upon the republican principles, that Dr Johnson suddenly took fire; – he called back his

---

1. Baronet, Member of Parliament and political and social crony of Henry Thrale. Clerke was a member of the political opposition to Lord North's ministry. Broadly speaking, he was a Whig (liberal), whereas Johnson was a Tory (conservative).

recantation, – begged Mr Thrale *not* to vote for Sir Philip's Bill, and grew very animated against his antagonist.

'The Bill,' said he, 'ought to be opposed by all honest men! – in *itself*, and considered *simply*, it is equitable, and I would forward it; – but when we find what a *Faction* it is to support and encourage, it ought not to be listened to. All men should oppose it, who do not wish well to sedition!'

These, and several other expressions yet more strong, he made use of, and had Sir Philip had less unalterable politeness, I believe they would have had a vehement Quarrel. He maintained his Ground, however, with calmness and steadiness, though he had niether argument nor wit at all equal to such an opponent.

Dr Johnson pursued him with unabating vigour and dexterity, – and, at length, – though he could not convince, he so entirely baffled him, that Sir Philip was self-compelled to be quiet; which, with a very good grace, he confessed. Dr Johnson then recollecting himself, and thinking, as he owned afterwards, that the dispute grew too serious, with a skill all his own, suddenly and unexpectedly turned it to Burlesque, – and taking Sir Philip by the Hand at the moment we arose after supper, and were separating for the night: – 'Sir Philip,' said he, 'you are too liberal a man for the Party to which you belong! – I shall have much pride in the Honour of converting you; for I really believe, if you were not spoilt by bad Company, the spirit of faction would not have possest you. Go then, Sir, to the House; – but make not your motion! – give up your Bill, and surprise the World by turning to the side of Truth and Reason. Rise, Sir, when they least expect you, and address your fellow Patriots[2] to this purpose; – Gentlemen, – I have, for many a weary Day, been deceived and seduced by you; – I have now opened my Eyes, – I see that you are all scoundrels, – the subversion of all government is your aim; – Gentlemen, I will no longer herd among Rascals in whose infamy my Name and Character must be included; – I therefore renounce you all, Gentlemen, as you deserve to be renounced.' Then, shaking his Hand heartily he added, 'Go, Sir, go to Bed, – meditate upon this recantation, and rise in the morning a more honest man than you laid down.'

---

2. Johnson had these 'Patriots' i.e. liberal or radical politicians, specifically in mind, when he made his oft-misapplied remark that 'Patriotism is the last refuge of a scoundrel' (*Life of Johnson*, ii. 348).

53. From Journal Letter to Susanna Burney *21–27 May 1779*

Streatham,
Friday, 21 May

O – but – shall I tell you something? – Yes, though you won't care a fig, – but I have had my first Lesson in Latin, – Dr Johnson tutored Miss Thrale while I was with you, and was set off for Litchfield before I came; but Mrs Thrale attended the Lecture, and has told me every word of it she could recollect: so we must both be ready for him against his return. I heartily wish I rejoiced more sincerely in this *Classical plan*; but the truth is, I have more fear of the malignity which will follow its being known, than delight in what advantages it may afford. All *my* delight, indeed, is that this great and good man should think me worthy his instructions.[1]

Brighthelmstone,
May 26th

I have not had a moment for writing, my dear Susy, since I came hither, till now, – for we have been perpetually engaged either with *sights* or *Company*, – for notwithstanding this is not the *season*, here are folks enough to fill up Time from morning to Evening.

The Road from Streatham hither is beautiful: Mr, Mrs, Miss Thrale, and Miss Susan Thrale[2] and I Travelled in the Coach, with 4 Horses, and 2 of the servants in a chaise, besides two men on Horseback: so we were obliged to stop for some Time at 3 places on the Road.

Reigate, the 1st Town, is a very old, half ruined Borough, in a most neglected condition: a high Hill, leading to it, afforded a very fine Prospect, of the *Malvern* Hill Nature, though inferior. We amused ourselves, while we waited here, at a Bookseller's shop, where Mrs Thrale enquired if they had got the *Book* she had recommended to them? 'Yes, Ma'am,' was the answer; 'and it's always *out*,– the Ladies like it vastly.'

I suppose I need not tell you what it was?

We went very near Epsom, before we came to this Town, and I made out dear Chesington with my Glass, – I sent off a Pacquet to my Daddy

---

1. FB studied Latin under Johnson's tutelage at least till the end of the year, but stopped because of CB's disapproval. The contemporary prejudice was that Latin was a 'masculine' subject wasted on women.
2. Susanna Arabella Thrale, the second daughter, nine years old.

there before I left Streatham, and shall expect a few Lines to know how he goes on very soon.

At Cuckfield, which is in Sussex, and but 14 miles hence, we Dined. It is a clean and pretty Town, and we passed all the Time we *rescued* from Eating in the Church Yard, where I copied 4 Epitaphs in my Tablets, – and you shall have them.

I

Lord, thou hast pointed out my Life
In length much like a span;
My Age was nothing unto thee,
So Vain is every man.

The 2d was

An indulgent Husband, and Friend sincere,
And a Neighbourly man lies buried here.

The 3d was upon a Young Wife.

Not 12 months were past after our Wedding Day,
But Death in come, and from a loving Husband took me away.

The 4th, upon a Young Couple who both died soon after marriage.

Repent in Time, make no delay,
We after each other were soon called away.

So, you see, the Dablers have not been idle in the noble Town of Cuckfield.

The View of the South Downs from Cuckfield to *this* place is very curious and singular. We got Home by about 9 o'clock [22 May]. Mr Thrale's House is in West Street, which is the *Court* end of the Town here as well as in London. 'Tis a neat, small House, and I have a snug comfortable Room to myself. The sea is not many Yards from our Windows. Our Journey was delightfully pleasant, the Day being heavenly, the roads in fine order, the Prospects charming, and every body good humoured and chearful.

We found Sophy Thrale[3] perfectly well, and the whooping Cough entirely gone. The next morning, Whitsunday, we went to the Brighthelmstone Church, – and, entering, from the Carriage, a Door at the Top of a Hill, I was not a little surprised to find myself already in the Gallery, without

3. Sophia Thrale, eight years old, had evidently been sent to Brighton beforehand for her health.

ascending one step: but the Church is built by the side of a declivity which is made answer the purpose of stairs. It reminded me of the Houses in Brixham, Devonshire, where they are so built by the sides of Hills, that the Top of them generally leads to a different part of the Town from the bottom: and, in the *upper* streets, they are entered from the Garrets. We had a sermon preached by Dr Hinchcliffe,[4] Bishop of Peterborough; – a plain and sensible Discourse.

After Church, Miss Thrale and I proceeded to the Steyn [Steine], which is the great public Walk: – the Parade, where the folks stroll, is *pretty enough*; open to the sea at one side, and bounded by high Hills on the other. She then took me to the Cliff, which has the best view of the sea, and sauntered about the Town with me till the heat drove us home.

The Sussex militia, of which the Duke of Richmond is Colonel, is now here. Mr Fuller, a very intimate young friend of Mr Thrale, who is Captain of a Company belonging to it, Dined with us. He is a Young man of a very large Fortune, remarkably handsome, and very gay, sensible, unaffected and agreeable.

At Tea we had more Company; Major Holroyd, his Lady, and Miss Firth,[5] who is on a visit at her House. The 1st of these is major of the militia, a very rich Sussex Gentleman, and *agreeable enough*, – It was *he*, who, you may remember, Mrs Thrale said told her he had Dined at Sir Joshua Reynold's with the Father of the *celebrated Lady who writ Evelina*, – and congratulated her about *knowing* me. I suppose he gave me a good stare, but as I did not, at the Time, recollect this circumstance, I did not heed him. His Lady is Tall, genteel, rather sensible, but terribly gossiping and full of the scandal of the place. Miss Firth is, in every thing, like her.

They took us to the Parade before Tea, to see the soldiers mustered, a ceremony the officers are obliged to go through every night. We then returned here, and had a chatty and comfortable Evening.

Monday [24 May] was a *Field Day*, and Captain Fuller invited us to Breakfast with him, before we proceeded to the Downs. We did so, – that is, Mrs and Miss T. and I, for Mr Thrale was not up in Time. Captain Fuller's apartments are on the Steyn, and he had his men all drawn out before the House, and *under arms*, against we came. He is a very pleasing young man, and I like him very much. He gave us *Eggs*, Tea and Chocolate

4. John Hinchliffe, DD, later Dean of Durham.
5. John Baker Holroyd, later Earl of Sheffield; a close friend of the historian Edward Gibbon, he edited Gibbon's papers. Ann Firth was live-in companion to Mrs Abigail Holroyd.

for Break fast: he told us that *Eggs* made the fashionable *officer's Breakfast* at Brighthelmstone, as being *good for the Voice*, which they are obliged to exercise as much as their persons, in giving *the Word*, and so forth.

After this, Mrs Holroyd called in her Carriage to take us to the Downs; where was to be the *shew*. Captain Fuller escorted us on Foot. He belongs to the light Infantry, and was pretty well worked, I believe, with the heat and the exercise before he had done.

Alltogether, the morning was pleasant. Major Holroyd, who acted as the General, was extremely polite, and attentive, and came to us between every evolution, to explain and talk over the manoeuvres. Captain Fuller, too, whenever he was at liberty, favoured us with his Company, – so we were very grand, and very military.

On our return, we went to the Major's. His House is on the Steyn, and the best, I believe, in the Town, both for situation and fitting up. After this, Mrs and Miss Thrale paraded me about the Town, and took me to the principal shops, *to see the World*.

When we came Home, Capt. Fuller called to excuse himself from Dining here, on account of Business with his men. He got into chat, however, and stayed more than an Hour. He wanted me violently to play to him, – but I am less able than ever so to do, as I literally *never* touch a key, lest I should be heard.

We drank Tea and spent the Evening at Major Holroyd's. They took us to the Parade, to see the *muster*, and there we were joined by Capt. Fuller, who went with us to the Major's. There were, also, 3 other officers, Mr Lucius Concannon, an Irish Lieutenant, a staring, smiling man, of few words; Mr Godfrey, a very handsome, conceited Youth, and Mr John Fuller, a heavy, *Sussex Headed* young man.

Captain Fuller was, again, quite vehement with me to play, – and I had great difficulty, indeed, to escape, – he said he would *watch* me the whole Time I remained here, and set *spys* to watch if I was not to be caught, privately, at the Piano Forte; 'And I have 75 servants here,' he said, 'all in my Livery, –' meaning his *Company*, as you probably guess! – Mrs Holroyd and Miss Thrale both performed, – and then I was assaulted, and re-assaulted, and the Major said he would Head a File of musqueteers against me – upon which, all the Officers arose, and came to me in a body, joining in the Petition, – I tried to *run* for it, but was stopt by a *detachment*, – Mrs Thrale joined with them, till, taking my Hand, she found I actually *shook*, and then she got me off.

Tuesday I accompanied Mrs and Miss Thrale to Lewes, a Town about

8 miles from Brighthelmstone, where we went to see Mrs Shelley, a Cousin of Mrs Thrale. But found her not at Home. We then proceeded to Dr Delap, a clergyman, of whom I expect to have more to say in a Day or 2, as he is to visit us, and bring a M.S. *play* with him! – Mr Shelley met us in our way,[6] and invited us back to his House, – and, while we were returning, Captain Fuller came up to the Coach Door, and invited himself to Dine with us. He was at Lewes, with all the Sussex officers, to wait upon the Duke of Richmond; Mrs Thrale offered him the vacant seat in the Coach, and we went on to the Shelleys.

They have a large and charming House in this Town; Mrs Shelley is just a *good sort of Woman*, she has a great family, of very fine Children. We spent all the morning with them, and then, with our Captain, came Home, and had a most agreeable Ride.

The Country about this place has a most singular appearance; there is not a Tree within several miles, but Hill rises above Hill in quantity innumerable. The sea is the great object from all parts.

In the Evening of Tuesday we had a large party, consisting of the Bishop of Peterborough, his Lady, the Holroyds, Miss Firth, and our light Infantry Captain.

The Bishop is a man of very mild manners, and most courteous demeanour; his Lady is pretty and lively. They, Mr Thrale and Mrs Holroyd, played at Cards from Tea to supper, and the rest of us formed into occasional little parties.

54. From Journal Letter to Susanna Burney *29 May 1779*

Peggy Pitches,[1] who is the greatest little Coquet in Sussex, fixed her Eyes, and aimed her dart, at Captain Fuller, – she smiled, tittered, lisped, languished, and *played pretty* all the Evening, – but the Captain was totally insensible, – he has, indeed, so little passion for flirtation, that he would rather listen to Mr Murphy,[2] the Bishop, or Mrs Thrale, than either speak to, or look at, the most celebrated *Toast* in the kingdom.

But Peggy, who thought a red Coat a certain prognostick of gallantry,

---

6. Philadelphia and Henry Shelley and their six children; John Delap, poet and playwright.

1. Margaret ('Peggy') Pitches, nineteen years old, daughter of Abraham Pitches, wealthy merchant; married Viscount Deerhurst in 1783.

2. Arthur Murphy was also on a visit to Brighton.

was not easily to be discouraged: when she found her little graces not merely *ineffectual*, but wholly *unobserved*, she began to set down her cards, in a pretty, affected, manner, protesting she did not know how to play, and begging his advice: – nothing, however, ensued from this, but that, by his inattention and indifference, I fancy he thought her a Fool.

When it came to her turn to deal, she mixed the cards, let them drop, tittered, and flung herself into sundry attitudes, and then begged the Captain to shuffle and deal for her.

Captain Fuller, to Ridicule, I believe, her affectation, took the contrary extreme; he put on an awkward, clownish Countenance, shuffled the Cards with a ludicrous clumsiness, and making various vulgar grimaces, *licked his Thumb* in order to deal!

This failing, her next attempt was more spirited; she looked over his Hand, and, declaring all cheating was allowable at Commerce, snatched one of his Cards to make her own Hand better.

The Captain, however, had so little gallantry, that instead of regarding this theft as a favour, and offering her her choice of what she pleased, he insisted upon having his Card returned! – and when she resisted, recovered it, in an easy manner, by exposing all her Hand, and then, very composedly, proceeded with the Game without comment.

This determined insensibility made her give him up, – she blushed, and sat quiet the rest of the Evening.

55. From Journal Letter to Susanna Burney *15 June 1779*

Streatham

Now, my dear Susan, hard and fast let me write up to the present Time.

I left you all, as you truly say, on Saturday [12 June], in no very high spirits; Mrs Thrale's visible uneasiness and agitation quite alarmed me. I dared ask her no Questions, but, soon after we drove off, Sir Philip Clerke, gently and feelingly, led to the subject, and, in the course of our ride, got from her all the particulars of poor Mr Thrale's dreadful and terrifying attack.

I find, with true concern, that it was undoubtedly a paralytic stroke; he was taken ill at his sister's, Mrs Nesbitts,[1] – during Dinner; he did not

---

1. Susanna Thrale Nesbitt. Her husband, Arnold Nesbitt, a merchant and Member of Parliament, had recently died. Nesbitt's solicitor informed Thrale that he was liable for the repayment of

absolutely fall, but his Head sunk upon the Table, – and, as soon as he was able to raise it, they found that his reason had left him! He talked wildly, and seemed to know nobody; Mrs Nesbit brought him Home, – he was much better before Dr Bromfield[2] could be fetched, yet, for 3 Days afterwards, his senses, at intervals, were frightfully impaired. Poor Mrs Thrale had been in an Agony of horror and alarm almost incessantly from the Time of her seeing him.

The Saturday that I came, was the first Day that he had not once spoken incoherently, – no wonder, then, that Mrs Thrale was so little like herself!

She spoke in terms of highest praise of Mr Seward, who, indeed, has behaved upon this occasion in the most friendly and Zealous manner; and exerted his medicinal skill, which is very uncommon, with equal address and kindness.

When she had unburthened her full and anxious Heart, she began, insensibly, to recover her spirits, – and told us that the party of company for the 3 settled Days still held good, for 'Mr Thrale,' she said, 'desires not to have any body suppose he has been ill, but, on the contrary, wants all his friends to *see* how well he is. I met your handsome Captain [Fuller], Miss Burney, in the streets, and reminded him of his Engagement for to Day [12 June], Sunday and Monday, and he will certainly come, – but *how does Miss Burney do*? the rogue asked! – so *that* was uppermost in *his* Head.'

This drew on Sir Philip's rallery, and glad was I that my dear Mrs Thrale was capable of attempting any thing like sport and gaity.

When we stopt here, Sir Philip immediately went to Mr Thrale, but I ran past the Door, and up to my own Room, for I quite dreaded seeing him till I had prepared myself to meet him without any seeming concern, as I was told that he was extremely suspicious of being thought in any danger. I dawdled away about an Hour, and then, asked Miss Thrale to accompany me into the Parlour. Miss Thrale will do any thing for me.

Mr Thrale was there, with Sir Philip, Mr Seward and Captain Fuller. I endeavoured to enter and behave as if nothing had happened; I saw Mr Thrale fix his Eyes upon me, with an inquisitive and melancholy earnestness, as if to read my opinion: indeed his looks were vastly better than I expected,

---

£200,000 for which he had co-signed a bond with Nesbitt. Thrale collapsed shortly after, and over the next two years suffered a series of further strokes (see p. 171 note 1). Hester Thrale did not learn of this threat of bankruptcy until 1791, and then was convinced that the shock and terror had caused Thrale's initial stroke and eventual death.

2. William Bromfield was the Thrales' family surgeon.

but his evident dejection quite shocked me. I did not dare go up to him, for if he had offered to shake Hands with me, I believe I should have been unable to have disguised my concern, for indeed he has, of late, made himself a daily encreasing interest in my regard and kind wishes. I therefore turned short from him, and pretending earnest talk with Miss Thrale went to one of the Windows.

56. From Journal Letter to Susanna Burney *16 June 1779*

We had, at Breakfast, a scene of its *sort*, the most curious I ever saw.

The *Persons* were Sir Philip, Mr Seward, Dr Delap, Miss Streatfield,[1] Mrs and Miss Thrale and I.

The Discourse turning, I know not how, upon Miss Streatfield's Tears, Mrs Thrale said 'Ay, I made her Cry once for Miss Burney as pretty as could be; – but nobody *does* cry so pretty as the S.S. – I'm sure when she cried for Seward, I never saw her look half so lovely.'

'For Seward?' cried Sir Philip, 'did she cry for Seward? – what a happy Dog! – I hope she'll never cry for *me*, for if she does, I won't answer for the consequences!'

'Seward,' said Mrs Thrale, 'had affronted Johnson, and then Johnson affronted Seward, – and then the S.S. cried –'

'O,' cried Sir Philip, 'that I had but been here!'

'Nay,' answered Mrs Thrale, 'you'd only have seen how like 3 fools 3 sensible persons behaved; for my part, I was quite sick of it, – and of them too.'

Sir Philip. But what did Seward do? was he not *melted*?

Mrs Thrale. Not he; he was thinking only of his *own* affront, and taking fire at that.

Mr Seward. Why yes, I *did* take Fire, for I went and planted my back to it.

S.S. And Mrs Thrale kept stuffing *me* with Toast and Water.

Sir Philip. But what did *Seward* do with himself? Was not he in *extacy*? what did he do or say?

Mr Seward. O, I said pho, pho, don't let's have any more of this, – it's making it of too much consequence, – no more piping, pray.

---

1. Sophia Streatfeild, a noted beauty, was called 'the fair Grecian' because of her knowledge of Greek. Able to cry at will, as this episode shows, she was in love with a married clergyman (see p. 134 note 16) and never married. In the meantime she amused herself by ensnaring the hearts of men, including Thrale's, without, however, ever yielding her virtue.

Did you ever hear such a speech made before such a lady, in your Life? I actually put down my Tea, and held up my Hands in expression of wonder! – both at *his* making, and *her* enduring it.

Sir Philip. Well, I have heard so much of these Tears, that I would give the Universe to have a sight of them.

Mrs Thrale. Lord, she shall Cry again if you like it.

S.S. No, – pray, Mrs Thrale; –

Sir Philip. O pray do! – pray let *me* see a little of it! –

Mrs Thrale. Yes, *do* cry, a little, Sophy; – (in a wheedling Voice) *pray* do! – consider, now, you are going to Day, – and it's very hard if you won't *cry* a little; – indeed, S.S., you *ought* to cry –

Now for the wonder of wonders, – when Mrs Thrale, in a coaxing voice, suited to a Nurse soothing a Baby, had run on for some Time, – while all the rest of us, in Laughter, joined in the request, – two Crystal Tears came into the soft Eyes of the S.S., – and rolled gently down her Cheeks! – such a sight I never saw before, nor could I have believed; – she *offered* not to conceal, or dissipate them, – on the contrary, she really *contrived* to have them seen by every body. She looked, indeed, uncommonly handsome, for her *pretty Face* was not, like Chloes, *blubbered*,[2] it was smooth and elegant, and niether her Features or complexion were at all ruffled, – nay, indeed, she was *smiling* all the Time.

'Look, look!' cried Mrs Thrale, 'see if the Tears are not come already!'[3]

Loud and rude bursts of Laughter broke from us all at once; – how, indeed, could they be restrained? – Yet we all stared, and looked and re-looked again and again 20 Times ere we could believe our Eyes. Sir Philip I thought would have died in convulsions, for his Laughter and his politeness, struggling furiously with one another, made him almost black in the Face; Mr Seward looked half vexed that her Crying for *him* was now so much lowered in its flattery, yet *Grinned* incessantly; – Miss Thrale Laughed as much as *contempt* would allow her; – Mrs Thrale and I *rolled* on our Chairs; – but Dr Delap seemed *petrified* with astonishment.

When the violence of our mirth abated, Sir Philip, colouring violently with his efforts to speak, said 'I thank you, Ma'am, – I'm much obliged to you.' But I really believe he spoke without knowing what he was saying.

'What a wonderful command,' said Dr Delap, very gravely, 'that Lady must have over herself!'

2. Allusion to Matthew Prior, 'A Better Answer', l. 1.

3. Hester Thrale was very aware of her husband's infatuation with Streatfeild, and takes a small revenge here by urging her to be ridiculous.

'She has certainly 2 Bags well stored next her Eyes, – ' said Mr Seward.

She now took out a Handkerchief, and wiped her Eyes.

'Sir Philip,' cried Mr Seward, 'how can you suffer her to dry her own Eyes? – You, who sit next her?'

'I dare not dry them for her,' answered he, 'because I am not the *right man*, – '

'But if *I* sat next her,' returned he, 'she should not dry them herself.'

'I wish,' cried Dr Delap, 'I had a Bottle to put them in! – 'tis a thousand pities they should be wasted.'

'There, now,' said Mrs Thrale, 'she looks for all the World as if nothing had happened, – for, you know, nothing *has* happened!'

'Would *you* cry, Miss Burney,' said Sir Philip, 'if we ask'd you.'

'Lord,' cried Mrs Thrale, 'I would not do thus by Miss Burney for ten Worlds! – I dare say she would never speak to me again. I should think she'd be more likely to walk out of my House, than to *Cry* because I bid her.'

'I don't know how that is,' said Sir Philip, 'but I'm sure she is gentle enough.'

'She *can* cry, I doubt not,' said Mr Seward, 'on any proper occasion.'

'But I must know,' said I, 'what *for*.'

I did not say this loud enough for the S.S. to hear me; – but if I had, she would not have taken it for the reflection it *meant*; she seemed, the whole Time, totally insensible to the numerous strange, and, indeed, *impertinent* speeches which were made, and to be very well satisfied that she was only manifesting a tenderness of disposition that encreased her beauty of Countenance.

At least, *I* can put no other construction upon her conduct, which was, without exception, the strangest I ever saw! Without any *pretence* of affliction, to weep merely because she was *bid*, though *bid* in a manner to *for*bid any one else! – to be in good spirits all the Time, – to see the whole Company expiring of Laughter at her *Tears* without being at all offended, – and, at last, to dry them up, and go on with the same sort of Conversation she held before they started, – All this to do is too extraordinary for Comments.

What Sir Philip or Mr Seward privately thought of this incident, I know not yet; but Dr Delap has made me sick with Laughing, by his odd manner of speaking of it. 'Yes,' he says, 'she has pretty blue Eyes, – very pretty, indeed, – she's quite a wonderful miss! – if it had not been for that little Gush I don't know what would have become of me! It was very good natured of her, really, for she charms and uncharms in a moment; she is a *bane and an antidote* at the same Time.'

Then, after considering it more deeply, 'I declare,' he said, 'I was never so much surprised in my life! I should as soon have expected that the Dew would fall from Heaven because Mrs Thrale called for it, as that that Miss what d'ye call her would have cried just because she was asked! – But the thing is, *did* she Cry? – I declare I don't believe it! – yet I think, at this moment, I saw it, – only I know it could not be, – something of a mist, I suppose, was before my Eyes.'

57. From Journal Letter to Susanna Burney *late June 1779*

And now I cannot resist telling you of a dispute which Dr Johnson had with Mrs Thrale, the next morning, concerning me, which that sweet woman had the honesty and good sense to tell me. Dr Johnson was talking to her and Sir Philip Jennings of the amazing progress made of late years in Literature by the Women. He said he was himself all astonished at it, and told them he well remembered when a Woman who could spell a common Letter was regarded as all accomplished, – but that *now*, they vied with the men in *every* thing.

'I think, Sir,' said my friend Sir Philip, 'the young lady we have here is a very extraordinary proof of what you say.'

'*So* extraordinary, Sir,' answered he, 'that I know none like her, – nor do I believe there *is*, or there ever *was* a *man* who could write *such* a Book so young.'

They both stared, – no wonder, I am sure! – and Sir Philip said 'What do you think of *Pope*, Sir? could not *Pope* have written such a one?'

'Nay, nay,' cried Mrs Thrale, 'there is no need to talk of *Pope*, – a Book may be a clever Book and an excellent Book, and yet not want a *Pope* for its Author. I suppose he was no older than Miss Burney when he writ Windsor Forest;[1] and I suppose *Windsor Forest* is not equal to Evelina!'

'Windsor Forest,' repeated Dr Johnson, 'though so delightful a Poem, by no means required the knowledge of Life and manners, nor the accuracy of observation, nor the skill of penetration necessary for composing such a Work as Evelina: He who could *ever* write Windsor Forest, might as well write it Young as Old. Poetical abilities require not *age* to mature them; but

---

1. Alexander Pope claimed to have written the first part of *Windsor Forest* in 1704, when he was sixteen; it was published in expanded and revised form in 1713. A neo-georgic poem written in the tradition of Virgil's *Georgics* and Denham's *Cooper's Hill*, it owes more to a knowledge of these poems than it does to observation of 'the real world'.

Evelina seems a work that should result from long Experience and deep and intimate knowledge of the World; yet it has been written without either. Miss Burney is a real Wonder. What she is, she is intuitively. Dr Burney told me she had had the fewest advantages of any of his Daughters, from some peculiar circumstances.[2] And such has been her timidity, that he himself had not any suspicion of her powers.'

'Her modesty,' said Mrs Thrale – (as she told me) 'is really beyond bounds. It quite provokes me. And, in fact, I can never make out how the mind that could write that Book could be ignorant of its value.'

'That, Madam, is another Wonder,' answered my dear – dear Dr Johnson, 'for modesty with her is neither pretence nor decorum; 'Tis an ingredient of her Nature; for she who could part with such a Work for Twenty pounds, can know so little of its worth, or of her own, as to leave no possible doubt of her native humility.'[3]

58. From Journal Letter to Susanna Burney 5–20 July 1779

July 5th

In the Evening we took the Tour round the Grounds, and were met on the Lawn by the Pitches Family; poor Sophy[1] had not been well; she looked as pale as Death, and Peggy looked hardly any better: – yet little did I imagine the former had but one more Day to Live! – this was Friday Night [2 July], at about 9 o'clock, and she walked hither from Streatham Town; – and the next News I heard of her was on Sunday morning that she was *Dying*, – and on Sunday Noon that she was Dead! –

Though I knew her very little, and had never cultivated any acquaintance with, or entertained much kindness for her, – yet the so sudden and unexpected Death of a Young, pretty and innocent Girl, with whom I had been walking and conversing but 2 Evenings before, both astonished and shocked me.

The cause of this fatal catastrophe cannot be ascertained. She had not

---

2. One circumstance was that FB was kept at home in 1764 when CB sent her sisters Esther and Susanna abroad to France to improve their French. FB was extremely fond of her Catholic maternal grandmother Frances Sleepe, and CB was afraid that in a Catholic environment the impressionable twelve-year-old, unlike her sisters, might be seduced away from the Church of England.

3. Lowndes paid FB an additional £10 after the third edition.

1. Sophia Pitches, eighteen years old, almost certainly died from lead or mercury poisoning.

been quite well for some months, but had no Cough, nor any consumptive symptom; – she went to Bed on Friday Night early and more languid than usual; on Saturday she was siezed with Hysteric fits, – these grew stronger and stronger, and lasted all Day, – towards Night she was totally senseless; – on Sunday morning, Mrs Thrale saw her, – she then in a burning Fever, speechless, insensible, and convulsed, – Mrs Thrale sent instantly for Dr Jebb,[2] – she had had the Physicians here, – but finding her case desperate, the Apothecary ventured to give her some of James's Powders,[3] – the poor dying Girl had not swallowed them 2 minutes, ere the fatal hyccough was heard, and she expired.

Is not this dreadful? – the surviving Relations are all in the most bitter affliction. There are 2 conjectures concerning the latent cause of her Death: the first and most probable is Mrs Thrale's, that she was a martyr to the *Worms*, – the 2d is the Apothecary's, that she was in love with Mr Beresford,[4] – ruined her Constitution with fasting and pining, and then Died of the Illness resulting from indigestion and deep grief.

Certain it is, that the first Time I saw Mr Beresford, which was in Company with all the Pitches, he asked my opinion of the 3 sisters, – and when we discussed their several qualities, he said 'I *used* to like Sophy the best, and was always talking and prating with *her*, – and chatting nonsense, and so forth, – but I have quite done with her, for I found her so heavy that I grew quite tired of trying at her.'

If, therefore, this poor thing *had* any partiality for this man, she probably imagined he also had for her, and, when she found her mistake, and that he neglected her, she might possibly be cruelly disappointed and afflicted. However, I have not much, if any belief in this suggestion, though it is not incredible.

July 20th

A new light is, of late, thrown upon the Death of poor Sophy Pitches, – Dr Hervey, of Tooting, who attended her the Day before she expired, is of opinion that she killed herself by Quackery, – that is, by *cosmetics*, and preparations of lead or mercury, taken for her Complection, which, indeed, was almost unnaturally white: – he thinks, therefore, that this pernicious

2. Sir Richard Jebb, MD, was the Thrales' family physician.
3. Popular sweat-inducing remedy of the time.
4. The Revd Benjamin Beresford, a clergyman who the following year eloped with a rich heiress.

stuff got into her veins, and poisoned her! – Peggy Pitches, nearly as white as her sister, is suspected strongly of using the same beautifying methods of destroying herself; – but as Mrs Thrale has hinted this suspicion to her, and charged her to take care of herself, we hope she will be frightened and warned to her safety. Poor foolish Girls! – how dearly do they pay for the ambition of being fairer than their neighbours! I say *they*, for poor Peggy looks upon the point of Death already.

59. Letter to Dr Burney *c. 13 August 1779*

[St Martin's Street]
The fatal knell then, is knolled! and down among the Dead Men sink the poor Witlings, – for-ever and for-ever and for-ever! – [1]

I give a *sigh* whether I will or not to their memory, for, however worthless, they were *mes Enfans*,[2] and *one must do one's Nature*, as Mr Crisp will tell you of the Dog.

You, my dearest Sir, who enjoyed, I really think, even more than myself the astonishing success of my first attempt, would, I believe, even more than myself, be hurt at the failure of my second; – and I am sure I speak from the bottom of a very honest Heart when I most solemnly declare that upon *your* Account any disgrace would mortify and afflict me *more* than upon my own, – for what ever appears with your *knowledge*, will be naturally supposed to have met with your *approbation*, and perhaps with your *assistance*; – and therefore, though all *particular* censure would fall where it *ought*, upon *me*, – yet any *general* censure of the *whole*, and the *Plan*, would cruelly, but certainly, involve *you* in its severity.

Of this I have been sensible from the moment my *Authorshipness* was discovered, – and therefore, from that moment, I determined to have no *opinion* of my own in regard to what I should thenceforth part with out of

---

1. Urged to write a comedy by Johnson, Sheridan, Arthur Murphy and Mrs Thrale, FB had composed *The Witlings* in five acts and submitted it to the perusal of her family and friends. CB seems at first to have been generally favourable to it, but after a reading at Chessington he was persuaded by Crisp to forbid its production, probably out of fear its satire might offend the bluestockings. It remained unpublished (except for an excerpt) and unacted until 1994. FB wrote an equally dutiful and reproachful letter to Crisp. FB alludes to *Macbeth*, V. ix. 16 ('And so, his knell is knolled'); John Dyer's refrain 'Down among the Dead Men' in 'Toast: Here's a Health to the King'; and Pope's *Rape of the Lock*, III. 154 ('for-ever and for-ever'); all are allusions to the theme of loss.
2. *My children.*

my own Hands. I would, long since, have Burnt the 4th Act, upon your disapprobation of it, but that I waited, and was by Mrs Thrale so much *encouraged* to wait, for your finishing the Piece.

You *have* finished it, now, – in *every* sense of the Word, – *partial* faults may be corrected, but what I most wished was to know the general effect of the Whole, – and as *that* has so terribly failed, all petty criticisms would be needless. I shall wipe it all from my memory, and endeavour never to recollect that I ever writ it.

You bid me open my Heart to you, – and so, my dearest Sir, I will, – for it is the greatest happiness of my life that I *dare* be sincere to you, – I expected many Objections to be raised, a thousand errors to be pointed out, and a million of alterations to be proposed; – but – the *suppression of the piece* were words I did *not* expect, – indeed, after the warm approbation of Mrs Thrale, and the repeated commendations and flattery of Mr Murphy, how could I? –

I do not, therefore, pretend to *wish* you should think the decision for which I was so little prepared has given me no disturbance; – for I must be a far more egregious Witling than any of those I tried to draw to imagine you could ever credit that I writ without some remote hope of success *now*, though I literally did when I composed Evelina. But my mortification is not at throwing away the Characters, or the contrivance; – it is all at throwing away the *Time*, – which I with difficulty stole, and which I have Buried in the mere trouble of *writing*.

What my Daddy Crisp says, 'that it would be the best *policy*, but for pecuniary advantages, for me to write no more' – is exactly what I have always thought since Evelina was published; – but I will not *now* talk of putting it in practice, – for the best way I can take of shewing that I have a true and just sense of the *spirit* of your condemnation, is not to sink, sulky and dejected, under it, but to exert myself to the utmost of my power in endeavours to produce something less reprehensible. And this shall be the way I will pursue, as soon as my mind is more at ease about Hetty and Mrs Thrale,[3] – and as soon as I have *read* myself into a forgetfulness of my old Dramatis persona, – lest I should produce something else as *Witless* as the last.

Adieu, my dearest, kindest, truest, best *Friend*, – I will never proceed so *far* again without your counsel, and then I shall not only save *myself* so much useless trouble, but *you*, who so reluctantly blame, the kind pain which I am

3. Both of whom had been seriously ill.

sure must attend your disapprobation. The World will not always go well, as Mrs Sap.[4] might say, and I am sure I have long thought I have had more than my share of success already.

Once more, adieu, dearest Sir! – and never may my philosophy be put to the test of seeing any abatement of true kindness from *you*, – for *that* would never be decently endured by

Your own

Frances Burney

60. From Journal Letter to Susanna Burney *12 October 1779*

Brighthelmstone.[1]

Sunday [3 October] – we had Lady Lade[2] at Streatham. She did not leave us till the next Day. She and I are grown most prodigious friends; – she is really so entertaining and lively with those she thinks well of, that it is not often possible to pass Time more gayly than in her Company. Mr Stephen Fuller, the sensible but deaf old Gentleman I have formerly mentioned, Dined here also; – as did his Nephew, Rose,[3] whose trite, settled, tonish emptiness of Discourse is a never failing source of Laughter and diversion.

'Well, I say, what, Miss Burney, so you had a very good Party last Tuesday? – what we call the *Family Party*, in that sort of way? – Pray who had you?'

'Mr Chamier, – '

'Mr Chamier? – ay, – give me leave to tell you, Miss Burney, that Mr Chamier is what we call a very sensible man! – '

'Certainly. And Mr Pepys[4] – '

'Mr Pepys? – ay, very good! very good, in that sort of way. – I'm quite sorry I could not be here, – but I was so much indisposed – quite what we call the *Nursing Party*.'

---

4. Mrs Sapient, in *The Witlings*.

1. FB sent this letter from Brighton (Brighthelmstone), to which she had accompanied the Thrales. She begins it by concluding her account of her last days at Streatham, and continues with descriptions of various stops along the way.

2. Henry Thrale's sister.

3. Stephen Fuller, London merchant and friend of Thrale, and Rose Fuller, Streatham neighbour (Sharp is his dog).

4. William Weller Pepys, a master in chancery who was a frequenter of bluestocking parties. He became a close friend of FB.

'I'm very sorry, – but I hope little Sharp is well? –'

'Ma'am your most humble! – you're a very good lady, indeed! – quite what we call a good lady, – little Sharp is perfectly well, – that sort of attention, and things of that sort – the Bow-wow system is perfectly well. But pray, Miss Burney, give me leave to ask, in that sort of way, – had you any body else?'

'Yes, – Lady Lade and Mr Seward.'

'So, so! – quite the Family system! – Give me leave to tell you, Miss Burney, this commands attention! – what we call a respectable invitation! – I am sorry I could not come, indeed, – for we young men, Miss Burney, we make it what we call a sort of a rule to take Notice of this sort of attention, – but I was extremely indisposed, indeed, – what we call the Walnut system had quite – Pray what's the News, Miss Burney? – in that sort of way, is there any news?'

'None that I have heard. Have *you* heard any?'

'Why very bad! very bad, indeed! quite what we call poor old England! – I was told, in Town, – Fact! – Fact, I assure you! – that these Dons intend us an Invasion this month! – they and the Monsieurs intend us the respectable salute this very month, – the powder system, in that sort of way! – Give me leave to tell you, Miss Burney, this is what we call a disagreeable visit, in that sort of way![5] –'

I think, if possible, his Language looks more absurd upon Paper even than it sounds in conversation, from the perpetual recurrence of the same words and Expressions.

. . .

I need not tell you how sweet a Country for Travelling is Kent, as you know it so well. We stopt at Sevenoak, which is a remarkably well situated Town, – and here, while Dinner was preparing, my kind and sweet Friends took me to Knoll,[6] – though they had seen it repeatedly themselves.

The Park, which, it seems, is 7 miles in circumference, and has, as the Game keeper told us, 700 Head of Deer in it, is laid out in a most beautiful manner, – nearly, I think, equal to Hagley,[7] as far as belongs to the

---

5. England was at war with the United States, France and Spain at this time, and rumours were rampant of an imminent invasion by a combined Spanish and French fleet.

6. Knole Park, near Sevenoaks, Kent, was the seat of the Duke of Dorset. Its antique architecture, elegant furnishings and artistic treasures attracted many visitors every year.

7. Hagley Park, Worcestershire, seat of Baron Lyttelton. FB would have visited it during her stay at Worcester in 1777.

Disposition of the Trees, Hills, Dales, etc., – though, in regard to Temples, Obelisks, or any sort of Buildings, it will bear *no* comparison to that sweet place, – since nothing is there of that sort.

The House, which is very old, has the appearance of an Antique Chapel, or rather Cathedral; – 2 immense Gates, and 2 Court Yards precede the Entrance into the Dwelling part of the House. The Windows are all of the small old Casements, and the general Air of the place is monastic and gloomy. It was begun to be Built, as the Housekeeper told us, in the Reign of Harry the 2d, by Thomas a Becket: but the *modern* part was finished in the Time of Elizabeth! –

The Duke of Dorset was not there himself, but we were prevented seeing the Library, and 2 or 3 other modernised Rooms, because *Mademoiselle Bacelli*[8] was not to be disturbed. The House, however, is so very magnificently large, that we only coveted to see that part of it which was Hung with Pictures: – 3 state Rooms, however, were curious enough; – one of them had been fitted up by an *Earle of Dorsete* for the Bed Chamber of King James the first, when upon a visit at Knoll. It had all the gloomy grandeur, and solemn finery of that Time; – the second State Room, a later Earle had fitted up for James the 2d – – The 2 Charles's either never honoured Knoll with their presence, or else condescended to sleep in their Father and Grandfather's Bed; – well, this James the 2d's Room was more superb than his predecessors, flaming with Velvet Tissue, Tapestry, and what not? – – but the *third* state Room was magnificence itself! – it was fitted up for King William; – the Bed – Curtains, Tester, Quilt, and Valens, were all of the richest Gold flowers worked upon a silver Ground, – its value, even in those Days, was £7000! – The Table, a superb Cabinet, Frame of the looking Glass, and all the Ornaments, and I believe, all the *Furniture* in the Room, were of solid massive silver, curiously embossed! – Nothing could be more splendid.

But to leave all this shew, and come to what is a thousand Times more interesting – the *Pictures*, of which there is, indeed, a delicious Collection! – I could have spent a *Day* in looking at every Room, and yet have longed to see them again. – *I* can, however, give a very imperfect and lame account of them, as we were so hurried by the Housekeeper from Room to Room, and I was so anxious to miss nothing, that the merely *glancing* over so many beautiful Paintings has only left a faint remembrance in my Head of each particular Picture, though a very strong and deep impression of the pleasure they at the Time afforded me.

8. Italian dancer who was the Duke's mistress.

Among such as just now occur to me were a Lucretia, with a Dagger, a large whole length by Guido, – *extremely* beautiful; – purchased by the present Duke, in Italy: – a madonna and Child, small size, by Raphael, so lovely I could not turn from it till called repeatedly, – a virgin by Carlo Dolci that was *irresistably* attractive, – a Raphael by himself that was Noble, – Landscapes by Poussin, and 1 or 2 by Claude Lauraine[9] that were enchanting, – – But all this will be heavy reading, my dear Susy, – so I will say no more till I *say* it with my *voice*, – but that the Collection is *infinitely* superior indeed to any I had ever before seen, – and that, equally for Portraits, Historical Pieces, and Landscapes.

There are several Pictures of Sir Joshua Reynolds, and, though mixed in with those of the best old Painters, they are so bewitching, and finished in a style of Taste, Colouring, and expression so like their Companions, that it is not, at first view, easy to distinguish the New from the Old. The celebrated Ugolino Family is almost too horrible to be looked at, – yet I was glad to see it again;[10] – 2 Beggar Boys make an exceedingly pleasing Picture; – the Duke himself, by Sir Joshua, among the Portraits of his own Family, in a state Room, is, I think, by no means a likeness to flatter his Grace's vanity. – One Room is appropriated to Artists, – and among them 3 are by Sir Joshua, – Dr Johnson, Dr Goldsmith,[11] and Sacchini: – all charmingly done, and the 2 I know, extremely like.

One Noble Gallery is fitted up with Copies of Raphaels Cartoons, by Romana[12] – done so delightfully, I could have looked at them till now, – – but I believe I shall never tear myself away from this delicious Collection – I have almost writ myself back to Knoll – but lest I should have writ *you* to sleep – – I *will* have done; –

. . .

Amongst the Company,[13] I was most struck with, the *Hon. Mrs Wilson*, – she ran away with a Mr *Wilson*, a man nearly old enough to be her Father,

9. Claude Lorrain.

10. FB had seen *Count Hugolino and his Children in the Dungeon, as Described by Dante* either in Reynolds's studio or in the Royal Academy Exhibition of 1773.

11. Oliver Goldsmith, author and friend of Johnson.

12. Giulio Romano, an outstanding pupil of Raphael, but the cartoons at Knole are copies in oil by Daniel Mytens of some of Raphael's famous designs commissioned by Pope Leo X for tapestries hung in the Sistine Chapel. Not all of the attributions described by FB have been verified by modern scholarship.

13. The Thrales and FB had stopped at Tunbridge Wells, where they were visiting the public assembly rooms.

– and of most notorious bad character, – both as a sharper and a Libertine; – this Wretch was with her, – a most hackneyed, ill-looking, object as I ever saw; – and the foolish Girl, who seems scarce 16, and looks a raw school Girl, has an air of so much discontent, and seems in a state of such dismal melancholy, that it was not possible to look at her without compassionating a folly she has so many Years to Live regretting! – I would not wish a more striking warning to be given to other such forward, adventurous Damsels, than to place before them this miserable Runaway, – who has not only disgraced her Family and enraged her Friends, but rendered herself a repentant mourner for Life.[14]

. . .

We spent the whole afternoon and Evening at Mount [Ephraim,] and, at Mrs Thrale's request, Mrs Streatfield[15] invited *Miss Boone* to Tea, purposely that I might see her.

Miss Boone is the same Lady Mr Seward was invited to see by the S.S.; – you may want, therefore, to know what is her particular attraction, – why simply and merely SIZE! – She is *so Tall*, so fat, so large, that she might be shewn for *the great Woman* at any Fair in England. But with all this grossness of size, she is very Young, and very handsome! – –

In regard to *Character*, she is as much a Female Falstaff, as she is in regard to *Person*, – for she loves nothing so well as Eating and Drinking, and never of either seems to get enough, even when she empties every Dish and every Glass. – She is also very ingenious, – Draws, paints, takes likenesses, and cuts out Paper Figures and devices remarkably well. And though she was invited to divert me as some thing *strange* and *preposterous*, I found her so sensible and so intelligent, that the diversion she gave me was all such as redounded to her own Honour.

Mrs Streatfield's 2 sons made up our Party. The Eldest, Harry, is a very pretty sort of young man, – the Youngest, Richard, is somewhat *below par*.

When Mrs Streatfield told me of Miss Boone's ingenuity in cutting Paper, and I expressed some desire to see her perform, she very obligingly took out

14. Anne Townshend, daughter of a former Chancellor of the Exchequer and of Lady Greenwich, had eloped with Richard Wilson, an Irish adventurer. They had been married the previous March. Mrs Wilson was twenty-three. Wilson gained £2,000 by the misalliance. He was later accused of beating her and keeping a mistress in or near his house; in 1795 she eloped with a failed attorney.

15. Mother of Sophia Streatfeild. Anne Elizabeth Boone, thirty-four years old, was the eldest daughter of a Member of Parliament. Mrs Streatfeild's sons, Henry, twenty-two, and Richard, twenty, both became High Sheriffs.

her scissars, and desiring Harry Streatfield to sit sideways, she cut out his Face, – and that *without* first Drawing it, – and though it was not a striking likeness, it seemed extremely well done. Afterwards, by memory, she cut out the Duchess of Devonshire, in a riding Hat, and *very* like indeed.

She then expressed *her* desire to take *me*, – but though she was pleased to ask it as a *favour*, I begged to be excused, for I have no passionate inclination to propagate my Profile, – lest it should make every body hate their own! – ! – ! –

The Poor S.S. had a mortifying Tale to tell concerning Dr Vyse.[16] – That affair being totally at an End. – I am very sorry for her disappointment, but *Ladies* chusing openly for themselves, never appeared to me a *right* thing, – nor does it prove *prosperous*. –

Mrs Thrale begged her to Write to her soon, – and let her know how she went on; – saying 'Why when Miss Burney and I are parted for 2 or 3 Days, we write a score of Letters. –'

'O!' – cried Miss Boone, '*What* would I give to see them!'

'Ay,' said Mrs Streatfield, 'I should like to see my *little Dove's* Letters.'

'Dove?' repeated Miss Boone, – 'don't call her a *Dove*, – for I'm sure she has very near been my Death! –'

It was in vain I intreated an explanation of this accusation, – for she would give me none, – but, soon after, I heard her whispering Mrs Streatfield the danger she had been put in by reading Evelina *en Chemise*,[17] because she could not put it down after she got into Bed, etc. – – –

Some Time after, 'Ah!' cried Mrs Streatfield, 'how I see those *little Dove's Eyes* reading us all! – what would I give to know her real opinion of me! – She *glances* at me with such *enquiring Eyes*, that I die to know what they will tell her of me! –'

She *might* have known without much displeasure, for I really took to her quite kindly.

The next morning [8 October] we had the Company of 2 young Ladies at Break fast, – the S.S. and a Miss Birch, – a little Girl but 10 years old, who the S.S. invited, well foreseeing how much we should all be obliged to her.

---

16. Dr William Vyse was the clergyman with whom Sophia Streatfeild was infatuated (see p. 121 note 1). It was perhaps at this time that she learned of his secret marriage to a lower-class woman whom she had pensioned off.

17. *In her nightgown.*

This Miss Birch is a Niece of the charming Mrs Playdel[18] – and *so* like her, that I should have taken her for her Daughter, – yet she is not, now, quite so handsome, but as she will soon know how to display her Beauty to the utmost advantage, I fancy in a few years she will yet more resemble her lovely and most bewitching Aunt. '*Every body*,' she said, 'tells her how like she is to her Aunt Playdell.'

As you, therefore, have seen that sweet Woman, only imagine her Ten years old, and you will see her sweet Niece. Nor does the resemblance rest with the Person, – she *sings* like her, *Laughs* like her, *talks* like her, *Caresses* like her, and alternately softens and animates *just* like her.

Her Conversation is not merely like that of a *Woman* already, but like that of a most uncommonly *informed, cultivated,* and *sagacious* Woman, – and, at the same Time that her Understanding is thus wonderfully premature, she can, at pleasure, throw off all this rationality, and make herself a mere playing, giddy, romping Child. One moment, with mingled gravity and sarcasm she discusses Characters, and the next with school-Girl spirits, she jumps round the Room; – then, suddenly, she asks 'Do you know such or such a song?' and instantly, with mixed grace and buffoonery, she singles out an object, and sings it: – and then, before there has been Time to applaud her, she runs into the middle of the Room, to try some new step in a Dance; – and, after all this, without waiting till her vagaries grow tiresome, she flings herself, with an affectionate air, upon somebody's Lap, and there, composed and thoughtful, she continues quiet, till she again enters into rational Conversation.

Her Voice is really charming, – infinitely the most powerful as well as sweet I ever heard at her Age, – were she well and constantly taught, she might, I should think, do *any thing*; – for 2 or 3 Italian songs which she learnt out of only 5 months teaching by Parsons[19] she sung like a little angel, with respect to *Taste, feeling* and *Expression,* – but she now learns of Nobody, and is so fond of French songs, for the sake, she says, of the *sentiment,* – that I fear she will have her wonderful abilities all thrown away. O how I wish my Father had the charge of her! –

She has spent 4 years out of her little life in France, which has made her

18. Selina Birch was the daughter of a solicitor but married at the age of thirty a younger son of the Earl of Dundonald; she died the following year. Mrs Elizabeth Playdell was the daughter of a former governor of Bengal (Governor Holwell) who had survived the infamous Black Hole of Calcutta; her husband was the Superintendent of Police in Calcutta, but she had returned to England some years before. She had been a music student of CB.

19. William Parsons, well-known musician (see also pp. 235 note 2 and 284).

distractedly fond of the French Operas, – and she told us the *story* quite through of several I never heard of, always singing the *sujet*[20] when she came to the Airs, – and comically changing parts in the Duets. She speaks French with the same fluency as English, and every now and then, addressing herself to the S.S. she uttered some *tender cant*, such as 'Que je vous adore! – Ah! permetter que je me mette à vos pieds!'[21] – etc. with a *dying languor* that was equally *laughable* and *lovely*. When I found, by her *taught songs*, what a delightful singer she was capable of becoming, I really had not patience to hear her little French Airs, – and entreated her to give them up, – but the little Rogue instantly began *pestering* me with them, singing, one after another, with a comical sort of *malice*, and following me round the Room, when I said I would not *listen* to her, to say 'But is not *this* pretty? – and *this*? – and *this*?' singing away with all her might and main.

She sung without any accompaniment, as we had no Instrument, – but the S.S. says she *plays*, too, very well. Indeed I fancy she can do well whatever she pleases.

We hardly knew how to get away from her, when the Carriage was ready to take us from Tunbridge; – and Mrs Thrale was so much enchanted with her, that she went on the Pantiles,[22] and bought her a very beautiful Ink-stand – 'I don't mean, Miss Birch,' she said, when she gave it her, 'to present you this Toy as to a *Child*, but merely to beg you will do me the favour to accept something that may make you now and then remember us.'

She was much delighted with this Present, and told me in a whisper that she should put a *Drawing* of it in her *Journal*! –

So you see, Susy, *other* Children have had this Whim! – But something being said of *Novels*, the S.S. said 'Salina do you ever read them?' and, with a *sigh*, the little Girl answered 'But too often! – I wish I did not! – '

The only thing I did not like in this seducing little Creature was our *leave-taking*; – the S:S: had, as we expected, her fine Eyes suffused with Tears, – – and nothing would serve the little Salina, who admires the S.S. passionately, but that she, also, must weep! – and weep, therefore she did, and that in a manner as pretty to look at, as soft, as melting, and as little to her discomposure, As the weeping of her fair *Example-setter*! The *Child's* success in this pathetic Art made the Tears of *both appear*, to the whole party, to be lodged, as the English merchant says, '*very near the Eyes*. – '

20. *Subject*; here meaning the theme or principal phrase.

21. 'How I adore you! Ah! Permit me to throw myself at your feet!'

22. The Parade at Tunbridge Wells.

Doubtful as it is whether we shall ever see this sweet syren again, Nothing, as Mrs Thrale said to her, can be more certain than that we shall *hear* of her again, let her go whither she will.

Charmed as we all were with her, we all agreed that to have the *care* of her would be *distraction!* – 'She seems the Girl in the World,' Mrs Thrale wisely said, 'to attain the highest reach of human perfection as a man's *mistress!* – as *such*, she would be a 2d Cleopatra, and have the World at her command.'

Poor Thing – I hope to Heaven she will escape *such* sovereignty, and *such* Honours!

But it is high Time I should take leave of her, – the S.S. – and of Tunbridge.

61. From Journal Letter to Susanna Burney *post 12 October 1779*

One thing, however, proved quite disagreeable to me, – and that was the whole behaviour of the whole Tribe of the Cumberlands, – which I must explain.

Mr Cumberland,[1] when he saw Mrs Thrale, flew with eagerness to her, and made her take his seat, – and he talked to her with great friendliness and intimacy, as he has been always accustomed to do, – and enquired very particularly concerning her Daughter, expressing an earnest desire to see her; – but when, some Time after, Mrs Thrale said, 'O, – there *is* my Daughter,– with Miss Burney. –' He changed the Discourse abruptly, – never came near Miss Thrale, and niether then, nor since, when he has met Mrs T., has again mentioned her name: and, the whole Evening, he seemed determined to avoid us both! –

Mrs Cumberland contented herself with only *looking* at me, as at a Person she had no reason or business to know. –

The 2 Daughters, but especially the Eldest, as well as the *son*, were by no means so quiet; they stared at me every Time I came near them as if I had been a thing for a *shew*, surveyed me from head to foot, and then, *again* and *again* and *again* returned to my *Face* with so determined and so unabating a curiosity, that it really made me uncomfortable.

---

1. Richard Cumberland, dramatist, was author of *The West Indian* and other popular sentimental comedies of the day. These daughters were Elizabeth, later Lady Bentinck, and Sophia; the son was his eldest, Richard. Hester Thrale, Queeney and FB were attending a ball at Brighton here, and a ball and a play on two other occasions below.

All the folks here impute the whole of this conduct to its having transpired that I am to bring out a *Play* this season, – for Mr Cumberland, though in all other respects an Agreeable and a good man, is so notorious for hating and envying and *spiting* all *authors of the Dramatic line*, that he is hardly decent in his behaviour towards them.

He has little reason, at present, at least, to bear *me* any ill will, – but if he is *capable* of such weakness and malignity as to have taken an aversion to me merely because I can make use of Pen and Ink, he deserves not to hear of my having suppressed my play, or of anything else that can gratify so illiberal and contemptible a Disposition.

Dr Johnson, Mrs Cholmondeley, Mr and Mrs Thrale have all repeatedly said to me 'Cumberland no doubt hates you heartily by this Time,' – but it always appeared to me a speech of mingled *fun* and *flattery*, and I never Dreamed of its being *possible* to be true. However, – perhaps yet all this may be accidental, – so I will discuss the point no longer.

. . .

We all went to the Rooms. – There was a great deal of Company and among them the Cumberlands: the Eldest of the Girls quite turned round her whole Person every Time we approached to keep me in sight, and stare at me as long as possible, – so did her Brother, – I never saw any thing so ill bred and impertinent, – I protest I was ready to quit the Rooms to avoid them: till, at last, *Miss* Thrale, catching Miss Cumberland's Eye, gave her so full, determined, and *downing* a stare, that whether cured by *shame* or by *resentment*, she forebore from that Time, to look at either of us. Miss Thrale, with a sort of good natured dryness, said 'when ever you are disturbed by any of these starers, apply to *me*, – I'll warrant I'll cure them! – I dare say the Girl hates me for it, – but what shall I be the worse for that? – I would have served *Master Dickey* so too, only I could not for my Life catch his Eye.'

Mr Cumberland spoke with Mrs Thrale some Time, not when *I* was with her! – I am really very sorry for all this foolish stuff, – though Mrs Thrale says I ought to be *flattered* by it, – but I neither do, nor ever did, ambition the Honour and Glory of being hated and avoided by either the sons or Daughters of Parnassus.[2]

---

2. Parnassus is the mountain in Greece, sacred to Apollo and the Muses; hence, literature. Cumberland would get his just deserts this month with the opening in London of Sheridan's highly popular burlesque play *The Critic*, in which Sir Fretful Plagiary was widely regarded as a caricature of him.

. . .

In the Evening, we all went to the play, which was Mr Colman's Suicide. But that it was so ill performed that to judge of it would be very unfair; I should be tempted to speak hardly enough of it. The best part of our Entertainment was from a certain Tom Willet, a poor crazy fellow, who Lives here, and who, being not in his senses, yet not bad enough for a mad House, wanders about the Town, and amuses himself with making signs and Grimaces to the Company of the Place. As Mr Thrale, who has known him many years, encourages him some times by a Nod or a smile, he is certain to begin his *Gambols* as soon as he sees any of his Family: he was this Night in the Pit, – and smiled, and shook his first Finger and his Head at us, as often as any of us looked at him; but his attention to us was not sufficiently entertaining to himself to suffice for his Evening's amusement, and therefore he made his observations upon the Play aloud, commending, disapproving or adding at his pleasure: but though this was diverting enough to *us*, the Players by no means approved of it; and in the 2d Act, one of the Women, who had to say 'A servant should be Deaf and Dumb,' upon his adding aloud 'Ay, and blind too!' said to her fellow Comedian 'That man puts me out so, I don't know how to go on.' And then this fellow Comedian, coming forward, said 'Upon my word, Sir, if you talk so I can't recollect one word of my part!'

Poor Tom Willet, nodding at them, said 'Well, well, I won't! –' And again directed his chief attention to us. When the first act was over, he got into the orchestra to look over the music Books at his leisure; but the Fidlers, not being ambitious of his Company, turned him out. He then made a motion to come into our Box, – and being prevented, threw in a Letter: – which, as it is short, I will Copy

To Lord Robert Manners.
My Lord, I happy *ham* to think I am[3]

---

3. Unfortunately the top of the next manuscript sheet is cut away, and with it the rest of this mad letter. There *was* a well-known contemporary Lord Robert Manners, who was an army general and Member of Parliament.

62. From Journal Letter to Susanna Burney *28 October–3 November 1779*

October 28th

And now I must have the Honour to present to you a new Acquaintance, who this Day Dined here. Mr Blakeney.[1] – An Irish Gentleman, late a Commissary in Germany. He is between 60 and 70, but means to pass for about 30, – gallant, complaisant, obsequious and humble to the *Fair sex*, for whom he has an aweful reverence, – but, when not immediately addressing them, swaggering, blustering, puffing and domineering. These are his 2 *apparent* Characters, – but the *real* man is worthy, moral, religious, – though *empty*, conceited and parading.

He is as fond of Quotations as my poor Lady Smatter,[2] – and like her, knows little beyond a *song*, and always blunders about the *Author* of that. His Language greatly resembles Rose Fuller's, who, as Miss Thrale well says, when as old, will be much such another Personage. His whole Conversation consists in little French phrases, picked up during his residence Abroad, and in anecdotes and story telling, which are sure to be re-told Daily, and Daily in the same words.

Having given you this general sketch, I will endeavour to illustrate it by some specimens, – but you must excuse their being unconnected, and only such as I can readily recollect.

Speaking of the Ball in the Evening, to which we were all going, – 'Ah, Madam!' said he to Mrs Thrale, – 'there was a Time when – *tol de rol*! – tol de rol (rising and Dancing and singing) tol de rol – I could Dance with the best of them! – but now – a man forty and upwards, as my Lord Ligonier used to say, – but – tol de rol, – there *was* a Time! –'

'Ay, so there was, Mr Blakeney,' said Mrs Thrale, 'and I think you and I together made a very venerable appearance.'

'Ah! Madam, – I remember once at Bath, – I was called out to Dance with one of the finest young Ladies I ever saw, – I was just preparing to do my best, – when a Gentleman of my Acquaintance was so cruel as to whisper me Blakeney! – The Eyes of all Europe are upon you! – for that was the phrase of the Times, – Blakeney! says he, the Eyes of all Europe are upon you! – I vow, Ma'am, enough to make a man tremble! – tol de rol, –

---

1. Edward Blakeney, wealthy native of Ireland, had settled in Newman Street, London. Hester Thrale, confiding in her diary, called him 'Old Beau Blakeney a foolish Fellow enough' (*Thraliana*, i. 156).

2. Character in *The Witlings*.

tol de rol, – (Dancing) the Eyes of all Europe are upon you! – I declare, Ma'am, enough to put a man out of Countenance! – '

Dr Delap who was here, some Time after, in his gay way said 'Miss Burney, I could not find you any where this morning; – I went to the Steyn, – and to both the Bookseller's, – to look for you, – but I could see nothing of you; – so I picked up a Book. – – ' And then he repeated, to Mrs Thrale, some Lines of Horace, – I have looked for them, – and *these are they*, – in English, – –

> My Laligen I still will Love
> Who *softly speaks, and sweetly smiles.*[3]

He said them in *Latin*. – –

'Horace,' continued he, 'certainly saw Miss Burney in a Vision when he writ those Lines; – they are exactly prophetic of her. – '

'Well,' cried Mrs Thrale, 'I have often heard Horace was *inspired*, but I never before knew he was a prophet.'

'Ah, Madam,' cried Mr Blakeney, 'this Latin, – things of that kind, – we waste our Youth, Ma'am, in these vain studies, – for my part, I wish I had spent mine in studying French and Spanish, – more *useful*, Ma'am, – but, bless me, Ma'am, what Time have I had for that kind of thing? – Travelling here, over the ocean, – Hills and Dales, Ma'am! – Reading the great Book of the World! – Poor ignorant mortals, Ma'am! – no Time to do any thing! – '

'Ay, Mr Blakeney,' said Mrs Thrale, 'I remember how you downed Beauclerk and Hamilton, *the Wits*,[4] once at our House, – when they talked of *Ghosts*.'

'Ah, Ma'am, – give me a Brace of Pistols, and I warrant I'll manage a *Ghost* for you! – Not but Providence may please to send little spirits, – Guardian angels, Ma'am, – to watch us, – *that* I can't speak about, – it would be presumptuous, – For, Ma'am, what can a poor ignorant mortal know? – '

'Ay, so you told Beauclerk and Hamilton. – '

'Oh yes, Ma'am! – poor Human Beings! – can't account for any thing! – and call themselves Esprits forts![5] – I vow, presumptuous, Ma'am! – Esprits forts, indeed! – they can see no farther than their Noses! – poor ignorant

---

3. Horace, *Odes*, xxii. 23.
4. Topham Beauclerk and William Gerard Hamilton were fashionable men about town; Beauclerk was a close friend of Dr Johnson and Hamilton was a Member of Parliament. See also p. 183 note 7.
5. Strong minds.

mortals! – Here's an admiral, – and here's a Prince – and here's a General, – and here's a Dipper, and poor Smoker the Bather,[6] – Oh, Ma'am, what's all this? – strutting about – and that kind of thing – and then they can't account for a blade of Grass! – '

After this, Dr Johnson being mentioned, – 'Ay,' said he, 'I'm sorry he did not come down with you, – I liked him better than those others, – not much of a fine Gentleman, indeed, but a clever fellow, – a deal of knowledge, – got a deuced good understanding!' –

Dr Delap, rather abruptly, asked my Christian Name, – Mrs Thrale answered, – and Mr Blakeney *tenderly* repeated '*Fanny*! – a prodigious pretty Name! – and a pretty Lady that bears it, – Fanny! – ah, how beautiful is that song of Swifts –

> When Fanny blooming fair
> First caught my ravish'd sight,
> Struck with her mien and air – '[7]

'Her *Face* and air,' interrupted Mrs Thrale, – 'for *mien* and air we hold to be much the same thing.'

'Right, Ma'am, right! – you, Madam, – Why, Ma'am, you know every thing! – but as to me, – to be sure I *began* with studying, – the old Greek and Latin, Ma'am, – but then Travelling, Ma'am, – going through Germany and then France, – and Spain, Ma'am, – and dipping at Brighthelmstone, – over Hills and Dales, – reading the great Book of the World, – – ay, – a little Poetry now and then to be sure I have picked up, –

> My Phoebe and I
> O'er Hills and o'er Dales and o'er Valleys will fly,
> And Love shall be by, –[8]

'But, as you say, Ma'am,

> Struck with her Face and Air,
> I felt a strange delight, –

'How pretty that is! – how *progressive* from the first sight of her! – Ah, Swift was a fine man!'

---

6. A dipper was an assistant who helped people bathe in the sea; presumably 'Smoker the Bather' smoked while he bathed.

7. Correctly, 'with her shape and air'. The popular air was not by Swift or Chesterfield (see below), but probably by Thomas Philips, an obscure writer.

8. This poem has not been traced.

'Why, Sir, I don't think it's Printed in his Works?' said Dr Delap. –

'No,' said Mrs Thrale, 'because 'tis Chesterfield's.'

'Ay, right! right, Ma'am! so it is!' – –

Now if I had heard all this *before* I writ my Play, would you not have thought I had borrowed the hint of my Witlings from Mr Blakeney? –

'I am glad, Mr Thrale,' continued this Hero, – 'you have got your Fire place altered, – Why, Ma'am, there used to be such a wind there was no sitting here; – admirable Dinners, – excellent Company, – *tres bon*[9] fare, – and all the Time *Signor Vento*[10] coming down the Chimney! – Do you remember, Miss Thrale, how one Day at Dinner, you burst out a Laughing, because I said a *tres bon* Goose – '

But if I have not now given you some idea of Mr Blakeney's Conversation, I *never* can, – for I have written almost as many words as he ever uses, – and given you *almost* as many *ideas* as he ever starts! – And as he almost *Lives* here, it is fitting I let you know some thing of him.

. . .

All that did not Dance soon retired into the Card Room, except Miss Thrale and me, – and Mr Shelly begged us to keep still, that his Daughters might occasionally join us; – this was very fatiguing, as they are *abominably* ignorant, flippant and conceited Girls, – however, when I found it impossible to get rid of them, I solaced myself by making sport from talking nonsense to them. Yet so little were they aware that I *meant* any sport, that they took every thing *à la Lettre*,[11] – to the mutual diversion of Miss Thrale and myself.

The Eldest Miss Shelly had for a Partner one of the young Finch's, – a most odiously vulgar young man, – short, thick, and totally underbred; 'I, wonder,' said she to me, between one of the Dances, 'what my Partner's Name is, – do you know?' –

'I am not sure,' quoth I, 'but I fancy Mr Squab.'[12]

'Mr Squab?' repeated she, – 'well, I don't like him at all. – Pray do you know who that Gentleman is that jumps so?' pointing to Mr Cure. –

'Yes,' answered I, – ' 'tis a Mr Kill.'

'Well,' cried she, 'I don't like his Dancing at all. I wonder who that officer is?' –pointing to a fat, coarse sort of a man, who stooped immoderately.

---

9. *Very good.*

10. *Mr Wind* (Italian).

11. *To the letter* (literally), i.e. to be true.

12. Among many meanings 'Squab' can denote a short, thickset person, a young pigeon and a fledgling bird (FB plays on 'Finch').

'Captain Slouch,' quoth I.

'Well,' said she, 'I think the people here have very odd Names! – '

And thus, though the Names I gave them were merely and markingly Descriptive of their Persons, did this little Noodle and her sister instantly believe them, – though I Laughed myself sick all the Time.

When the Dancing was over, and we walked about, Mr Cure, with his usual obsequiousness, came to speak to me, and, for a while joined us: – and these Girls, who Penned me between them, Tittered, and pinched me, and whispered observations upon *Mr Kill*, till I was obliged to assume the most steady gravity to prevent his discovering how free I had made with him.

Just before we came away, Mr Shelly came up to his Daughter, and said 'Pray, my dear, who was the Gentleman you Danced with?'

'Mr Squab, Papa.' answered she.

'A good tight young man,' said Mr Shelley, – 'I must go and make a Bow to him before we go.' –

Did you ever know such *innocents*? – to hear such a Name without suspicion, or any emotion? – I did not think it worth while to undeceive them, – though poor Mr Finch must have been rather surprised if Mr Shelly accosted him with 'your servant, Mr Squab!' – however, I am pretty sure they did not meet.

November 3d

As he [Mr Blakeney] is notorious for his contempt of all *Artists*, whom he looks upon with little more respect than upon Day Labourers the other Day, when *Painting* was discussed, he *downed* Sir Joshua Reynolds as if he had been upon a level with a Carpenter or Farrier! –

'Did you ever,' said Mrs Thrale, 'see his Nativity?' –

'No, Madam: – but I know his Pictures very well; I knew him many Years ago, in Minorca, – he Drew my Picture there, – and then he knew how to take a moderate Price, – but now, – I vow to God, Ma'am, 'tis scandalous! – scandalous indeed! – to pay a fellow here 70 Guineas for scratching out a Head! –'

'Sir,' cried Dr Delap, (who is here perpetually,) 'you must not run down Sir Joshua Reynolds, because he is Miss Burney's Friend. – '

'Sir,' answered he, 'I don't want to run the man down; – I like him well enough, in his proper place, – he is as decent as any man of that sort I ever knew, – but for all that, Sir, his Prices are shameful! – Why he would not –

(looking at the poor Doctor with an enraged contempt) he would not do *your* Head, under 70 Guineas!'

'Well,' said Mrs Thrale, 'he had *one* Portrait at the last Exhibition, that I think hardly *could* be paid enough for, – it was of a Mr Stuart, – I had never done admiring it.'[13]

'What stuff is this, Ma'am!' cried Mr Blakeney, 'how can 2 or 3 Dabs of Paint ever be worth such a sum as that!' –

'Sir,' said Mr Selwyn[14] (always willing to draw him out,) 'you know not how much he is improved since you knew him in Minorca; he is now the finest Painter, perhaps, in the World.'

'Pho, pho, – Sir, –' cried he, 'how can *you* talk so? – you, Mr Selwyn, who have seen so many capital Pictures abroad? –'

'Come, come, Sir,' said the ever odd Dr Delap, 'you must not go on so undervaluing him, for, I tell you, he is a Friend of Miss Burneys.'

'Sir,' said Mr Blakeney, 'I tell you again I have no objection to the man, – I have Dined in his Company 2 or 3 Times, – a very decent man he is, – fit to keep Company with Gentlemen; – but, Lord God, Ma'am! – what are all your modern Dablers put together to one ancient? – Nothing! – a set of – Not a Rubens among them! – I vow to God, Ma'am, not a Rubens among them!' – –

How flattered would Sir Joshua be by such commendation, *fit Company for a Gentleman – a decent man.* – But perhaps his contempt of Dr Delap's plea that he was *my* Friend, may make you suppose I am not in his good graces, – whereas I assure you, 'tis not so, – for the other Evening, when they were all at Cards, I left the Room for some Time, – and, on my return, Mr Selwin said 'Miss Burney do not your Cheeks *Tingle?* –' 'No,' quoth I, – 'why should they? –' 'From the conversation that has just passed,' answered he; – and afterwards, I heard from Mrs Thrale that Mr Blakeney had been singing my praises, and pronouncing me *a dear little Charmante.*[15]

63. From Journal Letter to Susanna Burney *8 November 1779*

However, I have never yet told you his [Mr Blakeney's] most favourite story, though we have regularly heard it 3 or 4 Times a Day! – And this is about his *Health.*

---

13. At the annual exhibition of the Royal Academy in London; the portrait was of Andrew Stuart, MP .

14. Charles Selwyn, wealthy gentleman who had been a prominent banker in Paris.

15. *Charmer.*

'Some years ago,' he says, – 'let's see, how many? – in the year 71. – Ay, 71, 72, – thereabouts, I was taken very ill, – and, by d—d ill luck, I was persuaded to ask advice of one of these Dr Gallipots,[1] – O how I hate them all! – Sir, they are the vilest pick-pockets, – know nothing, Sir! – nothing in the World! – poor ignorant mortals! – and then they pretend – In short, Sir, I hate them all! – I have suffered so much by them, Sir, – lost 4 years of the happiness of my life, – let's see, 71 – 72 – 73 – 74 – ay, 4 years, Sir! – mistook my Case, Sir! – and all that kind of thing, – why, Sir, my feet swelled as big as two Horses Heads! – I vow I'll never consult one of those Dr Gallipots while I live again! – lost me, Sir, 4 Years of the happiness of my Life! – Why I grew quite an object! – You would hardly have known me! – lost all the Calves of my Legs! – had not an ounce of Flesh left, and as to the *Rouge* – why my Face was the Colour of that Candle! – Those deuced Gallipot fellows! – why they rob'd me of 4 years – let me see, ay, – 71 – 72 – etc. – '

And then it all goes over again!

This story is almost *always* Apropos; – if *Health* is mentioned, it is Instanced to shew its precariousness; – if *Life*, – to bewail what he has lost of it; – if *pain* – to relate what he has suffered; – if *pleasure*, to recapitulate what he has been deprived of; – but – if a *Physician* is hinted at – eagerly indeed is the opportunity siezed of inveighing against the whole Faculty.

64. From Letter to Samuel Crisp *22 January 1780*

I am sure you must have been grieved for poor Capt. Cooke, – how hard, after so many dangers, so much toil, – to Die in so shocking a Manner – in an Island he had himself discovered, – among savages he had himself, in his first visit to them, civilised, and rendered kind and hospitable.

He was, besides, the most moderate, humane and gentle Circum-Navigator who ever went out upon Discoveries, agreed the best with all the Indians, and till this fateful Time, never failed, however hostilly they *met*, to *leave* them his Friends.[1]

1. A kind of earthen glazed pot used for ointments and medicines by apothecaries; thus a contemptuous term for apothecaries.

1. News had just been received in England of Cook's death in Hawaii the preceding February. There had been increasing tension between the English and the natives, and he had gone ashore with a detachment of marines to repossess a boat which the natives had taken. Having fired upon them and killed one or two, the outnumbered English were set upon with clubs. James Burney, from aboard ship through a telescope, saw Cook clubbed from behind and fall into the water.

65. Journal Letter to Susanna Burney *7 April 1780*

Bath.[1]

The Journey was very comfortable; Mr Thrale was charmingly well and in very good spirits, and *Mrs* Thrale *must* be charming, well or ill. We only went to Maidenhead Bridge the first Night. The 2d Day we slept at Speen Hill, and the 3d Day we reached the Devizes.

And here, Mrs Thrale and I were much pleased with our Hostess, Mrs Lawrence, who seemed something above her station in her Inn:[2] – but, while we were at Cards before supper, we were much surprised by the sound of a Piano Forte; – I jumped up and ran to listen whence it proceeded; I found it came from the next Room, where the Overture to the Buona Figliuola[3] was performing. The Playing was very decent, – I returned to finish the Rubber; – don't I begin to talk in a good old Cattish manner of Cards? – Well, another Deal was hardly played, ere we heard the sound of a *voice*, – and out I ran again, – the singing, however, detained me not long, as it was equally tasteless and powerless, – and so back I whisked: but the performance, however indifferent in itself, yet surprised us at *the Bear at the Devizes*, and therefore Mrs Thrale determined to know from whom it came: accordingly, she tapped at the Door; – a very handsome Girl, about 13 years Old, with fine Dark Hair upon a finely formed Forehead, opened it; Mrs Thrale made an apology for her intrusion, but the poor Girl Blushed and retreated into a Corner of the Room; – *another* Girl, however, advanced, and obligingly and gracefully invited us in, and gave us all Chairs. She was just 16, extremely pretty, and with a Countenance better than her Features, though those were also very good. Mrs Thrale made her many Compliments, which she received with a mingled modesty and pleasure both becoming and interesting. She was, indeed, a sweetly pleasing Girl. We found they were both Daughters of our Hostess. We were extremely pleased with them, and made them a long visit which I wished to have been longer. But though these pretty Girls struck us so much, the Wonder of the Family was yet to be produced, – this was their Brother, a most lovely Boy of 10

1. FB had gone to Bath for an extended stay as guest of the Thrales.
2. Mrs Lucy Lawrence, whose husband owned the well-known Black Bear hostelry on the Bath road, her daughters Anne and Lucy and her son Thomas, who would grow up to become the famous Sir Thomas Lawrence, the leading portrait painter of his day and President of the Royal Society.
3. Popular comic opera by Niccolò Piccinni.

years of Age, who seems to be not merely the wonder of their Family, but of the Times for his astonishing skill in Drawing. They protest he has never had any instruction, yet shewed us some of his productions that were really beautiful; – those that were *copies* were delightful – those of his own composition amazing, though far inferior. I was equally struck with the Boy and his works, – he has just such sweet, expressive, soft, intelligent Eyes as his *Brother Wonder* our Edward,[4] and all his other Features are *infinitely* handsomer.

We found that he had been taken to Town, and that all the Painters had been very kind to him, and Sir Joshua Reynolds had pronounced him, the mother said, the most promising Genius he had ever met with. This House was full of Books, as well as of Paintings, Drawing and Music, – and all the Family seem not only ingenious and industrious, but amiable, – added to which they are strikingly handsome.

I shall now skip to our arrival at this beautiful City, – . The Houses are so elegant, the streets are so beautiful, the Prospects so enchanting! – I could fill whole Pages upon the general beauty of the Place and Country, but that I have niether Time for *myself*, nor incitement for *you*, as I know nothing tires so much as Description.

We alighted at York House and Mrs Thrale sent immediately to Sir Philip Jennings Clerke, who spent the Easter Holydays here. He came instantly, with his usual alacrity to oblige, and told us of Lodgings upon the South Parade, whither, in the Afternoon, we all hied, – and Mr Thrale immediately hired a House at the left Hand Corner. It is most deliciously situated, – we have meadows, Hills, Prior Park,[5] the *soft flowing Avon*,[6] – whatever Nature has to offer, I think, always in our view. My Room commands all these, – and more luxury for the Eye I cannot form a notion of.

We spent Saturday Morn [1 April] in removing hither: and then immediately followed an Engagement! – it was to spend the Afternoon with some Relations of Mrs T. –

Our Afternoon was horribly wearrying.

When we came away, Mrs Thrale ordered our Chairs to the Play House; Mr Thrale would not accompany us. We were just in Time for the Padlock,[7] – which was almost as bad to me as the Company I had just left. Yet the

4. Edward Francesco Burney, himself a talented artist.
5. Well-known estate picturesquely situated on a hillside overlooking Bath.
6. FB echoes a popular air, the words by Garrick and the music by Arne.
7. Comic opera by Isaac Bickerstaffe.

Performers here are uncommonly good: *some* of them as good as almost any we have in Town.[8]

Sunday We went to St James's Church, – heard a very indifferent Preacher, and returned to read better sermons of our own chusing.

In the Evening we had again an Engagement. This, however, was far more agreeable than our last. It was at Mrs Lambert's. Mrs Lambert is a widow of General Lambert, and a sister of Sir Philip Jennings. She is an easy, chatty, sensible Woman of the World. There was a good deal of Company, among them, all that I much observed were 2 Clergymen and a Miss Lewis. Mr Evans, one of the Clergymen, repeatedly attacked Miss Thrale, who, I assure you, grows very handsome, – but she was in violent spirits, and kept prating away to me at such a rate that I was almost ashamed of hearing her, for her Tongue never rested a minute, – though she answered Mr Evans with an abruptness nothing short of rudeness. She is very strange, but I am not without hopes that she will greatly improve.

Mr Evans, who appears to be a *Dangler*, again tried at her, – but with no better success.

The other Clergyman was Mr Whaley, a Young man who has a House on the Crescent.[9] He is immensely Tall, thin and handsome, but affected, delicate, and sentimentally pathetic, – and his Conversation about his own *feelings*, about *amiable motives*, and about the Wind, which, at the Crescent, he said in a tone of dying horror, *blowed in a manner really frightful*! diverted me the whole Evening, – but Miss Thrale, not content with private diversion, Laughed out at his Expressions till I am sure he perceived and understood her merriment.

I would have expostulated, but it was in vain, – she always pursues her own humour: at length, however, Mr Whaley, in speaking of some very young Lady, said, in a very pointed manner, 'that *she* behaved with great modesty and propriety.'

'Better be quiet now,' quoth I, in a low voice, 'for I am sure this praise is meant as a sarcasm for *you*.' And so I am sure it was, – but she only laughed the more. 'Tis simple to set people thus wantonly at defiance.

The Young Lady, Miss Lewis, is a Daughter of the Dean of Ossory; she is very handsome; and mighty gay and giddy, half tonish, and half hoydenish: – and every other word she utters is '*horrible*!'

8. One of the company was the soon-to-be-famous Sarah Siddons.

9. Thomas Sedgwick Whaley, Rector of Hagworthingham, Lincolnshire, and Prebendary of Wells, later attained some fame as a poet and traveller. His *Journals and Correspondence* were published posthumously in 1863.

Well, – I must now to Monday. –

In the morning Miss Gregory called;[10] she is here with Mrs Montagu. She made a long visit, and was pleased to take to *me*, of the sudden, very violently.

In the Evening we had Company at Home, – Mrs Lambert, Miss Gregory, and Mrs Montagu.

Mrs Montagu was in very good spirits, and extremely civil to me, taking my Hand, and expressing herself well pleased that I had accompanied Mrs Thrale hither. She was very flashy, and talked away all the Evening, but Miss Gregory was as much disposed to talk herself, and therefore I could scarce hear a word that Mrs Montagu said.

66. From Journal Letter to Susanna Burney *8 April 1780*

Saturday [8 April]. We went to the Lower Rooms, where a master of the Ceremonies was Electing.[1] We found them violently Crowded, and parties running very high for the various Candidates. And a very disagreeable circumstance happened to us. Miss Cooper had called here in the morning, and had had a long conversation with me concerning Mrs Macartney, an unmarried sister of Mrs Greville, who resides at Bath.[2] She told me that she was one of the worst women Breathing; a Drunkard notoriously, an assistant to the vices of others, and an infamous Practicer of all species of them herself. I had, indeed, heard much the same Character of her from the S:S: before I left Town. But Miss Cooper added that, as she kept a superb House, and gave most elegant Entertainments, she contrived to get Company to her Mansion, and to be Countenanced by People of Character and Rank. And she related to me stories and Circumstances of her actions really terrible. Mrs Thrale happened, during this Conversation, to be engaged in Discourse herself, and so heard it not. Well, – at the Lower Rooms we saw

---

10. Dorothea Gregory was companion of Elizabeth Montagu, who had practically adopted her as her own daughter. Her father's book, *A Father's Legacy to His Daughters* (1774), was an extremely popular book of etiquette for young women.

1. There were two fashionable sets of assembly rooms in Bath, called the Old (or Lower) Rooms and the New (or Upper) Rooms. Each had its own master of ceremonies, elected by the subscribers.

2. Alicia Macartney was the eldest sister of Frances Greville, FB's godmother. She was a woman of notoriously vicious character, and had attained great wealth and influence by dint of usury, blackmail and the selling of information.

this Woman, – whose Face carries an affirmation of all this account, – it is bold, hardened, painted, snuft, leering and impudent! – Her Dress, too, was of the same cast, a thin muslin short sacque and Coat lined throughout with Pink, – a *modesty bit*[3] – and something of a *very* short cloak half concealed about half of her old wrinkled Neck – the rest was visible to disgust the Beholders, – red Bows and Ribbons in abundance, a Gauze Bonnet tipt on to the top of her Head, and a pair of Mittens! – We were all curious to see this Queen of Bath, as she is called, on account of the expensive Entertainments she makes, and therefore we got very near to her. She was haranguing with much warmth in favour of Mr Tyson, her protected Candidate, and, in a few Minutes, as we were jostled together by the Crowd, finding we attended to her, she addressed herself to Mrs Thrale; I was rather vexed at this, and got aloof, with Miss Thrale and Miss Willis, who took hold of my Arm, and *Bored* me the whole morning dreadfully, – but in a few minutes, Mrs Thrale, open and communicative herself, was drawn into a very intimate conversation with this gay lady, and entered into her affairs and views, and listened to her complaints of ill usage with the utmost sociability and interest: – Soon after, Mr Thrale approaching us, Mrs Thrale presented him to Mrs Macartney, who immediately solicited his Vote for Mr Tyson, concerning whom she was quite vehement. Mr Thrale, however, voted for nobody to avoid ill will or squabling. After this, Mrs Macartney invited them both to her House to a great Entertainment next Saturday; Mrs Thrale frankly accepted the invitation, and begged leave to introduce Miss Thrale and me to Her, – which was done, and the Invitation immediately extended to us. All this Time I was inwardly fretting at the whole affair, – the dreadful Character I had heard of this Woman made me shrink from the very notion of visiting her, nor could I bear that one of Mrs Thrale's Fame and celebrity and purity of mind and conduct should countenance a Wretch notorious for all manner of evil: a wretch who, Miss Bowdler has told me, endeavours as much, by dispersing obscene Books, to corrupt youth, as to assist already corrupted maturity in the prosecution of vice! When we came Home, I determined to *expound* the matter, and as Mrs Thrale came to sit with me while I was Dressing, she opened the Cause by saying, 'Well, we shall now visit this Bath Queen.'

'Ay, Ma'am,' quoth I, – 'and for *her* it is a very good Thing.'

This introduced an explanation, when I found that she had mistaken this

---

3. Small piece of light cloth to fill in a low-cut neckline.

Woman for Mrs *Catherine* Macartney, another sister of Mrs Greville, and one whose conduct has always been irreproachable!

We then talked the affair through, and agreed that it was totally improper to make such an acquaintance, and that some method must be devised to put an end to it *without* making the visit. We were exactly of the same opinion from the moment we had the same information. But not well-knowing how to break off without being Lampooned for our pains, as the poor S.S: was in the Morning Post, we settled upon acquainting Mrs Montagu of the scrape, and begging her advice: for this Creature, whose nick Name here is Mrs MacDevil will not, it seems, be slighted with impunity, and she put that mortifying paragraph into the Morning Post about the *lovely Grecian* merely for her refusing to visit her!

67. Letter to Samuel Johnson *26 April 1780*

So mix our Studies, and so join our Names.

Do you not, Sir, recollect how often in sport you have repeated this Line to me?[1] But what will You say when I tell You that *something of that there sort*, in Mr Norman's[2] phrase, is actually coming to pass? – and that in a stained Drawing designed from a Scene in Evelina, a Print of Dr Johnson is hung up in the Study of Mr Villars?[3] – I half fear that not all the kindness with which you honour me, nor all the partiality with which you exalt my Book will enable You to bear this with complacency. Nothing, however, is farther from my thoughts than any intention of offering to prevail with the Young Artist, Mr Edward Burney, to suppress the Drawing, – no, – I am much too proud of our appearing together thus in Public, – for it is meant to be Exhibited at the opening of the Royal Academy in Somerset House – to daintify away my own satisfaction. And indeed should I neglect an opportunity so inviting of joining our Names, none other may offer till we write an Account of our Travels to the Hebrides,[4] to Lapland, or to the peak of

1. Alexander Pope, *Epistle to Mr Jervas*, l. 10.
2. FB mocks the vulgar speech of James Norman, wealthy retired timber merchant who was one of the Streatham set.
3. The drawing was one of three illustrating scenes from *Evelina* by Edward Francesco Burney; they were entered in the annual Royal Academy Exhibition, which opened on 1 May. Mr Villars is the guardian and mentor of Evelina.
4. Allusion to Johnson's tour to the Hebrides undertaken with Boswell in 1773, which became the subject of books both by Boswell and by Johnson (posthumous).

Teneriffe, – and to wait so long demands more patience than I am willing to exert, for I think when we last talked upon this subject, we agreed that it would be most prudent to defer beginning our long projected Journeys till we have peace with America.[5] Ah this American War! – where will be the end to the evils it occasions?

One thing, however, yet remains to us, and dares to baffle all the wickedness of the Ministry, the tyranny of the Crown, and the various horrours of these ruinous Times, – Manuscript Tragedies are yet Handed about to be read, and Country Parsons are yet left to Write them. One of these we had last Night the happiness of hearing, – the Author is Tutor to a Nephew of Sir Philip Clerke, – I shall not pretend either to praise or to censure his Piece, but content myself with giving You a specimen of his ingenuousness, – 'If,' says he, 'any one asserts that my Play is barren of incident, – it is no more than I know already, – but I can't help it, – for I could find none in The History from which I took it.' It is called, from its Hero, Timoleon.[6]

> I am Dear Sir, with the greatest Respect,
> Your most obedt Servant
> Frances Burney.

68. From Journal Letter to Susanna Burney *30 April 1780*

We had much talk among us of *Chatterton*,[1] and, as he was best known in this part of the world, I attended particularly to the opinion of Dr Harrington concerning him; and the more particularly because he is uncommonly well versed in the knowledge of English Antiquities, – therefore was I much surprised to find it *his* opinion that Chatterton was no Imposter, and that the Poems were authentic and Rowley's. Much, indeed, he said, they had been modernised in his Copies, not by design, but from the difficulty

---

5. The American War of Independence (1776–83) meant that it was unsafe for British citizens to sail abroad because of American privateers (and by 1779 France and Spain had allied with America).

6. Ancient Greek hero. The Author was the Revd George Butt.

1. Thomas Chatterton, a native of Bristol, was a precocious young poet who poisoned himself in 1770, at the age of eighteen. He had forged poems which he alleged were by a fifteenth-century Bristol monk named Thomas Rowley. Immediately detected by the poets William Mason and Thomas Gray, he continued to have defenders such as Dr Henry Harington, Bath physician, musician and antiquary, and Dr Jeremiah Milles, Dean of Exeter.

which attended reading the old manuscript; a difficulty which the genius of Chatterton urged him not to *confess*, but to *redress*. A Book, however, is now publishing, that is to entirely clear up this so long disputed and very mysterious affair, by Dr Mills, Dean of Exeter.

69. From Journal Letter to Susanna Burney *June 1780*

Mrs Lambart beg'd to speak to me: she was upon a sofa with *Miss White*, who, it seemed, desired much to be introduced to me,[1] – and so I took a Chair Facing them.

Miss White is young and pleasing in her appearance, not pretty, but agreeable in her Face, and soft, gentle and well bred in her manners. Our Conversation, for some Time, was upon the common Bath topics, – but when Mrs Lambart left us, – called to receive more Company, we went, insensibly, into graver matters.

As I soon found, by the looks and Expressions of this young lady that she was of a *peculiar cast*, I left all choice of subjects to herself, determined quietly to follow as she led. And very soon, and I am sure I know not how, we had for topics the follies and Vices of mankind, – and indeed she spared not for lashing them! – The *women* she rather excused than defended, laying to the Door of the *men* their faults and imperfections; – but the *men*, she said, were *all* bad, – *all*, in one word, and without exception, *sensualists*.

I stared much at a severity of speech for which her softness of manner had so ill prepared me, – and she, perceiving my surprise, said 'I am sure I ought to apologise for speaking *my* opinion to *you*, – *you*, who have so just and so uncommon a knowledge of human Nature, – I have long wished ardently to have the honour of conversing with you, – but your Party has, altogether, been regarded as so formidable, that I have not had courage to approach it.'

I made, as what could I do else, disqualifying speeches, and she then led to discoursing of happiness and misery; – the *latter* she held to be the *invariable* lot of us all, – and '*one* word,' she added, 'we have in our Language, and in all other, for which there is never any essential necessity, – and that is *pleasure*.' And her Eyes filled with Tears as she spoke.

1. Lydia Rogers White, later a well-known London hostess, was under the misconception that FB was the author of *The Sylph* (see above, p. 108 and note 6), which brands all men, save 'the sylph', as predatory sensualists.

'How you amaze me!' cried I: 'I have met with *misanthropes* before, but never with so complete a one, – and I can hardly think I hear right when I see how young you are.'

She then, in rather indirect terms, gave me to understand that she was miserable *at Home*, – and in *very direct* terms that she was wretched *abroad*, and openly said that to affliction she was Born, and in affliction she must die, for that the World was so vilely formed as to render happiness *impossible* for its Inhabitants.

There was something in this freedom of repining that I could by no means approve, and as I found by all her manner that she had a disposition to even *respect* whatever I said, why I now grew very serious, and frankly told her that I could not think it consistent with either truth or religion to cherish such notions.

'One thing,' answered she, 'there is which I believe *might* make me happy, – but for that I have no inclination; – it is an amourous disposition. But that I do not possess; I can make myself no happiness by Intrigue.'

'I hope not, indeed!' cried I, almost confounded by her extraordinary notions and speeches, – 'but surely there are worthier subjects of happiness attainable.' –

'No, I believe there are not, – and the reason the men are happier than us, is because they are more sensual.'

'I would not *think such thoughts*,' cried I, clasping my Hands with an involuntary vehemence, 'for Worlds!' –

The Miss Caldwells then interrupted us, and seated themselves next to us, – but Miss White paid them little attention at first, and soon after none at all, but, in a low voice, continued her Discourse with me; recurring to the same subject of happiness and misery, upon which, after again asserting the folly of ever hoping for the former, she made this speech –

'There may be, indeed, *one moment* of happiness, – which must be the finding one worthy of exciting a Passion which one should dare own to himself! *That* would, indeed, be a moment worth Living for! but that can never happen, – I am sure not to *me*, – the men are so low, so vicious, – so worthless! – no, there is not one such to be found.'

What a strange Girl! I could do little more than listen to her, from surprise at all she said.

'If, however,' she continued, 'I had *your* talents, I could, bad as this world is, be happy in it – there is nothing, there is nobody I envy like *you*, – with such resources as yours, there can never be *ennui*; the mind may always be employed, and always be gay. O if I could Write as *you* write! –'

'*Try*,' cried I, '*that* is all that is wanting, – *try*, and you will soon do much better things.'

'O no, – I *have* tried, – but I cannot succeed.'

'Perhaps you are too diffident. But is it possible you can be serious in so dreadful an assertion as that you are *never* happy? Are you sure that some *real* misfortune would not shew you that your present misery is *imaginary*?'

'I don't know,' answered she, looking down, – 'perhaps it is so, – but in that case, 'tis a misery so much the harder to be cured.'

'You surprise me more and more,' cried I; – 'is it possible you can so rationally *see* the disease of a disordered Imagination, and yet allow it such power over your mind?'

'Yes, for it is the only source from which I draw any shadow of felicity! Sometimes, when in the Country, I give way to my Imagination whole Days, – and then I forget the World and its cares, and feel some enjoyment of existence.'

'Tell me what is *then* your notion of felicity? Whither does your Castle-Building carry you?'

'O – quite out of the World, – I know not where, – but I am surrounded with *sylphs*, – and I forget every thing besides!'

'Well, – you are a most extraordinary Character indeed! I must confess I have seen *nothing like you*!'

'I hope, however, *I* shall find something like myself, – and, like the magnet rolling in the Dust, attract some metal as I go.'

'That you may *attract* what you please, is of all things most likely; – but if you wait to be happy for a friend resembling *yourself*, I shall no longer wonder at your despondency.'

'O!' cried she, raising her Eyes in extacy, '*could* I find such a one! – Male or Female, – for sex would be indifferent to me, With such a one I would go to *Live* directly.'

I half Laughed, – but was perplexed in my own mind whether to be *sad* or *merry* at such a speech.

'But then,' she continued, 'after *making* – should I *lose* such a friend – I would not survive!'

'Not survive?' repeated I; 'what can you mean?'

She looked down, but said nothing.

'Surely you cannot mean,' said I, *very* gravely indeed, 'to put a violent end to your Life?'

'I should not,' said she, again looking up, 'hesitate a moment.'

I was quite thunderstruck, – and for some Time could not say a Word; –

but when I *did* speak, it was in a style of exhortation so serious and earnest I am ashamed to write it to you lest you should think it too much.

She gave me an attention that was even *respectful*, but when I urged her to tell me by what *right* she thought herself entitled to *rush unlicensed on Eternity*,[2] she said – 'By the right of believing I shall be *extinct*.'

I really felt *horror'd*!

'Where, for Heaven's sake,' I cried, 'where have you picked up such dreadful reasoning?'

'In *Hume*,'[3] said she; – 'I have read his Essays repeatedly.'

'I am sorry to find they have power to do so much mischief; you should not have read them, at least, till a man equal to Hume in *abilities* had answered him. Have you read any more Infidel Writers?'

'Yes, – Bolingbroke,[4] – the divinest of all Writers!'

'And do you read nothing upon the *right* side?'

'Yes, – the Bible, till I was sick to Death of it, every Sunday Evening to my Mother.'

'Have you read Beattie on the immutability of Truth?'[5]

'No.'

'Give me leave, then, to recommend it to you. After *Hume's Essays*, you *ought* to read it. And even, for *lighter* reading, if you were to look at Mason's Elegy on Lady Coventry,[6] it might be of no disservice to you.'

And then I could not forbear repeating to her from that beautiful Poem.

> Know, vain *Skeptics*, know, th'almighty mind
> That Breath'd on man a portion of his Fire,
> Bad his free soul, by Earth nor Time confin'd,
> To Heaven, to Immortality aspire!
> Nor shall the pile of Hope his Mercy rear'd
> By vain Philosophy be e'er destroyed;
> Eternity – by all or *wish'd*, or *fear'd*,
> Shall be by All or *suffer'd*, – or *enjoy'd*!

This was the chief of our Conversation, – which indeed made an Impression upon me I shall not easily get rid of, a young and agreeable *Infidel* is

2. FB echoes a line by Mason in his poem *Elfrida*.
3. David Hume, philosopher and historian.
4. Henry St John, Viscount Bolingbroke, deist and freethinker.
5. James Beattie, *Essay on the Nature and Immutability of Truth, in Opposition to Sophistry and Scepticism*.
6. Mason, *On the Death of a Lady*.

even a shocking sight, – and with her romantic, flighty and unguarded turn of mind, what could happen to her that could surprise?

Poor misguided Girl! I heartily indeed wish she was in good Hands. She is in a very dangerous situation with ideas so loose of Religion, and so enthusiastic of Love. What, indeed, is there to restrain an Infidel, who has no belief in a future state, from sin and evil of *any* sort?

. . .

Thursday [8 June]. We went to Bath Easton: as it was impossible without gross rudeness and pointed antipathy to leave Bath entirely without one visit, – for both Lady Miller has been here, and left us a Card for each, and Sir John.[7]

Mrs Lambart went with us.

The House is charmingly situated, well fitted up, convenient and pleasant and Not large, but commodious and elegant. Thursday is still their public Day for Company, though the Business of the Vase is over for this season.

The Room into which we were conducted was so much Crowded we could hardly make our way, – Lady Miller came to the Door, and, as she had first done to the rest of us, took my Hand, and led me up to a most prodigious fat and frolicking old lady, and introduced me to her. This old Woman was Mrs Riggs, her Ladyship's Mother, who seems to have Bath Easton and its owners under her feet.

I was smiled upon with a graciousness *designedly* marked, – and seemed most uncommonly welcome, – Mrs Riggs looked as if she could have *shouted* for Joy at sight of me! She is mighty merry and facetious. Sir John was very quiet, but very civil.

I saw the place appropriated for the Vase, but at this Time it was removed. As it was hot, Sir John Miller offered us to Walk round the House, and see his Green House, etc., – so away we set off, Harriet Bowdler accompanying me, and some others following.

We had not strolled far, ere we were overtaken by another party, and among them I perceived Miss White, my new *Sceptical Friend*; she joined me immediately, and I found she was by no means in so sad a humour as when I saw her last; on the contrary, she seemed flightily *gay*. –

7. Lady Miller, wife of Sir John Riggs Miller, presided over a literary circle at Batheaston. Visitors were invited to place verses of their own composition in a classical urn, and she published them in an annual volume. The custom was regarded with good-natured amusement or open contempt by connoisseurs such as Horace Walpole. The Millers' daughter, Jane Elizabeth – 'Miss Miller' below – married (1804) John Wheatley.

'Were you never here before?' she asked me.

'No.' – 'No! – why what an Acquisition you are then! – I suppose you will contribute to the Vase?'

'No, indeed. – '

'No more you ought; you are quite too good for it.'

'No, not that, – but I have no great passion for making the Trial. *You*, I suppose, *have* contributed?'

'No, never, – I *can't*, – I have tried, – but I could never write Verses in my Life, – never get beyond *Cupid* and *stupid*.'

'Did *Cupid*, then *always* come in your way? – what a mischievous Urchin!'

'No, – he has not been very mischievous to me this Year. – '

'Not *this* Year? – O, very well! – he has spared you, then, for a whole twelve month!'

She Laughed, – and we were interrupted by more Company.

Some Time after, while I was talking with Miss White and Harriet Bowdler, *Mrs Riggs* came up to us, and with an expression of comical admiration, fixed her Eyes upon me, and for some Time amused herself with apparently watching me; – Mrs Lambart, who was at Cards, turned round and begged me to give her her Cloak, for she felt Rheumatic; – I could not readily find it, and after looking some Time, was obliged to give her my own; – but while I was hunting, Mrs Riggs followed me, Laughing, nodding, and looking much delighted, – and every now and then saying '*That's right, Evelina! ah, look for it, Evelina! – Evelina always did so, – she always looked for people's Cloaks*, and *was obliging* and *well bred*! – '

I Grin'd a little, to be sure, but tried to escape her, by again getting between Miss White and Harriet Bowdler; – but Mrs Riggs still kept opposite to me, expressing from Time to Time by uplifted Hands and Eyes comical applause.

At length Lady Miller herself approached our Groupe; and then Mrs Riggs beckoning to her, said '*Evelina* won't speak to me!'

'Oh what a Book!' cried Lady Miller, coming up to me; 'I never read so sweet a Book in my Life! – Give me leave, Miss Burney, to tell you how much I have been delighted with it.'

'There never *was* such a Book,' cried Mrs Riggs, 'no, never, – but how you should write it! – such characters! such knowledge of the World! – where could you *get* it? How came you *by* it? O you are a fine Girl indeed!'

'So much *wit*,' cried Lady Miller, – 'so much *sport*, such *humour*, such *Life*, – I never Laughed so much since I was Born, – I was *sick* with Laughing, I never was so much entertained with any Book I ever read. Sir John! do come hither, – come and tell Miss Burney how you were charmed with Evelina!'

Did you ever hear the like? I Bowed, and Laughed, and thanked, and disclaimed, and did what I could, but the Torrent was too brisk to be stopt, and I had almost a mind to have recourse to *flight*, – only in a Crowded Room that was not very easy.

Sir John instantly obeyed, – and came up, and Bowing most obsequiously, made very fine speeches, but with rather more moderation and delicacy than the *Ladies* used.

'O there is *genius* in every line!' cried Mrs Riggs, 'but such knowledge of *Life*! – '

'So much *natural* wit,' cried Lady Miller, – 'and *that* is so very rare! – nothing so rare as *natural* Wit, – but why have we not *another*?'

'Another?' cried Mrs Riggs, 'why should you have another? Can't you read that again and again?'

'Why I *have*, – I *have* read it again and again.'

'Well, and so do on; *I* shall keep reading it till I see another by the same Hand. Ah! such a Girl!' Then coming up and clapping her Hand on my shoulder, she added with a loud Laugh 'you are a Devil of a Girl indeed!'

I now disentangled myself from them – almost *knocked down* by their unrestrained violence of flattery, – and Miss Thrale came giggling up to ask me *how I did*? – 'You have been receiving Tribute,' said Miss White, 'and *just* Tribute to your merit; your Book is indeed a wonderful performance, – I believe you have more real Wit than any body living.'

There's a *closer* for you! what you may call a *clincher*! Harriet Bowdler modestly mumbled some praise, but addressed it to Miss Thrale, – I begged a *Truce*, and retired to a Chair in a Corner at the request of Miss White, to have a Téte à Téte. For which, however, her strange levity gave me no great desire.

She begged to know if I had written any thing else. I assured her *never*. 'The *Sylph*,' said she, 'I was told was yours.'

'I had nothing at all to do with that or any thing else that ever was published but Evelina; – *You*, I suppose, read the Sylph for its *name* sake?'

'No; I never read Novels, – I hate them; I never read Evelina till I was quite persecuted by hearing it talked of. Sir Charles Grandison I tried once, – but could not bear it, – Sir Charles for a *Lover*! – no Lover for *me*! – for a *Guardian*, or the *Trustee* of an Estate, he might do very well, – but for a *Lover*! – '

'What, – when he *Bows upon your Hand*! would not that do?'

'O Lord no! when he goes so far, I think he might go further!' (And *gaity* is no word for the *wantonness* with which she spoke this.)

Upon my word I began to be quite disgusted with this new acquaintance, and half ashamed of being thus selected for her private sentiment hearer – however, she kept me by her side a full Hour, and we again talked over our former Conversation; and I enquired what had *first* led her seeking Infidel Books? – *Pope*, she said, he was himself a *Deist*, she believed, and his praise of *Bolingbroke* made her mad to read his Works, – and then the rest followed easily. She also gave me an account of her private and domestic Life; of her *misery* at Home, her search of Dissipation, and her incapability of happiness.

Poor Girl! I am really sorry for her, – she has strong and lively parts, but I think her in the high road of lasting destruction! She waits but to *Love* in order to be infamous, and she thinks about *Religion* only to persuade herself there is none! – I recommended to her all the good Books I could think of, – and scrupled not to express warmly and most seriously my surprise and horror at her way of thinking. It was easy to me to see that she attended to my opinions with curiosity, and yet easier to discover that had she not respected me as Author of a Book she happened to be fond of, she would have rallied them unmercifully; however, that consideration gave weight to what I said, and evidently disposed her to be pleased with me.

Our Conversation would have lasted till leave taking, but for our being interrupted by Miss Miller, a most beautiful little Girl of 10 years old. Miss White begged her to sing us a French song, – she Coqueted, – but Mrs Riggs came to us, and said if *I* wished it, I did her Grand Daughter great honour, and she insisted upon her obedience. The little Girl Laughed and complied, – and we went into another Room to hear her, followed by the Miss Caldwells. She sung in a pretty Childish manner enough. Mrs Riggs again said fine things to me, – and afterwards Miss Arabella Caldwell, the *fat* sister, came and joined Miss White and me; and then a conversation took place which completed the offence I had already taken to Miss White; it was upon *Beaux*, – and they were both so loose in their opinions, so indelicate in their expressions, and so licentious in their principles, that I could soon bear niether of them; Arabella, too, who seems a Girl of very ordinary intellects, seemed *corrupt* without any sensibility of what was better, Miss White seemed half ashamed when I looked at her, and I believe wished her Companion away; but I grew sick of them both, and turning from them, gave all my attention to the lovely little Miss Miller: who, when we became more intimate, said 'Ma'am I have a great favour to request of you, if you please!' –

I begged to know what it was, and assured her I would grant it: and to be out of the way of these Misses, I led her to the Window; 'Ma'am,' said the little Girl, 'will you then be so good as to tell me where Evelina is now?'

I was a little surprised at the Question, and told her I had not heard lately.

'O Ma'am, but I am sure you know!' cried she, 'for you know you writ it! – and Mama was so good as to let me hear her read it, – and *pray*, Ma'am, do tell me where she is? and whether Miss Brangton and Miss Polly went to see her when she was married to Lord Orville?'

I promised her I would enquire, and let her know.

'And pray, Ma'am, is Madame Duval with her now?'

And several other Questions she asked me, with a childish simplicity that was very diverting. She took the whole for a true story, and was quite eager to know what was become of all the people. And when I said I would enquire, and *tell* her when we next met, 'O but, Ma'am,' she said, 'had not you better write it down because then there would be more of it, you know.'

She told me repeatedly how sorry she was that I had not come to Bath Easton in *Vase Time*, and how sorry her Mama had been.

When we were coming away, and Lady Miller and Sir John had both taken very civil leave of me, I courtsied in passing Mrs Riggs, and she rose, and called after me 'set about another!' – – – –

70. Letter to Dr Burney *9–10 June 1780*

Bath, June 9th

My dearest Sir,

How are you? – where are you – and what is to come next? – these are the Questions I am dying with anxiety to have Daily answered, – the Accounts from Town are so frightful that I am uneasy not only for the City at large, but for every Individual I know in it, – I hope to Heaven that ere you receive this all will be once more quiet, – but till we *hear* that it is so, I cannot be a moment in peace.[1]

---

1. FB was worried about the safety of her family after the so-called 'Gordon Riots' had broken out in London. The riots, which began on 2 June, were incited by Lord George Gordon, a virulent anti-Catholic opposed to an Act of Parliament in 1778 which had eased legal restrictions against Catholics in England. Thousands of rioters marched through the streets, attacking the residences and carriages of prominent Catholics and suspected Catholic sympathizers. Over 10,000 militia and regular troops had been called out to quell the disturbance, but by the time of FB's letter the danger in London was mainly past.

Does this *Martial Law* confine you quite to the House? – folks here say that it must, and that no Business of any kind can be transacted, – O what dreadful Times! –

A private Letter to Bull the Bookseller brought Word this morning that much slaughter has been made by the military among the mob, – never, I am sure, can any set of wretches less deserve quarter or pity; yet it is impossible not to shudder at hearing of their destruction. Nothing less, however, would do; – they were too outrageous and powerful for civil power.

But what is it they want? who is going to turn *Papist*? Who, indeed, is thinking in an *alarming* way of *any* Religion? this pious mob, and Lord George Gordon excepted! –

I am *very* anxious indeed about our *dea Etty*, – such a disturbance in her Neighbourhood I fear must have greatly terrified her; – and I am sure she is not in a situation or state of Health to bear terror. I have writ and beg'd to hear from her.[2]

All the stage Coaches that come into Bath from London are chalked over with *No Popery*, and Dr Harrington called here just now, and says the same was chalked this morning upon his Door, and is scrawled in several places about the Town. Wagers have been laid that the Popish Chapel here will be pulled or burnt down in a few Days, – but I believe not a Word of the matter, nor do I find that any body is at all alarmed. Bath, indeed, ought to be held sacred as a sanctuary for Invalides, – and I doubt not but the News of the *Firing* in *Town* will prevent all tumults out of it.

Now if, after all the intolerable provocation given by the mob, after all the lenity and forbearance of the ministry, and after the *shrinking* of the minority,[3] – we shall by and by hear that this firing was a *massacre* – will it not be villainous and horrible? – And yet, as soon as safety *is* secured, though by this means alone *all* now agree it *can* be secured – nothing would less surprise me than to hear the seekers of Popularity make this assertion.

Will you, Dear Sir, make Charlotte answer this Letter by your directions? and tell me how the World goes? We are sure, here, of hearing too much or too little. – Mr Grenville says he knows not whether *any thing* can be done to Lord George, – and that quite shocks me, as it is certain in all equity, nay common sense, that he is either mad enough for Moorfields,

2. Esther Burney had a miscarriage after the riots were over.
3. From helping to quell the riot.

or wicked enough for the Tower, and therefore that to one of those places he *ought* to go.[4]

Friday Night. –

The above I writ this morning, before I recollected this was not Post Day, – and all is altered here since, – the threats I despised were but too well grounded, – for, to our utter amazement and consternation, the new Roman Catholic Chapel in this Town was set on Fire at about 9 o'clock, – it is now Burning with a fury that is dreadful, – and the House of the Priest belonging to it is in Flames also! – the poor persecuted man himself has I believe escaped with *Life*, though pelted, followed, and very ill used. Mrs Thrale and I have been walking about, with the Foot men, several Times, – the whole Town is still and orderly, – the Rioters do their work with great composure, and though there are knots of people in every corner, all execrating the Authors of such outrages, Nobody dares oppose them! – An attempt, indeed, was made, but it was ill conducted, faintly followed, and soon put an end to by secret fear of exciting vengeance.

Alas! to what have we all Lived! – the poor Invalides here will probably lose all chance of Life from terror, – Mr Hay, our apothecary, has been attending the removal of 2, who were confined to their Beds in the street where the Chapel is Burning: – the Catholics throughout the place are all threatened with destruction, – and we met several Porters, between 10 and 11 at Night, privately removing Goods.

I firmly believe, by the deliberate villainy with which this riot is conducted, that it will go on in the same desperate way as in Town, and only be stopt by the same desperate means. Our plan for going to Bristol is at an end, – We are told it would be madness, as there are 7 Romish Chapels in it, – but we are determined upon removing *some where* to-morrow, – for why should we who *can* go, stay to witness such horrid scenes? –

Saturday afternoon – 10th *June*

I was most cruelly disappointed in not having one word to Day – I am half crazy with doubt and disturbance in not hearing, – every body here is

---

4. Gordon was imprisoned in the Tower, but when he was tried for high treason in the House of Commons in February 1781, he was acquitted on the grounds that he had had no treasonable intentions. In 1788 he was convicted of libelling Marie Antoinette and sentenced to Newgate Prison, where he died in 1793.

terrified to Death – we have intelligence that Mr Thrale's Home in Town is filled with soldiers, – and threatened by the mob with destruction, – perhaps he may himself be a marked man for their fury;[5] – we are going directly from Bath, and intend to stop only at villages; – This place is now well guarded, – but still we dare not wait the event of to Night, – all the Catholics in the Town have privately escaped. –

I know not now *when* I shall hear from you, – I am in agony for news! – our Head Quarters will be Brighthelmstone, – where I do most humbly and most fervantly entreat you to write – do, dearest Sir! write! if but one word, if but only your *Name yourself*! – nothing but your own Hand can now tranquilize me – the reports about London here quite distract me, – if it were possible to send me a line by the *Diligence*,[6] to Brighton how grateful I should be for such an indulgence! I should then find it there upon our arrival, – Charlotte I am sure will make it in a sham parcel, – and Susy will write for you. – All but the Name.

God bless – defend – preserve you! my dearest Father, – Life is no Life to me while I fear for your safety! –

God bless and save you all! – I shall write to-morrow from where ever we may be, – nay, *every* Day I shall write, for you will all soon be as anxious for news from the *Country* as I have long been for it from Town. – Some infamous villain has put it into the papers here that Mr Thrale is a Papist! –

71. From Letter to Hester Lynch Thrale *1 July 1780*

[St Martin's Street]

Nothing here is talked of but the Trial of the Rioters: most people among those who are able to appear as Witnesses are so fearful of incurring the future resentment of the mob, that Evidence is very difficult to be obtained, even where guilt is undoubted: by this means Numbers are Daily discharged who had offended against all Laws, though they can be punished by none. I am glad, however, to see the moderation of those who might now, perhaps, extirpate all power but their own, for niether art nor authority is used to blacken the crimes of the accused, or force into light

---

5. Thrale was falsely rumoured to be a Catholic, and both his house and brewery in Southwark were threatened by the mob.
6. A public stagecoach.

the designs of the suspected. Nothing has yet appeared that indicates any Plot – except of general plunder; – nor have any of the *Conspirators* who have yet been examined seemed to have confederated for any *deeper* purpose than to Drink hard, shout loud, and make their Betters Houseless as themselves.

72. From Letter to Hester Lynch Thrale *8 July 1780*

Pacchierotti left London Yesterday morning,[1] – we all miss him much, myself particularly, because, *for all Dr Johnson*, he is not only the first, most finished and most delightful of singers, but an amiable, rational and intelligent Creature, who has given to himself a literary Education, and who has not only a mind superior to his own Profession, which he never names but with regret in spite of the excellence to which he has risen, but he has also, I will venture to say, Talents and an Understanding that would have fitted him for almost any other, had they, instead of being crushed under every possible disadvantage, been encouraged and improved. Had you seen as much of him as I have done, I think, in defiance of prejudice, you would be of the same opinion.

73. From Letter to Hester Lynch Thrale *16 August 1780*

Dr Johnson has delighted me with another Volume of his Lives,[1] – that which contains Blackmore, Congreve, etc., – which he tells me You have had. O what a Writer he is! what instruction, spirit, intelligence and vigour in almost every Paragraph! – Addison I think equal to *any* in the former *Batch*: but he is rather too hard upon Prior, and makes Gay, I think, too insignificant. *Some* of the little Poems of Prior seem to me as charming as any little Poems can be, – and Gay's Pastorals I had hoped to have seen praised more liberally.

1. He returned to Italy, but would come back to England a year later.

1. Johnson's magisterial *Lives of the Poets* had begun appearing in 1779. FB names Sir Richard Blackmore, William Congreve, Joseph Addison, Matthew Prior and John Gay.

74. From Letter to Hester Lynch Thrale *24 August 1780*

Chesington,

Here at length we are, – arrived just in Time to witness poor Daddy Crisp's misery upon receiving intelligence of our late very dreadful loss, – good Heaven, what a terrible blow! – Our Prophet here, who, however, is always a *croaking* Prophet, foretells nothing but utter destruction for its inevitable consequence. *You*, dearest Madam, who are *as* croaking a Prophetess, what say you? *Must* Jamaica, *must* all the West Indies be lost? – or have You some *Words of Comfort* to give us?[1]

Baretti met Mr Greville and Mr Sastris[2] at our House the Evening before we left Town, and *assured* us, peremptorily and with furious vehemence, that the War would be finished in another Year, and France, Spain and America would make what terms we pleased! Perhaps, as he found every body else foreboding ill, he thought it something for the *benefit of mankind* to forebode good: but you would have Laughed to have seen the little respect he paid to the opposition and opinions of the great Mr Greville, the arrogance with which he 'downed' whatever he advanced, and the fury with which he answered him when contradicted in his assertions. I really expected every moment to hear him exclaim 'it is that you are an impenetrable Blockhead,' and I could not get out of my Head the rage with which Mr Greville would have heard such a Compliment. As it was, the astonishment that siezed him when he saw the violence and contempt of Baretti was sufficiently comical; he had never before spoke a word to him, though he had accidentally met with him, and I fancy he expected, by his tonish grandeur, to have instantly silenced and intimidated him: but when he found Baretti *stout*, and that the more he resisted, the more he *Bullyed* him, he could only stare! – and look around at us all, with an expression that said *am I awake?*[3]

---

1. The outward bound East India and West India fleets had been captured by the combined fleets of France and Spain (see p. 130 note 5): 55 out of 63 vessels were taken, a major commercial loss to Britain.

2. Giuseppe Baretti and Francesco Sastres, Italian writers, teachers and translators, were friends of Johnson, the Thrales and the Burneys. Fulke Greville had been CB's patron in the early days; his wife was Frances (see p. 150 note 2).

3. The proud and aristocratic Greville would have felt it beneath him to respond more vigorously to the irascible Baretti, who had once stabbed to death an assailant in the streets of London. FB recalls the rudeness of another Italian, Vincenzio Martinelli, who had once boasted to the Burneys: 'I hear the nobleman talk – I give him great attention – I make him low Bow – & I

75. From Letter to Samuel Crisp *10 October 1780*

Our Jem is at last come, – and I have quitted Streatham to visit him; – So now all our long anxieties and fears are over, and we are all, thank Heaven, happy and at peace.[1] He has brought us Home an admirable Journal, of which I have yet only read one Year, but I have found it full of entertainment and matters of curiosity, and really *very* well written, concise, pertinent, and rational. You will be quite delighted with it, and he means to lend it you of *his own accord.*

He does not yet know when he shall be able to get to Chesington, as his Ship is not paid off, and till that ceremony is over he is obliged to visit it every other Day. We have not yet seen any of his curiosities, but I believe he has brought Home no small quantity.[2]

. . .

Mr Thrale, I believe, is gone to Day to the Discovery, to see Jem on Board. Dr Johnson also intends visiting him in his Ship. And he has had an invitation to Streatham, whither he means to accompany me when I go next.

Are you not delighted at this charming News from America, of Lord Cornwallis's victory?[3] Captains Gore and King are made Post: and Williamson, 2d Lieut. of the Discovery, is made Master and Commander as well as Jem. Capt. King is a very agreeable young Man, – Gore I have not seen.

---

say my Lord! you are a very great man – but, for all that – a Blockhead!' (*EJL*, i. 168–9). Such a remark from a fellow nobleman might well have ended in a duel.

1. James Burney had returned from his voyage around the world with Captain Cook's expedition. He had assumed command of the *Discovery*, which docked at Woolwich on 7 October.

2. Including a monkey as a pet for Dick Burney, and native cloth for his sisters and lady acquaintances.

3. In August the British forces under Lord Cornwallis had won a major battle near Camden, South Carolina, over the army of General Horatio Gates. FB next mentions the promotions of various of James Burney's fellow officers.

76. From Letter to Susanna Burney *c. 7 January 1781*

I have not yet settled about my return; the truth is it is Time, but I am *afraid* of seeing my Father.[1] Think of a whole Volume not yet *settled*, not yet begun! – and that so important a one as the last! – O that I could defer the publication, and relieve my Mind from this vile solicitude which does but shackle it, and disturbs my rest so abominably, that I cannot sleep half the Night for planning what to write next Day, – and then next Day am half dead for want of rest!

77. Letter to Esther Burney *8 January 1781*

Your Letter to Mr Crisp, my sweet Hetty, which I *made* him communicate to me, has indeed given me the most Heart felt concern, nor can I get it at all out of my Head. – Hard, indeed, is it upon You to have thus eternally these cruel struggles with such various difficulties and distress! – O my dear sister! that I had it but in my power to assist you! – a *little*, some time hence, I hope I shall, – *much*, I fear never![1]

I go on but indifferently, – I don't write as I did, the certainty of being known, the high success of Evelina, which, as Mr Crisp says, to fail in a 2d would *tarnish*, – these thoughts worry and depress me, – and a desire to do more than I have been able, by writing at unseasonable Hours, and never letting my Brains rest even when my *Corporeal Machine* was *succumbent*, – these things, joined to a Cold, have brought on a Fever of which I fear I shall some Time feel the ill effects in weakness and an horrid tendency to an Head ache, which disables me from all employment.

Your commission, my dear love, concerning the suspected coldness of my Daddy, I have executed to the best of my power, – but I do assure you most faithfully, your Name has only to be mentioned to bring on your *eloge*,

---

1. FB had been staying with Crisp at Chessington, trying to make significant progress in the writing of her second novel, *Cecilia* (1782). CB was pressing her to finish it so that publication would coincide with the appearance of the second volume of his *General History of Music*.

1. Esther and Charles Burney were perennially in straitened financial circumstances, and she had evidently written to Crisp describing their current situation. In addition, she had just learned that she was pregnant again for the ninth or tenth time, and was probably hoping for an invitation to Chessington for her health, which was always precarious during pregnancy; she had suffered at least two miscarriages.

– which is made most liberally and affectionately by every opportunity. Kitty [Cooke], too, talks of you with the warmest kindness. I have not, therefore, hinted at your suspicions, as, in truth, I could not without appearing absurd, and as you desired I would be guarded: but I have *beat about the Bush* with all the dexterity I have been able, and the result is to feel perfectly satisfied that You are as high in favour as ever, and so is Mr Burney. – I am not idly trying to soothe or deceive you, nor, when seriously employed by you, would I, – on the contrary, I will honestly tell what I myself *conjecture* to be the cause of less warmth in his *Invitations*, – he thinks you are never happy without your Children around you, – and he *dreads* Children in almost a *Childish* way.

This, however, is but a surmize.

Your Letter he received very kindly, and you were very right in being so open to him; he has, since, been casting about in his Head to think of some way to give serviceable advice, and he has been quite grieved at your account, though evidently pleased with its openness.

Keep up your spirits, dearest Hetty! – never mind one more Bantling, – 'tis better for your Health than those vile miscarriages, and poor little Harriet left a vacancy that there is no deferring longer to have occupied.[2] I thank God you will be under Dr Bromfield's care, for I think of him most highly. I am sure nobody can *look* at your Sweet Children, and think the *World*, at least, can have too many such. Be better, therefore, and doubt not but ere long all will go better. Remember, I *bespeak* to be Godmother to this in an *Honourable* way, as I intend to prepare for the same by *Lying in first*![3] – Adieu, my dear Love, – and believe me, to the last Breath I shall Breathe, yours with the most sisterly fondness and Sincerity

F: Burney

78. Letter to Hester Lynch Thrale *4 April 1781*

You bid me Write to you, and so I will, – you bid me pray for you, and so indeed I do, – for the restoration of your sweet peace of mind I pray, for your resignation to this hard blow, for the continued union and exertion of your Virtues with your Talents, and for the happiest reward their exertion can meet with in the gratitude and prosperity of your Chil-

2. Esther's infant daughter Harriet had died at Chessington in 1778.
3. To 'deliver' *Cecilia.*

dren![1] These are my prayers for my beloved Mrs Thrale, but these are not my only ones, – no, the unfailing warmth of her kindness for myself I have rarely, for a long Time past, slept without first petitioning.

I ran away without seeing you again when I found you repented that sweet compliance with my request which I had won from you. For the World would I not have pursued you had I first seen your prohibition, nor could I endure to owe that Consent to teizing which I only solicited from tenderness. Still, however, I think you had better have suffered me to follow you: I might have been of some use, – I hardly *could* have been in your way, but I grieve now to have forced you to an interview which I would have spared myself as well as you had I foreseen how little it would have answered my purpose.

Yet though I cannot help feeling disappointed, I am not surprised, for in any case at all similar I am sure I should have the same eagerness for solitude.

I tell you nothing of how sincerely I simpathise in your affliction, – yet do I believe that Mr Crutchley[2] and Dr Johnson alone do more earnestly: and I have some melancholy comfort in flattering myself that, allowing for the difference of our Characters, that true regard which I felt was as truly returned. Nothing but kindness did I ever meet with – he ever loved to have me not merely with his family, but with himself, – and gratefully shall I ever remember a thousand kind expressions of esteem and good opinion which are now crowding upon my memory.

Ah dearest Madam! you had better have accepted me, – I am sure if unfit for *you*, I am at this Time unfit for every body. Adieu, and Heaven preserve my Heart's Dearest Friend! – don't torment yourself to write to me, – nor will I even ask Queeny, though she is good, and I believe would not deny me, – but what can you say but that you are sad and comfortless, and do I not know that far too well? – I will write again to you, and a thousand Times again – for nothing am I more truly than Your

F.B

1. Henry Thrale, who had recently bought a new house in Grosvenor Square, London, had died there of a rapid series of strokes on 4 April. Hester Thrale shortly left it for Streatham. FB had gone to comfort her friend, either in Grosvenor Square or at Streatham, and Hester Thrale departed the same day with Queeney for Brighton, both to escape 'officious' friends in London and to seek the company of Mr Scrase, an old family friend (*Thraliana*, i. 490). It was not customary for women to attend funerals.

2. Jeremiah Crutchley, an intimate friend of the Thrales wh Hester Thrale believed to be her husband's natural son, was one of Thrale's executors.

79. From Journal Letter to Susanna Burney and Charlotte Ann Burney *June 1781*

[Streatham]

The long War which has been proclaimed among the Wits concerning Lord Lyttelton's Life by Dr Johnson, and which a whole tribe of *Blues*, with Mrs Montagu at their Head, have Vowed to execrate and revenge, now broke out with all the fury of the first actual hostilities, stimulated by long concerted schemes and much spiteful information: Mr Pepys, Dr Johnson well knew was one of Mrs Montagu's steadiest Abettors, and therefore, as he had some Time determined to defend himself with the first of them he met, this Day he fell the sacrifice to his Wrath.[1]

In a long Tête à Tête which I accidentally had with Mr Pepys before the Company was assembled, he told me his apprehensions of an attack, and entreated me earnestly to endeavour to prevent it, modestly avowing he was no antagonist for Dr Johnson, and yet declaring his personal friendship for Lord Lyttelton made him so much hurt by the Life, that he feared he could not discuss the matter without a Quarrel, which, especially in the House of Mrs Thrale, he wished to avoid.

It was utterly, however, impossible for me to serve him. I could have stopt Mrs Thrale with ease, and Mr Seward with a hint, had either of them begun the subject; but, unfortunately, in the middle of Dinner it was begun by Dr Johnson himself, to oppose whom, especially as he spoke with great anger, would have been madness and folly.

Never before have I seen Dr Johnson speak with so much passion; 'Mr Pepys,' he cried, in a voice the most enraged, 'I understand you are offended by my Life of Lord Lyttelton, what is it you have to say against it? come forth, Man! Here am I! ready to answer any charge you can bring.'

'No, Sir,' cried Mr Pepys, 'not at present; I must beg leave to decline the subject; I told Miss Burney before Dinner that I hoped it would not be started.'

I was quite frightened to hear my own Name mentioned in a debate which began so seriously; but Dr Johnson made not to this any Answer; he repeated his attack and his Challenge, and a violent disputation ensued, in which this great, but *mortal* man did, to own the truth, appear unreasonably

---

1. Johnson had written a disparaging account of George, first Baron Lyttelton, in *Lives of the Poets*. Lyttelton was a favourite of Elizabeth Montagu and other bluestockings.

furious and grossly severe: I never saw him so before, and I heartily hope I never shall again. He has been long provoked, and justly enough, at the *sneaking* complaints and murmurs of the Lytteltonians, and therefore his long excited wrath, which hitherto had met no Object, now burst forth with a vehemence and bitterness almost incredible.

Mr Pepys mean time never appeared to so much advantage; he preserved his Temper, uttered all that belonged merely to himself with modesty, and all that more immediately related to Lord Lyttelton with spirit. Indeed Dr Johnson, in the very midst of the dispute, had the candour and liberality to make him a personal Compliment, by saying 'Sir all that you say, while you are vindicating one who cannot thank you, makes me only think the better of you than I ever did before: yet still I think you do *me* wrong, – ' etc. etc.

Some Time after, in the heat of the Argument, he called out 'The more my Lord Lytelton is enquired after, the worse he will appear; Mr Seward has just heard 2 stories of him, which corroborate all I have related.'

He then desired Mr Seward to repeat them. Poor Mr Seward looked almost as frightened as myself at the very mention of his Name; but he quietly and immediately told the stories, which consisted of fresh Instances, from good authorities, of Lord Lytelton's illiberal behaviour to Shenstone;[2] and then he flung himself back in his Chair, and spoke no more during the whole debate, which I am sure he was ready to *Vote a bore.*

One happy circumstance, however, attended the quarrel, which was the presence of Mr Cator,[3] who would by no means be prevented talking himself, either by reverence of Dr Johnson, or ignorance of the subject in question; on the contrary, he gave his opinion quite uncalled, upon every thing that was said by either party, and that with an importance and pomposity, yet with an emptyness and *verbosity* that rendered the whole dispute, when in his Hands, nothing more than ridiculous, and compelled even the disputants themselves, all inflamed as they were, to Laugh. To give a specimen, – one speech will do for a thousand. 'As to this here question of Lord Lytelton I can't speak to it to the purpose, as I have not read his Life, for I have only read the Life of Pope: I have got the Books, though, for I sent for them last Week, and they came to me on Wednesday, and then I

2. Johnson had also written a life of William Shenstone, who like Lyttelton was both a poet and a landscape designer, in which he alleged that Lyttelton was pettily jealous of Shenstone's landscaping.
3. John Cator was a retired timber merchant, a Member of Parliament and an executor of Thrale's will.

began them; but I have not yet read Lord Lytelton. Pope I have begun, and that is what I am now reading. But what I have to say about Lord Lytelton is this here; Mr Seward says that Lord Lytelton's steward dunned Mr Shenstone for his Rent, by which I understand he was a Tenant of Lord Lytelton's, Well, if he was a Tenant of Lord Lytelton's, why should not he pay his Rent?'

Who could contradict this?

When Dinner was quite over, and we left the men to their Wine, we hoped they would finish the affair; but Dr Johnson was determined to talk it through, and make a Battle of it, though Mr Pepys tried to be off continually; when they were all summoned to Tea, they entered still warm and violent: Mr Cator had the Book in his Hand, and was reading the Life of Lytelton, that he might better, he said, understand the Cause, – though not a Creature cared if he had never heard of it!

Mr Pepys came up to me, and said 'Just what I had so much wished to avoid! – I have been crushed in the very onset.'

I could make him no Answer, for Dr Johnson immediately called him off, and harangued and attacked him with a vehemence and *continuity* that quite concerned both Mrs Thrale and myself, and that made Mr Pepys, at last, resolutely silent, however called upon.

This now grew more unpleasant than ever; till Mr Cator, having some Time studied his Book, exclaimed 'What I am now going to say, as I have not yet read the Life of Lord Lytelton quite through, must be considered as being only said aside, because what I am going to say –'

'I wish, Sir,' cried Mrs Thrale, 'it had been all said Aside! here is too much about it indeed, and I should be very glad to hear no more of it.'

This speech, which she made with great spirit and dignity, had an admirable effect: every body was silenced. Mr Cator, thus interrupted in the midst of his proposition, looked quite amazed; Mr Pepys was much gratified by the interference; and Dr Johnson, after a pause, said 'Well, Madam, you *shall* hear no more of it: yet I will defend myself in every part, and in every atom!'

And from this Time the subject was wholly dropt. This dear violent Doctor was conscious he had been wrong, and therefore he most candidly bore the reproof.

When the leave taking Time arrived, Dr Johnson called to Mr Pepys to shake Hands, an invitation which was most coldly and forcibly accepted.

Thursday morning Dr Johnson went to Town for some Days; but not before Mrs Thrale read him a very serious Lecture upon giving way to such violence, which he bore with a patience and quietness that even more than made his peace with me; for *such* a man's confessing himself wrong, is almost more amiable than another man's being steadily right.

80. From Journal Letter to Susanna Burney *c. 10–12 August 1781*

Mr Pepys had *desired* this meeting, by way of a sort of reconciliation after the Lytelton Quarrel: and Dr Johnson now made amends for his former violence; as he advanced to him as soon as he came in, and holding out his Hand to him, received him with a cordiality he had never shewn him before. Indeed he told me himself that 'he thought the better of Mr Pepys for all that had passed.' He is as great a *souled* man, as a *Bodyed* one, and, were he less furious in his passions, he would be demi-divine. Mr Pepys, *also*, behaved extremely well, politely casting aside all reserve or coldness that might be attributed to a lurking ill will for what had passed.

81. From Journal Letter to Susanna Burney and Charlotte Ann Burney *late August 1781*

While we were alone one Evening we made an extempore Elegy, Dr Johnson, Mrs Thrale and myself *spouting* it out alternately, for Miss Thrale is no versifier, not even in this miserable way. The *occasion* was to *make fun* of an Elegy in a Trumpery Book we had just been reading, so I will try to recollect it.

> Here's a Woman of the Town,
> Lies as Dead as any Nail!
> She was once of high renown, –
> And so here begins my Tale.

> She was once as Cherry plump,
> Red her Cheek as Cath'rine Pear,
> Toss'd her Nose, and shook her Rump,
> Till she made her Neighbours stare.

> But there came a Country 'Squire
> He was a seducing Pug!
> Took her from her friends and sire,
> To his own House her did Lug.

There she soon became a Jilt,
Rambling often to and fro',
All her life was nought but guilt,
Till Purse and Carcase both were low.

Black her Eye with many a Blow,
Hot her Breath with many a Dram,
Now she lies exceeding low,
And as quiet as a Lamb.

So if any 3 people can do worse – let them! –

82. From Letter to Dr Burney *c. 5 September 1781*

Dr Johnson has been very unwell indeed. Once I was quite frightened about him, – but he continues his strange discipline, starving, mercury, opium, – and though for a Time half demolished by its severity, he always, in the end, rises superior both to the disease, and the remedy, – which commonly is the most alarming of the two. His Kindness for me I think, if possible, still increased; – he actually bores every body so about me, that the folks even complain of it, – I must, however, acknowledge I feel but little pity for their fatigue.

83. From Letter to Hester Lynch Thrale *2 December 1781*

And now, in return for your anecdotes from Brighton, let me give you a touch of the Morals of Chesington. Master Mumford, a Farmer who lives within half a mile from this House, a Man as eminent for the low vices of drinking, swearing and quarrelling, as any Dean's or Lord's Son for those of higher horrour, having broke the Heart of one Wife, and almost the Bones, of another, met with a third who to the courage necessary for encountering him, joined the admirable prudence of formally binding him, under a penalty of £100, payable to a Tradesman at Kingston, not to beat her! Do you often hear of a lady's greater discretion in disposing of herself? Yet, to shew the utter vanity of all human precautions for happiness, Master Mumford, though the first year of their marriage is not over, contrives at once to evade the Law, and gratify his old propensities, by siezing both her

Wrists, and making her thump her own Face and Neck! So to which will you give the palm for rural Ingenuity? How can any one endure the Town, after seeing the artless simplicity of the Country?[1]

1. Hester Thrale responded: 'Your Farmer is a Hero, and I am glad he has found any method of beating his Ideot Wife' (undated letter in Berg Collection).

1782–1786

Cecilia *and Prelude to the Court*

84. From Letter to Samuel Crisp *15 March 1782*

Your Letter, my dear Daddy, which I have just received, has given me so much uneasiness that I may as well answer it immediately, as I can do nothing for thinking of it.

The conflict scene for Cecilia, between the mother and son, to which you so warmly object, is the very scene for which I wrote the whole Book! and so entirely does my plan hang upon it, that I must abide by its reception in the World, or put the whole behind the Fire.[1]

You will believe then, with the opinion I have of your judgment, and the anxious desire I have to do nothing quite contrary to your approbation, if I can now be very easy. I would it were in my power to defer the whole publication to another spring, – but I am sure my Father would run crazy if I made such a proposal.

Let me not, however, be sentenced without making my defence, and at least explaining to you my own meaning in the part you censure.

I meant in Mrs Delvile to draw a great, but not a perfect character: I meant, on the contrary, to blend upon paper, as I have frequently seen blended in life, noble and rare qualities, with striking and incurable defects. I meant, also, to shew how the greatest virtues and excellencies, may be totally obscured by the indulgence of violent passions, and the ascendancy of favourite prejudices.

This scene has yet been read by no human Creature but yourself and Charlotte, who would not let me rest till I let her go through the Book: upon Charlotte's opinion you will easily believe I put no solid reliance, but yet I mention to you the effect it had on her, because, as you told me about dear

---

1. FB would retain this scene (Bk. VIII, ch. 6 in the published work), in which Augusta Delvile so strenuously urges her son Mortimer to give up Cecilia that she bursts a blood vessel.

Kitty Cooke, the natural feelings of untaught hearers ought never to be slighted, – and Dr Johnson has told me the same a thousand Times: well – she prefers it to any part of the Book, and cried over it so vehemently, that she could Eat no Dinner, and had a violent Head ache all Day.

I would rather, however, have had one good word from you, than all the Tears of the Tender, and all the praises of the civil.

The Character of Mrs Delvile struck you in so favourable a light, that you sunk, as I remember I privately noticed to myself, when you mentioned her, all the passages to her disadvantage previous to this conflict. Else it would have appeared to you less inconsistent, for the way is paved for it in several places. But indeed you read the whole to cruel disadvantage: the bad writing, the haste, the rough Copy, all were against me. Your anger at Mrs Delvile's violence and obduracy is nothing but what I *meant* to excite; – your thinking it *unnatural* is all that disturbs me.

Yet, when I look about me in the World, such strange inconsistencies as I see, such astonishing contrariety of opinions, and so bigotted an adherence of all *marked* Characters to their own way of thinking, I really know not how to give up this point.

Another thing gives me some comfort: the part you have selected to like best, Vauxhall, is what I read to you myself, and the whole of the residence of Delvile Castle,[2] which I also read to you, I remember well you were pleased with more than with any other part of the Book. I cannot, therefore, but hope the bad Copy, and difficulty of reading, did me as much mischief as the bad and unusual composition.

But what are you thinking of, my dear Daddy, when you desire me to send you the 2 last vol.'s immediately? Did I not tell you I am still actually at Work upon the 2d? – and as to sending you again the rough Draught, it would both be *soliciting* and *establishing* your disapprobation.

The first volume seems to *grow*, by recollection, both on my Father and Mrs Thrale. It is not to be expressed how fond they are of it, – especially my Father.

Every body knows that I am about something, and the moment I put my Head out of Doors, I am sure to be attacked and catechised. Oh that I were but as sure of the *success*, as of the *sale* of this Book! but indeed I am now more discomfited and alarmed than I have ever been yet. Adieu, my dear Daddy, – I would I could do better; – but to love you and your most kind

2. Bk. V, ch. 12 (Vauxhall), in which Mr Harrel, one of Cecilia's legal guardians and a hopeless spendthrift, shoots himself in despair over his debts; and Bk. VI, chs. 3–11.

sincerity more truly is not possible: never, therefore, spare it, till you cease to love or cease to esteem your ever affectionate

[F.B.]

85. From Journal Letter to Susanna Phillips[1] *early July 1782*

At length, my ever dearest Susan, my long neglected Journal, and long promised renewal behold at Your Feet! for thither shall I speed them with all the expedition in my power.

So much has passed since I lost you – for I cannot use any other word! – that I hardly know what first to *record*; but I think 'tis best to begin with what is uppermost in my mind, Mr Burke.

Among the many I have been obliged to shirk this year, for the sake of living almost solely with *Cecilia*, none have had less patience with my retirement than Miss Palmer, who, bitterly, believing, I intended never to visit her again, has forborne sending me any invitations: but, about 3 Weeks ago, my Father had a Note from Sir Joshua Reynolds, to ask him to Dine, at Richmond, and meet the Bishop of St Asaph:[2] and therefore, to make my peace, I scribbled a note to Miss Palmer to this purpose, –

After the many kind invitations I have been obliged to refuse, will you, my dear Miss Palmer, should I *offer* to accompany my Father to-morrow, bid me remember the old Proverb

Those who will not when they may

When they will, they shall have nay? – F.B.

This was graciously received, and the next morning Sir Joshua and Miss Palmer called for my Father and me, accompanied by Lord Corke.[3] We had a mighty pleasant ride, Miss Palmer and I *made up*, though she scolded most violently about my long absence, and attacked me about *the Book* without mercy. The Book, in short, to my great consternation, I find is talked of and expected all the Town over. My dear Father himself, I do verily believe, mentions it to every body; he is fond of it to enthusiasm, and does not fore-see the danger of raising such general expectation, which fills *me* with the horrors every time I am tormented with the thought.

1. In January 1782 Susanna Burney had married Molesworth Phillips, career officer in the Royal Marines and shipmate of James Burney on the Cook expedition.
2. Revd Dr Jonathan Shipley. His daughter, Georgiana, married (1783) Francis Hare-Naylor.
3. Edmund Boyle, Earl of Cork. His wife was Anne, Lady Cork.

Lord Corke is ugly and unpleasing; and I had heard so much to his disadvantage, with regard to his behaviour to his lady, before I saw him, that he must have been nothing short of an Angel to have appeared to me handsome or attractive.

Sir Joshua's House is delightfully situated, almost at the top of Richmond Hill. We walked till near dinner Time upon the Terrace, and there met Mr Richard Burke,[4] the Brother of the Orator. Miss Palmer, stopping him, said 'Are you coming to Dine with us?' 'No,' he answered, 'I shall Dine at the Star and Garter.'

'How did you come, with Mrs Burke or alone?'

'Alone.'

'What, on Horseback?'

'Ay, sure!' cried he, Laughing, '*up* and *ride*! now's the Time.' And he made a fine flourish with his Hand, and past us. He is just made under secretary at the Treasury. He is a Tall and handsome man, and seems to have much dry drollery; but we saw no more of him.

After our return to the House, and while Sir Joshua and I were Tête à Tête, Lord Corke and my Father being still walking, and Miss Palmer having, I suppose, some orders to give about the Dinner, the *Knight of Plympton*[5] was desiring my opinion of the prospect from his Window, and comparing it with Mr Burkes, as he told me after I had spoken it, – when the Bishop of St Asaph and his Daughter, Miss Georgiana Shipley, were announced. Sir Joshua, to divert himself, in introducing me to the Bishop, said 'Miss Burney, my lord; – otherwise Evelina.'

The Bishop is a well looking man, and seemed grave, quiet, and sensible. I have *heard* much more of him, but nothing more appeared. Miss Georgiana, however, was shewy enough for *two*. She is a very Tall, and rather handsome Girl, but the expression of her Face is, to me, uncommonly and insufferably disagreeable, she has almost a constant smile, – but not of softness, nor of insipidity, but of self-sufficiency, and internal satisfaction. She is very much accomplished, and her fame for Painting and for scholarship I know you are well acquainted with; I believe her to have very good parts, and much quickness; but she is so conceited, so forward, so full of herself, so earnest to obtain notice, and so happy in her confidence of deserving it, that I have not less been charmed with any young lady I have seen for many a Day. I have met with her before, at Mrs Pepys, but never before was introduced to her.

---

4. Attorney. Mrs Burke below is Edmund Burke's wife.
5. Sir Joshua was a native of Plympton, Devon, where he had once served a term as mayor.

Miss Palmer soon joined us; and, in a short Time, entered more Company, – 3 Gentlemen, and one lady; but there was no more ceremony used of introductions. The lady I concluded was Mrs Burke, wife of *The* Mr Burke, and I was not mistaken; one of the Gentlemen I recollected to be young Burke, her son, whom I once met at Sir Joshua's in Town, and another of them I knew for Mr [Edward] Gibbon: but the third, I had never seen before. I had been told that *The* Burke was not expected, – yet I could conclude this Gentleman to be no other; – he had just the air, the manner, the appearance, I had prepared myself to look for in him, and there was an evident, a striking superiority in his demeanour, his Eye, his motions, that announced him *no common man*.

I could not get at Miss Palmer to satisfy my doubts, and we were soon called down stairs to Dinner. Sir Joshua and the *unknown* stopt to speak with one another upon the stairs; and when they followed us, Sir Joshua, in taking his place at the Table, asked me to sit next him; I willingly complied, 'And then,' he added, 'Mr Burke shall sit on the other side of you.' 'O no, indeed!' cried Miss Georgiana, who, also, had placed herself next Sir Joshua, 'I won't consent to that, Mr Burke must sit next *me*; I won't agree to part with him. Pray come and sit down quiet, Mr Burke.'

Mr Burke, – for Him it was, – smiled and obeyed.

'I only meant,' said Sir Joshua, 'to have made my peace with Mr Burke, by giving him that place, because he has been scolding me for not introducing him to Miss Burney. However, I must do it now; – Mr Burke! – Miss Burney! –'

We both half rose, and Mr Burke said 'I have been complaining to Sir Joshua that he left me wholly to my own sagacity; – however, it did not, here, deceive me.'

'O Dear, then,' said Miss Georgiana, looking a little *consternated*, 'perhaps you won't thank me for calling you to this place!'

Nothing was said. *And so*, – we all began Dinner, Young Burke making himself my next Neighbour.

Captain Phillips knows Mr Burke; has he, or has he not told you how delightful a Creature he is? – if he has *not*, pray in my Name, abuse him without mercy, – if he *has*, pray ask if he will subscribe to my account of him, which *here with* shall follow, –

He is Tall, his figure is noble, his air commanding, his address graceful: his Voice is clear, penetrating, sonorous and powerful; his Language is copious, various, and eloquent; his manners are attractive; his conversation is delightful! – What says Capt. Phillips? – have I chanced to see him *in his happiest Hour*! or is he all this in common? Since we lost Garrick, I have seen nobody so enchanting; nor to Garrick himself is he in any thing inferior.

I can give You, however, very little of what was said, for the conversation was not *suivie*,[6] Mr Burke darting from subject to subject with as much rapidity as entertainment: neither is the charm of his discourse more in the matter than the manner; all, therefore, that is related *from* him, loses half its effect in not being related *by* him. Such little sketches as I can recollect, take, however.

From the Windows of the Dining Parlour, Sir Joshua directed us to look at a mighty pretty white House, which belonged to Lady Di Beauclerk; 'I am extremely glad,' said Mr Burke, 'to see her, at last, so well Housed; poor Woman! the Bowl has long rolled in misery; I rejoice that it has now found its balance. I never, myself, so much enjoyed the sight of happiness in another, as in that Woman, when I first saw her after the Death of her Husband. It was really enlivening to behold her placed in that sweet House, released from all her cares, a thousand pound a Year at her own disposal; *and* – her Husband was Dead! – O it was pleasant; it was delightful to see her enjoyment of her situation!'[7]

'But, without considering the circumstances,' said Mr Gibbon, 'this may appear very strange, though, when they are fairly stated, it is perfectly rational and unavoidable.'

'Very true,' said Mr Burke, 'if the circumstances are not considered, Lady Di may seem highly reprehensible.' He then, addressing himself particularly to me, as the person least likely to be acquainted with the character of Mr Beauclerk, drew it himself, in strong and marked expressions, describing the misery he gave his Wife, his singular ill treatment of her, and the *necessary* relief the death of such a man must give.

He then reminded Sir Joshua of a Day in which they had Dined at Mr Beauclerks, soon after his marriage with Lord Bolingbroke's divorced Wife, in company with Goldsmith, and told a new story of poor Goldsmith's eternal blundering.[8]

My sweetest Susy – no further was I got than this, when dear Pacchierotti came in, and I had hardly left off to receive him, and make some Tea, when your sweet Captain joined us: think if I was not gay and happy, – no *sulky*

6. *Followed*, i.e. sustained on a given topic.

7. Lady Diana Beauclerk's husband, Topham, had died in 1780. His ill-tempered abuse of her had been general knowledge. She had been divorced by her first husband, Lord Bolingbroke, for adultery with Beauclerk.

8. Goldsmith had probably blurted out something about the adultery and divorce.

madre envying me, nor repressing my enjoyment![9] and think if I wished not for my Susy! – Oh almost with an earnestness of regret to destroy my happiness.

86. From Letter to Dr Burney *17 July 1782*

Miss Palmer and Capt. King called upon me yesterday to insist upon my Dining at Sir Joshua's, to meet Dr Johnson and Mrs Cholmondeley; but I had already refused the Pepys, and did not dare, – no answer, however, would satisfy them, and they worked at me with unremitting violence till they forced a promise from me to come to Tea.

I found Mrs Cholmondeley and her 2 Daughters, Mr Metcalf, Mrs Reynoldes,[1] Sir Joshua, Miss Palmer and the dear Dr Johnson, who had been puffing off my Book till the moment of my arrival. Capt. Phillips also went with me. I had no talk with the Dr all the Evening, as I was not near him, but I had many kind looks, which were not thrown away upon *Miss Reynolds*, whose comments were very diverting: however, Mrs Cholmondely attacked me in *all* ways, – gayly, and seriously, – with elegance and with absurdity, – with flattery and with threats, – and in as many modes and voices, and with as much variety of look and action, as if she had been performing some highly written part upon the stage.

Miss Palmer, who had read night and Day, was the only person who had finished Cecilia, for Mrs Cholmondeley had not yet got it, as her Bookseller had parted with every Copy he had received, and was himself waiting for more before he could supply her; and the circulating library people, Mrs Reynolds told me, have had it bespoken by old Customers for months to come, and cannot get enough to at all stop people's mouths. Miss Palmer is mad with fondness for Young Delvile, and so struck with Albany that he is never a moment out of her Head. – Sir Joshua, who is still only in the first Vol: says he foresees Monckton will be the victor, by his deep designing Character; but *he* seems most diverted by Miss Leeson, whose '*Yes, ma'am*,' '*no, ma'am*,' '*I don't know*,' and '*I can't tell*,' he quoted perpetually. Dr Johnson

9. FB alludes to the perennial ill feelings of her stepmother, who felt herself shut out by the Burney children.

1. Philip Metcalfe was a friend of Johnson and Reynolds and one of Reynolds's executors. Frances Reynolds, whom FB alternately styles 'Mrs' and 'Miss', was Sir Joshua's sister and a painter herself. (It was common practice in the eighteenth century to call older unmarried women 'Mrs'.)

supports Hobson at the Head of the tribe, and says it is a very *perfect* Character; – and Simkins and Miss Larolles are very highly in his favour.[2] Just as I was coming away, and passing him, he took my Hand, and, with sundry *kind* words, too tender for a *third person*, he said 'I have again read Harrel's Death, – it is finely done, – it is *very* finely done, –' with a very emphatic voice and manner.

I hear, through Capt. King, that all the Burkes are reading it; and he has negociated another meeting for me with Mrs Burke, whom I am to call upon to-morrow.

I have now lent Mr Hutton my first Vol. but have not seen him since he has had it. Miss Palmer tells me it is reported about Town I have had £1000 for the Copy![3] Mrs Cholmondeley told me she understood I had behaved like a *poor simple thing* again, and had a Father *no wiser than myself*! – I wonder what *would* content the people! – Miss Reynolds has not yet begun, but kept drolly *anticipating* Compliments, and exclamations of wonder and delight all the Evening.

87. From Letter to Susanna Phillips *31 August 1782*

My Father is now in Town: and since his absence, the Lady,[1] kept in no order, has been so flippant and facetious, and Mr Crisp, wanting the curb of my Father's presence, has been so openly disgusted and forbidding, that I have Daily expected a declaration of War. She still, however, *means* to Court him, though she has not the skill to know how; and *he means* to be very civil, though his distaste and aversion break out continually and involuntarily. Kitty and I were both quite frightened Yesterday at Dinner, by his looks, dry sneers, and almost groans of weariness: and she [Kitty] resolved upon Giving him a *Triming*; therefore as soon as the lady retired, she began. 'Upon my word, Mr Crisp, you carr. it too fur; to be sure she's

2. *Cecilia* had been published on 12 July. Albany is an 'old crazy moralist' (FB to Samuel Crisp, May 1782, *EJL* (forthcoming)); Moncton is Cecilia's neighbour and false counsellor, who hopes to gain her estate by marrying her; Miss Leeson and Miss Larolles are two 'TON [fashionable] Misses', the former 'silent, scornful, languid, and affected', the latter 'flirting, communicative, restless, and familiar' (*Cecilia*, Bk. I, ch. 5); the fat Hobson and the thin Simkens are comical tradesmen.

3. FB received £250 for the copyright from her publishers.

1. Elizabeth Burney. This letter, written from Chessington, shows Crisp's aversion to her. He and the Burney children considered her rude and vulgar, but were always careful to hide their feelings from CB, who truly loved his wife.

a nasty old Cat, for a Woman of sense, that sees the World, but for all that the poor Doctor can't help her being such a hobby Horse of Hound's flesh, and so its quite ung*i*nerous to an old fr*i*nd not to take up with it sometimes; to be sure, I'm as sorry as you can be that the old sow did not pop off, when she was so nigh it,[2] but there's no helping them things, for I dare say she'll live to be an hundred, she takes such a plaguy deal of care of herself, with her handsome Legs, that she's always a talking of, and shewing, as if I cared for seeing such things, or her Husband either, an indelicate Beast! How *s*ever, for all that, the woman behaves very well to you, so none of your sighing, my Lad, nor weeping nor wapping, for she'll live to plague you a great while yet, I can tell you that, with her nasty pole of gray stumps, tiffing herself up for a gay young thing: howsever there's no need to make bad worse, by all them speeches and gruntings, – behaving with that reserve to give her a slap bang upon everything she says!' This expostulation, though much resisted when pronounced, produced an excellent effect; and my Daddy for the Evening behaved with more decency than he has ever done since my arrival. But Edward [Burney], who seems much pleased with his quarters here, and myself Laugh ourselves quite sick at this good natured, worthy, loveable, blundering, Kitty's original and most singular conversation.

88. From Letter to Susanna Phillips *14 September 1782*

You will be sorry, I am sure, at what I must hint to You of sweet Edward[1] – You know, very well, his former and early partiality – and I have told you how absolutely I saw it was lately conquered: nothing, however, could be more apparent than its revival during this sojourn at Chesington: where it has been remarked by Kitty Cooke, Mrs Gast, and Ham [Mrs Hamilton] to me: though I saw it not ever myself till about a Week before my departure: when, one Evening, I purposely avoided him, after having almost constantly taken a stroll with him, merely from thinking he wanted more exercise than walking with *me* could give him. Kitty, however, then came to me, and said 'Is your Cousin well? he's leaning his Head against the Chimney, and doing nothing.'

2. Elizabeth Burney had been very ill recently.

1. This letter confirms an oral tradition in the Burney family, reported by Annie Raine Ellis in the late nineteenth century, that Edward Francesco Burney had been in love with FB. On three different occasions he painted portraits of her which she considered to be too flattering.

I then went and inquired if he was ill, he only laughed, but was much embarassed: I advised him to take a long run, and he instantly went out: but at supper, when I asked how many miles he had strolled, he told me he had only been sitting in the mount. All this *might* be accident, though it was not very like it: however, the next Night I gave him the same advice, with the same effect, for he stirred not from the short Gravel Walk before the House, and was so dejected and so apparently miserable, that every body in the House noticed it. I then walked with him again, the 3d Night, – and then again he was in excellent spirits and seemed very happy. The Day, however, before I left Chesington, he seemed in a state of wretchedness that it was hardly possible to see without participating: I knew not what to make of it, nor *know*, indeed, can I, – but Kitty, who had long given me hints upon the subject, took me aside at Night, and said 'Why your poor Cousin's quite over head and Ears! he's a very pretty young fellow, – I'm sure I don't think the age so much signifies,[2] – it's quite a *slap bangum* to him your going away – if you'll believe me, the Tears are in his Eyes, – ' I have no room for further particulars, but I am sorry at my Heart for the sweet Lad, who is more amiable, and worthy, and ingenious than almost any body. The next morning I had settled to go to Kingston with William;[3] but Kitty, eager to give pleasure to every body, proposed to Edward that he also should accompany me, and Charlotte desired to be of the party: this was agreed to, and so revived him, that all the way he was even *jovial* in his spirits. But Charlotte writes me word it was not the same upon their return, and that he had been utterly dejected from that moment of my departure to his own. I am sure you will be sorry, but such is the World!

89. From Letter to Hester Lynch Thrale *11 October 1782*

[St Martin's Street]

Thanks, ever dearest Madam, for both your sweet and most confidential Letters: but what to say about coming to you, further than how *much* I wish it, I yet know not,[1] – poor Susanna has by no means been so rapid in recovering as we hoped, – on the contrary, she has had a Fever to

2. Edward was eight years younger than FB.
3. A servant.

1. Hester Thrale was in Brighton.

frighten us all, and was yesterday so ill that I was cruelly terrified indeed.[2] To Day, however, she is, thank Heaven, considerably better, and if she has no relapse, my earnest wishes to be again under the roof with my dear Mrs Thrale will yet take place.

But now let me tell you what made her so very ill yesterday: about Noon there was a violent knocking at the Door, and, in 2 Minutes, into the Room scampered Mrs Meeke,[3] – without any introduction, without waiting to make any enquiry into the state of the family, and without any previous knowledge on our part that she had the smallest design of coming to England! Unthinking, giddy, good humoured and impetuous, she merely asked if any of the family were at Home, and, without waiting any answer, ran up to see herself whom she could find. Susan was in no condition for such hurry, vehemence, and surprise, and though I hastened her down stairs with all the expedition I could decently use, she was thrown into a *palpitation somewhere about the Heart,* that brought a violent fever in a very few minutes.

This poor little Girl, who is extremely affectionate and good-natured, so little meant to do any harm, that I have concealed from her this mischief. She cried with joy at sight of us, and was so earnest to pass some Time here, that I gave up to her all the Day I could possibly spare from poor Susy, and kept her till this morning, when Capt. Phillips accompanied her to Chesington: her eagerness to see my mother by no means inducing her to go sooner. Indeed both she and Mrs Rishton always loved my father and his family a thousand times more than their own Relations. Her plan in coming seems likely to see her English friends, among whom she means to pass the Winter: though, probably, as she will next month be of age, it may be necessary she should shew herself, as she is a Ward in Chancery: but of this I know nothing. Mr Meeke attended her to Calais, and then trusted her to a friend. His own affairs prevented his coming further.[4] She is extremely improved indeed, since her marriage, and is a *very* pleasing young Woman, and of an uncommon character and very singular manners: a sort of mixture of the Mrs Fitzgerald I have described to you, and your favourite Henrietta Belfield, for she is as fond of mischief, as great a Rattle, as perpetual a laugher, and as careless, easy and negligent as Mrs F: while she is as gentle

---

2. Susanna Phillips had just given birth to her first child, Frances. FB stood as godmother at the infant's christening on 4 February 1783.

3. Elizabeth Allen had eloped to Europe in 1777 at the age of sixteen with an adventurer, Samuel Meeke.

4. Probably because of debts owed in England.

in her speech, as innocent in her Heart, and as affectionate in her disposition as poor Henrietta.[5]

90. From Letter to Samuel Crisp *15 October 1782*

I am very sorry you could not come to Streatham at the Time Mrs Thrale hoped to see you, for when shall we be likely to meet there again? You would have been much pleased, I am sure, by meeting with General Paoli,[1] who spent the Day there, and was extremely communicative and agreeable. I had seen him in large Companies, but was never made known to him before; nevertheless he conversed with me as if well acquainted not only with myself, but my connections, – enquiring of me when I had last seen Mrs Montagu, and calling Sir Joshua Reynolds, when he spoke of him, *my friend*. He is a very pleasing man, Tall and genteel in his person, remarkably well bred, and very mild and soft in his manners. I will try to give you a little specimen of his conversation, because I know you love to hear particulars of all *out of the way Persons*. His English is blundering, but not *un*pretty.

Speaking of his first acquaintance with Mr Boswell;[2] 'He came,' he said, 'to my Country, and he *fetched* me some Letter of *recommending him*; but I was of the belief he might be an impostor, and I supposed, in my *mente*, he was an *Espy*;[3] for I look away from him, and, in a moment, I look to him again, and I behold his Tablets! – Oh! he was to the work of writing *down* all I say! – Indeed I was angry! But soon I discover he was no imposter, and no *Espy*, and I only find I was myself the monster he was come to discern. O, – is a very good man; I love him, indeed; – so chearful! so gay! so pleasant! – but, at the first, Oh! I was indeed angry.'

After this, he told us a story of an expectation he had had of being robbed, and of the protection he found from a very large Dog, that he is very fond

5. In 1776 FB had described Mary Fitzgerald to Crisp as 'as droll a sort of piece of Goods, (to use your expression) as one might wish to know' (*EJL*, ii. 211). Henrietta Belfield, in *Cecilia*, is in love with Mortimer Delvile.

1. Pascal Paoli was a famous Corsican general and patriot who had been driven off the island by the French in 1769. He settled in England where he was given a pension of £1,200 a year and became a friend of Johnson, Reynolds and Burke and a member of Johnson's club.
2. Boswell had sought out Paoli in Corsica and upon his return to England published the first biography of him in 1768.
3. Mind (Italian); Spy (Paoli combines English 'spy' with French 'espion').

of. 'I walk out,' he said, 'in the Night; I go towards the Field; – I behold a man; – Oh! ugly one! – I proceed, – he follow, – I go on, – he address me, You have one Dog, he says, – Yes, say I to him, – Is a fierce Dog, he says, is he fiery? – Yes, reply I, he can bite! – I would not attack in the Night, says he, a House to have such Dog in it. – Then I conclude he was a *breaker*; so I turn to him; – Oh very rough! not gentle, – and I say, very fierce, He shall destroy You, if You are Ten!'

Afterwards, speaking of the Irish Giant who is now shewn in Town, he said 'He is so large, I am as a Baby! I look at him, – Oh! I find myself so little as a Child! – indeed my indignation it rises, when I see him hold up his Hand so high; – I am as nothing! and I find myself in the power of a man who *fetches* from me half a Crown! – '

This Language, which is all spoke very pompously by him, sounds comical from himself, though I know not how it may read.

91. From Letter to Susanna Phillips *31 October 1782*

Poor Mr Pepys had, however, real cause to bemoan my escape; for the little set was broken up by my retreat, and he joined Dr Johnson, with whom he entered into an argument upon some lines of Gray, and upon Pope's definition of Wit, in which he was so roughly confuted, and so severely ridiculed, that he was hurt and piqued beyond all power of disguise, and in the midst of the discourse, suddenly turned from him, and wishing Mrs Thrale good night, very abruptly withdrew. Dr Johnson was certainly right and *most* right with respect to the argument, and to reason, but his opposition was so warm, and his wit so satirical and exulting, that I was really quite grieved to see how unamiable he appeared, and how greatly he made himself dreaded by all, and by many abhorred. What pity that he will not curb the *vehemence* of his love of victory and superiority! The sum of the dispute was this. Wit being talked of, Mr Pepys repeated

> True wit is Nature to advantage Dress'd,
> What oft was thought, but ne'er so well expressed.[1]

That, Sir, cried Dr Johnson, is a definition both *false* and *foolish*. Let Wit be *Dressed* how it will, it will equally be wit, and neither the more nor the less for any advantage Dress can give it.

1. Pope, *Essay on Criticism*, ll. 297–8.

Mr P. But sir, may not Wit be so ill expressed, and so obscure, by a bad speaker, as to be lost?

Dr J. The fault, then, Sir, must be with the *Hearer*. If a man cannot distinguish *wit* from *Words*, he little deserves to hear it.

Mr P. But Sir, what Pope means –

Dr J. Sir what Pope means, if he means what he says, is both *false* and *foolish*. In the first place, *what oft was thought*, is all the worse for being *often* thought, because to be *wit*, it ought to be *newly* thought. –

Mr P. But, Sir, 'tis the *expression* makes it new –

Dr J. How can the Expression make it new? It may make it *clear*, or may make it *elegant*; but How *new*? You are confounding words with things.

Mr P. But, Sir, if one man says a thing *very* ill, may not another man say it so much better that –

Dr J. That other man, Sir, deserves but small praise for the amendment; he is but the Taylor to the first man's thoughts.

Mr P. True, Sir, he may be but the Taylor, – but then the difference is as great as between a man in a gold lace suit, and a man in a Blanket.

Dr J. Just so, Sir, I thank you for that! the difference is precisely such, since it consists neither in the gold lace suit nor the blanket, but in the *man* by whom they are worn.

This was the summary; the various contemptuous sarcasms intermixed would fill, and very unpleasantly, a quire.

92. From Journal Letter to Susanna Phillips *December 1782*

[8 December] Then came in Sir Joshua Reynolds, and he soon drew a Chair near mine, and from that Time I was never without some friend at my Elbow.[1]

'Have you seen,' said he, 'Mrs Montagu lately?'

'No, not very lately.' 'But within these few months?'

'No, not since last year.' 'O, – you must see her, then! – you *ought* to see and to hear her! – 'Twill be worth your while. Have you heard of the fine long Letter she has written?'

'Yes, – but I have not met with it.'

'I have.' 'And who is it to?'

'The old Duchess of Portland. She desired Mrs Montagu's opinion of

---

1. FB had attended a large assembly at the residence of the Hon. Miss Mary Monckton.

Cecilia, and she has written it at full length. I was in a party at her Grace's, and heard of nothing but *you*, – she is so delighted, and so sensibly, so rationally, that I only wish you could have heard her. And old Mrs Delany[2] had been *forced* to begin it, though she had said she should never read any more, – however, when we met, she was reading it already for the 3d Time! Indeed I wish you had been there; there was a very fine discourse upon it.'

Pray tell my Daddy to rejoice for me in this conquest of the Duchess, his old friend, and Mrs Delany, his sister's.[3] Sir Joshua is extremely kind; he is always picking up some anecdote of this sort for me, yet, most delicately, never lets me hear his *own* praises but through others. He looks vastly well, and as if he had never been ill.

. . .

Monday [9 December]. I spent the morning at Mr Bogles,[4] very little to my liking. He and his Wife have so *persecuted* me to sit for my picture, that, not wholly to disoblige them, I have been compelled to consent, with this compromise, that he would give up his *first* request and plan, which was to put it into the Exhibition,[5] to which I will *not* consent.

. . .

[17 December] Pacchierotti called, and most earnestly begged me to write a note to him the next morning, with my opinion of Mrs Siddons, and he was so serious, that I could not deny him, though not very fond of the task: I will try, however, now, to recollect what I said, as the opinion I gave was a very honest one.

To Mr Pacchierotti.

'I must confess my admiration of Mrs Siddons does not keep pace with that of the Town; yet I think her a pleasing and elegant Actress. Her Countenance is intelligent, and full of sensibility, her voice is penetrating and affecting, her attitudes, upon striking occasions, are very noble, though, in general, her arms are awkward. I think her neither *great* nor *astonishing*; her manner seems to me monotonous, her Walk

---

2. Mary Delany, widow of the Revd Patrick Delany, was a special friend of Margaret Cavendish Bentinck, widow of the second Duke of Portland. She would soon become a close friend of FB and be instrumental in bringing her to Court.
3. Ann Crisp, who had died in 1776.
4. John Bogle, miniature portrait painter, old friend of the Burneys. His miniature of FB is the cover illustration of this volume.
5. At the Royal Academy.

mean, her air wants spirit, and her dignity is studied. Upon the whole, I think she has much merit and but few defects yet, alltogether, something through-out, is wanting to produce upon me much effect.'

This was the purpose of what I wrote, and what I think.

. . .

[24 December] I went in the Evening to call on Mrs Thrale, and tore myself away from her to go to *Bolt Court*, to see Dr Johnson, who is very unwell. He received me with great kindness, and bid me come oftener; which I will try to contrive. He told me he heard of nothing but *me*, call upon him who would, and though he pretended to *growl*, he was evidently delighted for me. His usual set, Mrs Williams and Mrs De Mullins,[6] were with him, and some queer man of a Parson, who after grinning at me some Time, said 'Pray, Mrs De Mullins, is the 5th volume of Cecilia at Home yet? – Dr Johnson made me read it, ma'am.'

'Sir, – he did it much honour. – '

'*Made* you, sir?' said the Doctor, 'You give an ill account of your own taste, or understanding, if you wanted any *making* to read such a Book as Cecilia.'

'O, sir, I don't mean that, – for I am sure I left every thing in the World to go on with it.'

A shilling was now wanted, for some purpose or other, and none of them happened to have one; I begged that I might lend one, – 'Ay, do,' said the Doctor, 'I will borrow of *you*, – Authors are like Privateers, always fair game for one another.'

'True, sir,' said the Parson, 'One Author is always robbing another – '

'I don't know that, sir,' cried the Doctor, – '*there* sits an author who, to *my* knowledge, has robbed nobody. I have never once caught her at a Theft. The Rogue keeps her resources to herself!'

I was then told that Mr Wyndham of Norfolk[7] had called in the morning, and that Dr Johnson had talked over the whole Book with him, – and said *such* things! – O me, in what must all this end!

. . .

6. Anna Williams and Elizabeth Desmoulins.
7. William Windham of Felbrigg Hall, Norfolk, devoted younger friend of Johnson and outstanding scholar and mathematician; later Member of Parliament and secretary at war.

[26 December] Our Evening was really a charming one, – the 2 Mr Cambridges came at about 8 o'clock, and the good Mr Hoole[8] was here; my Father came down stairs to them, in high spirits and good humour, and he and the elder Mr Cambridge not only talked *enough* for us all, but so well and so pleasantly that no person present had even a *wish* to speak for her/ himself; – Mr Cambridge has the best stock of good stories I almost ever heard, and, though a little too precise in his manner, and rather posing in his conversation, he is always well bred, and *almost* always entertaining. Our sweet Father kept up the Ball with him admirably, whether in anecdotes, serious disquisitions, philosophy or fun, for all which Mr Cambridge has both talents and inclination. The son rises extremely in my opinion and liking: There was something in his manner that, at first, I thought a little pedantic, but that notion entirely wears away upon further acquaintance. He is sensible, rational, and highly cultivated; very modest in all he asserts, and attentive and pleasing in his behaviour, and he is wholly free from the coxcombical airs, either of impertinence or negligence and *non-chalence*, that almost all the young men I meet, except, also, young Burke, are tainted with. What chiefly, however, pleased me in him was observing that he quite adores his Father. He attended to all his stories with a Face that never told he had heard them before, and though he spoke but little himself, he seemed as well entertained as if he had been the leading person in the company; – a Post which, nevertheless, I believe he could extremely well sustain, and, no doubt, much the better for being in no haste to aspire to it. I have seldom, alltogether, had an Evening with which I have been better pleased. Young Cambridge, a little oddly, said to me 'You don't go to Mrs Ord's to-morrow?' 'Yes, I do.' 'I shall have, then, the pleasure of seeing You.' Now Mrs Ord has, since, told my Father that, at his own desire, she *invited* him professedly to meet me: that is, she had *promised* him to let him know when I came. I am glad, however, that the *interview* took place before I knew this, which made it less formidable and far more agreeable.

. . .

[27 December] Mrs Ord received us with her usual good breeding. Mr Pepys was the most eager to attack me, but finding himself followed by Mrs Chapone,[9] he soon retreated, for his rage for Tete à Tetes unfits him for all

---

8. Richard Owen Cambridge, his son George Owen Cambridge and John Hoole, scholar and friend of Johnson.

9. Hester Chapone, writer.

other conversation. Mrs Chapone was more civil than ever, and after a little general discourse, she asked me if I had yet heard that *Swift's Mrs Delany*[10] was among my unknown friends. 'I have a Letter,' she said, 'which I must beg to shew you from her, for I think it will be worth your running over. It is in answer to one I wrote, begging to know whether she had met with Cecilia. – She tells me that both she and the old Duchess of Portland are reading it for the 3d time, and that they desire nothing so much as an acquaintance with the amiable Writer.'

There, Miss Susanna! there daddy! – the *old Wits* have *begun* the charge! – this was very pleasant to me indeed, for if *they* have the curiosity as well as *I*, we shall all have some end to answer in meeting.

93. From Journal Letter to Susanna Phillips *January 1783*

[11 January] Mr Jerningham,[1] though he talked to me very much, never did it while the Pac[chierotti] was singing, or while any thing else was going forward that was worth attention. Two specimens of his conversation, which, in their different ways, were equally curious; I must give you. And my Daddy, who used to be much regaled by the account of his *Harping* at Bath, will be glad to hear more of him. One of them, indeed, does him so little honour, that if I had the smallest regard for him, I should sink it; but as that is not the case, I am content to give you the same ill impression of him which he himself gave to me. The *first* was merely a preposterous stretch of affectation. He has lately been at Paris, and was full of French communications. 'There is a Book,' he said, 'lately come out *here*, which I find all *les Gens comme il faut*[2] endeavouring to read at Paris: its particular friend there is Madame la princesse du Bouillon, who says that for want of *10* Volumes, which she wished to have been its length, she was forced to make 10 of *5*, by instantly re-reading it, when she had first finished it. She is praying earnestly for peace,[3] as that is all she waits for to make a Tour to England: and then, she says, her first Object will be to seek out *you*. – She hopes to put herself under your protection.'

---

10. Mary Delany and her late husband had been friends of Swift in Ireland.

1. Edward Jerningham, poet and playwright, whom FB had described playing the harp in a highly affected manner.

2. *The fashionable people*. Jerningham is referring of course to *Cecilia*.

3. England and France were still at war; a peace treaty would be signed the following year.

There! – *my protection*! – Ha! Ha! – troppo baddo![4] – and quite solemnly seriously did he say it.

The 2d will require no comment. –

'Have you read,' he said, 'the new Book that has had such a run in France, "Les Liaisons dangereuses"? – '[5]

'No,' answered I, not much pleased at the Name, 'I have *not* even heard of it.'

'Indeed? – it has made so much noise in France I am quite surprised at that. It is not, indeed, a work that recommends very strict morality, but *you*, we all know, may look into *any* work without being hurt by it.'

I felt hurt *then*, however, and very gravely answered, 'I cannot give *myself* that praise, as I never look into any Books that *could* hurt me.'

He Bowed, and smiled, and said *that was* '*very right*,' and added – 'This Book is written by an officer;[6] and he says there are no characters nor situations in it that he has not himself seen.'

'That, then,' cried I, 'will with me always be a reason to as little desire seeing the Officer, as his Book.'

He looked a little simple at this, but pretended to approve it very much. However, I fancy it will save him the trouble of enquiring into my readings any more. I was really provoked with him, however, and though he was most obsequiously civil to me, I only spoke to him in answer, after this little Dialogue.

. . .

[18 January] Pacchierotti called, very grave, but very sweet. Mr George Cambridge asked if he spoke English? 'O, very well,' cried I, 'Pray try him, – he is very amiable, and I fancy you will like him.'

Pacchierotti began with complaining of the variable Weather, 'I cannot,' he said, 'be well, such an inconsistent Day!'

We Laughed at the Word *inconsistent*, and Mr Cambridge said 'It is curious to see what new modes all languages may take in the Hands of foreigners. The Natives *dare* not try such experiments, and therefore we all talk pretty much alike: but a Foreigner is *obliged* to hazard new expressions, and very often he shews us a force of power in our Words, by an

---

4. Too bad. FB may be echoing an Italian acquaintance mixing Italian and English.

5. *Dangerous Affairs*, novel by Choderlos de Laclos about a black-hearted seducer of women, Valmont, and his accomplice in debauchery, Mme de Merteuil. Published in 1782 in France – and instantly notorious.

6. De Laclos was an artillery officer.

unusual adaptation of them, that we were not ourselves aware they would admit.'

And then, to draw Pacchierotti out; he began a dispute of the different merits of Italy and England, defending his own Country merely to make him abuse it, while Pacchierotti most eagerly took up the Gauntlet on the part of Italy. 'This is a Climate,' said Pacchierotti, 'never in the same case for half an Hour at a Time; it shall be fair, and wet, and dry, and humid, 40 Times in a morning, *in the least.* I am tired to be so played with, Sir, by your Climate.'

'We have one thing, however, Mr Pacchierotti,' he answered, 'which I hope you allow makes some amends, and that is our verdure; – in Italy you cannot boast *that.*'

'But it seem to me, Sir, to be of no utility so much ever-green! – is rather *too* much, for my humble opinion.'

'And then your *Insects*, Mr Pacchierotti; – these alone are a most dreadful draw back upon the comfort of your fine Climate.'

'I must own,' said Pacchierotti, 'is rather disagreeable for the Insects; but is not better, Sir, than an atmosphere so bad as they cannot live in it?'

'Why as I can't defend our atmosphere, I must shift my Ground, and talk to you of our societies –'

'O, indeed, good Sir, are not very invigorating! – Twenty people of your Gentlemen and Ladies, to sit about not to pronounce one Word! – is very dull! –'

We Laughed heartily at this retort courteous, and Mr G. C. was so much pleased with it, that he kept up a sportive conversation with him the whole Time he stayed, much to my satisfaction, as most of the people the poor Pac. meets with here, affect a *superiority* to conversing with him, though he has more intelligence, ay, and cultivation too, than half of them.

Pacchierotti took leave. I then made his *eloge* to Mr G. C., who said 'I was very glad to meet with him; I had heard he applied very much to our language; – there is a softness in his manner, and at the same Time a spirit in his opinions, untimely engaging as well as entertaining.'

You may believe I did not *down* him for this notion.

Sunday, Jan. 19. And now for Mrs Delany. How fertile in adventures for my Susy has this spring proved! A Journal could never be more worth keeping in such sort of life as ours.

I spent one Hour with Mrs Thrale, and then called for Mrs Chapone, and we proceeded together to St James's Place.

Mrs Delany was alone, in her Drawing Room, which is entirely hung round with Pictures of her own painting, and ornaments of her own designing. She came to the Door to receive us. She is still Tall, though some of her height may be lost; not much, however, for she is remarkably upright. She has no remains of beauty in *Feature*, but in *Countenance* I never but once saw *more*, – and that was in my sweet Grand mother Sleepe; benevolence, softness, piety, and gentleness are all *resident* in her Face; and the resemblance with which she struck me to my dear Grand mother in her first appearance, grew so much stronger from all that came from her *mind*, which seems to contain nothing but purity and native humility, that I almost longed to Embrace her, and I am sure if I had, the recollection of that saint-like woman would have been so strong, that I should never have refrained from crying over her.

Mrs Chapone presented me to her, and, taking my Hand, she said 'You must pardon me if I give you an old-fashioned reception, for I know nothing new. – ' And she saluted me.[7]

'Can you forgive, Miss Burney,' she continued, 'this great liberty I have taken with you of asking for your Company to Dinner? – I wished so impatiently to see one from whom I have received such very extraordinary pleasure, that, as I could not be alone this morning, I could not bear to put it off to another Day. And if You had been so good to come in the Evening, I might perhaps have had Company, – and I hear so ill, that I cannot, as I wish to do, attend to more than one at a Time, – for age makes me stupid even more than I am by Nature, – and how grieved and mortified I must have been to know I had Miss Burney in the Room, and not to hear her!' –

I don't write you my own Bows and Thanks, because you can so well suppose them:

She then mentioned her regret that we could not stay and spend the Evening with her, which had been told her in our Card of accepting her invitation, as we were both engaged: which for *my* part I heartily regretted.

'I am particularly sorry,' she added, 'on account of the Dutchess Dowager of Portland, who is so good as to come to me in an Evening, as she knows I am too infirm to wait upon her Grace myself; and she wished so much to see Miss Burney, – but she said she would come as early as possible, and you won't, I hope, want to go very soon?'

My Time, I answered, was Mrs Chapone's, and Mrs Chapone said she could not stay later than half past seven.

7. I.e. she kissed FB.

'Fie! fie!' cried Mrs Delany, smiling, 'why *Miss Larolles* would not for the World go before 8! – However, the Dutchess will be here by seven, I dare say, for she said nothing should detain her.'

Mrs Chapone then made me look at the Paintings, which I greatly admired: particularly a Copy of Saccharissa from Vandyke.[8] There was also a portrait of Madame de Sevigné,[9] which struck me very much –

Soon after we went to Dinner, which was plain, neat, well cooked, and elegantly served.

. . .

We went up stairs, and then Mrs Delany shewed me the *new art* which she has invented. It is staining paper of all possible Colours, and then cutting it out, so finely and delicately, that when it is pasted on Paper or Vellum, it has all the appearance of being *Pencilled*, except that, by being raised, it has still a richer and more natural appearance. The effect is extremely beautiful. She invented it at 75! – She told me she did 4 Flowers the first Year, – 16 the second, and the 3d 160. – And after that many more. They are all from Nature, and consist of the most curious flowers, plants and weeds that are to be found. She has been supplied with *Patterns* from all the great Gardens, and all the great Florists in the kingdom. Her Plan was to finish 1000, – but alas! her Eyes now fail her, though she has only 20 undone of her task! – [10]

At about 7 o'clock, the Dutchess Dowager of Portland came. She is not near so old as Mrs Delany, nor, to me, is her face by any means so pleasing; but yet there is sweetness, and dignity, and intelligence in it. Mrs Delany received her with the same respectful ceremony as if it was her first visit, though she regularly goes to her every Evening. But what she at first took as an *Honour* and condendsion, she has so much true humility of mind that no use can make her see in any other light. She immediately presented me to her. Her Grace Courtsied and smiled with the most flattering air of pleasure, and said she was particularly happy in meeting with me.

We then took our places, and Mrs Delany said 'Miss Burney, ma'am, is acquainted with Mr Crisp, whom your Grace knew so well; and she tells me he and his sister have been so good as to remember *me*, and to mention me to her.'

8. Portrait of Lady Dorothy Sidney by Sir Anthony Van Dyck; 'Saccharissa' was the poetical name given her by Edmund Waller.

9. Seventeenth-century French letter writer.

10. The manuscript volumes of Mary Delany's 'paper mosaics', as she called her new art form, are in the British Library.

The Dutchess instantly asked me a thousand questions about him: where he lived, how he had his Health, and whether his fondness for the polite arts still continued. She said he was one of the most ingenious and agreeable men she had ever known, and regretted his having sequestered himself so much from the society of his former friends.

In the course of this Conversation, I found her very charming. High bred, courteous, sensible, and spirited: not merely free from *pride*, but free from *affability*, its most mortifying *deputy*.

After this, she asked me if I had seen Mrs Siddons, and what I thought of her. I answered in guarded terms, that I admired her very much. And this is constantly my answer, and, while it goes no further, is very true. For the World would I not have any critique of mine run about the Town in her disfavour. She is certainly by far the *best* Actress we have, and as to her not fulfilling all *my* ideas, nobody, after Garrick, I suppose ever could.

'If Miss Burney approves her,' said the Dutchess, 'no approbation, I am sure, can do her so much credit, for no one can so perfectly judge of Characters or of Human Nature.'

'Ah, ma'am!' cried Mrs Delany, 'and does your Grace remember protesting you would *never* read Cecilia?'

'Yes,' said she, Laughing, 'I declared that *5 volumes* could never be attacked! – but since I began, I have read it 3 Times.'

'O terrible!' cried I, – 'to make them *fiveteen*! –'

'The reason,' continued she, 'I held out so long against reading them, was remembering the cry there was in favour of Clarissa[11] and Sir Charles Grandison, when *they* came out; and those I never could read! – I was teized into trying both of them, but I was disgusted with their tediousness, and could not read Eleven Letters, with all the effort I could make: so much about my sisters and my Brothers, and all my Uncles and my Aunts! –'

'But if your Grace had gone on,' said Mrs Chapone, 'the latter part must certainly have affected you.'

'O I hate any thing so dismal! Every body that *did* read had melancholy faces for a Week! *Cecilia* is as pathetic as I can bear, – and *more*, sometimes; – yet, in the midst of the sorrow, there is a spirit in the Writing, a fire in the Whole Composition, that keep off that heavy depression given by Richardson. Cry, to be sure, we did, – O Mrs Delany, shall you ever *forget* how we cried? – but then we had so *much* Laughter to make us amends! – we were never left to *sink* under our concern.'

11. Richardson's novel *Clarissa*.

'For my part,' said Mrs Chapone, 'when I *first* read it, I did not cry at all; I was in an agitation that half killed me, – that shook all my Nerves, and made me unable to sleep at Nights, from the suspence I was in; but I could not Cry for excess of eagerness; the *second* Time, however, when I knew the *sum total*, I cried at the distress ready to break my Heart!'

. . .

'Ah ma'am,' said Mrs Delany, 'how hard your Grace was upon Mrs Delvile! so elegant, so sensible, so judicious, so charming a Woman – '

'O I hate her!' cried the Dutchess, – 'resisting that sweet Cecilia! – *coaxing* her, too, all the Time, with such hypocritical flattery – '

'O no,' cried Mrs Chapone, 'indeed she is no hypocrite, she shews, in all things but that *name*, how really and unaffectedly fond she is of Cecilia.'[12]

'Ah!' said the Dutchess, 'that silly name! – '

'I shall never forget,' said Mrs Delany, 'your Grace's earnestness when we came to that part where Mrs Delvile bursts a blood vessel; down dropt the Book, and just with the same energy as if your Grace had heard some real and important news, you called out "I'm glad of it with all my Heart"!'

'*I* have heard many people,' said Mrs Chapone, 'of high family themselves, say that nothing could have been so *base* and so *dirty* as for the Delviles to give up their Name: and others say nothing could be so preposterous as Cecilia's giving up her Fortune to gratify them: – but, for my part, I always say that where the Husband of her Choice was in question, all that could have been *base* and *dirty* would have been keeping the fortune in *preference* to him.'

'What disputes, too,' said Mrs Chapone, 'there are about Briggs![13] – I was in a Room some time ago, where somebody said there could be no such Character, – and a poor little mean City man, who was there, started up, and said "But there is, though, for *I'se* one myself!"'

'He diverts me extremely,' said Mrs Delany.

'What most amazes me,' said the Dutchess, 'is to hear people pretend to criticise the Character of old Delvile![14] Why I personally know *three* myself! and one is so *very* like, talks so exactly in the same manner of his occupations,

---

12. Cecilia is heiress to a large fortune provided that whoever she marries forfeits his family name and takes hers instead. Mrs Delvile opposes her son's marriage to Cecilia because of this condition.

13. Cecilia's miserly guardian.

14. Mr Delvile, Cecilia's guardian (with Briggs and Harrel), represents excessive family pride, as Briggs represents miserliness and Harrel extravagant living.

his family, his Estates, and his importance, that I always have him present to me when I read old Delvile's speeches. – How admirably is *young* Delvile supported! he has just what he *ought* to have of the pride and prejudice of his Family, just what Education and Example must necessarily give him; and *no more*. A Character more consistent, yet more uncommon, was never drawn.'

'The Harrels, – O then the Harrels!' cried Mrs Delany.

'If you speak of the *Harrels*, and of the *morality* of the Book,' cried the Dutchess, with a solemn sort of voice, 'we shall indeed never give Miss Burney her due! So striking, so pure, so genuine, so instinctive! –'

'Yes,' cried Mrs Chapone, 'let us complain how we will of the torture she has given our nerves, we must all join in saying she has *bettered* us by every line.'

'*No* Book,' said Mrs Delany, 'ever *was* so *useful* as this, because none other that is so *good*, was ever so much *read*.'

'It should be read,' cried the Dutchess, 'with energy, forever! it should be the *study of Youth*! both for precept and example I know nothing to compare with it. It seems to me, indeed, in *all* respects, one of the first Books in the World! And it ought to be put in every *Nursery*, it is so innocent and so pure, and if *I* had the care of any young people, it should be the first Book I would put in their Hands.'

The Dutchess had the good sense and judgment to feel she had drawn up her panegyric to a climax, and therefore here she stopt. So, however, did not *we*, for our Coach was ready, and when I set Mrs Chapone down I went to Mrs Ord. She had sent to me in the morning, that she was not well, and begged to speak with me.

94. From Journal Letter to Susanna Phillips *19 June 1783*

[St Martin's Street]

We heard today that Dr Johnson had been taken ill in a way that gave a dreadful shock to himself, and a most anxious alarm to his Friends. Mr Seward brought the news here, and my Father and I instantly went to his House. He had earnestly desired me, when we lived so much together at Streatham, *to see him frequently if he should be ill*. He saw my Father, but he had medical people with him, and could not admit me up stairs, but sent me down a most kind message, that he thanked me for calling, and when he *was* better, should hope to see me *often*. I had the satisfaction to hear from

Mrs Williams that the Physician had pronounced him to be in no danger, and expected a speedy recovery. The stroke was confined to his *Tongue*. Mrs Williams told me a most striking and touching circumstance that attended the attack; it was at about 4 o'clock in the morning; he found himself seized with a *paralytic affection*; – he rose, and composed in his own mind a Latin Prayer to the Almighty, 'that whatever were the sufferings for which he must prepare himself, it would please him, through the grace and mediation of Our Blessed Saviour, to spare his Intellects, and let them all fall upon his body!' When he had composed this, – internally, – he endeavoured to speak it, – aloud, – but found his voice was gone! – alas! how afflicting!

It soon, however, in some degree, returned, though with very imperfect articulation. Yet how delightful, how edifying, Dearest Susy, this awful testimony of the true and unfeigned *orthodoxy* of the very first man in the World! –

95. Letter to Hester Lynch Thrale *late June 1784*

What can I say to You, Dearest Madam, but that I do indeed Love, and indeed Pray for you? I tremble at the Final answer you are to give,[1] – ah, *think* a little before you utter it! – You will say you have been thinking all this Time, – no, dear Madam, you have *never* thought, – you have distressed and harassed yourself not about *changing* your plan, but merely in a wild anxiety to obtain approbation for it. That approbation will *forever* be withheld! The Mother of 5 Children, 3 of them as Tall as herself, will never be forgiven for shewing so great an ascendance of passion over Reason. *Somebody*, you say, shall be made happy, – ah, that *somebody* will not be you! – the still small voice within will tell you, when all your contrasts are settled, and you are no longer struggling to obtain your immediate way, that you have wilfully deprived yourself of all hope of happiness but one, – that one so uncertain! so *inadequate* to such a sacrifice. 'Tis probably for the last Time that I now speak out, since when your Final Answer is given – I must be silent. I would to Heaven you would *now* consider what I have said, or that hereafter it might never occur to you! This, I fear, will be reversed, – you will consider it *now* only to disapprove, – and hereafter to regret! –

1. Hester Thrale was on the verge of accepting the marriage proposal of her children's former music master, Gabriel Piozzi. An Italian singer and composer with whom she had fallen in love, he was regarded by FB, Johnson and most of London society as totally unsuitable for the well-born and wealthy widow.

How, you will say, can you sacrifice a Man to whom you have given such hopes? – but *how*, dear Madam, can you sacrifice to that Man *all else?* your hopes about Miss Thrale are romantic – talk with her, and you will find they are.[2] Nothing should tear from me such words as these, but the greatness of your present danger, and my own firm conviction of your future repentance. But all is at stake, and for what? – a gratification that no one can *esteem*, not even he for whom you feel it, however gratefully or honourably he may conduct himself.

O reflect a little before this fatal final answer with which you terrify me is given! –

Children – Religion, Friends, Country, Character, – – What on Earth can compensate the loss of all these?

You will think this cruel, – it is nothing less, my opinion has been uniform, and I have *said* all this repeatedly, at various Times, – but now, at last, I write it, that its last chance of being heeded may be tried. Heaven bless and direct you, ever dearest Madam, – my very Heart bleeds for your sufferings, when I think you *hesitate*; – when I see you *fixed*, my blame combats my sorrow! – We were not Born for ourselves, and I have regularly practiced, as far as occasion offered, the forbearance I recommend.

Once more Heaven bless, strengthen and direct you, most dear Madam! – at this most critical period of your life!

I may trust, I hope, that you will not shew this Letter, – not written in enmity to Piozzi of whom I think ever *highly*, but who to me is nothing, while you are almost every thing.[3]

96. From Journal Letter to Susanna Phillips *28 November 1784*

Last Thursday, November 25th my Father set me down at Bolt Court, while he went on upon business. I was anxious to again see poor Dr Johnson, who

---

2. Queeney Thrale would never forgive her mother for the marriage.

3. FB later annotated this letter:

What effect it produced on the reading F.B. never knew – Mrs Thrale brought it back herself to the Writer almost instantly, – & putting it into her hand, agitatedly, said 'you charge me not to shew it – &, that I may not be tempted, I return it you. – ' She then ran out of the Room, & the House –

Hester Thrale and Piozzi were married by a Roman Catholic chaplain on 23 July, and two days later repeated their vows before an Anglican priest. FB's disapproval of the match spelled the end of her friendship with Hester Thrale, who never fully forgave her, though they would meet briefly in 1790 and again many years later after Piozzi's death. Despite dire predictions, the marriage was a happy one.

has had terrible Health since his return from Litchfield. He let me in, though very ill. He was alone, which I much rejoiced at, for I had a longer and more satisfactory conversation with him than I have had for many months. He was in rather better spirits, too, than I have lately seen him: but he told me he was going to try what sleeping out of Town might do for him. 'I remember,' said he, 'that my Wife, when she was near her end, poor woman, was also advised to sleep out of Town:[1] and when she was carried to the Lodgings that had been prepared for her, she complained that the stair-case was in very bad condition, for the plaister was beaten off the Walls in many places. "O," said the man of the House, "that's nothing but by the knocks against it of the Coffins of the poor souls that have died in the Lodgings!"' He laughed, though not without apparent secret anguish in telling me this. I felt extremely shocked, but, willing to confine my words at least to the literal story. I only exclaimed against the unfeeling absurdity of such a confession. 'Such a confession,' cried he, 'to a person then coming to try his Lodging for her Health contains *more* absurdity than we can well lay our accounts for.' I had seen Miss Thrale the Day before. 'So,' said he, 'did I.' I then said 'Do You ever, sir, hear from her mother?' 'No,' cried he, 'nor write to her! I drive her quite from my mind. She has disgraced herself, disgraced her friends and connections, disgraced her sex, and disgraced all the expectations of mankind! If I meet with one of her Letters I burn it instantly. I have burnt all I can find. I never speak of her, and I desire never to hear of her more. I drive her, as I said, wholly from my mind.' Yet this poor infatuated woman assured me she was upon good terms with him! and When I asked, I expected to hear they were in some sort of correspondence.

Wholly to change this discourse, I gave him a history of the *Bristol milk woman*[2] and told him the tales I had heard of her writing so wonderfully, though she had read nothing but Young and Milton:[3] 'though those,' I continued, 'could never possibly, I should think, be the *first* authors with any body. Would Children understand them? and *grown* people who have not read, are Children in literature.'

'Doubtless;' said he, 'but there is nothing so little comprehended among mankind as what is *Genius*. They give it to it all, when it *can* be but a *part*.

1. Elizabeth ('Tetty') Johnson had died in 1752.
2. Ann Yearsley, working-class woman championed by Hannah More, who edited her verses and got them published in 1784. With only a rudimentary education, she was thought to be a 'natural' poet.
3. Edward Young and John Milton.

Genius is nothing more than knowing the *use of Tools*, but there must *be* tools for it to use. A man who has spent all his life in this Room, will give a poor account of what is in the next.'

'Certainly, sir, yet there *is* such a thing as *Invention*? Shakespeare could never have seen a Caliban?'[4]

'No; but he had seen a *man* and knew, therefore, how to vary him to a monster. A man who would draw a monstrous *Cow*, must first know what a Cow commonly is, or how can he tell that to give her an Ape's Head, or Elephant's Tusk, will make her monstrous? Suppose you shew me a man who is a very expert Carpenter; another will say He was Born to be a Carpenter; – but what if he had never seen any Wood? Let two men, one with Genius, the other with none, look at an overturned waggon; He who has no genius will think of the Waggon only as he sees it, over-turned, and walk on; He who has genius will paint it to himself before it was over turned, standing still, and moving on, and heavy loaded, and empty: but both must see the Waggon, to think of it at all.'

How just and true all this, my dear Susy? He then animated, and talked on, upon this milk Woman, upon a once as famous shoe-maker, and upon our immortal Shakespeare, with as much fire, spirit, wit, and truth of criticism and Judgment, as ever yet I have heard him: how delightfully bright are his faculties, though the poor and infirm machine that contains them seems alarmingly giving way! Yet all brilliant as he was, I saw him growing worse; and offered to go, which, for the first time I ever remember, he did not oppose: but, most kindly pressing *both* my Hands, 'Be not,' he said, in a voice of even tenderness, 'be not longer in coming again for my letting you go now! – ' I assured him I would be the sooner, and was running off, but he called to me back, in a solemn voice, and, in a manner the most energetic said 'Remember me in your prayers! – ' I longed to ask *him* to remember *me*! but did not dare. I gave him my promise, and, very heavily indeed, I left him. Great, good, and excellent that he is, how short a time will he be our boast! – Ah, my dear Susy, I see he is going! – this Winter will never conduct Him to a more genial season Here, – *elsewhere*, Who shall hope fairer? – I wish I *had* bid him pray for *me*? – but it seemed to me presumptuous, – though this repetition of so kind a condescendsion might, I think, have encouraged me.

---

4. Monstrous character in Shakespeare's *Tempest*.

97. From Journal Letter to Susanna Phillips *December 1784*

Wednesday [8 December]. I went in the Evening to poor Dr Johnson, – Frank[1] told me he was very ill, but let me in. He would have taken me up stairs; but I would not see him without his direct permission. I desired Frank to tell him I called to pay my Respects to him, but not to disturb him, if he was not well enough to see me. Mr Straghan, a Clergyman, he said was with him alone. In a few minutes, this Mr Straghan, came to me himself. He told me Dr Johnson was very ill, very much obliged to me for coming; but so weak and bad, he hoped I would excuse his not seeing me. I was much disappointed, – Dear – Dear and much reverenced Dr Johnson! *how* ill or *how* low must he be to decline seeing a Creature he has so constantly, and fondly called about him? – If I do *not* see him again, I shall be truly afflicted. – And I fear, – I almost know I cannot! –

Next Day we heard still worse accounts! – –

Friday Dec. 10th. – At Night, my Father brought us the most dismal tidings of Dear Dr Johnson. Dr Warren had seen him, and told him to take what opium he pleased! – he had thanked and taken leave of all his Physicians, – alas! – I shall lose – and he will take no leave of me! – My Father was deeply depressed, – he has himself tried in vain for admission this Week. – Yet some people see him; – but then they must be in the *House* watching for one moment whole Hours. I hear from every one he is now perfectly resigned to his approaching fate, and no longer in terror of Death. I am thankfully happy in hearing that. He speaks himself now of the change his mind has undergone from its dark hour, and says 'he feels the irradiation of Hope! – ' Good and pious and excellent Christian, who shall feel it if not he? –

Dec. 11th We had a party to Dinner, by long appointment, for which indeed none of us were well disposed, the apprehension of hearing News only of Death being hard upon us all. – The Day could not be well, – but mark the Night. – My Father in the morning saw this First of men! – and had not his account till Bed time; – he feared over-setting me. He would not, he said, but have seen him for Worlds! He happened to be better, and admitted him. He was up, and very composed. He took his Hand very *kindly*, asked after all his family, and then, in particular, *How Fanny did*? 'I hope,' he said, '*Fanny* did not take it amiss that I did not see her? I was very bad!' Amiss! – What a Word! – O that I had been present to have answered

1. Frank Barber, Johnson's servant.

it! – My Father stayed, I suppose, half an Hour, and then was coming away. He again took his hand, and encouraged him to come again to him. – And when he was taking leave, said 'Tell Fanny to pray for me! – ' Ah! Dear Dr Johnson! – might I but have *Your* prayers! – After which, still grasping his Hand, he made a prayer for himself, the most fervent, pious, humble, eloquent, and touching, my Father says, that ever was composed. – O would I had heard it! – He ended it with Amen! in which my Father joined, and was ecchoed by all present. And again, when my Father was leaving him, he brightened up, something of his arch look returned, and he said 'I think I shall throw the Ball at Fanny yet! – '

Little more passed ere my Father came away.

This most earnestly increased my desire to see him: this kind of frequent mention of me melted me into double sorrow and regret. – I would give the World I had but gone to him that Day! It was, however, impossible, and the Day was over before I knew he had said what I look upon as a Call to me. This morning [12 December], after Church time, I went, – Frank said he was very ill, and saw nobody; I told him I had understood by my Father the Day before that he *meant* to see me. He then let me in. I went into his Room up stairs, – he was in his Bed Room. I saw it crowded, and ran hastily down, – Frank told me his master had refused seeing even Mr Langhton,[2] I told him merely to say I had called, but by no means to press my admission. His own feelings were all that should be consulted, his tenderness I knew would be equal whether he was able to see me or not. I went into the Parlour, preferring being alone in the cold to any Company with a Fire. Here I waited long, – here and upon the stairs, which I ascended and descended to meet again with Frank, and make enquiries: but I met him not. At last, upon Dr Johnson's ringing his Bell, I saw Frank enter his Room, and Mr Langhton follow. 'Who's that? – ' I heard him say, – they answered Mr Langhton; and I found he did not return.

Soon after, all the rest went away but a Mrs Davis, a good sort of woman, whom this truly charitable soul had sent for to take a dinner at his House. I then went and waited, with her, by the Fire: it was, however, between 3 and 4 o'clock before I got any answer, Mr Langhton then came himself. He could not look at me, – and I turned away from him. – Mrs Davis asked how the Dr was – 'Going on to Death very fast! – ' was his mournful answer. 'Has he taken,' said she, 'anything?' 'Nothing at all! – we carried him some Bread and milk, – he refused it, and said *The less the better.* – ' She asked more

2. Bennet Langton, Johnson's close friend.

questions, by which I found his faculties perfect, his mind composed, and his dissolution quick drawing on. –

I could not immediately go on, and it is now long since I have written at all, – but I will go back to this afflicting theme, which I can now better bear.

Mr Langhton was, I believe, a quarter of a Hour in the room before I suspected he meant to speak to me, – never looking near me, – at last he said 'This poor man, I understand, ma'am, desired yesterday to see you?'

'*My* understanding that, sir, brought me to Day. –'

'Poor man! it is pity he did not know himself better, – and that you should have had this trouble. –'

'Trouble!' cried I, – 'I would come 100 times, to see him the hundredth and first!'

'He hopes, now, you will excuse him – he is very sorry not to see you, – but he desired me to come and speak to you myself, and tell *You* he hopes you will excuse him, for he feels himself too weak for such an interview. –'

I hastily got up, left him my most affectionate Respects, and every good wish I could half utter, and ran back to the Coach. – Ah my Susy, – I have never been to Bolt Court since! –[3]

98. From Journal Letter to Susanna Phillips *January 1785*[1]

If – as his third visit *forced* me to re-believe, he is attached to me, – O God. – How sincerely, how *inwardly* do I forgive him! – if *not*, Who, my Susy, – upon *Earth* – at least except on a Death-Bed, – could, or can pardon such wanton – such accumulating – such endless deceit and treachery? – I can use no other words; his conduct has long past all mere impeachment of *trifling*, – it has seemed irrepressibly attached to me, – it has been deemed Honourably serious by all our mutual Acquaintances.

You see, my sweetest Susan, – repository of all my most secret feelings! – You see that however unhappy I have been made, – I have not been blinded. Let this give You, with myself, to hope that another change of opinion, – its first shock being over, will make me drive him from my thoughts: – only *let* it be a *change* not merely a *wavering*. –

3. Johnson died the next day, 13 December.

1. This and the following excerpt show FB's distress over the '*wavering*' behaviour of George Owen Cambridge. He had shown her attentions which led her family and acquaintances to assume him to be a serious suitor, but he may have ultimately been put off by his own family and by FB's pride and sensitivity.

99. From Journal Letter to Susanna Phillips *March 1785*

I am now lightened effectually with respect to all future solicitude as to any meetings with Mr George Cambridge. We are now upon decided terms, of courteous civility and uneventful good will. His behaviour through-out this visit was of the most singular and delicate propriety. His attentions to me were such as he had never shewn me before *under that roof*,[1] but they were of a sort he might always have shewn with safety under any. In losing their variability and inconsistency, they have lost also their danger and perplexity; they were respectful without flattery, and pleasant from their uniformity. I will not deny he has appeared to me more interesting, but I have never seen him more amiable, more desirous to oblige, more affectionate to his family, or more gentle in his manners.

How happily ends here, then, this long and cruel perplexity! We are again friends, – not such as we were, perhaps, but such as we may always remain. What his engagements may be I am still in the dark, but since we have met thus amicably and properly, my curiosity has lost its impatience.[2]

100. From Letter to Dr Burney *24 September 1785*

The Queen has told Mrs Delany, upon her expressing her thanks to her Majesty for her new house, and saying how very comfortable a dwelling she found it, that she wished it was larger, that she might be able to accomodate her friend Burney – in it. – [1]

Seriously, my dearest Padre, how sweet and gracious this was! – Nor here has the matter rested; by another Letter from Windsor, which I received 2 Days ago, I find Mrs Delany has explained to the Queen that her House is large enough for that not quite gigantic person, and, Miss Port[2] now tells

---

1. I.e. in the home of Richard Owen Cambridge, George's father.
2. FB suspected him of being engaged to another. He did not marry until 1795, two years after FB's marriage. Despite the seeming stoicism of this letter, her feelings for him seem not to have completely abated until her own wedding. (In later years as Archdeacon of Middlesex he would be a particularly good friend to FB and her son during her widowhood.)

1. The Duchess of Portland had died suddenly in July. Through her Mary Delany had met and become a great favourite of the King and Queen, and now they gave her a small house in Windsor to live in and a pension of £200 a year.
2. Georgiana Port, later Mrs Waddington, Mary Delany's great-niece.

me that – her Aunt desires her to acquaint me that her Majesty has been enquiring when I shall come. –!!

This most sweet attention that dear Mrs Delany should have every thing of every sort that can possibly contribute to her ease or comfort, raises this charming Queen higher and higher in my most loyal veneration. Mrs Delany, when we parted, had told me she must consider herself so much the absolute Guest of their Majesties, while residing in their House, and under their immediate protection, that she should never venture to having any *sleeping* Guests of her own, but with their permission: – a delicacy they have well shewn themselves to deserve by so quickly finding out who Mrs Delany was likely to desire.

101. From Journal Letter to Dr Burney and
Susanna Phillips *December 1785*

[Windsor]

Dec. *16th Friday.* Yesterday morning we had a much better account of the Princess Elizabeth;[1] and Mrs Delany said to me '*Now* you will escape no longer, for if their [the King and Queen's] uneasiness ceases, I am sure they will send for you, when they come next.' To be *sent* for, I confessed to her, would really be more formidable than to be surprised; but to *pretend* to be surprised would answer no purpose in making the meeting easy to me, and therefore I preferred letting the matter take its chance.

After Dinner, while Mrs Delany was left alone, as usual, to take a little rest, – for *sleep* it but seldom proves, Mr Bernard Dewes, his little daughter,[2] Miss Port and myself went into the Drawing Room. And here, while, to pass the time, I was amusing the little Girl with teaching her some Christmas Games, in which her Father and Cousin joined, Mrs Delany came in; – we were all in the middle of the Room, and in some confusion; but she had but just come up to us, to enquire what was going forwards, and I was disentangling myself from Miss Dewes, to be ready to fly off if any one knocked at the street Door, – when the Door of the Drawing Room was again

---

1. Third daughter of the King and Queen, now fifteen years old. She may have been suffering an attack of acute intermittent porphyria, a hereditary disorder that also afflicted her father, resulting in the manic behaviour misdiagnosed as 'madness' in 1788–9. (She lived until 1840.)

2. Bernard Dewes, Mary Delany's nephew, and his daughter Anne, seven years old.

opened, and a large man, in deep mourning,[3] appeared at it, – entering, and shutting it, himself, without speaking.

A Ghost could not more have scared me when I discerned, by its glitter on the black, a star![4] – The general disorder had prevented his being seen, except by myself, who was always on the watch; – till Miss Port, turning round, exclaimed 'The King! – Aunt, – the King! –'

O mercy! thought I, that I were but out of the Room! which way shall I escape? and how pass him unnoticed? – There is but the single Door at which he entered in the Room! – Every one scampered out of the way, – Miss Port to stand next the Door, Mr Bernard Dewes to a corner opposite it, – his little Girl clung to me, and Mrs Delany advanced to meet his Majesty, – who, after quietly looking on till she saw him; approached, and enquired how she did.

He then spoke to Mr Bernard, whom he had already met two or three times here. –

I had now retreated to the Wall, and purposed gliding softly, though speedily, out of the Room, – but before I had taken a single step, the King, in a loud whisper to Mrs Delany, said 'Is that Miss Burney? –' and on her answering, 'Yes, sir,' He Bowed, and with a Countenance of the most perfect good humour, came close up to me.

A most profound reverence on my part arrested the progress of my intended retreat, 'How long have you been come back, Miss Burney? –'

'Two Days, sir. –' Unluckily, he did not hear me, – and repeated his question, and whether the second time he heard me or not, I don't know, but he made a little civil inclination of his Head, and went back to Mrs Delany.

He insisted she should sit down, though he stood himself, and began to give her an account of the Princess Elizabeth, who, once again, was recovering, and trying, at present, James's Powders. She had been blooded, he said, 12 times in this last fortnight, and had lost 75 ounces of blood, besides undergoing blistering, and other discipline. He spoke of her illness with the strongest emotion, and seemed quite filled with concern for her danger and sufferings.

Mrs Delany next enquired for the younger Children. They had all, he said, the whooping Cough, and were soon to be removed to Kew. 'Not,'

3. George III was in mourning for his brother-in-law, Prince George of Mecklenburg-Strelitz, youngest brother of the Queen; he had died in November.
4. The Order of the Garter.

added he, 'for any other reason than change of air for themselves; though I am pretty certain I have never had the distemper myself, and the Queen thinks she has not had it either: – we shall take that chance. When the two eldest had it, I sent them away, and would not see them till it was over; – but now, there are so many of them, that there would be no end to separations; so I let it take its course.'

Mrs Delany expressed a good deal of concern at his running this risk, but he laughed at it, and said he was much more afraid of *catching the rheumatism*, which has been threatening one of his shoulders lately. However, he added, he should hunt the next morning, in defiance of it.

A good deal of talk then followed about his own Health, and the extreme temperance by which he preserved it. The fault of his Constitution, he said, was a tendency to excessive fat, which he kept, however, in order, by the most vigourous exercise, and the strictest attention to a simple Diet.

When Mrs Delany was beginning to praise his forbearance, he stopped her, – 'No, no' he cried, ' 'tis no virtue; I only prefer eating plain and little, to growing diseased and infirm.'

During this discourse, I stood quietly in the place where he had first spoken to me.

His quitting me so soon, and conversing so freely and easily with Mrs Delany, proved so delightful a relief to me, that I no longer wished myself away; and the moment my first panic, from the surprise, was over, I diverted myself with a thousand ridiculous notions of my own situation.

It seemed to me we were *acting a Play*; there is something so little like common and real life, in every body's standing, while talking, in a Room full of Chairs, and standing, too, so aloof from each other, that I almost thought myself upon a stage, assisting in the representation of a Tragedy, in which the King played his own part, of The King; Mrs Delany that of a venerable confident, Mr Bernard, his respectful attendant; Miss Port, a suppliant virgin, waiting encouragement to bring forward some petition; Miss Dewes, a young Orphan, intended to move the Royal compassion; and myself, – a very solemn, sober, and decent *Mute*.

These fancies, however, only regaled me while I continued a quiet spectator, and without expectation of being called into play. But the King, I have reason to think, meant only to give me time to recover from my first embarrassment, – and I feel myself infinitely obliged to his good breeding and consideration; – which perfectly answered, for before he returned to me, I was entirely recruited.

When the discourse upon Health and strength was over, the King went up to the Table, and looked at a Book of Prints, from Claude Lorraine, which had been brought down for Miss Dewes: but Mrs Delany, by mistake, told him they were for me. – He turned over a leaf or two, and then said 'Pray – does Miss Burney *draw*, too? – ' The *too*, was pronounced very civilly.

'I believe not, sir,' answered Mrs Delany; 'at least, she does not *tell*.'

'O!' cried he, laughing, 'that's nothing! She is not apt to *tell*; she never *does tell*, you know! – Her Father *told* me that himself. He told me the whole history of her Evelina. – And I shall never forget his face when he spoke of his feelings at first taking up the Book! – he looked quite *frightened*, – just as if he was doing it that moment! – – I never can forget his face while I live! – '

Then, coming up close to me, he said 'But what? – what? – how was it? – '

'Sir?' cried I, – not well understanding him, –

'How come you – how happened it – what? – what? – '

'I – I only wrote, sir, for my own amusement: – only in some odd, idle Hours, – '

'But your publishing – your printing, – how was that?'

'That was only, sir – only because – '

I hesitated most abominably, not knowing how to tell him a long story, and growing terribly confused at these questions, – besides, – to say the truth, his own *What? What?* so reminded me of those vile probationary odes,[5] that, in the midst of all my flutter, I was really hardly able to keep my Countenance.

The *What?* was then repeated, with so earnest a look that, forced to say some thing, I stammeringly answered –

'I thought – sir – it would look very well in Print! – '

I do really flatter myself this is the silliest speech I *ever* made! I am quite provoked with myself for it, but a fear of laughing made me eager to utter any thing; and by no means conscious, till I had spoken, of what I was saying –

He laughed very heartily himself, – well he might! – and walked away to enjoy it, crying out 'Very fair indeed! that's being very fair and honest! – '

Then, returning to me again, he said 'But your Father – ? how came you not to shew him what you wrote? – '

'I was too much ashamed of it, sir, *seriously*.'

---

5. *Probationary Odes by the Various Candidates for the Office of Poet Laureat to His Majesty*, satirical verses prompted by the death of the poet laureate, William Whitehead, in April 1785. FB was thinking in particular of lines attributed to John Scott, Member of Parliament: 'What? – what? – what? / Scott! Scott! Scott!'

Literal truth that, I am sure! –

'And how did he find it out?'

'I don't know myself, sir. He never would tell me.'

Literal truth again, my dear Father, as you can testify –

'But how did you get it printed? – '

'I sent it, sir, to a Bookseller my Father never employed, and that I never had seen myself, Mr Lowndes, in full hope by that means he never would hear of it.'

'But how could you manage that?'

'By means of a Brother [Charles], sir.'

'O, – you confided in a Brother, *then*?'

'Yes, sir, – that is for the publication.'

'What entertainment you must have had from hearing people's conjectures, before you were known! – Do you remember any of them – ?'

'Yes, Sir, many – '

'And what? – '

'I heard that Mr Baretti laid a wager it was written by a *man*, – for no *woman*, he said, could have kept her own counsil.'

This diverted him extremely.

'But how was it,' he continued, 'You thought most likely for your Father to discover you?'

'Sometimes, sir, I have supposed I must have dropt some of the manuscript; sometimes, that one of my sisters betrayed me.'

'O, – your sister? – what, not your Brother? – '

'No, sir; – he could not, for – '

I was going on, but he laughed so much I could not be heard, exclaiming 'Vastly well! – I see you are of Mr Baretti's mind! – You think your Brother could keep your secret, and not your sister! – '

'Well, but,' cried he presently, 'how was it first known to You you were betrayed?'

'By a Letter, sir, from a sister; I was very ill, and in the Country; and she wrote me word that my Father had taken up a Review, in which the Book was mentioned, and had put his finger upon its name, and said – contrive to get that Book for me. – '

'And when he got it,' cried the King, 'he told me he was afraid of looking at it! – and never can I forget his face when he mentioned his first opening it! – But, pray, – You have not kept your Pen unemployed all this time?'

'Indeed I have, Sir.'

'But why? – '

'I – I believe I have exhausted myself, sir! – '

He Laughed aloud at this, and went and told it to Mrs Delany, civilly treating a plain fact as a mere bon mot.

Then, returning to me again, he said, more seriously, 'But you have not determined against writing any more?'

'N – o, sir. – '

'You have made no vow? – no real resolution of that sort?'

'No, sir.'

'You only wait for inclination?'

'No, Sir – '

A very civil little Bow spoke him pleased with this answer, and he went again to the middle of the Room, where he chiefly stood, and, addressing us in general, talked upon the different motives of writing, concluding with 'I believe there is no constraint to be put upon real Genius; nothing but inclination can set it to work: – Miss Burney however, knows best; – ' and then, hastily returning to me, he cried '*What? what? –* '

'No, sir, – I – I believe not, – certainly – ' quoth I, very awkwardly, for I seemed taking a violent Compliment only as my due; but I knew not how to put him off as I would another Person.

I was, also, kept in a very great fright by the little Miss Dewes, who, having heard the probationary odes quoted, was dying to Laugh at the What? what? and constantly looked up in my face every time it was said in hopes of some excuse for tittering, as well as to watch how I took it.

In the King, it is a mere habit, got from a disposition to stammer, which it seems something to relieve. What pity that no one dare tell him of it! The Queen, who alone could take such a liberty, is probably too much accustomed to it to be more sensible when he says it than he is himself.

When he does not, however, say it quite involuntarily, it seems meant as an injunction to his Hearer to proceed, and explain more at large what is discussing. To me he never used it but evidently in that manner, and as if merely to shorten the expression *what have you to say to that?*

He then made some enquiries concerning the Pictures with which the Room is hung, and which were all Mrs Delany's own painting; and a little discourse followed upon some of the masters whose pictures she has copied.

This was all with her; for nobody ever answers him without being immediately addressed by him.

He then came to me again; – and said 'Is your Father about any thing at present?'

'Yes, sir; he goes on, when he has time, with his History.'

'Does he write quick?'

'Yes, sir, when he writes from himself; but in his History, he has so many Books to consult, that sometimes he spends 3 Days in finding authorities for a single passage.'

'Very true; that must be unavoidable.'

He pursued these enquiries some time, and then went again to his general station, before the fire, and Mrs Delany enquired if he meant to hunt the next Day. Yes, he answered; and, a little pointedly, Mrs Delany said – 'I would the Hunt*ed* could but feel as much pleasure as the Hunt*er!*'

The King understood her, and, with some quickness, called out 'Pray what did *you* hunt? – '

Then, looking round at us all 'Did you know,' he said, 'that Mrs Delany once hunted herself? – And in a long Gown, and a great Hoop? – '

It seems she had told his majesty an adventure of that sort which had befallen her, in her Youth, from some accident in which her will had no share.

While this was talking over, a violent Thunder was made at the Door; – I was almost certain it was the Queen. Once more, I would have given anything to escape; – but in vain, – I had been informed that nobody ever quitted the royal presence, after having been conversed with, till motioned to withdraw.

Miss Port, according to established etiquette on these occasions, opened the Door which she stood next, by putting her Hand behind her, and slid out, backwards, into the Hall, to light the Queen in. The Door soon opened again, – and her Majesty entered.

Immediately seeing the King, she made him a low Courtsie, and cried 'O! your majesty is here! – '

'Yes,' he cried, 'I ran here, without speaking to any body.'

The Queen had been at the lower Lodge, to see the Princess Elizabeth: as the King had before told us.

She then hastened up to Mrs Delany, with both her Hands held out, saying 'My dear Mrs Delany, how are you? – '

Instantly after, I *felt* her Eye on my Face: I *believe*, too, she courtsied to me; but though I saw the bend, I was too near sighted to be sure it was intended for me. I was hardly ever in a situation more embarassing; I dared not return what I was not certain I had received; yet considered myself as appearing quite a *monster*, to stand stiff necked, if really meant.

Almost at the same moment, she spoke to Mr Bernard, and then nodded to my little clinging Girl.

I was now really ready to sink, with horrid uncertainty of what I was doing, or what I should do; – when his Majesty, who I fancy saw my distress, most good-humouredly said to the Queen something – but I was too much flurried to remember what, except these words – '*I have been telling Miss Burney* –'

Relieved from so painful a dilemma, I immediately dropped a Courtsie; – she made one to me in the same moment, and with a very smiling countenance, came up to me. But she could not speak, for the King went on talking eagerly, and very gayly, repeating to her every word I had said during our conversation, upon Evelina, its publication, etc. etc.

When he told her of Baretti's wager, saying 'But she heard of a great many conjectures about the author, before it was known; – and of Baretti an admirable thing! – he laid a bet it must be a *man*, as no woman, he said could have kept her own counsel!' The Queen, laughing a little, exclaimed 'O! that is quite too bad an affront to us! – Don't you think so?' – addressing herself to me, with great gentleness of voice and manner.

I assented; and the King continued his relation, which she listened to with a look of some interest; but when he told her some particulars of my secresy, she again spoke to me; – 'But your sister was your confident, was she not?'

'Yes, ma'am.'

My sister*s* I might have said; but I was always glad to have done.

'O yes!' cried the King, laughing, 'but I assure You she is of Baretti's opinion herself; for I asked her if she thought it was her sister or her Brother that betrayed her to her Father, and she says her *sister*, she thinks.'

Poor Esther! – but I shall make her amends by what follows; for the Queen, again addressing me, said 'But to betray to a *Father* is no *crime*; don't you think so? –'

I agreed; – and plainly saw she thought Esther – if Esther it was, had only done *right*.

The King then went on, and when he had done his narration, the Queen took her seat.

She made Mrs Delany sit next her, and Miss Port brought her some Tea.

The King, mean while, came to me again, and said 'Are you musical?'

'Not a performer, sir.'

Then, going from me to the Queen, he said – 'She does not play!'

I did not hear what the Queen answered: she spoke in a low voice, and seemed much out of spirits.

They now talked together a little while about the Princess Elizabeth; and the King mentioned having had a very promising account from her Physician, Sir George Baker; and the Queen soon brightened up.

The King then returned to me, and said 'Are you sure you never play? – Never touch the Keys at all? – '

'Never to acknowledge it, sir' –

'O! that's it! – ' cried he, and flying to the Queen, cried 'she does play, – but not to *acknowledge* it! – '

I was now in a most horrible panic once more; pushed so very home, I could answer no other than I did, for these categorical questions almost constrain categorical answers: and here, at Windsor, it seems an absolute point that whatever they ask, must be told, and whatever they desire, must be done: Think but then of my consternation in expecting their commands to perform! My dear Father, pity me!

The eager air with which he returned to me fully explained what was to follow; I hastily, therefore, spoke first, in order to stop him, crying 'I *never*, sir, played to any body, but myself! – never! – ' I spoke almost convulsively.

'No?' cried he, looking incredulous, 'What, not to – '

'Not even to *me*, sir!' cried my kind Mrs Delany, who saw what was threatening me. –

'No? – are you sure? – ' cried he, disappointed, – 'but – but you'll – '

'I have never, sir,' cried I, very earnestly, 'played in my life, but when I could hear no body else, – quite alone, and from a mere love of any musical sounds.'

He repeated all this to the Queen, whose answers I never heard; but when he once more came back, with a face that looked unwilling to give it up, in my fright, I had recourse to dumb shew, and raised my Hands in a supplicating fold, with a most begging Countenance to be excused. This, luckily, succeeded; he understood me very readily, and laughed a little, but made a sort of desisting, or rather, *complying* little Bow, and said no more about it.

I felt very much obliged to him, for I saw his curiosity was all alive. I wished I could have kissed his hand.

He still, however, kept me in talk, and still upon music: 'To me,' said he, 'it appears quite as strange to meet with people who have no Ear for music, and cannot distinguish one air from another, as to meet with people who are dumb. Lady Bell Finch once told me that she had *heard* there was some difference between a Psalm, a Minuet, and a Country Dance, but she declared they all sounded alike to her! There are people, too, who have no

Eye for difference of Colour. The Duke of Marlborough actually cannot tell scarlet from Green! – '

He then told me an anecdote of his mistaking those colours for another, which was very laughable: but I do not remember it clearly enough to write it. How unfortunate for *true* virtuosi that such an Eye should possess objects worthy the most discerning! the treasures of Blenheim![6]

'I do not find, though,' added his Majesty, 'that this defect runs in his family; for Lady Dye Beauclerk draws very finely.'

He then went to Mr Bernard Dewes.

Almost instantly upon his leaving me, a very gentle voice called out 'Miss Burney! – '

It was the Queen's. I walked a little nearer her, and a gracious inclination of her Head made me go quite up to her. 'You have been,' she said, 'at Mrs Walsingham's?'[7]

'Yes, ma'am.'

'Has not she lately made some improvements?'

'Yes, ma'am; she has built a conservatory.'

Then followed some questions about its situation during which, the King came up to us: and she then, ceasing to address me in particular, began a general sort of conversation with a spirit of animation that I had not at all expected, and which seemed the result of the great and benevolent pleasure she took in giving entertainment to Mrs Delany.

The subject was the last Drawing Room, which she had been in Town to keep on Thursday, during the dense Fog.

'I assure You, ma'am,' cried she, to Mrs Delany, 'it was so dark, there was no seeing any thing, and knowing any body. And Lady Harcourt could be of no help to tell me who they were, for when it is light, she can't see; and now it was dark, I could not see myself.[8] So it was in vain for me to go on, in that manner, without knowing which I had spoken to, and which was waiting for me; so I said to Lady Harcourt, We had better stop, and stand quite still, for I don't know any body, no more than you do. But if we stand still they will all come up in the end, and we must ask them who they are, and if I have spoke to them yet, or not: for it is very odd to do it, but what else can we manage?'

Her accent is a little foreign, and very prettily so; and her emphasis has

6. The seat of the Duke of Marlborough.
7. Mrs Charlotte Boyle Walsingham, granddaughter of the Earl of Coningsby.
8. Lady Harcourt was one of the Queen's ladies of the Bedchamber.

that sort of changeability which gives an interest to every thing she utters. But her language is rather peculiar than Foreign.

'Besides,' added she, with a very significant look, 'if we go on here in the dark, may be I shall push against somebody; or, somebody will push against *me*! – which is the more likely to happen!' –

She then gave an account of some circumstances which attended the darkness, in a manner not only extremely lively, but mixed, at times, with an archness and humour that made it very entertaining. She chiefly addressed herself to Mrs Delany; and to me, certainly, she would not, separately, have been so communicative; but she continued, with great delicacy, to include me in the little party, by frequently looking at me, and always with an expression that invited my participation in the conversation. And indeed, though I did not join in words, I shared very openly in the pleasure of her recital.

'Well,' she continued, 'so there was standing by me a man that I could not see in the Face; but I saw the Twisting of his Bow; and I said to Lady Harcourt – I am sure that must be nobody but the Duke of Dorset. – Dear! she says, how can you tell that! – only ask, said I, – and so, it proved he. – '

'Yes,' cried the King, 'he is pretty well again; he can *smile* again, now! – ' It seems his features had appeared to be fixed, or stiffened. – It is said he has been obliged to hold his Hand to his mouth, to hide it, ever since his stroke; which he refuses to acknowledge was paralytic.

The Queen looked as if some comic notion had struck her, and, after smiling a little while to herself, said, with a sort of innocent archness very pleasing, 'To be sure – it is very wrong to laugh at such things, – I know that! – but yet, – I could not help thinking, when his mouth was in that way, that it was very lucky People's happiness did not *depend upon his smiles*! – '

Afterwards, she named another person whose behaviour and manners pointed them, out to her, in defiance of obscurity.

'A Lady,' said she, 'came up to me, that I could not see, so I was forced to ask who she was, – immediately she burst into a laugh, – O, says I, – that can be only Mrs De Rolles![9] – and so it proved.'

Methinks, by this trait, she should be a near relation to *my* Miss *La*rolles! When these, and some more anecdotes, which I do not so clearly remember, were told, the King left us, and went to Mr Bernard Dewes. A pause ensuing, I, too, drew back, meaning to return to my original station; which, being opposite the fire, was never a bad one. But the moment I began retreating,

9. Mrs Christabella Dayrolles, wife of Solomon Dayrolles, diplomat.

the Queen, bending forward, and speaking in a very low voice, said 'Miss Burney! – ' and, upon my coming up to her, almost in a whisper, cried 'But – shall we have *no* more? – *nothing* more? – '

I could not but understand her, – and only shook my Head.

The Queen then, as if she thought she had said too much, with great sweetness and condescension, drew back herself, and, very deliberately, said 'To be sure, it is, I own, a very home question, – for one who has not the pleasure to know you. – '

I was quite ashamed of this apology, but did not know what to say to it. – But how amiable a simplicity in *her* speaking of herself in such a style, – '*for one who has not the pleasure to know you.*'

'But, indeed,' continued she, presently, 'I would not say it, only that, I think, – from what *has* been done, – there is a power to do so much *good*; – and good to *young* people, – which is so *very* good a thing, – that I cannot help *wishing* it could be. – '

I felt very grateful for this speech, and for the very soft manner in which she said it; and very much wished to thank her, – and was trying to mutter something, though not very intelligibly, when the King, suddenly coming up to us, enquired what was going forward.

The Queen readily repeated her kind speech.

The King, who looked much pleased that this subject was started, eagerly undertook to make my answer for me, – crying 'O, – but she *will* write! – she only waits for *inclination*, – she told me so. – ' Then, speaking to me, – he said '*What*? – Is it not so? – '

I only laughed a little; – and he again said to the Queen – 'she *will* write! – she told me, just now, she had made no *vow* against it.'

'No, no,' cried the Queen, 'I hope not, indeed! – '

'A vow!' cried dear Mrs Delany, 'no, indeed, I hope she would not be so wicked, – she who can *so* do what she does!'

'But she has *not*,' said the King, earnestly, 'she has owned that to me already.' What excessive condescendsion, my dear Padre! –

'I only wish,' cried Mrs Delany, 'it could be as easily done, as it is earnestly and universally desired.'

'I doubt it not to be so desired. – ' said the Queen.

I was quite ashamed of all this, and quite sorry to make no acknowledgement of their great condescendsion in pressing such a subject, and pressing it so much in earnest. But I really could get out nothing, – so that's the truth; and I wish I could give a better account of my eloquence, my dear Padre and Susan –

I cannot, however, in justice any more than in inclination, go on, till I stop to admire the sweetness of the Queen, and the consideration of the King, in each making me a party in their general conversation before they made any particular address to me.

They afterwards spoke of Mr Webb, a Windsor Musician, who is Master to the young Princess, and who has a Nose, from some strange calamity, of so enormous a size that it covers all the middle of his Face. I never saw so frightful a deformity. Mrs Delany told the Queen I had met with him, accidentally, when he came to give a lesson to Miss Port, and had been quite startled by him.

'I dare say so;' said her Majesty. 'I must tell Miss Burney a little trait of Sophia about Mr Webb.'

A small Table was before the Queen, who always has it brought when she is seated, to put her Tea, or work,[10] upon, or, when she has neither, to *look comfortable*, I believe; for certainly it takes off much formality in a standing Circle. And close to this, by the gracious motion of her Head, she kept me.

'When first,' continued she, 'Mr Webb was to come to Sophia, I told her he had had some accident to disfigure his whole face, by making him an enormous Nose; but I desired her to remember this was a misfortune, for which he ought to be pitied, and that she must be sure not to laugh at it, nor stare at it. And she minded this very well, and behaved always very properly. But, while Lady Cremorne was at the Lodge, she was with Sophia when Mr Webb came to give her a lesson. As soon as he was named, she coloured very red, and ran up to Lady Cremorne, and said to her, in a Whisper, "Lady Cremorne, Mr Webb has got a very great nose, but that is only to be pitied, so mind you don't Laugh!" – '

This little Princess is just 9 years old!

The King joined us while the Queen was telling this, and added 'Poor Mr Webb was very much discountenanced when he first saw me, and tried to hide his nose, by a great nosegay, or I believe only a Branch, which he held before it: but really that had so odd a look, that it was worse and more ridiculous than his nose. However, I hope he does not mind me, now, for I have seen him four or five times.'

After this, Mrs Delany mentioned Madame La Fîte,[11] and her son –

'Yes,' said the Queen, 'he is a pretty little Boy; and when he goes to school, – it will do him good.'

10. Needlework.
11. Madame Marie-Elisabeth de la Fîte, Reader to the Queen in French and German and French governess to Princess Elizabeth.

'Where will she send him?' said the King.

The Queen, looking at me with a smile, answered, 'To the school where Mr Lock[12] puts his sons: – I know that! – '

'And where is that?'

'Indeed I can't tell; – where is it, Miss Burney?'

'At Cheam, ma'am.'

'O, at Young Gilpin's?'[13] cried the King.

'Is it near Mr Lock's?'

'Yes, sir; within about six miles – I believe.'

The Queen, then, with a little arch smile that seemed to premise she should make me stare, said – 'It was there – at Mr Lock's, your sister laid in? – '

'O yes, ma'am?' cried I, out of breath with surprise.

The King repeated my *O yes*! and said 'I fancy – by that *O* – you were frightened a little for her? – What? – '

I could not but assent to that; and the King, who seemed a good deal diverted at the accident – for he loves little Babies too well to look upon it, as most people would, to be a shocking business, – questioned me on about it. 'How,' said he 'was it? how happened it? Could not she get Home?'

'It was so sudden, sir, and so unexpected, there was no time.'

'I dare say,' said the sweet Queen, 'Mrs Lock was only very happy to have it at her House. – '

'Indeed, ma'am,' cried I, 'her kindness, and Mr Lock would make any body think so! – but they are *all* kindness and goodness. – '

'I have heard, indeed,' said the Queen, 'that they are all sensible, and amiable, and ingenious, in that family.'

'They are indeed,' cried I, 'and as exemplary as they are accomplished.'

'I have never seen Mrs Lock,' said the King, 'since she was that high – ' pointing to little Miss Dewes.

'And I,' said the Queen, 'I have never seen her in my life; but for all that, from what I hear of her, I cannot help feeling interested whenever I only hear her name.'

This, with a good deal of animation, she said directly to me.

'Mr William Lock, ma'am,' said Mrs Delany, 'I understand, from Miss

---

12. William Locke of Norbury Park, Mickleham, Surrey, and his wife Frederica ('Fredy') were neighbours and close friends of Susanna and Molesworth Phillips. FB had met them in 1784.
13. William Gilpin, Jr had succeeded his father William Gilpin, miscellaneous writer, as master of Cheam School.

Burney, is now making the same wonderful progress in painting, that he had done before in drawing.'[14]

'I have seen some of his drawings,' said the Queen, 'which were charming.'

'How old is he?' said the King.

'18, sir.'

'Eighteen?' repeated the King; – – 'how Time flies! –'

'Oh! for *me*,' cried the Queen, 'I am always quarrelling with Time! It is so short to do something, and so long to do nothing!'

She has now and then something foreign to our idiom, that has a very pretty effect.

'Time,' said the King, 'always seems long when we are young, and short when we begin to grow old.'

'But nothing makes me so angry,' said the Queen, 'as to hear people not know what to do! For *me*, I never have half time enough for things. But what makes me most angry still, is to see people go up to a window, and say *What a bad Day! Dear! what shall we do such a Day as this!* What? I say; why employ yourselves! – and then, what signifies the bad Day?'

Afterwards, there was some talk upon sermons; and the Queen wished the Bishop of Chester[15] would publish another volume.

'No, no,' said the King, 'you must not expect a man, while he continues preaching, to go on publishing. Every sermon printed, diminishes his stock for the pulpit.'

'Very true;' said the Queen, 'but I believe the Bishop of Chester has enough to spare.'

The King then praised Carr's sermons;[16] and said he liked none but what were plain and unadorned.

'Nor I neither,' said the Queen, – 'but, for *me*, it is, I suppose, because the others I don't understand!'

The King then, looking at his watch, said 'It is 8 o'clock, and if we don't go now, the Children will be sent to the other House.'

'Yes, *your Majesty*. –' cried the Queen, instantly rising.

Mrs Delany put on her Majesty's Cloak; and she took a very kind leave of her. She then curtsied separately to us all, and the King Handed her to the Carriage.

14. William Locke, Jr was a student and friend of Henry Fuseli and would distinguish himself as an amateur artist. His father was a noted connoisseur and collector of art.

15. Beilby Porteus, later Bishop of London.

16. The sermons of the Revd George Carr were published posthumously in 1777.

It is the custom for every body they speak to, to attend them out: but they would not suffer Mrs Delany to move: Miss Port, Mr Dewes and his little Daughter and myself all accompanied them, – and saw them in their Coach, and received their last gracious nods.

When they were gone, Mrs Delany confessed she had heard the King's knock at the Door, before she came into the Drawing Room, but would not avow it, that I might not run away. Well! being *over* was so good a thing, that I could not but be content.

The Queen, indeed, is a most charming Woman. She appears to me full of sense and graciousness, mingled with delicacy of mind and liveliness of Temper. She speaks English almost perfectly well, with great choice and copiousness of language, though now and then with foreign idiom, and frequently with a foreign accent. Her manners have an easy dignity, with a most engaging simplicity; and she has all that fine high breeding which the mind, not the station, gives, of carefully avoiding to distress those who converse with her, or studiously removing the embarrassment she cannot prevent.

The King, however he may have power, in the Cabinet, to command himself, has, in private, the appearance of a character the most open and sincere. He speaks his opinions without reserve, and seems to trust them intuitively to his Hearers from a belief they will make no ill use of them. His Countenance is full of enquiry, to gain information without asking it, probably from believing that to be the nearest road to Truth. All I saw of Both was the most perfect good humour, good spirits, ease, and pleasantness.

Their behaviour to each other speaks the most cordial confidence and happiness. The King seems to admire as much as he enjoys her conversation, and to covet her participation in every thing he either sees or hears. The Queen appears to feel the most grateful regard for him, and to make it her chief study to raise his consequence with others, by always marking that she considers herself, though Queen to the Nation, only, to him, the first and most obedient of subjects.

. . .

Monday [19 December] continued.[17]

[The King] spoke of Voltaire, and talked a little of his works, concluding with this strong condemnation of their *tendency*, '*I*,' cried he, 'think him a *monster*! I own it fairly.'[18]

17. FB describes an evening visit of the King to Mary Delany, Miss Port and herself.
18. The King is reacting to the French writer's deism and political liberalism. He would have been especially horrified by Voltaire's condemnation of organized religion.

Nobody answered, Mrs Delany did not quite hear him, and I knew too little of his Works to have courage to say any thing about them.

He next named Rousseau, whom he seemed to think of with more favour, though by no means with approbation. Here, too, I had read too little to talk at all, though his Majesty frequently applied to me. Mrs Delany told several anecdotes which had come to her immediate knowledge, of him, while he was in England,[19] at which time, he had spent some Days with her Brother, Mr Granville, at Calwich. The King, too, told others, which had come to his own Ears, all charging him with savage pride and insolent ingratitude.

Here, however, I ventured to interfere: for as I knew he had had a pension from the King, I could not but wish his Majesty should be informed he was grateful to *him*. And as *you*, my dear Father, were my authority, I thought it but common justice to the memory of poor Rousseau to acquaint the King of his personal respect for him.

'Some Gratitude, sir,' said I, 'he was not without. When my Father was in Paris, which was after Rousseau had been in England, he visited him, in his Garret, – and the first thing he shewed him was Your Majesty's portrait over his Chimney.'[20]

The King paused a little while upon this, – but nothing more was said of Rousseau.

The sermon of the Day before was then talked over. Mrs Delany had not heard it, and the King said 'twas no great loss. He asked me what I had thought of it, and we agreed perfectly, to the no great exaltation of poor Dr Lockman.[21]

Some time afterwards, the King said he found, by the News-Papers, Mrs Clive was Dead.[22]

Do you read the News-Papers! thought I. – O King! You must then have the most unvexing Temper in the World, not to run wild.[23]

This led on to more Players. He was sorry, he said, for Henderson,[24] and

---

19. Jean-Jacques Rousseau had come to England in 1765 as the guest of David Hume, the philosopher. He was already suffering from a persecution mania that caused him to alienate virtually everyone he met. He had died in 1778.

20. The King had awarded Rousseau a pension for his services to literature. CB visited him in Paris in 1770.

21. The Revd Dr John Lockman was a Canon of Windsor.

22. Catherine ('Kitty') Clive, famous actress, had died on 7 December, aged seventy-four.

23. London newspapers run by the political opposition were full of vituperative attacks on the King, not to mention scathing political satires and caricatures that were freely circulated.

24. John Henderson, actor regarded by his contemporaries as second only to Garrick, had died on 25 November, aged thirty-eight.

the more, as Mrs Siddons had wished to have him play at the same House with herself. Then Mrs Siddons took her turn, and with the warmest praise. 'I am an *Enthusiast* for her,' cried the King, 'quite an Enthusiast; I think there was never *any* player, in my time, so excellent, not Garrick himself; – I own it! – ' Then, coming close to me, who was silent, he said 'What? – what? – ' meaning *what say you?* – but I still said nothing; I could not concur, where I thought so differently, and to enter into an argument was quite impossible; for every little thing I said, the King listened to with an eagerness that made me always ashamed of its insignificancy. And indeed, but for that, I should have talked to him with much greater fluency, as well as ease.

From players, he went to plays: and complained of the great want of good modern Comedies, and of the extreme immorality of most of the old ones.[25] 'And they pretend,' cried he, 'to mend them; but it is not possible. Do you think it is? – *what?* – '

'No, sir, not often; – I believe; – the fault, commonly, is in the very foundation.'

'Yes; – or they might mend the mere speeches; – but the Characters are all bad from the beginning to the end.'[26]

Then he specified several; but I had read none of them, and consequently could say nothing about the matter: till, at last, he came to Shakespeare. 'Was there ever,' cried he, 'such stuff as great part of Shakespeare? only one must not say so! – but What think you? – *What?* – Is there not sad stuff? – *What? what?*'

'Yes, indeed, I think so, sir, – though mixed with such excellencies that – '

'O!' cried he, laughing good humouredly, 'I know it is not to be said! – but it's *true*. Only it's *Shakespeare*, and nobody dare abuse him. – ' Then he enumerated many of the Characters and parts of plays that he objected to, and when he had run them over, finished with again laughing, and exclaiming 'But one should be stoned for saying so! – '[27]

'Madame De Genlis, sir,' said I, 'had taken such an impression of the

---

25. The King is referring particularly to the Restoration comedies of playwrights like William Wycherley and George Etherege.

26. It was theatrical practice to alter old plays to suit contemporary taste, sometimes by the suppression of entire scenes or the writing of new ones; speeches were often freely modified or new ones inserted.

27. Popular veneration of Shakespeare in the eighteenth century had reached its apogee with the Shakespeare Jubilee of 1769, held at Stratford and orchestrated by Garrick. Johnson's critical edition of Shakespeare (1765) had provided a corrective to ignorant idolatry by calling attention to deficiencies as well as excellencies in the Bard's works.

English Theatre, that she told me she thought no woman ought to go to any of our comedies.'[28]

This, – which, indeed, is a very overstrained censure of our Dramas, made him draw back, and vindicate the stage from a sentence so severe: which, however, she had pronounced to me, as if she looked upon it to be an opinion in which I should join as a thing past dispute.

The King approved such a denunciation no more than his little subject and he vindicated the stage from so hard an aspersion with a warmth not wholly free from indignation.

This led on to a good deal more dramatic criticism; but what was said was too little followed up to be remembered for writing.

102. Letter to Esther Burney *17 December 1785*[1]

Windsor

My dearest Hetty

I am sorry I could not more immediately write, but I really have not had a moment since your last –

Now I know what you next want is to hear accounts of Kings, Queens, and such Royal Personages. – O ho! do you so? – Well, – –

Shall I tell you a few matters of fact? – or had you rather a few matters of etiquette? – O, matters of Etiquette, you cry, – for matters of fact are short and stupid, – and any body can tell, and every body is tired with them. –

Very well, take your own Choices – –

To begin, then, with the beginning.

You know I told you, in my last, my various difficulties what sort of preferment to turn my thoughts to; and concluded with just starting a young budding notion of decision, by suggesting that a handsome Pension for nothing at all would be as well as working night and day for a Salary.

This blossom of an idea, the more I dwelt upon, the more I liked: Thinking served it for a Hot-house and it came out into full blow as I ruminated upon my Pillow. Delighted that thus all my contradictory and wayward fancies were overcome, and my mind was peaceably settled what

---

28. Madame de Genlis, French author, had visited England in July 1785.

1. Copy in the hand of Charlotte Barrett, FB's niece, literary executor and first editor.

to wish and to demand, I gave over all further meditation upon Choice of Elevation, and had nothing more to do but to make my election known.

My next business, therefore, was to be presented.

This could be no difficulty; my coming hither had been their own desire and they had earnestly pressed its execution. I had only to *prepare myself for the rencounter*.

You would never believe – you, who, distant from Courts and Courtiers, know nothing of their ways, – the many things to be studied for appearing with a *proper propriety* before crowned Heads. Heads without Crowns are quite other sort of rotundas. Now, then, to the Etiquette. I enquired into every particular, that no error might be committed. And as there is no saying what may happen in this mortal life, I shall give you those instructions I have received myself, that, should you find yourself in the Royal presence you may know how to comport yourself.

> *Directions for Coughing, sneezing, or moving*
> *before the King and Queen.*

In the first place, you must not Cough. If you find a cough tickling in your throat, you must arrest it from making any sound: if you find yourself choacking with the forbearance, you must choak: But not cough.

In the 2d place, you must not sneeze. If you have a vehement Cold, you must take no notice of it; if your Nose membranes feel a great irritation, you must hold your breath; if a sneeze still insists upon making its way, you must oppose it by keeping your teeth grinding together; if the violence of the repulse breaks some blood-vessel, you must break the blood-vessel: But not sneeze.

In the 3d place, you must not, upon any account, stir either hand or foot. If, by chance, a black pin runs into your Head, you must not take it out: If the pain is very great, you must be sure to bear it without wincing; If it brings the Tears into your Eyes, you must not wipe them off; If they give you a tingling by running down your Cheeks, you must look as if nothing was the matter. If the blood should gush from your Head by means of the black pin, you must let it gush; If you are uneasy to think of making such a blurred appearance, you must be uneasy; but you must say nothing about it. If, however, the agony is very great, you may, privately, bite the inside of your Cheek, or of your lips, for a little relief; taking care, meanwhile, to do it so cautiously as to make no apparent dent outwardly. And, with that precaution, if you even gnaw a piece out, it will not be minded, only be sure either to swallow it, or commit it to a corner of the inside of your mouth till they are gone, – for, You must not spit.

I have many other Directions, but no more paper: I will endeavour however, to have them ready for you in Time. Perhaps, meanwhile, you would be glad to know if I have myself had opportunity to put in practice these receipts? –

How can I answer in this little space? – – My Love to Mr Burney and the Little ones. – And remember me kindly to Coz: Edward – and believe me

My dearest Esther,

most affectionately yours

FB.

103. From Letter to Charlotte Cambridge[1] *12 June 1786*

Yesterday Evening, while I was with Mrs Delany, Mr Smelt[2] arrived from Windsor, and desired a private conference with her; and, when it was over, a separate one with me: surprising me not a little, by entreating me to suffer some very home questions from him, with respect to my future life. At first I only laughed: but my merriment a little failed me, when he gave me to understand he was commissioned to make these enquiries by a great personage, who had conceived so favourable an opinion of me as to be desirous of undoubted information whether or not there was a probability she might permanently attach me to herself and her family.

You can not easily, my dear Miss Cambridge, picture to yourself the consternation with which I received this intimation. It was such that the good and kind Mr Smelt, perceiving it, had the indulgence to instantly offer me his services first in forbearing to mention even to my Father his commission, and next in fabricating and carrying back for me a respectful excuse. And I must always consider myself the more obliged to him, as I saw in his own face the utmost astonishment and disappointment at this reception of his embassy.

I could not, however, reconcile to myself concealing from my dear Father a matter that ought to be settled by himself: yet I frankly owned to Mr Smelt that no situation of that sort was suited to my own taste, or promising to my own happiness.

He seemed equally sorry and surprised: he expatiated warmly upon the

---

1. Sister of George Owen Cambridge. The manuscript is a draft of the letter actually sent.
2. Leonard Smelt, formerly sub-governor to the Prince of Wales and the Duke of York, who by his own choice remained at Court without further appointment, preferring to be known simply as 'the King's friend' (*JL*, i. 94 n. 18).

sweetness of Character of all the Royal Family and then begged me to consider the very distinction shewn me that unsolicited, unsought, I had been marked out with such personal favour by the Queen herself, as a person with whom she had been so singularly pleased, as to wish to settle me with one of the Princesses, in preference to the thousands of offered Candidates, of high birth and rank but small fortunes, who were waiting and supplicating for places in the new forming establishment. – Her Majesty, he said, proposed giving me apartments in the Palace, making me belong to the Table of Mrs Schwellenberg,[3] with whom all her own visitors – Bishops, Lords or Commons, always Dine, keeping me a footman, and settling on me 200 a year. 'And in such a situation,' he added, 'so respectably *offered*, not *solicited*, – you may have opportunities of serving your particular friends, especially your father, – such as scarce any other could afford you.'

My dear Miss Cambridge will easily feel that this was a plea not to be answered, – yet the attendance upon this Princess was to be incessant – the confinement to the Court continual, – I was scarce ever to be spared for a single visit from the palaces, nor to receive any body in them but with permission, – O my dear Miss Cambridge, what a life for me, who have friends so dear to me, and to whom friendship is the balm, the comfort, the very support of existence! –

Don't think me ungrateful, mean while, to the sweet Queen, for thus singling out and distinguishing an obscure and most unambitious Individual – no indeed, I am quite penetrated with her partial and most unexpected condescendsion: but yet, – let me go through, for Her sake, my tasks with what chearfulness I may, the deprivations I must suffer would inevitably keep me from all possibility of happiness.

Though I said but little, – my dear Mrs Delany was disturbed, and good Mr Smelt much mortified, that a proposition which had appeared to them the most flattering and honourable, should be heard only with dejection: – I cast, however, the whole into my Father's disposal and pleasure: – –

But I have time for no more detail, than merely to say that till the offer comes *in form*, no positive answer need be given, and therefore that I am yet at liberty. Write to me, then, my dearest Miss Cambridge, with all your fullest honesty, and let me know which you wish to strengthen, my courage in making my real sentiments openly known, or my fortitude in concealing what it may be right I should endure.

The moment this affair is decided, – as I shall then strive to make the

3. Elizabeth Juliana Schwellenberg, Keeper of the Robes to Queen Charlotte.

best of it whatever be my decision, I shall entreat you to return me this Letter, or commit it to the flames. The measles will keep off any meetings at Windsor for sometime: I hope, therefore, to receive your answer before I am obliged to speak finally.

Can you forgive all this trouble? – if matters take the turn I so much dread, I shall not give you much more! –

If it should be in my power, I intend till all this is arranged to defer my journey to Windsor.

Adieu, my dearest Miss Cambridge – I am sorry to send you a Letter written in such confusion of mind –

Monday Night. I have now to add that the zealous Mr Smelt is just returned from Windsor whither he went again this morning purposely to talk the matter over with her Majesty – What passed I know not – but the result is that she has desired an interview with me herself, – it is to take place next Saturday at Windsor. – I now see the end – I see it next to inevitable – I can suggest nothing upon Earth that I dare say for myself in an audience so generously meant. I cannot even to my Father utter my reluctance, – I see him so much delighted at the prospect of an establishment he looks upon as so honourable – but for the Queen's own word *permanent* – but for her declared desire to *attach me entirely* to her Family – I should share in his pleasure, – but what can make *me* amends for all I shall forfeit? – *but* I must do the best I can – write me a comforting and a strengthening Letter, my dearest Miss Cambridge, – I have no heart to write to Mickleham or Norbury[4] – I know how they will grieve. They have expected me to spend the Whole summer with them. –

My greatest terror is lest the Queen – from what Mr Smelt hinted – should make me promise myself to her for a length of Years – What can I do to avoid that? – any thing that has a period is endurable – but what can I object that will not sound ungrateful to the honour she is doing me and meaning me? – she has given the most highly flattering reasons for making this application in preference to listening to that of others – she has put it upon terms of commendation the most soothing – she is indeed one of the sweetest characters in the World – will *you*, too, condemn me, then, that I feel thus oppressed by her proposal? – I *hope* not – I *think* not, – but be very honest if you really do. I wish I could see you! – It is not from nervousness, – I have always and uniformly had a horrour of a life of attendance and dependence.

4. To the Phillipses or to the Lockes.

Don't be uneasy about me, however – for this one week of conflict over, I shall set all my faculties at work to *do* the best – and *think* the *least* I can. – And till that time comes, I must not venture to write to my poor Susan. – She and Mrs Locke have long feared this – I thought their fears so vain! so partial, so almost absurd, – that I never heeded them – yet, I now hear the Queen has been forming this plan ever since I had first the honour of seeing her – and she has even been making the minutest inquiries from that time into my conduct – disposition – and all that belongs to me. How little did I suspect it! – Could I but save myself from a *lasting bond*, – from a *promised devotion*! – that is the great point of all, my dearest Miss Cambridge – in which if you can help me to suggest something that will not sound disrespectful or improper you will serve me indeed!

104. From Letter to Dr Burney *19 June 1786*

Monday

How great must have been your impatience, Dearest Sir! – but my Interview has only this morning taken place. Every thing is settled, – and to-morrow morning I go to the Queen's Lodge to see the apartments, and to receive my instructions.

I must confess myself extremely frightened and full of alarms at a change of situation so great, so unexpected, so unthought of. Whether I shall suit it or not Heaven only knows, but I have a thousand doubts. – Yet nothing could be sweeter than the Queen – more encouraging, more gentle, or more delicate. She did not ask me one question concerning my qualifications for the charge, – she only said, with the most condescending softness, 'I am sure, Miss Burney, *we shall suit one another very well.* –' And another time, 'I am sure we *shall do very well together.* –'

And what is it, Dear Sir, you suppose to be my business? – not to attend *any* of the Princesses, – but the Queen herself! – This, indeed, was a delightful hearing, reverencing and admiring her as I have so sincerely done ever since I first saw her. – And in this, my amazement is proportioned to my satisfaction, for the Place designed me is that of *Mrs Haggerdorn*,[1] who came with her from Germany: and it will put me more immediately and

---

1. Johanna Louisa Hagedorn had been joint Keeper of the Robes to Queen Charlotte ever since they had arrived together from Germany in 1761. She had resigned owing to ill health, and would return to Germany the following month.

more constantly in her presence than any other place, but that of Mrs Schwellenberg, in the Court. The prepossetion the Queen has taken in my favour is truly extraordinary, for it seems as if her real view was, as Mr Smelt hinted, to attach me to her person. She has been long, she told Mrs Delany, looking out for me to supply the place of Mrs H., whose ill Health forces her back to Germany: – 'and I was led to think of Miss Burney first by her Books; – then by seeing her; then by always hearing how she was loved by her friends; – but chiefly by *your* friendship for her. – '[2]

2. FB's appointment to the Court of George III, as Second Keeper of the Robes to Queen Charlotte, was an offer she could not refuse. Beyond the financial security of a life appointment worth £200 a year, it would give her an opportunity to help her family. Her brother Charles was still seeking ordination in the Church despite having been expelled from Cambridge for stealing books from the University Library in October 1777, and her brother James had been forced into retirement from active service in the navy in 1785 because of insubordination to a superior officer (in the event FB would be unable to help either during her five years at Court). The appointment was also probably intended as recompense to CB for his having been passed over for the position of Master of the King's Band, a post the King himself had promised him (but which went to William Parsons).

1786–1791

The Court Years

105. From Journal Letter to Susanna Phillips *July 1786*

Once more I take up my Pen, to give my beloved Susan a Journal of my proceedings. I have been advised against it, but I do not see why; a simple account of inoffensive actions can have no more to fear from the reader than from the listener; and while I never make the most distant allusion to politics, to the Royal family's private transactions or opinions, nor to any state affairs of any kind, I see not why I must be deprived of my long accustomed confidence in the Dearest and sweetest of Sisters, whose never failing discretion, honour, and fidelity have always called for my trust from the earliest time I have had any thing to communicate.

. . .

Queen's Lodge, Windsor.

I am more than a week in arrears; but I have kept memorandums in my pocket Book, and I shall continue the same practice, and draw out my accounts for my Susan from them, when ever I can find leisure. I go now to

Monday, July 17th. With what hurry of mind and body did I rise this morning! – Every thing had already been arranged for Mrs Ord's carrying us to Windsor, and my Father's carriage was merely to go as Baggage Waggon for my Cloaths. But I wept not then. – I left no one behind me to regret; my dear Father accompanied me, and all my dear sisters had already taken their flight, never more to return. Even poor little Sarah,[1] whom I love very dearly, was at Chesington. –

Between 9 and 10 o'clock we set off. Poor Nanny,[2] who had expected to follow me when ever I quitted Home, could hardly bear the disappointment

1. FB's half-sister Sarah Harriet ('Sally') Burney, future novelist, aged fourteen. Considered 'odd' by the family, she was chronically neglected by her mother.
2. Family servant.

at the last; but I have promised that if she can but leave my mother satisfied with a successor I will immediately take her. I am sure I long for the good and faithful Creature, who would here be truly a Treasure to me.

We changed Carriage in Queen Ann Street, and Mrs Ord conveyed us thence to Windsor. With a struggling Heart I kept myself tolerably tranquil during the little journey: My dear Father was quite happy, and Mrs Ord felt the joy of a Mother, in relinquishing me to the protection of a Queen so universally reverenced. Had I been in better spirits, their extacy would have been unbounded: but alas – what I was approaching was not in my mind; what I was leaving had taken possession of it solely! –

Miss Port flew out to us, as the carriage stopt, – the youthful blush of pleasure heightening her complection, and every feature shewing her kind happiness. – Mrs Delany, she said, was gone out with the Queen. I took leave of my good Mrs Ord, whose Eyes overflowed with maternal feelings – chiefly of contentment, – in the parting. Mrs Delany, my dear, my most loved Mrs Delany, came Home in about an Hour – – a chastened satisfaction was hers; – she rejoiced in the prospects before me, she was happy we should now so much be united, – but she felt for my deprivations, she saw the hard conflict within me, and the tenderest pity checked her delight.

It was now debated whether I was immediately to go to the Lodge, or wait for orders. The accustomed method, for those who have their Majesty's commands to come to them, is to present themselves to the people in waiting, and by them to be announced. My Heart, however, was already sinking, and my spirits every moment were growing more agitated, and my sweet Mrs Delany determined to spare me the additional task of passing through such awe-striking formalities. She therefore employed my dear Father, delighted with the employment, – to write a Note, in her name, –

'Mrs Delany presents her most humble Duty to the Queen; she found Dr Burney and his Daughter at her House, – Miss Burney waits the honour of her Majesty's commands.'

This, though unceremonious and unusual, she was sure the Queen would pardon, and verbal answer came, that I was to go to the Lodge immediately.

O my dear Susan! in what an *agony* of mind did I obey the summons! I was still in my travelling Dress, but could not stay to change it. My Father accompanied me, – Mrs Delany anxiously, and full of mixed sensations, gave me her blessing, – we walked; the Queen's Lodge is not 50 yards from Mrs Delany's Door. My dear Father's own courage all failed him in this little step; for as I was now on the point of entering, – probably for-ever! – into an entire new way of life, and of fore-going by it – all my most favourite schemes – and every dear expectation my Fancy had ever indulged of happiness adapted to its taste, – as now, all was to be given up, – I could disguise my trepidation no longer, – indeed I never had *disguised*, I had only forborn *proclaiming* it, – but my dear Father now, sweet soul, felt it all, as I held by his arm, without power to say one word, but that if he did not hurry along, I should drop by the way. I heard in his kind voice that he was now really alarmed; he would have slackened his pace or have made me stop to breathe: but I could not, my breath seemed gone, and I could only hasten with all my might lest my strength should go too.

A Page was in waiting at the Gate, who shewed us into Mrs Haggerdorn's Room, which was empty. My dear Father endeavoured here to compose my spirits, – but I could have no other command over them than to forbear letting him know the afflicted state of all within, and to suffer him to keep to his own conclusions, that my emotion was all from fear of the approaching audience.

Indeed was it not! – I could hardly even think of it. All that I was *resigning* — there, and there only went every fear and all reluctance. –

The Page came in a minute or two to summon me to the Queen. – I just begged my kind Father to return to Mrs Delany, and followed the Page.

The Queen was in her Dressing Room. Mrs Schwellenberg was standing behind her, Nobody else present.

She received me with a most gracious bow of the head, and a smile that was all sweetness. She saw me much agitated, and attributed it, no doubt, to the awe of her presence. O she little knew my mind had no *room* in it for feelings of that sort! She talked to me of my Journey, my Father, my Sisters, and my Brothers, – the weather, the Roads, – and Mrs Delany; – any, every thing she could suggest, that could best tend to compose and to make me easy: and when I had been with her about a quarter of an Hour, she desired Mrs Schwellenberg to shew me my Apartment, and, with another graceful bow, motioned my retiring.

Not only to the sweet Queen, but to myself let me here do justice, in declaring, that though I entered her presence with a heart filled with every thing but herself, I quitted it with much-softened sensations. The condescendsion of her efforts to quiet me, and the elegance of her receiving me, thus, as a visitor, without giving me the smallest employment, without naming to me a single direction, without even the most distant hint of business, struck me to shew so much delicacy, as well as graciousness, that I quitted her with a very deep sense of her goodness, and a very strong conviction that she merited every exertion on my part to deserve it.

Mrs Schwellenberg left me at the Room Door, where my dear Father was still waiting for me, too anxious to depart till he again saw me. Mrs Schwellenberg asked me who he was. I told her, and she invited him to see her, and quitted us.

We spent a short time together, – in which I assured him I would, from that moment, take all the happiness in my power, and banish all the regret. I told him how gratifying had been my reception, and I omitted nothing I could think of to remove the uneasiness that This Day seemed first to awaken in him. Thank God! I had the fullest success; his hopes and gay expectations were all within call, and they ran back at the first beckoning.

This settled, and his dear countenance all fresh illumined with returning content, we went together to Mrs Schwellenberg, where we made a visit of about an Hour, in which I had the pleasure of seeing them upon very amicable terms; and then we had one more Tête à Tête, all in the same chearing style, and he left me to Dress, and went to Dine with Mrs Delany.

Left to myself, – I did not dare stop to *think*, nor look round upon my new abode, nor consider for how long I was taking possession; – I rang for my new maid, and immediately Dressed for Dinner.

My maid, whose name is Scourfield, has been recommended to me by Mrs Ord: I shall hope, therefore, to keep her till I can have my good Nanny, though she neither suits the place, which requires the most vigilant punctuality and diligence, nor the mistress, who wishes for a chearful and obliging Character. She is conceited and unpleasant; but as I hope to part with her, it is no matter.

I now took the most vigourous resolutions to observe the promise I had made my dear Father. I needed no monitor to tell me it would be foolish, useless, even *wicked* not to reconcile myself to my destiny.

The many now wishing for just the same – – O could they look within me! —

I am *married*, my dearest Susan, – I look upon it in that light. – I was averse to forming the union, and I endeavoured to escape it; but my friends interfered, – they prevailed – and the knot is tied. What, then, now remains, but to make the best Wife in my power? I am bound to it in Duty, and I will strain every Nerve to succeed.

. . .

Tuesday, July 18. My Windsor Apartment is extremely comfortable. I have a large *Drawing Room*, as they call it, which is on the Ground Floor, as are all the Queen's Rooms, and which faces the Castle, and the venerable round Tower, and opens at the further side, from the Windows, to the little Park. It is airy, pleasant, clean and healthy. My Bed Room is small, but neat and comfortable. It is next the Drawing Room, and looks to the Garden. These two Rooms are delightfully independant of all the rest of the House, and contain every thing I can desire for my convenience and comfort.

. . .

Monday, July 24th. To Day finished the First Week of my residence at the Queen's Lodge.

Having now Journalised for one complete Week, let me endeavour to give you, more connectedly, a concise abstract of the *general method of passing the Day*; that then I may only write what varies and occurs occasionally.

I rise at six o'clock, Dress in a morning Gown and Cap, and wait my first summons, which is at all times from 7 to near 8; but commonly in the exact half hour between them. What time I gain before I am called, I devote to settling Drawers, Dress and my Room, and giving directions to my man and maid, whom I am obliged to watch and instruct as if they were my Children, as I feel myself answerable for their good behaviour.

The Queen never sends for me till her Hair is Dressed. This, in a morning, is always done by her Wardrobe Woman, Mrs Thielky, A German, but who speaks English perfectly well.

Mrs Schwellenberg, since the first week, has never come down in a morning at all. The Queen's Dress is finished by Mrs Thielky and myself. No Maid ever enters the Room while the Queen is in it. Mrs Thielky hands the things to me, and I put them on. Tis fortunate for me I have not the handing them! I should never know which to take first, embarrassed as I am, and should run a prodigious risk of giving the Gown before the Hoop, and the Fan before the Neck Handkerchief.

By 8 o'clock, or a little after, for she is extremely expeditious, she is dressed. She then goes out, to join the King, and be joined by the Princesses, and they all proceed to the King's Chapel in the Castle, to Prayers, attended by the Governesses of the Princesses, and the King's Equery. Various others at times, attend; but only these indispensably.

I then return to my own Room, to Breakfast.

I make this meal the most pleasant part of the Day; I have a Book for my companion, and I allow myself an Hour for it.

My present Book is *Gilpin's Description of the Lakes of Cumberland and Westmore-*

land.[3] Mrs Delany has lent it me. It is the most picturesque reading I ever met with; it shews me Landscapes of every sort with Tints so bright and lively, I forget I am but reading, and fancy I see them before me, Coloured by the hand of Nature.

At 9 o'clock I send off my Breakfast things, and relinquish my Book, to make a serious and steady examination of every thing I have upon my Hands in the way of *business*; in which *preparations for Dress* are always included, – not for the present Day alone, but for the Court Days, which require a particular Dress, for the next arriving Birth Day of any of the Royal family, every one of which requires new apparel, – for Kew, where the Dress is plainest, and for going on here, where the Dress is very pleasant to me, requiring no shew nor finiry, but merely to be neat, not inelegant, and moderately fashionable.

That over, I have my time at my own disposal till a quarter before 12, except on Wednesday and Saturdays, when I have it only to a quarter before Eleven.

My rummages and business sometimes occupy me uninterruptedly to those Hours. When they do not, I give till 10 to *necessary Letters*, – of Duty, Ceremony, or long arrears; – and, *now*, from 10 to the times I have mentioned, I devote to walking.

These times mentioned call me to the irksome and quick returning labours of the Toilette. The Hour advanced on the Wednesdays and Saturdays is for curling and craping the Hair, which it now requires twice a Week.

A quarter before one is the usual time for the Queen to begin Dressing for the Day. Mrs Schwellenberg then constantly attends; so do I. Mrs Thielky of course at all times. We help her off with her Gown, and on with her powdering things, and then the Hair Dresser is admitted. She generally reads the news-papers during that operation.

When she observes that I have run to her but half Dressed, she constantly gives me leave to return and finish as soon as she is seated. If she is grave, and reads steadily on, she dismisses me, whether I am Dressed or not; but at *all* times, she never forgets to send me away while she is powdering, with a consideration not to spoil my Cloaths that one would not expect belonged to her high station. Neither does she ever detain me, without making a point of reading here and there some little paragraph aloud.

When I return, I finish, if any thing is undone, my Dress, and then take

3. William Gilpin, *Observations on . . . the Mountains and Lakes of Cumberland and Westmoreland* (1786).

Baretti's Dialogues,[4] my dearest Fredy's Tablet of memory,[5] or some such *disjointed* matter, for the few minutes that elapse ere I am again summoned.

I find her then always removed to her state Dressing Room, – if any Room in this private mansion can have the Epithet of state. There in a very short time, her Dress is finished. She then says she won't detain me, – and I hear and see no more of her till Bed time.

It is commonly 3 o'clock when I am thus set at large. And I have then two Hours quite at my own disposal: – but, in the *natural course of things*, not a moment after! –

These dear and quiet two Hours, – my only quite sure and undisturbed time in the whole Day, after Breakfast is over, I shall, henceforward, devote to thus talking with my beloved Susan, – my Fredy, – my *other* sisters, – my dear Father, or Miss Cambridge; – with my Brothers, Cousins, Mrs Ord, and other friends, in such turns as these two Hours will occasionally allow me.

Henceforward, I say, – for hitherto, – dejection of spirits, with uncertainty how long my time might last, have made me waste moment after moment as sadly as unprofitably.

At 5 we have Dinner. Mrs Schwellenberg and I meet in the Eating Room. We are commonly Tête à Tête: when there is any body added, it is from her invitation only. Whatever right my place might afford me, of also inviting my friends to the Table, I have now totally lost, by want of courage and spirits to claim it originally.

From this time, *naturally*, I belong to Mrs Schwellenberg wholly. And indeed I think myself fortunate in a high degree, that I resisted her invitations to sit with her sometimes in a *morning*, – for the morning, except what is given of it to the Queen herself, is sacred.

When we have Dined, we go up stairs to her Apartment, which is directly over mine. Here we have Coffee. Only by ourselves, *of course*, but Major Price,[6] who loves society, invites himself, I fancy, when ever he is without other Gentlemen, to drink coffee with Mrs Schwellenberg.

Here we sit, *when I behave as I ought to do*, till half past 6, when the Major goes to attend the King to the Terrace. And *here we sit*, also, when, also, *I behave as I ought to do*, till the Terracing is over; this is at about 8 o'clock. Our

4. Giuseppe Baretti, *Easy Phraseology for the Use of Young Ladies, Who Intend to Learn the Colloquial Part of the Italian Language* (1775), which was written for Queeney Thrale.
5. *The Tablet of Memory* was an annual memorandum book containing a chronology of memorable events. FB had presumably received her copy as a gift from Frederica Locke.
6. Major William Price, Equerry to George III.

Tête à Tête then finishes, and we come down again to the Eating Room. There Major Price comes to Tea constantly, and with him any Gentlemen that the King or Queen have invited for the Evening: and when Tea is over, he conducts them, and goes himself, to the Concert Room.

This is commonly about 9 o'clock.

From that time, if Mrs Schwellenberg is alone, I never quit her for a minute, till I come to my little supper, at near Eleven. If she has any body to play at Cards, I steal away for 5 minutes at a time, into my own Room, – which is close by, though not leading to, the Eating Room.

My supper time I spend in a little reading, when not too much tired; which is often the case.

Between Eleven and 12 my last summons usually takes place. Earlier and later occasionally.

Twenty minutes is the customary time then spent with the Queen: Half an Hour I believe is seldom exceeded.

I then come back, and after doing whatever I can to forward my Dress for the next morning, I go to Bed. – And to *sleep*, too, believe me, – the early rising, and a long Day's attention to new affairs and occupations, cause a fatigue so bodily, that nothing mental stands against it, and to sleep I fall the moment I have put out my Candle and laid down my Head.

Such is the Day to your F.B. in her new situation at Windsor: such, I mean, is its usual destination, and its intended course. I make it take now and then another Channel, but never stray far enough not to return to the original stream after a little meandering about and about it.

. . .

Tuesday, July 25. We were now to go to Kew, there to remain till Friday. Mrs Schwellenberg, Miss Planta[7] and myself travelled to Kew together.

I have two Rooms there; both small, and up two pair of stairs; but tidy and comfortable enough. Indeed all the apartments but the King's and Queen's, and one of Mrs Schwellenberg's, are small, dark and old fashioned. There are stair-Cases in every passage, and Passages to every Closet. I lost myself continually, only in passing from my own Room to the Queen's.

. . .

Thursday, July 27th. This being a Court Day, we went to Town. The Queen Dresses her Head at Kew, and puts on her Drawing Room apparel

7. Margaret Planta, English teacher and companion to the Princesses.

at St James's. Her new humble attendant dresses all at Kew, except Tippet[8] and long Ruffles, which she carries in Paper, to save from dusty Roads. I forgot to tell you, I believe, that at St James's I can never appear, even though I have nothing to do with the Drawing Room, except in a sacque.[9] 'Tis the Etiquette of my place.

Mrs Schwellenberg, Miss Planta and myself went about an Hour before the King and Queen. Mrs Schwellenberg went to the Queen's Dressing Room, to give orders about the Dress, Miss Planta went to the Princesses' Room for the same purpose, and I was shewn to mine, for *no* purpose, by Mrs Moore, the Necessary woman.[10]

Mine are two small Rooms, newly and handsomely furnished, one of which has a view of the Park over the stable yard, and the other only of the passage to the Park from St James's Street.

I had now the great satisfaction to find that there was a private stair-Case, from that same passage, that leads straight up to my apartments and also that I may appoint any friend to meet me in them on the Court Days. I hope never to be there again without making use of this privilege.

106. From Journal Letter to Susanna Phillips *2 August 1786*

[Windsor]

I went into my own Room for my Cloak, and, as usual, found Madame La Fîte just waiting for me. She was all emotion, – she seized my Hand, – 'Have you heard? – O mon Dieu! – O le bon Roi! – O Miss Burney! – What an horreur! – '[1]

I was very much startled, but soon ceased to wonder at her perturbation; – she had been in the Room with the Princess Elizabeth, and there heard, from Miss Goldsworthy,[2] that an attempt had just been made upon the life of the King! –

I was almost petrified with horror at the intelligence. If This King is not safe, – good, pious, beneficent as he is, – if His life is in danger, from his own Subjects, of violence, – What is to guard the Throne, and which way is a monarch to be secure? –

---

8. Cape covering the neck and shoulders.
9. Silk train.
10. In charge of cleaning and supplying services.

1. 'Oh my God! – Oh the good King! . . . a horror!'
2. Martha Caroline Goldsworthy, sub-governess to the younger Princes and Princesses.

Miss Goldsworthy had taken every possible precaution so to tell the matter to the Princess Elizabeth as least to alarm her, lest it might occasion a return of her spasms: but, fortunately, she cried so exceedingly that it was hoped the vent of her Tears would save her from those terrible convulsions.

Madame La Fîte had heard of the attempt only, not the particulars: but I was afterwards informed of them in the most interesting manner, – namely, how they were related to the Queen. And as the news-papers will have told you all else, I shall only and briefly tell that.

No information arrived here of the matter before his Majesty's return, at the usual hour in the afternoon, from the Levee. The Spanish Minister[3] had hurried off instantly to Windsor, and was in waiting, at Lady Charlotte Finch's,[4] to be ready to assure her Majesty of the King's safety, in case any report anticipated his return.

The Queen had the two Eldest Princesses, the Dutchess of Ancaster, and Lady Charlotte Bertie[5] with her when the King came in. He hastened up to her, with a countenance of striking vivacity, and said 'Here I am! – safe and well, – as you see! – but I have very narrowly escaped being stabbed! – '

His own conscious safety, and the pleasure he felt in thus personally shewing it to the Queen, made him not aware of the effect of so abrupt a communication; the Queen was seized with a consternation that at first almost stupified her, and, after a most painful silence, the first words she could articulate, were, in looking round at the Dutchess and Lady Charlotte, who had both burst into Tears, – 'I envy you! – I can't cry! – '

The two Princesses were for a little while in the same state; but the Tears of the Dutchess proved infectious, and they then wept even with violence.

The King, with the gayest good-humour, did his utmost to comfort them: and then gave a relation of the affair, with a calmness and unconcern that, had any one but himself been his Hero, would have been regarded as totally unfeeling.

You may have heard it wrong; I will concisely tell it right. His Carriage had just stopt at the Garden Door, at St James's, and he had just alighted from it, when a decently Dressed woman, who had been waiting for him some time, approached him with a Petition. It was rolled up, and had the normal superscription For the King's most excellent Majesty. She presented

---

3. Bernardo, Marquès del Campo.

4. Former governess to the Prince of Wales.

5. Princesses Charlotte and Augusta; Mary, Duchess of Ancaster, Mistress of the Robes to Queen Charlotte, and her daughter Lady Georgiana Charlotte Bertie. The Princesses were (from eldest) Charlotte, Augusta, Elizabeth, Mary, Sophia and Amelia.

it with her right hand, – and, at the same moment that the King bent forward to take it, she drew from it, with her left hand, a knife with which she aimed strait at his Heart! –

The fortunate awkwardness of taking the Instrument with the left Hand made her design perceived before it could be executed; – the King started back, scarce believing the testimony of his own Eyes; and the woman made a second thrust, which just touched his waistcoat, before he had time to prevent her; – and at that moment, one of the attendents, seeing her horrible intent, wrenched the knife from her Hand.

'Has she cut my Waistcoat?' cried he, in telling it, – 'look! for I have had no time to examine.'

Thank Heaven, however, the poor wretch had not gone quite so far. 'Though nothing,' added the King, in giving his relation, 'could have been sooner done, for there was nothing for her to go through, but a thin Linen and Fat!'

While the Guards and his own people now surrounded the King, the Assassin was seized by the populace, who were tearing her away, no doubt to fall the instant sacrifice of her murtherous purpose, when the King, the only calm and moderate person then present, called aloud to the Mob 'The poor Creature is mad! – do not hurt her! She has not hurt *me*!'

He then came forward, and shewed himself to all the people, declaring he was perfectly safe and unhurt; and then gave positive orders that the woman should be taken care of,[6] and went into the Palace, and had his Levee.

There is something in the whole of his behaviour upon this occasion, that strikes me as proof indisputable of a true and noble courage: for in a moment so extraordinary, an attack, in this Country, unheard of before, to settle so instantly that it was the effect of insanity, to feel no apprehension of private plot or latent conspiracy, to stay out, fearlessly, among his people, and so benevolently to see himself to the safety of one, who had raised her arm against his life, – these little traits, all impulsive, and therefore to be trusted, have given me an impression of respect and reverence to the intrinsic worth of their operator that I can never forget, and never think of but with fresh admiration.

If that love of prerogative, so falsely assigned, were true,[7] what an

6. The assailant, Margaret Nicholson, a servant woman, was judged insane and committed to St Mary of Bethlehem Hospital ('Bedlam'), where she died in 1828.

7. The King's political enemies maintained that he and his ministers aimed to extend the King's powers ('the royal prerogative') beyond their constitutional limit.

opportunity was here offered to exert it! had he instantly taken refuge in his Palace, ordered out his Guards, stopt every avenue to St James's, and issued his commands that every Individual present at this scene should be secured and examined – who would have dared murmur, or even blame such measures? –

The insanity of the woman has now fully been proved; but that noble confidence which gave that instant excuse for her, was then all his own.

Nor did he rest here; notwithstanding the excess of terror for his safety, and doubt of further mischief, with which all his family and all his household were seized, he still maintained the most chearful composure, and insisted upon walking on the Terrace, with no other attendant than his single Equery.

The poor Queen went with him, pale and silent, – the Princesses followed, scarce yet commanding their Tears.

In the Evening, just as usual, the King had his Concert: but it was an Evening of grief and horror to his family; nothing was listened to, scarce a word was spoken; the Princesses wept continually; – the Queen, still more deeply struck, could only, from time to time, hold out her hand to the King, and say '*I have you yet!*' –

When I went to the Queen at night, she scarce once opened her lips. Indeed I could not look at her without feeling the Tears ready to start into my Eyes. But I was very glad to hear again the voice of the King, though only from the next Apartment, and calling to one of his Dogs.

107. From Letter to Susanna Phillips *20 August 1786* [1]

When may I see you here Susan?

Let me *know*, for God's sake, lest I miss you also.[2] – If to you, alone, I shew myself in these dark colours, can you blame the plan that I have intentionally been forming, namely – *To wean myself from myself*; – *to lessen all my affections, – to Curb all my wishes, to deaden all my sensations?* – This design, my Susan, I formed so long ago as the first day my dear Father accepted my offered Appointment: I thought that what demanded a compleat New system of Life required, if attainable, a new set of feelings for all enjoyment of New prospects, and for lessening regrets at what were quitted – or lost: –

---

1. Copy in the hand of Charlotte Barrett.
2. FB had been away from Windsor and missed a visit of William and Frederica Locke.

Such being my primitive idea, merely from my grief of separation. – Imagine but how it was strengthened and confirmed when the interior of my position became known to me! – When I saw myself expected by Mrs Schwellenberg, not to be her Colleague but her dependent Deputy! not to be her visitor at my own option, but her Companion, her Humble Companion, at her own command!

This has given so new a character to the place I had accepted under such different auspices, that nothing but my horror of disappointing, – perhaps displeasing my dearest Father, has deterred me, from the moment that I made this mortifying discovery, from soliciting his leave to resign. But oh my Susan, – kind, good, indulgent, as he is to me, I have not the Heart so cruelly to thwart his Hopes, – his views, – his Happiness in the honours he conceived awaiting my so unsolicited appointment. – The Queen, too, is all sweetness, encouragement, and gracious goodness to me – and I cannot endure to complain to her of her old servant. You see, then, my situation; *Here I must remain*! – The die is cast; and that struggle is no more: – to keep off every other, – to support the loss of the dearest Friends, and best society, and bear, in exchange, the tyranny, the *exigeance*, the *ennui*, and attempted indignities of their greatest contrast, – this must be my constant endeavour.

Amongst my sources of unhappiness in this extraordinary case is, the very favour that, in any other, might counteract it, – namely, that of the Queen: for while in a manner the most attractive she seems inviting my confidence and deigning to wish my happiness, she redoubles my conflicts never to shock her with murmurs against one who, however to me noxious and persecuting, is to Her a faithful and truly devoted servant. This will prevent my ever having my distress and disturbance redressed; for they can never be disclosed. – Could I have, as my dear Father conceived, all the Time to myself, my Friends, my Leisure, or my own Occupations, that is not devoted to my official duties, how different would be my feelings, how far more easily accomodated to my privations and sacrifices! Little does the Queen know the slavery I must either resist or endure. And so frightful is hostility, that I know not which part is hardest to perform.

What erasures! Can you read me? I blot, and rewrite – yet know not how to alter or what to send. I so fear to alarm your tender kindness.

108. From Journal Letter to Susanna Phillips *29 November 1786*

The Queen in looking over some Books while I was in waiting one morning, met with *The Mysterious Mother*, Mr Walpole's Tragedy: which he printed at Strawberry Hill, and gave to a few friends, but has never suffered to be published.[1] I expressed, by looks, I suppose, my wishes, for she most graciously offered to lend it me. I had long desired to read it, from so well knowing, and so much liking the Author: and he had promised me, if I would come a second time to Strawberry Hill,[2] that I should have it: all excursions of that sort being now totally over for me! – I was particularly glad of this only chance for gratifying my curiosity.

I had had it in my possession some Days, without reading it; – I had named it to Mr and Mrs Smelt, and they were eager to see it: the loan, however, being private, and the Book, having been lent to her Majesty by Lord Harcourt, I knew not under what restrictions, I could not produce it without leave: This morning I asked, and obtained it; and promised to my two Guests, who dined with me, that as soon as the party broke up after Tea, it should be forth coming.

We waited, however, in vain to be alone: neither Mr De Guiffardiere nor Mr De Luc[3] were summoned, and neither of them seemed disposed to retire to their own affairs. They are both, nevertheless, so high in favour, that I ventured to extend my Licence to them, and proposed concluding our Evening with my Tragedy.

Mr De Guiffardiere seemed delighted with the proposal: Mr De Luc made a wry face, and declared *he loved not all that pretence to unhappiness*; – but his objections were over-ruled by a large majority, and I brought forth the Play.

The opening of the play contains a description of *superstitious fear* extremely well, and feelingly, and naturally depicted: it begins, too, in an uncommon style, promising of interest and novelty: – but my praise will soon be ended! swallowed up all in the heaviest censure.

---

1. FB had met Horace Walpole, writer, wit and connoisseur, in 1783. He had printed fifty copies of *The Mysterious Mother* at his private press at Strawberry Hill, his seat in Twickenham, in 1768, for his friends. The announcement of another edition printed by James Dodsley in 1781 forestalled unauthorized reprints, and Walpole decided not to publish, distributing these copies among further acquaintances, including Lord Harcourt, who lent his to the Queen.
2. FB had visited the famous Gothic castle Strawberry Hill in September 1785.
3. The Revd Charles de Guiffardière, teacher of French to the Princesses, and Jean André de Luc, Reader to the Queen.

Dreadful was the whole! truly dreadful! a story of so much horror, from attrocious and voluntary guilt, never did I hear![4] Mrs Smelt and myself heartily regretted that it had come in our way, and mutually agreed that we felt ourselves *ill-used* in having ever heard it. She protested she would never do herself so much wrong as to acknowledge she had suffered the hearing so wicked a tale, and declared she would drive it from her thoughts as she would the recollection of what-ever was most baneful to them.

For myself, I felt a sort of indignant aversion rise fast and warm in my mind against the wilful Author of a story so horrible: all the entertainment and pleasure I had received from Mr Walpole seemed extinguished by this lecture, which almost made me regard him as the Patron of the vices he had been pleased to record.

Mr De Luc had escaped from the latter part of this hateful Tragedy, protesting, afterwards, he saw what was coming, and would not stay to hear it out.

Mr Smelt confessed, with me, it was a lasting Disgrace to Mr Walpole to have chosen such a subject, and thought him deserving even of punishment for such a painting of Human wickedness: and the more, as the story through-out was forced and improbable.

But the whole of all that could be said on this subject was summed up in one sentence by Mr Guiffardiere, which, for its masterly strength and justice brought to my mind my ever revered Dr Johnson. – 'Mr Walpole,' cried he, 'has chosen a plan of which nothing can equal the abomination – – but the absurdity!' –

And now I think you have enough of it! and when I returned it to the Queen, I professed myself earnest in my hopes that she would never deign to cast her Eye upon it.

109. From Journal Letter to Susanna Phillips *15 August 1787*

In the afternoon, while I was drinking Coffee with Mrs Schwellenberg, – or, rather, *looking at it*, since I rarely swallow any, – Her Majesty came into the Room, and, soon after a little German discourse with Mrs Schwellenberg, told me Mrs Siddons had been ordered to the Lodge, to read a Play, and desired I would receive her in my Room.

I felt a little queer in the office; I had only seen her twice or thrice in large

4. Set in the early days of the Reformation, its theme is double incest.

Assemblies, and never had been introduced to her, nor spoken with her. However, in this dead and tame life I now lead, such an interview was by no means undesireable.

I had just got to the bottom of the stairs, when she entered the Message-Gallery. I took her into the Tea Room, and endeavoured to make amends for former distance and taciturnity, by an open and chearful reception: I had heard from sundry people, in *old Days*, that she wished to make the Acquaintance; but I thought it, then, one of too conspicuous a sort for the quietness I had so much difficulty to preserve in my ever encreasing connections. Here all was changed; I received her by the Queen's commands, and was perfectly well inclined to reap some pleasure from the meeting. –

But – now that we came so near, – I was much disappointed in my expectations. I know not if my dear Fredy has met with her in private, but I fancy approximation is not highly in her favour. I found her the Heroine of a Tragedy, – sublime, elevated, and solemn. In Face and person, truly noble and commanding; in manners, quiet and stiff; in voice, deep and dragging; and in conversation, formal, sententious, calm, and dry. –

I expected her to have been all that is interesting; the delicacy and sweetness with which she seizes every opportunity to strike and to captivate upon the Stage, had persuaded me that her mind was formed with that peculiar susceptibility that, in different modes, must give equal powers to attract and to delight in common life. But I was very much mistaken; as a stranger, I must have admired her noble appearance and beautiful countenance, and have regretted that nothing in her conversation kept pace with their promise; and, as a celebrated actress, I had still only to do the same.

Whether Fame and success have spoiled her, – in making her imagine That to *speak* alone is enough, from Her, to *charm*, or whether she only possesses the skill of representing and embellishing materials with which she is furnished by others, I know not. But still I remain disappointed.

She was scarcely seated, and a little general discourse begun, before she told me – all at once – that *There was no Part she had ever so much wished to Act as that of Cecilia.* –

I made some small little acknowledgement, – and hurried to ask when she had seen Sir Joshua Reynolds –, Miss Palmer, – and others with whom I knew her acquainted.

The Play she was to read was 'the Provoked Husband.'[1] She appeared

---

1. By Sir John Vanbrugh and Colley Cibber (1728).

neither alarmed nor elated by her summons, but calmly to look up it as a thing of course from her celebrity.

She left me to go to Lady Harcourt, through whose interest she was brought hither.

110. From Journal Letter to Susanna Phillips *17 September 1787*

On the Evening that they left me – my ever kind Mrs Delany carried me, with Miss Port, to Dr Herschall's.[1] Mme La Fîte said, afterwards, that nothing remaining *upon Earth* good enough to console me for *Les Lockes and Mrs Phillips*, I was fain to *travel to the Moon* for comfort. I think it was very well said.

And, indeed, I really found myself much pleased with the little excursion. Dr Herschall is a delightful Man, so unassuming, with his great knowledge, so willing to dispense it to the ignorant, and so chearful and easy in his general manners, that were he no Genius, it would be impossible not to remark him as a pleasing and sensible man.

I was equally pleased with his Sister, whom I had wished to see very much, for her great celebrity in her Brother's Science. She is very little, very gentle, very modest, and very ingenuous: and her manners are those of a Person unhackneyed and unawed by the World, yet desirous to meet, and to return its smiles. I love not the philosophy that braves it: this Brother and Sister seem gratified with its favour, at the same time that their own pursuit is all-sufficient to them without it.

I enquired of Miss Herschall if she was still comet-hunting, or content now with the Moon? The Brother answered that *He* had the charge of the Moon, but he left to his Sister to sweep the Heavens for Comets.

Their manner of working together is most ingenious and curious. While he makes his observations without Doors, he has a method of communicating them to his Sister so immediately, that she can instantly commit them to paper, with the precise moment in which they are made. By this means, he loses not a Minute, when there is any thing particularly worth observing, in writing it down, but can still proceed, yet still have his accounts and calculations exact. The methods he has contrived to facilitate this commerce

1. William and Frederica Locke and Susanna Phillips had visited FB at Windsor from 10 to 17 September. Sir William Herschel, the eminent astronomer, lived at Slough with his sister Caroline. He was already famous for his discovery of the planet Uranus in 1781.

I have not the terms to explain though his simple manner of shewing them made me fully, at the time, comprehend them.

The Night, very unfortunately, was dark, and I could not see the Moon with the famous new Telescope.[2] I saw Saturn, however, and his Satellites, very distinctly, and their appearance was very beautiful.

III. From Journal Letter to Susanna Phillips and Frederica Locke *November 1787*

Tuesday, 27th. I had a terrible journey indeed to Town, Mrs Schwellenberg finding it expedient to have the Glass down on my side, whence there blew in a sharp wind, which so painfully attacked my Eyes, that they were inflamed even before we arrived in Town. Mr De Luc and Miss Planta both looked uneasy, but no one durst speak; and for me, 'twas among the evils that I can always best bear. Yet, before the Evening, I grew so ill, that I could not propose going to Chelsea,[1] lest I should be utterly unfitted for Thursday's Drawing Room.

The next Day, however, I received a consolation that has been some ease to my Mind ever since. My dear Father spent the Evening with me, and was so incensed at the state of my Eyes, which were now as piteous to behold as to feel, and at the relation of their usage, that he charged me, another time, to draw up my Glass in defiance of all opposition and to abide by all consequences, since my place was wholly immaterial when put in competition with my Health.

I was truly glad of this *permission to rebel*; and it has given me an *internal hardiness* in all similar assaults, that has at least relieved my Mind from the terror of giving mortal offence, where most I owe implicit obedience, should provocation overpower my capacity of forbearance.

We wrote jointly to our good and dear Mr Twining; though I was so blind, that my Pen went almost its own way. And for the rest of the Evening, my dear Father read me papers, Letters, manuscripts innumerable.

On the Thursday I was obliged to Dress just as if nothing was the matter. –

The next Day, when we assembled to return to Windsor, Mr De Luc was

2. A reflecting telescope of 20 feet focal length. Herschel was constructing a much larger instrument of 40 feet focal length.

1. Where her father had rooms as resident organist of Chelsea College.

in a real consternation at sight of my Eyes; and I saw an indignant glare at my Coadjutrix that could scarce content itself without being understood. Miss Planta ventured not at such a glance, but a most indignant whisper broke out, as we were descending the stairs, expressive of horrour against the same poor person – *poor* person, indeed, to exercise a power productive only of abhorence to those that view, as well as those that feel it! –

Some business of Mrs Schwellenberg's occasioned a delay of the journey, and we all retreated back: and when I returned to my Room, Miller, the old head Housemaid, came to me, with a little neat tin saucepan in her Hand, saying 'Pray, ma'am, use this for your Eyes, 'tis Milk and butter, *such as I used to make for Madame Haggerdorn*, when she Travelled in the Winter with Mrs Schwellenberg.'

Good Heavens! – I really shuddered, – when she added, that all that poor woman's misfortunes with her Eyes, which, from inflamation after inflamation grew nearly blind, were attributed by herself to these journies, in which she was forced to have the Glass down at her side, in all Weathers, though so tender in that tender part, and frequently *behind* her also! –

Upon my word this account of my Predecessor was the least exhilarating intelligence I could receive! Goter[2] told me, afterwards, that all the servants in the House had remarked I *was going just the same way*! –

Miss Planta presently ran into my Room, to say she had hopes we should travel without this amiable being – and she had left me but a moment, when Mrs Stainforth[3] succeeded her, exclaiming 'O for God's sake – don't leave her behind! – for God's sake, Miss Burney, take her with you!'

'Twas impossible not to laugh at these opposite interests, both, from agony of fear, breaking through all restraint.

Soon after, however, we all assembled again, and got into the Coach. Mr De Luc, who was my vis à vis,[4] instantly pulled up the Glass.

'Put down that Glass!' was the immediate order.

He affected not to hear her; and began conversing. She enraged quite tremendously, calling aloud to be obeyed without delay. He looked compassionately at me, and shrugged his Shoulders, and said 'But – ma'am –'

'Do it, Mr De Luc, when I tell you! I *will* have it! – when you been too cold, you might bear it! –'

'It is not for *me*, Ma'am – but poor Miss Burney –'

---

2. Elizabeth Goter, FB's maidservant at Court.
3. Elizabeth Stainforth, Housekeeper at the Queen's House (Buckingham House).
4. Literally, face to face, i.e. sitting opposite.

'O, poor Miss Burney might bear it the same! – put it down, Mr De Luc! – without, I will get out! – Put it down, when I tell you! – It is *my* Coach! – I will have it selfs! – I might go alone in it! – or with one – or with what you call nobody, when I please!'

Frightened for good Mr De Luc, and the more for being much obliged to him, I now interfered, and begged him to let down the Glass. Very reluctantly he complied, and I lent back in the coach, and held up my Muff to my Eyes.

What a Journey ensued! – To see that Face when lighted up with Fury, is a sight for Horrour! – I was glad to exclude it by my Muff.

Miss Planta alone attempted to speak. I did not think it incumbent on me to *make the agreable* thus used; I was therefore wholly dumb: for not a word not an apology, not one expression of being sorry for what I suffered, was uttered. The most horrible ill humour, violence, and rudeness, were all that were shewn. Mr De Luc was too much provoked to take his usual methods of passing all off by constant talk: and as I had never seen him venture to appear provoked before, I felt a great obligation to his kindness.

When we were about half way, we stopt to water the Horses. He then again pulled up the Glass, as if from absence. A voice of fury exclaimed 'Let it down! without I won't go!'

'I am sure,' cried he, 'all *Mrs Luc's* plants will be killed by this Frost! – '

For the Frost was very severe indeed.

Then he proposed my changing places with Miss Planta, who sat opposite Mrs Schwellenberg, and consequently on the sheltered side. 'Yes!' cried Mrs Sc. – 'Miss Burney might sit here, and so she ought!' –

I told her, briefly, I was always sick, in riding back wards.

'O, ver well! when you don't like it! – what did the poor Haggerdorn bear it! – when the blood was all running down from her Eyes! – '

This was too much! – '*I* must take, then,' I cried, 'the more warning!' And after that, I spoke not a Word.

I ruminated all the rest of the way upon my dear Father's recent charge and permission – I was upon the point continually of availing myself of both: but alas! – I felt the deep disappointment I should give him – and I felt the most cruel repugnance to owe a resignation to a quarrel.

These reflections powerfully forbid the rebellion to which this unequalled arrogance and cruelty excited me: – and, after revolving them again and again, I – *accepted a bit of Cake* which she suddenly offered me as we reached Windsor, – and determined, since I submitted to my monastic destiny from motives my serious thoughts deemed right, I would not be prompted to oppose it from mere feelings of resentment to one who, strictly, merited only contempt.

112. From Journal Letter to Susanna Phillips *January 1788*

I spent one Evening at my dearest Mrs Delany's, with Lady Bute and Mrs Ord: and Miss Port shewed me a news paper paragraph which had been lent her, for that purpose, by Colonel Goldsworthy.[1] He is a collecter of these Diurnal squibs. – Lo, and Behold it! –

'Miss Burney, we are told, is directing her thoughts to the Composition of a Novel, of which a *married Woman* is the Heroine. As her aim is always moral, this production will no doubt prove extremely useful: for though the fair sex do not appear to want instruction with regard to their conduct in a single state, it is to be regretted that too many of them are deficient in that affection and goodness which constitute the chief part of conjugal duty.'

There! *ye fair married Dames*! what say ye to this? – do you think me qualified for this office? or will you say 'Go and First make trial of yourself? – '

I seized the paper, and bid her say That as it was the first I had heard of the Design, I must beg to keep it, as a memorandum for its execution.

113. From Journal Letter to Susanna Phillips *February 1788*

February 13th. The Trial, so long impending, of Mr Hastings, opened to Day.[1] The Queen, yesterday, asked me if I wished to be present at the beginning, or had rather take another Day. I was greatly obliged by her condescendsion, and preferred the opening. I thought it would give me a general view of the Court, and the manner of proceeding, and that I might read, hereafter, the speeches and evidence.

1. Colonel Philip Goldsworthy, Equerry to the King and Member of Parliament, and brother of Martha. The newspaper item is an example of the kind of false rumours that circulated about FB while she was sequestered at Court.

1. Warren Hastings, Governor General of India, was brought to trial in Westminster Hall on charges of maladministration and abuse of power. The trial was engineered by Hastings's personal enemies in the East India Company together with the Parliamentary opposition led by Charles James Fox; Fox, Edmund Burke and Sheridan were the principal managers of the impeachment proceedings. The trial would drag on for seven years, when Hastings was completely acquitted. As a loyal subject of the King, FB sympathized entirely with Hastings and the King's government under William Pitt which supported him.

She then told me she had 6 Tickets, from Sir Peter Burrel, the Grand Chamberlain, for every Day: that 3 were for his Box, and 3 for his Gallery. She asked me who I would go with, and promised me a Box Ticket not only for myself, but my Companion. Nor was this consideration all she shewed me, for she added that as I might naturally wish my Father, she would have me send him my other Ticket.

I thanked her very gratefully, and, after Dinner, went to St Martin's Street: but all there was embarrassing; my Father could not go; he was averse to be present at the Trial, and he was a little lame from a fall: in the end, I sent an Express to Hammersmith, to desire Charles to come to me the next morning by 8 o'Clock.[2]

I was very sorry not to have my Father, as he had been named by the Queen; but I was glad to have Charles, upon such an occasion, for many reasons.

I told her Majesty, at Night, the step I had ventured to take, and she was perfectly content with it. 'But I must trouble you,' she said, 'with Miss Gomme,[3] – who has no other way to go.'

I assured her I should be very happy in her for a Companion. This morning, she dispensed with all attendance from me, after her first Dressing, that I might haste away. Mrs Schwellenberg was fortunately well enough to take the whole Duty, and the sweet Queen not only hurried me off, but sent me some Cakes from her own Breakfast Table, that I might carry them in my pocket, lest I should have no time for Eating before I went.

Charles was not in Time, but we all did well in the end. We got to Westminster Hall between 9 and 10 o'clock; and as I know my dear Susan, like myself, was never at any Trial, I will give some account of the place and arrangements: Whether the description be new to her, or old, my partial Fredy will not blame it.

The Grand Chamberlain's Box is in the centre of the upper end of the Hall; there we sat, Miss Gomme and myself, immediately behind the Chair placed for Sir Peter Burrel.

To the left, on the same level, were the Green Benches for the House of Commons, which occupied a third of the upper end of the Hall, and the whole of the left side; – To the right of us, on the same level, was the Grand Chamberlain's Gallery.

The left side opposite to the Green Benches for the Commons, was appropriated to the Peeresses, and Peer's Daughters.

2. Her brother Charles kept a school there.
3. Jane Gomm, English teacher to the younger Princesses.

The Bottom of the Hall, contained the Royal Family's Box and the Lord High Steward's. Above which was a large Gallery, appointed for receiving Company with Peer's Tickets.

A Gallery also was run along the left side of the Hall, above the Green Benches, which is called the Duke of Newcastle's Box. The center of which was railed off into a separate Apartment for the reception of the Queen, and 4 eldest Princesses, who were there *incognito*, not chusing to appear in state, and in their own Box.

Along the right side of the Hall, ran another Gallery, over the seats of the Peeresses; and this was divided into Boxes for various people: the Lord Chamberlain, not the *Great* Chamberlain, the surveyor, architect, etc. –

So much for all the raised Buildings.

Now for the disposition of the Hall itself, or Ground.

In the middle of it was placed a large Table, and at the Head of it the seat for the Chancellor, and round it seats for the Judges, the Masters in Chancery, the Clerks, and all who belonged to the Law.

The upper end, and the right side of the Room was allotted to the Peers, in their Robes.

The left side to the Bishops and Archbishops.

Immediately below the Great Chamberlain's Box was the Place allotted for the Prisoner! – On his right side was a Box for his own Counsel, on his left, the Box for the Managers, or Committee, for the Prosecution. – And these 3, most important of all divisions in the Hall, were all directly adjoining to where I was seated. –

Almost the moment I entered, I was spoken to by a Lady I did not recollect, but found, afterwards, to be Lady Claremont,[4] and this proved very agreeable, for she took Sir Peter's place, and said she would occupy it till he claimed it: and then, when just before me, she named to me all the Boxes, all the order of the Buildings, and all the Company, pointing out every distinguished Power, and most obligingly desiring me to ask her any questions I wanted to have solved, as she knew, she said, '*All those Creatures* that filled the Green Benches, looking so little like Gentlemen, and so much like Hair-Dressers. –' These were the Commons. In truth, she did the honours of the Hall to me, with as much good-nature and good breeding, as if I had been a foreigner of distinction, – to whom she had dedicated her time and attention.

4. Frances, Lady Clermont.

My Acquaintance with her had been made, formerly, at Mrs Vesey's.[5]

The Business did not begin till near 12 o'clock. The opening to the whole then took place by the entrance of the *Managers of the Prosecution*; – all the Company were already long in their Boxes or Galleries.

I shuddered, – and drew involuntarily back, – when, as the Doors were flying open, I saw Mr Burke, as Head of the Committee, make his solemn entry; – he held a scroll in his Hand, and walked alone, his Brow knit with corroding Care and deep labouring Thought: – a Brow how different to that which had proved so alluring to my warmest admiration when first I met him! – so highly as he had been my favourite, so captivating as I had found his manners and conversation, in our first Acquaintance, – and so much as I had owed to his zeal and kindness to me and my affairs in its progress, – how did I grieve to behold him now, the cruel Prosecuter – such to me he appeared – of an injured and innocent man! – Mr Fox followed next, – Mr Sheridan, Mr Wyndham, Messieurs Anstruther, Gray, Adam, Michael Angelo Taylor, Pelham, Col. North, Mr Frederick Montagu, Sir Gilbert Elliot, General Burgoigne, Dudley Long,[6] &c.

They were all named over to me by Lady Claremont, or I should not have recollected, even those of my Acquaintance, from the shortness of my Sight.

When the Committee Box was filled, the House of Commons at large took their seats on their Green Benches, which stretched, as I have said, along the whole left side of the Hall, and, taking in a third of the upper End, joined to the Great Chamberlain's Box, from which nothing separated them but a partition of about 2 foot in height.

Then began the Procession, – the Clerks entering first, then the Lawyers, according to their Rank, and the Peers, Bishops, and officers, all in their Coronation Robes, – concluding with the Princes of the Blood, – Prince William, son to the Duke of Gloucester, coming first, – then the Dukes of Cumberland, Gloucester, and York, then the Prince of Wales;[7] – and the whole ending by the Chancellor with his train borne.

They then all took their seats.

A Serjeant at Arms arose, and commanded silence in the Court, on pain of imprisonment.

5. Elizabeth Vesey, bluestocking hostess.
6. Sheridan, Windham, John Anstruther, Charles Grey, William Adam, Taylor, Thomas Pelham, George Augustus North, Montagu, Elliot, John Burgoyne and Long were all opposition Members of Parliament and adherents of Fox.
7. Later George IV.

Then some other officer, in a loud voice, called out, as well as I can recollect, words to this purpose. 'Warren Hastings Esquire, come forth! – Answer to the Charges brought against you; save your Bail, or forfeit your recognizance! –'

Indeed I trembled at these words, – and hardly could keep my place when I found Mr Hastings was being brought to the Bar; – he came forth from some place immediately under the Great Chamberlain's Box, and was preceded by Sir Francis Molyneux, Gentleman Usher of the Black Rod; and at each side of him walked his Bail, Messrs Sulivan and Sumner.[8]

The moment he came in sight, – which was not for full 10 minutes after his aweful summons, he made a low Bow to the Chancellor and Court facing him. I saw not his Face, as he was directly under me. He moved on, slowly, and, I think, supported between his two Bails, to the opening of his own Box, – there, lower still, he Bowed again; – and then, advancing to the Bar, he leant his Hands upon it, and dropt on his knees, but a voice, in the same moment, proclaiming he had leave to rise, he stood up almost instantaneously, and a third time, profoundly Bowed to the Court.

What an aweful moment this for such a man! – a man fallen from such height of power, to a situation so humiliating, – from the almost unlimitted command of so large a part of the Eastern World, to be cast at the feet of his Enemies, – of the great Tribunal of his Country – and of the Nation at large, assembled thus in a Body to try and to Judge him! – Could even his Prosecutors, at that moment, look on, – and not shudder, at least, – if they did not blush? –

The *Cryer*, I think it was, made, in a loud and hollow voice, a public proclamation, 'That Warren Hastings Esquire, late Governor General of Bengal, was now on his Trial, for High Crimes and misdemeanours, with which he was charged by the Commons of Great Britain; and that all Persons whatsoever who had aught to alledge against him, were now to stand forth.'

A general silence followed, and the Chanceller, Lord Thurlow, now made his speech. I will give it you to the best of my power from memory, – the newspapers have printed it far less acurately than I have retained it, though I am by no means exact or secure.

'Warren Hastings, – You are now brought into this Court to answer to

---

8. Richard Sulivan, Member of Parliament, and George Sumner, Member of Parliament and son of William Brightwell Sumner, an old friend of Hastings who had been a member of the Bengal council.

the charges brought against you by the Knights, Esquires, Burgesses, and Commons of Great Britain: charges now standing only as allegations, by *them* to be legally proved, or, by *you*, to be disproved. Bring forth your Answers and defence with that seriousness, respect, and truth, due to Accusers so respectable. Time has been allowed you for preparation, proportioned to the intricacies in which the transactions are involved, and to the remote distances whence your documents may have been searched and required. You will still be allowed Bail, for the better forwarding your defence, and whatever you can require will still be yours, of Time, witnesses, and all things else you may hold necessary. This is not granted you as Any indulgence; it is entirely your due; it is the privilege which every British subject has a right to claim, – and which is due to every one who is brought before this high Tribunal.'

This speech, uttered in a calm, equal, solemn manner, and in a voice mellow and penetrating, with Eyes keen and black, yet softened into some degree of tenderness while fastened full upon the Prisoner, – This speech, its occasion, its portent, and its object, had an effect upon every Hearer of producing the most respectful attention, and, out of the Committee Box at least, the strongest emotions in the cause of Mr Hastings.

Again Mr Hastings made the lowest Reverence to the Court, and, leaning over the Box, answered – with much agitation, through evident efforts to suppress it, – 'My Lords, – Impressed, – deeply impressed – I come before Your Lordships, – equally confident in my own integrity, and in the Justice of the Court before which I am to clear it.'

Impressed, and *deeply* impressed too, was my mind by this short, yet comprehensive speech: and all my best wishes for his clearance and redress, rose warmer than ever in my Heart.

A general silence again ensued; and then one of the Lawyers opened the Cause. He began by reading, from an immense roll of Parchment, the general Charges against Mr Hastings; but he read in so monotonous a Chaunt that nothing more could I hear, or understand, than now and then the name of Warren Hastings.

During this reading, to which I vainly sent all my attention, Mr Hastings, finding it, I presume, equally impossible to hear a word, began to cast his Eyes around the House: and, having taken a survey of all in front and at the sides, he turned about, and looked up — pale looked his Face, – pale, ill, and altered! – I was much affected by the sight of that dreadful harrass which was written on his Countenance; – had I looked at him without restraint, it could not have been without Tears. – I felt shocked, too, –

shocked and ashamed to be seen by him in that place, – I had wished to be present, from an eminent interest in the business, joined to a firm confidence in his powers of defence; but *His* Eyes were not those I wished to meet in Westminster Hall! – I called upon Miss Gomme and Charles to assist me in looking another way, and in conversing with me as I turned aside; and I kept as much aloof as possible, till he had taken his survey, and placed himself again in front. Whether he saw me or not I cannot be certain; I rather believe he did: but I was the more anxious to avoid him, because I could not endure he should suppose I shirked acknowledging his Acquaintance in this Hour of suspence, yet thought it utterly improper to Courtsie to him in such a situation, where the Eyes of so many hundred people were following and watching all his motions.

From this time, however, he frequently looked round, and I was soon without a doubt that he must see me: – Not very desireable to me, therefore, was a civility I next received from one of the managers, – one, too, placed in the front of the Committee, and on a line with the Prisoner; – it was Mr Frederick Montagu, who recognized, and Bowed to me. –

He is a most intimate friend of Mrs Delany, and a man of excellence in all parts of his Character, save politics, – and there he is always against the administration! Why will any man of principle join any party? – why not be open to all, yet belong to none? –

Mr Fred: Montagu looked so gloomy and uncomfortable, that but for the assistance of Lady Claremont, I should not have recollected him: at Mrs Delany's he had seemed all gaiety and good-humour! – Lady Claremont herself remarked to me 'that Mr Montagu looked as if engaged in a business he did not approve. –' If so, – doubly is he censurable for adherance to opposition.

I hope Mr Hastings did not see us; – but, in a few minutes more, while this reading was still continued, I perceived Sir Joshua Reynolds in the midst of the Committee! – he, at the same moment, saw me, also, and not only Bowed, but smiled and nodded, with his usual good-humour and intimacy: making, at the same time, a sign to his Ear, by which I understood he had no Trumpet: whether he had forgotten, or lost it, I know not.

I would rather have answered all this dumb shew any where else, as my last ambition was that of being noticed from such a Box. I again entreated aid in turning away; but Miss Gomme, who is a friend of Sir Gilbert Elliot, one of the managers, and an ill wisher, for his sake, to the opposite Cause, would only laugh, and ask why I should *not* be owned by them? –

I did not, however, like it; – but had no choice, from my near situation:

and, in a few seconds, I had again a Bow, – and a profound one: – and again, very ridiculously, I was obliged to enquire of Lady Claremont who my own Acquaintance might be! *Mr Richard Burke Senior*, she answered. He is Brother of the Great – Great in defiance of all draw-backs – Edmund Burke.

Notice from *any* Burke was particularly distressing to me at such a time; but I courtsied, and we were both satisfied.

I now redoubled my diligence to cast my Eyes every other way, from a serious apprehension that I might be recollected by the Two Leaders in the Prosecution, Mr Burke and Mr Sheridan: and I could not have offended either of them by declining their notice, – which heretofore I had so much wished, – nor could I endure to have Mr Hastings perceive me associate with them.

I assure you it was a very painful feeling; – I had better have been placed in any other part of the Hall.

Another Lawyer now arose, and read – so exactly in the same manner, that it was utterly impossible to discover even whether it was a Charge, or an answer! –

Such reading as this, you may well suppose, set every body pretty much at their ease: and, but for the interest I took, in looking from time to time at Mr Hastings, and watching his Countenance, I might as well have been away. He seemed composed, after the first half Hour, and calm. But he looked with a species of indignant contempt towards the Box of his accusers, that could not, I think, have been worn, had his defence been doubtful. Many there are who fear for him; – for me, I own myself wholly confident in his acquital.

. . .

[16 February] The second time that the Queen, who saw my wishes, indulged me with one of her Tickets and a permission of absence for the Trial, was to hear Mr Burke; for whom my curiosity and my interest stood the highest.

. . .

At length, the Peer's procession closed, the Prisoner was brought in, and Mr Burke began his speech.

It was the second Day of his Harangue; the first I had not been able to attend.

All I had heard of his eloquence, and all I had conceived of his great abilities, was more than answered by his performance. Nervous, clear, and striking, was almost all that he uttered; the main business, indeed, of his coming forth, was frequently neglected, and not seldom wholly lost; but his excursions were so fanciful and so entertaining, and so ingenious, that no miscellaneous Hearer, like myself, would blame them. It is true, he was unequal; but his inequality produced an effect which, in so long a speech, was perhaps preferable to greater consistency, since though it lost attention in its falling off, it recovered it with additional energy by some ascent unexpected and wonderful. When he narrated, he was easy, flowing, and natural; when he declaimed, energetic, warm, and brilliant; the sentiments he interspersed were as nobly conceived as they were highly coloured; his satire had a poignancy of wit that made it as entertaining as it was penetrating; his allusions and quotations, as far as they were English and within my reach, were apt and ingenious, and the wild and sudden flights of his Fancy, bursting forth from his creative Imagination in Language fluent, forcible, and varied, had a charm for my Ear and my attention wholly new and perfectly irresistible.

Were talents such as these excercised in the service of Truth, unbiassed by party and prejudice, how could we sufficiently applaud their exalted Possessor? But though frequently he made me tremble by his strong and horrible representations, his violence recovered me, by stigmatizing his assertions with personal ill-will, and designing illiberality. Yet, at times, I confess, with all that I felt, wished, and thought, concerning Mr Hastings, the whirlwind of his eloquence nearly drew me into its vortex.

I give no particulars of the speech, because they will all be printed.

. . .

I was now most eager to depart from a circumstance that made me feel infinitely awkward.

Mr Burke himself was just come forward, to speak to a lady a little below me; in a minute, however, Mr Burke himself saw me; – and he Bowed with the most marked civility of manner; my Courtsie was the most ungrateful; distant and cold; – I could not do otherwise; so hurt I felt to see him the Head of such a Cause, so impossible I found it to utter one word of admiration for a performance whose nobleness was so disgraced by its tenour, and so conscious was I the whole time, that at such a moment to say nothing must seem almost an affront, that I hardly knew which way to look, or what to do with myself. How happy, and how proud, would any distinction from such a man have made me, had he been engaged in a pursuit of which I could have thought as highly as I think of the abilities with which he has conducted it? –

. . .

[22 February] And now for my Third Westminster Hall, which, by the Queen's own indulgent Tickets and order, was with dear Charlotte and Sarah.

. . .

Mr Fox spoke 5 Hours! and with a violence that did not make me forget what I had heard of his being in such a *fury*. But I shall never give any account of these speeches, as they will all be printed: I shall only say a word of the speakers, as far as relates to my own feelings about them: and that briefly will be to say that I adhere to Mr Burke, whose oratorical powers appeared to me far more Gentlemanlike, scholar-like, and fraught with Genius, than those of Mr Fox. It may be I am prejudiced by old kindnesses of Mr Burke, – and it may be, that the Countenance of Mr Fox may have turned me against him; for it struck me to have a boldness in it quite hard and offensive: however, 'tis little matter how much my judgement in this point may err: with you, my dear Friends, I have nothing further to do, than simply to give it: – and even should it be wrong, it will not very essentially injure you in your politics.

. . .

Again, on the Fourth Time of my attendance at Westminster Hall, honest James was my Esquire.

. . .

I then began upon Mr Burke; but I must give you a very brief summary of *my* speech, as it could only be intelligible at full length from your having heard *his*: I told him [William Windham], that his *opening* had struck me with the highest admiration of his powers, from the eloquence, the imagination, the fire, the diversity of expression, and the ready flow of language, with which he seemed gifted, in a most superior manner, for any and every purpose to which rhetorick could lead. 'And when he came to his two narratives,' – I continued, – 'when he related the particulars of those dreadful murders,[9] – he interested, – he engaged, – he at last over powered

9. On 16 February Burke implicated Hastings in two plots: by the Nawab of Bengal, Mir Jaffier, to murder the crown prince of the Grand Mogul, and by Jaffier's son-in-law, Cossim Ali Khan,

me, – I felt my Cause lost! – I could hardly keep on my seat, – my Eyes dreaded a single glance towards a man so accused as Mr Hastings, – I wanted to sink on the floor, that they might be saved so painful a sight, – I had no hope he could clear himself, – not another wish in his favour remained! – But, when from this narration, Mr Burke proceeded to his own comments, – and Declamation, – and when the charges of rapacity, cruelty, tyranny, were general, and made with all the violence of personal detestation, and continued and aggravated, without any further fact or illustration, – then there appeared more of study, than of truth, more of invective, than of justice, – and, in short, so little of proof, to so much of passion, – that, in a very short time, I began to lift up my Head, – my seat was no longer uneasy, – my Eyes were indifferent which way they looked, or what object caught them; and, before I was myself aware of the declension of Mr Burke's powers over my feelings – I found myself a mere spectator in a public place, and looking all around it, with my Opera Glass in my Hand! – '

I next began upon Mr Fox; and I ran through the general matter of *his* speech, with such observations as had occurred to me in hearing it. His violence, I said, had that sort of monotony that seemed to result from its being factitious; and I felt less pardon for that, than for any extravagance in Mr Burke, whose excesses seemed at least to be *unaffected*, and, if they spoke against his judgement, spared his probity. Mr Fox appeared to have no such excuse; he looked all good humour and negligent ease, the instant before he began a speech of uninterrupted passion and vehemence; and he wore the same careless and disengaged air the very instant he had finished. A display of talents in which the *inward man* took so little share, could have no powers of persuasion to those who saw them in that light: and therefore, however their brilliancy might be admired, they were useless to their Cause, for they left the mind of the hearer in the same state that they found it.

After a short vindication of his friends, – he [Mr Windham] said 'you have never heard Pitt? – *You* would like him, – beyond any other competitor.'

And then he made his panegyric, in very strong terms, allowing him to be *equal, ready*, splendid, – *wonderful*! – he was in constant astonishment himself at his powers and success; – his youth and inexperience never seemed against him, though he mounted to his present height after – and

to murder Jaffier (*Speeches of the Managers and Counsel in the Trial of Warren Hastings*, ed. E. A. Bond, 1859–61, i. 52–4, 61).

in opposition to such a Vortex of *splendid abilities*; – yet, alone and unsup-
ported, he coped with them all! And then, with conscious generosity, he
finished a most noble eloge, with these Words 'Take, you *may* take, the
testimony of an Enemy! – a very confirmed Enemy of Mr Pitt's! –'

Not *very* confirmed, I hope! a Man so liberal can harbour no enmity of
that dreadful malignancy that sets mitigation at defiance for-ever.

114. From Journal Letter to Susanna Phillips and
Frederica Locke *April 1788*

I have scarce a memorandum of this fatal month, in which I was bereft of
the most revered of Friends – and perhaps the most perfect of Women![1] –
The two excellent persons to whom I write this will be the first to subscribe
to her worth, – nearest to it themselves, they are least conscious of the
resemblance – but how consolatory to *me* is it to see, and to feel it! –

I am yet scarce able to settle whether to glide – silently and resignedly –
as far as I *can*! – past all this melancholy deprivation, – or whether to go
back, once more, to the ever remembered ever-sacred scene that closed the
Earthly pilgrimage of my venerable – my sainted Friend; – my beloved
Susan and Fredy I believe know it all, – I had so recently parted with that
sweet Fredy, – and my Susan – was waiting for me as I quitted the dying
Angel – just on the almost very moment of her beatitude! – What a support
to me was she in that aweful – Heart- piercing minute! – What a consolation,
what a *blessing* on the following mourning Day! –

I believe I heard the last words she uttered – I cannot learn that she spoke
after my reluctant departure, – she finished with that chearful resignation,
that lively hope, which always broke forth when this last – aweful – but, to
Her, most happy change seemed approaching – Poor Miss Port and myself
were kneeling by her Bed side, – she had just given me her soft Hand, –
without power to see either of us, she felt, – and knew us, – O never can I
cease to cherish the remembrance of the sweet – benign – the *holy* voice
with which she pronounced a blessing upon us both! – we kissed her – and
with a smile all beaming – I thought it so – of Heaven, she seemed then to
have taken leave of all Earthly solicitudes, – yet then, even then, – short as
was her time on Earth, the same soft human sensibility filled her for poor
human objects, – she would not bid us farewell – would not tell us she

---

1. Mary Delany died on 15 April 1788 at her house in St James's Place, London.

should speak with us no more, – she only said – as she turned gently away from us, 'And now – *I'll go to sleep*! – ' But O in what a voice she said it! – I felt what the sleep would be! – so did poor Miss Port – Poor sweet unfortunate Girl! – what deluges of Tears did she shed over me! – I promised her, in that solemn moment, my eternal regard – and she accepted this – my *first* protestation of any kind made to her, as some solace to her sufferings – sacred shall I hold it! – sacred to my last Hour. – I believe, indeed, that angelic Being had no other wish equally fervent. –

How full of Days, and full of Honours was Her exit! – I should blush at the affliction of my Heart in losing her, could I ever believe Excellence was given us *here* to Love and to revere, yet gladly to relinquish. No – I cannot think it, – the deprivation may be a *chastisement*, but not a *Joy*, – we may submit to it with patience; but we cannot have felt it with warmth, where we lose it without pain. Outrageously to murmur, or sullenly to refuse consolation, – there, indeed, we are rebels against the dispensations of Providence, – and Rebels yet more weak than wicked, for what and whom is it we resist? What and Whom are *We* for such resistance? –

She bid me – how often did she bid me – not to grieve to lose her! – yet she said, in my absence, she knew I must, – and sweetly regretted how much I must miss her! – I teach myself what I can to think of Her Felicity, – and I never dwell upon that, without faithfully feeling I would not desire her return – but – in every other channel in which my thoughts and feelings turn – I miss her with so sad a void! – She was All that I dearly loved that remained within my reach, – she was become the bosom repository of all the live-long Days's transactions, reflections, feelings, and wishes! – her own exalted mind was all expanded when we met; – I do not think she concealed from me the most secret thought of her Heart, – and while every word that fell from her spoke wisdom, piety, and instruction, her manner had an endearment – her spirits a native gaiety, – and her smile, to those she loved, a tenderness so animated, – O why do I go on – entering into these details! – Believe me, my dear Friends, – now – now that the bitterness of the first blow is over, – and that the dreary chasm becomes more familiar to me – I *think* – and *trust* I would not call her back –! –

115. From Journal Letter to Susanna Phillips *26 July 1788*

[Cheltenham][1]

About 12 o'clock, I was reading in my private loan Book, when hearing the step of Miss Planta on the stairs, I put it back in my Work Box, and was just taking thence some other employment, when her voice struck my Ear, almost in a scream, '*Good God, Mr Digby!*'[2]

My own with difficulty refrained ecchoing it, when I heard *his* voice answer her; – and, in a few minutes, they parted, – and he rapt at the Door, and entered my little Parlour! –

He came in hobbling, leaning on a stick, and with a large Cloth shoe over one of his feet, which was double the size of the other.[3]

I assured him *I did not believe it could be him*! – he was smiling, and in good spirits, and said that, finding the pain go off, though not the swelling, he had determined to try the effect of air and Exercise.

I was afraid this was not very prudent; but I was too glad to see him not to give him a most pleased and sincere welcome.

We sat down together; and he soon enquired what I had done with his little Book.

I had only, I answered, read two more Letters.

'*Have* you read two?' he cried, in a voice rather disappointed: and I found he was actually come to devote the morning, which he knew to be unappropriated, on my part, to reading it on to me himself.

Much as I was gratified by this desire of participating in the pleasure these Letters would give me, I was almost too much astonished, after Colonel Gwynn's[4] account of his seizure, to venture to put the Book in his hands.

He protested himself, however, quite free from pain, and that his coming out might, perhaps, drive the Gout away from his foot.

1. The King and Queen and their entourage had gone to Cheltenham Spa in order for the King to take the waters there after he had suffered a bilious attack. They were staying at the summer residence of Lord Fauconberg.
2. Colonel the Honourable Stephen Digby, Vice-Chamberlain to the Queen. He had lent FB a copy of an anonymous novel entitled *Original Love Letters, Between a Lady of Quality and a Person of Inferior Station* (1784).
3. Digby was suffering from gout in his foot. Miss Planta's and FB's astonishment was over both his venturing forth at all, and his visiting FB when he had declared himself incapable of attending the Queen.
4. Colonel Francis Edward Gwynn, Equerry to the King.

'But *whither*,' cried I, 'may it be driven?'[5]

He understood me, and smiled, but made no immediate answer; though, after a little reflexion, he said, with some quickness 'What can it matter, whether what *must* be, should happen 10 years hence – or happen in 10 Minutes?'

This led to a discourse on long life, to which he seems to have an averseness – and then he took up the Book, and read on from the 5th. Letter.

And charming Letters are they indeed! –

But he read, at first, with evident uneasiness, throwing down the Book at every noise, and stopping to listen at every sound. At last, he asked me if any body was likely to come?

Not a Soul, I said, that I knew, or expected.

He laughed a little at his question, and apparent anxiety, but, with an openness that singularly marks his character, he frankly added 'I must put the Book away, pure as it is, if any one comes, – or, without knowing a word of the contents, they will run away with the title alone exclaiming *Mr* Digby reading Love Letters *to Miss Burney*! – a fine story that would make! –'

'Pon Honour, thought I, I would not hear such a tale for the World! However, he now pursued his reading more at his ease.

. . .

I believe Mr Digby to possess from nature high animal spirits, though now curbed by misfortune;[6] and a fine vein of satire, though constantly kept in order by genuine benevolence. He is still, in mixed Company, gay, shrewd, and arch, foremost in *badinage*, and readiest for what-ever may promote general entertainment. But in chosen society, his spirits do not rise above chearfulness; he delights in moral discourse, on grave and instructive subjects, and though always ready to be led to the politics or business of the Day, in which he is constantly well versed and informing, I never observe him to lead himself but to themes of Religion, Litterature, or moral life.[7]

---

5. In eighteenth-century medical practice it was commonly believed that the 'flying gout' might be fatal if the disease lodged in a vital organ.

6. Digby's wife, Lady Lucy Fox-Strangeways, had died of cancer the previous summer, leaving him with four children.

7. FB's high opinion of Digby would alter. His frequent visits led to widespread rumours that he was courting her, but Digby was at the same time pursuing Charlotte Gunning, Maid of Honour to the Queen, whom he would marry in 1790.

116. From Journal Letter to Susanna Phillips and
Frederica Locke *16 August 1788*

We left Cheltenham early this morning.

Melancholy, most melancholy, was the return to Windsor, – destitute of all that could solace, compose, or delight, – replete with what-ever could fatigue, harrass, and depress! – Ease, leisure, elegant society, and interesting communication, were now to give place to arrogant manners, – contentious disputation, – and arbitrary ignorance![1] – Oh Heaven, my dearest Friends, what scales could have held and have weighed the Heart of your F.B. as she drove past the Door of her revered – lost Comforter,[2] – to enter the apartment inhabited by such qualities! –

Let me not, however, appear more discontented than I am; one soothing circumstance remains from this late relief, though the relief itself is at an end: I think, and believe, there rests with me from it the permanent benefit of a new and most estimable Friend, worthy to be ranked amongst my most chosen set, if I am not deceived in supposing such his desire.[3]

117. From Journal Letter to Susanna Phillips *October 1788*

[Kew]

Sunday – Oct. 19. The Windsor Journey is again postponed, and the King is but very indifferent – Heaven preserve him! – there is something unspeakably alarming in his smallest indisposition.

. . .

We are to stay here some time longer – and so unprepared were we for more than a Day or two, that our distresses are prodigious, even for Cloaths to wear: – and as to Books, – there are not 3 amongst us! – and for company only Mr De Luc and Miss Planta. And so, – in mere desperation for employment – I have just begun a *Tragedy*![1] – – We are now in so spiritless a situation, that my mind would bend to nothing less sad, even in fiction.

1. Referring to Mrs Schwellenberg.
2. Mary Delany.
3. Referring to Digby.

1. *Edwy and Elgiva*, a five-act blank verse tragedy: see pp. 298 and 375–7.

But I am very glad something of this kind has occurred to me: it may wile away the tediousness of this unsettled – unoccupied – unpleasant – period. –

. . .

Thursday, 23d. The King continues to mend, thank God. Saturday we hope to return to Windsor. Had not this *Composition* fit seized me, *societyless* and *Bookless*, and *viewless* as I am, I know not how I could have wiled away my being. But my Tragedy goes on, and fills up all vacancies.

118. From Journal Letter to Susanna Phillips and Frederica Locke *November 1788*

Saturday 1st. Our King does not advance in amendment: he grows so weak, that he walks like a gouty man, yet has such spirits, that he has talked away his voice, and is so hoarse, it is painful to hear him. The Queen is evidently in great uneasiness. – God send him better![1] –

. . .

Wednesday, 5th November. O Dreadful Day! – my very Heart has so sickened in looking over my memorandums, that I was forced to go to other employments. – I will not, however, omit its narration: 'tis too interesting ever to escape my own memory, – and my dear Friends have never yet had the beginning of the Thread which led to all the terrible scenes of which they have variously heard. –

. . .

O my dear Friends, what an history! – The King at Dinner had broken forth into positive Delirium, which long had been menacing all who saw him most closely; and the Queen was so overpowered, as to fall into violent Hysterics. –

All the Princesses were in misery, – and the Prince of Wales had burst into Tears. No one knew what was to follow – no one could conjecture the event!

. . .

1. The King's attack of acute intermittent porphyria (see p. 211 note 1) would not abate until the following March, and then despite of, rather than because of, the various treatments given him.

Thursday Nov. 6th. I rose at Six, – Dressed in haste, by Candle light, and unable to wait for my summons, in a suspence so aweful, I stole along the Passage, in the Dark, a thick fog intercepting all faint light, to see if I could meet with Sandys,[2] or any one, to tell me how the Night had passed.

When I came to the little Dressing Room, I stopt, irresolute what to do. I heard Men's voices: I was seized with the most cruel alarm at such a sound in her Majesty's Dressing Room; – I waited some time – and then the Door opened; and I saw Colonel Goldsworthy and Dr Batterscomb.[3] I was relieved from my first apprehension, yet shocked enough to see them there, at this early Hour. They had both sat up there all Night, as well as Sandys. Every Page, both of the King and Queen, had also sat up, dispersed in the passages and anti-rooms! and O what horrour in every Face I met! –

I waited here, amongst them, till Sandys was ordered by the Queen to carry her a pair of Gloves. I could not resist the opportunity to venture myself before her. I glided into the Room, – but stopt at the Door; she was in Bed, sitting up; – Miss Goldsworthy was on a stool by her side.

I feared approaching without permission, yet could not prevail with myself to retreat. She was looking down, and did not see me.

Miss Goldsworthy, turning round, said ' 'Tis Miss Burney, Ma'am.' –

She leant her Head forward, and in a most soft manner said 'Miss Burney? – how are you? – '

Surprised, and most deeply affected, I hastened up to her, but, in trying to speak, burst into an irresistible torrent of Tears, –

My dearest Friends – I do it at this moment again – and can hardly write for them – yet I wish you to know all this piercing history right: –

She looked like Death – colourless and wan, – but *Nature* is infectious, the Tears gushed from her own Eyes, and a perfect agony of weeping ensued, which, once began, she could not stop. – She did not, indeed, try; for when it subsided, and she wiped her Eyes, she said 'I thank you, Miss Burney, – you have made me cry! – it is a great relief to me. I had not been able to cry before all this Night long! – '

O what a scene followed! – what a scene was related! – The King, in the middle of the Night, had insisted upon seeing if his Queen was not removed from the House: and he had come into her Room, with a Candle in his

---

2. Mrs Sandys, one of the Queen's wardrobe-women.
3. Robert Battiscombe, Windsor apothecary.

Hand, opened the Bed Curtains, and satisfied himself she was there, and Miss Goldsworthy by her side. This observance of his directions had much soothed him: but he stayed a full half Hour – and the depth of terror during that time no words can paint! –

The fear of such another entrance was now so strongly upon the nerves of the poor Queen, that she could hardly support herself.

The King – the Royal Sufferer, – was still in the next Room, – attended by Sir George Baker and Dr Heberden,[4] and his Pages, with Colonel Goldsworthy occasionally, and as he called for him. He kept talking unceasingly, – his voice was so lost, in hoarseness and weakness, it was rendered almost inarticulate; – but its tone was still all benevolence – all kindness – all touching graciousness! –

It was thought adviseable the Queen should not rise, lest the King should be offended that she did not go to him: at present, he was content, because he conceived her to be nursing for her illness.

But what a situation for Her! –

. . .

Friday Nov. 7th. It was now arrived at a sort of settled regularity of life more melancholy than can possibly be described. I rose at 6, Dressed and hastened to the Queen's Apartments, uncalled, and there waited, in silence and in the dark, till I heard her move, or speak with Miss Goldsworthy, and then presented myself to the sad Bed-side of the unhappy Queen. She sent Miss Goldsworthy early every morning to make enquiry what sort of Night his Majesty had passed, – and, in the middle of the Night, she commonly also sent for news, by the Wardrobe Woman.

She dismissed Miss Goldsworthy, on my arrival, to dress herself. Lady Elizabeth Waldegrave[5] accommodated her with her own room for that purpose.

I had then a long conference with this most patient sufferer: and equal forbearance and quietness, during a period of suspensive unhappiness, never have I seen, never could I have imagined!

At noon, now, I never saw her, – which I greatly regretted, – but she kept on her Dressing Gown all Day, and the Princes were continually about the passages, so that no one, unsummoned, dared approach the Queen's apartments.

4. William Heberden, distinguished physician.
5. Lady of the Bedchamber to the Princess Royal.

It was only, therefore, at Night and morning I could see her. – But my Heart was with her, the livelong Day! – And *how* long, – good Heaven! – *how* long that Day became! – Endless I used to think it, – for nothing could I do; – to wait, and to watch – starting at every sound, – yet revived by every noise, – this was my life. –

. . .

Saturday, Nov. 8th. From this time, as the poor King grew worse, general hope seemed universally to abate: and the Prince of Wales now took the government of the House into his own Hands. Nothing was done but by his orders, and he was applied to in every difficulty. The Queen interfered not in any thing; she lived wholly in her two new Rooms, and spent the whole Day in patient sorrow and retirement, with her Daughters.

The next news that reached me, through Mr De Luc, was that the Prince had sent his commands to the Porter to admit only 4 Persons into the House on any pretence whatever; these were Mr Majendie, Mr Guiffardiere, General Harcourt,[6] and Mr De Luc himself: and these were ordered to repair immediately to the Equery Room below stairs, while no one whatsoever was to be allowed to go to any other apartment.

From this time commenced a total banishment from all intercourse out of the House, and an unremitting confinement within its Walls!

I had now, all Tea-meetings being over, no means of gaining any particulars of what was passing, which added so much to the horror of the situation, that, by the Evening, I was almost petrified. –

. . .

Sunday, Nov. 9th. No one went to Church; not a Creature now quits the House: but I believe devotion never less required the aid and influence of public worship! – For me, I know, I spent almost my whole time between prayer and watching. – Even my melancholy resource, my Tragedy, was now thrown aside: misery so actual, living, and present, was knit too closely around me to allow my depressed imagination to fancy any use beyond what my Heart felt.

. . .

6. The Revd Henry William Majendie, Canon of Windsor, formerly Preceptor to Prince William (later King William IV). General the Honourable William Harcourt, Groom of the Bedchamber to the King. (He was the brother-in-law of Lady Harcourt.)

Wednesday, Nov. 19. The account of the dear King this Morning was rather better.

Sir Lucas Pepys was now called in, and added to Dr Warren, Dr Heberden, and Sir George Baker. I earnestly wished to see him, and I found my poor Royal Mistress was secretly anxious to know his opinion. I sent to beg to speak with him, as soon as the consultation was over, – determined, however, to make that request no more if he was as shy of information as Dr Warren.

The moment we were alone, Sir Lucas opened upon the subject in the most comfortable manner: he assured me there was nothing desponding in the case, and that His Royal Patient would *certainly recover*, though not immediately.

Sir Lucas was very open and comforting; – how many sad meetings have I had with him heretofore! first in the alarming attacks of poor Mr Thrale, and next in the agonizing fluctuations of his unhappy Widow, whose reason and Life seemed alternately endangered by her most unfortunate vehemence of passions![7] –

Ah, my Dearest Friends – whom shall we pity so much as Those who neglect to habituate those imperious assaulters of all virtue and all self-denial, *The Passions*, to the controul of Patience? – For that, I begin to think, is more properly their superior than Reason, which, in many cases, finds it hard not to join with them.

. . .

Thursday, Nov. 20th. Poor Miss Goldsworthy was now quite ill, and forced to retire, and nurse. No wonder, for she had suffered the worst sort of fatigue, that of *fearing to sleep*, from the apprehension the Queen might speak, and want her. For though the Queen was all graciousness and consideration, the situation could not admit of ease and repose.

Lady Elizabeth Waldegrave now took her place, of sleeping in the Queen's Room; but the office of going for early intelligence how His Majesty had passed the Night devolved upon me.

Exactly at 7 o'Clock I now went to the Queen's Apartment. Lady Elizabeth then rose, and went to her own Room to Dress, and I received the Queen's commands for my enquiries.

I could not, however, go myself into the Room where they assembled,

---

7. Sir Lucas had treated Hester Thrale when she suffered a virtual nervous breakdown in attempting to suppress her love for Piozzi.

which Miss Goldsworthy, who always applied to her Brother, had very properly done. I sent in a message, to beg to speak with General Budé,[8] or whoever could bring an account.

Mr Charles Hawkins[9] came. He had sat up – O how terrible a narrative did he drily give of the Night! – short, abrupt, peremtorily bad, and indubitably hopeless! –

I did not dare alter, but I greatly softened this relation, in giving it to my poor Queen: I had been, indeed, too much shocked by the hard way in which I had been told it to deliver it in the same manner. Neither did I, in my own Heart, despair; – I thank Heaven! –

I saw Sir Lucas afterwards, who encouraged all my more sanguine opinions. He told me many new regulations had been made. His Majesty was to be kept as quiet as possible, and see only Physicians, except for a short and stated period in every Day, during which he might summon such amongst his Gentlemen as he pleased.

The rest of the Day was comfortless; my Coadjutrix was now grown so fretful and affronting, that though we only met at Dinner, it was hard to support her most unprovoked harshness. –

. . .

Friday, 28th. How woeful – how bitter a Day, in every part, was this! –

My early account was from the King's Page, Mr Stillingfleet: and the night had been extremely bad! –

I dared not sink the truth to my poor Queen, though I mixt in it whatever I could devise of chear and hope; – and she bore it with the most wonderful calmness, and kept me with her a full half Hour, after Breakfast was called, talking over Hunter's Lectures,[10] and other religious Books, – with some other more confidential matters.

Dr Addington[11] was now called in; A very old Physician, but peculiarly experienced in disorders such as afflicted our poor King, though not professedly a practitioner in them.

Sir Lucas made me a visit, and informed me of all the medical proceedings, – and told me, in confidence, we were to go to Kew to-morrow! – though the Queen herself had not yet concurred in the measure! – but the physicians joined to desire it, and they were supported by the Princes. The

---

8. General Jacob de Budé, Hanoverian officer, former governor to Prince William.
9. Serjeant-surgeon to the King.
10. Henry Hunter, DD, *Sacred Biography* (1783–92).
11. Dr Anthony Addington had retired from practice and lived at Reading.

difficulty how to get the King away from his favourite abode was all that rested. If they even attempted force, they had not a doubt but his smallest resistance would call up the whole Country to his fancied rescue! – Yet how, at such a time, prevail by persuasion?

He moved me even to Tears, by telling me That none of their own lives would be safe, if the King did not recover, so prodigiously high ran the tyde of affection and loyalty. All the Physicians received threatening Letters Daily, to answer for the safety of their monarch with their lives! – Sir George Baker had already been stopt in his carriage by the mob, to give an account of the King, – and when he said it was a bad one, they had furiously exclaimed 'The more shame for *you*!'

A privy Council was held at the Castle, with the Prince of Wales, – the Chancellor,[12] Mr Pitt, and all the officers of state were summoned, to sign a permission for the King's removal. – The poor Queen gave an audience to the Chancellor, – it was necessary to sanctify their proceedings. – The Princess Royal and Lady Courtown[13] attended her, and he was presented by Mr Digby. It was a tragedy the most dismal! –

The Queen's knowledge of the King's aversion to Kew made her consent to this measure with the extremest reluctance, – yet it was not to be opposed, – it was stated as much the best for him, on account of the Garden; as here there is none but what is public to spectators from the Terrace, or tops of Houses. I believe they were perfectly right, though the removal was so tremendous.

The Physicians were summoned to the privy Council, to give their opinions, upon oath, that this step was necessary.

Inexpressible was the alarm of every one, lest the King, if he recovered, should bear a lasting resentment against the authors and promoters of this journey.

To give it, therefore, every possible sanction, it was decreed that he should be seen both by the Chancellor and Mr Pitt. –

The Chancellor went into his presence with a tremor such as, before, he had been only occasioned to inspire; and when he came out, he was so extremely affected by the state in which he saw his Royal Master and Patron that the Tears ran down his Cheeks, and his feet had difficulty to support him. –

Mr Pitt was more composed, – but expressed his grief with so much

12. Lord Thurlow.
13. Lady in Waiting to the Queen.

respect and attachment, that it added new weight to the universal admiration with which he is here beheld. –

All these circumstances, with various others, of equal sadness, which I must not relate, came to my knowledge through Sir Lucas, Mr De Luc, and my noon attendance upon her Majesty, who was compelled to Dress for her Audience of the Chancellor.

119. From Journal Letter to Susanna Phillips *4 December 1788*

Dr Willis,[1] a physician of Lincoln, of peculiar skill and practice in intellectual maladies, had been sent for by Express, – the poor Queen had most painfully concurred in a measure which seemed to fix the Nature of the King's attack in the face of the World; – but the necessity, and strong advice, had prevailed over her repugnance.

How interesting – how fearfully interesting to me was this event, and all its details! –

120. From Journal Letter to Susanna Phillips *3 January 1789*

I have the great pleasure, now, of a change in my morning's Historiographers; I have made acquaintance with Dr Willis and his son, and they have desired me to summon one of them constantly for my information.

I am extremely struck with both these physicians. Dr Willis is a man of Ten Thousand; open, honest, dauntless, light-Hearted, innocent, and high-minded. – I see him impressed with the most animated reverence and affection for his Royal Patient; but it is wholly for his Character, — *not a whit* for his Rank. –

Dr John, his Eldest son, is extremely handsome, and inherits, in a milder degree, all the qualities of his Father; but living more in the general World, and having his Fame and Fortune still to settle, he has not yet acquired the same courage, nor is he, by Nature, quite so sanguine in his opinions.[1] The manners of both are extremely pleasing, and they both proceed their own way, not merely unacquainted with court etiquette, but wholly, and most artlessly, unambitious to form any such acquaintance.

---

1. Dr Francis Willis, specialist in mental illness.

1. Dr John Willis would attend the King alone again in 1811 after his father's death.

121. From Journal Letter to Susanna Phillips *February 1789*

Monday 2d. What an adventure had I this morning! one that has occasioned me the severest personal terror I ever experienced in my life.

Sir Lucas Pepys still persisting that excercise and Air were absolutely necessary to save me from illness, I have continued my Walks, varying my Gardens from Richmond to Kew, according to the accounts I received of the movements of the King. For this I had her Majesty's permission, on the representation of Sir Lucas.

This morning, when I received my intelligence of the King, from Dr John Willis, I begged to know where I might walk in safety? In Kew Garden, he said, as the King would be in Richmond.

'Should any unfortunate circumstance,' I cried, 'at any time, occasion my being seen by His Majesty, do not mention my name, but let me run off, without call or notice.'

This he promised. Every body, indeed, is ordered to keep out of sight.

Taking, therefore, the time I had most at command, I strolled into the Garden; I had proceeded, in my quick way, nearly half the round, when I suddenly perceived, through some Trees, two or three figures. Relying on the instructions of Dr John, I concluded them to be workmen, and Gardeners; – yet tried to look sharp, – and in so doing, as they were less shaded, I thought I saw the Person of his Majesty!

Alarmed past all possible expression, I waited not to know more, but turning back, ran off with all my might – But what was my terror to hear myself pursued! – to hear the voice of the King himself, loudly and hoarsely calling after me 'Miss Burney! Miss Burney! –'

I protest I was ready to die; – I knew not in what state he might be at the time; I only knew the orders to keep out of his way were universal; that the Queen would highly disapprove any unauthorised meeting, and that the very action of my running away might deeply, in his present irritable state, offend him.

Nevertheless, on I ran, – too terrified to stop, and in search of some short passage, for the Garden is full of little labyrinths, by which I might escape.

The steps still pursued me, and still the poor hoarse and altered voice rang in my Ears: – more and more foot steps resounded frightfully behind me, – the attendants all running, to catch their eager master, and the voices of the two Doctor Willis's loudly exhorting him not to heat himself so unmercifully.

Heavens how I ran! – I do not think I should have felt the hot Lava from Vesuvius, – at least not the hot Cinders, had I so ran during its Eruption. My feet were not sensible that they even touched the Ground.

Soon after, I heard other voices, shriller though less nervous, call out 'Stop! Stop! – Stop! – '

I could by no means consent, – I knew not what was purposed, – but I recollected fully my agreement with Dr John that very morning, that I should decamp if surprised, and not be named.

My own fears and repugnance, also, after a flight and disobedience like this, were doubled in the thought of not escaping; I knew not to what I might be exposed, should the malady be then high, and take the turn of resentment.

Still, therefore, on I flew, – and such was my speed, so almost incredible to relate, or recollect, that I fairly believe no one of the whole party could have overtaken me, if these words, from one of the Attendants, had not reached me 'Dr Willis begs you to stop! – '

'I cannot! – I cannot! – ' I answered, still flying on, – when he called out 'You *must*, ma'am, it hurts the King to run. – '

Then, indeed, I stopt! – in a state of fear really amounting to agony! – I turned round, – I saw the two Doctors had got the King between them, and about 8 Attendants of Dr Willis's were hovering about. They all slacked their pace, as they saw me stand still, – but such was the excess of my alarm, that I was wholly insensible to the effects of a race which, at any other time, would have required an Hour's recruit.

As they approached, some little presence of mind happily came to my command; it occurred to me that, to appease the wrath of my flight, I must now shew some confidence; I therefore faced them as undauntedly as I was able, – only charging the nearest of the Attendants to stand by my side.

When they were within a few yards of me, the King called out 'Why did you run away? – '

Shocked at a question impossible to answer, yet a little assured by the mild tone of his voice, I instantly forced myself forward, to meet him – though the internal sensation which satisfied me this was a step the most proper, to appease his suspicions and displeasure, was so violently combatted by the tremor of my nerves, that I fairly think I may reckon it the greatest effort of personal courage I have ever made.

The effort answered, – I looked up, and met all his wonted benignity of Countenance, though something still of wildness in his Eyes. Think, however, of my surprise, to feel him put both his Hands round my two shoulders, and then kiss my Cheek! – I wonder I did not really sink, so exquisite was my affright when I saw him spread out his arms! – Involuntarily, I concluded he meant to crush me: – but the Willis's, who have never seen him till this fatal illness, not knowing how very extraordinary an action this was from him, simply smiled and looked pleased, supposing, perhaps, it was his customary salutation!

I have reason, however, to believe it was but the joy of a Heart unbridled, now, by the forms and proprieties of established custom, and sober Reason. He looked almost in *rapture* at the meeting, from the moment I advanced; and to see any of his Household thus by accident, seemed such a near approach to liberty and recovery, that who can wonder it should serve rather to elate than lessen what yet remains of his disorder? –

He now spoke in such terms of his pleasure in seeing me, that I soon lost the whole of my terror, though it had threatened to almost lose *me*: astonishment to find him so nearly *well*, and gratification to see him so pleased, removed every uneasy feeling, and the joy that succeeded, in my conviction of his recovery, made me ready to throw myself at his feet to express it.

What a Conversation followed! – when he saw me fearless, he grew more and more alive, and made me walk close by his side, away from the Attendants, and even the Willis's themselves, who, to indulge him, retreated. I own myself not completely *composed*, but *alarm* I could entertain no more. –

Every thing that came uppermost in his mind he mentioned; he seemed to have just such remains of his flightiness, as heated his imagination, without deranging his Reason, and robbed him of all control over his speech, though nearly in his perfect state of mind as to his opinions.

What did he not say! – He opened his whole Heart to me, – expounded all his sentiments, and acquainted me with all his intentions.

The heads of his discourse I must give you, briefly, as I am sure you will be highly curious to hear them, and as no accident can render of much consequence what a man says in such a state of physical intoxication.

He assured me he was *quite well*, as well as he had ever been in his life: and then enquired *how I did*, and *how I went on*? and whether I was *more comfortable*?

If these questions, in their implication, surprised me, imagine but how that surprise must encrease when he proceeded to explain them! – he asked after the *Coadjutrix*, laughing, and saying '*Never mind her*! – – *don't be oppressed,* – *I am your Friend*! – don't let her cast you down! – I know you have a hard time of it, – but don't mind her! –'

Almost thunderstruck with astonishment, I merely courtsied to his kind '*I am your Friend*' and said nothing.

Then presently he added 'Stick to your Father, – stick to your own family, – let them be your object.' –

How readily I assented! –

Again he repeated all I have just written, nearly in the same words, but ended it more seriously; he suddenly stopt, and held me to stop too, and putting his Hand on his Breast, in the most solemn manner, he gravely and slowly said '*I* will protect you! – I promise you that, – therefore depend upon *me*! – '

I thanked him; and the Willis's, thinking him rather too elevated, came to propose my walking on. 'No, no, no,' he cried, an hundred times in a Breath; – and their good humour prevailed, and they let him again walk on with his new companion.

He then gave me a history of his Pages, animating almost into a rage, as he related his subjects of displeasure with them; particularly with Mr *Ernst*,[1] whom he told me had been brought up by himself; – I hope his ideas upon these men are the result of the mistakes of his malady.

Then he asked me some questions that very greatly distressed me, relating to information given him in his illness, from various motives, but which he suspected to be false, and which I knew he had reason to suspect; yet it was most dangerous to set any thing right, as I was not aware what might be the views of their having been stated wrong. I was as discreet as I knew how to be, and I hope I did no mischief, but this was the worst part of the Dialogue.

He next talked to me a great deal of my dear Father, and made a thousand enquiries concerning his history of music. This brought him to his favourite theme, Handel;[2] and he told me innumerable anecdotes of him, and particularly that celebrated tale of Handel's saying of himself, when a Boy, 'While that Boy lives, my music will never want a protector – ' And this, he said, I might relate to my Father.

Then he ran over most of his Oratorios, attempting to sing the subjects of several airs and choruses, but so dreadfully hoarse, that the sound was terrible.

Dr Willis, quite alarmed at this exertion, feared he would do himself

---

1. George Ernst, Page of the Backstairs, was dismissed from service later this year. He had threatened to make a public disclosure of private details of the King's illness.
2. George Frederick Handel, German composer; his music was highly favoured by both George II and George III.

harm, and again proposed a separation. 'No! no! no!' he exclaimed, 'not yet, – I have something I must just mention first.'

Dr Willis, delighted to comply, even when uneasy at compliance, again gave way.

The good King then greatly affected me, – he began upon my revered old Friend, Mrs Delany! – and he spoke of her with such warmth, such kindness: – 'She was my *Friend*!' he cried, 'and I *loved* her as a Friend! – I have made a memorandum when I lost her! – I will shew it you –'

He pulled out a pocket-Book, and rummaged some Time, but to no purpose –

The Tears stood in his Eyes, – he wiped them, – and Dr Willis again became very anxious, – 'Come, Sir,' he cried, 'now do you come in, and let the lady go on her walk, – come, now you have talked a long while, – so will go in, – if your Majesty pleases.'

'No! – no! –' he cried, 'I want to ask her a few questions, – I have lived so long out of the World, I know nothing! –'

This touched me to the Heart, – we walked on together, and he enquired after various people, – particularly Mrs Boscawen,[3] *because she was Mrs Delany's Friend*!

Then, for the same reason, after Mr Frederick Montagu, of whom he kindly said 'I know he has a great regard for *me*, for all he joined the opposition.' Lord Grey de Wilton, Sir Watkin Wynn, the Duke of Beaufort, and various others, followed.

He then told me he was much dissatisfied with several of his state officers, and meant to form an entire new Establishment. He took a paper out of his Pocket Book, and shewed me his new List.

This was the wildest thing that passed; and Dr John Willis now seriously urged our separating; but he would not consent; he had only 3 more words to say, he declared; and again he conquered.

He now spoke of my Father, with still more kindness, and told me he *ought* to have had the post of Master of the Band, and not that little poor musician *Parsons*, who was not fit for it: 'but Lord Salisbury,' he cried, 'used your Father very ill in that business – and so he did *me*! however, I have dashed out his name, – and I shall put your Father's in, – *as soon as I get loose again*! –'

This again – how affecting was this! –

'And what,' cried he, 'has your Father got, at last? – nothing but that

3. Anne Boscawen was a Maid of Honour to the Queen.

poor thing at Chelsea?[4] – O fie! – fie! – fie! – But never mind! *I* will take care of him! – – *I* will do it *myself*! – '

Then presently he added, 'As to Lord Salisbury, he is out already,[5] – as this memorandum will shew you, – and so are many more, – I shall be much better served, – and when once I get away – I shall rule with a rod of Iron! – '

This was very *un*like himself, and startled the two good Doctors, who could not bear to cross him, and were exulting at my seeing his great amendment, but yet grew quite uneasy at his earnestness and volubility.

Finding we now must part, he stopt to take leave, – and renewed again his charges about the Coadjutrix. 'Never mind her!' he cried, 'Depend upon *me*! – *I* will be your *Friend* – as long as I live! – I here pledge myself to be your Friend! – ' And then, he saluted me again, just as at the meeting, and suffered me to go on.

What a scene! how variously was I affected by it! – but, upon the whole, how inexpressibly thankful to see him so nearly himself! so little removed from recovery.

I went very soon after to the Queen, to whom I was most eager to avow the meeting, and how little I could help it. Her astonishment, and her earnestness to hear every particular, were very great. I told her almost all, – some few things, relating to the distressing questions, I could not repeat; nor many things said of Mrs Schwellenberg, which would much, and very needlessly, have hurt her.

This interview – and the circumstances belonging to it, excited general curiosity, and all the House watched for opportunities to beg a relation of it. How delighted was I to tell them all my happy prognostics!

. . .

Friday, 13th. This Morning there was a great alarm in the House, by the appearance of two Mad-men! – I heard it from Columb:[6] Mr Smelt was so engaged in consultation about them, that he did not even come up stairs: and I remained in the most anxious uncertainty till noon, when my ever ready and kind Informant, Mr Digby found his way to me.

'I am come,' he cried, 'only for a moment, to acquaint you with the state of things below.' He then repeated all the particulars: but as the adventure

4. See p. 253 and note 1.

5. Lord Salisbury, Lord Chamberlain of the Household, kept his post until 1804.

6. Jacob Columb (or Colomb), FB's manservant. No other record has been found of these intruders.

was local, I shall not Write more of it than that one of these men, after a long examination by all the Gentlemen, was dismissed, and the other sent to the office of Lord Sydney, Secretary of State.

Nothing so strange as the eternal rage of these unhappy lunatics to pursue the Royal Family.

He enquired if I had done with the Letters![7] No; I had not looked at them. – He had promised them, he said, to a lady. –

– I should like to have asked if he was to read them to her, also? and if he *goes about* reading such Letters.

I assured him I could dispense with a second perusal, well as I liked them; but he said the lady was not *pressed*, and positively refused to let me get them.

He then gave me the particulars of the progress of the Regency Bill,[8] which direful topic lasted while he stayed. O how dreadful will be the Day when that unhappy Bill takes place! – I cannot approve the plan of it, – the King is *too well* to make such a step right. It will break his spirits, if not his Heart, when he hears and understands such a deposition.

122. From Journal Letter to Susanna Phillips *March 1789*

Sunday, 1st. What a pleasure was mine this morning! how solemn, but how grateful! The Queen gave me the Prayer of Thanksgiving upon the King's Recovery! – It was this morning read in all the Churches throughout the Metropolis, and by this Day Week it will reach every Church in the kingdom. – It kept me in Tears all the morning, – That such a moment should actually arrive! after fears so dreadful, scenes so terrible! –

The Queen gave me a dozen, to distribute among the female servants: but I reserved one of them for dear Mr Smelt, who took it from me in speechless extacy – his fine and feeling Eyes swimming in Tears of joy.

There is no describing – and I will not attempt it, – the fullness, the almost over whelming fullness of this morning's thankful feelings! –

I had the great gratification to see the honoured object of this joy, for a few minutes, in the Queen's Dressing Room. He was all calmness, and benevolent graciousness: I fancy my strong emotion had disfigured me; –

7. See p. 269 and note 2.
8. A bill had been introduced in Parliament to make the Prince of Wales Regent. It was dropped with the King's recovery.

or perhaps the whole of this long confinement, and most affecting Winter, may have somewhat marked my countenance; for the King presently said to me 'Pray, *are* you quite well to day?' 'I think not quite, sir,' I answered. 'She does not *look* well,' – said he, to the Queen, – 'she looks a little – *yellow*, I think. – '

How kind and condescending, to think of *any* body and their looks, at this first moment of re-appearance!

. . .

Tuesday, 10th. Intelligence of remarks has reached me the most disagreeable in themselves, and the hardest to conquer. They are all from Goter.

First, she complained that Columb had not been civil to Mrs Lovel, Mrs Schwellenberg's maid, who had told her she met much more civility in her last place, which was living with Lady Digby,[1] where she had always been waited upon herself by a footman, *as Mr Digby*, she said, *could tell Miss Burney.*

'Indeed,' I gravely answered, 'I never heard any thing upon the subject.'

'O ma'am,' cried Goter, Colouring, 'but Mrs Lovel says if ever I should see Sherborne Castle,[2] I shall know it to be true, for there are 3 footmen waiting at the Housekeeper's Table, where Mrs Lovel Dined. – '

'And what makes you think of seeing Sherborne Castle? – '

'Why, ma'am, because – because, ma'am, Mr Westerholds[3] says I'm much the most likely to get off, of any of the other maids here. – '

'How get off? – '

'Why, ma'am, – if you was to marry, he says. – '

Enquiring a little further into this, she plainly owned her meaning, *and Mr Westerholds*, that *Mr Digby came a courting to me!* –

'And all the maids, ma'am, and Columb, and every body says so!' –

'Then all the maids,' cried I, 'and Columb, and every body are much mistaken. I desire you will tell them so. I only see Mr Digby as a Friend and acquaintance; – for any thing further, – I should as soon think of the Man in the Moon.'

I thought this quite necessary, and quite within full comprehension for its expression! She looked extremely disappointed, but presently said 'Columb always says, ma'am, that it won't be, – because he says it's only Mr Digby – and not you, ma'am, – for he's sure, he says, you would not be such a fool. – '

1. Mary, Lady Digby, sister-in-law of Stephen Digby.
2. Seat of Lord Digby.
3. Mrs Schwellenberg's manservant.

Pretty plain language in return! I could not forbear heartily laughing, – which encouraged her to go on with renewed spirits.

'Columb don't like Mr Digby at all, ma'am, – he says he comes in and out, just as if he was his master, and he says he shan't be that, for he'd sooner go away. He says he knows his reasons why he don't like him. And he says, as to his coming here so much, he knows others would like it just the same, only he has not such assurance. But he says he never calls you for him, and he never will, and he bid me not be so over-officious myself.'

I was surprised enough at all this; but only made a general answer, that it was the business of every servant to announce every visitor, and leave the choice to those who received them.

Another time, she began telling me Mr Digby desired his best Compliments to me. She had met him in the passage. She said she very often met him, and he always stopt her, to ask how I did, and whether I was in my room. And so he did to Columb too – and all the maids knew he would, and stopt her, when they saw him coming.

Amazing this, in Mr Digby! – Is it not? –

'But Columb,' she continued, 'says he never gives his messages, – nor he never will.'

'That is very wrong,' cried I, gravely; 'he ought to give every message from every body.'

'Yes, ma'am; but Mr Digby knows his way, I believe, for now he never asks him to call you; if he can't find me, he goes to Mrs Keene, Miss Planta's maid, and asks her to see for your servant; but he says, always *Miss Burney's maid*, if you please, *not her man!*'

How very inconsiderate! –

'Columb quite hates him, ma'am – when it rains, he always looks to see if he's out, and if he is, he says "Look, there's *my master*! he'll be wet to the skin! I'm glad of it! – "'

You may imagine the sort of answers I made.

'But Miss Planta, ma'am, always asks Mrs Keene what Company you keep, – and whether Mr Digby does not come; – and when she says she don't know, she says she's a fool, and bids her find out his voice, and know against another time. – '

Amazing! –

'And Mrs Schwellenberg, ma'am, always asks Mrs Arline[4] who's with you; and when I come for you, she says *I'm mighty alert about it*; and one Day

4. Mrs Schwellenberg's maid.

288

Mrs Arline went herself, and she asked who wanted you, and when Mrs Arline said she did not know, because Mr Digby told her to say somebody wanted you, – she said, what, are *you* turned Cupid's Mercury too, as well as that pert little Goter?'

Good Heaven, what hearings were these! –

'Mrs Arline, ma'am, always says she is sure it will be, and so does Mrs Sandys; – but Columb says he likes Colonel Greville,[5] a great deal the best, for he's the most the Gentleman among them. But he says you've a rare pack of old Gentlemen coming after you, as ever he see; – there's nobody but that old sniffling Gentleman, Mr Bryant, and old Mr Cambridge, and t'other old Gentleman with the Horn; that ever he sees – '[6]

This is Mr Hutton, who is deaf.

'And Columb told Mrs Keene, ma'am, never to see for you again, – he said if ever Mr Digby asked, the way was to say you were out, and nobody knew where. He said that was what he always did himself.'

I was now obliged to speak angrily of this liberty in Columb, and express my astonishment at his caring so much about my visitors, be they whom they might.

And then came out a curious discovery of what it all meant! – 'Because, ma'am, he says he knows why he hates him – '

'And why? – '

'Because, ma'am, he says he's a villain – '

Good God, how I started! – I desired her to explain –

'He says, ma'am, he knows very well, all the time that he is coming after you in this manner, Morning, Noon and Night, he pays his addresses to a Lady in Town – a very handsome lady, ma'am, and a Maid of Honour. – '

'Miss Gunning?' cried I –

'Yes, ma'am, that's the very name.'

I was very glad this was the clearance of the 'villain' – I assured her his acquaintance with me was not of a sort that need give Miss Gunning, or any other lady, any anxiety: and repeated my *Man of the Moon*.

Nevertheless, this communication has given me inexpressible vexation: I do not mean the latter part, – I attribute that solely to the old report, and hold Mr Digby as incapable of a duplicity so base almost as an angel of Heaven! – it serves, however, to exculpate poor Columb, who cannot believe this, and thinks too hardly of him –

5. Colonel Robert Fulke Greville, Equerry to the King.
6. Jacob Bryant, eminent antiquary, lived at Cypenham, near Windsor, and was a friend of the King and Queen and the Burney family; Richard Owen Cambridge; and James Hutton.

But these servants – their surmizes – their assertions, rather, and the extreme defiance of all conjecture in Mr Digby hurt – embarass – disturb me inexpressibly.

I cannot deny I feel disposed to be angry with Mr Digby and, with any thing short of the established opinion I feel of his high honour, – I should instantly resolve to break off all intercourse with him, except what is official. –

. . .

This was a Day of Happiness indeed! – a Day of such heart-felt public delight, as could not but suppress all private disturbance.

The King sent to open the House of Lords by commission.

The General Illumination of all London proved the universal joy of a thankful and most affectionate people, who have shewn so largely, on this trying occasion, how well they merited the monarch thus benignantly preserved from Earthly destruction.

The Queen, from her privy purse, gave private orders for a splendid Illumination at this Palace: Rebecca[7] painted a beautiful transparency, – and Mr Smelt had the regulation of the whole.

The King – Providence – Health, and Britannia, were displayed with elegant devices: the Queen and Princesses, all but the Youngest, went to Town, to see the illumination there; and Mr Smelt was to conduct the surprise.

It was magnificently beautiful.

When it was lighted and prepared, the Princess Amelia went to lead her Papa to the front window: but first she dropt on her knees, and presented him a Paper with these lines, – which, at the Queen's desire, I had scribbled in her name for the happy occasion.

To The King.

Amid a rapt'rous Nation's praise
That sees Thee to their pray'rs restor'd,
Turn gently from the gen'ral blaze –
Thy Charlotte wooes her bosom's Lord! –

Turn and behold where, bright and clear,
Depictur'd with transparent art,
The Emblems of her thoughts appear,
The Tribute of a grateful Heart.

---

7. Biagio Rebacca, Italian decorative artist.

> O small the tribute, were it weigh'd
> With all she feels, – or half she owes!
> But noble Minds are best repaid
> From the pure spring whence bounty flows.

> P.S. The little Bearer begs a Kiss
> From dear Papa for bringing this.

I need not, I think, tell you, the little Bearer begged not in vain. The King was extremely pleased. He came into a Room belonging to the Princesses, in which we had a party to look at the illuminations, and there he stayed above an Hour, – chearful, composed, and gracious! all that could merit the great national testimony to his worth this Day paid him.

Lady Effingham,[8] Major Price, and Dr Willis, – and Mr and Mrs Smelt, made the party; with the sweet little Princess, till her Bed-time, Miss Gomme, etc.

The Queen and Princesses did not return from Town till one in the morning; they were quite enchanted with the glorious scene they had been beholding.

. . .

Saturday, March 14th. This Morning we returned to Windsor. With what different sensations to those with which we left it! All illness over, all fears removed, all sorrows lightened! – The King was so well as to go on Horseback, – attended by a large party of Gentlemen.

Mrs Schwellenberg went to Town, to spend some Days. Miss Planta only accompanied me: Mr and Mrs Smelt, on invitation by the King, came also to Windsor, for a Week.

The Queen was all graciousness: every thing and every body were smiling and lively.

All Windsor came out to meet the King. It was a joy amounting to extacy, – I could not keep my Eyes dry all Day long. A scene so reversed! Sadness so sweetly exchanged for thankfulness and delight!

. . .

Thursday, 19th. This morning, their Majesties went to Kew, to receive addresses from the City on the King's Recovery.

---

8. First Lady of the Bedchamber to Queen Charlotte.

Mr Digby did not call for his intended *long leave-taking*; whether he was detained by the King till they all set out, — for they went at the same moment, – or whether he had no time, or something internal made him think it better to change his plan, I cannot tell, but he set off at 9 o'clock, with the Equerries, and without calling.

N.B. And here, my dear Friends, ends a minute and faithful narration of these busy and conflicting 4 months: As I now only wish to give you Facts, and clear up all ambiguity, and hasten to more modern times, I omit a world of comment and detailed *intentions*, which follow in my memorandums: I will simply speak, from them, the *result* of my opinion, – which was, that *His* [Digby's] *Heart was surely mine* – I come *to the point* for brevity's sake; – his conduct, his high Character, his solicitude for my confidence, his reproaches for my withholding it, – his *unfair*, yet flattering detention of my paper,[9] – in short, – an assiduity to secure my friendship, esteem, sympathy, and confidence, so unweariedly exercised for now so long a time, – since at Cheltenham it was particularly evident, – all this, concurred to satisfy me *His Heart was mine.* The various and strong obstacles in his way, of his family, the family of his late lady, his moderate fortune, his court connections, – numberless, numberless were the impediments I saw to the pursuance of an attachment founded on feelings of such extreme disinterestedness. I concluded, therefore, nothing less certain than his *power* to follow the bent of his partiality, though had I not believed he *thought* himself able to do it, I must have concluded him – all considered – a *Barbarian*. There seemed to me no medium, after a conduct so assiduously calculated to win *my* Heart, than that he must either believe himself in the road to claim it honourably, or be void of all integrity and all feeling.

Could I think *this* a moment? – no! – The other, therefore, became my fixed opinion. And with a reliance upon the steadiness of his Honour and his constancy, that painted him to me as a character modelled in the most genuine mould of Generosity, nobleness, and refinement.

All, therefore, that at this time oppressed *me*, my dearest Friends, was *myself*! – – *unworthy* I felt of him, *because not happy, ungrateful*, – O but for these drawbacks, – with what *rapture* should I, now, have looked forward to such a conclusion of my long confinement – incessant labours, – and perpetual indignities! – But such, I thought, *the condition of life* – this prospect, which seemed to me so undoubtedly open, would have made me too blessed, had

9. FB, urged by Digby, had reluctantly lent him a prayer she had written – which he delayed returning.

not these considerations given to me a secret dread that often made me wish it again closed! –

123. Letter to Dr Burney *13 July 1789*

Gloucester House, Weymouth

My Dearest Padre's kind Letter was most truly welcome to me. When I am so distant, the term of absence or of silence seems always doubly long to me.

The Bay here is most beautiful; the Sea never rough, generally calm and gentle, and the sands perfectly smooth and pleasant. I have not yet bathed, for I have had a cold in my Head, which I caught at Lindhurst,[1] and which makes me fear beginning; but I have hopes to be well enough to-morrow, and thence forward – to *ail nothing more*. It is my intention to cast away all superfluous complaints into the main Ocean, which I think quite sufficiently capacious to hold them: and really *my* little frame will find enough to carry and manage without them.

Colonel Goldsworthy has just sent me in a Newspaper, containing intelligence that Angelica Kauffman is making drawings from Evelina for the Empress of Russia! – Do you think the Empress of Russia hears of any thing now besides Turkey and the Emperor? – And is not Angelica Kauffman dead? –[2]

O what an *Oracle*! – for such is the Paper called.

His Majesty is in delightful Health, and much improved Spirits. All agree that he never looked better. The loyalty of all this place is excessive; they have dressed out every street with Labels of God Save the King; – All the Shops have it over the Doors; all the Children wear it in their Caps; all the Labourers in their Hats, and all the Sailors *in their voices*, for they never approach the House, without shouting it aloud, nor see the King, or his Shadow, without beginning to huzza, and going on to three Cheers.

The Bathing Machines make it their motto over all their Windows; – and those Bathers that belong to the Royal Dippers, wear it in *Bandeaus* on their

1. FB and the Royal Family had been at Lyndhurst, a village in the New Forest, from 25 to 30 June. They were now staying at Gloucester House, the Duke of Gloucester's residence on the Weymouth seafront.

2. Angelica Kauffmann, a professional artist, who had left England in 1781, was living in Rome, where she died in 1807. A report in a London newspaper, *The Oracle* (11 July 1789), claimed that she had 'nearly finished' some illustrations of *Evelina*, commissioned by Catherine the Great, Empress of Russia. No other reference to these illustrations has been found. Russia and Turkey were at war in 1789.

Bonnets, to go into the Sea; – and have it again, in large Letters, round their waists, to encounter the Waves! – Flannel Dresses, tucked up, and no shoes nor stockings, with Bandeaus and Girdles, have a most singular appearance; and when first I surveyed these loyal Nymphs, it was with some difficulty I kept my features in order.

Nor is this all; think but of the surprise of his Majesty, when, the first time of his Bathing, he had no sooner popt his Royal Head under water, than a Band of Music, concealed in a neighbouring Machine, struck up God Save Great George our King! –

One thing, however, was a little unlucky; when the Mayor and Burgesses came, with the address, they requested leave to Kiss Hands: this was graciously accorded: but the Mayor advancing in a common way, to *take the Queen's Hand*, as he might that of any Lady Mayoress, Colonel Gwynn, who stood by, whispered 'You must kneel, sir! – '

He found, however, that he took no notice of this hint, but Kissed the Queen's Hand Erect. – As he passed him, in his way back, the Colonel said 'You should have knelt, sir – !'

'Sir,' answered the poor Mayor, 'I cannot. – '

'Every body does, Sir!'

'Sir, – I have a wooden Leg! – '

Poor Man! – 'twas such a surprise! – and such an excuse, as no one could dispute.

But the absurdity of the matter followed, – all the rest did the same! taking the same privilege, by the example, without the same, or any cause! –

We have just got Mrs Piozzi's Book here.[3] My Royal Mistress is reading, and will then lend it me. Have you read it? –

124. Letter to Dr Burney *27 October 1789*

Queen's Lodge, Windsor

Most dear Sir,

We go on here amazingly well, though every day now presents some anniversary of such miseries as scarce any House ever knew before last year.[1] They call back to my Mind every circumstance, with Daily acuracy,

---

3. Hester Piozzi's *Observations and Reflections made in the Course of a Journey through France, Italy, and Germany* (1789), which FB described as 'Wild, entertaining, flighty, inconsistent, and clever' (*DL*, iv. 300).

1. I.e. the anniversary of George III's first bout of insanity.

and a sort of recollective melancholy that I find always ready to mix with the joy and thanksgiving of the most blessed deliverance and change. –

Nor is it possible to think more of *our escape*, than of the sudden adversity of the French. – Truly terrible and tremendous are revolutions such as these – There is nothing in old History that I shall any longer think fabulous; the destruction of the most ancient Empires on record has nothing more wonderful, nor of more *sounding* improbability, than the demolition of this Great Nation, which rises up, all against itself, for its own ruin – perhaps annihilation. Even the Amazons were but the poissardes[2] of the Day, – I no longer doubt their existence or their prowess – and name but some Leader amongst the destroyers of the Bastile,[3] and what is said of Hercules or Theseus[4] we need no longer discredit? – I only suppose those Two Heros were the many Headed mob of ancient Days.

125. From Journal Letter to Susanna Phillips *18–27 November 1789*

We were to go to Town: but while I was taking my hasty Breakfast, Miss Planta flew into the Room, eagerly exclaiming 'Have you heard the News? – '

I saw, instantly, by her Eyes and manner, what she meant, – and therefore answered 'I believe so.'

'Mr Digby is going to be married! – I resolved I would tell you. – '

'I heard the rumour,' I replied, 'the other Day, from Colonel Gwynn.'

'O it's true!' she cried; 'he has written to ask leave. – But for Heaven's sake don't say so! – '

I gave her my ready promise, for I believed not a syllable of the matter: but I would not tell her that, as it was impossible to me to explain why I doubted her.

Doubt, however, is no word to use; I *positively* and *completely* disbelieved the assertion. I felt there could be no medium between the utter falsehood of the report, or the total reverse of that basis of Honour and Goodness on which my friendship had been built; – and I found not even the power to hesitate which must be given up.

She looked much surprised at my steady coolness, and began *pitying poor*

2. Fishwives.

3. The symbol of the *ancien régime* during the French Revolution had fallen on 14 July 1789.

4. Theseus, famous for his martial exploits, was represented in Greek myth as a friend of Hercules, the greatest of all the heroes.

Mr Digby to have hit upon such a shocking choice, as Miss Gunning was made up of conceit and ill temper.

I took but slight notice of all this – I hardly, indeed, thought of it, except as shewing a vehement curiosity to devellope what I felt upon such a turn to his long assiduities: I believe she imagined she should surprise me into a little railing – but I must do her the justice to add, *I fear* – she had still an opinion internally that the intelligence would be kept off from a near approach *to the seat of life*, by the idea started by Mr Guiffardiere! The *justice*, I say, however provoking the suggestion: for I must own *without* it, her abruptness, and her investigation would have had no excuse – they would have been even inhuman. Even as it was, she appeared – and could not disguise it, extremely elated that one who had so long openly seemed partially attached, should take another Walk, – and seem not attached at all. – And this from no malevolence, for I believe she even thought me ready to *reject* any proposal if made – but simply to get rid of an obvious distinction, which she deemed *mortifying without use*. Thus, at least, it is that I read her eager exultation.

We went to Town not only for the Drawing Room[1] on the next Day, but also for the Play on this Wednesday Night:[2] and the party appointed to sit in the Queen's private Box, as, on these occasions, the Balcony Box opposite to the Royals is called, Dined with Mrs Schwellenberg: namely, Mrs Stainforth, Miss Planta, Mr De Luc and Mr Thomas Willis.

During Dinner, 'Poor Mr Digby is not well again,' cried Mr Willis, – 'he's in *my* way – going to be married!'

This, indeed, struck me, – !

'Yes, and very soon,' cried Miss Planta.

'Indeed?' quoth Mrs Stainforth.

'And to whom?' cried Mr De Luc, looking all amaze.

'To Miss Gunning!' *I* answered: merely, however, to join in the Dialogue, not from believing the thing even possible, though somewhat *stunned* in my disbelief, by the assertion coming from Mr Willis. I concluded the visit to Northampton[3] had awakened the report, and I imagined some great and full contradiction and explanation near at hand. For still its truth I thought utterly impossible.

1. A day devoted to formal receptions by the Royal Family.
2. Frederick Reynolds's comedy *The Dramatist*, performed at the Covent Garden Theatre. FB describes it as 'full of absurdities, yet laughable in the extreme' (*DL*, iv. 339).
3. Digby had visited Charlotte Gunning's father, Sir Robert Gunning, at his seat at Horton near Northampton.

. . .

A curious conversation, at Dinner, the following Day, I cannot refuse sketching: Mr Guiffardiere dined here, and, in the midst of the meal, said 'O – but Miss Burney – I must wish you joy, ma'am, of Mr Digby's marriage. – '

'For what wish you her joy?' cried Mrs Schwellenberg, disdainfully, 'does she know him? – '

Can you almost *believe* such a question as this, after the Kew history? – Yet, – in fact, I might have answered *No*, Ma'am, I know him not![4] –

Mr Guiffardiere and Miss Planta looked amazed: but I saw it was a sudden start of resentment at the *implied honour* of intimacy, and therefore would not notice it.

A little while after, Mr Guiffardiere spoke, not very flatteringly, of the lady; and added he must confess he had been greatly surprised at the News.

'For what surprised?' cried Mrs Schwellenberg; 'they been both whiny piney, says Mrs Harcourt,[5] and so they may do that together.'

'If that's all,' cried he, 'they will soon be tired, I can tell them! . . .' And then followed some further discussion. I mixt in it but sparingly. I would not at all, for many reasons, as I could not speak openly, but that I saw myself *waited* for: since, notwithstanding Mr Guiffardiere is quite fixed in his Dream of *Thames's Banks*,[6] and has a power over the mind of Miss Planta to fix *her* there also, – she yet concludes *something* there passed between Mr Digby and me, and in her extreme uncertainty what, she suffers evidently from mortified curiosity: while Mr Guiffardiere, satisfied in his private mind of his *Watery* conjecture, is yet persuaded, also, Mr Digby was somewhat beyond a common acquaintance with me, and I saw him dying to ask me a thousand questions.

He enquired of Mrs Schwellenberg when it was to be?

'Mr has got the Gout,' she answered, 'so Miss might wait.'

At Night, during picquet, Mrs Schwellenberg expressed her aversion to Mr Digby in every spiteful way she could suggest, and *her wonder at Miss Gunning*: though every one else reverses the wonder. 'But Mr Digby might be re-ely,' she cried, 'surprised; for he bin grown so white as possibil, what you call his Head, others, his Hair; and his Teeth been all gone, and his skin been so *yaller* as possibil – and he got 4 Children, what you call five, –

---

4. Alluding to Peter's denial of Jesus, foretold by Jesus in a parable.
5. Mary Harcourt, wife of General William Harcourt, aide-de-camp to George III.
6. Not identified.

and Miss Gunning has £10.000 and she loves him prodigious, what I hear! – '

The £10.000 surprised me: I had not imagined her so well portioned. I am not sure I *now* think money without its weight in those scales which held the balance of her merits! – A short time ago, I thought it light as air –

The next Day, my *former* friend, Major Price, arrived, to spend some time: I am sure I cannot say my *present* friend, for his distance is, if possible, encreased, – there was a large party the first Evening, and every one of it spoke to me except himself, who only Bowed! – Though, to soften off in the Eyes of others a *caution*, if caution it is, so unnecessary, I made it my business, by the first opportunity, to speak myself, and say I was glad to see him at Windsor again.

And so I always am: he is so gentle, and so pleasing, and I am persuaded he is so good, that I always rejoice to have him here: and as to shyness – I am now grown into honouring it.

None of them speak of Mr Digby; they had all avowed a distaste of Miss Gunning, who is very unpopular throughout the Household, and Mr Digby had so frequently and publicly disclaimed the report, that they now seem little pleased or interested about his proceedings.

The Queen *never* names him, *never*! –

126. From Journal Letter to Susanna Phillips and Frederica Locke *4–23 April 1790*

On Easter Sunday, the 4th of April, when I left my beloved Susan at St James's, I left with her all spirit for any voluntary employment, – and it occurred to me I could best wile away the leisure allowed me by returning to my long forgotten Tragedy.[1] This I have done, in those moments as yet given to Journal, and it is well I had so sad a resource, since any merrier I must have aimed at in vain.

It was a Year and 4 Months since I had looked at or thought of it. I found nothing but unconnected speeches and hints and ideas, though enough in quantity, perhaps, for a whole play. I have now begun planning and methodizing, and have written 3 or 4 regular scenes. I mention all these particulars of my progress, in answer to certain queries in the comments of my Susan and Fredy both, of old date.

---

1. *Edwy and Elgiva*, begun in October 1788 (see p. 271). FB completed the first draft in August 1790.

. . .

I go on, occasionally, with my Tragedy. It does not much enliven, but it soothes me. I am a little like my own Mr Lovel, *who 'has really no idea what sort of a Person he has,'*[2] – for I can fairly say I have no conception what sort of a composition this will prove.

127. Journal Letter to Susanna Phillips and Frederica Locke *2 May 1790*

This morning, in my way to Church, just as I arrived at the Iron Gate of our Court Yard, a well known voice called out 'Ah, there's Miss Burney! – '

I started, and looked round – and saw – Mrs Piozzi! –

I hastened up to her; – she met my held out hand with both hers, – Mr Piozzi and Cecilia[1] were with her – all smiling and good-humoured.

'You are going,' she cried, 'to Church? – so am I – I must run first to the Inn – I suppose one may sit – any where one pleases? – '

'Yes,' I cried, 'but you must be quick, or you will sit no where, there will be such a throng. – '

This was all; – she hurried on, – so did I. –

I received exceeding great satisfaction in this little and unexpected meeting.

She had been upon the Terrace, and was going to change her Hat, and haste on both sides prevented awkwardness on either.

Yet I saw she had taken in good part my concluding *Hand presentation* at my dear Mr Lock's:[2] she met me no more with that *fiérté*[3] of defiance – it was not – nor can it ever be, – with her old cordiality, but it was with some degree of pleasure, and that species of readiness which evinces a consciousness of meeting with a good reception.

I was *extremely* happy in this circumstance.

I shall now, on my own account, dread seeing her no more. What a

---

2. Alluding to Mr Lovel's remark in the penultimate chapter of *Evelina*: 'really, I have not the least notion what sort of person I am'.

1. Cecilia Margaretta Thrale, Hester Piozzi's youngest daughter, aged thirteen.
2. FB and Hester Piozzi had met on 17 March 1790 at Frederica Locke's assembly, the first encounter since their rupture over Hester's remarriage. FB refers only in passing to this 'long-wished, long-dreaded interview' (*DL*, iv. 361).
3. *Pride.*

weight of anxious apprehension, and comfortless uncertainty is now removed!

I was, however, afterwards, distressed enough. I knew it would be disapproved that any connection should be renewed, beyond a courtsie, in the Royal presence; and I feared that was just the time when I should be jealously watched for something more: however, fortunately, the Chapel was so near full, she and her party were carried to a great distance, and my near-sighted Eyes never once discerned them.

I was the more satisfied in now missing her, as Miss Planta, who sat next me, pointed her out as Dressed in a most ludicrous and fantastic manner. And when she was quitting the Chapel, a glimpse was sufficient to shew this representation but too true.

How was I ashamed, afterwards, when the Queen asked us both, during her Toilette, who was that *painted Foreigner*? Miss Planta instantly answered: – I really grew husky. It is truly vexatious she will descend to singularity so unbecoming. For the paint was nothing to the rest of the glare, though high enough for the Opera Stage.

I cleared her, as well as I was able, of every thing worse than injudiciousness: I *believe* it, indeed, the chief cause of all her errors.

128. Journal Letter to Susanna Phillips and Frederica Locke *18 May 1790*

This Morning I again went to the Trial of poor Mr Hastings. Heavens! Who can see him sit there unmoved! – not even those who think him *guilty*; – if they are *human*!

I took with me Mrs Bogle.[1] She had long since begged a Ticket for her Husband, which I could never before procure. We now went all three. And indeed, her original speeches and remarks made a great part of my entertainment.

Mr Hastings and his Counsel[2] were this Day most victorious. I never saw the Prosecutors so dismayed. Yet both Mr Burke and Mr Fox spoke, and, before the conclusion, so did Mr Windham. They were all in evident embarassment: Mr Hastings' Counsel finished the Day with a most noble appeal to Justice and Innocence, protesting that if his Client did not fairly

1. May Bogle.
2. Edward Law, who declared that if Hastings 'does not falsify every act of cruelty that the Hon. Managers shall attempt to prove upon him, May the hand of this House, and the hand of God light upon him!' (*DL*, iv. 383 n. 1).

claim the one, by proving the other, he wished himself that the Prosecutors – that the Lords – that the Nation at large – that The Hand of God might fall heavy upon him! –

This had a great and sudden effect – not a word was uttered – The Prosecutors looked dismayed and astonished – and the Day closed.

Mr Windham came up to speak to Miss Francis's,[3] about a *Dinner*, – but he only bowed to me, – and with a look so conscious – so much saying ' 'Tis *your* turn to triumph now!' – that I had not the spite to attack him.

But – when the Counsel had uttered this animated speech, Mrs Bogle was so much struck, she hastily arose, and clapping her Hands, called out; audibly, in a broad Scotch accent 'O Chaarming! – ' I could hardly quiet her – till I assured her we should make a paragraph for the news-papers! –

I had the pleasure to deliver this myself to their Majesties and the Princesses; and as I was called upon while it was fresh in my memory, I believe but little of the general energy was forgotten. It gave me great pleasure to repeat so striking an affirmation of the innocence of so high – so injured, I believe, a character. – The Queen eagerly declared *I should go again the next sitting.* –

129. Journal Letter to Susanna Phillips and Frederica Locke *28 May 1790*

And now, my dear Sisters! – to a subject and narration interesting to your kind affections, because important to my future life.

Friday the 28th. The Princess Augusta condescended to bring me a most gracious message from the King, desiring to know if I wished to go to Handel's Commemoration,[1] and if I should like 'the Messiah,' or prefer any other Day?

With my humble acknowledgements for his goodness, I fixed instantly on 'the Messiah'; and the very amiable Princess came, smiling, back to me, bringing me my Ticket from the King.

This would not, indeed, much have availed me, but that I fortunately knew my dear Father meant to go to the Abbey. I dispatched Collomb to Chelsea, and he promised to call for me the next morning.

---

3. The daughters of Philip Francis, whom FB describes as Hastings's 'worst foe' (*DL*, iv. 381).

1. A performance of Handel's *Messiah* at Westminster Abbey. A series of Handel festivals, featuring vast orchestras and choirs, was held there from 1784 to 1791.

My *visions*[2] I had meant to produce in a few Days, – and to know their chance, before I left Town for the summer. But I thought the present opportunity not to be slighted, for some little opening, that might lighten the task of the *exordium*[3] upon the Day of attempt.

He was all himself, – all his native self, – kind, sweet, gay, open, and full fraught with converse. –

Chance favoured me: we found so little room, that we were fain to accept two vacant places at once, though they separated us from my uncle, Mr Burney, and his Brother James,[4] who were all there, and all meant to be of the same party.

I might not, at another time, have rejoiced in this dis-union, but it was now most opportune: it gave me three Hours conference with my dearest Father, – the *only* conference of that length I have had in 4 Years!

Fortune again was kind, – for my Father began relating various anecdotes of attacks made upon him, for procuring to sundry strangers some acquaintance with his Daughter, – particularly, with the Duchesse de Biron, – and Mesdames de Boufflers,[5] – to whom he answered, he had *no power*, – but was somewhat struck by a question of Madame de Boufflers in return, who exclaimed 'Mais, Monsieur, est-ce possible! Mlle votre fille n'a-*t-elle point de vacance*?'[6]

This led to much interesting discussion, – and to many confessions and explanations, on my part, never made before: which induced him to enter more fully into the whole of the situation, and its circumstances, than he had ever yet had the leisure, or the spirits, to do and he repeated sundry speeches of discontent at my seclusion from the World.

All this, encouraged me to much detail, – I spoke my high and constant veneration for my Royal Mistress, her merits, her virtues, her condescendsion, and her even peculiar kindness towards me: but I owned the *species* of life distasteful to me, – I was lost to all private comfort, dead to all domestic endearment, – I was worn with want of rest, and fatigued with laborious watchfulness and attendance. My time was devoted to official duties, and all that in life was dearest to me – my friends – my chosen society – my best affections – lived now in my mind only by recollection, and rested upon that with nothing but bitter regret. – With Relations the most

---

2. FB's plans to retire from service at Court.

3. The introductory part of a discourse.

4. Richard Burney, CB's brother, and James Burney, his half-brother.

5. Marie de Saujon, Comtesse de Boufflers, and her daughter-in-law, Amélie de Boufflers.

6. 'But sir, is it possible! Does your daughter have *no time to herself*?'

deservedly dear, with Friends of almost unequalled goodness, I lived like an orphan! – like one who had no natural ties, and must make her way as she could by those that were factitious. Melancholy was the existence, where Happiness was excluded, though not a complaint could be made! where the illustrious Personages who were served professed almost all human excellence, – yet where those who were their servants, though treated with the most benevolent condescendsion, could never, in any part of the live-long Day, command Liberty, or social intercourse, or repose! –

The silence of my dearest Father now silencing myself, – I turned to look at him, – but how was I struck, to see his honoured Head bowed down, almost into his bosom, with dejection and discomfort! – We were both perfectly still a few moments, – but when he raised his Head, – I could hardly keep my seat, to see his eyes filled with Tears! – 'I have long,' he cried, 'been uneasy, – though I have not spoken, . . . but . . . if *you* wish to *resign* – my House – my Purse – my Arms – shall be open to receive you back! –'

The emotion of my whole Heart at this speech – this sweet, this generous speech – O my dear Friends – I need not say it! –

We were mutually forced to break up our conference, – I could only *instantly* accept his paternal offer, – and tell him it was my Guardian Angel, – it was Providence in its own benignity, that inspired him with such goodness. I begged him to love the Day in which he had given me such comfort, and assured him it would rest upon my Heart, with grateful pleasure, till it ceased to beat.

He promised to drink Tea with me before I left Town, and settle all our proceedings.

I acknowledged my intention – to have ventured to *solicit* this very permission of resigning, – 'But *I*,' cried he, smiling with the sweetest kindness, 'have spoken first myself!'

What a joy to me, what a relief this very circumstance! – it will *always* lighten any evil that may – unhappily – follow this proposed step! –

130. From Journal Letter to Susanna Phillips and Frederica Locke *August 1790*

Know, then, fair ladies – about the middle of this August – 90 – The Author finished the rough first Draught and Copy of her first Tragedy.

What species of a composition it may prove, she is very unable to tell: she only knows it was an almost spontaneous work, – and soothed the melancholy of Imagination for a while, – though afterwards it impressed it with a secret sensation of horrour, so like real woe, that she believes it contributed to the injury her sleep received about this period.

Nevertheless – whether well or ill, she is pleased to have done something, at last: she had so long lived in all ways as nothing.

You will smile, however, at my next trust – but scarce was this completed, as to design and scenery, I mean, for the whole is in its first rough state, and legible only to herself – scarce, however, had this done with Imagination, to be consigned over to correction – when Imagination seized upon another subject, for another Tragedy.[1]

The first, therefore, I have deposited in my strong Box, in all its imperfections, to attend to the other: I well know, *Correction* may always be summoned: *Imagination* never will come but by choice. I received her, therefore, a welcome Guest, – the best adapted for softening weary solitude, where only covetted to avoid irksome exertion.

131. From Journal Letter to Susanna Phillips and Frederica Locke *October 1790*

I was ill the whole of this month, though not once with sufficient seriousness for confinement: yet with a difficulty of proceeding as usual so great, that the Day was a burthen – or rather, myself a burthen to the Day. A languor so prodigious, with so great a failure of strength and spirit, augmented almost Hourly, that I several times thought I must be compelled to excuse my constancy of attendance. But there was no one to take my place, except Miss Planta, whose Health is insufficient for her own, and Mlle Montmollin,[1] to whom such an addition of duty is almost distraction. I could not therefore but work on while to work at any rate able.

I now drew up, however, my memorial, – or rather, shewed it now to my dearest Father: – He so much approved it, that he told me he would not have a *Comma* of it altered. I will Copy it for you. It is as respectful and as grateful as I had words at command to make it; and expressive of strong devotion and attachment: but it fairly and firmly states that my strength is

---

1. Having completed the first draft of *Edwy and Elgiva*, FB was now beginning work on her second tragedy, *Hubert De Vere*.

1. Julie de Montmollin, who taught French and needlework to the Princesses.

inadequate to the duties of my charge, and therefore that I humbly crave permission to resign it, and retire into domestic life. It was written in my Father's name and my own.

I had now that dear Father's desire to present it upon the first auspicious moment. – And O with what a mixture of impatience and dread unspeakable did I look forward to such an opportunity!

132. From Journal Letter to Susanna Phillips and Frederica Locke *October 1790*

And now for a Scene a little surprising.

The beautiful Chapel of St George, repaired and finished by the best Artists at an immense expence, which was now opened after a very long shutting up for its preparations, brought innumerable strangers to Windsor, and, among others, Mr Boswell.

This I heard in my way to the Chapel, from Mr Guiffardiere, who overtook me, and mentioned having met Mr Boswell at the Bishop of Carlisle's[1] the Evening before; he proposed bringing him to call upon me; but this I declined, certain how little satisfaction would be given here by the entrance of a man so famous for compiling Anecdotes! But yet I really wished to see him again, for old acquaintance' sake, and unavoidable amusement from his oddity and good humour, as well as respect for the object of his constant admiration, my revered Dr Johnson. I therefore told Mr Guiffardiere I should be extremely glad to speak with him after the service was over.

Accordingly, at the Gate of the Choir, Mr Guiffardiere brought him to me. We saluted with mutual glee; his comic serious face and manner have lost nothing of their wonted singularity: nor yet have his mind and language, as you will soon confess!

'I am extremely glad to see you, indeed,' he cried, 'but very sorry to see you here! – My dear ma'am, why do you stay? – it won't do! ma'am! – you must resign! – We can put up with it no longer. I told my good host the Bishop so last Night; we are all grown quite outrageous! –'

Whether I laughed the most, or stared the most, I am at a loss to say; but I hurried away from the Cathedral, not to have such treasonable declarations over heard; for we were surrounded by a multitude.

---

1. John Douglas, Bishop of Carlisle and Dean of Windsor.

He accompanied me, however, not losing one moment in continuing his exhortation: 'If you do not quit, ma'am, very soon, some violent measures, I assure you, will be taken! We shall address Dr Burney in a body! I am ready to make the Harangue myself! We shall call a National Assembly, and fall upon him all at once! – '

I stopt him to enquire about Sir Joshua;[2] he said he saw him very often, and that his spirits were very good. I asked about Mr Burke's Book – 'O,' cried he, 'it will come out next Week; 'tis the first Book in the World! – except my own! – And that's coming out also very soon;[3] only I want your help.'

'My help? – '

'Yes, Madam, – you must give me some of your choice little notes of the Doctor's, – we have seen him long enough upon stilts; I want to shew him in a new light. Grave Sam, and great Sam, and solemn Sam, and learned Sam, – all these he has appeared over and over; now I want to entwine a wreath of the Graces across his Brow, I want to shew him as Gay Sam, agreeable Sam, pleasant Sam! – so you must help me with some of his beautiful billets to yourself.'

I evaded this by declaring I had not any stores at hand. He proposed a thousand curious expedients to get at them, but I was invincible.

Then I was hurrying on, lest I should be too late. He followed eagerly, and again exclaimed 'But ma'am, as I tell you, this won't do! – you must resign off hand! – Why I would farm you out myself for double – treble the money! – I wish I had the regulation of such a farm! yet I am no Farmer-General! But I should like to Farm you! and so I will tell Dr Burney. I mean to address him. I have a speech ready for the first opportunity.'

He then told me his Life of Dr Johnson was nearly Printed: and took a proof sheet out of his pocket to shew me! with crowds passing and re-passing, knowing me well, and staring well at him! For we were now at the Iron Rails of the Queen's Lodge.

I stopt; I could not ask him in: I saw he expected it: and was reduced to apologise, and tell him I must attend the Queen immediately.

He uttered again stronger and stronger exhortations for my retreat, accompanied by expressions which I was obliged to check in their bud. But finding he had no chance for entering, he stopt me again at the Gate, and said he would read me a part of his work!

There was no refusing this: and he began, – with a Letter of Dr Johnson's

2. Sir Joshua Reynolds was in failing health; see p. 344.
3. Burke's *Reflections on the Revolution in France* was published in November 1790; Boswell's *Life of Johnson* in May 1791.

to himself: he read it in strong imitation of the Doctor's manner, very well, and not caricature. But Mrs Schwellenberg was at her Window – a crowd was gathering to stand round the Rails, – and the King and Queen and Royal Family now approached from the Terrace. – I made a rather quick apology; and with a step as quick as my now weakened limbs have left in my power, I hurried to my apartment.

You may suppose I had enquiries enough, from all round, of *who was the Gentleman I was talking to at the Rails?* And an *injunction* rather frank not to admit him beyond those limits!

However, I saw him again the next morning, in coming from early prayers, – and he again renewed his remonstrances, and his petition for my Letters of Dr Johnson.

I cannot consent to print private Letters, even of a man so justly celebrated, when addressed to myself: no, I shall hold sacred those revered and but too scarce testimonies of the high honour his kindness conferred upon me. *One* Letter I have from him that is a Master-piece of elegance and kindness united. 'Twas his last![4]

133. From Letter to Georgiana Waddington *23 November 1790*

I am myself entirely of Mrs Montagu's[1] opinion about Mr Burke's Book, – it is the noblest, deepest, most animated, and exalted work that I think I have ever read. I am charmed to hear its eloge from Mrs Montagu; it is a tribute to its excellence which reflects high honour on her own candour, as she was one of those the most vehemently irritated against its author but a short time since. How can man – with all his inequalities, be so little resembling to *himself* at different periods as this man? He is all ways a prodigy, – in fascinating talents, and incomprehensible inconsistencies.

When I read, however, such a Book as this, I am apt to imagine the whole of such a Being must be right, as well as the parts, – and that the time may come when the mists which obscure the motives or incentives to those actions and proceedings which seem incongruous, may be cleared away, and we may find the internal intention had never been faulty, however ill

4. His last letter to FB was dated 1 November 1784 and to CB 17 November. A few later letters to other correspondents are extant.

1. Elizabeth Montagu's praise of Burke's *Reflections* had apparently been conveyed to FB in a letter from Georgiana Waddington (called 'Marianne' by FB).

appearances had supported any claim to right. Have you read it? – You will find it to require so deep and so entire an attention, that perhaps you may delay it till in more established Health; but read it you will, and with an admiration you cannot often feel excited.

We do not *expect* to go to Town till a Day or two before the Birth Day, the 19th of January.[2] – Would that time suit my dear Marianne? – Indeed I would not for the World it should be deferred any later; and that time will suit *me*, I believe, as well as any part of the Year. You know the uncertainty of all things here?

134. From Journal Letter to Susanna Phillips and Frederica Locke *December 1790–March 1791*

Leaving a little longer in the lurch the late months, let me endeavour to give my beloved Friends some account of this conclusion of the year while yet in being. This month is as big and important, as most lately preceding it have been little and passive.

This little had I written before Christmas – and now, 3 months after, I must have recourse to my memory – as memorandums I have none, for endeavouring to recollect what then I meant to relate.

My loss of Health was now so notorious, that no part of the House could wholly avoid acknowledging it. – Yet was the terrible picquet the catastrophe of every Evening! though frequent pains in my side forced me 3 or 4 times in a Game to creep to my own Room for Hartshorn and for rest. And so weak and faint I was become, that I was compelled to put my Head out into the air, at all Hours, and in all weathers, from time to time, to recover the power of breathing, which seemed not seldom almost withdrawn.

Her Majesty was very kind during this time, and the Princesses interested themselves about me with a sweetness very grateful to me. Indeed the whole Household shewed compassion and regard; and a general opinion that I was falling into a decline ran through the Establishment. Miss Planta was particularly attentive and active to afford me help and advice; Mlle Montmollin's Eyes glistened when we met; Miss Goldsworthy declared she thought my looks so altered as scarcely to be known again; Lady Elizabeth Waldegrave enjoined me earnestly to ask leave for respite and recruit, lest

---

2. Queen Charlotte's official birthday, celebrated at St James's Palace in London. (Her actual birthday was on 19 May.)

the Queen should lose me *entirely* by longer delay; Miss Gomm honestly protested she thought it became a *folly* to struggle on any longer against strength and Nature; Mr De Luc was so much struck with the change as to tell the Queen herself that a short and complete retirement from attendance seemed essential to my restoration; and even Mr Guiffardiere himself called one Day upon me, and frankly counselled me to resign at once, for, in my present state, a life such as that I led, was enough to destroy me.

Thus there seemed about my little person a universal commotion: and it spread much further, amongst those I have never, or slightly mentioned; you will not, therefore, be surprised to hear that my true and faithful friend Mrs De Luc, partook so largely in the general alarm, as to come to me, with her kind Eyes over-flowing with Tears, to entreat me, without the risk of further delay, to relinquish a situation of which the fatigue would else prove fatal to me. There seemed, indeed, but one opinion; that resignation of place, or of life, was the only remaining alternative.

There seemed now no time to be lost; when I saw my dear Father, he recommended to me to be speedy, and my Mother was very kind in urgency for immediate measures. I could not, however, summon courage to present my memorial: my Heart always failed me, from seeing the Queen's entire freedom from such an expectation, for though I was frequently so ill in her presence that I could hardly stand, I saw she concluded me, while life remained, inevitably hers.

Finding my inability unconquerable, I at length determined upon consulting Mr Francis.[1] I wrote to Charlotte a faithful and minute account of myself, with all my attacks, – Cough, pain in the side, weakness, sleeplessness, etc. – at full length, and begged Mr Francis's opinion how I must proceed. Very kindly, he wrote directly to my Father, exhorting instantaneous resignation, as all that stood before me to avert some dangerous malady. – How right he proved! –

The dear Charlotte, at the same time, wrote to me, conjuring my prompt retreat with the most affecting earnestness.

The uneasiness that preyed upon my spirits in a task so dreadfully difficult to perform for myself, joined to my daily declension in health, was now so apparent, that – though I could go no further – I paved the way for an opening, by owning to the Queen that Mr Francis had been consulted upon my health.

The Queen now frequently enquired concerning his answer: but as I

1. FB's brother-in-law Clement Francis.

knew he had written to my Father, I deferred giving the result till I had had a final conference with that dear Parent. I told her Majesty my Father would shew me the Letter when I saw him.

This, I saw, raised, for the first time, a surmise that something was in agitation: though I am certain the suspicion did not exceed an expectation that leave would be requested for a short absence to recruit. I was glad, however, that any thing was apprehended, and I determined to improve the little opening, by making it lead to decisive avowals. But how ill I was, how very ill, both mind and body, as this catastrophe drew near, I can hardly describe.

My dearest Father – all kindness and goodness, yet all alarm, thought time could never be more favourable, – and when next I saw him at Chelsea, I prepared for presentation on the moment of my return. I knew I could never call myself forth, if not in his name, and immediately from himself. I wrote a second memorial that very Night, at Chelsea, to enclose the original one; which my dear Father would not have altered.

With a beating Heart, and every pulse throbbing, I returned, thus armed, to the Queen's House.

Mrs Schwellenberg sent for me to her Room. I could hardly articulate a word to her. My agitation was so great, that I was compelled to acknowledge something very aweful was impending in my affairs, and to beg she would make no present enquiries.

I had not meant to employ her in the business, nor to name it to her; but I was too much disturbed for concealment or evasion.

She seemed really sorry, and behaved with a humanity I had not had much reason to expect.

I spent a terrible time till I went to the Queen at night, spiriting myself up for my task, and yet finding apprehension gain ground every moment.

Mrs Schwellenberg had already been some time with Her Majesty when I was summoned. I am sure she had already mentioned the little she had gathered. I could hardly perform my customary offices, from excess of trepidation. The Queen looked at me with the most inquisitive solicitude. When left with her a moment, I tried vainly to make an opening: I could not. She was too much impressed herself by my manner to wait long. She soon enquired what answer had arrived from Mr Francis? –

That he could not, I said, *prescribe at a distance.*

I hoped this would be understood, and said no more. The Queen looked much perplext, but made no answer.

Mrs Schwellenberg returned, and stayed, as usual, till Her Majesty retired to her Bed Room, first very gently wishing me good Night.

The next morning, – I was half dead, with real illness, excessive nervousness, and the struggle of what I had to force myself to perform. The Queen again was struck with my appearance, which I believe indeed to have been shocking. When I was alone with her, she began upon Mr Francis, with more enquiry. I then tried to articulate that I had something, of deep consequence to myself, to lay before Her Majesty, but that I was so unequal, in my weakened state, to speak it, that I had ventured to commit it to writing, and entreated permission to produce it.

She could hardly hear me, yet understood enough to give immediate consent.

I then begged to know if I might present it myself, or whether I should give it to Mrs Schwellenberg.

'O, to *me*! to *me*!' she cried, with kind eagerness.

She added, however, *not then*, as she was going to Breakfast.

This done, was already some relief, terrible as was all that remained. But I now knew I must go on, and that all my fears and horrors were powerless to stop me.

This was a Drawing Room Day. I saw the King at St James's, and he made the most gracious enquiries about my Health. So did each of the Princesses. I found they were now all aware of its failure.

The Queen proposed to me to see Dr Gisburne.[2] The King seconded the proposition. There was no refusing; yet, just now, it was distressing to comply.

The Queen gave me no opportunity whatsoever in the course of this Day to present my tremendous paper. But I uttered sundry expressive sentences, which I flattered myself would damp surprise in its perusal.

The next morning, Friday, when again I was alone with the Queen, she named the subject, and told me she would rather I should give the Paper to the Schwellenberg, who had been lamenting to her my want of confidence in her, and saying I confided and told *every thing* to the Queen: 'I answered,' continued Her Majesty, 'that you were always very good, but that with regard to confiding, you seemed so happy with all your family, and to live so well together, that there was nothing to say.'

I now perceived Mrs Schwellenberg suspected some dissention at Home was the cause of my depression! I was sorry not to deliver my memorial to

2. Dr Thomas Gisborne, Physician-in-Ordinary to George III.

the Principal Person, and yet glad to have it to do where I felt so much less compunction in giving pain.

I now desired an Audience of Mrs Schwellenberg. – With what trembling agitation did I deliver her my Paper! requesting her to have the goodness to lay it at the Feet of the Queen, before Her Majesty left Town. We were then to set out for Windsor before 12 o'clock. Mrs Schwellenberg herself remained in Town.

Here let me copy the memorial.

Most humbly presented to Her Majesty

Madam,

With the deepest sense of your Majesty's goodness and condescendsion, – amounting even to sweetness – to kindness – who can wonder I should never have been able to say what I know not how to write – that I find my strength and health unequal to my duty.

Satisfied that I have regularly been spared and favoured by your Majesty's humane consideration to the utmost, I could never bring myself to the painful confession of my secret disquietude; but I have long felt creeping upon me a languor, a feebleness, that makes, at times, the most common attendance a degree of capital pain to me, and an exertion that I could scarce have made, but for the revived alacrity with which your Majesty's constant graciousness has inspired me, – and would still, I believe, inspire me, even to my latest Hour, while in your Majesty's immediate presence. I kept this to myself while I thought it might wear away, – or, at least, I only communicated it to obtain some medical advice: but the weakness, though it comes only in fits, has of late so much encreased, that I have hardly known how, many Days, to keep myself about, – or to rise up in the morning, or to stay up at Night.

At length, however, as my constitution itself seems slowly, yet surely, giving way – my Father became alarmed. –

I must not enter, here, upon his mortification and disappointment: the Health and preservation of his Daughter could alone be more precious to him than your Majesty's protection.

With my own feelings upon the subject it would ill become me to detain your Majesty, and the less, as I am fully sensible my place, in point of its real business, may easily be far better supplied; – in point of *sincere* devotion to Your Majesty I do not so readily yield.

I can only, therefore, most humbly entreat, that your Majesty will deign to accept from my Father and myself the most dutiful acknowledgements for the uniform benignity so graciously shewn to me during the whole of my attendance. My Father had originally been apprehensive of my inability with regard to strength, for sustaining any but the indulgence of a domestic life: but Your Majesty's justice and liberality will make every allowance for the flattered feelings of a Parent's Heart, which could not endure, untried, to relinquish for his Daughter so high an Honour as a personal office about your Majesty.

I dare not, Madam, presume to hope that your Majesty's condescendsion will reach to the smallest degree of concern at parting with me; but permit me, Madam, humbly, earnestly, and fervently to solicit that I may not be deprived of the mental benevolence of your Majesty, which so thankfully I have experienced, and so gratefully must for-ever remember.

That every blessing, every good, may light upon Your Majesties here, and await a future and happier period hereafter, will be always amongst the first prayers of Madam,

> Your Majesty's
>> ever devoted, ever grateful,
>> most attached, and most dutiful
>> subject and servant Frances Burney.

With this, though written so long ago, I only wrote an Explanatory Note to accompany it, – which I will also copy.

Madam, –

May I yet humbly presume to entreat your Majesty's patience for a few added lines – to say, that the address which I now most respectfully lay at your Majesty's feet, was drawn up two months ago, when first I felt so extreme a weakness as to render the smallest exertion a fatigue. While I waited, however, for firmness to present it, I took the Bark; and found myself, for some time, so much amended, that I put it aside, and my Father, perceiving me better, lost his anxious uneasiness for my trying a new mode of life. But the good effect has, of late, so wholly failed, that an entire change of air, and manner of living are strongly recommended, as the best chance for restoring my shattered Health. We hold it, therefore, a point of the grateful duty we owe to your Majesty's goodness and graciousness, to make this melancholy statement at once, rather than to stay till absolute incapacity might disable me from offering one small but sincere tribute of profound respect to your Majesty, – the only one in my power, – that of continuing the high Honour of attending your Majesty, till your Majesty's own choice, Time, and convenience, nominate a successor.

Mrs Schwellenberg took it, and promised me her services, but desired to know its contents. I begged vainly to be excused speaking them. She persisted, – and I then was compelled to own, they contained my resignation. –

How aghast she looked! – how inflamed with wrath! how petrified with astonishment! – It was truly a dreadful moment to me. –

She expostulated on such a step, as if it led to destruction; she offered to save me from it, as if the peace of my life depended on averting it, and she menaced me with its bad consequences, as if life itself, removed from these Walls, would become an evil. –

I plainly recapitulated the suffering state in which I had lived for the last 3 months; the difficulty with which I had waded through even the most common fatigues of the Day, the constraint of attendance, however honourable, to an invalid, and the impracticability of pursuing such a life, when thus enfeebled, with the smallest chance of ever recovering the Health and strength which it had demolished.

To all this she began a vehement eulogium on the superior happiness and blessing of my lot, while under such a protection, and angrily exhorted me not to forfeit what I could never regain.

I then frankly begged her to forbear so painful a discussion, and told her the memorial was from my Father, as well as myself, that I had no right or authority to hesitate in delivering it, that the Queen herself was prepared to expect it, and that I had promised my Father not to go again to Windsor till it was presented. I entreated her, therefore, to have the goodness to shew it at once.

This was unanswerable, and she left me, with the paper in her Hand, slowly conveying it to its place of destination.

Just as she was gone, – I was called to Dr Gisburne! or, rather, *without* being called, I found him in my room, as I returned to it.

Think if my mind, now, wanted not medicine the most! I told him, however, my *corporeal* complaints, – my sleeplessness, pain in the side, etc. – etc. – and he ordered me opium, and 3 Glasses of wine in the Day, and recommended rest to me, and an application to retire to my friends for some Weeks, as freedom from anxiety was as necessary to my restoration as freedom from attendance.

During this consultation, I was called to Mrs Schwellenberg. –

Do you think I breathed as I went along? – no!

She received me, nevertheless, with complacency and smiles; she began a laboured panegyric of her own friendly zeal and goodness, and then said she had a proposal to make me, which she considered as the most fortunate turn my affairs could take, and as a proof that I should find her the best friend I had in the World.

She then premised, that she had shewn the Paper, that the Queen had read it, and said it was *very modest*, and nothing improper.

Her proposal was, that I should have leave of absence for six weeks, to go about, and change the air, to Chelsea, and Norbury Park, and *Capitan* Phillips, and Mr Francis, and *Mr Cambrick*,[3] which would get me quite well; and during that time, *she* would engage Mlle Montmollin to perform my office.

I was much disturbed at this; and though rejoiced and relieved to understand that the Queen had read my memorial without displeasure, I was grieved to see it was not regarded as *final*. I only replied I would communicate her plan to my Father.

Soon after this, we set out for Windsor.

Here the first presenting myself before the Queen was a task the heaviest, if possible, of any. Yet I was ill enough, Heaven knows, to carry the apology of my retreat in my Countenance. However, it was a terrible effort. I could hardly enter her Room. She spoke, at once, and with infinite softness, asking me how I did after my journey? Not well, indeed! I simply answered. – 'But *better*?' she cried, – 'are you not a little better? – '

I only shook my Head, – I believe the rest of my frame shook without my aid!

'What, not a *little*? – not a *little bit* better?' she cried, in the most soothing voice: while her Eyes displayed the remains of many and many Tears that she had recently been shedding.

'To *Day*, ma'am,' I said, 'I did indeed not *expect* to be better!'

I then muttered something, indistinctly enough, of the pain I had suffered in what I had done: she opened however upon another subject immediately, and no more was said upon this. But she was kind and sweet and gentle, and all consideration with respect to my attendance.

I wrote the proposal to my poor Father.

I received, by return of post, the most truly tender Letter he ever wrote me.[4] He returns thanks for the clemency with which my melancholy memorial has been received, and is truly sensible of the high honour shewn me in the new proposition; but he sees my Health so impaired, my strength so decayed, my whole frame so nearly demolished, that he apprehends any thing short of permanent resignation, that would ensure lasting rest and recruit, might prove fatal. He quotes a Letter from Mr Francis, containing his opinion that I must even be *speedy* in my retiring, or risk the utmost

---

3. Richard Owen Cambridge.

4. CB's letter to FB of 13 December 1790, which will be published in vol. ii of *Letters of Charles Burney*.

danger, and he finishes a Letter filled with gratitude towards the Queen, and affection to his Daughter, with his decisive opinion that I cannot go on, and his prayers and blessings on my retreat.

The term *speedy*, in Mr Francis's opinion, deterred me from producing this Letter, as it seemed indelicate and unfair to hurry the Queen, after offering her the fullest time. The praise, also, lavishly bestowed by this dear Father on myself, made it hardly proper to be shewn. I therefore waited till Mrs Schwellenberg came to Windsor, before I made any report of my answer.

A scene almost horrible ensued, when I told Cerbera[5] the offer was declined. She was too much enraged for disguise, and uttered the most furious expressions of indignant contempt at our proceedings. I am sure she would gladly have confined us both in the Bastile, had England such a misery, as a fit place to bring us to ourselves, from a daring so outrageous against imperial wishes.

The further particulars of this difficult and grievous business, I think, my beloved Friends, I transmitted from time to time by Letters: and I am too much worn with what yet remains, to rummage my loaded memory for any detail not essential to clear your doubts. Tell me, therefore, if there is any thing you are still perplext about, and that I will write.

135. From Journal Letter to Susanna Phillips and Frederica Locke *January 1791*

Though I continued sensibly decreasing in health, strength, and spirit, and though it was remarked by all, I made no advance in my retreat. The Queen sedulously avoided the subject, though she was uniformly and even sweetly kind and confidential upon other matters: and Mrs Schwellenberg, though she became all gentleness and consideration, from the Era of the memorial's being pronounced irreversible, yet would not even hear an allusion the most distant relative to its execution.

You may suppose my recovery was not much forwarded by a Ball, given at the Castle, on Twelfth Day.[1] The Queen condescended to say, that I might go to Bed, and she would content herself with the Wardrobe Woman, in consideration of my weak state; but then she exhorted me not to make it known to the Schwellenberg, who would be quite *wretched* at such a thing.

---

5. The female form of the name Cerberus, the dog guarding the entrance to Hades.

1. 6 January, the twelfth day after Christmas, celebrating the festival of the Epiphany.

I returned my proper thanks, but declined the proposal, so circumstanced, assuring her Majesty that it would make *me* wretched to have an indulgence that could produce an impropriety which would make Mrs Schwellenberg so through my means.

Nor, indeed, situated as is my apartment, could I have executed such a clandestine scheme, had it been possible for me to have *rested* upon such terms.

I sat up, therefore, – and I will not tell you how I wiled away the Night: it was about 5, I believe, when I came to Bed; and from this time the pain in my side ceased to consist of flying stitches, it was fixt to one spot, though I never felt it but when coughing, sneezing, or in some particular motion: and then, indeed, it cut like a Razor.

And now, to enliven a little, what will you give me, fair Ladies, for a Copy of Verses written between The Queen of Great Britain, and your most small little Journalist?

The Morning of the Ball, the Queen sent for me, and said she had a fine pair of old fashioned Gloves, white, with stiff tops, and a deep Gold Fringe, which she meant to send to her new Master of the Horse, Lord Harcourt,[2] who was to be at the Dance. She wished to convey them in a Copy of Verses, of which she had composed 3 lines, but could not get on. – She told me her ideas, and I had the honour to help her in the Metre: and now, I have the honour to Copy them from her own Royal Hand.

To the Earl of Harcourt.

Go, happy Gloves, bedeck Earl Harcourt's hand,
And let him know they come from Fairy Land:
Where ancient customs still retain their reign;
To modernize them all attempts were vain.
Go, cries Queen Mab,[3] some noble owner seek,
Who has a proper taste for the antique.

Now no criticising, fair Ladies! – The assistant was neither allowed a pen, nor a moment, but called upon to help finish, as she might have been to hand a Fan. However, she graciously received the original writing, while a fairer Copy was sent to the Earl.

The Earl, you may suppose, was sufficiently enchanted: but I somewhat

2. George Simon, Earl Harcourt, Lord of the Bedchamber and Master of the Horse.
3. Characterized by Mercutio in *Romeo and Juliet* as 'the fairies' midwife' (I. iv. 54), Queen Mab became a popular figure in eighteenth-century children's stories.

fear, by what dropt from him in a visit afterwards to my Room, he suspected *me* of *the whole!* –

136. From Journal Letter to Susanna Phillips and Frederica Locke *April 1791*

Now though I have kept memorandums since the departure of my dear Fredy, they are not chronological, and therefore you must pardon the omission of my former regularity.

With respect to the great business of my resignation, I shall say almost nothing; when could I finish were I to enter into the detail of the difficulties perpetually re-curring? the afflictive repugnance, now manifested by the most conceding kindness, now obvious in the most killing coldness, of my Royal Mistress? the various impediments thrown in my way by Cerbera? – the endless cruel conflicts how to bring forward an event which ought long since to be past? Heaven send it all to end well, and amicably, at last, and then I may account less tediously, and less painfully than by writing, the innumerable circumstances still Daily occurring of distress, embarrassment, and alarm, from eternal obstructions to the straight and open path so decidedly avowed to be the only one I can take.

I have forgot to mention that, just before my grand seizure,[1] I had again a visit from Mrs Digby. I enquired after her Husband, and said some civil nothings of my inability to wait upon her. She brightened very much, and assured me she would not expect it, if she might, from time to time, call upon me. She said much of Mr Digby's excellent health and spirits since he married, and seemed solicitous to have his happiness fully comprehended.

I am told, by my Royal Mistress, he is the most assiduous of husbands, indulging and flattering her till all present are either laughing, or sick! – How injudicious and indelicate such public testimonies of regard! And how unlike all I had imagined of a character I once thought even peculiarly refined!

---

1. On 17 January 1791, but its precise nature is unknown.

137. From Journal Letter to Susanna Phillips and
Frederica Locke *May 1791*

Let me have the pleasure, for once, to begin with mentioning something that I know my dear partial Readers will read with satisfaction: last Month I commenced a new work:[1] I finish nothing; I can get time to read and revise nothing; but a spirit of composition has fortunately assailed me, in this suspensive period, which from time to time amuses my solitude, and beguiles my weariness. The melancholy life I lead in this perpetual conflict how to lead any other, would else, I think, since your absences and Charlotte's, quite have consumed me. But I can go on with nothing – my mind is uneasy and unsettled, and my inventive faculties fly from matter to matter, softening, soothing, and lightening my lonely Hours, but never arriving at what might stand any chance to better those of any other. Three works which I have now in hand seize me capriciously;[2] but I never reprove them; I give the play into their own direction, and am sufficiently thankful, in this wearing waste of existence, for so being seized at all.

. . .

That dear and valuable Mrs Ord will now very rarely come near me. She fears suspicion of influencing my proceedings. I assured her, as I did Miss Cambridge, how clear I had kept all manner of people from any involvement. She has used all possible means to do what I have rendered *im*possible; she could not bear to find I must stay for the Birth Day, and go through all that expence; yet retire before the next Quarter's salary.[3] I assured her I could not be dangerously distressed, though much the loser; but she conjured to be my *Banker*, my *mother*, in taking upon her all the charges of that Day, in a way so pressing so maternal, so tender, I had real difficulty to withstand her, and yet greater to satisfy her from being hurt that I succeeded. Another most kind plan she has since formed, which still remains unfixt: this is, to take me for a tour with her, for the effect of gentle travelling and change of air, this summer; and she said she would put the map of England in my Hand, if I agreed to her scheme, and make me mark

---

1. *The Siege of Pevensey*, FB's third tragic drama.
2. FB's first three tragedies.
3. George III's birthday, on 4 June. The second quarter's salary would be paid only at the end of June.

our route myself. Her goodness is indeed of the most genuine worth and sincerity, and I love her, now, as much as I have respected her always. What a treasure is such a friend! one who has grown in my esteem and affection by every added year of intimacy! In this first – this essence of human happiness, how peculiar has been my lot! – and how has it softened all other bitter ingredients in it.

As no notice whatever was taken, all this time, of my successor, or my retirement, it was settled by my dear Father that I should demand leave to give warning to my servants, as I had no further occasion for them, on the 5th of May, as the 5th of June was my appointed day of departure.

This, with much difficulty, I put in practice. I was ill heard, and sullenly averted: but I pressed for an answer, saying my servants would else be on my Hands. This was with Mrs Schwellenberg.

After very great harrass of suspence, and sundry attempts to conquer it, I had at length again a conference with my Royal Mistress. She was evidently displeased at again being called upon; but I took the courage to openly remind her, that the Birth Day was Her Majesty's *own time*, and that my Father conceived it to be the period of my attendance by her especial appointment. And this was a truth which flashed its own conviction on her recollection. She paused, and then, assentingly, said ' – certainly –' I then added, that as, after the Birth Day, their Majesties went to Windsor, and the early prayers began immediately, I must needs confess I felt myself wholly unequal to encountering the fatigue of rising for them, in my present weakened state.

She was now very gracious again, conscious all this was fair and true. She told me her own embarrassments concerning the successor, spoke confidentially of her reasons for not engaging an English-woman, and acknowledged a person was fixt upon, though something yet remained unarranged. She gave me, however, to understand that all would be expedited: and foreign Letters were dispatched, I know, immediately.

This painful task over, of thus frequently reminding my Royal Mistress that my services were ending, I grew easier, and she herself grew kinder. She renewed, in a short time, all her old confidence and social conde-scendsion, and appeared to treat me with no other alteration than a visible regret that I should quit her: shewn, rather than avowed, – or much indeed it would have distressed me.

Mrs Schwellenberg was now invariable in kindness. But with regard to my servants, I could obtain no other satisfaction, than that they must each have a month's wages, as her Majesty would not consent to making my resignation known. William,[4] she told me, might probably become the footman of my successor; poor little Goter has little chance! and I fear it will be a real tragedy, when she knows her doom. She now improves Daily, and I am quite sorry for her.

138. Journal Letter to Susanna Phillips and Frederica Locke *1–2 June 1791*

On the opening of this month, Her Majesty told me, that the next Day Mr Hastings was to make his Defence, and warmly added 'I would give the World you could go to it! – '

This was an expression so unusual in animation, that I instantly told her I would write to my Father, who could not possibly, in that case, hesitate.

'Surely,' she cried, 'you may wrap up, so as not to catch cold that once?'

I ventured then to remind her, that it was not fear of *cold*, but of *misconstruction* in the world, that had so entirely made me abstain from all going out, adding that in this case, I had the *only* desire for it I had felt the whole year; for it was the only exertion I felt interest or anxiety enough to wish making, in the present state of my Mind.

I wrote this to my dear Father. He sent me an answer, that if I felt well enough, he could not object, as *it was not upon us* the comments would fall, if excited, and we had honestly done our part to keep quiet and avoid them.

I only told her Majesty, that as my Father had never thought going out would be really prejudicial to my Health, he had only wished to have his motive laid fairly before her Majesty, and then to leave it to her own command. His and my fear of rumours and mischief might perhaps be groundless; and certainly, if I was looked at, as well as known to be abroad, my countenance, in my Father's own words, would tell its own Tale of the cause of my Resignation.

Her Majesty accepted this mode of consent, and gave me Tickets for Charles and Sarah[1] to accompany me, and gave leave, and another Ticket, for Mr Deluc to be of the party.

. . .

4. William Moss, previously a servant of Mrs Schwellenberg.

1. FB's brother Charles and Sarah Harriet Burney.

Thursday, June 2d – I went, once more, to Westminster Hall. Charles and Sarah came not to their time, and I left directions and Tickets, and set off with only Mr Deluc, to secure our own, and keep places for them.

The Hall was more crowded than on any Day since the trial commenced, except the first. Peers, Commoners, and Council, Peeresses, Commoneresses, and the numerous Indefinites, crowded every part, with a just and fair curiosity to hear one Day's Defence, after Seventy Three of Accusation!

Unfortunately, I sat too high up to hear the opening, and, when, afterwards, the departure of some of my obstacles removed me lower, I was just behind some of those unfeeling Enemies, who have not even the decorum due to themselves of appearing to listen to what is offered against their own side. I could only make out, that this great and persecuted man, upon a plan all his own, and at a risk impossible to ascertain, was formally making his own Defence, not with retaliating Declamation, but by a simple, concise, and most interesting statement of facts, and of the necessities accompanying them in the situation to which the House then impeaching had 5 times called him! He spoke with most gentlemanly temper of his accusers, his provocation considered, yet with a firmness of disdain of the injustice with which he had been treated, in return for his services, that was striking and affecting, though unadorned and manly.

His spirit, however, and the injuries which raised it, rested not quietly upon his particular Accusers: he arraigned the late Minister, Lord North, of ingratitude and double-dealing, and the present Minister, Mr Pitt, of unjustifiably and unworthily forbearing to sustain him.

Here Mr Fox, artfully enough, interrupted him, to say the *King's Ministers* were not to be arraigned for what passed in the House of Parliament.

Mr Burke rose also, to enter his protest –

But Mr Hastings then lost his patience and his Temper: he would not suffer the interruption; he had never, he said, interrupted *their long* speeches – and, when Mr Burke again attempted to speak, Mr Hastings, in an impassioned, but affecting manner, extended his arms, and called out, loudly 'I throw myself upon the Protection of your Lordships! – I am not used to public speaking, and cannot answer them – what I wish to submit to your Lordships, I have committed to Paper, – but – *if I am punished for what I say*, I *must* insist upon being heard! – I call upon you, my Lords, to protect me from this violence! –'

This animated appeal prevailed; the managers were silenced, by an almost universal cry of 'Hear! Hear! Hear!' from the Lords; and by the Lord

Kenyon,[2] who represented the Chancellor, and said 'Mr Hastings, Proceed!'

The angry orators, though with a very ill grace, were then silenced. They were little aware what a Compliment this intemperate eagerness was paying to Mr Hastings, who for so many long Days manifested that Fortitude against attack, and that Patience against abuse, which they could not muster, without any parallel in provocation, even for 3 short Hours!

I rejoiced with all my Heart to find Mr Windham was not in their Box. He did not enter with them in procession, nor appear as a manager, or party concerned, further than as a Member of the House of Commons. I could not distinguish him in so large a Group, and he either saw not, or knew not, me.

The Conclusion of the Defence I heard better, as Mr Hastings spoke considerably louder, from this time; the spirit of indignation animated his manner, and gave strength to his voice. You will have seen the chief parts of his discourse in the news-papers; and you cannot, I think, but grow more and more his friend as you peruse it. He called pathetically and solemnly for instant judgement; but the Lords, after an adjournment, decided to hear his Defence by Evidence, and in order, the next sessions.[3] How grievous such continual delay to a man past sixty,[4] and sighing for such a length of time for redress from a prosecution as yet unparallelled in our annals!

139. Journal Letter to Susanna Phillips and Frederica Locke *5 June 1791*

Notwithstanding my extreme unfitness for remaining in office, and my distinct hope that I had no more duty expected after the Birth Day, I was called upon to return again to Windsor. – I must be brief in all these retrospections, which I now love not to dwell upon.

My orders, which I punctually obeyed, of informing no one of my impending departure, were extremely painful to adhere to, as almost every body I saw advised me strenuously to beg leave of absence to recruit, and pressed so home to me the necessity of taking some step for my Health, that I was reduced to a thousand unpleasant evasions in my answers. But I was bound; and I never disengage *myself* from bonds imposed by others, if once I have agreed to them.

2. Lloyd, Lord Kenyon, Chief Justice of the King's Bench.
3. The next session of the trial would begin on 14 February 1792.
4. Hastings was fifty-eight.

Mr Guiffardiere out-stayed the Tea party one Evening not for his former rhodomontading, but to seriously and earnestly advise me to *resign*. My situation, he said, was evidently death to me. Thank Heaven, nothing upon Earth could be more peaceable, and friendly, and proper, than all my latter transactions with this excentric Character.

He was eager to enquire of me *Who was Mrs Lenox?* He had been reading, like all the rest of the World, Boswell's Life of Dr Johnson, and the preference there expressed of *Mrs Lenox* to all other females, had filled him with astonishment, as he had never even heard her name.[1]

These occasional sallies of Dr Johnson, uttered from local causes and circumstances, but all retailed verbatim by Mr Boswell, are filling all sorts of readers with amaze, except the small party to whom Dr Johnson was known, and who, by acquaintance with the power of the moment over his unguarded conversation, knew how little of his solid opinion was to be gathered from his accidental assertions.

The King, who was also now reading this work, applied to me for explanations without end. Every Night, at this period, he entered the Queen's Dressing Room, and detained her Majesty's proceedings, by a length of discourse with me upon this subject. All that flowed from himself was constantly full of the goodness and benevolence of his character; and I was never so happy as in the opportunity thus graciously given me of vindicating, in instances almost innumerable, the serious principles and various excellencies of my ever most revered Dr Johnson, from the clouds so frequently involving and darkening them, in narrations so little calculated for any Readers who were strangers to his intrinsic worth, and therefore worked upon and struck by what was faulty in his Temper and manners.

I regretted not having strength to read this Work to Her Majesty myself. It was an honour I should else have certainly received: for so much wanted clearing! so little was understood! – However, the Queen frequently condescended to read over passages and anecdotes which perplexed or offended her; and there were none I had not a fair power to soften or to justify. Dear and excellent Dr Johnson! I have never forgot nor neglected his injunction, given me when ill – to stand by him and support him, and not hear him abused, when he was no more, and could not defend himself! – but little –

---

1. Charlotte Lennox, novelist, translator and critic, was among the most famous English women writers before FB. In his *Life of Johnson*, Boswell records Johnson's declaration on 15 May 1784: 'I dined yesterday at Mrs Garrick's, with Mrs Carter, Miss Hannah More, and Miss Fanny Burney. Three such women are not to be found: I know not where I could find a fourth, except Mrs Lennox, who is superiour to them all' (iv. 275).

little did I think it would ever fall to my lot to vindicate him to his King and Queen. –

At this time Colonel Manners was in waiting, and Colonel Goldsworthy was on a visit, as was Mr Digby. They all little enough thought how near we were to a separation. Lords Chesterfield, Harrington, and Cathcart drank Tea with us almost constantly. The two latter I liked extremely, and shall be glad if hereafter I should meet them.

With Mr Digby I proceeded as usual, – distant, impenetrably distant, and cold, invincibly cold: he, too, proceeded as usual with me; attentive, submissive, serious, meditative, and vigilantly watchful for opportunities he never found. Once Mrs De Luc drank Tea with us; – she is near-sighted, and did not recollect him; but after he was gone, – 'Do tell me,' she cried, 'who that is, for I must love him – he so *venerates* you! – such a trait of reverence as that of his leaving his own Tea, to take that which he did not like, because it was weaker, merely on account of your having held one, and not the other – it was such a *trait of reverence*, with his look and whole air joined, that I shall never forget it! –'

Odd enough this! I could hardly tell her it was Mr Digby – she was so prepossessed it was one of our *single cavaliers*. – I believe this was the last Evening of our meeting. In all probability it will remain the last ever more.

Mrs Schwellenberg was in Town all this fortnight.

Her Majesty, the Day before we left Windsor, gave me to understand my attendance would be yet one more fortnight requisite, though no longer. I heard this with a fearful presentiment I should surely never go through another fortnight, in so weak and languishing and painful a state of Health. However, I could but accede – though I fear with no very courtly grace.

So melancholy, indeed, was the state of my mind, from the weakness of my frame, and the never-ending struggles for the rest I sighed after, that I was never alone but to form scenes of '*foreign woe*',[2] when my own disturbance did not ocupy me wholly. I began – almost whether I would or not – another Tragedy! The other three all unfinished! not one read! – and one of them, indeed, only generally sketched as to plan and character. – But I could go on with nothing; I could only suggest and invent. And the other work which I have mentioned is of another sort – in a style my dear friends all around will most wish me to cultivate: but that was not dismal enough,[3] –

---

2. Not identified.
3. The fourth tragedy, never completed, is 'Elberta'. The one 'only generally sketched' is her third, *The Siege of Pevensey*.

and away it went, from Pen, Hand, and Head, to give place to a plan of the deepest Tragedy, which first had occurred to me in the worst part of my illness in January, but which I had not thought of since my quitting my room.

The power of Composition has to me, indeed, proved a solace, a blessing! – When incapable of all else, that, unsolicited, unthought of, has presented itself to my solitary leisure, and beguiled me of *myself*, though it has not, of late, regaled me with gayer associates.

140. From Journal Letter to Susanna Phillips and Frederica Locke *July 1791*

I come now to write the last Week of my royal residence. The Queen honoured me with the most uniform graciousness, and though, as the time of separation approached, her cordiality rather diminished, and traces of internal displeasure appeared sometimes, arising, from an opinion I ought rather to have struggled on, live or die, than to quit her, – yet I am sure she saw how poor was my own chance, except by a change in the mode of life, and at least ceased to wonder, though she could not approve.

The King was more courteous, more communicative, more amiable, at every meeting; and he condescended to hold me in conversation with him by every opportunity; and with an air of such benevolence and goodness, that I never felt such ease and pleasure in his notice before. He talked over all Mr Boswell's Book – and I related to him sundry anecdotes of Dr Johnson, all highly to his honour, and such as I was eager to make known. He always heard me with the utmost complacency, and encouraged me to proceed in my accounts by every mark of attention and interest.

He told me once, laughing heartily, that having seen my name in the Index, he was eager to come to what was said of me; but when he found so little, he was surprised and disappointed.

I ventured to assure him how much I had myself been rejoiced at this very circumstance, and with what satisfaction I had reflected upon having very seldom met Mr Boswell, as I knew there was no other security against all manner of risks in his relations.

141. Journal Letter to Susanna Phillips and
Frederica Locke *4–5 July 1791*

This was my last Sunday, I think, at Windsor: and the next morning, Her Majesty sent the Princess Royal to summon me to her presence; and then informed me that my successor, Mlle Jacobi,[1] was arrived, and would be at Windsor in a few Hours. She spoke to me very graciously, and put various directions into my hands.

This was, alltogether, a very painful period to me. Rejoiced, relieved as I felt, that my long struggles now ended, I yet had much personal regret in quitting my *Royal Mistress* – though not *my place*! – But I must simply, now, write facts.

I had soon the pleasure to receive Mlle Jacobi. She brought with her a young German, as her maid, who proved to be her neice![2] but so poor, she could not live when her Aunt left Germany! Mr Best, a messenger of the King's, brought her to Windsor, and Mrs Best, his Wife, accompanied him.

I was extremely pleased with Mlle Jacobi, who is Tall, well made, and nearly handsome, and of a humour so gay, an understanding so lively, and manners so frank and ingenuous, that I felt an immediate regard for her, and we grew mutual good friends. She is the Daughter of a dignified Clergyman of Hanover,[3] high in fame theological.

They all dined with me: and, indeed, Mlle Jacobi wanting a thousand informations in her new situation, which I was most happy to give her, seldom quitted me an instant.

Tuesday morning, the sweet Princess Elizabeth fetched me to the Queen: – and then I had a conversation very long and very affecting to me with Her Majesty. I cannot pretend to detail it. I will only tell you, she began by speaking of Mlle Jacobi, whom I had the satisfaction to praise, as far as had appeared, very warmly; and then she led me to talk at large upon the nature and requisites and circumstances of the situation I was leaving. I said whatever I could suggest that would tend to render my successor more comfortable, and had the great happiness to represent with success the infinite consolation, and every innocent pleasure, she might reap from the society of the young Relation she had brought over, if she might be permitted

1. Caroline Jacobi of Hanover, who would hold the post of Second Keeper of the Robes to Queen Charlotte until October 1797.
2. Bettina Winkelmann.
3. Johann Friedrich Jacobi.

to treat her at once as a Companion, and not as a Servant. This was heard with the most humane complacency, and I had leave given me to forward the plan in various ways.

She then conversed upon sundry subjects, all of them confidential in their nature, for near an Hour, – and then, after a pause, said 'Do I owe you any thing, my dear Miss Burney? –'

I acquainted her with a Debt or two, amounting to near £70. – She said she would settle it in the Afternoon; and then paused again, – after which, with a look full of benignity, she very expressively said – 'As I don't know your plan – or what you propose – I cannot tell what would make you comfortable; – but – you know the size of my family —'

I comprehended her, and was immediately interrupting her, with assurances of my freedom from all expectation or claim, – but she stopt me, – saying 'You know what you now have from me – the half of that I mean to continue. –'[4]

Amazed and almost overpowered, by a munificence I had so little awaited or expected, or thought of, – I poured forth the most earnest disclaimings of such a mark of her graciousness, declaring I knew too well her innumerable calls to be easy in receiving it: and much more I uttered to this purpose, with the unaffected warmth that animated me at the moment. She heard me almost silently; but, in conclusion, simply, yet strongly, said 'I shall certainly do *that*!' with a stress on the *that* that seemed to kindly mean she would rather have done *more*.

The conference was in this stage, when the Princess Elizabeth came into the Room. The Queen then retired to the anti-chamber. My Eyes being full, and my Heart not very empty, I could not then forbear saying to her Royal Highness how much the goodness of the Queen had penetrated me. The sweet Princess spoke feelings I could not expect, by the immediate glistening of her soft Eyes: she condescended to express her concern at my retiring – but most kindly added 'However, Miss Burney, you have this to comfort you, go when you will – that your behaviour has been perfectly honourable.'

This, my last Day at Windsor, was filled with nothing but packing, leave-taking, Bills paying, and lessoning to Mlle Jacobi, who adhered to my side through every thing, and always with an interest that made its own way for her.

All the people I had to settle with, poured forth for my better Health good wishes without end.

4. I.e. a pension of £100 per annum.

142. Journal Letter to Susanna Phillips and Frederica Locke *7 July 1791*

This, my last Day of office, was big and busy, – joyful, yet affecting to me in a high degree.

In the morning, before I left Kew, I had my last interview with Mrs Schwellenberg. She was very kind in it, desiring to see me whenever I could in Town, during her residence at the Queen's House, and to hear from me by Letter meanwhile.

She then much surprised me, by an offer of succeeding to her own place, when it was vacated either by her retiring, or her Death![1] This was, indeed, a mark of favour and confidence I had not expected. I declined, however, to enter upon the subject, as the manner in which she opened it made it very solemn, and, to her, very affecting.

She would take no leave of me, but wished me better hastily, and saying we should soon meet, she hurried suddenly out of the Room.

Poor Woman! if her Temper were not so irascible, I really believe her Heart would be by no means wanting in kindness.

I then took leave of Mrs Sandys, giving her a token of remembrance, in return for her constant good behaviour. – And she shewed marks of regard and of even grief I was sorry to receive, as I could so ill return. –

But the Tragedy of Tragedies was parting with Goter! – that poor Girl did nothing but cry incessantly from the time she knew of our separation. I was very sorry to have no place to recommend her to, though I believe she may rather benefit by a vacation, that carries her to her excellent Father and mother, who teach her nothing but good. However, it was a scene, on her part, almost of agony, – when the last moment came, I did what I could to soften the blow, by every exertion in my power, in all ways: – for it was impossible to be unmoved at her violence of sorrow.

I then took leave of Kew Palace: the same party again accompanying me, for the last time, in a Royal Vehicle going by the name of *Miss Burney's Coach*. –

I should mention, that the Queen graciously put into my hands the power of giving every possible comfort and kind assurances of encouragement, to Mlle Jacobi and her poor little Bettina; and all was arranged in the best manner for their accomodation and ease. Her Majesty made me, also, the happy conveyer of various Presents to them both, and gave to me the regulation of their proceedings.

1. Mrs Schwellenberg's appointment as Keeper of the Robes lasted until her death in 1797.

When we arrived in Town, I took leave of M. De Luc. I believe he was as much inclined to be sorry as the visible necessity of the parting would permit him. For me, I hope to see every one of the Establishment hereafter far more comfortably than ever I have been able to do, during the fatigues of a life to which I was so ill-suited.

I come now near the close of my Court career.

At St James's all was graciousness, and my Royal Mistress gave me to understand she would have me stay to assist at her Toilette after the Drawing Room: and much delighted me by desiring my attendance on the Thursday fortnight, when she came again to Town. This lightened the last, and the parting, in the pleasentest manner possible.

During the Drawing Room, I considered of what had passed from Mrs Schwellenberg with respect to my succeeding her to her place; and however I was gratified in a proof so complete of the good opinion with which I was honoured, I found myself equally and steadily unwilling and incapable of living a Court Life. I therefore thought it best to prevent any application, that the pain and danger of a refusal might not hang on my mind, nor the expectation of an acceptance deceive or disappoint my Royal Mistress. When the Queen, therefore, summoned my last attendance, I gathered courage to resolve to speak sincerely and openly at once: and I entreated to be allowed a private audience before her departure for Kew.

She accorded it me most readily.

You may believe I was very much flurried, volunteer as I was in this business, during this *last of all*: – When the Queen commanded me to follow her to her Closet, I was, indeed, in much emotion; but I opened upon the business immediately. I told her, that as what had passed from Mrs Schwellenberg in the morning had given me to understand her Majesty was fixed in her munificient intention, notwithstanding what I had most unaffectedly urged against it –

'*Certainly*,' she interrupted, 'I shall certainly do it.'

'Yet so little,' I continued, 'had I thought it right to dwell upon such an expectation, that, in the belief your Majesty would yet take into further consideration, I had not even written it to my Father –'

'Your Father,' she again interrupted me, 'has nothing to do with it! it is solely from *Me* to *you*.'

'Let me then, humbly entreat,' I cried, 'still in some measure to be considered as a servant of your Majesty, – either as Reader, – or to assist, occasionally, if Mlle Jacobi should be ill –'

She looked most graciously pleased, and smiling, though through Eyes that were full of Tears, she immediately closed in with the proposal, saying 'When your Health is restored – perhaps sometimes. —'

I then fervently poured forth my thanks for all her goodness, and my prayers for her felicity. –

She had her Handkerchief in her Hand, or at her Eyes the whole time – I was so much moved by her condescending kindness, that as soon as I got out of the Closet I nearly sobbed. – I went to help Mlle Jacobi to put up the Jewels, that my emotion might the less be observed. The King then came into the Room. He immediately advanced to the window, where I stood, to speak to me. I was not then able to *comport myself* steadily. I was forced to turn my Head away from him. He stood still, and silent, for some minutes, waiting to see if I should turn about: but I could not recover myself sufficiently to face him, strange as it was to do otherwise; and perceiving me quite over-come, he walked away, – and I saw him no more.

His kindness, his goodness, his benignity, never shall I forget! never think of but with fresh gratitude and reverential affection.

They were now all going – I took, for the last time, the Cloak of the Queen – and putting it over her shoulders, slightly ventured to press them, earnestly, though in a low voice, saying 'God Almighty bless your Majesty! –'

She turned round, and putting her Hand upon my ungloved arm, pressed it with the greatest kindness, and said 'May you be happy! –'

She left me overwhelmed with tender gratitude – the 3 eldest Princesses were in the next Room – They ran in to me, the moment the Queen went onward; – Princess Augusta and Princess Elizabeth each took a Hand, – and the Princess Royal put hers over them. I could speak to none of them, – but they repeated 'I wish you happy! – I wish you Health!' again and again, with the sweetest eagerness. –

They then set off for Kew. –

Mlle Jacobi and Miss Planta followed, – the latter almost in hysterics with crying.

I took the same leave, in all ways, of Mrs Thielke[2] that I had done of Mrs Sandys, – and of poor William that I had done of Goter: save that I had the good fortune to settle William with Mlle Jacobi.

That good nature repeatedly brought me fine fruit, from the Table formerly mine, after I was at Chelsea.

. . .

2. A wardrobe-woman to Queen Charlotte.

My Thursday's final attendance at St James's, and the infinite graciousness of my reception by their Majesties, and by the Princesses, and my last
Cadeau from my Queen, of a Gold Necklace, etc etc – my beloved Susan
heard at the time: – and will tell to my Fredy.

Here, therefore, end

   My Court Annals.

After having lived in the service of

Her Majesty

Five Years

within

Ten Days:

From July 17 1786.
To July 7 1791.

1791–1792

London and the Western Tour

143. Journal Letter to Susanna Phillips and William and Frederica Locke *31 July 1791*

Chelsea College[1]

Once more I have the blessing to address my most beloved Friends from The Natal Home! – with a satisfaction, a serenity of heart immeasurable. All smaller evils shall now give way to the one great good, – and I shall not, I hope, be forgetful, when the World wags ill; that scarce any misfortune, scarce misery itself, can so wastefully desolate the very soul of my Existence as a banishment, even the most honourable, from those I love.

I write this moment at the side of my dearest Father, – What a delight that is to me You can only conceive by traversing back the Country in which I have lived an alien –

But I must haste to the present time, – and briefly give the few facts that occurred before my Susanna came to greet my restoration, and the few that preceded my journey South West afterwards, in

July.

My dear Father was waiting for me in my Apartment at St James's, when their Majesties and their fair Royal Daughters were gone. He brought me Home – and welcomed me most sweetly. – My Heart was a little sad, in spite of its contentment. My joy in quitting my Place extended not to quitting the King and Queen, and the final marks of their benign favour had deeply impressed me. My Mother received me according to my wishes, and Sarah most cordially.

---

1. FB returned to her father's rooms here.

My dear James and Charles speedily came to see me,[2] – and one precious half Day I was indulged with my kindest Mr Lock and his Fredy – If I had been stouter and stronger in health, I should then have been almost flightily happy. But the weakness of the Frame still kept the rest in order. My ever kind Miss Cambridge was also amongst the foremost to hasten with congratulations on my return to *my old ways*, – and to make me promise to visit Twickenham after my projected Tour with Mrs Ord: as well as to reiterate my early argument to make no disposal of my £100 annuity without her previous consent. – A foolish promise, which she will not give me back, though her view in exacting it is not easy to fathom.

I could myself undertake no visiting at this time; rest and quiet being quite essential to my recovery. But my Father did the honours for me amongst those who had been most interested in my resignation. He called instantly upon Sir Joshua Reynolds and Miss Palmer, and Mr Burke; And he wrote to Mr Walpole, Mr Seward, Mrs Crewe, Mr Windham, and my Worcester Uncle.[3] Mr Walpole wrote the most charming of answers, in the gallantry of *the old Court*, and with all its wit, concluding with a warm invitation to Strawberry Hill.[4] Sir Joshua and Miss Palmer sent me every species of kind exultation. Mr Burke was not in Town. Mr Seward wrote very heartily and cordially, – and came also, when my Susanna was here. Mrs Crewe immediately pressed me to come and recruit at Crewe-Hall in Cheshire, where she promised me repose and good air and good society, – every body wrote or sent, except Mr Windham, and for him, he shall speak for himself, in the Letter he sent my father the *last* Day of the Month.[5]

---

2. FB's stepmother, Sarah Harriet Burney and brothers.

3. Edmund Burke, Frances Anne Crewe (daughter of Fulke and Frances Greville) and Richard Burney, brother of CB.

4. Walpole's courtly letter to CB inviting FB and CB to Strawberry Hill is printed in *The Yale Edition of Horace Walpole's Correspondence*, ed. W. S. Lewis et al. (New Haven, Conn., 1937–83), xlii. 331–2. It was arranged for 4 January 1792, but FB was forced to break the engagement (*JL*, i. 108–10).

5. FB copied part of Windham's flattering letter to CB (30 July) here in her own letter to Susanna and the Lockes (*JL*, i. 4).

144. Journal Letter to Susanna Phillips and William and Frederica Locke *4–5 August 1791*[1]

Thursday, August 4   We proceeded to Breakfast at Romsey.[2] What a contrast this journey to that I took 2 years ago in attendance upon Her Majesty! the Roads now so empty, the Towns so quiet, – and then – what multitudes! what tumults of joy – and how graciously welcomed!

We went on to Dine at Salisbury, – a City which, with their Majesties, I could not see for People![3] It seemed to have neither Houses nor Walls, but to be composed solely of Faces. We strolled about the Town, but the Cathedral was shut up, to be repaired, – much to our regret.

Friday August 5   We went to see Stonehenge. – Here I was prodigiously disappointed, at first, by the little shape, or intelligence, of the huge masses of stone so unaccountably piled at the summit of Salisbury Plain. However, we alighted, and the longer I surveyed and considered them, the more augmented my Wonder, and diminished my disappointment. There is enough remnant to prove the form had been circular, and the pile a Temple; – but I shall enter into no disquisitions of what is nearly proved undisquisitionable – even though I spent *half an Hour* in examining the premises! – [4]

We then went on to Wilton – There I renewed my delight over the exquisite Vandykes,[5] and with Statues, Busts – and Pictures, which again I sighingly quitted, with a longing wish I might ever pass under that Roof time enough to see them more deliberately. We stopt in the Hans Holbein porch, and upon the Inigo Jones Bridge, as long as we could stand, after standing and staring and straining our Eyes, till our guide was quite fatigued. 'Tis a noble, noble collection: and how might it be enjoyed if – as an arch

---

1. Together with selection 146, part of FB's extensive journal letter recording her western tour.

2. Market town in the New Forest, where in June 1789 crowds celebrated the recovery of George III.

3. FB had also visited Salisbury with the Thrales in June 1780.

4. There was much debate in the eighteenth century about the origin and meaning of the standing stones at Stonehenge, eight miles north of Salisbury. In Burney's *The Wanderer* (1814) the heroine Juliet is 'struck with solemn wonder' on her first sight of the 'massy ruins' (ch. 83).

5. Wilton House, Wiltshire, estate of the Pembrokes. Juliet in *The Wanderer* (ch. 82) also admires the collection of paintings, sculptures and antiquities, and in particular Van Dyck's portrait of the children of Charles I. (The bridge was not designed by Jones, but by the ninth Earl of Pembroke.)

rustic old Labouring man told us, *fine folks lived as they ought to do*! How I wish my dear Susan to see Wilton. – My Fredy I am sure has been there.

I returned to Salisbury almost ill again with the exertion and fatigue of this great pleasure, from the strain of attention, joined to standing and walking.

145. Letter to Dr Burney *13 August 1791*

Sidmouth, Devon.

Most dear Padre,

The *'few pleasing words'*[1] were most acceptable indeed. I received them at Salisbury, just as we were departing. I trust you are now with Mrs Crewe,[2] and then, if well, I am sure you are happy. I must not, now, drop a word of how much the same sejour[3] would have agreed with me; – it would be graceless, at this time, when every thing possible is done to give every comfort where I am. And, in truth, I am fit only, as yet, for so indulgent a fellow traveller, who watches me continually and allows for all my weaknesses – *corporeal* ones, I mean – the *mental*, I have no intention to commit to such close investigation.

Just as I finished my hasty scrap at Winchester, a large party of French stopt at the Inn, intending to sleep there.[4] But the House was already so full, we had found great difficulty in getting *one Room* for Mrs Ord, her maid, and myself. And what became of the *Men* we concluded it best not to enquire. – The Judges were expected next day, and the Road and every Inn were filled, with people whom the Trials, or the Balls, called severally to be Hanged, or to Dance. The poor foreigners, therefore, had little chance, not chusing the first, as they were flying from *à la lanthorne*![5] and not being chosen for the second, though ready for it in the worst of times, *à ce qu'on dit*.[6] They could not comprehend this difficulty, a considerable while. From

---

1. Burney family catchphrase taken from the first sentence of CB's letter to FB of 10 August.
2. CB's lumbago had forced him to cancel his visit to Frances Crewe at Crewe Hall, Cheshire.
3. Stay.
4. The 'scrap' is apparently a note to CB, no longer extant. FB's description of the French refugees, the first she had encountered, reveals her natural sympathy for the victims of the Revolution. In her journal for 2 August 1791, she describes them in further detail (*JL*, i. 13–18).
5. *To the lantern!*: familiar street cry during the French Revolution, when the mob used ropes attached to street lanterns to hang its victims. (The Court of Assizes had met at Winchester on 3 August.)
6. *As they say.*

our windows, we saw them debating the matter, and then ordering fresh Horses to go on. They were in their own Coach, with 4 hack Horses, and their maids in a chaise, with outriders –

Horses were as scarce as Beds, – none could be procured.

They ordered their postillions, in broken English, to drive to the next stage.

The postilions declined obedience; they protested the Horses could go no further.

The poor Quadrupeds were then taken off; and the poor bipeds remained, at the Gate of the Inn, in the Horseless Carriages, shewing, by the most animated gestures, their indignant disbelief that such usage was unavoidable.

We pitied them – but – like true good Daughters of John Bull, passed them quietly, to take a survey of the City. Dr Warton, unluckily, was absent, on an excursion to the Isle of Wight.

When we had seen there was nothing to be seen, – except the Cathedral, which we reserved for the Morning, we returned to the Inn, – and saw there still the poor French Travellers, waiting for Horses, Beds, or even one Room to sit in, without success.

After a little deliberation, we now were touched to shake off a part of the John Bullism that had encrusted us, and to ask them to our sitting Room, to drink Tea: though a little still clung to us, in our debate which should be excused from making them the proposal.

I assured Mrs Ord it was her place; She assured me it must be my French; I assured her I had very little – and she assured me again she had none at all: so we ended the contest, by ordering a waiter to carry them our invitation.

They were by no means as long, or as fastidious, in arranging its acceptation. They alighted instantly – 2 ladies, and 2 Men.

A shower of French was poured upon us, *vehicling* thanks and compliments. We returned very modest little answers, having no more french than to serve that purpose.

They proved, however, very interesting; – they had been to see the Fleet, in hopes it was sailing to the relief of their *pauvre Roi*.[7] I assured them I wished their *pauvre Roi* every other Good, most cordially; but not that of involving a National War. They had been in England 2 Months. One of

---

7. *Poor King.* The other French in this and the following paragraph is *bêtes* ('animals'), *bien aristocrate* ('a true aristocrat'), *les plus jolis spectacles* ('the finest sights'), *les honnettes Gens* ('honest people') and *le peuple* ('the people').

the ladies spoke English tolerably, though comically; but I saw the rest of the party regarded her as a Being to wonder at, their own attainments in our language rendering them, as they said, mere *bêtes* in comparison. She was a Mlle de Beaufort. The other lady seemed exactly a French Character drawn by an English Author. She was characteristically National in the highest degree. She was *bien aristocrate*, she told me, and bewailed the situation of her King and Party with an emotion that almost made her sob as she spoke; – and the moment she had sighed deeply, and recovered, she eagerly demanded what were *les plus jolis spectacles* at Bath, whither she was going? –

She had scarcely exercised her complaisance in attending to my tame answer, when she vehemently broke forth with a detail of the calamitous state of the finest Country in the World, where none were safe, but of the reigning party, and where the gift of liberty to the people, had annihilated common security for *les honnettes Gens*, if their principles were even suspected to be opposite to those of the National Assembly: – All, she said, was confusion and horror, except for the Democrats: – and even their country Houses, whither they were wont to retire, when distressed, disturbed, or wearied at Paris, could now afford them no shelter, as the humour of *le peuple* must not be controverted; and if they were seized with a desire to enter any villa, and turn out its inhabitants, and burn all their Records and property, they must neither be stopt nor punished, till the mischief was done. – The Tears rolled from her large prominent Eyes as she painted this Picture, – which, however, almost instantly dispersing with a most expressive and animated smile, 'Ah, Mademoselle – ', she cried, 'and You have never seen France! ah! what pity! – I find London so little pretty to Paris! – Have the goodness to excuse me – – there is no comparison! – '

They stayed with us till our early Bed time: the Waiter then procured them a sitting Room. We asked him, afterwards, what they were to do? He sneeringly said 'They may have Horses about midnight: – but now they be got into one of our Rooms, they are all as merry as if they were going to Dance a Jig.'

They were detained for Horses till *Two* in the morning, – and then proceeded towards Oxford. – They left us their direction for town, which was Mme La Comtesse de Menage, in Gerrard Street. Mrs Ord gave them hers. I promised to meet them at her House. But they sent, after leaving us, for Mrs Ord's servant, and made him write down mine also, and my Name. How greatly they are to be pitied! I should much like to see them again.

So here is so much of French, I have no room left for English: – We travel very slowly, 30 miles being our furthest stretch, and 20, and even 14, or 15 our more common quantity. We stop to see all places in our way worth the trouble, as far as we can find them out – We have been to Wilton, Stonehenge, Milton abbey, Mr Portman's, Farnham Castle,[8] Salisbury – and Winchester Cathedrals –, and I continue gaining ground in general Health, and follow your directions to the best of my power in avoiding to *take sides*. My weakness still often surprises and disappoints me: but I have still fair hopes of becoming again my own *robustious self*.[9] We found ourselves tiring with continued motion, however gentle, and for *me* it grew wearisome: we have therefore settled ourselves here for a week's rest. – And have given up Plymouth, &c, to remove hence to Bristol.[10]

146. From Journal Letter to Susanna Phillips and William and Frederica Locke *20–31 August 1791*

Queen Square, Bath

Bath is extremely altered since I last visited it. Its circumference is perhaps trebled: but its buildings are so unfinished, so spread, so every where beginning, and no where ending, that it looks rather like a space of Ground lately fixed upon for creating a Town, than a Town itself, of so many years duration.

It is beautiful and wonderful through-out. The Hills are built up and down, and the vales so stocked with streets and Houses, that in some places, from the Ground floor on one side a street, you cross over to the attic of your opposite neighbour. The White stone, where clean, has a beautiful effect, and even where worn, a grand one. But I must not write a literal Bath Guide, – and a figurative one Anstey has all to himself.[1] I will only tell you, in brief, yet in truth, – It looks a City of Palaces – a Town of Hills, and a Hill of Towns.

O how have I thought – in patroling it – of my poor Mrs Thrale! – I went to look, and sigh at the sight, at the House on the North Parade where we

---

8. Elsewhere in her journal for August FB describes Milton Abbey, Dorset; Henry Portman's seat at Bryanston House, Dorset; and Farnham Castle, Surrey.

9. Alluding to CB's advice in his letter.

10. Instead of Bristol Hot Wells, the party went to Bath.

1. FB met Christopher Anstey, author of the celebrated *New Bath Guide* (1766), with the Thrales in May 1780. Oddly, one of her friends, Hannah Humphreys, had earlier suspected Anstey of being the author of *Evelina* (*EJL*, iii. 8).

dwelt,[2] – and almost every old place brings to my mind some scene in which we were engaged.

. . .

Not long after our settling at Bath, I found, upon returning from the Pump Room, cards left for me of the Bishop of Dunmore (Dr Percy) Mrs and the Miss Percys.[3] I had met them formerly once at Miss Reynolds, and once visited them, when Dr Percy was Dean of Carlile. The Collector and Editor of the beautiful reliques of ancient English Poetry I could not but be happy to again see. I returned the visit: they were out; but the Bishop soon after came when I was at home. I had a pleasant little chat with him. He told me he had heard of my arrival at Bath by Lady Spencer.[4] He renewed an acquaintance, after this, with Mrs Ord, and we have all visited and been visited by them.

The Bishop is perfectly easy and unassuming, very communicative, and though not very entertaining, because too prolix, he is otherwise intelligent and of good commerce. Poor Mrs Percy is ill, and cannot make visits, though she sends her name, and receives company at home. She is very cultivated, and ordinary in manners and conversation, but a good creature, and much delighted to talk over the Royal Family, to one of which she was formerly a Nurse. Miss Percy is a natural and very pleasing character.

147. Letter to Esther Burney *8 September 1791*

Queen Square, Bath

My dearest Esther[1] will I know rejoice to hear how well the Bath Water has agreed with Me. I am recovering apace, though by no means without severe occasional draw-backs. But you will probably have heard of me and my goings on through our Padre: from whom I have had accounts of yourself and co., which though only in *generals*, have satisfied me all essentials went on well.

---

2. FB has forgotten that, from March to June 1780, she lived with the Thrales on the South Parade; see *EJL*, iv. forthcoming.

3. Thomas Percy, editor of *Reliques of Ancient English Poetry*, was Dean of Carlisle (1778–82) and Bishop of Dromore from 1782 until his death in 1811. His wife, Anne, had been appointed nurse to Prince Edward in 1771. The daughters were Barbara and Elizabeth.

4. Margaret Georgiana, Countess Spencer, an acquaintance of FB at Bath.

1. Esther Burney lived in Portland Place, London.

Saturday the 10th I set forward for Mickelham: – and there, my dearest Esther, in the course of my *Month's confinement*, I shall hope to see you.[2] I think you will never be able to resist a little peep at our Nursery. Heaven send it prosperous! – I think with our dear Susan there is every possible good augur.

I would send you some News, only I know none.

I ought to give you, from this distance, a little flourish – only I have not *de quoi*[3] to compose one. I am certainly of opinion, after deeply thinking over the matter, that the Heliconian spring did *not* bring forth hot water. Apollo and the nine must have owed their spirit to streams of more bracing qualities.[4] The Hot water which I quaff here has, in this respect, wholly disappointed me, for it rather renders my ideas vapid than bright, notwithstanding the reasonable expectations I had entertained of its *whetting my wits*. And if it does not mend that, it has surely no chance to mend my *humour*; for how can what is moist contribute to what is dry? Thus you see, My dear sister, how small a chance you have to be a gainer by my Bath Beverage.

This City is so filled with Workmen, dust, and lime, that you really want two pair of Eyes to walk about in it, – one for being put out, and the other to see with afterwards. But as I, however, have only one pair, which are pretty much dedicated to the first purpose, you cannot, in reason, expect from me a very distinct description of it. Bath seems, now, rather a collection of small Towns, or of magnificent Villas, than one City. They are now building as if the World was but just beginning, and this was the only spot on which its Inhabitants could endure to reside. Nothing is secure from their architectural rage. They build upon the pinnacle of Hills that only to look up to breaks ones neck, – and they build in the deepest depths below, which only to look down upon makes one giddy. Even the streets round the Pump room are pulling down for new Edifices, and you can only drink from their choice stream, by wading through their chosen mud. Their plans seem all to be formed without the least reference to what adjoins or surrounds them, they are therefore high, low, broad, narrow, long, short, in manners the most unexpected, and by interruptions the most abrupt; – and some of their Houses are placed so zig-zag, in and out, you would suppose them built first, and then dropt, to *find* their own *foundation*. They seem seldom to attempt levelling the Ground for the sake of uniformity, but, very content-

---

2. FB was planning to visit Mickleham for a month to assist Susanna, who would give birth to a son, sooner than expected, on 12 September (*JL*, i. 65).

3. *What is needed.*

4. Apollo and the nine Muses were worshipped at Mount Helicon, with its sacred fountains.

edly, when they have raised one House on the spot where it could stand most conveniently, they raise the next upon its nearest and steepest aclivity, so precisely above it, that from the Garret of one, you *Mount* into the Kitchen of the other. One street, leading out of Laura Place, of a noble width, and with a broad handsome Pavement, pompously labelled at the corner *Johnson Street*, has in it – only one House: – nor can another be added, for it opens to Spring Gardens, and even its vis à vis is occupied by the dead wall belonging to a House in Laura Place. Nor can You make a visit from one street to another, without such an ascent, or such a declivity, that you must have the wheel of a carriage *locked* to go from neighbour to neighbour. – You will ask me if I mean to set you up with materials for making a model of Bath? but I am perfectly content with having given you a *Model* of Confusion.

Certainly, unless you are advised to come hither for *Health*, I should advise you not to see this place these 2 years, at least, for *pleasure*; as the avenues to the pump Rooms will not sooner be finished, and *walking* here in the winter must be next to impracticable. However, when all these works are compleated, and the Compleaters, with the usual gratitude of the world, are driven aloof, this City, already the most splendid of England, will be as noble as can well be conceived.

It is impossible to tell you how kind, good and considerate is our excellent Mrs Ord: yet we are Daily upon the point of a quarrel concerning my leaving her. 6 weeks is the appointed time for drinking these waters, and I shall just have halved *it*. However, I go to peace, good air, good Hours, and the best and dearest Society, and all those will more than compensate for Bath waters, as my worn strength and wasted spirit want more of time and care and patience and happiness for recruit, than medicine.

148. From Journal Letter to Susanna Phillips and Frederica Locke *October 1791*

[Chelsea College]

I have never been so pleasantly situated at Home since I lost the Sister of my Heart and my most affectionate Charlotte.[1] My Father is almost constantly within, and considerations there now are that occasion an *almost* total sparing of reproach for one who indulges herself with resorting to his apartment.[2]

---

1. FB's sisters Susanna and Charlotte, when they married.
2. Alluding to Elizabeth Burney, whose jealousy of FB was now in abeyance.

Indeed – I now live with him wholly; he has himself appropriated me a place, a seat, a desk, a table, and every convenience and comfort, and he never seemed yet so earnest to keep me about him. We read together, write together, chat – compare notes, communicate projects, and diversify each other's employments. He is all goodness, gaiety, and sweetest affection, – and his society and kindness are more precious to me than ever.

Fortunately, in this season of leisure and comfort, the Spirit of Composition proves active. The Day is never long enough, and I could employ two pens almost incessantly in merely scribbling what will not be repressed. This is a delight to my dear Father inexpressibly great: and though I have gone no further than to let him know, from time to time, the *species* of Matter that occupies me, he is perfectly contented, and patiently waits till something is quite finished, before he insists upon reading a Word. This 'suits my humour well,'[3] as my own industry is all gone, when once its intent is produced.

My little Ballad, indeed, *Willy*,[4] he was eager to see, conceiving it finished: but, upon reading it over myself, I found it much wanted revisal, in some places, though, in general, I have left it just as you have read it: but I have now added some Stanzas, and new written the denoüment, which my dearest Susanna most justly thought too abrupt, and which I had been entirely dissatisfied with myself, and I have prevailed with him to let me lock it up, till I have done something else, and, by forgetting it, in some measure enable myself to read it, again, as if it were the work of another Person.

For the rest, I have been going on with my third Tragedy.[5] I have two written, – but never yet have had opportunity to read them, which, of course, prevents their being corrected to the best of my power, and fitted for the perusal of less indulgent Eyes – or, rather, of Eyes less prejudiced.

Believe me, my dear friends, in the present composed and happy state of my mind, I could never have suggested these Tales of Woe; – but having only to connect, combine, contract, and finish, I will not leave them undone. Not, however, to sadden myself to the same point in which I began them, I read more than I write, and call for happier themes from others, to enliven my mind from the dolourous sketches whence I now draw of my own. The Library or study, in which we constantly sit, supplies such delightful variety

---

3. Not identified.

4. The original manuscript, completed on 23 October 1787, is missing. Two copies of an unpublished translation (*c.* 450 lines) by AA are extant (Berg and Osborn Collections). The conclusion is the spectacular near-drowning at sea of a young child, rescued through the courage of peasants and a dog, Flash.

5. *The Siege of Pevensey*. The 'two written' are *Edwy and Elgiva* and *Hubert De Vere*.

of food, that I have nothing to wish. – Thus, my beloved Sisters and Friends – You see me, at length, enjoying all that peace, ease, and chosen recreation and employment, for which so long I sighed in vain, and which, till very lately, I had reason to believe, even since attained, had been allowed me too late. I am more and more thankful every Night – every Morning – for the change in my destiny, and present blessings of my lot. – And you, my beloved Susan and Fredy, for whose prayers I have so often applied in my sadness, suffering and despondence, – afford me now the same community of thanks and acknowledgements. –

149. From Journal Letter to Susanna Phillips and Frederica Locke *November 1791*[1]

Chelsea College

Another evening, after visiting our Esther, my father took me to Sir Joshua Reynolds. I had long languished to see that kindly zealous friend, but his ill health had intimidated me from making the attempt; and now my dear father went upstairs alone, and inquired of Miss Palmer if her uncle was well enough to admit me. He returned for me immediately. I felt the utmost pleasure in again mounting his staircase.

Miss Palmer hastened forward and embraced me most cordially. I then shook hands with Sir Joshua. He had a bandage over one eye, and the other shaded with a green half-bonnet.[2] He seemed serious even to sadness, though extremely kind. 'I am very glad,' he said, in a meek voice and dejected accent, 'to see you again, and I wish I could see you better! but I have only one eye now, – and hardly that.'

I was really quite touched. The expectation of total blindness depressed him inexpressibly; not, however, inconceivably. I hardly knew how to express, either my concern for his altered situation since our meeting, or my joy in again being with him: but my difficulty was short; Miss Palmer eagerly drew me to herself, and recommended to Sir Joshua to go on with his cards. He had no spirit to oppose; probably, indeed, no inclination.

---

1. The manuscript of this journal letter is missing; the text is taken from *DL*.

2. Sir Joshua had lost the sight in his left eye in August 1789, and been forced to stop painting; now he was losing the sight in his other eye and declining in health. FB recorded his death on 23 February 1792 in her journal: 'He was always peculiarly kind & sweet to me – & he had worked at my deliverance from a life he conceived too laborious for me, as if I had been his own Daughter' (*JL*, i. 128).

Dr Lawrence, one of the counsel in the impeachment against Mr Hastings, and Miss Lawrence, his sister, Mr King, and Dr Blagden, were the company. Some days no one is admitted.

Mr King is brother to our lost Captain.[3]

One other time we called again, in a morning. Sir Joshua and his niece were alone, and that invaluable man was even more dejected than before. How grievous to me it is to see him thus changed!

150. From Journal Letter to Susanna Phillips and William and Frederica Locke *18 June 1792*

After many invitations and regulations, it was settled I was to accompany my Father on a visit of 3 Days to Mrs Crewe, at Hampstead.

I came from Chelsea with my Father, and was *landed* at our dear Esther's, – where I spent some part of every Day that brought me to London all the spring and summer. – – My Father and I were then taken to Hampstead, in Mrs Crewe's Carriage.

The little villa at Hampstead is small, but commodious; we were received by Mrs Crewe with much kindness. The Room was rather dark, and she had a veil to her Bonnet half down, and with this aid, she looked, still in a full blaze of beauty! I was wholly astonished. Her bloom, perfectly natural, is as high as that of Augusta Lock,[1] when in her best looks, and the form of her face is so exquisitely perfect, that my Eye never met it without fresh admiration. She is certainly, in my Eyes, infinitely the most completely a *Beauty* of any woman I ever saw. I know not, even now, any female in her first Youth who could bear the comparison. She *uglifies* every thing near her.

Her son was with her. He is just of age, and looks like her elder Brother! he is a heavy, old-looking young man. He is going to China with Lord Macartney.[2]

My former friend, young Burke,[3] was also there. I was glad to renew acquaintance with him; though I could see some little strangeness in him;

---

3. French Laurence, Esther Laurence, Walker King and Sir Charles Blagden. The 'lost Captain' is James King (friend of Captain Cook and of FB's brother James), who had died in 1784.

1. Mary Augusta Locke, elder daughter of William and Frederica Locke, was then only seventeen; Frances Crewe was forty-four.
2. John Crewe, aged twenty. George, Lord Macartney, Ambassador Extraordinary and Plenipotentiary to Peking, 1792–4.
3. Richard Burke, son of Edmund Burke.

which I impute to his observing me, from the Manager's Box, so sedulous in attendance to Mr Hastings' Defense. This strangeness, however, completely wore off before the Day was over.

Soon after, entered Mrs Burke, Miss French, a niece, and Mr Richard Burke, the comic, humourous, bold, queer Brother of The Mr Burke, who, they said, was soon coming, with Mr Elliot.[4]

The Burke family were invited by Mrs Crewe to meet us.

Mrs Burke was just what I have always seen her, soft, gentle, reasonable and obliging, and we met, I think, upon as good terms as if so many years had not parted us.

At length – Mr Burke appeared – accompanied by Mr Elliot.

He shook hands with my Father, as soon as he had paid his devoirs to Mrs Crewe, – but he returned my courtsie with so distant a Bow, that I concluded myself quite lost with him, from my evident solicitude in poor Mr Hastings' cause. I could not wish that less obvious, thinking as I think of it; but I felt infinitely grieved to lose the favour of a Man whom, in all other articles, I so much venerate: and who, indeed, I esteem and admire as the very first Man of true Genius now living in this Country.

Mrs Crewe introduced me to Mr Elliot – I am sure we were already well *personally* known to each other, for I have seen him perpetually in the Manager's Box, whence, as often, he must have seen me in the Great Chamberlain's. He is a tall thin young Man, plain in face, dress, and manner, but sensible – and possibly much besides: he was reserved, however, and little else appeared.

The moment, I was named – to my great joy I found Mr Burke had not recollected me. He is more near-sighted, considerably, than myself. 'Miss Burney!' he now exclaimed, coming forward, and, quite kindly, taking my hand – 'I did not see you –' and then he spoke very sweet words of the meeting, and of my looking far better than *while I was a Courtier*, and of how he *rejoiced* to see that I so little suited that station. – 'You look,' cried he, 'quite *renewed – revived – disengaged* – you seemed – when I conversed with you last, at the Trial, quite – *altered* – I never saw such a change for the better as *quitting a Court* has brought about!'

Ah! thought I, this is simply a mistake from reasoning according to your own feelings. I only seemed altered for the Worse at the Trial because I there looked coldly and distantly from distaste and disaffection to your

4. Burke's wife, Jane Mary Burke; his niece, Mary Cecilia French; his younger brother, Richard Burke, and his close friend William Elliot.

proceedings; and I here look changed for the better, only because I here meet you without the chill of disapprobation, and with the glow of my first admiration of you and your talents! –

Mrs Crewe gave him her place, and he sat by me, and entered into a most animated conversation, upon Lord Macartney and his Chinese expedition, and the two Chinese Youths who were to accompany it.[5] These last he described minutely, and spoke of the extent of the undertaking in high, and perhaps fanciful terms, but with allusions and anecdotes intermixed so full of general information, and brilliant ideas, that I soon felt the whole of my first enthusiasm return, and with it a sensation of pleasure that made the Day delicious to me.

After this, my Father joined us, and *politics* took the lead. He spoke then with an eagerness and vehemence that instantly banished the *Graces*, though it redoubled the *energies* of his discourse. The French Revolution, he said, which began by authorising and legalising Injustice, and which by rapid steps had proceeded to every species of Despotism except owning a Despot, was now menacing all the Universe, and all Mankind with the most violent concussion of principle and order.

My Father heartily joined, and I tacitly assented to his doctrines, though I feared not with his fears.

One speech I must repeat, for it is explanatory of his conduct, and *nobly* explanatory. When he had expatiated upon the present dangers even to *English* Liberty and Property, from the contagion of Havock and novelty, he earnestly exclaimed '*This* it is that has made *me* an abettor and supporter of Kings! Kings are *necessary*, and if we would preserve peace and prosperity, we must preserve *Them*. We must all put our shoulders to the Work! Aye, and stoutly, too!'

This subject lasted till Dinner.

At Dinner, Mr Burke sat next Mrs Crewe, and I had the happiness to be seated next Mr Burke. And my other neighbour was his amiable son.

The Dinner, and the Desert when the Servants were removed, were delightful. How I wish my dear Susanna and Fredy could meet this wonderful Man when he is easy, happy, and with people he cordially likes! – But Politics, even on his own side, must always be excluded: his irritability is so terrible on that Theme that it gives immediately to his Face the Expression of a Man who is going to defend himself from Murderers.

---

5. 'Paolo Cho and Jacobus Li, students for the priesthood at the Chinese College in Naples, who were to accompany the expedition as interpreters' (*JL*, i. 195 n. 35).

I can give you only a few little detached traits of what passed, as Detail would be endless.

Charles Fox being mentioned, Mrs Crewe told us that he had lately said, upon being shewn some passage in Mr Burke's Book which he had warmly opposed, but which had, in the event, made its own justification, very candidly ' – Well! – Burke is right – but Burke is *often* right, only he is right *too soon!* – '[6]

'Had Fox seen some things in that Book,' answered Mr Burke, *'as* soon, he would at this moment, in all probability, be first Minister of this Country!'

'What!' cried Mrs Crewe, 'with Pitt? – No! – no! – Pitt won't go out – and Charles Fox will never make a Coalition with Pitt.'

'And why not?' said Mr Burke, drily, 'why not *this* coalition as well as *other* coalitions?'[7]

Nobody tried to answer this.

'Charles Fox, however,' said Mr Burke afterwards, 'can never internally like the French Revolution. He is – entangled – but, in himself, if he should find no other objection to it, he has at least too much *taste* for such a Revolution.'

Mr Eliot related that he had lately been in a Company of some of the first and most distinguished Men of the French Nation, now fugitives here, and had asked them some questions about the new French Ministry;[8] they had answered That they knew them not even by Name till now! – 'Think,' cried he, 'what a Ministry that must be! Suppose a new administration formed here, of *English* men of whom we had never before heard the names? What Statesmen they must be! how prepared and fitted for Government! To *begin* by being at the helm!'

Mr Richard Burke related, very comically, various censures cast upon his Brother, accusing him of being the *Friend of Despots*, and The *abettor of Slavery*, because he had been shocked at the imprisonment of the King of France, and was anxious to preserve our own limitted Monarchy in the same state in which it so long had flourished.

6. Fox, formerly a friend of Burke, initially supported the French Revolution and condemned Burke's *Reflections on the Revolution in France*, with its clairvoyant predictions of extensive bloodshed.
7. William Pitt the Younger, Prime Minister since 1783, succeeded the short-lived coalition of Fox and Lord North; he and Fox were always bitter rivals. Burke is alluding to Pitt's efforts to draw Whigs into his ministry.
8. Still 'that of the Girondists, which, formed early in March 1792, was on the point of dissolving' (*JL*, i. 197 n. 37).

Mr Burke looked half alarmed at his Brother's opening, but when he had finished, he very good-humouredly poured out a Glass of Wine, and, turning to me, said 'Come, then – here's *Slavery for-ever!*'

This was well understood, and echoed round the Table with hearty laughter.

'This would do for you completely, Mr Burke,' said Mrs Crewe, 'if it could get into a News-paper! Mr Burke, they would say, had now *spoken out*; the truth has come to light unguardedly, and his real defection from the Cause of true Liberty is acknowledged. – I should like to draw up the paragraph! – '

'And add,' said Mr Burke, 'the Toast was addressed to Miss Burney, in order to pay court to the Queen! – '

This sport went on till, upon Mr Eliot's again mentioning France, and the rising Jacobins,[9] Mr Richard Burke loudly gave a new Toast. – 'Come!' cried he, 'here's Confusion to confusion.'

151. From Journal Letter to Susanna Phillips and William and Frederica Locke *27 June 1792*

We next proceeded to the Shakespeare Gallery,[1] which I had never seen. And here we met with an adventure that finished our morning's excursions.

There was a lady in the first Room, dressed rather singularly, quite alone, and extremely handsome, who was parading about, with a Nosegay in her hand, which she frequently held to her nose, in a manner that was evidently calculated to attract notice. We therefore passed on to the Inner Room, to avoid her. Here we had but just all taken our stand, opposite different pictures, when she, also, entered, and coming pretty close to my Father, snifted at her Flowers with a sort of extatic eagerness, and then let them fall. My Father picked them up, and, gravely, presented them to her. She courtsied to the ground in receiving them; and presently crossed over the Room, and brushing past Mrs Crewe, seated herself immediately by her Elbow. Mrs Crewe, not admiring this familiarity, moved away, giving her, at the same time, a look of dignified distance that was almost petrifying.

9. The Jacobins, radical activists in Revolutionary France, continued to grow in strength until the overthrow of Robespierre in July 1794.

1. John Boydell's Shakespeare Gallery in Pall Mall, displaying paintings and engravings of scenes from Shakespeare's plays, had opened in June 1789. It was at first a popular tourist attraction, but was forced to close, with Boydell facing bankruptcy, in 1804.

It did not prove so to this lady, who presently followed her to the next Picture, and sitting as close as she could to where Mrs Crewe stood, began singing various quick passages, without words or connection.

I saw Mrs Crewe much alarmed, and advanced to stand by her, meaning to whisper her that we had better leave the Room; and this idea was not checked by seeing that the *Flowers* were artificial.

By the looks we inter-changed, we soon mutually said, This is a Mad woman! – We feared irritating her by a sudden flight, but gently retreated, and soon got quietly into the large Room; when she bounced up with a great noise, and throwing the veil of her Bonnet violently back, as if fighting it, she looked after us, pointing at Mrs Crewe.

Seriously frightened, Mrs Crewe seizd my Father's arm, and hurried up two or three steps, into a small apartment, – – Here Mrs Crewe, addressing herself to an elderly Gentleman, asked if he could inform the people below that a Mad woman was terrifying the Company – and while he was receiving her commission with the most profound respect, and with an evident air of admiring astonishment at her beauty, – we heard a rustling – and looking round, saw the same figure hastily striding after us, and in an instant at our Elbows.

Mrs Crewe turned quite pale; it was palpable she was the object pursued, and she most civilly and meekly articulated 'I beg your pardon, ma'am,' as she hastily passed her, and hurried down the Steps.

We were going to run for our lives – when Miss Townshend[2] whispered Mrs Crewe it was only Mrs Wells, the actress![3] and said she was certainly only performing vagaries to *try effect*, which she was quite famous for doing.

It would have been food for a Painter to have seen Mrs Crewe during this explanation. All her terror instantly gave way to indignation – and scarcely any pencil could equal the high, vivid glow of her Cheeks. To find herself made the object of Game to the burlesque humour of a bold player, was an indignity she could not brook, and her mind was immediately at work how to assert herself against such unprovoked and unauthorised effrontery.

---

2. Earlier described as 'half Governess, half companion' to Emma Crewe (*JL*, i. 200).

3. FB had seen the actress Mary Wells, who performed 'admirably', in two productions at Weymouth on 17 July 1789: Garrick's *The Irish Widow* (1772) and Charles Coffey's *The Devil to Pay* (1731). She must also have seen Mary Wells's 'gambols' on the esplanade, designed to attract the attention of the Royal Family. See Philip Highfill et al., *A Biographical Dictionary of Actors . . . in London, 1660–1800* (Carbondale, Ill., 1973–93), xv. 348, which also notes Wells's 'reputation for unconventional and sometimes eccentric behavior, some of it brought on by incipient insanity and some of it by drink'.

The elderly Gentleman, who with great eagerness had followed Mrs Crewe, accompanied by a young Man, who was of his party, requested more particularly her commands. But before Mrs Crewe's astonishment and resentment found words, Mrs Wells, singing, and throwing herself into extravagant attitudes, again rushed down the steps, and fixed her Eyes on Mrs Crewe.

This, however, no longer served her purpose; Mrs Crewe fixed her in return, and, with a firm, composed, commanding air and look, that, though it did not make this strange Creature retreat, somewhat disconcerted her for a few minutes.

She then presently affected a violent Coughing, such a one as almost shook the Room, though such a forced and unnatural Noise as rather resembled howling than a Cold.

This over, and perceiving Mrs Crewe still steadily keeping her ground, she had the courage to come up to us, and, with a flippant air, said to the elderly Gentleman 'Pray, Sir, will you tell me what it is o'clock?'

He looked vexed to be called a moment from looking at Mrs Crewe, and with a forbidding gravity, answered tis 'about Two.'

'No offence, I hope, sir?' cried she, seeing him turn eagerly from her.

He bowed without looking at her, and she strutted away, still, however, keeping in sight, and playing various tricks, her Eyes perpetually turned towards Mrs Crewe, who as regularly met them, with an expression such as might have turned a softer Culprit to stone.

Our cabal was again renewed, and Mrs Crewe again told this Gentleman to make known to the proprietors of the Gallery, that this person was a Nuisance to the Company: when, suddenly re-approaching us, she called out 'Sir! Sir!' to the younger of our new protectors.

He coloured, and looked much alarmed, but only bowed.

'Pray, Sir' cried she, 'What's o'clock?'

He looked at his watch, and answered.

'You don't take it ill, I hope, sir?' she cried.

He only bowed.

'I do no harm, Sir,' said she; 'I never bite!'

The poor young man looked aghast, and bowed lower; but Mrs Crewe, addressing herself to the Elder, said, aloud, 'I beg you, sir, to go to Mr Boydell; – you may name me to him; Mrs Crewe.'

Mrs Wells, at this, walked away; yet still in Sight.

'You may tell him what has happened, sir, in all our Names. You may tell him Miss Burney – –'

'O no!' cried I, in a horrid fright, 'I beseech I may not be named! – – And indeed, Ma'am, it may be better to let it all alone. It will do no good: and it may all get into the News-papers.'

'And if it does,' cried Mrs Crewe, 'what is it to us? – We have done nothing; we have given no offence, and made no disturbance; this person has frightened us all wilfully, and utterly without provocation; and now she can frighten us no longer, she would brave us. Let her tell her own story, and how will it harm us?'

'If truth only were told, in these anecdotes, we should certainly fare very well: but that is rarely the case.'

'Surely, ma'am' said the Gentleman, to Mrs Crewe, 'this is a species of impertinence, a sort of liberty and insolence not to be put up with.'

'To me, sir,' said she, 'it is immaterial, as I shall probably come here no more; but this person would behave the same to those who have no protection from her affronts; and I do not like the *meum et tuum*[4] of escaping for ourselves and leaving others, less prepared, to similar attacks. You may tell Mr Boydell, therefore, sir, that Miss Burney, my Daughter, and myself, have all been equally alarmed.'

I fancy Mrs Wells gathered what was passing, for she now had taken a Gentleman's Arm and came our way; talking aloud, and saying 'It's very hard, very cruel indeed, to take such notice of people in public. The Public's open to us all, and we have all a right to behave how we please. And it's very hard, and very cruel in people to be so soon affronted. And one person is as good as another in a public place.'

I was really uneasy at the idea of any competition with this lady, and again I ventured to remonstrate with Mrs Crewe, saying she was a wild, half-crazy woman, accustomed to indulge herself in all her whims, as I had witnessed at Weymouth, where, absurdly as she behaved, she was opposed by nobody, and seemed always to regard herself as a priveleged person.

'O, pardon me! I have notion of that!' said Mrs Crewe; 'we do not molest her; she has no title to molest us. I don't understand such priveleges. If she assumes them as *hers*, what in the meantime, is to become of ours?'

'Still,' cried I, 'I must always fear being brought into any News-paper cabals. Let the fact be ever so much against her, she will think the circumstances all to her honour, if a paragraph comes out beginning *Mrs Crewe and Mrs Wells. –* '

Mrs Crewe liked this sound as little as I should have liked it in placing

4. *Mine and yours* (Latin): used to express rights of property.

my own name where I put hers. She hesitated a little what to do, and we all walked down Stairs; where, instantly, this bold woman followed us, paraded up and down the long shop with a dramatic air, while our group was in conference, and then, sitting down at the Clerk's Desk, and calling in a footman, she desired him to wait while she wrote a Note.

She scribbled a few lines, and read aloud her directions, 'To Mr Topham'.[5] – And giving the note to the Man, said 'Tell your Master that is something to make him laugh. Bid him not send to the Press till I see him.'

Now as Mr Topham is the Editor of 'The World', and notoriously her *protector*, as her having his footman acknowledged, this looked rather serious, and Mrs Crewe began to partake of my alarm. She therefore, to my infinite satisfaction, told her new friend that she desired he would name no names, but merely mention that some ladies had been frightened.

I was very glad indeed to gain this point, and the good Gentleman seemed enchanted with any change that occasioned a longer discourse.

We then got into Mrs Crewe's Carriage, and not till then would this facetious Mrs Wells quit the shop. And she walked in sight, dodging us, and playing antics of a tragic sort of gesture, till we drove out of her power to keep up with us. What a strange Creature!

---

5. Edward Topham, fashionable figure in London, by whom Mary Wells had borne four children. He had started *The World*, a daily paper, in 1787 partly as a promotional device for her. In 1792, he closed the paper and left Wells for another woman.

1793–1795

Courtship and Marriage

152. Letter to Dr Burney *28 January 1793*[1]

Norbury Park, Monday

My dearest Padre,

I have been wholly without spirit for writing, reading, working, or even walking or conversing, ever since the first Day of my arrival. The dreadful Tragedy acted in France has entirely absorbed me.[2] Except the period of the illness of our own inestimable King, I have never been so overcome with grief and dismay for any but personal and family calamities. O what a Tragedy! how implacable its villainy, and how severe its sorrows! You know, my dearest Father, how little I had believed such a catastrophe possible: with all the guilt, and all the daring already shewn, I had still thought this a height of enormity impracticable. And, indeed, without military Law through-out the wretched city, it had still not been perpetrated. – Good Heaven! – what must have been the sufferings of the few unhardened in crimes – who inhabit that city of horror! – – If *I* – an English person – have been so deeply afflicted that even this sweet House and society – even My Susan and her lovely Children, have been incapable to give me any species of pleasure, or keep me from a desponding low-spiritedness, what must be the feelings of all but the Culprits in France! –

M. de Narbonne and M. D'Arblay[3] have been almost annihilated – they are for-ever repining that they are French, and though two of the most

1. Annotated by FB: 'cruel slaughter of the King of France, Louis 16. 1st in introducing M. d'Arblay to Dr B.'
2. FB had arrived for an extended stay with the Lockes on 22 January. Louis XVI had been guillotined on 21 January, and the news would have reached FB a few days later.
3. FB had first heard about the 'Juniper colony' – the French Constitutionalists living at Juniper Hall, Mickelham, close to Norbury Park – in October 1792. They included the comte de Narbonne, the French Minister of War until March 1792, and his friend Alexandre Piochard d'Arblay, FB's future husband, exiled Adjutant-General of the Marquis de Lafayette.

accomplished and elegant Men I ever saw, they break our Hearts with the humiliation they feel for their guiltless *Birth* in that guilty Country – '*Est-ce-vrai*,' cries M. de Narbonne, 'que vous conserve encore quelque amitiè, M. Lock, pour ceux qui ont la honte et le malheur d'être nés françois?'[4] – Poor Man! – he has all the symptoms upon him of the Jaundice, – and M. D'Arblay from a very fine figure and good face, was changed as if by Magic in one night, by the receipt of this inexpiable news, into an appearance as black, as meagre, and as miserable as M. la Blancherie.[5]

We are all here expecting War every Day. This dear family has deferred its Town journey till next Wednesday.[6] I have not been at all at Mickleham, nor yet settled whether to return to Town with the Locks, or to pay my promised visit there first. All has been so dismal, so wretched, that I have scarce ceased to regret our living at such times, and not either sooner or later. These immediate French sufferers here interest us, and these alone have been able to interest me at all – We hear of a very bad tumult in Ireland – and near Captain Phillips. – Mr Brabanson[7] writes word it is very serious. Heaven guard us from insurrections! – What must be the feelings at the Queen's House – how acute, and how indignant! – Adieu, most dear Sir – I am sure we simpathise but too compleatly on this subject. My duty and love to my Mother and Sarah – I hope you are all well –

and am ever Your   F.B.

153. Letters to Frederica Locke *14, 16 February 1793*[1]

Thursday. Mickleham

I have no heart *not* to write and no time *to* write – I have been *scholaring* all day – and *mastering* too, – for our lessonings are mutual, and more entertaining than can easily be conceived.[2] My *Master of the Language* says he *dreams* of how much more *solemnly he shall write* to charming Mrs Lock after a little

---

4. '*Is it true* . . . that you still have some feelings of friendship, Mr Lock, for those who have the shame and misfortune to be born French?'

5. Flammès-Claude-Catherine de Lablancherie, French writer whom FB had first met at Court in July 1787.

6. 6 February.

7. Molesworth Phillips had extensive lands in County Louth. 'Probably Wallop Brabazon . . . who was distantly related to Molesworth Phillips and a close neighbour' (*JL*, ii. 9 n. 6).

1. These letters survive in copies by Charlotte Barrett.

2. FB preserved some of the 'themes' (exercises) that she wrote to AA in French and his in English; see *JL*, ii. 188–205.

more practice. Mme de Staël has written me two English notes, quite beautiful in *ideas*, and not very reprehensible in idiom.[3] But *English* has nothing to do with elegance such as theirs – at least, *little* and *rarely*. I am always exposing myself to the wrath of John Bull when this coterie come in competition. It is inconceivable what a convert M. de Talleyrand[4] has made of me; I think him now one of the first members, and one of the most charming, of this exquisite set. Susanna is as completely a prosilyte. His powers of entertainment are astonishing both in information and in raillery. We know nothing of how the rest of the World goes on. They are all coming to night. I have yet avoided – but with extreme difficulty, the change of abode – Mme de Staël however will not easily be parried, and how I may finally arrange I know not. Certainly I will not offend or hurt her, – but *otherwise*, I had rather be a visitor than a guest. –

. . .

                                                            Mickleham

My most dear Friends How do? – We go on here living upon *Junipere Be'ers*[5] most luxuriantly – and their flavour loses nothing by use. I never used to think them so exquisite. You will not wonder M. de Narbonne grows upon *me*, when I tell you he really seems softening more and more, though involuntarily, into my sentiments and mode of reasoning: the dread consequences and successful villainies which have followed the Revolution, and the murder of the innocent King, seem more and more deeply to affect him. Mme de Staël absolutely accuses him of *aristocracy*, and says she is sure *I* commend his English more than hers from that sympathy. – I told her I should be proud of such a cause of partiality. We are very good friends, you will imagine, by my daring at such *waggery*. M. d'Arblay is so, *so* good – I really want to beg *you* to help me to thank him: but I go on very miserably, in all but reading – Speak I cannot for my life, though I am ready to chastise myself with every species of severity for such folly of fear to those who can,

---

3. Letters from Madame de Staël to FB of 7–13 February and 8–14 February 1793; see *Correspondance générale de Madame de Staël*, ed. Béatrice W. Jasinski (Paris, 1962–), ii. pt. 2, 387–90. Germaine de Staël, fourteen years younger than FB but already a celebrated woman of letters, had arrived at Juniper Hall on 26 or 27 January.

4. Charles-Maurice de Talleyrand, formerly Bishop of Autun, who would become an influential foreign minister after the Terror, in 1797.

5. I.e. juniper berries, with their pungent flavour; alluding to the set at Juniper Hall.

now, expect no better than they would find: and I defy them to expect worse. Mme de Staël read the noble Tragedy of *Tancrede*[6] till she blinded us all round. – She is the most charming person, to use her own phrase, *that never I saw.*

Pray tell Mr Lock that '*the best of the Men*'[7] grows upon us at every meeting. We dined and stayed till midnight at *Junipere* on Friday, – and I would I could collect but the twentieth part of the excellent things that were said. Mme de Staël read us, the opening of the work '*Sur le bonheur*':[8] It seems to me admirable. M. de Talleyrand avowed he had met with nothing better thought or more ably expressed. It contains the most touching allusions to their Countrys calamities.

154. Letter to Dr Burney *16–19 February 1793*[1]

[Mickleham]

Have you not begun, Dearest Sir, to give me up as a lost sheep? Susanna's widowhood, however, has tempted me on,[2] and spelled me with a spell I know not how to break. It is long, long since we have passed any time so completely together. Her three lovely Children only knit us the closer. The widowhood, however, we expect now quickly to expire, and I had projected my return to my dearest Father for Wednesday next: which would complete my fortnight here. But some circumstances are intervening that incline me to postpone it another week.

Madame De Staël, Daughter of M. Necker, and wife of the Sweedish Ambassadour to France,[3] is now head of the little French Colony in this neighbourhood. M. de Staël, her Husband, is at present suspended in his Embassy, but not recalled; and it is yet uncertain whether the Regent

---

6. Voltaire's *Tancrède* (1761).

7. Quoting Madame de Staël's description of Talleyrand (see FB to Frederica Locke, *c.* 9 February 1793, *JL*, ii. 13), which echoes the phrase 'best of men' frequently applied by his family and acquaintances to the hero of Richardson's *Sir Charles Grandison*.

8. 'Evidently an early draft of *De l'influence des passions sur le bonheur des individus et des nations* (1796)' (*JL*. ii. 15 n. 3). In May 1793, AA transcribed the essay for Susanna Phillips and her friends.

1. Annotated by FB: 'Mme de Stael, M. d'Arblay M. de Narbonne M. de Talleyrand Opening intercourse of M. d'A & F.B., in reciprocating Themes'.

2. Phillips was absent in Colchester on a recruiting mission.

3. Jacques Necker, statesman and financier, and the Baron Eric de Staël-Holstein, Germaine de Staël's estranged husband.

Duke of Sudermania,[4] will send him to Paris, during the present horrible Convention, or order him home. He is now in Holland, waiting for commands. Mme de Staël, however, was *unsafe* in Paris, though an ambassadress, from the resentment owed her by the *Commune*, for having received and protected in her House[5] various destined victims of the 10th of August, and of the 2d September. – She was even, once, stopt in her Carriage, which they called *aristocratic*, because of its arms and ornaments, and threatened to be murdered; and only saved by one of the worst wretches of the Convention, *Tallien*,[6] who feared provoking a War with Sweeden from such an offence to the Wife of its Ambassadour. She was obliged to have this same Tallien to accompany her, to save her from massacre, for some miles from Paris, when compelled to quit it.

She is a woman of the first abilities, I think, I have ever seen. She is more in the style of Mrs Thrale than of any other celebrated Character; but she has infinitely more depth, and seems an even *profound* politician and metaphysician. She has suffered us to hear some of her works in mss. which are truly wonderful, for powers both of thinking and expression. She adores her Father – but is much alarmed at having had no news from him since he has heard of the massacre of the martyrred Louis – and who can wonder it should have overpowered him?[7]

Ever since her arrival, she has been pressing me to spend some time with her, before I return to Town – she wanted Susan and me to pass a Month with her; but finding that impossible, she bestowed all her entreaties upon me alone; and they are grown so urgent, upon my preparation for departing, and acquainting her my *furlough* of absence was over, that she not only insisted upon my writing to you, and telling why I deferred my return, but declares she will also *write herself*, to ask your permission for the visit. She exactly resembles Mrs Thrale in the ardour and warmth of her temper and partialities. I find her impossible to resist, and therefore, if your answer to her is such as I conclude it must be, I shall wait upon her for a week. She is only a short walk from hence, at Juniper Hall.

There can be nothing imagined more charming, more fascinating than

---

4. Charles, Duke of Sudermania, Regent of Sweden and Norway.

5. 'Madame de Staël's salon in the Swedish Embassy in the rue du Bac was a gathering place for the Constitutionnels in Paris and it was here that they met in the years 1791–2 to plan their political strategy' (*JL*, ii. 17 n. 6). Those saved by her included the comte de Narbonne.

6. Jean-Lambert Tallien, who had escorted Madame de Staël from Paris on 3 September 1792.

7. In a heavily deleted passage, FB wrote that Necker 'fell into a state of dejection' until he was given a copy of *Cecilia*, which, according to Madame de Staël, '*soothed and regaled* him'.

this Colony. Between their Sufferings and their *agrêmens*,[8] they occupy us almost wholly. M. de Narbonne, alas, has no £1000 a year! – he got over only £4000, at the beginning, from a most splendid fortune, – and – little foreseeing how all has turned out, he has lived, we fear, upon the principal! for he says if all remittance is withdrawn, on account of the War, he shall soon be as ruined as those companions of his misfortunes, with whom, as yet, he has shared his little all. He bears the highest character for goodness, parts, sweetness of manners, and ready wit: You could not keep your Heart from him, if you saw him only for half an Hour. He has not yet recovered from the black blow of the King's Death, but he is better, and less jaundiced: and he has had a Letter which, I hear, has comforted him, though at first, it was almost heart-breaking, informing him of the unabated regard for him of the truly saint-like Louis. This is communicated in a letter from M. de Malesherbes.[9]

M. D'Arblay is one of the most singularly interesting Characters that can ever have been formed. He has a sincerity, a frankness, an ingenious openness of nature that I had been injust enough to think could not belong to a French Man. With all this, which is his *Military portion*, he is passionately fond of literature, a most delicate critic in his own language, well versed in both Italian and German, and a very elegant Poet.[10] He has just undertaken to become my *French Master*, for pronunciation, and he gives me long daily lessons in reading. Pray expect wonderful improvements! In return I hear him in English, – and for his theme this Evening, he has been writing an English address *à Mr Burney*, (i. e. M. le Docteur) joining in Mme De Staël's request. I cannot send it you, because it is a precious morsel of elegant broken English, and I must keep it amongst my treasures: but I will produce it when I return, for your entertainment.

I hope your last Club[11] was more congenial? Mr de Tallyrand insists on conveying this Letter for you. He has been on a visit here, and returns again on Wednesday. He is a man of admirable conversation, quick, terse, *fin*,[12] and yet deep. They are a marvellous set for excess of agreeability.

Adieu, most dear Sir – Susanna sends her best Love, and the Fanni and

---

8. *Attractiveness, charm.*

9. From Chrétien-Guillaume de Malesherbes to Narbonne of 6 January 1793 (Berg Collection).

10. AA had published a pseudonymous collection of poetry, *Opuscules du Chevalier d'Anceny* (1787), and continued to write and translate poetry.

11. I.e. Johnson's club, of which CB had been an active member since Spring 1784.

12. *Sharp.*

Norbury kisses and sweet words[13] – I beg my love to my Mother, and hope she continues amending.

I am ever, ever, and ever my dearest Father's

F.B.

155. Letter to Frederica Locke *23 May 1793*[1]

Chesington

I have been quite enchanted to day by my dear Susan's intelligence that my three Convalescents walked to the Wood.[2] *Would* I had been there to meet and receive them!

I have regretted excessively the finishing so miserably an acquaintance begun with so much spirit and pleasure, and the *dépit*[3] I fear Mme de Staël must have experienced. I wish The World would take more care of itself and less of its neighbours. I should have been *very safe*, I trust, without such flights, and distances, and breaches! – But there seemed an absolute resolution[4] formed to crush this acquaintance, and compel me to appear its wilful renouncer. All I did, also, to clear the matter, and soften to Mme de Staël any pique or displeasure, unfortunately served only to increase both. Had I understood her disposition better, I should certainly have attempted no palliation, for I rather offended her pride than mollified her wrath. Yet I followed the Golden Rule – for how much should I prefer *any acknowledgement* of regret at such an apparent change, from any one I esteemed, to a seeming unconscious complacency in an unexplained caprice?

I am vexed, however, – very much vexed at the whole business. I hope she left Norbury Park with full satisfaction in its steady and more *comfortable* connection? I fear mine will pass for only a *fashionable* one.

Miss Kitty Cooke still amuses me very much by her incomparable dialect:

13. Susanna's daughter Frances and son Charles Norbury, aged eleven and eight.

1. Copy by Charlotte Barrett.

2. Susanna's letter of 22 May said that Frederica Locke and her two daughters, Mary Augusta and Amelia, who had been suffering from measles for a month, were now recovering. The 'Wood' is Norbury Park.

3. *Resentment.* Susanna's letter of 14 May describes Madame de Staël on being dropped by FB as 'on the point of being offended' and having 'a kind of *dépit* in her manner once or twice in speaking of you' (*DL*, v. 191).

4. The 'resolution' against FB's associating with de Staël (because of the latter's rumoured love affair with Narbonne) was taken by CB, in conjunction with Anna Ord, Edmund and Jane Burke, James Hutton and others.

and by her kindness and friendliness I am taken the best care of imaginable.

My poor Brother who will carry this to Mickleham, is grievously altered by the loss of his little Girl.[5] It has affected his spirits and his health and he is grown so thin and meagre that he looks ten years older than when I saw him last. I hope he will now revive, since the blow is over; – but it has been a very, – very hard one, after such earnest pains to escape it.

Did the Wood look very beautiful? I have figured it to myself with the three dear Convalescents, wandering in its winding paths and inhaling its freshness and salubrity, ever since I heard of this walk. I wanted prodigiously to have issued forth from some little green recess to have hailed your return. I hope Mr Lock had the pleasure of this sight. Is *Jenny*[6] capable of such a journey?

Do you know anything of a certain young lady who eludes all my enquiries, famous for having eight sisters, all of uncommon talents? I had formerly some intercourse with her, and she used to promise she would renew it whenever I pleased: but whether she is offended that I have slighted her offers so long, or whether she is fickle, or only whimsical, I know not, – all that is quite undoubted, is, that she has concealed herself so effectually from my researches, that I might as well look for Justice and Clemency in the French Convention, as for this former friend in the plains and lanes of Chesington, where, erst, she met me whether I would or no! —[7]

156. Letter to Susanna Phillips and William and Frederica Locke *31 May 1793*[1]

A safe[2]

Friday Morning
Chesington.

My Heart finally so smites me this Morning with making no answer to all I have been requested to weigh and decide, that I feel I cannot with any ease return to Town, without at least complying with *one* demand, which, just at

---

5. James's seven-year-old daughter Catherine had died in early May.
6. Quiet mare used for country rides by William Locke.
7. FB had composed parts of *Evelina* and *Cecilia* while at Chessington. There is of course no Muse of the Novel, so by 'a certain young lady' she perhaps meant Calliope, chief of the Muses and Muse of the Epic.

1. Annotated by FB: 'deeply distressing suspensive anxiety previous to Marriage'.
2. FB's code for requesting an acknowledgement that a letter had been safely received.

parting yesterday, besought me to write fully to *you*, if, *elsewhere*, I could not to my satisfaction.[3]

Much, indeed, in the course of last Night and this Morning, has occurred to me, that now renders my longer silence as to *Prospects* and *proceedings* unjustifiable to myself. I will therefore now address myself to both my beloved and most precious Confidents, and open to them all my thoughts, and entreat their own, with equal plainness, in return.

That my Fredy may be au fait[4] as to *judgement materials*, I enclose her the Letter which draws me thus forth.[5] She will have the goodness when she has read it, to send it me back by the post.

M. D'Arblay must know none of the detail of this Writing at present. I wish fully to discuss all with my dear Sisters before I venture at a word with him, beyond what may tolerably satisfy him in suspence. O God! – I would inflict Suspense on no human Being! – but you will find what now follows unfitted to offer him any consolation.

When you have read this Letter, my dear Fredy, and seen his serious and solemn call upon me to enter seriously and solemnly into definitive discussions, you will not wonder my passiveness ceases to be right in my own Eyes: though I hope you will make allowance for the thousand causes which absolutely prevented my complying with his desire to discourse upon the subject in the few minutes we chanced to be alone when he came hither for that purpose. I am ashamed to seem tiresome or trifling or dilatory – but so much is at stake – and my mind is *so* – *so* ill at ease! —— and I dare not add to *his* disturbance by telling him that!

To the point.

His last 3 Letters, as well as what he dropt to me yesterday, convince me he is desperately dejected when alone, and when perfectly natural. It is not that he wants patience; it seems to me a virtue he even eminently possesses: but he wants *rational expectation* of better times: expectation founded on something more than mere aerial *Hope* that builds one Day upon what the next blasts – and then has to build again – and again to be blasted.

What affects me the most, in this situation, is – that his time may as completely be lost, as another's peace, by waiting for the effects of distant

3. AA had visited FB at Chessington on the previous day, and been dissatisfied by her reluctance to speak frankly to him.

4. Conversant.

5. AA's letter to FB of 27 May (see *JL*, ii. 126–8).

events, vague, bewildering, and remote, and quite as likely to lead to ill as to good. The very waiting, indeed, with the Mind in such a state, is in itself an evil scarce to be recompensed.

All his dependence, he tells me forever, is upon Mr Lock[6] – so, too, would be mine, if Friendship and Goodness were all which such a dependance demanded. But he does not know as I do the difficulties attending all application for places, to *Natives*, and *claimants*: where, then, can stand the hope for an Emigré,[7] who is supposed to be here to Day, and gone to-morrow? and with the prejudice now reigning in the Court against all Constitutionels? I fairly confess I see *no prospect of success* in this *his* only hope! —— I think it, therefore, a cruel delusion, and painful as it is to me – past all expression – to bring such a subject forward, it seems indispensable to me – and I will therefore entreat my dearest Fredy to speak with Mr Lock. *Time* and *Patience*, in a war such as this, *may* do every thing, but they may also, and more probably, do nothing; and I cannot, thinking as I think of the chances, satisfy myself with seeing *them* trusted to, when I believe, in the end, it will be found that *exertion* must do every thing.

He believes his want of English his only impediment to Preferment, and he studies 6 Hours regularly every Day! I am *glad* of this – but cannot at all build upon it. What, in any application, can be urged for him, that will be believed? My Father, *if willing to act*, has no interest – nor do I know that Mr Lock has any sufficient. Here lies his flattering error. – But who, except just the very few, acquainted fully with his peculiar character, and his peculiar situation – will credit that he remains here except *perforce*? or that he will not fly away the moment a road is open to his own Country? a road that may be opened next Month – or be shut till the next Generation! – –

In justice, in Honour, in Conscience, these opinions and scruples call upon me to entreat a Counsel of the *three* best and wisest Friends that ever united to one object, and to entreat all this may be weighed, and the result sent me to Chelsea College. My mind is inexpressibly disturbed by seeing such reliance on what, to me, seem false expectations, – and I feel it a duty to take some step either to think better of them myself, or to crush them completely in another. – This, will, indeed, be a severe task – but if once convinced it *ought* to be done, I believe, I should rest no more till it was over.

*

6. AA believed (wrongly) that Locke had the influence at Court to find him a position of some kind.

7. During the Reign of Terror, Constitutionalists such as AA, who had initially supported the French Revolution, were much criticized in England and anathematized at Court.

My dearest Fredy, in the beginning of her knowledge of this transaction, told me that Mr Lock was of opinion that the £120 per annum[8] might *do*, as it does for many a *Curate*: M. D'Arblay – also, most solemnly and affectingly declares, That *la simple necessaire*[9] is *all* he requires, and here – in *your* vicinity, would unhesitatingly be preferred by him to the most brilliant fortune in another sejour –

If *he* can say that . . . what must *I* be not to eccho it? I, who, in the bosom of my own most chosen, most darling Friends, –

I need not enter more upon this – You all *must* know, that to *me* a crust of Bread, with a little Roof for shelter, and a *Fire* for warmth, *near you*, would bring me to peace, to happiness – to all that my Heart holds dear, or ever, in any situation, could prize – I cannot picture such a fate with dry Eyes – all else, but kindness and society, has to me, so *always* been nothing ——

It is certain, also, that – with peace of mind and retirement – I have resources that I could bring forward to amend the little situation[10] – as well as, that, once thus undoubtedly *established* and *naturalized*, M. D'Arblay would have claims for employment –

These reflections, with a mutual freedom from ambition, might lead to a quiet road, unbroken by the tortures of applications, expectations, attendance, disappointment, and time wasting hope and fears – if – there were not apprehensions the £100 might be withdrawn! — I do not think it *likely*, but it is a risk too serious in its consequences to be run – M. D'Arblay protests he could not answer to himself the hazard. —

How to ascertain this – to clear the doubt, or to know the fatal certainty, before it should be too late, exceeds my powers of suggestion –

His own idea, *to write to the Queen*, much as it has startled me, and wild as it seemed to me, is certainly *less* wild than to take the chance of such a blow in the dark.

Yet – such a Letter could not even reach her – his very name is probably only known to her, through myself – and Mr and Mrs Lock, by means of Mme La Fite and M. de Luc. –

In short, my dearest Friends, you will think for me, and let me know what occurs to you – and I will defer any answer till I hear your opinions.

Pray keep this communication, as from *me*, to yourselves, for the present

---

8. FB's pension from the Queen of £100, together with £20 that she received from the investment of the payment for *Cecilia*.

9. *Basic necessities*.

10. I.e. her potential earning power as novelist or dramatist.

– it would be misery to a *very* susceptible mind to know I had made it while all hangs suspended.

Heaven bless my dear and excellent Friends – by one by two by *three*.

157. Letter to Charles Burney *23 July 1793*

Norbury Park

My dear Carlos, –

I am anxious for intelligence of your safe arrival at your Home, and of your amendment – How very – very calamitous and sad an excursion![1] –

Without having first some news of you and your Health – it is difficult – and even distasteful to me to enter upon any concerns of my own; nevertheless, I must not here consult my wishes, but my situation – and my situation is critical; – and not, just now, under my immediate controul.

My dear Charles loves short Letters – yet it would be difficult in many long ones to state all I now desire to communicate to him. I must be, however, as *compact* as I can – and you – – must be as *comprehending*.

Were I with you, I should relieve myself from the extreme embarrassment of opening my own Cause by employing you in various conjectures, and keeping your imagination in play, till by skill or chance, you came near to my subject: – but at this distance, I have no such resource – I have no aid – I am forced to mount my Pegasus[2] without any Esquire –

My Pegasus? – No! – I have nothing to do with Poetics – nothing with fiction – all is plain truth – though perhaps you may not hold it to be plain – or common sense. –

In brief – and to give you – at once – some little scope for conjecture – Do you remember seeing, at a Concert in Titchfield Street, a Gentleman – whose Face, you said, looked *any thing* but French?[3] –

Now your Eye brows begin to arch – –

This Gentleman – if I am not of all women the most mistaken, is one of the noblest Characters now existing. – An Exile from patriotism and loyalty, he has been naturalized in the bosom of Norbury Park and Mickleham, amongst the dearest and best of my Friends – he wishes there, in that vicinity

---

1. 'Apparently Charles had taken his wife in late June or early July to Clifton or the Bristol Hotwells for her health, and there fell ill himself' (*JL*, ii. 174 n. 1).

2. The mythological winged horse, figurative for poetic genius.

3. During a visit to London, AA had apparently heard a concert at the home of Esther and Charles Rousseau Burney.

where he has found a new Home, new affections, new interests, and a new Country, to fix himself for life: he wishes, in that picture, to have a Companion – an English Companion, – with whom he may learn to forget in some measure his own misfortunes, or at least to sooth them.

Can you guess the Companion he would elect? –

I can enter now into no particulars – they are too diffuse, the tale is too long – and my spirits are too much agitated. I can only tell my dear Charles that if I should here give him another Brother – he will find him one whom he can no sooner know than he must love and respect.

My dear Father – alas! – from prudential scruples is coldly averse to this transaction – and my Heart is heavy from his evident ill will to it – yet he has not refused his consent – and circumstances are such, that I feel myself bound in honour – and even in necessity – to here fix my fate – or to relinquish for ever a Person the most peculiarly to my taste, and whom I think the most peculiarly formed for my happiness, of any Mortal I ever saw or ever knew in my life.

As this affair must be conveyed to the Queen – before it is made public, even among my friends, I entreat you to keep its design to *yourself* till you hear further. It is of the highest importance that no accidental information should anticipate my communication.

Pray write me a kind word – I send by this post similar Letters to my sisters and to James – but I spread my confidence no wider – for the reason I have just given.

God bless you, my dearest Carlos – may you have good news to send me of yourself with good wishes for

your truly affectionate

F. Burney

I hope poor Rosette[4] is better.

158. Letter to Georgiana Waddington *2 August 1793*

How in the world shall I begin this Letter to my dearest Marianne! – how save her from a surprise almost too strong for her weak nerves and tender Heart? –

After such an opening, perhaps *any* communication may be a relief – But it is surprise only I would guard against, – my present communication has

---

4. Charles's wife Sarah, née Rose ('Rosette').

nothing else to fear – it has nothing in it sad, melancholy, unhappy – but it has every thing that is marvellous and unexpected.

Do you recollect at all, when you were last in Town, my warm interest for the loyal part of the French Exiles? – do you remember my eloge of a French officer, in particular – a certain M. d'Arblay? –

Ah, my dear Marianne – you are quick as lightening – your sensitive apprehension will tell my tale for me now without any more aid than some details of circumstance.

The eloge I then made was with design to prepare you for an event I had reason to expect – such, however, was the uncertainty of my situation, from prudential obstacles, that I dared venture at no confidence, – though my Heart prompted it strongly to a Friend so sweetly simpathising in all my feelings and all my affairs – so constantly affectionate – so tenderly alive to all that interests and consumes me! – My dearest Marianne! – you will give me, I am sure, your Heart-felt wishes – your most fervent prayers. – The choice I have had the means to make appears to me all you could yourself wish to fall to my lot, all you could yourself have formed to have best accorded with your kind partiality. –

I had some hope you would have seen him that Evening we went together from Mrs M. Montagu to Mrs Lock's, for he was then a guest in Portland Place;[1] but some miserable circumstances, of which I knew nothing till after your departure, had just fallen out, and he had shut himself up in his Room.[2] He did not know we were there. – Many, indeed, have been the miserable circumstances that have, from time to time, alarmed and afflicted in turn, and seemed to render a renunciation indispensable. Those difficulties, however, have been conquered – and last Sunday – Mr and Mrs Lock – my sister and Captain Phillips, and my Brother Captain Burney – accompanied us to the Altar, in Mickleham Church. – Since which, the Ceremony has been repeated in the Chapel of the Sardinian Ambassadour,[3] that, if, by a Counter-revolution in France, M. d'Arblay recovers any of his rights, his wife may not be excluded from their participation.

You may be amazed not to see the name of my dear Father upon this solemn occasion: but his apprehensions from the smallness of our income

1. FB and Georgiana Waddington met at Elizabeth Montagu's house on 11 April 1793; see *JL*, ii. 74. AA was staying at the London residence of the Lockes.
2. On 19 April AA was in his room at Portland Place with a severe migraine and could not see visitors; see *JL*, ii. 89. (FB has conflated the events of 11 and 19 April.)
3. The Anglican wedding of 28 July at St Michael's Church, Mickleham, was followed by a Catholic ceremony at the chapel of the Sardinian Ambassador in London on 30 July.

have made him cold and averse – and though he granted his consent, I could not even solicit his presence; – I feel satisfied, however, that Time will convince him I have not been so imprudent as he now thinks me. Happiness is the great end of all our worldly views and proceedings; and no one can judge for another in what will produce it. To me, wealth and ambition would always be unavailing; I have lived in their most centrical possessions, – and I have always seen that the happiness of the Richest and the Greatest has been the moment of retiring from Riches and from Power. Domestic comfort and social affection have invariably been the sole as well as ultimate objects of my choice: and I have always been a stranger to any other species of felicity. M. d'Arblay has a taste for literature, and a passion for reading and writing as marked as my own; this is a simpathy to rob retirement of all superfluous leisure, and ensure to us both occupation constantly edifying or entertaining. He has seen so much of life, and has suffered so severely from its disappointments, that retreat, with a chosen Companion, is become his final desire.

Mr Lock has given M. d'Arblay a piece of Ground in his beautiful Park, upon which we shall build a little neat and plain Habitation.[4] We shall continue, mean while, in his neighbourhood, to superintend the little edifice, and enjoy the society of his exquisite House, and that of my beloved sister Phillips. We are now within two Miles of both, at a Farm House,[5] where we have what Apartments we require, and – no more, – in a most beautiful and healthy situation, a mile and a half from any Town. The nearest is Bookham. But I beg that my Letters may be directed to me at Captain Phillip's, Mickleham, as the Post does not come this way, and I may else miss them for a week. As I do not correspond with Mrs Montagu, and it would be awkward to begin upon such a theme, I beg that when you write you will say something for me.

One of my first pleasures, in our little intended Home, will be finding a place of Honour for the Legacy of my revered Mrs Delany.[6] What ever may be the general wonder, and perhaps blame, of general people, at this connexion, equally indiscreet in pecuniary points for us both, I feel sure that the truly liberal and truly intellectual judgement of that most venerated Character, would have accorded its sanction, when acquainted with the worthiness of the Object who would wish it. Adieu, my sweet Friend. Give

4. The plot in Norbury Park on which, in 1796–7, the d'Arblays would build Camilla Cottage.
5. Phenice Farm, at the summit of Blagden Hill.
6. Mary Delany had bequeathed to FB medallions of George III and Queen Charlotte, and a painting, *Saccharissa*, by herself.

my best Compliments to Mr Waddington – and give me your kind wishes – your kind prayers, my ever dear Marianne.

159. From Letter to Georgiana Waddington *19 September 1793*

The account of your surprise, my sweet Friend, was the last thing to create mine: I was well aware of general astonishment, – and of yours in particular. – My own, however, at my very extraordinary fate is singly greater than that of all my Friends united. I had never made any vow against Marriage, but I had long – long been firmly persuaded it was – *for me* – a state of too much hazard, and too little promise, to draw me from my individual plans and purposes. I remember, in playing at Questions and Commands, when I was thirteen, being asked *When I intended to Marry?* – – and surprising my playmates by solemnly replying 'When I think I shall be happier than I am in being single. – ' It is true, I imagined that time would never arrive; and I have pertinaciously adhered to trying no experiment upon any other hope – for many and mixed as are the ingredients which form what is generally considered as happiness, I was always fully convinced that Social Simpathy of character and taste could alone have any chance with *me*. All else I *always* thought – and now Know to be immaterial. I have only This peculiar – that what many contentedly assert, or adopt, in Theory – I have had the courage to be guided by in practice.

We are now removed to a very small House in the *suburbs* of a very small village, called Bookham.[1] We found it rather inconvenient to reside in another person's Dwelling, though our own Apartments were to ourselves. Our views are not so beautiful as from Phenice Farm, but our situation is totally free from neighbours and intrusion. We are about a Mile and an half from Norbury Park, and 2 miles from Mickleham. I am become already so stout a Walker, by use, and with the help of a very able supporter, that I go to those places and return Home, on foot, without fatigue, when the Weather is kind. – At other times, I condescend to accept a Carriage from Mr Lock; but it is always reluctantly, I so much prefer walking, where, as here, the Country and Prospects are inviting.

I thank you for your caution about building:[2] we shall certainly undertake

---

1. The d'Arblays had moved to a rented house in Great Bookham, after a few weeks at Phenice Farm.

2. In a letter to FB of 3 August 1793.

nothing but by contract: however, it would be truly mortifying to give up a House in Norbury Park; we defer the structure till the Spring, as it is to be so very slight, that Mr Lock says it will be best to have it hardened in its first stage by the summer's sun. It will be *very* small, – merely an Habitation for Three people, but in a situation truly beautiful, and within 5 minutes of either Mr Lock or my Sister Phillips. It is to be placed just between those two loved Houses.

My dearest Father, whose fears and draw backs have been my sole subject of regret, begins now to see I have not judged rashly, or with romance, in seeing my own road to my own felicity. And his restored chearful concurrence in my *constant principles*, though new station, leaves me, for myself, without a wish. *L'Ennui*,[3] which could alone infest our retreat, I have ever been a stranger to, except in tiresome company – and my Companion has every possible resource against either feeling or inspiring it.

As my Partner is a *French man*, I conclude the wonder raised by the connection may spread beyond my own private circle: but no wonder upon Earth can ever arrive near my own in having found such a Character from that Nation. – This is a prejudice certainly impertinent and very John Bullish, and very arrogant; but I only share it with all my Country men, and therefore – must needs forgive both them and myself! – I am convinced, however, from your tender solicitude for me in all ways, that you will be glad to hear that *The Queen and all the Royal Family* have deigned to send me wishes for my happiness, through Mrs Schwellenberg, who has written me *what you call* a very kind congratulation.

I long much for news of your being recovered from that terrible sickly state,[4] my dearest Marianne – Pray let me, if possible, hear a better account soon. Surely that cruel state cannot last – You were quite right in conjecturing I *wrote*, – certainly I could not have *spoken* to the Queen – on such a subject, had the person in question been of her own Court and first favour: however, before any engagement had passed between us – I had previously paved the way, by saying to her one Morning That I should cease to think Honour and integrity existed in the World, if ever I lost my opinion of their residing in M. D'Arblay. – This was too strong an assertion to be easily forgotten. I had already told his story and situation.

---

3. *Boredom.*
4. Referring to Georgiana Waddington's pregnancy.

160. Letter to Alexandre d'Arblay *c. 26 September 1793*[1]

Do not be astonished at my consternation – nor attribute it wholly to weakness – I had deceived myself into a belief that the Profession of blood was wholly relinquished – I had understood you that you had satisfied yourself, and might now, with a safe conscience, retire from public life. – If this had been my belief before I belonged to you – before I had experienced that perfect felicity which I hardly thought mortal, but which you have given to my existence – – – Judge the bitterness of my disappointment at this juncture! —

I know – and acknowledge the force of what you urge, but the strength of your arguments, however they may carry conviction to the judgement, – offer no peace, no consolation to a stroke so unexpected –

Nevertheless – I cannot endure that the tenderness of your Nature should be at variance with the severe calls of your Honour – You have generously said you would take no step without my consent – My Tongue refuses to pronounce it – but my Pen shall write it – Take it then, – my sad – but full – consent – which however reluctantly given I will never torment you with calling back – – *Do whatever you think right* – and only join in my prayer That Heaven may preserve to me the Husband of my Heart! –

F.A.D.

I promise you shall find me better when you come Home – but *pray* show this to nobody. –

161. Letter to Dr Burney *20 October 1793*[1]

Sunday Noon

My dearest Father will think I have been very long in doing the little I have done, – but my mind is so anxiously discomfitted by the continued suspense with regard to M. D'Arblay's proposition and wish – that it has not been

1. Annotated by FB: 'Written to the bravest, yet tenderest of Men on his project to join the Royal Army collecting at Toulon, a few months after our happy – happy marriage'. The project to gather Royalist forces at Toulon, however, proved abortive, and AA did not leave England at this time.

1. Annotated by FB: 'F.d'A's. Tract for the Emigrant Priests Now written & preparing for the Press'. CB had asked FB to support Frances Crewe, who was organizing charitable relief for the exiled French clergy, by writing a pamphlet on their behalf. FB's *Brief Reflections Relative to the Emigrant French Clergy* was published on 19 November 1793.

easy to me to weigh completely all I could say – and the fear of repeating what has already been offered upon the subject, has much restrained me, for I have seen none of the Tracts that may have appeared. However, it is a matter truly near my Heart, and though I have not done it rapidly, I have done it with my whole Mind, and – to own the truth, with a species of emotion, that has greatly affected me, for I could not deeply consider the situation of these venerable Men without feeling for them to the quick. If what I have written should have power to procure them *one more guinea*,[2] I shall be paid.

I shall send the scrawl to you by the stage on *Tuesday*. I have still to Copy it, – and But I have the pleasure to give you another Subscriber, *Mrs Hume*,[3] a Lady who has listened to the eloquence of Mrs Lock, who never sees any one without producing the Plan. Mrs Lock begs you to trust her for the guinea. Mr Lock enters into this business with the warmest approbation.

If you think what I have drawn up worth printing, I should suppose it might make a little 6d paper,[4] to be sold for the same purpose it is written. Or will it only do to be printed by the expence of the acting Ladies, and given Gratis? You must judge of this.

My duty and Love to my Mother and Sarah – I will now go and Copy with all my Might, as it must go to-morrow to Mickleham to be ready for the stage. We have here neither stage nor post.

Adieu, ever most and most dear Sir! –

M. D'Arblay charges me with his best Respects.

162. Letter to Dr Burney 27 *October 1793*[1]

Bookham

My most dear Father,

The terrible confirmation of this last act of savage hardness of Heart has wholly overset us again – M. D'Arblay had entirely discredited its probability, and, to the last moment, disbelieved the report: not from milder thoughts of the barbarous Rulers of his unhappy Country, but from seeing that the Death of the Queen could answer *no* purpose, helpless as she was

2. Subscribers were invited to contribute up to one guinea each.
3. Elizabeth Hume, wife of an Irish parson.
4. The pamphlet was sold for three times this amount (one shilling and sixpence).

1. Annotated by FB: 'Barbarous Execution of the Queen of France Marie Antoinette'. The Queen was guillotined on 16 October 1793.

to injure them, while her life *might* answer some, as an hostage with the Emperor.[2] Cruelty, however, such as theirs, seems to require no incitement whatever; its own horrible exercise appears sufficient both to prompt and to repay it. Good Heaven! that that wretched Princess should so finish sufferings so unexampled! –

With difficulties almost incredible, Mme de Stael has contrived, a second time, to save the lives of M. de Jaucourt and M. de Montmorenci,[3] who are just arrived in Swisserland, we know as yet none of the particulars; simply that they are saved is all: but they write in a style the most melancholy to M. de Narbonne, of the dreadful fanaticism of Licence, which they dare call Liberty, that still reigns, unsubdued, in France. And they have preserved nothing but their persons! – of their vast properties they could secure no more than pocket money for travelling in the most penurious manner. They are therefore in a state the most deplorable. Swisserland is filled with Gentlemen and Ladies of the very first families and rank, who are all starving, but those who have had the *good fortune* to procure, by disguising their quality, some menial office! —

No Answer comes from Mr Pitt; and we now expect none till Sir Gilbert Elliot makes his report of the state of Toulon, and of the *Toulonese*;[4] till which, probably, no decision will be formed whether the Constitutionals in England will be employed or not.

163. Letter to Dr Burney *10 August 1794*[1]

Bookham

It is just a Week since I had the greatest gratification, the most complete, the most exquisite joy I ever, I think, experienced – no – there was never so dear a thing done – so kind a thought – so sweet an execution – my dearest dear Father! how softly and soothingly it has rested upon my mind ever since! – *Abdolonime* has no regret but that his Garden was not in better

2. Francis II, Emperor of Austria and nephew of Marie-Antoinette.
3. Arnail-François de Jaucourt and Mathieu-Jean de Montmorency-Laval, both part of the Juniper Hall group.
4. AA had written to the Prime Minister offering his services for the Royalist forces to be gathered at Toulon, where Gilbert Elliot had been appointed Civil Commissioner on 25 September 1793. The project failed before AA received a reply.

1. Annotated by FB: 'After the First Visit – & by surprize – of Dr. Burney to the Hermitage of M. d'Arblay & F.d'A. at Bookham'.

order,[2] – he was a little *piquè* he confesses that you said it was not *very neat* – and *to be shor*! – but his passion is to do great Works, – he undertakes with pleasure, pursues with energy, and finishes with spirit – – but then, all is over! he thinks the business *once* done, *always* done, and to repair, and amend, and weed, and cleanse – O, these are drudgeries insupportable to him!

However, you should have seen the place before he began his operations, to do him justice: there was then *nothing else* but *mauvaises herbes*,[3] *now*, you must at least, allow, there is a *mixture* of flowers and grain! I wish you had seen him, yesterday, mowing down our Hedge – with his *Sabre*! – and with an air, and attitudes so military, that if he had been hewing down other legions than those he encountered – – i.e. of spiders – he could hardly have had a mien more tremendous, or have demanded an Arm more mighty. God knows – I am 'the most *contente personne*[4] in the World' to see his Sabre so employed!

You spirited me on in all ways, for this week past I have taken *tightly* to the *grand ouvrage*.[5] If I go on so a little longer, I doubt not but M. d'Arblay will begin settling where to have a new shelf for arranging it! – which is already in his rumination for *Metastasio*,[6] – he says he cannot possibly excuse you the *smallest tract*, much less memoirs of an author he so highly admires. – – I imagine you now seriously resuming that work. I hope to see *further sample* ere long.

We think with *very* great pleasure of accepting yours and my Mother's kind invitation for a few Days. I hope, and mean, if possible, to bring with *me* also a littel sample of something less in the dolourous style than what always causes your poor Shoulders a little Shrug.[7]

---

2. The gardener-hero of Bernard de Fontenelle's *Abdolonime, Roi de Sidon* (1725), and FB's pet-name for AA.

3. *Weeds*.

4. *Happiest person*.

5. *Great work. Camilla*, FB's third novel, which would be published in five volumes on 28 June 1796.

6. CB's *Memoirs of the Life and Writings of the Abate Metastasio*, which would be published in three volumes in February 1796.

7. I.e. FB's four tragedies, which her father disliked.

164. Letter to Georgiana Waddington *7 March 1795*

Ah my Marianne! — What an age since I have written! – what delight –
and what torture has filled up the interval – my Baby is all I can wish[1] – my
opening recovery was the most rapid I ever witnessed or heard of – but in
a fortnight the poor thing had the Thrush – communicated it to my Breast
– and in short – after torment upon torment, a milk fever ensued – an
abscess in the Breast followed – and till that broke, 4 Days ago, I suffered
so as to make life – even My happy life – scarce my wish to preserve! – need
I say more –

I am now fast recovering once more – living on Bark – Porter and raw
Eggs – incessantly poured down – much reduced, you may believe – but
free from pain and fever – Therefore in a fair way –

But – they have made me wean my Child! – O my Marianne! you who
are so tender a Mother can need no words to say what that has cost me!
But God be praised my Babe is well, and feeds, while he pines – adieu –
and Heaven bless you! I grieve sincerely for your cruel loss[2] – my poor dear
unfortunate young Friend! – may your children bless and repay all! prays
yours

F. d'A

165. Letter to Georgiana Waddington *15 April 1795*

Bookham

So dry a reproof from so dear a Friend? – – And do you, then, measure my
regard of Heart by my remissness of Hand? – Let me give you the short
History of my Tragedy[1] fairly and frankly.

I wrote it not, as your Acquaintance imagined, *for the Stage*, nor yet *for the
Press* – I began it at Kew Palace[2] – and, at odd Moments, I finished it at
Windsor; *without* the least idea of any species of publication.

Since I left the Royal Household, I ventured to let it be read by my

---

1. Alexander Charles Louis d'Arblay, born on 18 December 1794.
2. Georgiana Waddington's brother George Port had died of yellow fever in Antigua in June 1794.

1. *Edwy and Elgiva* had been played for a single night at Drury Lane on 25 March 1795. FB had been present.
2. See p. 271.

Father, Mr and Mrs Lock, my Sister Phillips, and – – of course, M. d'Arblay: and not another human Being. – Their opinions led to what followed – and my brother Dr Charles shewed it to Mr Kemble[3] while I was on my visit to my Father last October. He instantly and warmly pronounced for its acceptance, but I knew not when Mr Sheridan[4] would see it, and had not the smallest expectation of its appearing this year. However – just 3 Days before my beloved little Infant came into the World, an Express arrived from My Brother [Charles], that Mr Kemble wanted the Tragedy immediately, in order to shew it to Mr Sheridan, who had just heard of it, and had spoken in the most flattering terms of his good will for its reception.

Still, however, I was in doubt of its actual acceptance, till 3 Weeks after my confinement, when I had a visit from my Brother, who told me he was the next Morning to read the Piece in the Green Room.

This was a precipitance for which I was every way unprepared, as I had never made but one Copy of the Play, and had intended divers corrections and alterations: – absorbed, however, by my new charge, and then growing ill, I had a sort of indifference about the matter, which, in fact, has lasted ever since.

The moment I was then able to hold a pen, I wrote two short Letters to acknowledge the state of the affair to my Sisters[5] – and to one of these, I had an immediate laughing answer – informing me *my confidence* was somewhat of the latest, as the Subject of it *was already in all the News-papers!*[6] – I was extremely chagrined at this intelligence – but, from that time, thought it all too late to be the herald of my own Designs. And this, added to my natural and incurable dislike to enter upon these egoistical details unasked, has caused my silence to my dear Marianne – and to every Friend I possess. Indeed, speedily after, I had an illness so severe and so dangerous, that for full 7 Weeks the Tragedy was neither named nor thought of by M. d'Arblay or myself –

It was not my *Health enabled me to go to Town* – I was too much indisposed to make a single visit there, even to my sisters – I merely went, *one Night*, to alight at the Theatre, where I was met by my Sister Phillips, with whom, and M. d'Arblay and my Brother Dr Charles I sat, snug and retired and wrapt up in a Bonnet and immense Pelice, in Mr Sheridan's Box to see Mrs

3. John Philip Kemble, actor-manager of Drury Lane Theatre.

4. Sheridan was the proprietor of Drury Lane Theatre.

5. Probably Esther and Charlotte Francis; the letters and replies are not extant.

6. Advertisements for the production had begun appearing in the London newspapers on 6 March.

376

Siddons and Mr Kemble in *Edwy and Elgiva*.[7] And except this once, and for this purpose, I entered not London. I could not risk my Babe there, and I would not leave him, thus early, for a single Night upon any consideration, except eminent danger to a dear friend. I spent near 3 Weeks in the pure air of Greenwich, at my Brothers,[8] with M. d'Arblay and our little inseparable, and there my family visited me, and Mr and Mrs Lock, but I was too much an Invalide to receive *any others*.

The Piece was represented to the utmost disadvantage, save only Mrs Siddons and Mr Kemble, – for it was not written with any idea of the stage, and my illness and weakness and constant *absorbment* in the time of its preparation, occasioned it to appear with so many *undramatic* effects, from my inexperience of Theatrical requisites and demands, that when I saw it, I perceived myself a thousand things I wished to *change*. The Performers, too, were cruelly imperfect, and made blunders I blush to have pass for mine, – added to what belong to me – the most important Character, after the Hero and Heroine, had *but 2 lines* of his part by Heart![9] he made all the rest at random – and such nonsense as put all the other actors out as much as himself – so that a more wretched performance, except Mrs Siddons, Mr Kemble and Mr Bensley,[10] could not be exhibited in a Barn. All this concurred to make it very desirable to *withdraw the Piece for alterations*[11] – which I have done.

And now you have the whole history – and now – are you appeased?

---

7. As Elgiva and Edwy, and Sarah Siddons spoke the epilogue.
8. At Charles's house, where she stayed from 21 March to 11 April.
9. The newspaper reviewers also condemned the actors, and particularly John Palmer, who played the part of Bishop Aldhelm.
10. Robert Bensley, who played the part of Dunstan.
11. Kemble said the play was being 'withdrawn for alterations' at the end of the performance, and this was greeted with applause from the audience. Unlike FB, the newspaper reviewers took the applause to express relief that the play was being withdrawn, not that it was being altered.

1796–1802

Camilla *and Camilla Cottage*

166. Journal Letter to Dr Burney *10–17 July 1796*[1]

WINDSORIANA, Part I

Bookham, July 10th

The Books were ready at 11 or 12 – but not so *The Taylor!*[2] – the 3 Miss Thrales[3] came to a short but cordial *handshaking* at the last minute, by appointment, – and, at about ½ past 3 we set forward. I had written the Day before to my worthy old friend, Mrs Agnew,[4] the Housekeeper, erst, of my revered Mrs Delaney, to secure us rooms for one Day and night, – and to Miss Planta, to make known I could not set out till late.

When we came into Windsor, at 7 o'clock, the way to Mrs Agnew's was so intricate, that we could not find it, – till one of the King's footmen – recollecting me, I imagine, – came forward, a volunteer, and walked by the side of the Chaise to shew the Postillion the House. N.B. No bad omen to worldly Augurers!

Arrived, Mrs Agnew came forth with faithful attachment – to conduct us to our destined lodgings. I wrote hastily to Miss Planta, to announce to the Queen that I was waiting the high honour of Her Majesty's commands, – and then began preparing for my appearance the next Morning, when I expected a summons: but Miss Planta came instantly herself, *from The Queen*, with orders of immediate attendance, – as her Majesty would see me

1. Annotated by FB: 'on the Presentation of Camilla to the Queen'. FB entitled the journal, written in five parts between 10 July and 13 August, 'WINDSORIANA': the first two parts, describing the events of 5 July, are printed here.
2. Presumably the one responsible for her or for AA's court dress.
3. Hester Maria, Susanna Arabella and Sophia Thrale. (The youngest daughter, Cecilia, had married in June 1795.)
4. Anne Agnew, Mary Delany's waiting gentlewoman.

directly! The King was just gone upon the Terrace, but Her Majesty did not walk that Evening.

I cannot express to you my delight at this most flattering condescendsion of readiness – Mrs Agnew was my maid – Miss Planta, my Arranger – My Landlord, who was a Hair Dresser, came to my head – and M. d'Arblay was general superintendent – the haste and the joy went hand in hand, and I was soon equipped, though shocked at my own precipitance in sending before I was already *visible*. Who, however, could have expected such prompt admission? And in an *Evening*?

M. d'Arblay helped to carry the Books as far as to the Gates. The lodgings were as near to them as possible. At the first entry towards the Queen's Lodge, we encountered Dr Fisher, and his lady[5] – the sight of *me* there – in a dress announcing indisputably whither I was hying, was such an astonishment, that they looked at me rather as a recollected spectre, than a renewed acquaintance. – When we came to the Iron Rails, poor Miss Planta, in much fidget, begged to take the Books from M. d'Arblay, terrified I imagine, lest *French feet* should contaminate the Gravel within! – while he, innocent of her fears, was insisting upon carrying them as far as to the house – till he saw I took part with Miss Planta, and he then was compelled to let us *lug* in 10 Volumes as we could.

The King was already returned from the Terrace, the page in waiting told us; – 'O, then,' said, Miss Planta, 'you are too late!' I went into my old Dining Parlour, – while she said she would see if any one could obtain the Queen's commands for another time. – I did not stay 5 minutes – ruminating upon the *Dinners* – 'gone where the Chickens,'[6] etc. when Miss Planta returned, and told me The Queen would see me instantly. This second surprise really agitated me with so much gratitude and pleasure, that it lost me wholly my voice, when I arrived in the Royal presence. Miss Planta had *orders* to help me in with the Books – which shewed that they were all to be presented.

The Queen was in her Dressing Room, and with only the Princess Elizabeth. Her reception was the most gracious imaginable – yet, when she saw my emotion in thus meeting her again, she was herself by no means quite unmoved, – I presented my little – yet not *small* offering, upon one Knee, placing them, as she directed, upon a Table by her side, and expressing, as well as I could, my devoted gratitude for her invariable goodness to

5. John Fisher, Canon of Windsor, and his wife Dorothea.
6. Swift, 'On Poetry: A Rhapsody' (1733), l. 70: 'Gone, where the *Chickens* went before'.

me. She then began a conversation – in her old style – upon various things and people, with all her former graciousness of manner, which soon, as she perceived my strong sense of her indulgence, grew into even all its former kindness. Particulars I have now no room for – but when, in about half an Hour, she said 'How long do you intend to stay here, Madame d'Arblay? –' and I answered – 'we have no intentions, Ma'am! –' she repeated, laughing, 'You have no intentions? – Well, then, if you can come again to-morrow morning, you shall see the Princesses. –'

Can you paint to yourself a higher satisfaction than this? –

She then said she would not detain me at present – and, encouraged by her extreme condescendsion in all that had passed, I asked if I might presume to put at the Door of the King's Apartment a copy of my little work? – She hesitated – but with smiles the most propitious – then told me to fetch the Books – and whispered something to the Princess Elizabeth, who left the room by another Door at the same moment that I retired for the other set –

Here ends part the First. Part the second must wait a future Letter from dearest dearest Sir your

F. d'A.

WINDSORIANA, Part II

Almost immediately upon my return to The Queen and The Princess Elizabeth, – The King entered the Apartment! – and entered it to receive himself my little offering! – How did I long to present it to him, as to The Queen, upon one knee! – but, as it was not dedicated to him, I had not courage. But my very Heart bowed down to him, in gratitude for this kind condescendsion.

'Madame d'Arblay,' said her Majesty, 'tells me that Mrs Boscawen[7] is to have the – *third* set, – but the *First* – your Majesty will excuse me! – is mine!'

This sweetness was not, you will believe, thrown away upon me; The King, smiling, said 'Mrs Boscawen, I hear, has been very zealous?'

I confirmed this, and the Princess Elizabeth eagerly called out 'Yes, Sir! and while Mrs Boscawen kept a Book for Madame d'Arblay, the Duchess of Beaufort kept one for Mrs Boscawen.'

---

7. Frances Boscawen, foremost among the group of ladies who raised subscriptions for *Camilla*, was aided by her daughter, the Duchess of Beaufort, who brought them in from the highest ranks of the aristocracy, including nine dukes and duchesses; see *JL*, iii. 143.

This led to a little discourse upon the business, in which the King's countenance seemed to speak a benign interest, and the Queen then said 'This book was begun *here*, Sir,' which already I had mentioned.

'And what did you write of it here?' he cried; – 'how far did you go? – did you finish any part? or only form the – skeleton?'

'Just that, Sir;' I answered; 'The skeleton was formed here, but nothing was completed. I worked it up in my little Cottage.'

'And about what time did you give to it?'

'*All* my time, sir! – from the period I planned publishing it, I devoted myself to it wholly; – I had no Episode – but a little baby! – My subject grew upon me, and encreased my materials to a bulk – that, I am afraid, will be still more laborious to wade through for the Readers, than for the Writer! – '

'Are you much frightened? – ' cried he, smiling? – 'As much frightened as you were before?'

'I have hardly had time to know, yet, Sir! – I received the fair sheets of the last volume only last night. I have, therefore, had no leisure for fear. – And sure I am, happen what may to the Book from the Critics, – it can never cause me pain in any proportion with the pleasure and happiness I owe to it! – '

I am sure I spoke most sincerely, and he looked kindly to believe me.

He asked if *Mr Locke* had seen it: and when I said no, seemed comically pleased, as if desirous to have it in its *first state*: he asked next if *Dr Burney* had overlooked it, – and, upon the same answer, – looked with the same satisfaction. He did not imagine how it would have *passed current* with my dearest Father! – he appeared only to be glad it would be a *genuine work*: but laughingly said 'So you kept it quite snug? – '

'Not intentionally, sir, but from my situation and my haste; I should else have been very happy to have consulted my Father and Mr Locke; but I had so much, to the last moment, to *write*, that I literally had not a moment to hear what could be *said*! The work is longer by the whole fifth Volume than I had first planned: – and I am almost ashamed to look at its size! – and afraid my Readers would have been more obliged to me if I had left so much out – than for putting so much in! – '

He laughed – and enquired who corrected my proofs? Only myself, I answered. 'Why some Authors have told me,' cried he, 'that they are the last to do that work for themselves. They know so well by heart what *ought* to be, that they run on, without seeing what *is*. They have told me, besides, that a mere *plodding head* is best and surest for that work, – and that the livlier the imagination, the less it should be trusted to it.'

*

I must not go on thus minutely, or my 4 parts will be 40 – but a full half Hour of graciousness, I could almost call kindness, was accorded me, though the King came from the Concert to grant it – it broke up by the Queen's saying 'I have told Madame d'Arblay that if she can come again to-morrow, she shall see the Princesses.'

The King bowed gently to my grateful obeisance for this sweet offer, and told me I should not know the Princess Amelia, she was so much grown, adding 'She is taller than you! – '

I expressed warmly my delight in the permission of seeing their Royal Highnesses; and their Majesties, then, with looks and manners of the most indulgent softness and goodness, returned to the Concert Room. The Princess Elizabeth stayed – and flew up to me, crying 'How glad I am to see you here again, my dear Miss Burney! – I beg your pardon, Madame d'Arblay, I mean – but I always call all my friends by their maiden names, when I first see them after they are married.'

I warmly now opened upon my happiness in this return to all their sights, – and the condescendsion and sweetness with which it was granted me, – and confessed I could hardly behave *prettily* and *properly* at my first entrance, after so long an absence. 'And, I assure you I felt for you!' cried she; 'I thought you must be agitated – it was so *natural* to you to come here! – to *Mama*! – '

You will believe, my dearest Father, how light-hearted and full of glee I went back to my Expecting Companion: Miss Planta accompanied me, and stayed the greatest part of the little remaining Evening, promising to let me know at what hour I should wait upon their Royal Highnesses.

The next Morning, at 8 or 9 o'clock – my old footman, Moss[8] came with Mlle Jacobi's compliments to *Monsieur* and *Madame* d'Arblay, and an invitation to Dine at the Queen's Lodge. I could scarce believe my Ears – my Senses! – I made Mrs Agnew run down to him, and enquire if it were not a mistake – but he was gone – and I could only resolve to visit Mlle Jacobi *first*, and make certain whether or not Monsieur were really invited to The Queen's Lodge!

End of Part 2d

8. Possibly William Moss, a chairman; see *JL*, iii. 178 n. 5.

Sunday morn.[9]

I have just received my beloved Father's Letter,[10] which I have just room to express my most warm thanks for – and my extreme delight my *little large Work* has met with that approbation I *most* prize of all approbations in this lower sphere – dear to me and interesting as are many others – indeed I am quite seriously thankful for it, and receive it rather as a *blessing* than a *pleasure*.

167. Letter to Georgiana Waddington *2 October–11 November 1796*

You allow so little, my dear Marianne, to even the Manual labour of bringing forth the 5 huge volumes with which I have burthened so many shelves, that I must plead a wearied hand no more – though I will not promise you will no more feel its consequences. I thank you for the honesty of your confession. When I cease to prize sincerity, how must I be metamorphosed! I have not, however, any great philosophy to boast in sustaining heroically partial censors, while the Public reception is beyond all possible expectation. The sale has been one of the most rapid ever known for a Guinea Book: it is 4 times that of Evelina, and nearly double that of Cecilia. Of the First Edition, containing the immense quantity of 4000, 500 only remain: and it has been printed but 3 Months.[1] —

We have parted with the Copy right, – very reluctantly, as guarding it was our motive to the subscription: but all our friends interfered, representing our ignorance of money concerns, and the risks we should run from piracies and double dealings. The Publishers give 1000 pounds for the Copy[2] – but this you must not mention from me at present, as they desire to keep it secret, from affirming a similar price has never yet been given, and fearing to offend cotemporaries. I doubt not, however, it will soon be known, as the very extraordinary quick sale will make the Purchasers think it incumbent upon their characters to proclaim an extraordinary price. We know not, yet, what the subscription will prove, from certain non-payments, and

9. 17 July.
10. CB wrote two enthusiastic letters to FB about *Camilla* (12 and 14 July).

1. Despite the initial sales, the remaining 500 sold out only in 1802, when a (revised) second edition of *Camilla* was finally published.
2. There had been considerable debate among the Burneys about selling the copyright of *Camilla*; £1,000 was unprecedented for a novel.

various expences not yet settled: but we have reason to believe it will nearly, if not wholly, clear another thousand.[3]

I confide what I am sure will be highly interesting to you without scruple; and now I will go back to your Letters.

I am truly delighted with the account you give me of your health, and I hope the little *excess* of which you were guilty in overstraining your strength is already forgotten. 'Tis the only excess to which I am myself ever tempted, and certainly were I in the circle of your beautiful Welsh Mountains, I should not be more likely to escape it. The description of your little Girls is all alive, and brings them forcibly to my view and knowledge. Fanny seems, by it, *la plus aimable* – Emily, *la plus aimée*[4] – not from your partiality, but from the very construction of their characters.

Nov. 11. – Thus much has been written this Month – and I meant to have added some little account that might have been interesting to you of my visit to Windsor with my little big work – but circumstances have stopt my writing – The papers will have announced to you the late fatal end at Chelsea[5] – it took me instantly to my dearest Father, with whom I spent a fortnight – and for the few days since my return I have not had a moment from my Hermit or my Bambino – a bewitching little suducer of time! – or Norbury park, even to add these few miserable words which hasten – thus tardily – to assure you of my constant affectionate tenderness through all absence and all silence –

F. d'A.

All Mr Lock's charming family are well, and always love you.

168. Letter to Dr Burney *14 October 1796*[1]

Friday, Bookham –

How well I know – and feel the pang of this cruel Day to my beloved Father![2] my Heart seems visiting him almost every minute in grief and

---

3. With 1,060 subscribers paying a guinea per copy, FB should have cleared about £1,000, after settling the printing expenses of £183. 6s.

4. Frances Waddington, aged five, 'the most loveable', and her sister Emelia, aged two, 'the most loved'.

5. The death of Elizabeth Burney on 20 October was announced in the London papers.

1. Annotated by FB: 'Mrs. Phillips. astonishing Sale of Camilla'.

2. The day Susanna was to leave England to settle in Ireland with her husband. The sisters would never meet again.

participation. Yet I was happy to see it open with a smiling aspect, and encourage a superstition of hoping it portentous of a good conclusion. All here are persuaded that the Major is *already* tired of Ireland. This dear Soul, therefore, we suppose taken to *lighten* to him his banishment, by making him a *chez lui*;[3] and raising his credit by his but too excellent choice. That he loves her I still believe, though with a selfishness so imperious, tyrannical, and absorbing, that not one mark of regard can break out of the adamantine fortifications of his egotism that could oppose, or restrain, his own smallest will or wish. – –

I am almost afraid to ask how my poor Mother bore the last farewell – indeed I hope She was *virtuously* cheated of a leave-taking. I advised Susan to avoid it if possible, as the parting impression would be lighter by such management; and, much as she is recovered from her *very* terrible state, she cannot be too cautious of emotions, of almost any sort – much less of such a separation. Our sorrow, however, here, has very considerably been diminished by the Major's voluntary promises to Mrs Locke of certain and speedy return. I shall expect him *at the Peace*! – not before. I cannot think it possible he should appear here during the War[4] – except, as now, merely to fetch his family.

But I meant to have begun with our thanks for my dear kind Father's indulgence of our extreme curiosity and interest in the sight of the Reviews. I am quite happy in what I have escaped of greater severity, though my Mate cannot bear that the palm should be contested by Evelina and Cecilia, his partiality rates the *last* as so much the highest. So does the News paper I have mentioned, of which I long to send you a Copy.[5] But those immense Men whose single praise was Fame and Security, who established, by a Word, the two elder sisters, are now silent – Dr Johnson and Sir Joshua are no more – and Mr Burke is ill, or otherwise engrossed.[6] Yet, – even without their powerful influence, to which I owe such unspeakable obligation, the *essential* success of Camilla *exceeds* that of the Elders: the sale is truly astonishing, – Charles has just sent to me that 500 only remains of 4000! – and it has appeared barely 3 Months! –

The first Edition of Evelina was of 800. – The second of 500 – and the 3d. of 1000. – What the following have been I have never heard. The sale from that period became more flourishing than the generous Publisher

3. (*His*) home.
4. Britain had been at war with France since 1793.
5. Not identified.
6. Edmund Burke would die within a year, in July 1797.

cared to announce.[7] Of Cecilia the first Edition was reckoned *enormous* at 2000. – And as a part of payment was reserved for it, I remember our dear Daddy Crisp thought it very *unfair*. It was printed, like this, in July, and sold in October, – to every one's wonder. Here, however, the Sale is encreased in rapidity more than a third. Charles says

> Now heed no more what Critics thought 'em
> Since this you know – All People bought 'em. – – [8]

We have resumed our original plan, and are going immediately to build a little Cottage for ourselves. We shall make it as small and as cheap as will accord with its being warm and comfortable. We have relinquished, however, the very kind offer of Mr Locke, which he has renewed, for his Park: we mean to make this a property *salable* or *lettable* for our Alec – and in Mr Locke's park we could not encroach any Tenant, if the youth's circumstances, profession, or inclination should make him not chuse the Spot for his own residence. M. d'Arblay, therefore, has fixed upon a field of Mr Locke's, which he will rent, and of which Mr Locke will grant him a lease of 90 years.[9] By this means, we shall leave the little Alex: a little property besides what will be in the Funds, and a property likely to rise in value, as the situation of the field is remarkably beautiful. It is in the valley, between Mr Locke's park and Dorking, and where Land is so scarce, that there is not another possessor within many Miles who would part, upon any term, with half an Acre. My kindest Father will come and give it, I trust, his benediction. I am now almost *jealous* of Bookham for having received it. – Imagine but the extacy of M. d'Arblay in framing All his own way an entire new Garden! He dreams now of Cabbage Walks – potatoe Beds – Bean perfumes and peas' blossoms. My Mother should send him a little sketch to help his Flower Garden, which will be his second favourite object. Alex has made no progress in *phrases*, but pronounces single words, a few more – adieu, most dear Sir,

My Love to my Mother and to Clarentine[10] – I hope to see her in the next paccellone[11] –

> ever most dutifully and most affectionately your
> F. d'A

7. Lowndes, who had, in FB's view, underpaid her for the several editions of *Evelina*.

8. Paraphrase of Swift, *Verses on the Death of Dr Swift* (1731), ll. 311–12.

9. AA was disastrously mistaken in the lease; see below, p. 463 note 5.

10. Sarah Harriet Burney, whose first novel *Clarentine* had been published in July 1796, a few days before *Camilla*.

11. Apparently a humorous corruption of the Italian *pacchetto*, meaning 'packet' or 'small parcel'.

169. Letter to Dr Burney *8 November 1796*[1]

Bookham

I had intended writing to my dearest Father by a *return of Goods*; but I find it impossible to defer the overflowings of my Heart at his most kind and generous indignation with the Reviewer.[2] What Censure can ever so much hurt as such compensation can heal? And, in fact, the praise is so strong, that, were it neatly put together, the writer might challenge my best Enthusiasts to find it insufficient; the truth, however, is, that the criticisms come forward, and the panegyric is entangled, and so blended with blame, as to lose almost all effect. What of *verbal* criticisms are fair, I shall certainly and gladly attend to in the second edition:[3] but most of them are of another class, and mark a *desire* to find them that astonishes me; for I have no consciousness of any enemy, and yet only to enmity can attribute the possibility of supposing 'A man and Horse *was* sent off –' could be other than an error of the press. A Chambermaid, *now adays*, would have written *were*. 'An *admirable* good joke,' also, is the cant of Clermont, not of the author; who might as well be accountable for the slip slops of Dubster.[4] '*Nor* have I *no* great disposition' – must be an *invention*, I should think. Certainly I never wrote it, whether it be in the Book or not. I had not time for an errata – which might, methinks, have been observed, in some candid supposition that, otherwise, a few of the verbal errours might have been corrected.

The Reviews, however, as they have not *made*, will not, I trust, *mar* me. Evelina made its way all by itself: it was well spoken of, indeed, in all the Reviews, compared with general Novels; but it was undistinguished by any quotation, and only put in the Monthly Catalogue, and only allowed a short single paragraph.[5] It was circulated only by the general public, till it reached through that unbiassed medium, Dr Johnson – and Mr Burke – and thence

1. Annotated by FB: 'On the Reviewers on Camilla – after a visit of Condolence to Dr. B on the Death of Mrs. Burney his 2d Wife'.
2. CB's letter to FB of 2 November 1796 denounced the review of *Camilla* in the October *Monthly Review*; see *DL*, v. 296–7. It was by William Enfield, with concluding paragraphs supplied by CB's old friend Ralph Griffiths, the founding editor of the periodical.
3. For the second edition of *Camilla*, FB corrected many of the grammatical errors pointed out in the *Monthly Review*, as well as others in a friendly critique by CB's friend the Revd Thomas Twining sent to CB on 1 June 1797.
4. Clermont Lynmere is the irresponsible young man intended by Sir Hugh Tyrold as husband for his niece Eugenia, Camilla's sister; Mr Dubster is a self-important would-be gentleman.
5. *Evelina* received a brief notice in the 'Monthly Catalogue' section of the *Monthly Review* for April 1778 (lvii, 316).

it wanted no patron. This circumstance made me easy about Cecilia, which, however, was extremely well treated, though not by them, but by Dr Johnson and Mr Burke brought forward to the high station its supporters have claimed for it. Camilla, also, will live or die by more general means. Works of this kind are judged always by the *many*: works of science, History and philosophy and voyages and travels, and poetry, frequently owe their fate to the sentiments of the first Critics who brand or extol them.

Miss Cambridge[6] asked me, early, if I should not take some care about the Reviews? No, I said, none. There are two species of Composition which may nearly brave them; Politics and Novels: for these will be sought and will be judged by the various Multitude, not the fastidious few. With the latter, indeed, they may be Aided, or injured, by Criticism; but it will not stop their being read, though it may prejudice their Readers. They want no Recommendation for being handed about but that of being new, and they frequently become established, or sink into oblivion, before that high Literary Tribunal has brought them to a Trial. She laughed at my composure; but, though I am a good deal chagrined, it is not broken. If I had begun by such a perusal, I might indeed have been disturbed: but it has succeeded to so much solace and encouragement, that it cannot penetrate deeply. The respected opinion of Mr Langhton, the perpetual praise of Mr Cambridge,[7] the continual histories of three readings, the triumphal criterion of nearly 4000 Copies soled in 4 Months – and the unbounded kindness of my dearest Father, – more dear to me than all else – have surely ill played their parts, if they have not braced me for a little castigation, though I affect not to say they have rendered me invulnerable.

But I wanted to write a Whole Letter upon my earnestness that my beloved Father would find some new *Canons*;[8] I sigh at the picture of his lowness. I long to be with him again – in aid of Sally, – I know how my dearest Father accepts from All the offerings of affection. – But how could he name the journies that saved me from an anxiety I should have found insupportable? and that gave me the comfort of witnessing his mild fortitude in sorrow, and the *self-consolation* his reflections on all that is past with the poor departed Sufferer in his constant indulgent kindness *must* and *do* occasion him – with a reception so sweet it still soothes me – how could I have purchased a hundredth part of such satisfaction any other way? When

6. One of the women responsible for gathering subscriptions for *Camilla*.

7. Langton's praise had been reported in a letter from CB to FB of 6 August; Richard Owen Cambridge.

8. Such as the *XII Canzonetti a due voci in Canone* (1790).

I peep at you again, I must bring my little Boy, – *for he is worth us all* as a Consoler, and he begins now to grow manageable without a Maid. I hope the melancholy Inventory[9] has been made? I know what a *lift* the News of our Susanne's safety will prove. She has sent me a little Letter, her *second* – for she was sure her *First* would be spread in Town through my dearest Father. My Chevalier almost lives in his Field. Lady Rothes, Sir Lucas Pepys and Lady Hariet Leslie have been to see it.[10] No Water yet in the Well! – yet 60 feet deep![11] – I want to say something of a *Dictionary of Music* – it would be an unrivalled work in your hands.[12] My kind Love to Sally – I shall write to her soon – we go on slow, from resolving to read together, – I like her Book very much[13] – so does M. d'Arblay – but it is well worth a Letter to herself.

170. From Letter to Dr Burney *14 November 1796*

I covet much to hear that the melancholy task of ransacking, examining, depositing, or demolishing regretful records is over. Sometimes I wish this search could be mixed with collecting for Copying your numerous – and so many of them beautiful – manuscript poems.[1] Some particular pursuit is absolutely necessary. How I wish we could engage in any conjointly! – If Mr Twining – and 2 or 3 other such – (only where are they to be found?) – would bear a part, I know nothing that might better interest my dearest Father, nor in which he would more, and in a thousand ways, excel, than superintending some periodical work.[2]

Upon a second reading the Monthly Review upon Camilla, I am far in better humour with it, and willing to *confess the Case* to the criticisms, if I may claim by that concession any right to the eulogies. They are stronger and more important, upon re-perusal, than I had imagined, in the panic of a

---

9. CB's correspondence with his late wife, most of which he was destroying after her death.
10. Jane Pepys, Countess of Rothes, her husband and their daughter Lady Harriet Leslie.
11. The well would at last produce water, on 25 November, at a depth of over 100 feet; see *JL*, iii. 240.
12. CB did not take up this suggestion.
13. *Clarentine*.

1. CB carried out this project; a collection of manuscript poems copied in his hand is extant in the Osborn Collection.
2. CB did not collaborate with Twining on editing a periodical, but CB did later undertake to provide the articles on music for Abraham Rees's 45-volume *Cyclopaedia of the Arts and Sciences* (1802–20).

first survey, and an unprepared for disappointment in any thing like severity from so friendly an Editor. The recommendation at the conclusion of the Book as a warning Guide to Youth would recompense me, upon the least reflection, to whatever strictures might precede it.[3] I hope my kind Father has not suffered his generous – and to me most *cordial* – indignation against the Review to interfere with his intended answer to the affectionate Letter of Dr Griffiths?[4]

171. Letter to Susanna Phillips *14 March 1797*

What an age since I began this![1] and how I long to hear if my most loved Susan is well again – and all hers and how they are. – How she does in all respects, and if she has ever received a pacquet in which we all writ, and which has induced me to defer finishing this sheet till I could recount a history in which she will take nearly the same interest as myself. I would not awaken useless inquietude in your kind bosom by telling you our fixed design of innoculating our little love this spring – but Mr Ansell[2] was bespoke a Week before this Letter was begun, and the last Day of last month he came – and performed the dreaded operation. The dear little soul sat on my lap, and he gave him some Barley sugar; this made him consent to have his Frock taken off. Mr Ansell pressed me to relinquish him to Betty;[3] but I could not to any one but his Father, who was at his field. When the Lancet was produced, Betty held him a favourite Toy, of which I began discoursing with him. It was a maimed young Drummer, of whose loss of Eyes, Nose, Chin and Hair he always hears with the tenderest interest. But, while listening attentively, he felt Mr Ansell grasp his arm to hold it steady – he turned quick away from his Drummer, and seeing the Lancet, shrunk back. Mr Ansell bid me help to hold him tight, – he then shriekt, and forcibly disengaged his arm from my hand – but, to my utter astonishment, held it out himself very quietly, and looked on, and suffered the incision to be made

3. Griffiths singled out for special praise the sermon-letter written for Camilla by her father, the Revd Augustus Tyrold (*Camilla*, Bk. V, ch. 5).

4. Griffiths's letter of condolence is missing, but CB's reply (2 November) is extant.

1. Part of a journal letter which FB had begun on 27 February.

2. William Ansell, Dorking surgeon and apothecary specializing in inoculations against smallpox, described by FB as 'the first man for such business in this neighbourhood' (*JL*, iii. 279). He had delivered Alexander.

3. Elizabeth Parker, Alexander's nursemaid.

without a cry, or any resistance, only raising his Eyes from his arm to Mr
Ansel, with an expression of the most superlative wonder at his proceedings.
Mr Ansel forced out the blood repeatedly, and played upon it with the
Lancet for some minutes, fearing, he said, if particular caution was not used,
the little soul was so pure his blood could not be infected. The Child still
made no resistance, but looked at the blood with great curiosity, in the most
profound silent rumination. Mr Ansel still was apprehensive the disorder
might not be imbided, from the excessive strictness of his whole life's diet:
he therefore asked my leave to innoculate the other arm also. I left it to his
own decision; – and he took off the shirt from the other arm. – The little
Creature fixed him very attentively, and then turned to me, as if for some
explanation of such conduct; but still made not the smallest resistance, and
without being held *at all*, permitted the second wound. — I own I could
hardly endure the absence of his Father, to whom the actual view of this
infantine courage and firmness would have been such exquisite delight. Mr
Ansel confessed he had met no similar instance. – You will not, I believe,
expect an equal history of his Mother's intrepidity – and therefore I pass
that bye. But she behaved *very well indeed* before Company! —

This beloved little object had taken – with me – his leave of Norbury
Park the Day before, for the fine little Baby Emily Frederica[4] was there,
and, of course, must be guarded as he himself has been guarded hitherto.
He had one double tooth just pierced, and 3 teeth threatening – but we
could not defer our purpose, as the season was advancing, and would have
been lost by waiting. But one very material comfort immediately preceded
the experiment; he had shewn the power of repeating sounds, and could
make us understand when he wished to drink or eat.

This stroke was given on the Tuesday; and on the following Sunday, after
Breakfasting with us in a gaiety the most animating, and with Eyes and
Cheeks brilliant with health and spirits, he suddenly drooped, became pale,
languid, hot and short breathed. This continued all Day, and towards
evening increased into a restlessness that soon became misery – he refused
any food – his Eyes became red, dull, and heavy, his breath feverish, and
his limbs in almost convulsive tribulation. His starts were so violent, it was
difficult to hold him during his short sleeps, and his cries from pain and
nameless sufferings grew incessant. – I expected a fit – and indeed my
terrour was horrible – but his Father – my support – made me put his feet
in warm water at about 10 o'clock at Night, and he fell into a soft slumber,

4. Emily Frederica Locke, daughter of the Lockes' son Charles, born on 12 December 1796.

which lasted 4 Hours. This was a relief that made the renewed pain with which he awoke better endured, and he again slept some Hours afterwards. The Night was far better than the Day which followed, which was a repetition of that I have described. – But so was also the succeeding Night of similar relief. The spots began to appear, but yet Tuesday also was very suffering – however, I will not go on with this triste[5] journal, but tell my dearest dear Susan that *now* all is deliciously well! They began to turn yesterday, and this Day, which makes but the fortnight from the operation, many of them are already fading away, – his appetite is returned, his gaiety is revived, all fever is over, and if his face was not changed, the disorder would not be suspected. I know how you will feel for our excessive joy at this conquest of a dread that has hung cruelly over our best happiness. We have been so much frightened, that we would have compromised with fate for the loss of all his personal recommendation, to have *ensured* his life. Yet Mr Ansel says there never was a better sort, and that all my apprehensions have been groundless. He yesterday took from his little Arm *4 Lancets of matter* – and the dear darling Hero suffered the 4 cuts unmoved, except, as before, by astonishment and curiosity. He would not be held, and his Father, this time, had the satisfaction to see I have not spoiled his race. – Mr Ansel then took his leave, giving me general directions, and assuring me all was safely and happily over as to the distemper. –

Thank God! repeat for me thank God, my own dearest Susan. And read of his prowess to his dear little Cousins.

You will not wonder this subject should engross both me and my paper, – but I could fill another such with his opening powers of elocution – which have begun, like his Mother's reading, all at once, and familiarly. But this must rest for my next folio. He will be but slightly, if at all, marked, though he has more than he will yet let me count of these frightful boutons.[6] Only one, however, has risen in order; the rest come up half way, and seem dying off for want of nourishment: Mr Ansel says this is the recompence of his state of blood. He has 13 upon his Face; 3 upon his Nose, in particular, which disfigure it most comically. They give him, his Father says, the air d'un petit Ivrogne[7] – I fear this feature will never recover entirely from this triple association to destroy its delicacy; but I could bear, just now, to see him turned negro without positive repining. He is thinner and paler

5. Sad.
6. Spots.
7. Of a little drunkard.

considerably, and his Hair I have been forced to chop rather than cut in a way that helps the alteration most unfavourably. My poor Partner will tell you his own history[8] – I grow very anxious for yours, my own darling Susan!

172. Letter to Hester Maria Thrale[1] *July 1798*

Westhamble

Your kind idea of ornamenting my little cottage with some of the work of your own hands, gave me great pleasure, and as I do not fear being obliged by you, after the long test of the many years our friendship has stood unbroken though battered at by Time, absence, silence, and various events, – Why I will not lose the gratification merely because I cannot return it: though that, I confess, is ordinarily sufficient reason with me for starting even insuperable objections. – Alas – I regret, at this moment, I did not make them *insuperable* to the continual exertions of this sort of Mrs Piozzi from the commencement of our acquaintance to its most unprovocked breach! But she pertinaciously loaded me with obligations, which, even at the time, were oppressive to me, dearly as I loved her; and which, even then, when I considered and believed her fondness to be unalterable, I thought the least pleasant part of it, from an inherent dislike to all sort of presents, and from an innate spirit of contentment with what I naturally possessed, however small its proportion to what surrounded me. The things, indeed, from her were trifles, her affluence considered, – but my pride was dearer to me than her gifts, which were forced upon me, whether I would or not, and which hurt me inexpressibly, even, in private, to tears of vexation, as sometimes they were accompanied with a raillery that shewed she discredited the sincerity of my resistance. But I valued her friendship too much for any *serious* dispute and all other she sturdily over-powered. – What she can invent to amuse her fancy with in fashioning any just enmity towards me, I cannot devise. That *he* should be offended that I opposed his marriage with all my might, is natural enough, though unjust and unwise; for I could mean him no harm – I thought not of him, personally at all: it was She I thought of; and I ran all risks to serve, not to disoblige. But I am convinced that from the moment of their Nuptials, she shewed him all my

8. AA added a paragraph.

1. Letter Book copy by AA.

letters, and probably attributed to me every obstacle that he had found in his way. It is the common mode upon such occasions, by which the 'fond married dames'[2] repair their cruelties and hesitations; and the counsellors who, however urged to openness, have declared adverse sentiments, are almost uniformly sacrificed at the hymeneal shrine. Of this I was aware, generally speaking, all the time I worked so strongly against the match: but I thought her so superior to such common, poor, paltry, fifteen years old Girlishness, that I never abated my courage. – And indeed, she bore all my opposition, which was regularly the strongest that the utmost efforts of my stretched faculties could give, with a gentleness nay a *deference* the most touching to me, till the marriage was over – And then, – to my never ending astonishment, in return to the constrained and painful letter I forced myself to write of my good wishes, she sent me a cold, piqued, reproachful answer, in entirely a new style to any I had ever received from her, to upbraid me that my *congratulations were not hearty*! As if I could write *congratulations* at all! or *meant* to write them! How gross must have been such hypocrisy! – And for what? Not to please *her*, for she must have seen their falsehood and despised them. – And had *he* any claim upon me? – Had any human being, indeed, a claim upon my veracity?

I wrote then, indeed, an answer somewhat high, for I felt injured, and far from averse to letting her see my resentment. She sent me a reply *all kindness and returning affection*. To that, you may believe I wrote with warmth and friendship,[3] – but I *never* have heard from her since, in any way good or bad! And sometimes I have thought, as my next news was that she had left England, that my letter was some how lost, as she was continually changing place, and had a maid, as I have heard from Mr Seward, who used to sometimes keep or destroy her letters, to save foreign postage.

I did not mean to let this grievous subject swallow up all my paper – but it is one always near my heart when it recurs, and I am not sorry to have you know how the strange total breach of intercourse began, as far as I know it myself. She must have motives of her own which I cannot fathom, or our acquaintance never could have dropt, though its pristine warmth and pleasure could no more have been revived. —

---

2. Alluding to a song, 'Ye fair married dames', written by Garrick for Arthur Murphy's comedy *The Way to Keep Him*; see EJL, ii. 199 and n. 21.

3. FB's 'painful letter' of good wishes is missing. For Hester Piozzi's 'reproachful answer' (6 August), FB's 'somewhat high' response (10 August) and Hester Piozzi's reassuring letter (13 August), see *The Piozzi Letters*, ed. Edward A. Bloom and Lillian D. Bloom (Newark, N.J., 1989–), i. 107–8. FB's final letter is missing.

173. Letter to Esther Burney *19 November 1799*

turn over cautiously

West Hamble

My dearest Etty,

'Tis my turn now to have the dear commission of spreading news from our beloved Susanna. I have this Day a Letter, dated *November 11th*, with an assurance she is greatly mended, and unremitting in hopes and preparations and Nursings for her journey: but she still names no Day for its commencement, but repeats she shall remain some time at Dublin, where she hopes much benefit from the skill and kindness of Mr Keirnan,[1] who will have charge of her. She again gives her direction at Mrs Cartland's,[2] but does not press for any Letter, and would have none of a private nature, I believe, ventured; as all her motions are precarious. Her eagerness to arrive seems augmenting every moment – 'O my God!' she cries, 'to be once again in England – with you all – will pay me for all I have suffered – will *over*-pay me! –' What affecting words! and what do they not convey both of what she has gone through, and of her tender love for us? – Dearest Soul! I now indeed look forward with a beating Heart to a speedy meeting. Her chief anxiety seems lest the Major should perceive, on his arrival, the disgust he has excited in us, and the chief purport of her Letter is to beseech us all to repress such feelings, and all apparent resentment, that he may *leave her behind in peace and amity*. She dreads some new outrage from his vindictive temper, should he receive any mortification; and when I write, which will be very soon, I shall venture to promise for us all the utmost forbearance. She wishes only to be directed to at Mrs Cartland's, hoping to be there before an answer could reach Belcotton:[3] but not advising or pressing writing at all at present. However, as I can do it gratis, I shall say nothing that might not be published at Charing Cross, and then I am sure it will be a great comfort to her to hear me individualize every one of her family for health and welfare. She commissions me distribute her *bulletin*. She has missed 2 Letters from me – and one had begged her own directions about

1. George Kiernan, Molesworth Phillips's brother-in-law, apothecary.
2. Elizabeth Cartland, friend of Phillips and resident of Dublin.
3. Phillips's estate in County Louth.

our meeting. I shall write for them again, and tell her again your most hospitable invitation, which it will be *hers* to accept or postpone for us, though *ours* to give Our cordial thanks, in either case.

I have written to our dear Padre – and shall to Charles. This is all I have to glean for you from my short Letter. When you write next, pray enclose another ½ of a *ten* and the fellow, the next time of writing.[4]

Now to other matters.

Your extreme contempt, Mrs Hetty, of my dealings with low tradespeople[5] shall not dishearten me from continuing them; shall I give you a dialogue, which past previous to the delivery of the goods, and will put you into a little hot water, for a punishment for your haughtiness? Yes, I will; but *read it alone*. – So here turn to t'other side in a spare room.

Scene St James's Street

Enter Agent and Upholsterer, *meeting*.

Ag. I was just going to beat up your quarters.

Up. I am glad to save you the trouble.

Ag. I want to speak to you upon a little business. A Lady – a relation of Mine – has written a play – Will you act it?

Up. A Lady? – Is it your sister? –

Ag. Suppose it is – Will you Act it?

Up. If I see nothing that seems positively against its succeeding, certainly. But – – You must let me have it.

Ag. When you please.

Up. Immediately.

Ag. It is at her hermitage. I will send for it.

Up. Do, and directly. But, – have you read it?

Ag. I – don't – know!

Up. Pho, – what do you think of it?

Ag. I – don't know. –

Up. Pho, – that's worse still!

Ag. I am no judge.

Up. Pshaw –

Ag. Besides – a lady – my sister – how can I speak?

---

4. I.e. half of a £10 note, referring to financial transactions between FB and Esther made with a view to aiding Susanna.

5. Codeword in the Burney family for theatre managers. FB had recently given her second comedy, *Love and Fashion*, to Thomas Harris, manager of Covent Garden Theatre, with her brother Charles acting as go-between. In a letter of 30 October, Charles had told her that Harris 'admires the Fable' and would produce it in March 1800 (Berg Collection).

Up. Well, that's true. Let me have it in two days.

Ag. All she urges is secresy. She is bent upon making the attempt unknown.

Up. And why? – A *good* play *will* succeed, – and sometimes a bad one – but if there be a circumstance, as here, that will strongly prepare the public in its favour, – why should we lose that circumstance?

Ag. I will speak to her about that: but be very secret meanwhile, especially if you decline it, as it is then her intention to try the other house,[6] – and it *must* not be blown upon.

The result of this dialogue, was sending the Goods forthwith, as soon as fair Copied, to the Upholsterer, but with reiterated charges to secresy, from a firm persuasion the chances are better *without* than *with* expectation.

Therefore, if you meet Agent, be upon your guard, as *he* will make confidents if he knows *I* have, and otherwise is perfectly compliant. – What sweet weather is this, if our beloved may avail herself of it! she seems to have only her health to combat, no more caprices in the Major who is now all *gentle attention*! –

174. Letter to Dr Burney *10 February 1800*[1]

Monday

I hasten to tell you, dearest Sir, Mr Harris has at length, listened to our petitions, and has returned me my poor ill fated – wholly relinquishing all claim to and for this season. He has promised also to do his utmost, as far as his influence extends to keep the news papers totally silent in future.[2] We demand therefore no contradicting paragraph as the report must needs die when the *reality* no more exists. Nobody has believed it from the beginning on account of the premature moment when it was advertised. This release gives me present repose which indeed I much wanted – for to combat your – to me – unaccountable but most afflicting displeasure, in the midst of my own panics and disturbance, would have been ample punishment to me, had I been guilty of a crime in doing what I have all my life been urged to,

---

6. Drury Lane Theatre, where *Edwy and Elgiva* had been performed.

1. Copy by AA.

2. The tragic death of Susanna on 6 January, days after her return from Ireland, had made CB determined to put a stop to the impending production of *Love and Fashion*, which had already been announced in newspapers. FB had thus asked Harris to return the manuscript to her, and to use his influence to prevent further newspaper reports.

and all my life intended, writing a Comedy. Your goodness, your kindness, your regard for my fame, I know have caused both your trepidation, which doomed me to *certain* failure; and your displeasure that I ran, what you thought, a wanton risk. But it is *not* wanton, my dearest Father. My imagination is not at my own controll, or I would always have continued in the walk you approved. The combinations for another long work did not occur to me. Incidents and effects for a Dramma did. I thought the field more than open – inviting to me. The chance held out golden dreams. The risk could be only our own for – permit me to say, appear when it will, you will find nothing in the principles, the moral, or the language that will make you blush for me. *A failure*, upon those points only, can bring *Disgrace* – upon mere control or want of dramatic powers, it can only cause *disappointment*.

I hope, therefore, my dearest Father, in thinking this over, you will cease to nourish such terrors and disgust at an essay so natural, and rather say to yourself with an internal smile, 'After all – 'tis but *like Father like Child* – for to what walk do I confine myself? – She took my example in writing – She takes it in ranging – Why, then, after all, should I lock her up in one paddock, well as she has fed there, if she says she finds nothing more to nibble – while I find all the Earth unequal to my ambition, and mount the skies to content it?[3] Come on then, poor Fan – The World has acknowledged you my offspring – and I will *disencourage*[4] you no more. Leap the pales of your paddock – let us pursue our career – and while you frisk from novel to Comedy, I, quitting Music and Prose, will try a race with Poetry and the Stars.'

I am sure, my dear Father, will not infer, from this appeal, I mean to parallel our Works – no one more truly measures their own inferiority, which with respect to yours has always been my pride; – I only mean to shew, that if my Muse loves a little variety – She has an hereditary claim to try it.

F. B.

---

3. Alluding to the twelve-book poem on astronomy which CB had been composing for several years.

4. Burney family catchword taken from Cecilia Arne, wife of Thomas Arne.

175. Letter to Dr Burney *22 March 1800*[1]

West Hamble

Day after Day I have meant to write to my dearest Father – but I have been unwell ever since our return,[2] and that has not added to my being sprightly. I have not once crossed the threshold since I re-entered the house, till to day, when Mr and Mrs Locke almost insisted upon taking me an airing. I am glad of it, for it has done me good, and broken a kind of spell that made me unwilling to stir. M. d'Arblay has worked most laboriously in his garden; but his misfortunes there, during our absence, might *melt a Heart of stone.* – The Horses of our next neighbouring Farmer broke through our Hedges, and have made a kind of bog of our Meadow, by scampering in it during the wet; the sheep followed, who have eaten up All our Greens – Every sprout and Cabbage and Lettuce, destined for the Winter – while the Horses dug up our Turnips and carrots, and the swine, pursuing such examples, have trod down all the young plants, besides devouring whatever the others left of vegetables! our potatoes, left – from our abrupt departure, in the Ground, are all rotten or frost-bitten – and utterly spoilt; and not a single thing has our whole Ground produced us since we came home. A few dried Carrots, which remain from the in-doors collection, are all we have to temper our viands. What think you of this for people who make it a rule to owe a third of their sustenance to the Garden? Poor Mr d'Arblay's renewal of toils to supply future times is exemplary to behold, after such discouragement. But he works as if nothing had failed, such is his patience as well as industry.

My Alex, I am sure you will be kindly glad to hear, is entirely well – and looks so blooming no Rose can be fresher. I am encouraging back his *spouting* propensity, to fit him for his royal interview with the sweet and gay young Princess who has demanded him, who will, I know, be diverted with his speeches and gestures. We must present ourselves before Easter, as the Court then adjourns to Windsor for 10 days.[3] My Gardener will not again leave his Grounds to the four footed marauders, – and our stay, therefore, will be the *very* shortest we can possibly make it: for though we love

1. Annotated by FB: 'M. d'Arblays losses & Misadventures in his Garden after its neglect from our absence & fatal Calamity'.
2. The d'Arblays had been in London since 9 January, and returned home *c.* 27 February.
3. Alexander would entertain Princess Amelia with his set-piece declamations on 10 April; see *JL*, iv. 413.

retirement, we do not like solitude. I long for some further account of you, dearest Sir, and how you bear the mixture of business and Company, of *fag and frolic*, as Charlotte used to phrase it. –

Our assemblage of poor here at Dorking, by hundreds, about the price of bread,[4] forced the magistrates to allow to each man 1s a week while it continues so high! –

176. Letter to Charles Burney *18 November 1800*

My dearest Carluci –

M. d'Arblay has just left Westhamble – to set sail for the Continent –

I know I need say nothing to excite your interest in such a step – I will only briefly narrate its cause.

It is now nearly a year since he has been erased from the list of Emigrants[1] – and consequently at liberty to revisit his Country and native Friends – but he had early determined against ever taking that measure while France was at war with England. – A few days since, however, he received a Letter[2] to inform him some little part of his property was yet unsold – and might be re-claimed – , now he was erased, if he went over immediately or sent his *procuration* to his nearest surviving Relation,[3] from some country *not at War with France* – but it must be *signed* – *sealed* – and *witnessed* in such a country, or his friends would be personally endangered for even receiving it. The sum in question does not quite amount to £1000 – but that – for us – is a capital object – and therefore he unhesitatingly resolved to go to Holland instantly. He went to Town to make enquiries concerning passport and passage – and returned on Sunday to arrange *our joint* departure – for I could not consent not to share his fate through-out be it what it might – but – after innumerable discussions and cruel conflicts – we finally fixed he should go alone, from fears of the sea in two voyages at such a season for our Alex – and from drawbacks to the *object* which carries him, in the added expense – the more than doubled expense of our all going. – He left me Monday – yesterday morning – meaning to go to Chelsea – *You* – Mr Lock

4. On 3 March, some 300 labourers had gathered in Dorking to protest against the exorbitant price of bread; see *JL*, iv. 401.

1. By decree of the Consuls, AA's name had been struck from the list of émigrés on 21 April 1800; see *JL*, iv. 459 n. 2.

2. The letter from AA's friend Pierre-Auguste Lajard is missing.

3. AA's beloved uncle, Jean-Baptiste-Gabriel Bazille.

at Woodlands – Beaumont Street[4] – etc. but he heard immediately of a vessel new going to sail – and this morning I have a few hasty lines from him, charging me to explain his situation to you all, for that the suddeness of the sailing gave him barely time to exchange money for dutch currency, and prepare some warm covering – particularly a *peruke* – for the cold voyage –

I am not very gay, my dear Charles – nor shall I feel a peaceful moment until I have news from *abroad*.

But I am amazed – and rather frightened – you have not given me the word *Safe* for my parcel[5] – I should be vexed indescribably if it is not arrived, as I have laboured very seriously in its preparation, and inserted all the amendments, verbal, of Mr Twining, and all the Reviews, besides whatever I could devise to Abridge and ameliorate the whole. It has taken me a great deal of time, as will, I trust, be visible in its amendment. Hurry alone, I hope, has kept back the Safe I begged.

I have a beautiful drawing of Mr William Lock which, if they thought it worth engraving *well*, I would send you – but not else. It is the parting of Camilla from her Father when she goes to Mrs Berlinton, in the 5th volume. – And he has given to the two figures, Mr Tyrold and Camilla, a strong resemblance to Mr Lock and Amelia, though not a *portrait* of them, or designed likeness.[6]

I know how vexed my beloved Traveller will be he could not get to you – *particularly* vexed, as *particularly* he loves you – warmly – *fondly* – The kind and good M. Bourdois accompanied him to town to help about passport &c – and is with him yet, probably, at Gravesend – to which place he was to go this Morning. *Maria* is quite well – she was here just now, blooming and lively.[7] My Alex is very prosperous – and says, when we conn Latin – 'Mama, I think the *accusative case* is the kindest – for that says amo magistratum, I *love* the Master.' So I, too, am for the accusative case, for I *love* the Master (of Greenwich School)[8] with all my Heart and soul. Witness F. d'Arblay.

---

4. I.e. visits to CB at Chelsea College, Charles Burney, William Locke at Woodlands (the Blackheath home of his recently married daughter Amelia Angerstein) and Esther Burney at Beaumont Street.

5. The package containing FB's extensive manuscript revisions for the second edition of *Camilla*, which Charles was to give to the publishers, Payne, Cadell and Davies, arrived safely.

6. The illustration, for *Camilla*, Bk. IX, ch. 11 ('The Workings of Sorrow'), is missing. It was not engraved for the second edition.

7. Lambert Bourdois de Bréviande had accompanied his friend AA to the port on the Thames, and had recently married Hannah Maria Burney, daughter of FB's sister Esther.

8. Charles Burney.

Love to Carlos – and best Compliments to Mrs Bicknel.[9]
I have never had any letter from Payne or Cadell and Davies.[10]

177. Letter to Charles Burney *16 December 1800*

I know the postage will be *cheap* that shall tell my dearest Carlos my best of all friends – dear and excellent as are my others – is returned! – to my unspeakable joy and gratitude and surprise, I have this Morning a letter dated *Gravesend*! The weight it has taken off my soul almost revives it to – once more – pleasure, as well as thankfulness and satisfaction. I know Rosette and Carluc – and Mrs Bicknel will rejoice – but few on Earth perhaps more cordially – if *as* – as my dearest Charles. –

I will write about the *monish*[1] when I have seen him – I hope he will arrive to keep his son's 6th Birthday, the 18th. He is detained now for his passport, which must be sent him from London[2] – his letter was begun on board the vessel on *Friday*, and finished on Sunday – he was out from Gravesend one day short of 3 weeks in all. What he has been able to do, I have yet no account. Probably merely to forward a properly witnessed and authenticated *procuration*.

178. Letter to Dr Burney *3 October 1801*[1]

West Hamble

God avert mischief from this Peace,[2] my dearest Father! – for in our Hermitage you may imagine, more readily than I can express, the hopes and happiness it excites – M. d'Arblay now feels paid for his long forbearance, his kind patience, and compliance with my earnest wishes not to re-visit his native Land while we were at War with it. He can now go with honour as

9. Charles Burney's son Charles Parr, and his housekeeper, Sabrina Bicknell.
10. FB was waiting for a new letter from the publishers about when the second edition would appear. They had asked her for her revisions in early April 1799; see *JL*, iv. 274.

1. Burney family catchword for 'money'; FB is referring to banking transactions with Charles (*JL*, iv. 463).
2. As an alien, AA needed a special passport to travel inland from the port of disembarkation.

1. Annotated by FB: 'Peace, & projected visit to France'.
2. Preliminaries to the Treaty of Amiens, establishing peace between France and Britain, Spain, and Holland, were signed on 1 October and ratified in London on 10 October.

well as propriety, for every body, even the highest personages, will rather expect he should make the journey, as a thing of course, than hear of it as a proposition for deliberation. He will now have his heart's desire granted, in again seeing his loved and respectable Uncle, – and many Relations, and more friends, and his own native Town, as well as soil: and he will have the delight of presenting to that uncle, and those friends, his little Pet Alex.

With all this gratification to one whose endurance of such a length of suspence, and repetition of disappointment, I have observed with gratitude, and felt with sympathy, must not I, too, find pleasure? – Though, on my side, many are the draw-backs – but I ought not, and must not listen to them. We shall arrange our affairs with all the speed in our power, after the ratification is arrived, for saving the cold and windy weather – but the approach of winter is unlucky, as it will lengthen our stay, to avoid travelling, and voyaging, during its severity – unless, indeed, any internal movement, or the menace of any, should make frost and snow secondary fears, and induce us to scamper off. But the present is a season less liable, in all appearance, to storms, than the seasons that may follow. *Fêtes*, joy, and pleasure, will, probably, for some months, occupy the public in France, and it will not be till those rejoicings are past, that they will set about weighing Causes of new commotion, the rights of their Governors, or the means, or desirability of changing them. I would far rather go immediately, than 6 months hence.

I hope, too, this so long wished view of friends and Country gratified, my life's Partner will feel a tranquility without which, even our little Hermitage, and Great Book Room[3] cannot make him completely happy. –

179. Letter to Dr Burney *11 November 1801*[1]

West Hamble

I did not purpose writing to my dearest Father till my suspense and inquietude were happily removed by a Letter from France – but as I find he is already anxious himself, I will now relate all I yet know of my dearest Traveller's history. On Wednesday the 28th of October he set off for Gravesend. A Vessel, he was told, was ready for sailing; and would set off the following Day. He secured his passage, and took up his abode at an end,

3. The library at Camilla Cottage, the d'Arblays' favourite room.

1. Annotated by FB: 'M. d'Arblay set out for France Tempest Danger – M. le Duc de Duras'.

whence he wrote me a very long Letter,[2] – in full hope his next would be from his own Country. But Thursday came – and no sailing – though the wind was fair, and the weather, then calm; he amused his disappointment as well as he could, by visiting divers *Gardeners*, and taking sundry lessons for nursing and managing Asparagress, – Friday, also, came – and still no sailing! – he was more and more vexed – but had recourse, then, to a *Chymist*, with whom he revived much of his early knowledge; Saturday followed, – no sailing! – and he found the people waited on and on, in hopes of more passengers, though never avowing their purpose. His patience was now nearly exhausted, and he went and made such *vif remonstrances*,[3] that he almost startled the managers. They pretended the ballast was all they stayed for: he offered to aid that himself – and actually went to work, and never rested till the Vessel was absolutely ready: – orders *enfin*,[4] were given for sailing next morning, – though he fears, with all his skill, and all his eloquence, and all his aiding, they were more owing to the arrival of 4 new passengers, than to his exertions. That Night, October the 31st he went on board, – November the first, he set sail, at 5 o'clock in the morning. –

You know how high a wind arose on Sunday the 1st – and how dreadful a storm succeeded, lasting all Night – all Monday, – and all Night again – How thankful – how grateful am I to have heard of his safety since so terrifying a period! – they got on, with infinite difficulty and danger, as far as Margate[5] – they there took anchor, – and my kind voyager got a Letter for me sent on shore, '*moyennant un Shilling*.'[6] To tell you my gratitude in knowing him safe after that Tempest – no! I cannot! –– Your warm affections, my dearest Father, will easily paint to you my thankfulness. –

Next, they go on to Deal – and here anchored again – for the Winds, though they abated on shore, kept violent and dangerous near the Coast. Some of the Passengers went on shore – and put two Letters for me in the Post – assuring me all was safe. These two Passengers who merely meant to dine on shore, and see the town, – were left behind! – the Sea rose so high, no Boat could put off to bring them back, and though the Captain hoisted a flag, to announce he was sailing, there was no redress. They had not proceeded a league, before the sea grew yet more rough and perillous – and

---

2. See AA's letter to FB, 30 October 1801, *JL*, v. 21–4.

3. *Animated objections.*

4. *At last.*

5. Port on the north-east coast of Kent. Deal is about twenty miles south of Margate, and Dover eight miles south of Deal.

6. *At a charge of a shilling.*

the Captain was forced to hoist a flag of distress! – every thing in the Vessel was overset – My poor M. d'Arblay's provision Basket flung down, and its contents demolished, – his Bottle of wine broke by another toss, and violent fall – and he was nearly famished! – The Water now began to get into the Ship – all hands were at work that could work – and he – my poor Voyager, gave his whole noble strength to the pump, till he was so exhausted, so fatigued, so weakened, that with difficulty he could hold a Pen to repeat that still – I might be *tranquille*, for all danger was again over! – A Pilot came out to them from Dover, for 7 Guineas, which the higher of the Passengers subscribed for – (and here Poor M. d'Arblay was reckoned of that Class!) and the Vessel was got into the Port at Dover, and the Pilot – *moyennant un autre shilling*,[7] put me again a Letter, with all these particulars, into the Post. –

This was Thursday the 5th the sea still so boisterous, the Vessel was unable to cross the Water. The magistrates at Dover permitted the poor passengers all to land – and M. d'Arblay wrote to me again, from the Inn, after being regaled with an excellent dinner, of which he had been much in want. Here they met again the Passengers lost at Deal – who, in hopes of this circumstance, had travelled post from thence to Dover. Here, too, M. d'Arblay met the Duke de Duras[8] – an hereditary officer of the Crown – but who told him, since Peace was made, and all hope seemed chaced of a proper return to his Country, he was going, *incognito*, to visit a beloved old Mother, whom he had not seen for 11 years. 'I have no passport,' he said, 'for France – but I mean to avow myself to the Commissary at Calais; and tell him I know I am not *erazed*,[9] nor do I demand to be so – I only solicit an interview with a venerable Parent, – send to Paris, to beg leave for it – you may put me in prison till the answer arrives – but, for Mercy, for humanity's sake, suffer me to wait in France till then! – Guarded as you please! – – ' This is his purposed address – which my Mr d'Arblay says he heard *avec les larmes aux yeux*[10] – I shall long to hear the event. On Friday, Nov. 6th M. D'Arblay wrote me two lines –

'Nov. 6. 1801. Je pars![11] – the wind is excellent –
au revoir – '

This is dated 10 o'clock in the morning. –

---

7. *For another shilling.*
8. Amédée-Bretagne-Malo de Durfort, duc de Duras.
9. I.e. struck from the list of emigrants.
10. *With tears in his eyes.*
11. I am leaving.

I have not had a word since! though he said he would write back by his Captain, who was to return immediately. I pray God to end this anxious suspence! – This is my full account, my dearest Father. I thank you a thousand times for your most kind invite to Chelsea, but my Alex, though recovered from all danger, is still in want of all my attention, regular hours, regimen, and constant exercise in this pure air. Surely, the instant I hear, I will write again – Heaven bless and preserve my dearest Father!
prays his most dutiful and affectionate

F. d'Arblay.

A thousand thanks to my dearest Fanny for her kind Letter and kind words and news of Norbury.[12] Mr and Mrs Charles Lock are just arrived,[13] with their 3 children. They were in the last tremendous storm and barely saved!

180. Letter to Dr Burney *12 November 1801*[1]

With what joy – my dearest Father, do I tell You I have just now received a Letter from M. d'Arblay, dated *Calais*, Nov. 7th[2] – He has had a terrific voyage – in so much as to bless Heaven for the illness of the Child, since it was the cause that he and I were not in similar danger! He was 3 Days without food – the fury of the Storm overturned his Basket of provisions – which, I suppose, were trod under foot, and he says he could get none to eat – and his bottle of wine was broken – He was called up in the middle of the night, with cries that the Ship was driving over the anchor – he was then sick to death – but *instantly cured*, and sprung up, and worked harder than any sailor – till the ship got into Port – 6 days and a half out of 8 were spent in storm! Thank God, he is now safe! As I had written all the enclosed Yesterday,[3] though too late for the post I think you would rather have it than let me burn it for 4d.[4] – Heaven bless you, dearest Sir – I am still agitated – though with joy –

---

12. Frances and Charles Norbury Phillips.
13. From Naples, where Charles Locke had resigned his post as British Consul.

1. Annotated by FB: 'M. d'Arblay's arrival at Paris after a dreadful storm'.
2. See *JL*, v. 36–8.
3. Selection 179.
4. The cost of the postage, paid by the recipient.

181. Letter to Margaret Planta *11 February 1802*[1]

A most unexpected – and, to me, severe event, draws from me now an account I had hoped to have reserved for a far happier communication – but which I must beg you to endeavour to seek some leisure moment for making known, with the utmost humility, to my most gracious Royal Mistress, whose true benevolence always finds room for some little interest in the concerns of Her Majesty's humble, but ever grateful and devoted servant.

Upon the total failure of every effort M. d'Arblay could make to recover any part of his natural inheritance, he was advised by his friends to apply to the French Government for half pay, upon the claims of his former military services. He drew up a memoir, openly stating his attachment and loyalty to his late King, and appealing for this justice, after undeserved proscription. His Right was admitted; but he was informed it could only be made good by his re-entering the army; and a proposal to that effect was sent him by Berthier,[2] the Minister at War.

The disturbance of his mind at an offer which so many existing circumstances forbade his foreseeing, was indiscribable. He had purposed, faithfully retiring to his Hermitage, with his fellow-Hermit, for the remainder of his life; and nothing upon Earth could ever induce him to bear Arms against the Country which had given him asylum, as well as birth to his wife and Child; – and yet, a military spirit of Honour, born and bred in him, made it repugnant to all his feelings to demand even retribution from the Government of his own Country, yet refuse to serve it. – Finally, therefore, he resolved to accept the offer Conditionally; – to accompany the expedition to St Domingo,[3] for the restoration of order in the French Colonies, and then, restored thus to his rank in the army, to claim his *retraite*.[4] This he declared to the Minister at War, annexing a further clause of receiving his instructions immediately from the Government.

---

1. Annotated by FB: 'Letter written for Her Majesty but addressed to Miss Planta. On M.d'A's fixed departure for the West Indies. Orders of Napoleon, for St Domingo'.

2. Louis-Alexandre Berthier, whose dealings with AA's claims for a pension are summarized in *JL*, v. 450–67.

3. The French colony, now Haiti, where Pierre-Dominique Toussaint L'Ouverture, leader of an army of native soldiers, was attempting to create an independent state. A French army of 20,000 troops, led by Napoleon's brother-in-law Victor-Emmanuel Leclerc, had been sent in December 1801 to quell the rebellion and restore slavery.

4. *Retirement.*

The Minister's answer to this was That these conditions were impossible.

Relieved rather than resigned – though dejected to find himself thus thrown out of *every* promise of prosperity, M. d'Arblay hastened back to his Cottage,[5] to the inexpressible satisfaction of the Recluse he had left there. – Short, however, has been its duration! – a pacquet has just followed him, containing a Letter from Berthier, to tell him that his appointment was made out according to his own demands! and enclosing another Letter to the Commander in Chief, Le clerc, with the orders of Government for employing him, delivered in terms the most distinguished of his professional character. ——

All hesitation, therefore, now, necessarily ends; and nothing remains for M. d'Arblay but acquiescence and dispatch, – while his best consolation is in the assurance he has universally received that this expedition has the good wishes and sanction of England. – And, to avert any misconception, or misrepresentation, he has, this Day, delivered to M. Otto a Letter addressed immediately to the first Consul,[6] acknowledging the flattering manner in which he has been called forth, but decidedly and clearly repeating, what he had already declared to the War minister, that though he would faithfully fulfil the engagement into which he was entering, it was his inalterable resolution never to take up arms against the British Government.

I presume to hope this little detail may, at some convenient moment, meet Her Majesty's Eyes – with every expression of my profoundest devotion.

I am etc.

My own plans, during the absence of M. D'Arblay are yet undetermined. – I am, at present, wholly consigned to aiding his preparations – to me, I own, a most melancholy task, – but which I have the consolation to find gives pleasure to our mutual Friends, glad to have him, for a while, upon such conditions, quit his spade and his Cabbages.

5. AA landed at Dover on 24 January 1802.

6. AA's letter of 10 February 1802 to the First Consul Napoleon Bonaparte, delivered to Ludwig Wilhelm Otto, put an end to the San Domingo commission and to AA's military career in Napoleonic France; see *JL*, v. 147 n. 7, and FB's subsequent letter. AA would hear of Napoleon's response, through Berthier and others, within a few days.

182. Letter to Esther Burney *22 March 1802*

West Hamble

I know well how my dearest Esther will feel for the mingled sensations – yet Joy which predominates over them all – when I tell her M. d'Arblay writes me word[1] his *commission has been annulled*, in consequence of his own positive declaration, that though he would re-enter the army to fight against all *other* of his Country's Foes, he would *never bear arms against England.* They will listen, they say, to no *conditions* in the service, and therefore he must take his chance against *all* nations, or *renonçer à Jamais au service de France.*[2]

The generous sacrifice thus made to me, of interest, profit, honours, (not *Honour*, dieu Merci![3]) I feel more strongly than any language can express – and shall think my whole life well spent in manifesting my gratitude; for, God knows, had he acted otherwise, I think I must have *buried myself alive*, had a new war broken out, and *he* commanded an expedition against This Country! –

Yet many are *my* drawbacks in *his* to comfort, and far enough has this transaction removed him from the tranquility he enjoyed before his first journey to Paris: the fatigue, – hopes – fears – struggles he has suffered – the disappointment of his renovated views to Fame and Fortune – and the enormous, now wholly useless expences he has incurred,[4] which, so far from ultimately *adding*, as he had believed, to our income, now diminish it considerably, have chagrined him so as nearly to put him in a state of despondence. He is now, however, somewhat rising from it, and if once I see him recovered in spirits, God knows how little I shall ever think of our losses, and how *nothingly* they are – even at this moment, compared with the ease and peace which now result from them: for indeed, my dearest Esther, the expedition was every way frightful to me – not only for the *contention*, with a ferocious set of irritated, and probably ill used Africans, but the risks of the stormy Voyage, and the far greater risks of the pestilential climate – for such, to *bilious* constitutions, it generally proves[5] – Yet – I dare not feel

1. In a letter of 2 March 1802; see *JL*, v. 160–63.
2. *Renounce forever his services to France.*
3. Thank God!
4. In a letter to Lafayette of 3 March 1802, AA complained of having spent a large sum (220 louis) in expenses in the quest to receive his pension; see *JL*, v. 172–3.
5. By 14 October 1802, 24,000 of 34,000 French troops sent to San Domingo had died; see *JL*, v. 112 n. 6.

even now secure – as he waits upon the spot, to see if they will change, and determines there to abide for a year! – he desires Alex and Me to go over to him – in company with Maria and Bood,[6] if they go speedily; if not, to find some other means, that we may hasten to him, as he will form no plan, no scheme, and enter into no agreements, etc., till we meet, and can consult together how we shall best spend the year – at Paris, Joigny,[7] or *where*, and *how*. I need not tell you how this consideration will hasten my motions. Yet I own I am very cowardly in the scheme, – and love not quitting my dear Father – *you* – and my other dear Friends and Family for so long a time – but say not this to Maria! – and, indeed, draw back as this is to my happiness, I yet would, and eagerly, follow him to the furthest corner of the Earth, if so only I could live with him. But after such hopes of living with *him*, and yet in the bosom of my other friends, and native land – this change will needs be grievous!

I had a note from Mrs Bishopp[8] just now about the Cottage, which her friend declines. She thinks it, I doubt not, too dear; but the price was fixed by an Appraiser,[9] who told me he would take upon himself the responsibility of its fairness. I shall now put the affair into his hands as much as possible. I have been doing, and am still doing, much to finish the furniture, and am setting about putting the garden, also, into order. Mr Lock advises this; and though it will cost a good deal of money at the instant, he is persuaded it will well pay it. How happy I am in the counsel of such a friend! whom I revere as much as I love! I cannot more. M. Bourdois was but just returned to Paris from Joigny *March 11th*, when Maria last heard from him. God send the business may be finished at St Domingo before the signing the Definitive Treaty![10] – I dread else, lest, when all war and talk of it with this Country is over, M. d'Arblay may be still called upon to serve in the French Colonies! – *Five Artillery Superior Officers* are at this Moment demanded from the first Consul by the Commander in Chief at St Domingo![11] – – – I may too easily be alarmed – but who, after What has twice happened to me within 2 Months, upon a subject so close to my *vitals*,

---

6. Bourdois de Bréviande ('Bood') and his wife set out for Paris on 10 April.

7. AA's birthplace, and the home of his uncle Bazille.

8. Elizabeth Rebecca Bisshopp, whose friend has not been identified.

9. George Morris of Dorking; see *JL*, v. 181 n. 4.

10. The Peace of Amiens, signed on 25 March 1802.

11. The translation of a letter from General Leclerc to Napoleon, complaining that French officers commissioned for service in San Domingo had not arrived, was printed in *The Times* for 20 March; see *JL*, v. 186 n. 2.

can wonder I shall be ill at rest till St Domingo is subdued? – My dear Friends at Norbury Park desire their kind Love to you – I am but little there just now, yet see or hear from them Daily.

1802–1812

Ten Years in France

183. Letter to Alexandre d'Arblay *15 April 1802*

J'arrivè, *mon ami*! mon Cher – Cher ami! frightened – harrassed – embarrassed – but eager, happy, and with a whole soul beating with trueest
tenderness, *J'arrive* pour ne jamais vous quitter, j'èspere, encore pour la vie![1]
Amen!

Dover, Thursday Night, April 14.

This, as you enjoin, is ready to put to the post at Calais when we Land –

If I could be fetched by a safe Messenger to you from the Inn – near the
palais Royale[2] – I should *rather* be received by you – after this eventful
separation – in our apartment alone – but you must do as you think best –
whatever may be my preference of an uninterrupted meeting, *all* must be
solacing and delightful – Adrienne[3] and Alex are quite well –

Est-ce – bien vrai?! –

Voyez[4] what your Letter and injunction and eagerness has made me
enterprise! – I cross the sea to-morrow – an element I so dread – with 2
Children, and not a soul that knows me, or to whom I am known! –

---

1. I am coming, *my friend*! my dear – dear friend! . . . *I am coming* never to leave you again, I hope,
for the rest of my life! ·
2. The inn where the Calais stagecoach alighted.
3. Adrienne de Chavagnac, aged six, had been left in the care of the Lockes while her parents
were in France; FB was now restoring her to her family in Paris.
4. Is it – really true?! See.

184. Letter to Margaret Planta *21 April 1802*[1]

Paris

My dear friend,

As I have just received a message that a Gentleman, M. Huber,[2] is going back to England to-morrow, by whom I may write to my Father, I seize the opportunity of enclosing you a few lines, which I shall beg him to direct and forward.

We arrived yesterday about Noon – M. D'Arblay was eagerly awaiting us. He has taken me a little apartment in Rue Miromenil which, though up two pair of stairs, is really very pretty, and just new papered and furnished. The view from the windows is very pleasant, open to the Country, and airy and healthy. I have a good sized (*for me*) little neat Drawing room, a small ante-room which we make our Dining Parlour, a tidy Bed Chamber, and a closet within it for Alexander. This, with a kitchen and a bit of a bed-room for my Maid, all on the same floor, compose my habitation. M. D'Arblay had taken the utmost pains to prepare every thing clean and neat that could make me comfortable, knowing that to be what I least expected, yet most desired. He had made a female friend hire me a femme de chambre,[3] who is to make me *fit to be seen*, by various manoeuvres, which I don't rightly understand, but which are to metamorphose me from a rustic Hermit into a figure that may appear in this celebrated capital without causing convulsions or fainting fits to its inhabitants. How this is to be brought about; I don't yet know, but if by such means as I have seen represented, or heard described, I foresee my young Abigail[4] will find me too refractory for a convert. Mean while, the very idea of such an attempt amuses me doubly from recollecting how much Miss Rose[5] diverted herself with the thought of seeing me return in the light Parisienne Drapery so much talked of, and in vogue. However, I am at present so extremely fatigued, I can make no experiments. I had fully meant to wait upon Mlle de Mortemar[6] to Day,

1. Annotated by FB: 'This letter was never sent à son addresse as Mr. Huber, who was to carry it, missed it – I forget *how*'.
2. Barthélemy Huber, Swiss banker living in England and friend of Hannah More.
3. Lady's maid.
4. Standard name for a maid.
5. Princess Augusta. With Margaret Planta FB used botanical code names for the King and Queen and their daughters; see *JL*, v. 360–61.
6. Catherine-Victurnienne de Mortemart, émigrée, had returned from England on the same ship as AA.

but I woke with so violent a head ache – and, indeed, an *every* ache, for I feel bruised all over, – that I am utterly unable to go abroad, and only rose at five o'clock. My voyage was cruelly long, from a dead calm, which kept the vessel motionless for 8 Hours, just after we had sailed from the Port of Dover. We were a whole Day, and a whole Night at sea, and I was sick nearly without intermission all the time, and quite terrified for my poor Alexander who was so ill, and so pale and exhausted, I thought he would have been demolished. Adrienne, my other little charge, was, on the contrary, perfectly well, and gay as a Lark. M. D'arblay sent instantly to inform her Father and Grandmother of her arrival. They came hither directly. The poor little child, who had never seen her Father since she could remember, nor Mme de Montecler at all, nor her little Brother, who accompanied them, nor a young lady, just married, of about 12 years old! – who is a Relation,[7] and was of their party, was quite confounded by their first appearance, but soon reconciled to accompany them, by their fond caresses and endearments. They have all been here again this morning, to see me; but I was inevitably invisible, except to little Adrienne, who came to my Bedside, and brought me a Letter she had written for her *mama Lock*, whose Name she cannot hear without bursting into tears, from tender gratitude and regret. I doubt not, however, she will soon be happy, as her Relations are good and respectable, and delight to have her restored to her family.

I cannot express to you with what emotion I heard, while Dining, at Calais, a band of music, that came to the windows of the Hotel, strike up God save the King. The surprise and pleasure were of the best kind I ever experienced. As we were forced to remain some time in that Town, we walked about it, to refresh ourselves after the long confinement, and the dress of the females amused the Children inexpressibly; all the women, without exception, wore large Gold Earings, though under immensely wide winged French night Caps, which seemed intended to cover the cheeks, but were always flying wide open, to display this ornament. The Girls who were scrubbing the floors at the Inn, women with large baskets on their heads, young creatures draggled, dirty, and sweeping the streets, old ones, wrinkled, bent-double, and carrying Babies at their backs, – all still had these huge shewy dropping Earings, and many of them Gold necklaces round their throats. I observed, also, with some surprise, that most of them were fair,

---

7. Adrienne de Chavagnac's mother had died in 1798; her father was Louis-Vigile, comte de Chavagnac. She had never met her maternal grandmother, her brother Henri or her relation Eugénie-Henriette de Montecler, who was twenty; see *JL*, v. 244 n. 6.

and that the youthful were commonly very handsome: in mentioning this to an English Gentleman here, he *modestly* accounted for it, by saying Calais was so long in the possession of the English, that our race must still subsist in it. –

Pardon this Paper and vile writing; I am forced to scribble on as fast as possible, not to lose so good an opportunity. I hope you received a few words I sent from Dover. I had no time to tell you a quarter of that Fable, but could not forbear what I mentioned, as my only means ever to obtain any satisfactory information of a Tree I hold in such natural reverence as the Oak, or a Plant of which I have always found the perfume so delicious as the Magnolia,[8] as well as of the bloom of the other sweet Flowers I enumerated.

I found the people quite enchanted throughout the whole Country from Calais to Paris, by the restoration of The Dimanche.[9] One poor old woman, where we changed Horses, at Claremont, said that le bon Dieu[10] had been lost for Ten years – but Bonaparte had now found him: and another further on, told us, They could bear all their sufferings and hardships now, for they might now hear mass, and their souls would be saved.

Adieu, my dear friend – You will endeavour to speak for me where you know I most fervently covet not to be forgotten[11] – and believe me ever

Your affectionate friend and servant

F. D'arblay.

185. From Journal Letter to Frederica Locke *mid or late May 1802*[1]

As I think there is no one my beloved friends will feel more interest to hear about, after M. De Narbonne[2] than the Lady they know so particularly in England, I shall now give them the whole narration of all that I should recount to them were we to meet.

---

8. I.e. George III and Queen Charlotte.

9. As part of Napoleon's Concordat of 8 April 1802, restoring Catholicism in France, Sunday was to be kept as a day of religious rest.

10. The good Lord.

11. I.e. the Royal Family, and especially the Queen.

1. Copy in an unknown hand. The letter was probably written in Paris or Monceaux, about a month after the events it describes.

2. Formerly the lover of Mme de Staël (whose marriage had ended in 1800), Narbonne was now living in Paris with the vicomtesse de Laval.

M. D'Arblay was informed, by a friend,[3] that, as soon as she heard of my arrival, she expected I should wait upon her: but finding I did not, she applied again to that friend, and, hearing, probably, of the visits I had received from divers ladies, said 'Croyez vous que Mme D'Arblay me reçévra avec amitié?'[4] Adding, 'if you think she will, I will go to her, notwithstanding it is not the Custom of *les dames francoises*[5] to make the first visit.' – Our Friend (a lady) hesitated, rather *discouragingly*: – She perceived it, and, firing with proud – yet most natural resentment, said 'Eh bien, donc! soit! – qu'est ce que c'est pour *Moi que Mme D'Arblay*!'[6] Here it dropt, and I was well content a first indignation should suffice for my acquittal of expectation – my whole mind being strongly bent, as you will know, against renewing an acquaintance which had already cost me so much pain and difficulty.

In a few days, however, her anger subsided; for among the fine qualities which try to balance their opponents must always be reckoned a complete freedom from malice or vengeance. She spoke again to that Friend, and said that, as she found other Ladies had *begun first*, she would not hold out, but either call or send her carte. Our Friend counselled the latter; her advice was taken, and, during my little Boy's first illness, came a Carte Mme de Staël-Holstein, née Necker – I was too much disturbed at that time to think upon the subject, but when he grew better, I wanted a Carte in return, – but feared it might too grossly repulse an acquaintance, unhappily, already made, in my own country: while we loitered in hesitation, however, from fear of going too far – imagine my surprise, to receive the billet I shall here copy: 'À Mme D'Arblay. Je voudrois vous témoigner mon empressement, Madame, et je crains d'etre indiscrette; j'espore que vous aurez la bonté de me faire dire quand vous serez assez remise de fatigues de votre voyage pour que je puisse avoir l'honneur de vous voir sans vous importuner.[7] Necker Staël de Holstein.'

This excess of concession, – after avoidance so marked, and coldness so undisguised, was inexpressibly painful to me. This I am sure you will concieve, from the same recollections which made it so. I will copy you the

---

3. Vicomtesse de Laval.

4. 'Do you think that Mme d'Arblay will give me a friendly reception?'

5. *French ladies.*

6. 'So be it! and what is *this Mme d'Arblay to me*?'

7. 'To Mme d'Arblay. I should like to show you my alacrity, Madame, but I fear to be indiscreet; I hope that you will be good enough to let me know when you have recovered sufficiently from the fatigue of your journey, that I might have the honour of seeing you without troubling you.'

answer which M. D'arblay drew up for me: 'Mme d'arblay ne peut qu'être infiniment flattré de l'extreme bonté de Mme la comtesse de Staël. Elle aura certainement l'honneur de se presenter chez Mme de Staël – aussitôt que possible. –'[8] You will feel the courage it required thus to decline all appointment, as well as the more than coldness of the *ne peut qu'être* but you will feel, also, my increased dread of the interview, from such unequivocal demonstration how much it was desired. We all concluded that so supercilious an answer to so humble a note, would awaken all the fierté[9] of the high spirit to which it was addressed, and terminate the affair; and our friend thought the *ne peut qu'être* quite too repulsive, and almost impertinent: however it did not prove so! – for you will be surprised to hear, that, in a few days afterwards, she came in person. Fortunately, on account of a hint she had enabled our friend to give us of her intention, we had been upon our guard, and the Portiere had previous orders to say my child was still unwell, and I was not visible: a message was sent up to desire to see M. D'arblay but he was *in dishabille*,[10] and – not chusing to indulge every body with that view as he does his friends of Norbury Park, – he only returned an excuse – Upon the consultation which ensued after this grand stroke, it was decreed that to return the visit was indispensable: though it was also resolved that she should only be on the list for the day on which I was to make my first general round for payment of all such debts. Before this day, however, arrived, Our friend received a note from this – I doubt not *unhappy* persecutrix – with all her talents, all her consciousness of them, all her good qualities, and all her bad ones, *unhappy*! persecutrix, announcing that she was quitting Paris. We thought, nevertheless, it would be right to leave our names, – or rather, wrong *not* to leave them: and on a morning which I had filled from 11 to 5 by incessant calls, I finished my Career at the door of her grand Hotêl:[11] – Paint to yourselves, my dearest friends, what were my feelings, and how great was my consternation, when, as we were preparing, without enquiry, to give our *Cartes* to the *Portiere*, we heard the Lady was still in Paris, and *at Home*! How sick I turned! the reproaches I expected – my inability to speak one word that might clear them – the intimacy formed with a dear departed Angel[12] in ignorance of all that has

---

8. 'Mme d'Arblay cannot but be infinitely flattered by the extreme kindness of Mme la comtesse de Staël. She will certainly have the honour to visit Mme de Staël – as soon as possible. –'
9. Pride.
10. *In undress*, i.e. everyday garments.
11. Town-house.
12. Susanna Phillips.

since been so repulsive – all crowded upon me, and like a culprit for terror
lest the whole should end in unavoidable reconciliation, I had just given my
hand to M. D'arblay who was nearly as much disturbed as myself, to
descend from our voiture[13] when a person came out to say that Madame,
though still in Paris, was just gone out, unknown to the Portiere. We escaped
as fast as possible – I heard afterwards that the next morning she left Paris.
Thus ends, in nothing thank Heaven, a little history that menaced me so
much pain, embarrassment, unjust judgements from others, and cruel
feelings in myself. I thought you would like it all thus concentrated, my
dearest Friends, as I have not been able to let you know, from time to time,
how the matter proceeded. – You will I am sure, more than any one,
concieve, how irksome to myself has been the seemingly, ungrateful, Nay,
insolent part I have appeared to act, towards one whom all the world
admires, and whom we have All – once – been so disposed to love – But I
need not write those comments you can so well make. She left Paris to join
– I know not for what reason, her husband – and immediately upon their
reunion, their meeting I should say, he was so obliging, according to report
– as to reward her conjugal attention by sudden liberty – or rather, by the
open property of that blessing.[14] People here are extremely witty upon this
subject: and I, amongst the rest, find some benefit from it, as it is conjectured
the widowhood will be passed out of France. Will she venture again into a
state of so much thraldom?

186. From Journal Letter to Dr Burney *5–6 May 1802*[1]

At length, the two human hedges were finally formed, the door of the
Audience Chamber[2] was thrown wide open with a commanding crash, a
vivacious officer-Centinel! – or I know not what, nimbly descended the
three steps into our Apartment, and, placing himself at the side of the door,
with one hand spread as high as possible above his head, and the other
extended horizontally, called out, in a loud and authoritative voice, 'Le
Premier Consul!' You will easily believe nothing more was necessary to

13. Carriage.
14. Baron de Staël-Holstein died on 8 May, three days after Mme de Staël's departure from
Paris.

1. Annotated by FB: 'Grand Review at the Thuilleries' and 'Grand Review continued'.
2. The d'Arblays had been given tickets to watch Napoleon review the troops on the parade-
ground of the Tuileries Palace; FB was stationed at a window of the Audience Chamber.

obtain attention; not a soul either spoke or stirred as he and his suite passed along; which was so quickly, that had I not been placed so near the door, and had not all about me facilitated my standing foremost and least crowd-obstructed, I could hardly have seen him: as it was, I had a view so near, though so brief, of his face, as to be very much struck by it: it is of a deeply impressive cast, pale even to sallowness, while not only in the Eye, but in every feature, Care, Thought, Melancholy, and Meditation are strongly marked, with so much of character, nay, Genius, and so penetrating a seriousness – or rather sadness, as powerfully to sink into an observer's mind: – yet, though the Busts and Medallions I have seen are, in general, such good resemblances, that I think I should have known him untold, he has by no means the look to be expected from Bonaparte, – but rather that of a profoundly studious and contemplative Man, who, 'o'er Books consumes' – not only the 'midnight oil,' but his own daily strength, and 'wastes the puny body to decay'[3] by abstruse speculations, and theoretic plans, or, rather, visions, ingenious, but not practicable. But the look of the Commander who heads his own army, who fights his own Battles, who conquers every difficulty by personal exertion, who executes all he plans, who performs even all he suggests – whose ambition is of the most enterprizing, and whose bravery of the most daring cast – This, which is the look to be expected from his situation, and the exploits which have led to it, the spectator watches for in vain. The plainness, also, of his dress, so conspicuously contrasted by the finery of all around him, conspires forcibly with his countenance, so 'Sicklied o'er with the pale hue of Thought,'[4] to give him far more the air of a Student than of a Warrior.

The intense attention with which I fixed him, in this short, but complete view, made me entirely forget the lady[5] who had promised me to hold him in conference; when he was passed, however, she told me it was upon his return she should address him, as he was too much hurried to be talked with at the moment of going to the Parade. I was glad to find my chance not over, and infinitely curious to know what was to follow. – The Review I shall attempt no description of; I have no knowledge of the subject, and no fondness for its object: it was far more superb than any thing I had ever

3. John Gay, Introduction to *Fables* (1727), l. 16: 'O'er books consum'd the midnight oil'; John Dryden, *Absalom and Achitophel* (1681), l. 157: 'Fretted the pigmy body to decay'.

4. Shakespeare, *Hamlet*, III. i. 85: 'Is sicklied o'er with the pale cast of thought'.

5. The wife of a 'Tall Grenadier' previously described by FB, who calls her husband 'Ma Mie' (my dear).

beheld – but while – with all the 'Pomp and circumstance of War – '[6] it animated all others – it only saddened me! – and all of past reflection – and all of future dread – made the whole of the grandeur of the martial scene, and all the delusive seduction of the martial music, fill my Eyes frequently with Tears – but not regale my poor Muscles with one single Smile! Buonaparte, mounting a beautiful and spirited white Horse, closely encircled by his glittering Aid-de-Camps, and accompanied by his Generals, rode round the ranks, holding his bridle indifferently in either hand, and seeming utterly careless of the prancing, rearing, or other freaks of his horse; in so much as to strike some with a notion he is a bad Horse-man; I am the last to be a *Judge* upon this subject, but as a *Remarker*, he appeared to me a Man who knew so well he could manage his Animal when he pleased, that he did not deem it worth his while to keep constantly in order what he knew – if urged or provoked, – he could subdue in a moment. Precisely opposite to the Window at which I was so civilly placed, the Chief Consul stationed himself, after making his round, and there he presented some swords of Honour – spreading out one Arm, with an air and mein which, during that action, changed, to my view, his look from that of Scholastic severity, to one that was highly military and commanding.

Just as the Consular band – with their brazen Drums, as well as Trumpets, marched facing the First Consul, the Sun broke suddenly out from the clouds which had obscured it all the morning – and the effect was so abrupt, and so dazzling, that I could not help observing it to my friend, the Wife of *Ma Mie*, – who, eyeing me with great surprise, not unmixt with the compassion of contempt, said 'Est-ce que vous ne savez pas cela, Madame? Dès que le premier Consul vient à la Parade, le soleil vient aussi! – il a beau pleuvoir tout le matin; – c'est egal; le premier Consul n'a qu'à paroître, et tout de suite il fait beau'[7]!!! – I apologised humbly for my ignorance, but doubt whether it was forgiven.

187. Letter to Georgiana Waddington *27 July 1802*

I know not by what strange fatality it happens, loving you my ever dear Marianne, as tenderly and as faithfully as I love you, that I seem destined

---

6. Shakespeare, *Othello*, III. iii. 360: 'Pride, pomp, and circumstance of glorious war!'
7. 'Don't you know, Madam? As soon as the First Consul comes to the Parade, the sun comes too! – it might have been raining all morning; – it makes no difference; the First Consul has only to appear, and at once the weather is fine.'

never to begin a Letter to you but as a Culprit – Do not, however, imagine because the blame is all mine, the fault is so also; your reproaches upon my scraps of paper, and little Letters, have made me, these last 3 or 4 Years, put by writing to you, till I could build, in some sort, upon a clear Hour or two for that purpose: – and how seldom have I so much time without expected interruption! – you can hardly imagine the little leisure a *ménage*[1] narrow as mine allows, with a Child whom I have no right to detain from school but by being myself his constant instructress. General causes, however, though constant in their effects, I must now put aside, to give you a narration of my peculiar situation, and never ending difficulties, since last October, when – I am pained to recollect, I last wrote to you. Inconceivable is it to myself to reflect, notwithstanding all my obstacles, that it can have been so long. – Forgive it, my dear Marianne – *if possible*! I am almost hopeless of doing better, for my epistolary spirit is flown! – try, therefore, to forgive it; and to bear with me *as I am*, confident my love and friendship for you can never a moment waver; – do not, then, be hard-hearted enough to resent I am not *what I was*, or what you *would have me* — Letter writing is become a severe task to me; and I cannot but regret the time past, when, without the hint of a reprimand, you so kindly gave me 3 or 4 Letters for one, as a thing of course. You, certainly, are now older, and have more cares. – But I, Marianne, am I younger? or have I fewer? –

Weigh a little all this, in your moments of sweetness and kindness, not of *exigeance* and resentment, and then read, and answer, my little history.

In October, as you know, the preliminaries of peace with France were signed and published. M. D'arblay, who had resisted till that epoch every wish for returning to his own country – always dearer than all things to his heart, except his Child and its Mother, – now decided upon immediately visiting it. He meant to take with him his small family, and I began my preparations, – but when I had spent a fortnight in diligent exertions to get ready, my poor little Boy was seized with a fever, which, though not of long continuance, nor, perhaps, really dangerous, left him so much Thinner and weaker, that we were both too much alarmed to suffer him to take a voyage so near as it then was to November, especially as M. D'arblay had no intention to stay above a Month or two on the Continent. It was impossible for me, you will easily conceive, to offer to leave him in so delicate a state – in *any*, I might, perhaps say, but that I have since found, upon another trial, the contrary, – M. D'arblay therefore now settled to make an excursion of

1. *Household.*

only 3 Weeks in all, merely to see his Country, his Relations – and still surviving Friends, and then to return for the rest of the winter to our Hermitage, and make a longer visit in France early in the summer, with us all. He went – and you will say why not then, when alone and disengaged, write me an account of such an event? — Never was I less capable, – never! the anxiety of my mind during his absence unfitted me for every occupation, but close attendance on my Boy. First, I feared the Voyage – he did not set out till the end of October, – the winds were then in their most direful conflicts – and though we had obtained, in fact, a passport for us all from Lord Pelham,[2] by Dover – it arrived the day after M. D'arblay had set sail, while despairing of procuring it, from Gravesend. – The weather was never more boisterous – and instead of seeing him return, as he meant, and I hoped, in 3 weeks – 3 weeks had separated us nearly when he got to Calais. As every leaf that shook was to me, in that period, a storm, you may suppose my solace upon my first Letter from France – Well, *then*, you cry, why not write? – – O, that was a *solace*, it is true, but not ease! not peace! – how he might be received in Paris – after an exile so long – you have, I am sure, an imagination to fully paint the various evils my doubts pictured to myself, if you will give it leave to dwell a while upon the subjects of uneasiness open at such a crisis. A fortnight elapsed ere I had any intelligence at all; the post not being settled, I could only hear by chance conveyances; and nothing very explicit could be written, so that I was kept in a most restless suspence as to his situation, till – at the very moment I was expecting his return, after various unaccounted for delays, he desired Mr Lock to come to me, and prepare me for receiving the tydings of his re-entering his profession, and – instead of returning to his Hermitage, – setting sail for the West Indies according to his rank in the army! – I leave you to judge my feelings – I could not trust myself to them in my now abandoned solitude, and I flew, therefore, with my Boy, to seek refuge from lonely terror and sorrow in the bosoms of my faithful and sympathising friends, with whom I kept alive my shaken existence for about 3 weeks, and whose tender consolations are engraven upon my heart, and were doubly enabled to sustain me, from my conviction of their full knowledge and appreciation of the value of that safety which I thought endangered: – January of this Year was just closing, in these dark scenes, when one morning, at 8 o'clock, Mrs Lock, in her Bed Gown and night Cap, came suddenly to my Apartment, breathless with a Joy that brightened every feature of her fine face, and told me Mr Lock had

2. Lord Pelham, Home Secretary from 1801 to 1803.

that moment opened a Letter from M. D'arblay, to acquaint him a new turn in his affairs had changed his measures, and he was relinquishing St Domingo for England! – My beloved Mr Lock, in his powdering Gown, and half shaved, followed, to congratulate me – and my sweet Amelia hurried to me to pour forth her soft participation in my revival – Augusta – Mrs Charles – Mr William – his wife[3] – all the house followed, in affectionate succession; and, to crown this morning's recompense of so many Weeks of suffering, a packet of no less than 7 Letters were delivered to me, which various accidents had withheld till they arrived all together, confirming to me, from M. D'arblay, the intelligence so much covetted. – – Yet thus relieved, and in this joy, you will cry, you did not write? – No, I could not, – I was in joy, in thankfulness, – but I had not a moment to spare, – I scarcely breakfasted at Norbury Park, before I abruptly left it, to prepare my deserted home for its expected Master. In a few days he arrived – and we only spent a few more together, – amongst the shortest of my life – when we left our Cottage to see my Father and Brethren – and, in less than a week, while we were at Dr Charles's at Greenwich – a Letter arrived from abroad, acquainting M. d'Arblay the conditions which he had exacted, but which had been refused, were now granted – and that he had only to prepare himself for his embarkation. – I will not attempt to write you one word upon this sudden reverse – all pleading against it was ineffectual – the acceptance was deemed a point of honour, and a dismal 10 Days were devoted to procuring passports, making purchases of Linnen, Bedding, Weapons, etc. etc. – fitted for hot climates, and – in the middle of February, I was again widowed – though not till I had offered to leave even my Boy – to his Uncle Charles's care – and go myself to St Domingo – This crowded Sheet shall now be packed off, and I will *try* to send you another as soon as I hear this is received – I dare not promise – yet I think I may –

I won't ask you to send me your free pardon till I have communicated all I have to urge in my *excuse* – I won't say *justification*, except of my faithful and ever affectionate regard – and friendship – to which witness my hand and seal

F D'Arblay

---

3. Mary Augusta Locke, Cecilia Margaret Locke (wife of Charles), William Locke, Jr and his wife, Elizabeth Catherine.

188. From Journal Letter to Frederica Locke *20 August 1802*[1]

I now go on, preparing, with all the comfort of having had good and dear news from my most beloved Friends.

When first I was presented to *des Dames françoises*, upon their giving me a cheek, I kissed it, and drew back, satisfied to the full with such a mark of affection upon first sight: but as they regularly held forward the other cheek, I was fain to salute it also, not uninformed of the custom, but always taken unawares in its practice; – till at length, I received so many bobs of the face, in return for my kisses, that I began to – grow upon my guard, and only give bob for bob. Even this however I found, in the progress of my initiation into the minutiae of this affectionate ceremony, was more than was perfectly correct, the intention being only that the two mouths of the two meeting persons should advance merely to retreat, and that then each party should present the right cheek, for the sole purpose of drawing it hastily away, that each may present the left, which, with the same rapidity, approaches only to retire. My education upon this point being tolerably complete before my visit to Mme de Beaufremont, I acquitted myself with scrupulous exactness, both in apparent desire, and real avoidance of *embrassades*:[2] but when, as the mother quitted me, the Daughter, Mme de Listenois,[3] took her place, the excess of eagerness with which she seemed almost dancing into my arms, the pleasure dimpling round her lips, and the lively rapture of her eye, made me conclude her youth yet unformed to the vague ceremony I have described, or her character too ardent for its insipidity: unwilling, therefore, to check what seemed genuine, though enthusiastic partiality, my lips were once more prompt to what seemed their bidden office, – but their execution, though immediate, and in a certain degree, cordial, was of none effect – they encountered nothing – the presented cheek having darted, rather than slipt away; yet, as another cheek, with the same apparent vehemence of affection, was jutted into its place, I was again not proof against an air, look, and manner of such determined devotion and again my lips manifested my pleased acknowledgement of her extraordinary kindness, the other cheek, however, as rapid in its motions as its sister, was snatched away ere touched, and twice within the same half moment, I tenderly kissed the air. The

1. Copy in an unknown hand.
2. *Kissing.*
3. Princess de Bauffremont-Listenois and her twenty-year-old daughter, Hortense, who seemed 'about 17' to FB (*JL*, v. 344).

Nymph, meanwhile, whose Airy Form and flying motions were truly Nymph-like, was seated in an instant, utterly unconscious, – I trust! – of my *bourgeoise* disappointment. From this time, however, you may easily, my dear Friends, believe, a similar plebeianism cannot disgrace me.

189. From Letter to Georgiana Waddington *22 March 1803*

– What you say of your sister's abilities is indeed surprising;[1] but what I see you wish me to write about, is Mrs Piozzi. – Alas, my dear Mary, that, to me, is a melancholy subject, for though she was never a character approaching to any of those ideas of perfection my mind had formed – and which so few like Mrs Delany, Mrs Lock, and my lost Angel sister fulfilled – yet, with all her errors and exentricities about her, she had once a fond possession of my sincere and ardent friendship. — For though she was always vain of her talents, and proud of her pedigree, she was ever the first to laugh at her own vanity, and expose and mock her own pride, even while she cherished them. She was warm-hearted, generous, sweet-tempered, and full of active zeal for her friends, and of fervant devotion in religion. She was replete with wit and pleasantry, and her powers of entertainment exceeded those of almost any woman I ever knew. But her manners were flaunting, her voice was loud, and she had no peace, and allowed none to others, but in the display of her talents. With draw backs such as these to her better parts, you will not suppose I could ever have *chosen* her for my friend, – yet, being by her chosen, she conceived for me so enthusiastic a regard, that it nearly amounted to a species of idolatry. She was never contented when I was out of her house, never happy when away from her sight. All she did that was singular, and had better have been left undone, all she said, that was strange, and had better have been left unsaid, she suffered me to point out, and with a frankness the most extraordinary would acknowledge she had been wrong, and make, if it were in her power, reparation, either by some change of measures, or softenings of speech. Her whole conduct to me, during the whole time of our intimacy, was of a nature the most endearing that can be conceived; but her marriage annulled, at once, the connexion. She did not trust me with her design, till she had bound herself to carry it into execution. Even then, it was accident brought it forth, for she could not doubt my

1. In her letter to FB, no longer extant, Georgiana Waddington had apparently written about her sister Louisa Port (and inquired about FB's friendship with Hester Piozzi).

entire dislike of so unaccountable a choice, nor my sincerity in speaking it. It was from the abbé Gerard's synonimes[2] that the discovery was made to me, and from the article Songer, penser, rêver[3] – But though the detection, and its avowal were subjects of true grief of heart to me in those days, when my feelings were so tenderly involved in hers and her affairs, I did not dream of relinquishing our friendship on that account: she was not my ward – far otherwise, – I had no right over her actions, and however ill advised and imprudent – and perhaps improper her decision, it yet was not criminal: I kept up, therefore, the same connexion, and felt as much of the same affection as the change of esteem into pity could sustain – but as various circumstances relative to her Children, which occurred, retarded her plan, and at times made her seem to waver in its ultimate execution, I scrupled not expressing my earnest wishes it might be given up – and O what Scenes followed! – sometimes I prevailed entirely – then she repented her compliance – then she repented her engagement – then her senses seemed to fail her – then she raved – then she was seized with a sort of stupor – then she used to fall suddenly asleep, and talk aloud – frightful period! – I had no peace or rest, if I conciliated for restoring her tranquility, I felt as if accessory to what seemed to me a degradation of all sorts, – for Piozzi was more beneath her in understanding and in Mind than in education and birth – and if I opposed in the hope to prevent so ill-judged an alliance, the sufferings of her health or her senses menaced me with shortening or embittering her existence. Yet, during all this time, her kindness, her sweetness, her fondness never wavered, never abated – imagine therefore, my surprise when, upon her marriage actually taking place, she suddenly wrote me a Letter of reproach for the want of cordiality in my congratulations! –! as if it were possible to rejoice in what I so deeply lamented! or as if a change from sincerity to hypocrisy ought not have been as despicable to her as it would have been detestable in me! I wrote her for my sole reply that I committed to Time and her own Recollections my answer. She then sent me some very kind words, but very short, saying she was immediately setting off for Italy. I wrote an immediate promise to forget the only *un*kind words that had ever dropt from her, and added all I thought most soothing: but I have never heard from her since. Whether, as she was departing, my Letter did not reach her, or whether she deemed our friend-

2. FB, Dr Johnson and Hester Thrale had been reading Gabriel Girard's *La Justesse de la langue françoise* (1718) together when FB discovered Hester Thrale's passion for Piozzi; see *JL*, v. 427–8 n. 6.

3. 'Muse upon, think about, dream about'.

ship a fitting sacrifice to offer up to her new engagements, I know not. Certainly as to *him*, I never was his enemy; *he* was not in fault; and deserved not any blame. She was neither of an Age nor a disposition to be seduced – though how she could so be bewitched, I have never been able to fathom. He was an itinerant musician, admirable in his profession, but without any other recommendation. And she cared not for Music! — I have known nothing of her, except two or three accidental sights, since her marriage; I hear from all quarters how much she is altered – and your account gave me real pain. – How differently would you have described her in the days of her triumph and of Streatham! — I never without extreme reluctance enter upon a subject which calls forth so much regret. Dr Johnson's opinion of her in those days did her but justice. I can only attribute all I am told of her spirits and conduct, to a determination she has taken to hide her consciousness of her fall, by seeming content to let it pass that she never held herself above her present circle. Basta![4] —

190. Letter to Dr Burney *14 May 1803*[1]

My dearest – dearest Father!

The enclosed[2] missed the opportunity for which it was written – and now – the ambassadour is gone! – I am offered a place for this in a conveyance that follows him – and it is well something was ready – for I am incapable of writing now – further than of expressing my ceaseless prayers for a speedy restoration of Peace! – my dearest dearest Father! – how impossible to describe my distress! – Had I any other Partner upon Earth, I could hardly support it at all – but he suffers nearly as much as myself – He has just received the *Retraite*[3] – which proves but £62 10.0 or 1500 francs, *per annum*! – He expected double – ! but 'tis a mark of being under Government protection, and that is so much! – you will easily, however, conceive how

4. Enough! (Italian)

1. Annotated by FB: 'Last Letter of This Year sent by the Last Courier of the Ambassadour Lord Whitworth'. (The first part of the letter, in French, is by AA.)

2. A letter to CB of 23 March 1803. Both it and the present letter were taken to England by the Revd Edward Hodgson, chaplain to the British Embassy, who left France on 19 May, a week after the ambassador, Lord Whitworth. Britain officially declared war on France on 16 May, making it impossible for FB, an Englishwoman, to leave the country.

3. AA's military pension, the only source of income for the family, since FB had no access to her pension.

completely it makes it impossible for him to quit his Country during a War – I need write nothing explanatory, and I cannot – in the disordered state of my nerves from this bitter stroke, do more now than pray Heaven to bless and preserve my beloved – dearest Father – and to restore the Nations to peace – and Me to his arms! – and to assure him whatever *can* solace a period so cruel falls at least to my lot, in the truest and tenderest sympathy of one who merits his kindest paternal blessing and affection in the same degree as it is prayed for – by his truly devoted – dutiful and affectionate Daughter

F. d'A.

191. Letter to Dr Burney 5 May 1805[1]

Passy, Rue basse.

Ah my dearest – dearest Father, what a melancholy length of time has elapsed since I have seen your beloved hand! – Do you ever write, and do I lose your Letters? or does no opportunity ever occur?[2] This by which I now have the satisfaction once more to address you has offered so suddenly, and allows so little time, that I can scarcely breathe while I hold my pen.[3] Yet 'tis with joy I seize it – in addressing you, I seem again to see you – I hope again to hear from you. M. d'Arblay is most unfortunately at Paris, and misses this conveyance: but if I may dare judge my beloved Father by myself, any thing that shews life and speaks of health will be acceptable after a silence so terrible. We live in such complete retirement, that I never hear of any means for writing. There are, nevertheless, some who assert that even the common post is at times open. If my dearest Father would try it? – o what an extacy to me would be its success should a word from him arrive!

We live always at Passy, the retirement suits our inclinations very well, and our purses better. I shall enter more fully into our affairs by another conveyance that is promised me by an American lady who purposes to travel and visit England in about 6 weeks.[4] As I shall not then be so hurried, I will prepare for her, and let you know how we go on. The constitution of

---

1. Annotated by FB: 'Misery of broken off intercourse with England. Alex & his Works'.
2. Unknown to FB, CB would not write to her for fear of endangering AA; see *JL*, vi. 513 n. 2.
3. The comte de Lally-Tolendal would take the letter to Frankfurt, from where it would be sent to England. He was an old friend of the d'Arblays, who had met him frequently at Norbury Park.
4. Catherine de Cadignan, née Hunter.

our Alex is still very unfixed, and occasions us continual alarms, though not of long duration. He is otherwise very much and very nearly all we can wish. He would write if he were permitted. He is never so happy as with a pen in his hand. I mean to send you, in my next, a list of his works. – Or rather fragments, or commencements –

Has my dearest Father yet heard that he is named a member of the Institute?[5] And that his History of Music is here in high estimation by its most savant Members, who have studied that art? The secretary general,[6] a very amiable Man, and perfectly well principled, spoke of this to M. d'Arblay about a week ago. I am too much hurried to enter into further particulars just now. M. Morellet[7] I met not long since at a dinner, and he talked to me much of my dear Father and his works.

192. Letter to Dr Burney *1 May 1810*[1]

Rue d'Anjou,
No 13. Paris.

A happy May Day to my dearest Father! sweet scented be the cowslips which approach his Nostrils, lovely and rosy the Milk maids that greet his Eyes, and animating as they are noisy the Marrow bones and Cleavers that salute his Ears![2] Dear, and even touching are these anniversary recollections where distance and absence give them existence only in the memory! And, at this moment, to hear and see them, I would exchange all the Raphaels in our museum, and the new and beautiful composition of Paesiello in the Chapel.[3] The pleasure of admiration is so relative that no intrinsic merit can awaken it like our proper interests. Yet I need not fear *You* will think me insensible to the noble works here exhibited – Oh no! You, my dearest Father, will unfold all my meaning, and enter into every feeling that makes even excellence vapid which we can only witness through separation from these we love.

---

5. FB was mistaken; CB would be named a member of the Institut de France only in November 1810.
6. Joachim Le Breton.
7. André Morellet, an old friend of CB.

1. Annotated by FB: 'agitated misery at stoppage of all intercourse'.
2. Alluding to the rural English tradition of playing music on primitive instruments on May Day.
3. Paintings by Raphael at the Louvre and a *Te Deum* for Napoleon's coronation by Giovanni Paisiello, Italian composer and formerly director of the 'Musique de la Chapelle'.

Could you but send me a little food for the Hope now in private circulation that the new alliance of the Emperor may perhaps extend to a general alliance of all Europe[4] – ah Heaven! how would that brighten my faculties of enjoyment! I should run about to see all I have hitherto omitted to seek with the ardent curiosity of a traveller newly arrived; and I should hasten to re-view and consider all I have already beheld with an alertness of vivacity that would draw information from every object I have as yet looked at with undiscerning tameness. – Oh, such a gleam of light would new-model – or re-model me, and I should make you present to all my sights, and partake of all the wonders that surround me.

Were not this cruel obscurity so darkening to my views, and so depressing to my spirits, I could tell my dearest Father many things that might amuse him, and detail to him, in particular, my great and rare happiness in a point the most essential, after domestic comforts, to peace of mind and chearfulness, namely my good fortune in my adopted friends in this my adopted country. The society in which I mix – when I can prevail with myself to quit my yet dearer Fire-side – is all that can be wished, whether for Wit, Wisdom, intelligence, gaiety or politeness. The individuals with whom I chiefly mix, from being admired at first for their talents or amiability, are now sincerely loved for their kindness and goodness. Could I write more frequently, or with more security that I write not to the Winds and the Waves, I would characterise the whole set to you, and try to make us yet shake hands in the same party. I have heard of this opportunity[5] so suddenly that I have not a moment for extending my use of it to my dear Sisters, Brothers, and Friends – except through your goodness, which must again fabricate messages to all and everyone, from the materials you well know to be in my heart, and which no one can draw forth and disseminate with equal justness. M. d'Arblay is at his office,[6] and knows nothing of this offer; he is well, but thinner, *much*, and over-worked, terribly, at this moment – Alex is writing on the same Table, but not quite so familiarly, nor so glibly, for he is preparing 20 lines of Euripides for his Master.

Heaven bless my ever most dear Father! prays his

F B d'Arblay.

---

4. Napoleon married the Archduchess of Austria, Marie-Louise, on 2 April 1810.
5. The opportunity to send a letter, possibly through the banker Jacques Lafitte; see *JL*, vi. 583 n. 2.
6. Since May 1803, AA had held a position as editor at the Ministère de l'Intérieur.

193. Journal Letter to Esther Burney *22 March–June 1812*[1]

Separated as I have now so long – long been from my dearest Father – Brothers – Sisters – Nieces, and Native Friends, I would spare, at least, their kind hearts any grief for me but what they must inevitably feel in reflecting upon the sorrow of such an absence to one so tenderly attached to all her first and for-ever so dear and regretted ties – nevertheless, if they should hear that I have been dangerously ill from any hand but my own, they might have doubts of my perfect recovery which my own alone can obviate. And how can I hope they will escape hearing what has reached Seville to the South, and Constantinople to the East? from both I have had messages – yet nothing could urge me to this communication till I heard that M. de Boinville[2] had written it to his Wife, without any precaution, because in ignorance of my plan of silence. Still I must hope it may never travel to my dearest Father – But to You, my beloved Esther, who, living more in the World, will surely hear it ere long, to you I will write the whole history, certain that, from the moment you know any evil has befallen me your kind kind heart will be constantly anxious to learn its extent and its circumstances, as well as its termination.

About August, in the year 1810, I began to be annoyed by a small pain in my breast, which went on augmenting from week to week, yet, being rather heavy than acute, without causing me any uneasiness with respect to consequences: Alas, 'what was the ignorance?'[3] The most sympathising of Partners, however, was more disturbed: not a start, not a wry face, not a movement that indicated pain was unobserved, and he early conceived apprehensions to which I was a stranger. He pressed me to see some Surgeon; I revolted from the idea, and hoped, by care and warmth, to make all succour unnecessary. Thus passed some months, during which Madame de Maisonneuve,[4] my particularly intimate friend, joined with M. d'Arblay to press me to consent to an examination. I thought their fears groundless, and could not make so great a conquest over my repugnance. I relate this

---

1. The first sheet of this account of FB's mastectomy of 30 September 1811 is dated 22 March 1812; the remainder was completed by June. Annotated on the cover sheet by FB: 'Account from Paris of a terrible operation – 1812 – '. An outer cover enclosing the letter, a later copy and other documents, is annotated by FB: 'Breast operation Respect this & beware not to injure it!!! This Letter announces – Operation of M. Le Baron de Larrey. The medical account. The police permission for Straw'.
2. Jean-Baptiste Chastel de Boinville, husband of an old friend Harriet Collins.
3. Not identified.
4. Marie Françoise de Maisonneuve.

false confidence, now, as a warning to my dear Esther – my Sisters and Nieces, should any similar sensations excite similar alarm. M. d'Arblay now revealed his uneasiness to another of our kind friends, Mme de Tracy,[5] who wrote to me a long and eloquent Letter upon the subject, that began to awaken very unpleasant surmizes; and a conference with her ensued, in which her urgency and representations, aided by her long experience of disease, and most miserable existence by art, subdued me, and, most painfully and reluctantly, I ceased to object, and M. d'Arblay summoned a physician – M. Bourdois? Maria will cry; – No, my dear Maria, I would not give your beau frere[6] that trouble; not him, but Dr Jouart, the physician of Miss Potts.[7] Thinking but slightly of my statement, he gave me some directions that produced no fruit – on the contrary, I grew worse, and M. d'Arblay now would take no denial to my consulting M. Dubois,[8] who had already attended and cured me in an abscess of which Maria, my dearest Esther, can give you the history. M. Dubois, the most celebrated surgeon of France, was then appointed accoucheur to the Empress, and already lodged in the Tuilleries, and in constant attendance: but nothing could slacken the ardour of M. d'Arblay to obtain the first advice. Fortunately for his kind wishes, M. Dubois had retained a partial regard for me from the time of his former attendance, and, when applied to through a third person, he took the first moment of liberty, granted by a *promenade* taken by the Empress, to come to me. It was now I began to perceive my real danger, M. Dubois gave me a prescription to be pursued for a month, during which time he could not undertake to see me again, and pronounced nothing – but uttered so many charges to me to be tranquil, and to suffer no uneasiness, that I could not but suspect there was room for terrible inquietude. My alarm was encreased by the non-appearance of M. d'Arblay after his departure. They had remained together some time in the Book room, and M. d'Arblay did not return – till, unable to bear the suspence, I begged him to come back. He, also, sought then to tranquilize me – but in words only; his looks were shocking! his features, his whole face displayed the bitterest woe. I had not, therefore, much difficulty in telling myself what he endeavoured not to tell me – that a small operation would be necessary

---

5. Émilie Destutt de Tracy.

6. Brother-in-law. Edmé-Joachim Bourdois de la Motte was a fashionable physician and the brother-in-law of Hannah Maria Bourdois.

7. Gabriel Jouard and Anna Potts.

8. Antoine Dubois, whom FB had consulted in 1806–7; see *JL*, vi. 599 n. 7. At this time he was attending the Empress Marie-Louise, who gave birth to a son on 20 March 1811.

to avert evil consequences! – Ah, my dearest Esther, for this I felt no courage – my dread and repugnance, from a thousand reasons *besides* the pain, almost shook all my faculties, and, for some time, I was rather confounded and stupified than affrighted. – Direful, however, was the effect of this interview; the pains became quicker and more violent, and the hardness of the spot affected encreased. I took, but vainly, my proscription, and every symtom grew more serious. At this time, M. de Narbonne spoke to M. d'Arblay of a Surgeon of great eminence, M. Larrey,[9] who had cured a polonoise[10] lady of his acquaintance of a similar malady; and, as my horror of an operation was insuperable, M. de Narbonne strongly recommended that I should have recourse to M. Larrey. I thankfully caught at any hope; and another friend of M. d'Arblay gave the same counsel at the same instant, which other, M. Barbier Neuville,[11] has an influence irresistible over this M. Larrey, to whom he wrote the most earnest injunction that he would use every exertion to rescue me from what I so much dreaded. M. Larrey came, though very unwillingly, and full of scruples concerning M. Dubois; nor would he give me his services till I wrote myself to state my affright at the delay of attendance occasioned by the present high office and royal confinement of M. Dubois, and requesting that I might be made over to M. Larrey. An answer such as might be expected arrived, and I was now put upon a new *regime*, and animated by the fairest hopes. – M. Larrey has proved one of the worthiest, most disinterested, and singularly excellent of men, endowed with real Genius in his profession, though with an ignorance of the World and its usages that induces a *naiveté* that leads those who do not see him thoroughly to think him not alone simple, but weak. They are mistaken; but his attention and thoughts having exclusively turned one way, he is hardly awake any other. His directions seemed all to succeed, for though I had still cruel seizures of terrible pain, the fits were shorter and more rare, and my spirits revived, and I went out almost daily, and quite daily received in my Apartment some friend or intimate acquaintance, contrarily to my usual mode of *sauvagerie*[12] – and what friends have I found! what kind, consoling, zealous friends during all this painful period! In fine, I was much better, and every symptom of alarm abated. My good M. Larrey was enchanted, yet so anxious, that he forced me to see le Docteur Ribe,[13]

9. Baron Dominique-Jean Larrey, celebrated army surgeon.
10. Polish.
11. Jean-Pierre Barbier de Neuville.
12. *Unsociability.*
13. François Ribes, anatomist and surgeon, and colleague of Baron Larrey.

the first anatomist, he said, in France, from his own fear lest he was under
any delusion, from the excess of his desire to save me. I was as rebellious to
the first visit of this famous anatomist as Maria will tell you I had been to
that of M. Dubois, so odious to me was this sort of process: however, I was
obliged to submit: and M. Ribe confirmed our best hopes – Here, my
dearest Esther, I must grow brief, for my theme becomes less pleasant –
Sundry circumstances, too long to detail, combined to counter-act all my
flattering expectations, and all the skill, and all the cares of my assiduous
and excellent Surgeon. The principal of these evils were – the death, broke
to me by a newspaper! of the lovely and loved Princess Amelia – the illness
of her venerated Father[14] – and the sudden loss of my nearly adored – my
Susan's nearly worshipped Mr Lock[15] – which terrible calamity reached me
in *a few lines* from Fanny Waddington, when I knew not of any illness or
fear! – Oh my Esther, I must indeed here be brief, for I am not yet strong
enough for sorrow. – The good M. Larrey, when he came to me next after
the last of these trials, was quite thrown into a consternation, so changed he
found all for the worse – 'Et qu'est il donc arrive?'[16] he cried, and presently,
sadly announced his hope of dissolving the hardness were nearly extinguished. M. Ribe was now again called in – but he only corroborated the
terrible judgement: yet they allowed to my pleadings some further essays,
and the more easily as the weather was not propitious to any operation. My
Exercise, at this time, though always useful and chearing, occasioned me
great suffering in its conclusion, from mounting up three pair of stairs: my
tenderest Partner, therefore, removed me to La Rue Mirmenil,[17] where I
began my Paris residence nearly 10 Years ago! – *quite* 10 next Month! Here
we are *au premier*[18] – but alas – to no effect! once only have I yet descended
the short flight of steps from which I had entertained new hopes. A Physician
was now called in, Dr Moreau,[19] to hear if he could suggest any new means:
but Dr Larrey had left him no resources untried. A formal consultation now
was held, of Larrey, Ribe, and Moreau – and, in fine, I was formally
condemned to an operation by all Three. I was as much astonished as
disappointed – for the poor breast was no where discoloured, and not much

14. Princess Amelia died at the age of 27 on 2 November 1810. George III had suffered his most
recent attack of porphyria in October 1810 (and did not recover).
15. William Locke died on 5 October 1810, as FB had heard from Georgiana Waddington's
daughter.
16. 'And so, what is going on?'
17. The d'Arblays had lived on the rue de Miroménil from April to October 1802.
18. *On the first floor.*
19. Jacques-Louis Moreau de la Sarthe.

larger than its healthy neighbour. Yet I felt the evil to be deep, so deep, that I often thought if it could not be dissolved, it could only with life be extirpated. I called up, however, all the reason I possessed, or could assume, and told them that – if they saw no other alternative, I would not resist their opinion and experience: – the good Dr Larrey, who, during his long attendance had conceived for me the warmest friendship, had now tears in his Eyes; from my dread he had expected resistance. He proposed again calling in M. Dubois. No, I told him, if I could not by himself be saved, I had no sort of hope elsewhere, and, if it must be, what I wanted in courage should be supplied by Confidence. The good man was now dissatisfied with himself, and declared I ought to have the First and most eminent advice his Country could afford; 'Vous êtes si considerée,' Madame, said he, 'ici, que le public même sera mecontent si vous n'avez pas tout le secour que nous avons à vous offrir. – '[20] Yet this modest man is premier chirugien de la Garde Imperiale,[21] and had been lately created a Baron for his eminent services! – M. Dubois, he added, from his super-skill and experience, might yet, perhaps, suggest some cure. This conquered me quickly, ah – Send for him! Send for him! I cried – and Dr Moreau received the commission to consult with him. – What an interval was this! Yet my poor M. d'Arblay was more to be pitied than myself, though he knew not the terrible idea I had internally annexed to the trial – but Oh what he suffered! – and with what exquisite tenderness he solaced all I had to bear! My poor Alex I kept as much as possible, and as long, ignorant of my situation. – M. Dubois behaved extremely well, no pique intervened with the interest he had professed in my well-doing, and his conduct was manly and generous. It was difficult still to see him, but he appointed the earliest day in his power for a general and final consultation. I was informed of it only on the Same day, to avoid useless agitation. He met here Drs Larrey, Ribe, and Moreau. The case, I saw, offered uncommon difficulties, or presented eminent danger, but the examination over, they desired to consult together. I left them – what an half hour I passed alone! – M. d'Arblay was at his office. Dr Larrey then came to summon me. He did not speak, but looked very like my dear Brother James, to whom he has a personal resemblance that has struck M. d'Arblay as well as myself. I came back, and took my seat, with what calmness I was able. All were silent, and Dr Larrey, I saw, hid

---

20. 'You are so esteemed here, Madam, that the public itself would be unhappy if you did not receive all the help that we have to offer. –'

21. First surgeon of the Imperial Guard.

himself nearly behind my Sofa. My heart beat fast: I saw all hope was over. I called upon them to speak. M. Dubois then, after a long and unintelligible harangue, from his own disturbance, pronounced my doom. I now saw it was inevitable, and abstained from any further effort. They received my formal consent, and retired to fix a day.

All hope of escaping this evil now at an end, I could only console or employ my Mind in considering how to render it less dreadful to M. d'Arblay. M. Dubois had pronounced 'il faut s'attendre à souffrir, Je ne veux pas vous tromper – Vous Souffrirez – vous souffrirez *beaucoup*! –'[22] M. Ribe had *charged* me to cry! to withhold or restrain myself might have seriously bad consequences, he said. M. Moreau, in ecchoing this injunction, enquired whether I had cried or screamed at the birth of Alexander – Alas, I told him, it had not been possible to do otherwise; Oh then, he answered, there is no fear! – What terrible inferences were here to be drawn! I desired, therefore, that M. d'Arblay might be kept in ignorance of the day till the operation should be over. To this they agreed, except M. Larrey, with high approbation: M. Larrey looked dissentient, but was silent. M. Dubois protested he would not undertake to act, after what he had seen of the agitated spirits of M. d'Arblay if he were present: nor would he suffer me to know the time myself over night; I obtained with difficulty a promise of 4 hours warning, which were essential to me for sundry regulations.

From this time, I assumed the best spirits in my power, *to meet the coming blow*; – and support my too sympathising Partner. They would let me make no preparations, refusing to inform me what would be necessary; I have known, since, that Mme de Tessé,[23] an admirable old friend of M. d'Arblay, now mine, equally, and one of the first of her sex, in any country, for uncommon abilities, and nearly universal knowledge, had insisted upon sending me all that might be necessary, and of keeping me in ignorance. M. d'Arblay filled a Closet with Charpie,[24] compresses, and bandages – All that to *me* was owned, as wanting, was an arm Chair and some Towels. – Many things, however, joined to the depth of my pains, assured me the business was not without danger. I therefore made my Will – unknown, to this moment, to M. d'Arblay, and entrusted it privately to M. La Tour Maubourg,[25] without even letting my friend his Sister, Mme de Maison-

---

22. 'You must expect to suffer, I do not want to deceive you – you will suffer – you will suffer *very much*! –'

23. Adrienne-Catherine, comtesse de Tessé, aged seventy.

24. Linen, used for surgical dressings.

25. César, comte de Latour-Maubourg, an old friend of AA from Passy.

neuve, share the secret. M. de Maubourg conveyed it for me to Maria's excellent M. Gillet,[26] from whom M. de Maubourg brought me directions. As soon as I am able to go out I shall reveal this clandestine affair to M. d'Arblay – till then, it might still affect him. Mme de Maisonneuve desired to be present at the operation; – but I would not inflict such pain. Mme de Chastel belle soeur de Mme de Boinville,[27] would also have sustained the shock; but I secured two Guards, one of whom is known to my two dear Charlottes,[28] Mme Soubiren, portière de l'Hotel Marengo:[29] a very good Creature, who often amuses me by repeating '*ver. vell, Mawm;*' which she tells me she learnt of Charlotte the younger, whom she never names but with rapture, The other is a workwoman whom I have often employed. The kindnesses I received at this period would have made me for-ever love France, had I hitherto been hard enough of heart to hate it – but Mme d'Henin[30] – the tenderness she shewed me surpasses all description. Twice she came to Paris from the Country, to see, watch and sit with me; there is nothing that can be suggested of use or comfort that she omitted. She loves me not only from her kind heart, but also from her love of Mrs Lock, often, often, exclaiming 'Ah! si votre angelique amie étoit ici! – '[31] But I must force myself from these episodes, though my dearest Esther will not think them *de trop*.[32]

After sentence thus passed, I was in hourly expectation of a summons to execution; judge, then, my surprise to be suffered to go on full 3 Weeks in the same state! M. Larrey from time to time visited me, but pronounced nothing, and was always melancholy. At length, M. d'Arblay was told that he waited himself for a Summons! and that, a formal one, and in writing! *I* could not give one. A *consent* was my utmost effort. But poor M. d'Arblay wrote a desire that the operation, if necessary, might take place without further delay. In my own mind, I had all this time been persuaded there were hopes of a cure: why else, I thought, let me know my doom thus long? But here I must account for this apparently useless, and therefore cruel measure, though I only learnt it myself 2 months afterwards. M. Dubois

---

26. Antoine-Louis Gillet, notary who had worked for Hannah Maria Bourdois in 1806.

27. Catherine-Françoise Chastel, sister-in-law of Harriet de Boinville.

28. FB's sister Charlotte Broome and her daughter Charlotte Barrett.

29. The doorkeeper at the Hotel Marengo had much admired FB's niece Charlotte Barrett when she visited FB in 1802; see *JL*, v. 436–7.

30. The former princesse d'Hénin, who had met FB as an exile in England and became a close friend during FB's stay in France. She was also a friend of the comte de Lally-Tolendal.

31. 'Ah! if your angelic friend were here! –'

32. *Excessive, superfluous.*

had given his opinion that the evil was too far advanced for any remedy; that the cancer was already internally declared; that I was inevitably destined to that most frightful of deaths, and that an operation would but accellerate my dissolution. Poor M. Larrey was so deeply affected by this sentence, that – as he has lately told me, he regretted to his Soul ever having known me, and was upon the point of demanding a commission to the furthest end of France in order to force me into other hands. I had said, however, he remembered, once, that I would far rather suffer a quick end without, than a lingering life with this dreadfullest of maladies: he finally, therefore, considered it might be possible to save me by the trial, but that without it my case was desperate, and resolved to make the attempt. Nevertheless, the responsibility was too great to rest upon his own head entirely; and therefore he waited the formal summons. – In fine, One morning – the last of September, 1811, while I was still in Bed, and M. d'Arblay was arranging some papers for his office, I received a Letter written by M. de Lally to a Journalist, in vindication of the honoured memory of his Father against the assertions of Mme du Deffand.[33] I read it aloud to My Alexanders, with tears of admiration and sympathy, and then sent it by Alex. to its excellent Author, as I had promised the preceding evening. I then dressed, aided, as usual for many months, by my maid, my right arm being condemned to total inaction; but not yet was the grand business over, when another Letter was delivered to me – another, indeed! – 'twas from M. Larrey, to acquaint me that at 10 o'clock he should be with me, properly accompanied, and to exhort me to rely as much upon his sensibility and his prudence, as upon his dexterity and his experience; he charged to secure the absence of M. d'Arblay and told me that the young Physician who would deliver me this *announce*, would prepare for the operation, in which he must lend his aid: and also that it had been the decision of the consultation to allow me but two hours notice. – Judge, my Esther, if I read this unmoved! – yet I had to disguise my sensations and intentions from M. d'Arblay! – Dr Aumont,[34] the Messenger and terrible Herald, was in waiting; M. d'Arblay stood by my bed side; I affected to be long reading the Note, to gain time for forming some plan, and such was my terror of involving M. d'Arblay in

33. Marie du Deffand had written to Horace Walpole in 1766, when the comte de Lally-Tolendal's father was executed for treason, supporting the punishment, which de Lally would have read in the 1811 edition of du Deffand's letters to Walpole. De Lally responded by defending his father in the letter that he showed to FB.
34. Philippe-Éléonor-Godefroy Aumond.

the unavailing wretchedness of witnessing what I must go through, that it
conquered every other, and gave me the force to act as if I were directing
some third person. The detail would be too *Wordy*, as James says, but the
wholesale is – I called Alex. to my Bed side, and sent him to inform M. Barbier
Neuville, chef du division du Bureau[35] de M. d'Arblay that *the moment was
come*, and I entreated him to write a summons upon urgent business for
M. d'Arblay and to detain him till all should be over. Speechless and
appalled, off went Alex, and, as I have since heard, was forced to sit down
and sob in executing his commission. I then, by the Maid, sent word to the
young Dr Aumont that I could not be ready till one o'clock: and I finished
my breakfast, and – not with much appetite, you will believe! forced down
a crust of bread, and hurried off, under various pretences, M. d'Arblay. He
was scarcely gone, when M. Du Bois arrived: I renewed my request for one
o'clock: the rest came; all were fain to consent to the delay, for I had an
apartment to prepare for my banished Mate. This arrangement, and those
for myself, occupied me completely. Two engaged nurses were out of the
way – I had a bed, Curtains, and heaven knows what to prepare – but
business was good for my nerves. I was obliged to quit my room to have it
put in order: – Dr Aumont would not leave the house; he remained in the
Sallon, folding linen! – He had demanded 4 or 5 old and fine left off under
Garments – I glided to our Book Cabinet: sundry necessary works and
orders filled up my time entirely till One O'clock, When all was ready – but
Dr Moreau then arrived, with news that M. Dubois could not attend till
three. Dr Aumont went away – and the Coast was clear. This, indeed, was
a dreadful interval. I had no longer any thing to do – I had only to think –
Two Hours thus spent seemed never-ending. I would fain have written to
my dearest Father – to You, my Esther – to Charlotte James – Charles –
Amelia Lock – but my arm prohibited me: I strolled to the Sallon – I saw it
fitted with preparations, and I recoiled – But I soon returned; to what effect
disguise from myself what I must so soon know? – yet the sight of the
immense quantity of bandages, compresses, spunges, Lint – – Made me a
little sick: – I walked backwards and forwards till I quieted all emotion,
and became by degrees, nearly stupid – torpid, without sentiment or
consciousness; – and thus I remained till the Clock struck three. A sudden
spirit of exertion then returned, – I defied my poor arm, no longer worth
sparing, and took my long banished pen to write a few words to M. d'Arblay
– and a few more for Alex, in case of a fatal result. These short billets I

35. Divisional head of the Office.

could only deposit safely, when the Cabriolets[36] – one – two – three – four – succeeded rapidly to each other in stopping at the door. Dr Moreau instantly entered my room, to see if I were alive. He gave me a wine cordial, and went to the Sallon. I rang for my Maid and Nurses, – but before I could speak to them, my room, without previous message, was entered by 7 Men in black, Dr Larry, M. Dubois, Dr Moreau, Dr Aumont, Dr Ribe, and a pupil of Dr Larry, and another of M. Dubois. I was now awakened from my stupor – and by a sort of indignation – Why so many? and without leave? – But I could not utter a syllable. M. Dubois acted as Commander in Chief. Dr Larry kept out of sight; M. Dubois ordered a Bed stead into the middle of the room. Astonished, I turned to Dr Larry, who had promised that an Arm Chair would suffice; but he hung his head, and would not look at me. Two *old mattrasses* M. Dubois then demanded, and an old Sheet. I now began to tremble violently, more with distaste and horrour of the preparations even than of the pain. These arranged to his liking, he desired me to mount the Bed stead. I stood suspended, for a moment, whether I should not abruptly escape – I looked at the door, the windows – I felt desperate – but it was only for a moment, my reason then took the command, and my fears and feelings struggled vainly against it. I called to my maid – she was crying, and the two Nurses stood, transfixed, at the door. 'Let those women all go!' cried M. Dubois. This order recovered me my Voice – 'No,' I cried, 'let them stay! *qu'elles restent!*'[37] This occasioned a little dispute, that re-animated me – The Maid, however, and one of the nurses ran off – I charged the other to approach, and she obeyed. M. Dubois now tried to issue his commands *en militaire*,[38] but I resisted all that were resistable – I was compelled, however, to submit to taking off my long robe de Chambre,[39] which I had meant to retain – Ah, then, how did I think of My Sisters! – not one, at so dreadful an instant, at hand, to protect – adjust – guard me – I regretted that I had refused Mme de Maisonneuve – Mme Chastel – no one upon whom I could rely – my departed Angel![40] – how did I think of her! – how did I long – long for my Esther – my Charlotte! – My distress was, I suppose, apparent, though not my Wishes, for M. Dubois himself now softened, and spoke soothingly. 'Can *You*,' I cried, 'feel for an operation that, to *You*, must seem so trivial?' – 'Trivial?' he repeated – taking up a bit

36. Light, one-horse carriages.
37. *Let them stay.*
38. *In military manner.*
39. Dressing gown.
40. Susanna Phillips.

of paper, which he tore, unconsciously, into a million pieces, *'oui – c'est peu de chose – mais –'*[41] he stammered, and could not go on. No one else attempted to speak, but I was softened myself, when I saw even M. Dubois grow agitated, while Dr Larry kept always aloof, yet a glance shewed me he was pale as ashes. I knew not, positively, then, the immediate danger, but every thing convinced me danger was hovering about me, and that this experiment could alone save me from its jaws. I mounted, therefore, unbidden, the Bed stead – and M. Dubois placed me upon the Mattrass, and spread a cambric handkerchief upon my face. It was transparent, however, and I saw, through it, that the bed stead was instantly surrounded by the 7 men and my nurse. I refused to be held; but when, Bright through the cambric, I saw the glitter of polished Steel – I closed my Eyes. I would not trust to convulsive fear the sight of the terrible incision. A silence the most profound ensued, which lasted for some minutes, during which, I imagine, they took their orders by signs, and made their examination – Oh what a horrible suspension! – I did not breathe – and M. Dubois tried vainly to find any pulse. This pause, at length, was broken by Dr Larry, who in a voice of solemn melancholy, said 'Qui me tiendra ce sein? – '[42]

No one answered; at least not verbally; but this aroused me from my passively submissive state, for I feared they imagined the whole breast infected – feared it too justly, – for, again through the Cambric, I saw the hand of M. Dubois held up, while his fore finger first described a straight line from top to bottom of the breast, secondly a Cross, and thirdly a circle; intimating that the Whole was to be taken off. Excited by this idea, I started up, threw off my veil, and, in answer to the demand 'Qui me tiendra ce sein?' cried 'C'est moi, Monsieur!'[43] and I held My hand under it, and explained the nature of my sufferings, which all sprang from one point, though they darted into every part. I was heard attentively, but in utter silence, and M. Dubois then, re-placed me as before, and, as before, spread my veil over my face. How vain, alas, my representation! immediately again I saw the fatal finger describe the Cross – and the circle – Hopeless, then, desperate, and self-given up, I closed once more my Eyes, relinquishing all watching, all resistance, all interference, and sadly resolute to be wholly resigned.

My dearest Esther, – and all my dears to whom she communicates this

---

41. *'Yes – it's a small thing – but –'.*
42. 'Who will hold this breast for me? –'
43. 'I will, Sir!'

doleful ditty, will rejoice to hear that this resolution once taken, was firmly
adhered to, in defiance of a terror that surpasses all description, and the
most torturing pain. Yet – when the dreadful steel was plunged into the
breast – cutting through veins – arteries – flesh – nerves – I needed
no injunctions not to restrain my cries. I began a scream that lasted
unintermittingly during the whole time of the incision – and I almost marvel
that it rings not in my Ears still! so excruciating was the agony. When the
wound was made, and the instrument was withdrawn, the pain seemed
undiminished, for the air that suddenly rushed into those delicate parts felt
like a mass of minute but sharp and forked poniards, that were tearing the
edges of the wound – but when again I felt the instrument – describing a
curve – cutting against the grain, if I may so say, while the flesh resisted in
a manner so forcible as to oppose and tire the hand of the operator, who
was forced to change from the right to the left – then, indeed, I thought I
must have expired. I attempted no more to open my Eyes, – they felt as if
hermetically shut, and so firmly closed, that the Eyelids seemed indented
into the Cheeks. The instrument this second time withdrawn, I concluded
the operation over, – Oh no! presently the terrible cutting was renewed –
and worse than ever, to separate the bottom, the foundation of this dreadful
gland from the parts to which it adhered – Again all description would be
baffled – yet again all was not over, – Dr Larry rested but his own hand,
and – Oh Heaven! – I then felt the Knife rackling against the breast bone
– scraping it! – This performed, while I yet remained in utterly speechless
torture, I heard the Voice of Mr Larry, – (all others guarded a dead silence)
in a tone nearly tragic, desire every one present to pronounce if anything
more remained to be done; or if he thought the operation complete. The
general voice was Yes, – but the finger of Mr Dubois – which I literally *felt*
elevated over the wound, though I saw nothing, and though he touched
nothing, so indescribably sensitive was the spot – pointed to some further
requisition – and again began the scraping! – and, after this, Dr Moreau
thought he discerned a peccant attom[44] – and still, and still, M. Dubois
demanded attom after attom – My dearest Esther, not for days, not for
Weeks, but for Months I could not speak of this terrible business without
nearly again going through it! I could not *think* of it with impunity! I was
sick, I was disordered by a single question – even now, 9 months after it is
over,[45] I have a head ache from going on with the account! and this miserable

44. I.e. fragments of diseased (peccant) breast tissue.
45. I.e. June 1812.

account, which I began 3 Months ago, at least, I dare not revise, nor read, the recollection is still so painful.

To conclude, the evil was so profound, the case so delicate, and the precautions necessary for preventing a return so numerous, that the operation, including the treatment and the dressing, lasted 20 minutes! a time, for sufferings so acute, that was hardly supportable – However, I bore it with all the courage I could exert, and never moved, nor stopt them, nor resisted, nor remonstrated, nor spoke – except once or twice, during the dressings, to say 'Ah Messieurs! que je vous plains! – '[46] for indeed I was sensible to the feeling concern with which they all saw what I endured, though my speech was principally – *very* principally meant for Dr Larry. Except this, I uttered not a syllable, save, when so often they re-commenced, calling out 'Avertissez moi, Messieurs! avertissez moi! – '[47] Twice, I believe, I fainted; at least, I have two total chasms in my memory of this transaction, that impede my tying together what passed. When all was done, and they lifted me up that I might be put to bed, my strength was so totally annihilated, that I was obliged to be carried, and could not even sustain my hands and arms, which hung as if I had been lifeless; while my face, as the Nurse has told me, was utterly colourless. This removal made me open my Eyes – and I then saw my good Dr Larry, pale nearly as myself, his face streaked with blood, and its expression depicting grief, apprehension, and almost horrour.

When I was in bed, – my poor M. d'Arblay – who ought to write you himself his own history of this Morning – was called to me – and afterwards our Alex. –

[Alexandre d'Arblay begins:]

No! No my dearest and ever more dear friends, I shall not make *a fruitless* attempt. No language could convey what I felt in the deadly course of these seven hours. Nevertheless, every one *of you, my dearest dearest friends*, can guess, must even know it. Alexandre had no less feeling, but showed more fortitude. He, perhaps, will be more able to describe to you, nearly at least, the torturing state of my poor heart and soul. Besides, I must own, to you, that these details which were, till just now, quite unknown to me, have almost killed me, and I am only able to thank God that this more than half Angel has had the sublime courage to deny herself the comfort I might have

46. 'Ah Sirs! how I pity you! –'
47. 'Warn me, Sirs! warn me!'

offered her, to spare me, not the sharing of her excruciating pains, that was impossible, but the witnessing so terrific a scene, and perhaps the remorse to have rendered it more tragic. For I don't flatter my self I could have got through it – I must confess it.

Thank Heaven! She is now surprisingly well, and in good spirits, and we hope to have many many still happy days. May that of peace soon arrive, and enable me to embrace better than with my pen my beloved and ever ever more dear friends of the town and country. Amen. Amen!

[Frances Burney resumes:]
God bless my dearest Esther – I fear this is all written – confusedly, but I cannot read it – and I can write it no more, therefore I entreat you to let all my dear Brethren male and female take a perusal – and that you will lend it also to my tender and most beloved Mrs Angerstein, who will pardon, I well know, my sparing myself – which is sparing her, a separate letter upon such a theme. My dearest Father and my dearest Mrs Locke live so little in the world, that I flatter myself they will never hear of this adventure. I earnestly desire it may never reach them. My kind Miss Cambridge and Miss Baker,[48] also, may easily escape it. I leave all others, and all else, to your own decision.

I ought to have mentioned Sarah when I regretted and sighed for my Sisters, for I am sure she would gladly and affectionately have nursed me had she been at hand: but at that critical moment I only thought of those who had already – and so often – had opportunity as well as Soul to demonstrate their tenderness. – and She who is gone is ever, and on all occasions, still present to me. Adieu, adieu, my beloved Esther –

P.S.[49] I have promised my dearest Esther a Volume – and here it is: I am at this moment quite Well – So are my Alexanders. Read, therefore, this Narrative at your leisure, and without emotion – for all has ended happily. I will send the rest by the very first opportunity: I seize this present with eagerness – oh let none – none pass by that may bring me a return! – I have no more yet written. March 22d – 1812

---

48. Charlotte Cambridge's companion Sarah Baker.
49. This postscript is written at the top of the first page and would thus have been read before the body of the letter.

194. Journal *before July 1812*

The intense desire of Bonaparté to conquer not only universal Dominion, but universal suffrage, and the arts of sagacity for the latter, which abetted his martial skill for the former, is strongly portrayed in the two following Facts.

The celebrated David[1] was appointed to paint him on a large and grand scale, for some national exhibition, where, and of what nature, I have forgotten. The Painter consulted with him upon the choice of a subject. Bonaparté paused but a moment, and then said, 'Faits moi calme, posé, tranquil – sur un Cheval fougeux. – '[2]

The Artist, quickly comprehending, executed the idea admirably. I have seen the picture. I was shewn it by the Painter's Wife.[3] And the imperturbable composure of Bonaparté, who seems absorbed in ruminations so abstruse that they lift him up above all personal care, and give him a contempt of all personal danger, contrasted with the fiery spirit and uncontrollable vigour of the wildly unruly animal, produces an effect so striking between The Horse and the Rider, that France seems depicted as retaining all its martial ardour, while governed by a Chief who owes his power and command to his own fearless self-possession.

The 2d Fact shews the same discriminating penetration for working out his own purposes.

A British Nobleman contrived, during the most violent animosity of the War, to send over an order to David for an original Picture of the Emperor, for which, if he could find means to paint it, the Nobleman, the Marquis of Douglas,[4] would convey to him through a trusty Banker, a thousand pounds. David, who was frequently admitted to the presence, because frequently employed by Bonaparté, put the Letter into his hands. He did not immediately answer; but some time after, said he would not impede the receipt of a sum so unheard of in France for a Portrait, and consented to sit: David saw in his compliance an undisguised pleasure in so splendid a mark of the

---

1. Jacques-Louis David, formerly a friend of Robespierre and a prominent Republican; now the official court painter for Napoleon. His equestrian portrait, *Bonaparte au Mont Saint-Bernard*, was painted in 1800 on a commission from Napoleon.
2. 'Show me as calm, sober, tranquil – on a fiery horse. –'
3. Marguerite-Charlotte David.
4. Alexander Hamilton-Douglas, Marquess of Douglas and Clydesdale. The painting was entitled *L'Empereur debout dans son cabinet* (*The Emperor standing in his office*).

favour of a British Peer: but something deeper than what merely touched his vanity was soon indicated, though not proclaimed, as will appear from a description of the Picture, which I shall draw up to the best of my recollection, and of which every circumstance was executed from the Emperor's own orders.

He is taken full length, and standing, in his Morning and most undressed military uniform. His Table and scrutore,[5] are covered with Maps, and some others, of immense dimensions, are rolled up in different parts of the room. He appears to have been solitarily occupied in Nocturnal studies, and ruminations all Night. The clock is, I think, upon the stroke of 5: but he only seems to have been roused to the lateness of the hour by the near extinction of his lamp, which causes a gloomy but picturesque effect in the chamber. He is very carelessly arrayed, his cravat off, or falling, and one stocking down at heel: though the Artist has not omitted so to fasten the other as to exhibit a well shaped leg. A spacious Globe has marks of having been studiously pored over. His Chair, however, and a corner that is just in view of a Bed or sopha, are covered with the richest crimson Velvet, and the Cornices are magnificent in Gold Embroidery.

This, I suppose, as a display not merely personal, he left to the Artist; as well as the peeping out, on a Corner of the Table, of an Imperial Diadem: but, what belonged to himself individually was by himself indicated: his face, therefore, has an expression as simple, as unaffected, and as unassuming as his attire, and, with the fall of his hands, which are very finely finished, he seems to mean making an appeal to the British Nation, through the British Nobleman for whom this Representation of their renowned Antagonist is designed, that shall cry out: 'Look at me, Britons! survey me well! What have you to fear, or doubt? What is there to excite such deadly hatred, in a Man as soberly and modestly arrayed as the plainest John Bull among yourselves, and as philosophically employed, without state or attendance? – '

The burthen of this appeal was '*Why should You not make Peace with me?*'

For, though the last desire of his turbulent ambition was to *Keep* Peace, the First was to *Make* it, as stamping for Posterity the recognition of his Imperial title by the British Legislature.

These two famous Pictures, both of them executed in David's best manner, and highest style, were shewn to me, in the year 1812, by Madame David, with the consent, no doubt, and possibly by the desire of her Husband: for I had made no solicitation, and, indeed, of the Picture for

5. I.e. 'scrutoire', writing-desk.

England I had not even heard. I was carried to the House by La Baronne de Larrey,[6] wife of the most eminent surgeon of France – which formerly would have meant of Europe, to whom I owed my almost restoration to life, through the skill, courage, and Judgement with which he performed a difficult and doubtful operation against an incipient cancer in opposition to the opinion of his Rival, Dubois, that the evil was too deep for extirpation. This brave Man, who conceived a zeal in my service, during his attendance, that soon, from the ardour of his character, was heightened into an almost enthusiastic regard, had excited in his Wife a desire of my acquaintance that made his first request upon my recovery bring us together. She was a woman of family, whom the Revolution had ruined, of remarkably pleasing and well bred manners, and full of talents.

Madame David was alone to receive us, and continued so during our stay. She was a woman of no sort of elegance, either of person or attire; and if ever she had possessed any beauty, it had deserted her at an early period, and without leaving any mark, either in her face or Form, That there it once had been. Yet she was by no means old; though also by no means young. But if he could not, like another Rubens, impart his conjugal Beauty to the World,[7] he had taken care to appropriate something more permanently beneficial to himself, in the intellectual endowments of his Mate. Mme David appeared to me to be shrewd, penetrating, sagacious and sarcastic. These are qualities very likely to be congenial to the taste of David – who, in return, was to her palpably and sincerely an object of adoration.

He was away, and I was sorry to miss seeing him; for ill as I accord with him in politics, or conducts, I was not without curiosity to behold a Man of such true Genius in so exquisite an art. He is Authour, I believe, of an entire new school.

I would I had been as able to merit by knowledge, as to enjoy from admiration, the treasures which, in the painting study of David, were now entrusted to my view. Entrusted I say, for though he was completely, and I fancy faithfully now devoted to Bonaparté, he had been so vehement a Republican, and his principles and his taste were so outrageously democratic, that his private Work Shop contained specimens of Designs, and of sketches that would Now to the *Emperor* have been as little congenial as they

---

6. Élisabeth-Charlotte Larrey.

7. Ten years before his death in 1640, Rubens (aged fifty-three) married the sixteen-year-old Hélène Fourment, who became the subject of many of his late paintings.

could have proved to any of the Bourbons in the Days of Anarchy when they were executed. Whatever was monarchical his very heart execrated; and I had been told tales of his lawless passion for Licence, not Liberty, that lessened my pleasure in the wonders of his skill, though they could not diminish my visual conviction of its pre-eminence. What chiefly attracted my notice and my curiosity, were the Portraits of innumerable personages painted in the various Historical Groups that were dispersed about the Chamber, and allowed to be striking likenesses of celebrated characters who had only had time to raise their Name and their fame, to have both, in rapid succession, immolated by Revolutionary fury.

I viewed them with that interest which so lively a representation of what so lately had been a living scene could not but inspire; but though I asked various questions, not to seem dangerously concentrated, I hazarded not a single comment, nor the smallest observation, save upon the splendid talent which all before me displayed. I could by no means consider myself upon safe ground, while I saw the sharp black Eyes of Madame David always directed to my face, even while most earnestly conversing with Madame Larrey; and though she had seemed to invite from me some sarcasm upon Bonaparté by openly acknowledging to me his own orders, which implied his own motives, for the subjects of the two Pictures which she had exhibited; I could not but imagine that my opinions, if gathered, would not rest with herself.

Nevertheless, I do not by any means suspect that she had the baseness to invite in order to devellop and betray me; on the contrary, I believe her, according to her own maxims, a woman of severe probity; and her personal regard for the good and gentle Madame Larrey, who, in her revolutionary distresses, had become a house pupil of David, would alone have sufficed to save me from such treachery: but my private notion of this courtesey was, that both the Artist and his mate were curious to know what would be the sentiments of an Englishwoman upon the subjects of these two celebrated Pictures, in which, with such a characteristic mixture of intrepidity and sagacity, the Emperor displayed himself as the magnanimous Master of the French, and the pacific Inviter to Fraternity from the English.

Finding me, however, deliberately silent, though so sincerely struck with the merit of the works before me that my silence, probably, was rather piquant than offensive, Madame David, as I was taking a last glance at the Portrait for the Marquis of Douglas, Mme David suddenly came up to me, and abruptly asked me how I thought Ces Messrs les Anglais[8] would like

8. Those fine English gentlemen.

that Picture? Surprized off my guard, I ingenuously answered her that they would like it but too well! She was extremely gratified: – much more than I was myself by this implied acknowledgement that Bonaparté had well understood how to conquer John Bull's opinion for the attainment of British popularity. The words *too well*, which visited her features with a sort of sarcastic exultation, that said: So *you* do not wish his success, yet nevertheless believe in it! were reported, I doubt not, to David, as demonstrative that his work was a Masterpiece. And that as such it was received and seen by the Marquis of Douglas I infer, from the information I have since had, that he kept it carefully under Lock and Key, and never ventured to exhibit it but Individually to confidential Friends.

Madame David, who, like her husband, was a rank Republican, could not herself be a thorough Votary of Bonaparte; though she wished his prosperity because he was the powerful protector of her Mate, and because he had crushed, at least, all Legitimate sovereignty. And she was probably also softened to him the more sincerely, by considering that though he was a Monarch, he was a Usurper.

195. From Journal for *July–August 1812*[1]

Our Journey – Alexander's and mine, – from Paris to Dunkirk[2] was sad, from the cruel separation which it exacted, and the fearful uncertainty of impending events; though I was animated at times into the liveliest sensations, in the prospect of again beholding my Father, my Friends, and my Country.

General d'Arblay, through his assiduous researches, aided by those of M. de Boinville[3] and some others, found that a vessel was preparing to sail from Dunkirk to Dover, under American Colours, and with American passports and License, and, after privately landing such of its passengers as meant but to cross the Channel to proceed to the Western continent. M. d'Arblay found, at the same time, 6 or 7 persons of his acquaintance, who were to be of this Voyage, Madame and Mlle de Cocherolle, Madame de Carboniere; Mme de Roncherolle – Madame de

---

1. This was written *c.* 1825.
2. 4–6 July 1812.
3. De Boinville had also counselled FB on an abortive attempt to leave France in 1810; see *JL*, vi. 705–6.

Caillebot and her Son and Daughter; the two Miss Potts and Mrs Gregory.[4]

We all met, and severally visited at Dunkirk – where I was compelled, through the mismanagement and misconduct of the Captain of the Vessel,[5] to spend the most painfully wearisome – though far from the most acutely afflicting – 6 Weeks of my life; for they kept me alike from all that was dearest to me either in France or in England; save my Alexander. I was 20 times on the point of returning to Paris; but whenever I made known that design, the Captain promised to sail the next Morning. The truth is, he postponed the Voyage from Day to Day, and from Week to Week, in the hope of obtaining more passengers; and, as the clandestine visit he meant to make to Dover, *in his way to America*, was whispered about, re-inforcements very frequently encouraged his cupidity.

The *ennui* of having no positive occupation was now for the first time known to me; for though the peculiarly first object of my active cares was with me, it was not as if that object had been a Daughter, and always at my side; it was a youth of 17, who, with my free consent, sought whatever entertainment the place could afford, to while away fatigue. He ran, therefore, wildly about, at his pleasure, to the Quay, the Dockyard, the sea, the suburbs, the surrounding country; frequently visited the Miss Potts; found a favourite School fellow, who was waiting to sail with us, and accepted whatever other recreation came in his way; but chiefly his time was spent in skipping to the Marianne, our destined vessel, and seeing its preparations for departure. Indeed he almost lived in making the examination for the ship amused him by its novelty; and to enter it seemed always something like expediting our liberation.

To stroll about the town, to call upon my fellow sufferers, among the females, to visit the principal shops, and to talk with the good Dutch people while I made slight purchases, was all I could devize to do that required action: and in that there was little exertion, and little reward; the town had nothing in it Noble or splendid, beautiful or curious; the Tower, indeed, I mounted;[6] but its innumerable steps, up a round small stair case, turned me so giddy I could scarcely reach the top; where the view, though vast, had no particular beauty; and in descending I with difficulty could keep my

---

4. Françoise-Charlotte de Cocherel and her daughter Virginie; Henriette de Carbonnière; Louise-Élisabeth de Roncherolles, daughter of Mme de Cocherel; Anne de Caillebot, her children Armand and Marie; Anna and Caroline Potts; and Jeanne Gregory.

5. John Risbrough.

6. The Gothic belfry of Dunkirk; 'some 231 feet high, it contained a spiral staircase of 264 steps' (*JL*, vi. 715 n. 39).

feet from failing me, the Winding was so close, so narrow, and so dizzily circular.

The two Inhabitants of the Town with whom I had sufficient converse to make any acquaintance, I found full of worthiness, probity, hospitality, and affectionate simplicity. I left amongst them, I am persuaded, some cordial good wishers, and some who had even conceived a friendship for me that was anxious for manifestation, and that led them to suggest sundry kind offices by which I benefitted during my stay.

But while all this was common, I have two things to relate that were certainly Singular.

When I found our stay thus indefinitely protracted, it occurred to me that if I had the papers of a Work which I had then in hand, they might afford me an occupation to while away my truly vapid and uninteresting leisure. I wrote this idea to my *Partner in All* – as the famous M. de Taleyrand had early called M. d'Arblay! – and, with a spirit that was always in its first youth where any service was to be performed, he waited on M. de Saulnier,[7] at the Police Office and made a request that my manuscripts might be sent after me, with a permission that I might, also, be allowed to carry them with me on board the Ship. He durst not say to England, whither no vessel was supposed to sail, but he would not to M. de Saulnier, who palpably connived at my plan and purpose, say America. M. de Saulnier made many inquiries relative to these papers; but on being assured, upon his Honour, that the Work had nothing in it political, nor even National, nor possibly offensive to the Government, he took the single Word of M. d'Arblay, whose noble countenance, and dauntless openness of manner were guarantees of sincerity that wanted neither seals nor bonds, and invested him with the power to send me what papers he pleased, without demanding to examine, or even to see them: a trust so confiding and so generous, that I have regretted a thousand times the want of means to acknowledge it according to its merit.

The Work was The Wanderer, or Female Difficulties; of which nearly 3 Volumes – were finished;[8] They filled a small portmanteau, in which M. d'Arblay packed them up with as much delicacy of care as if every page had been a Bank note.

They arrived, nevertheless, vainly for any purpose at Dunkirk; the disturbance of my suspensive state incapacitating me for any composition, save of

7. Pierre Saulnier, Secretary-General of the police in Paris.
8. FB had begun writing her final novel, *The Wanderer*, before 1800, according to the preface. She wrote the last two volumes after her return to England, completing it in draft form by 21 August 1813; see *JL*, vii. 163.

Letters to my best Friend; to whom I wrote, or dictated by Alexander, every Day; and every Day was only supported by the same kind diurnal return. But when, at length, we were summoned to the Vessel, and our Goods and Chattels were conveyed to the Custom House – which was close to the place of embarcation on the Wharf, but – which had rather the look of a Barn than of a public office; and when the little portmanteau was produced, and found to be filled with Manuscripts, the police officer who opened it, began a rant of indignation and amazement, at a sight so unexpected and prohibited, that made him incapable to enquire, or to hear the meaning of such a freight. He sputtered at the Mouth, and stamped with his feet, so forcibly and vociferously, that no endeavours I could use could palliate the supposed offence sufficiently to induce him to stop his accusations of traiterous designs, till tired of the attempt, I ceased both explanation and entreaty, and stood before him with calm taciturnity. Wanting then the fresh fuel of interruption or opposition, his fire and fury evaporated into curiosity to know what I could offer. Yet even then, though my account staggered his violence into some degree of civility, he evidently deemed it, from its very nature, incredible; and this Fourth Child of my Brain had undoubtedly been destroyed ere it was Born, had I not had recourse to an English Merchant, Mr Gregory,[9] long settled at Dunkirk, to whom, happily, I had been recommended, as to a person capable, in any emergence, to afford me assistance. Great was now the suspence, and powerful the assistance: he undertook the responsibility; and the Letter of M. d'Arblay containing the Licence of M. de Saulnier was then all sufficient for my manuscripts and their embarcation.

Such an event, however, is truly memorable, as well as singular, during a period of such unexampled strictness of Police Discipline with respect to Letters or Papers, between the two Nations.

And this permission, also, like the Passport for myself and *my son* would never, I am fully convinced, have been obtained during the residence in Paris of Buonaparte. But he was now advancing into Russia, and struggling by every means in his power to obtain a Battle; which he imagined, and probably with reason, would have been decisive in his favour.

The Second peculiar event I have to relate I never even yet recollect without an inward shuddering.

In our Walks out of the town, on the borders of the Ocean, after passing beyond the Dock yard, or Wharf, we frequently met a large party of Spanish

9. David Gregory, husband of Jeanne Gregory.

Prisoners, well escorted by *Gens d'Armes*,[10] and either going to their hard destined labour, or returning from it for Repast or Repose. I felt deeply interested by them, knowing they were Men with and for whom our own English and the Immortal Wellington[11] were then fighting: and this interest induced me to walk on the Bank, by which they were paraded to and fro', as often as I could engage Alexander, from his other pursuits, to accompany me. Their appearance was highly in their favour, as well as their situation: They had a look calmly intrepid, of concentrated resentment, yet inalterable patience. They were mostly strong built and vigorous, of solemn, almost stately Deportment, and with fine dark Eyes, full of meaning, rolling around them as if in watchfull Expectation of insult.

My looks, I doubt not, in our frequent encounters, shewed them it was not from me, at least, they had insult to dread; and, in a short time, they certainly caught from my countenance an air of sympathy, for they gave me, in return, as we passed one another, a glance that spoke grateful consciousness. I followed them to the place of their labour; though my short-sightedness would not let me distinguish what they were about, whether mending Fortifications, Dykes, Banks, Parapets, or what not; and I durst not use my Glass, lest I should be suspected as a Spy. We only strolled about in their vicinity, as if merely visiting and viewing the sea.

The Weather – it was now August – was so intensely hot, the place was so completely without shade, and their work was so violent, that they changed hands every two hours, and those who were sent off to recruit, were allowed to cast themselves upon the burnt and straw-like Grass, to await their alternate summons. This they did in small Groups, but without venturing to solace their rest by any species of social intercourse. They were as taciturn with one another as with their keepers and Task Masters.

One among them there was, who wore an air of superiority, grave and composed, yet decided, to which they all appeared to bow down with willing subserviency, though the distinction was only demonstrated by an air of profound respect whenever they approached, or passed him; for discourse held they none. One Morning, when I observed him seated at a greater distance than usual from his overseers, during his Hour of release, I turned suddenly from my Walk, as if with a view to find my way Homewards, but contrived, while talking with Alexander, and looking another way, to slant

---

10. I.e. *gendarmes*, military police.
11. The Duke of Wellington, commander of the British army fighting the French in Spain, had won the Battle of Salamanca on 22 July 1812.

my steps close to where he sat, surrounded by his mute adherents, and to drop a handful of small coin nearly under the Elbow upon which, wearily, he was reclining. We proceeded with alertness, and talking together aloud: but Alexander perceived this apparent Chief evidently moved by what I had done, though forbearing to touch the little offering, which, however, his companions immediately secured.

After this, I never met him that he did not make me a slight, but expressive Bow. This encouraged me to repeat the poor little tribute of compassion, which I soon found he distributed, as far as it would go, to the whole set, by the kindly looks with which every one, thenceforward, greeted me upon every meeting. Yet he whom we supposed to be some Chief, and who palpably discovered it was himself I meant to distinguish, never touched the money, nor examined what was taken up by the others; who, on their part, nevertheless, seemed but to take charge of it in trust.

We were now such good friends, that this became more than ever my favourite walk; and these poor unhappy captives never saw me without brightening up into a vivacity of pleasure that was to me a real exhilaration.

We had been at Dunkirk above 5 Weeks, when one Evening, having a Letter of consequence to send to Paris, I begged Alexander to carry it to the Post himself, and proposed our making our walk that way. But the distance being great, and the Streets hot and disagreeable, in the midst of August, I requested him to deposit me upon the Quay, and there to join me. As the Weather was very fine, I stood near the Sea, wistfully regarding the Element on which depended all my present hopes and views, and examining also the shipping, which was there in abundance, at the Mouth of the Harbour; but not chusing to walk from the spot at which he left me, as I saw only Men, and did not ambition to be remarked as a Female Wanderer. But presently my meditations were interrupted, and my thoughts diverted from mere self, by the sudden entrance, in a large body, of my friends the Spanish Prisoners, who all bore down to the very place where I was stationed, evidently recognizing me, and eagerly shewing that it was not without extreme satisfaction.

I saw their approach in return, with lively pleasure, for, the Quay being, I suppose, a place of certain Security, they were unincumbered by their usual *Turnkeys*, the Gens d'Armes; and this freedom, joined to their surprise at my sight, put them, also, off their guard, and they flocked round, though not near me, and hailed me with smiles, Bows, and hands put upon their Breasts. I now took courage to speak to them, partly in French, partly in English, for I found they understood a little of both those languages. I enquired whence they came, and whether they knew General Wellington. They smiled and nodded at his Name, and expressed infinite delight in finding I was English; but though they all, by their head movements, entered into discourse, my friend the Chief was the only one who attempted to answer me, which he did with such an expansion of physiognomy, such an opening to natural feelings and excited confidence, that his countenance beamed with an expression so changed in his favour, so full of noble trust and grateful ardour, that I felt an earnest wish I could have cultivated his friendship, and a thorough conviction that my own best Friend would have taken him to his heart.

When I first went to France, and, from having never practiced speaking, though I had always loved Reading French, being continually embarrassed for terms, I used constantly to apply to M. d'Arblay for aid, till Madame de Tessé, in a peremtory, though high bred manner, customary to *Les Dames de Condition*, after *Un certain Âge*, in France, charged him to be quiet, saying that my looks filled up what my words left short, '*de sorte que*,' she added, '*nous la dévinons*:'[12] this was the case between my Spaniards and myself, and we *deviné*-d one another so much to our mutual satisfaction, that while this was the converse the most to my taste of any I had had at Dunkirk, it was, also, probably, the most to theirs of any that had fallen to their lot since they had been torn from their native country.

While this was going on, I was privately drawing from my Purse all that it contained of small money, to distribute to my new and completely dilapidated Friends; carefully observant, while my head presented it to my Chief, that my hands should part with it to his associates; not to shock a dignity which he seemed to sustain amongst them by common accord: but at this same moment, a sudden change in the countenance of the chief, from looks of grateful feelings, to an expression of austerity, checked my purpose, and, sorry and alarmed lest he had taken offence, I hastily drew my empty hand from my Ridicule.[13] I then saw that the change of expression was not simply to austerity from pleasure, but to consternation from serenity; and I perceived, which my near-sightedness prevented more immediately, that it was not to me the altered visage was directed; the Eye pointed beyond me, and over my head: startled, I turned round – and what, then, was my own consternation, when I beheld an Officer of the Police, in full gold trappings, and wearing his Badge of authority, and his head covered, and

---

12. *Ladies of quality* (after) *a certain age . . . 'so that . . . we divine it'*.
13. I.e. reticule, a small bag.

half a yard beyond it, with an enormous Gold Laced cocked Hat, furiously darting forward from a small house at the entrance upon the Quay, which I afterwards learned was his official dwelling! When he came within two yards of us, he stopt short, and stood still, mute and Erect; but with an air of dreadful menace, his Eyes scowling, first upon the Chief, then upon me, then upon the whole Group, and then upon me again, with looks that seemed diving into some conspiracy, and which mingled in their ire a ferocious joy of anticipated vengeance.

My alarm was extreme; my imprudence and its danger, in conversing thus aloof with these unhappy Captives struck me all at once with foreboding terrour of ill consequences. To be aware, however, of the peril I had incurred, imbued me instantly with resolution to seek to ward off the threatening blow; and the instances innumerable that rushed upon my memory of the happy effects of courage, and the disastrous ones of timidity, impelled me to resist my affright, and to summon sufficient presence of mind to meet the Eyes of my Antagonist with a look that shewed surprise rather than apprehension at his wrath.

This was not without some effect. Accustomed, probably, to scrutinize and to penetrate into secret plots, he might be an Adept in distinguishing the fear of ill-treatment from the fear of detection; The latter I certainly could not manifest, as my compassion had shown no outward mark beyond a little Charity; but the former I tried vainly, perhaps, to subdue for I well knew that pity towards a Spaniard would be deemed suspicious, at least – if not culpable.

We were all silent, and all motionless; but when the Man, having fixed upon me his Eyes, with intention to petrify me, saw that I fixed him in return, with an open, though probably not very composed Face, he spoke – and with a Voice of Thunder! vociferating Reproach, Accusation, and Condemnation all in one. His Words I could not distinguish, they were so confused and rapid from rage. Compared to him, the Custom house officer had been mild.

This violence, though it secretly affrighted me even to the soul, I tried to meet with simple astonishment making no sort of answer, or interruption to his invectives: When he observed my steadiness, and that he excited none of the humiliation of discovered guilt, he stopt short; and after a pause, gruffly said: 'Qui est Vous?'[14]

A thousand reasons made this a question I was unwilling to answer; but

14. 'Who are you?'

a thousand more told me the danger of either evasion or delay; and I therefore compelled myself to say

'Je me nomme d'Arblay.'

'Est Vous Mariée?'

'Oui.'

'Où est Votre Mari? – '

'A Paris.'

'Qui est il?'

'Il travaille aux Bureaux de l'Interieur.'

'Pourquoi le quittez Vous?'[15]

I was here sensibly embarrassed. I durst not avow I was going to England: – I could not assert I was really going to America: I hesitated; and the sight of his Eyes brightening up with the hope of mischief, abated my firmness; and, while he seemed to be staring me through, I gave an account very imperfect, indeed, and far from clear, though true, that I came to Dunquerque to embark on Board the Mary Ann Vessel.

'Ah ha!' exclaimed he, 'Vous êtes Anglaise?'

Then, tossing back his head with an air of triumphant victory, 'Suivez moi! – '[16] he added, and walked away, fast, and fierce, but looking back every minute to see that I followed.

Never can I forget the terrour with which I was seized at this Command: it could only be equalled by the evident consternation and sorrow that struck me, as I turned my head around to see where I was, in my poor Chief and his Group, who, I am sure, were only withheld from offering me their protection by the view of the tremendous Belt of my assailant, which was furnished, conspicuously, with Pistols and Daggers. Follow I did, though not less perforce than if I had been dragged by chains; but when I saw him arrive at the Gate of the little Dwelling I have mentioned, which I now perceived to belong to him officially; I impulsively, involuntarily, stopt. To enter a police office with so ferocious a Wretch; – alone, helpless, unprotected, unknown; to be probably charged with planning some conspiracy with the Enemies of the State; – my poor Alexander away, and not knowing what must have become of me; – my breath was gone, – my power of movement ceased; my Head – or Understanding, seemed a Chaos, bereft of every distinct or discriminating idea; – and my Feet, as if those of a

---

15. 'My name is d'Arblay.' 'Are you married?' 'Yes.' 'Where is your husband? –' 'In Paris.' 'Who is he?' 'He works at the Ministry of the Interior.' 'Why are you leaving him?'

16. 'You are English?' . . . 'Follow me! –'

Statue, felt rivetted to the Ground, from a vague, but overwhelming belief I was destined to incarceration in some Dungeon, where I might sink ere I could make known my situation to my friends, while Alex, thus unaccountably abandoned, might be driven to Despair, or become the prey to nameless mischiefs.

Again the Tyger vociferated a 'Suivez moi!' but finding it no longer obeyed, he turned full round, as he stood upon his Threshold, and perceiving my motionless and speechless dismay, looked at me for two or three seconds in scornful, but investigating taciturnity. Then, again tossing back his head with an air of derisive exultation, and putting his arms a kembo, he said, in lower, but more taunting accents, '*Vous ne le juger donc pas aprôpos de me suivre?*'[17]

This was followed by a sneering sardonic grin that seemed anticipating the enjoyment of using compulsion.

The most remote apprehension of any thing so horrible as that – compulsion! – produced a revolution in my sense and feelings that brought back the use of my Judgement, which told me at the same moment the danger of betraying my fears, and the uselessness of resistance: on, therefore, I again forced myself, and, though, as I reached and crossed the Threshold, my heart sunk with a deadly weight, I once more felt sufficiently the importance of courage to assume its semblance, and with tolerable composure I said, 'Je n'ai rien, Monsieur, Je crois, à faire ici?'

'Nous verrons!'[18] he answered, bluffly, and led the way into a small Hovel, – I thought, – rather than parlour; and then haughtily seated himself at a Table, – on which were Pen, Ink, and Paper, and, while I stood before him, began an Interrogation, with the decided asperity of examining a detected Criminal, of whom he was to draw up the *procès Verbal*.[19]

When I perceived this, my every fear, feeling, nay thought, concentrated in Alexander, to whom I had determined not to allude, while I had any hope of self-escape, to avoid, for us both, the greatest of all perils, that of an accusation of intending to evade the ensuing Conscription, for which though Alex was yet too young, he was fast advancing to be amenable.

But Now, that I was enclosed from his sight, and there was danger every moment of giving him the horror of suddenly missing me, I felt that our only chance of safety must be in my naming him before he should return: With all the composure, therefore, that I could assume, I said that I was

---

17. '*So you're not disposed to follow me?*'
18. 'I have no need, Sir, to be here, I believe.' 'We shall see!'
19. *Police report.*

come to Dunkirk with my son, to embark in the Mary Ann, an American Vessel, with a passport from M. de Saulnier, secretary to the Duke de Rovigo, Minister of the Police.

And what had I done with this Son?

I had sent him to the Post office with a Letter for his Father

At that instant I perceived Alexander wildly running past the Window.

This moment was critical. I instantly cried 'Sir, there is my Son!'

The Man rose, and went to the door, calling out 'Jeune homme!'[20]

Alex approached, and was questioned, and, though much amazed, gave answers perfectly agreeing with mine.

I now recovered my poor affrighted faculties, and calmly said, that if he had any doubt of our veracity, I begged he would send for Mr Gregory, who knew us well.

This, a Second time, was a most happy reference. Mr Gregory was of the highest respectability, and he was near at hand. There could be no doubt of the authenticity of such an appeal. The brow of my ferocious assailant was presently unbent. I siezed the favourable omen to assure him, with apparent indifference that I had no objection to being accompanied, or preceded to l'Hotel Sauvage, where I resided, nor to giving him the Key of my Portmanteaux and portfolio, if it were possible I had excited any suspicion by merely speaking, from curiosity, to the Spanish Prisoners.

No, he answered, he would not disturb me, And then, having entered the Name of Alexander by the side of Mine, he let us depart.

Speechless was my joy, and speechless was the surprise of Alexander, and we walked Home in utter silence.

This adventure, in the terrours to which it gave rise, was one of the most severe to my apprehensions, during several minutes, that I have ever experienced in my life.

Happily, this incident occurred but just before we set sail, for with it terminated my greatest solace at Dunkirk, the seeing and consoling those unhappy Prisoners, and the regale of wandering by the sea Coast.

6 Weeks completely we consumed in wasteful weariness at Dunkirk: and our passage, when, at last, we set sail, was equally, in its proportion, toilsome and tedious. Involved in a sickening Calm, we could make no way, but lingered two days and two nights in this long-short passage.[21] The second Night, indeed, might have been spared me, as it was spared to all my

20. 'Young man!'
21. 13–15 August 1812.

fellow-Voyagers: but, when we cast anchor, I was so exhausted by the unremitting sufferings I had endured, that I was literally and utterly unable to rise from my Hammock.

Yet was there a circumstance capable to have aroused me from any torpidity, save the demolishing ravage of sea-sickness: for scarcely were we at Anchor, when Alex, who had been till then, in a state of much bodily misery himself, instantly reviving, and capering up to the Deck, descended with yet more velocity than he had mounted, to exclaim 'Oh Maman! there are two British Officers now upon Deck!'

But, finding that even this could not make me recover Speech or Motion, he ran back again to this new and delighting sight, and again returning, cried out, in a tone of rapture 'Maman, we are taken by the British! We are all captured by British Officers!'[22]

Even in my immoveable, and nearly insensible state, this juvenile ardour excited by so new and strange an adventure, afforded me some amusement. It did not, however, afford me strength for so utterly dislocated did I feel, that I could not rise, though I heard that every other passenger was removed. Every attempt that I made was productive of such severe, such annihilating effects, that even my poor vehement young companion gave over his exhortations and his entreaties, and I remained, almost lifeless, and quite alone, in the Cabin and my Hammock the whole Night.

With difficulty, even the next morning, I crawled upon the Deck. And There I had been but a short time, when Lieutenant Harford[23] came on Board, to take possession of the Vessel: not as French, but American booty, War having been declared against America the preceding Week.

Mr Harford, hearing my name, most courteously addressed me, with congratulation, upon my safe arrival in England. These were words to re-waken all the happiest purposes of my expedition, and they recovered me from the nerveless, sinking state into which my exhaustion had cast me as if by miracle. My Father – my Brothers – my Sisters and all my Heart dear Friends, seemed rising to my view and springing to my embraces, with all the rapturous joy of renovating re-Union. I thankfully accepted his obliging offer to carry me on shore in his own Boat; but when I turned round, and called upon Alexander to follow us, Mr Harford, assuming a commanding air, said 'No, Madam – I cannot take that young man. No

---

22. The United States had declared war on Britain on 18 June, so the ship, owned by an American, Captain Risbrough, was subject to seizure.

23. Possibly Lieutenant Charles Halford; see *JL*, vi. 726 n. 52.

French person can come into my Boat without a passport and permission from Government.'

My air, now a little corresponded with his own, as I answered 'He was Born, Sir, in England!'

'O!' cried he; 'that's quite another matter! Come along, Sir! we'll all go to-gether.'

I now found we were rowing to Deal, not Dover, to which town we had been destined by our engagement: but we had been captured, it seems, *chemin faisant*,[24] though so gently, and with such utter helplessness of opposition, that I had become a Prisoner without any suspicion of my captivity, from the disordering sufferings which left one no faculties but for themselves.

We had anchored about half a mile, I imagine, from the shore; which I no sooner touched, than, drawing away my arm from Mr Harford, I took up, on one knee, with irrepressible transport, the nearest bright pebble, to press to my lips, in grateful joy at touching again the land of my Nativity, after an absence nearly hopeless of more than 10 Years.

24. *In making our way.*

1812–1814

Interlude in England: The Wanderer

196. Letter to James Burney *15 August 1812*

[Deal]

Who will be more sincerely rejoiced – except myself – than my dear kind James to meet again a so long lost sister? – no one, I firmly believe, no one! – and I can let no creature rob me of the pleasure of telling him that I am actually in good – dear old England! – I seized a pebble to kiss when I touched the shore, and I shall guard it all my life – But alas – what is perfect? – the best and dearest of partners could not accompany me! – I have Alex, however, in raptures – Distribute my love – I shall spend to-morrow here to rest – for I have passed 3 Nights with my cloaths on, and I must recruit in strength for supporting my approaching happiness.

197. Journal Letter to Alexandre d'Arblay *18 August 1812*[1]

Still no Charles: Lady Lucy[2] warmly pressed me to stay on; but I only passed the morning with her, and then, sure there was some mistake, set off the 19th for Canterbury, where we slept, and on the 20th proceeded towards Chelsea. While, upon some Common, we stopt to water the Horses, a Gentleman on Horse back passed us twice, and then, looking in, pronounced my name: and I saw it was Charles! – dear Charles! who had been watching for us several hours, and *3 nights* following, through a mistake.[3]

Thence we proceeded to Chelsea, where we arrived at 9 o'clock at night.

---

1. Annotated by FB: 'Detail of arrival in England after Ten year's absence'. The journal covers the events of 12–22 August; only the entry for 18 August is printed here.
2. Lady Lucy Anne Foley, an old friend of FB, now a resident of Deal, who had entertained FB there.
3. Charles Burney had been waiting for FB at Dover.

I was in a state almost breathless. John, the man servant, was in the courtyard looking for us; Becky[4] came down, – but I could not speak to any of them; I could only demand to see my dear Father alone: fortunately, he had the same feeling, and had charged all the family to stay away, and all the World to be denied. I found him, therefore, in his Library, by himself – – but oh my dearest Friend! very much altered indeed! – weak, weak and changed! – his head almost always hanging down, and his hearing most cruelly impaired. – I was terribly affected, – but most grateful to God, for my arrival. Our meeting, you may be sure, was very tender, though I roused myself as quickly as possible to be gay and cheering. He was extremely kind to Alex, and said, in a tone the most impressive, 'I should have been very glad to have seen M. d'Arblay! –' In discourse, however, he re-animated, and was, at times, all himself. But he now admits scarcely a creature but of his Family, and will only see for a short time even his Children. He likes quietly reading, and lies almost constantly upon the sofa, and will never eat but alone! –! –! – What a change! —

198. Letter to Dr Burney *10 December 1812*[1]

Deptford Rectory[2]

Two Letters from my dearest Padre! – what sweet kindness! and O – what rare news is the news at this moment exciting it![3] – I hardly yet breathe from the various and blessed hopes – mixt nevertheless with nameless terrours which it has put into agitation. The first Letter greeted me on Sunday morning at Norbury Park,[4] where, indeed, such cheering intelligence was peculiarly seasonable, for most cruelly melancholy was the change in all my feelings at that loved spot compared with what formerly I had experienced. The virtuous and accomplished Chief is missed every moment. – Yet William is a truly worthy successor,[5] – but William was there *besides*! And *Mrs* Lock, my constant, cherished and cherishing Friend, *she* also, was

---

4. Rebecca More, CB's cook.

1. Annotated by FB: 'Perfect state of long shut up Goods in closets at dear happy – lost West Hamble!'
2. The home of Charles Burney, who was Vicar of St Paul's, Deptford.
3. Napoleon's enforced retreat from Moscow, which led to his withdrawal from Russia.
4. On 6 December, two days after she arrived at Norbury Park.
5. William Locke and his son William. FB's 'attitude toward [the latter] was to change when, in the process of selling Norbury Park, he forced the sale of Camilla Cottage in 1814' (*JL*, vii. 60 n. 4).

there *besides*! Nothing, therefore, fills up the void[6] – – But I had meant to keep to more chearful themes, and I have so great, so unexpected a delight to give to Mr d'Arblay, that I am sure you will rejoice for him with all your heart, – i.e. – I have visited the shut up Closet of Books at West Hamble, which contained our whole Library *in these parts*, and which he had prepared himself to hear was a mass of moths, mildew, cobwebs, and insects.[7] — I have visited it, my dearest Father, after an absence of Ten years and a half, during which period the door has never once been opened, and I have not found a single Book injured! – the few that were new, and handsomely bound, are as bright as if just bought; the many which he had himself sewed in various coloured paper, are dry, sound, and clean: Not a pamphlet has a single leaf curled at the corner; not a label of the hundreds neatly written with his own hand, has dropt off, or is effaced. All the virtuous toils of his diligent leisure are now amply repaid. After the great and grand and incomparable good news which You have sped to me, there is none, perhaps, in the world – save what concerns his bosom affections – that will give him such glee, such warmth such glowing satisfaction as this intelligence. Ah, when can I send it him! –

My Cloaths, too, that I expected to find half eaten by the Worms, and the other half in a wet, blue, mouldy, sticky, tatter demallion state, are in perfect repair. I, therefore, am as much bodily, as He is intellectually richer than our joint hopes ventured to make us.

I long to see you again, dearest Sir, but I went through so much in this visit that I want a little refitting. I hope to Heaven the Cough is better? –

Adieu, most dear Padre, ever most dutifully

your affectionate Daughter –

FB. d'A

all hence send love and duty.

My Alex is well – I saw him for a moment yesterday.[8]

My kind love to dear Sarah –

I had not time to tell you, in my multiplicity of tellings, that the Princess Elizabeth spoke to me in high terms of Sally's last work, and with much praise, though not equal, of Clarentine.[9]

---

6. Caused by Susanna Burney's death.

7. In a letter to AA of 23 March 1802, FB had described her plan to pack their books in a closet at Camilla Cottage and then to have the door papered over, 'so as to leave an appearance of no door at all' (*JL*, v. 191).

8. At Greenwich School, where he had been accepted as a pupil by FB's brother Charles.

9. Sarah Harriet Burney had published her third novel, *Traits of Nature*, in April 1812. Princess Elizabeth preferred her first.

199. Letter to Queen Charlotte *16 March 1813*[1]

Madam

Most humbly – yet with that chering confidence which your Majesty's ever gracious goodness has long mingled with my respect and awe, I now venture to write my happiness – Dr Davy[2] has just been brought to me by my Brother, to announce – what he goodnaturedly insisted upon acquainting me with himself, my Son's election.

The opponent, it seems, withdrew his petition.

All the Electors, therefore, voted for Alexander, even Dr Fisher and Mr Hargrave.[3]

The certificate of his Birth at Gt Bookham Surry, sworn by Mr Ansell, my surgeon, before the Earl of Rothes, was formally read.[4] My dear Mrs Lock was not called upon or she would have come, she says, from her retreat, to take her oath of this fact to the whole University, – nay to the whole Universe, rather than My Boy should have lost the blessing of his Birth right.

I feel sure of your Majesty's forgiveness that I write this joy of my heart – Alas! your Majesty would fain see such joy – all springing from your Majesty's own benificient graciousness, – more frequently. Where, indeed, would be sorrow if success to the suppliant hung only upon the wishes of your Majesty? And such has always been to me – hereditary almost like their virtues – the condesendsion of Their Royal Highnesses the Princesses, that my heart now glows doubly in the trust that their Royal Highnesses will not disdain to take some share in my delight. Most humbly, and with soul-felt grateful attachment

I presume to sign myself Madam

1. This letter survives in draft form.
2. The Revd Martin Davy, Master of Gonville and Caius College, Cambridge, where Alexander had just been awarded the Tancred Scholarship, worth £120 a year for three years.
3. Philip Fisher, Master of Charterhouse School, and Francis Hargrave, Treasurer of Lincoln's Inn. There were seven electors in all. FB had canvassed many people, including Queen Charlotte, to use their interest with the electors.
4. Supporters of the rival candidate had falsely declared that Alexander was born in Calais and therefore ineligible for the Tancred, reserved for British Anglicans in financial need.

200. Letter to Charles Burney *22 March 1813*

My dearest Carlucci,

Since we make use – than which nothing can be so right, – of the name of my dear absentee, why not do it according to his real idea? – which is, That he would have the offer be put fairly *to Auction?*[1]

If not, in applying from one to another, the work will seem, to all who come second, bandied about, and rejected!!!

I would wish a short kind of circular Letter, to this effect –

That you shall have shortly *a work* to dispose of for your sister, which, as well as she can judge by the uncopied and yet not quite finished ms. will be about the length of her Cecilia; and which, you frankly make known, you shall commit fairly to the highest bidder – or bidders.

––––––––

Now this will admit no cavil, for 'tis the honest fact. And no one can be affronted, where all are treated alike.

I would wish it to go to Longman, Murray, Colborn, Robinson – Payne, White, Rees, Rivington, Williams, Hurst, Orme, Brown – Richardson, Hookham, Leigh, Mathews, Booker, Hatchard[2] – and as many more as you will; the more the merrier.

If you see this well, Charlotte will copy, and I will send the Billets, *all at the same moment.*

One or two a day, and one after another, will certainly incur an idea that the work is *under examination,* or *has* been, and is offered about *in Succession.*

I would say nothing of *printing* for myself, though if dissatisfied I may *do* it:[3] but I hate all that looks like menace.

I know no other way than this that will really satisfy M. d'Arblay that *the best has been done:* –

That we may not hear of some man who would have given £100 more than the rest, when it shall be too late.

1. I.e. the opportunity to become publisher of *The Wanderer.*

2. For information on these booksellers, see *JL*, vii. 567–8. The company chosen would be Longman, Hurst, Rees, Orme and Brown.

3. FB wished to avoid the risks and additional labour that printing for the author entailed: instead, she wanted to sell the copyright of the manuscript for the highest possible sum.

Colborn[4] has been so civil and respectful, I would not affront him by leaving him out: and he is very obliging to my Father, in lending him Books *Gratis*.

This is a great stake to me! very great indeed, in its consequences!

I have taken these names from only one weeks news papers. I hope you can add some others.

Almost every work now, I see, even a play, has 5 or 6 publishers.

The more, for Me, the better, because the pay comes quicker and easier.

To Mr *Payne*,[5] perhaps, it may be more proper you should *tell* than write this plan.

As I am not ready, I should not be in haste, but for your lost[6] – and indeed, when I *am* ready, I have no time to lose, since I wish ardently to superintend the Press.

Pray call it a work: I am passed the time to endure being supposed to write a Love-tale. I will abide by the consequence.

And also say nothing of its purposes, and all that. It looks like Puff.

They will take it – or They Will let it alone, from public expectation – be its purpose etc. what it may.

If you have not written already to Longman, pray don't till *all the other* Billets are ready for the *same post*.

201. From Letter to Georgiana Waddington *26 August 1813*

I am truly glad you had a gratification you so earnestly covetted, that of seeing Mme de Staël. Your account of her was extremely interesting to me. As to myself – I have not seen her at all. Various causes have kept me in utter retirement. And, in truth, with respect to Mme de Staël my situation is really embarrassing. It is too long, and difficult, to write upon, – nor do I recollect whether I ever communicated to you our original acquaintance, which, at first, was *intimate*. I shall always, internally, be grateful, for the partiality with which she sought me out upon her arrival in this Country before my marriage: and still, and far more, if she can forgive my *dropping*

4. Henry Colburn, who would correspond with FB about publishing *The Wanderer* and whom she would have chosen. Her brother Charles, however, persuaded her to go to Longman; see *JL*, vii. 153–5.

5. Thomas Payne, James Burney's brother-in-law and one of the publishers of *Camilla*.

6. Apparently alluding to a letter from Charles no longer extant, in which he may be regretting time 'lost' by FB's delays in completing the novel.

her, which I could not help; for none of my friends, at that time, would suffer me to keep up the intercourse! I had messages – remonstrances – entreaties – representations Letters and Conferences, till I could resist no longer, though I had found her so charming, that I fought the hardest battle I dared fight against almost all my best connexions! – She is now received by all mankind – but that, indeed, she always was – all womankind, I should say, with distinction and pleasure. – I wish much to see her Essay on suicide:[1] but it has not yet fallen in my way. When will the work come out for which she was, she says, *chassée de la France?*[2] – Where did your Fanny hear her a whole evening? She is, indeed, most uncommonly entertaining; and animating, as well as animated, almost beyond any body. 'Les Memoires de Mme de Staal'[3] I *have* read, long ago, and with singular interest and eagerness. They are so attaching, so evidently original, and natural, that they stand very high indeed, in reading that has given me most pleasure. – My Boy has just left me for Greenwich. He goes in October to Cambridge. I wish to install him there myself. My last Letter from Paris gives me to the end of October to stay in England. There is a wish the present campaign should be over before my return, that I may go by Calais or Dunquerque. I dread inexpressibly the long passage by Morlaix[4] – Adieu, my ever dear Mary – Heaven grant you may be enabled to send me better news of your own – and your poor sweet Emily's health![5]

202. From Letter to Dr Burney *post 23 September 1813*

Let me steal a Moment to relate a singular gratification, and, in truth, a real and great Honour I have had to rejoice in.[1] You know, my Padre, probably

---

1. *Réflexions sur le suicide* (1813), translated as *Reflections on Suicide* (1813).
2. *De l'Allemagne* had been printed in Paris in 1810 but suppressed, on the grounds that it was hostile to France, by Napoleon, who ordered that Mme de Staël be sent into exile (*chassée de la France*). It would be published in London, with the English translation *On Germany*, in October 1813.
3. *De l'influence des passions sur le bonheur des individus et des nations* (1796), translated as *A Treatise on the Influence of the Passions upon the Happiness of Individuals and of Nations* (1798).
4. FB had earlier expressed her dread of the crossing from Plymouth to Morlaix (111 miles), five times the length of the Dover–Calais crossing; see *JL,* vii. 101.
5. Her invalid daughter Emelia would die in 1819, aged twenty-five.

1. FB's meeting with William Wilberforce, leader of the anti-slavery movement, took place on 19 September, when she was visiting her brother Charles. Her account was added much later, in her hand of the 1820s or 1830s; see *JL,* vii. 180.

that Marian Francis[2] was commissioned by Mr Wilberforce to bring about an acquaintance with your F.D'A – and that, though highly susceptible to such a desire, my usual shyness – or rather consciousness of inability to merit the expectations that must have made him seek me, induced my declining an Interview – Eh bien[3] – at Church at Sandgate, the Day after my arrival, I saw this justly celebrated Man, and was introduced to him in the Church yard, after the service, by Charles. The Ramparts and Martellos around us became naturally our Theme, and Mr Wilberforce proposed shewing them to me. I readily accepted the offer, and Charles and Sarah, and Mrs Wilberforce and Mrs Barrett, went away in their several carriages, while Mr Barrett alone remained,[4] and Mr Wilberforce gave me his arm – and, in short, we walked the round from one to Five o'clock! 4 Hours of the best conversation I have, nearly, ever enjoyed. He was anxious for a full and true account of Paris, and particularly of Religion and Infidelity, and of Buonaparté and the Wars, and of all and every Thing that had occurred during my Ten years seclusion in France: and I had so much to communicate, and his drawing out, and comments, and Episodes, were all so judicious, so spirited, so full of information, yet so benignly unassuming, that my shyness all flew away, and I felt to be his confidential Friend, opening to him upon every occurrence, and every sentiment, with the frankness that is usually won by years of intercourse. I was really and truly delighted and enlightened by him. I desire nothing more than to renew the acquaintance, and cultivate it to intimacy – But, helas,[5] he was going away next Morning. That his discourse should be edifying could not, certainly surprize me; I expected from him all that was elevated in instruction; but there was a mixture of simplicity and Vivacity in his manner that I had not expected, and found really Captivating. In contemplating the Opposite – and alas hostile shore, which to our Fancy's Eye, at least, was visible, – I could not forbear wafting over to it a partial blessing – nor refuse myself beseeching one from Mr Wilberforce, and the smiling benevolence with which he complied has won my heart forever. Encore

adio, Padre mio.[6]

2. FB's niece Marianne Francis.
3. Well.
4. Charles's wife Sarah, Wilberforce's wife Barbara Ann, Charlotte and Henry Barrett.
5. Alas.
6. Again goodbye, dear Father (Italian).

203. Letters to William Lowndes *22 January and 5 February 1814*

Madame d'Arblay returns Mr Lowndes[1] thanks for the Copy which he has sent her of Evelina.[2] She cannot be so ungrateful as to take ill a preliminary account that is meant so well; but she would have been far more pleased that the history of her Life should have awaited her death. There are many errours in the relation; beginning with the very first line; but none that are material.

She will accept with pleasure the obliging offer of Mr Lowndes for two more copies: one for M. d'Arblay, in France, another, for her Son, at Cambridge.

Chelsea College

Madame d'Arblay is much obliged to Mr Lowndes for the setts which he has sent her of Evelina: but she must entirely decline correcting any mistakes in Memoirs which she so little wishes authenticated, or printed, as those which would bring her very obscure life before the public.

Chelsea College

204. Letters to Longman, Hurst, Rees, Orme and Brown *2 and 6 February 1814*

Madame d'Arblay acquaints Messrs Longman and Co. that a rumour which has for some time alarmed her, has to day been confirmed to her for fact – that the first volume of her work is now in reading in various circles! –! How this has been brought to bear she knows not: she has regularly refused to shew even a page of it: even her Father, even her Brothers have not read one line: but she is now in the deepest uneasiness at the offence that must

---

1. William Lowndes, bookseller, son of Thomas Lowndes.
2. The 1810 edition of *Evelina*, published by Rivington, Lowndes and others, as part of the *British Novelists* series. In the first line of the preface, by Anna Laetitia Barbauld, FB is referred to as 'Mrs d'Arblay', which offended her. In April 1817, she reproached her brother Charles for addressing her thus; see *JL*, ix. 367.

necessarily be given amongst her best friends, by a refusal on her part which seems to exclude those only who ought least to have been excluded. The work must unavoidably risk unfair censures by being seen thus partially; and the sale will undoubtedly be injured by thus prematurely satisfying curiosity.

She begs leave, also, to observe, that the Critics, and very able judges, into whose hands she is informed that the first Volume is fallen, are the last who ought to see it in an unfinished state. Their approbation is the most difficult to obtain; and their censure stamps disgrace: She is peculiarly, therefore, vexed that the reading should have been begun under such disadvantages by Sir James Mackintosh, Madame de Staël, and Lord Holland.[1]

Finally, Mme d'Arblay assures Messrs Longman and Co. that the prefatory pages of which she has spoken, will lose all their purpose in being read After the work which they are written to precede.[2]

Her other works she had the uncontested privilege of presenting to her own family and friends, before they were seen by those of her publishers, Messrs Payne and Cadell.

She solemnly, therefore, entreats that they will call back the Volume, or Volumes, which they have lent out; and not suffer another to go forth, till the Work, in its proper state, shall be delivered to the public at large.

Mme d'Arblay forbore making this remonstrance to Messrs Longman till she had made enquiries of the Printer,[3] who has positively protested that from his house not a Copy has ever been sent, or lent, except to Messrs Longman.

If this application should be too late, and the Copy, or Copies, cannot be withdrawn, Mme d'Arblay must, at least, beg to have some of the 1st Volumes designed for her own connexions and friends forwarded to her without delay; that she may soften the reproach of what is thought her undue reserve, which, in 5 Letters, from separate quarters, has reached her already.

It would be needless for Mme d'Arblay to add how much she has been flattered, nevertheless, by this eagerness. Her cautions are the mere effect

---

1. Mackintosh was a lawyer, philosopher and reviewer; Henry Fox, Lord Holland, was an admirer of Napoleon. For others given advance copies of the first volume, see selection 213, and Lancelot Baugh Allen, a friend of Georgiana Waddington; see *JL*, vii. 237 n. 1.
2. The advance copies had evidently been printed without the dedication to CB, which is dated 14 March and which the publishers had not yet seen.
3. Andrew Strahan.

of her solicitude to run less risk of ending it in disappointment and disapprobation: for, if this premature communication be not checked, all the interest of the narration will be broken; all illusion will be abolished; and the Work will be born old.

Madame d'Arblay is overwhelmed with confusion and gratitude by the perusal of the letter of Sir James Mackintosh. Could she have foreseen such an honour, her nervousness would have been changed into [pleasure]. And if she may hope – as Sir James politely intimates – for the favourable opinion of the other two distinguished characters, who have occasioned her – so much alarm, she is perfectly conscious of the kindness of his observation upon so flattering an introduction of her new work to the public. Nor is she less satisfied with the justice of Sir James's remark that the truth will acquit her of any blame towards her own friends – who must find some other appellation if they will not rather rejoice at, than merely forgive, a loss of the precedence redounding, by its event, so singularly to her advantage.

Neither Sir James Mackintosh, nevertheless, nor Madame de Staël can be surprised at her late affright, when they hear that the Ms. had never been shown to her Father's best Friend, Lady Crewe, nor to her own, Mrs Lock: two ladies whose merits and claims they can peculiarly appreciate.

Mme d'Arblay, nevertheless, recommends to Messrs Longman not to repeat so hazardous an experiment; for the lenity and candour with which this 'fragment' of her work has here been judged are nearly as rare as the talents and genius which give them weight.

She hopes Messrs Longman will permit her to keep the Note of Sir James, that it may be found, hereafter, by her son, in contact with similar marks of favour bestowed upon her earlier productions by Dr Johnson and Mr Burke.

205. Letter to Charles Burney *2 April 1814*

Your Letter,[1] my dearest Charles, arrived just as I was setting forth to the Queen's House; on Thursday, – where I spent not only the day, but the night. And the next day, I went thence to Brother James's – from whom I did not return till very late. Two posts were thus inevitably and unavoidably lost: and this morning, Saturday, arrives your sett at Chelsea, ere I had had

---

1. Charles had apparently offered to escort FB to Windsor to present the Queen with a set of *The Wanderer*, published in five volumes on 28 March.

a moment to order it to your Rectory. It must therefore there wait, till you have the grace and the duty to present yourself there in person.

I have been labelling for distribution my whole 30 setts – though they must wait opportunities for delivery as I have very small means of finding them.

I am charmed with your kind project relative to Windsor. The Queen's sett is the only one not yet arrived. The 4 princesses are already here. They came with yours, and my Father's: which latter, as it is pill day, I defer presenting. Our dearest Father is weak and suffering; but I hope and trust from a passing complaint.

News from France is expected every hour of some decision respecting Peace[2] – Oh how will my heart glow when that Peace, shall be announced!

I hear you have made a noble and spirited attack upon the seizure of my property by certain purloiners: Is this true?[3]

But – put on a Wig! That will warm the dear brains, and keep them clear and vigorous. And you cannot be a Bishop without one:[4] and it will look *de bon augure*[5] –

Besides –

I have news for you that would lift it up! though, now, it must be content to make your own natural ringlets stand on end: –

i.e. viz. –

The Longman's have sent to beg me to prepare my 2d Edition! –

The orders are so vast, it must soon be wanted! –![6]

How stands the Hair?

Not quite in elevation?

Well, then, – a bit more

Martin[7] hies to me from Longman's this morning, with the incredible tidings – That the whole edition – of 3000 Copies – is already all gone! – by the enormous orders sent from all the Booksellers, joined to their own customers, through out the Kingdom! –

!!!!

What say the Curls? –

---

2. The allied armies had entered Paris on 31 March, and on 20 April Napoleon would be exiled to Elba, paving the way for the long-awaited peace.

3. This 'attack' has not been identified.

4. Charles's desire for a bishopric was the subject of much family discussion.

5. *Auspicious.*

6. The second edition of 1,000 copies would be published, with minor corrections, on 15 April.

7. Martin Charles Burney, son of FB's brother James.

Oh put on that Wig!

Here's yet another mounter: –

They entreat me to forbear seeing Revizes, or proofs; not to check the sail: For – not only the whole is gone 2 days before publication – but more-over, They have already orders for 800 more! – [8]

Astonishing! incredible! impossible!

I was quite overpowered – Martin shed tears of delight and pride – crying: 'If my uncle and I had fore-seen this, you should not have had less than £4000 – and ought not!'[9] – Am I really dear Carlos, Awake? They must print, they say, the two next Editions together! –![10]

206. Letter to Georgiana Waddington *between 12 and 28 April 1814*

Alas – my dear – fervant – but too precipitate Friend – if you have written such a Letter, you have undone us all![1] – – M. d'Arblay belongs to the National guard,[2] and he has written me word that Honour keeps him to his post till a proper moment for giving in his resignation! Judge, then, what sort of consolation I should receive from his presence, when I should know that he would ever after – if he found me tolerably well, repent having taken such a Treason!

Be not uneasy for me, my tender friend – My affliction is heavy, but not acute: my beloved Father had been spared to us something beyond the verge of the prayer for his preservation which you must have read[3] – for

8. FB's optimism here proved false: unfavourable reviews caused many of the advance orders to be cancelled, and after mid 1814 sales slowed to a trickle. In 1824, the publishers disposed of the 465 remaining copies as 'waste'; see *JL*, xii. 639–40.

9. Martin Charles Burney together with his uncle Charles had negotiated with Longman's on FB's behalf. The contract specified a maximum payment of £3,000 if *The Wanderer* went through six editions. In the event, FB received £2,000, her payment for the first two editions.

10. These editions – if indeed printed – were never published. On 29 April 1814, FB wrote to AA that 'the 3d Edition is already printed and in sale' (*JL*, vii. 327), but see note 8 above. In July 1815, she reminded her brother Charles that the printer had told Martin that third and fourth editions of the novel had been printed in readiness for future sales (*JL*, viii. 334); both may have confused the publishers' intention for fact.

1. Georgiana Waddington apparently did write a letter to AA urging him to return to England post haste to console FB on the death of her father. CB died on 12 April, a week before his 88th birthday; AA arrived for a four-week visit on 28 April, and this letter was written between those dates.

2. With the overthrow of Napoleon, AA could resume his military career in France.

3. Alluding to the final words of FB's dedication of *The Wanderer*, in which she hopes that CB's life might be prolonged 'to the utmost verge of enjoyable mortality' (p. 10).

already his sufferings had far surpassed his enjoyments! I could not have wished him so to linger! – though I indulged almost to the last hour a hope he might yet recover, and live to comfort. — I last of all gave him up! – but never wished his duration such as I saw him on the last few days. Dear blessed Parent! how blest am I that I came over to him while he was yet susceptible of pleasure – of happiness! — Many thought I had given 10 years more to his life! — alas! — my best comfort in my grief – in his loss – is that I watched by his revered side the last night – and hovered over him 2 hours after he breathed no more – for though much suffering had *preceded* the last hours, they were so quiet, and the final exit was so soft, that I had not perceived it, though I was sitting by his Bedside –! – and I would not believe it – when all around announced it —

I forced them to let me stay by him, and his reverend form became stiff before I could persuade myself to believe he was gone hence for-ever ——

Yet neither then, nor now, has there been any violence, any thing to fear from my grief – his loss was too indubitably to be expected – he had been granted too long to our indulgence, to allow any species of repining to mingle with my sorrow – and it is repining that makes sorrow too hard to bear with resignation – Oh! I have known it! – – –

You will easily believe with what pain I must have torn myself from my retirement in little more than a week – in 11 days – after this separation, to enter into the very midst of the World, to be presented to Mme la Duchesse d'Angouleme.[4] — But those who ought best to know remonstrated against my repugnance, and assured me it might be lastingly injurious to Mr d'Arblay, since every body who had any pretence to that Honour came eagerly forward. I found the effort however, less trouble than I had expected, for though the Crowd was immense, and I was kept in it all day, it was of new faces – I met no one, save Lady Crewe, who took me, that I had ever beheld in the same apartment with my dearest Father. Nothing, therefore, called forth his image save my own constant recollection.

Adieu – dearest Mary! – you have frightened me into writing – but I am better, not worse for it. I have now had 6 Letters from M. d'Arblay –

---

4. FB records her attendance at a large salon held by the Duchess, at which she was presented to Louis XVIII, in her journal for 22 April; see *JL*, vii. 295–317.

207. Letter to Georgiana Waddington *13–18 October 1814*

Richmond, October 13

Eh bien, mes chères amies? are you becoming a little Englishised? or are you still tout à fait Parisiennes? In either case, donnez moi, je vous en prie, de vos Nouvelles.[1] – Did not my fair namesake give me to understand that she had a *hundred little details* to communicate that she knew would be interesting? – I have let a month pass away without any demand, sure that the fondest of mothers could not require less for her own private, though never selfish information: but now, I may venture, I hope, to put in my claim for some intelligence, both *general* and *particular*, of this delightful excursion.

I wish, too, passionately, my dearest Mary, for a full and faithful development of the points at which you hint in the folding of your Letter – namely, Cambridge and Alexander. He never, you say, can succeed at Cambridge — unriddle to me, I beg, what that never means? and tell me honestly what the Cambridge Men you have seen, those expected after your Letter, as well as those who had preceded it, have related or imagined upon this too interesting subject.[2] It is now that to know the *whole truth* may be useful; for now, just now the conflict is at the height which must subside by our fixing to which of his two native Countries – that of his Birth or that of his Ancestors – he will finally belong. Had I fears he would *never* succeed, all my influence would take a new turn. – M. d'Arblay's *own* affairs, indeed, must ultimately biass us both, as from our Alexander neither of us will be parted; but even for the instant such a belief as yours would make me struggle hard against his return —

Monday – October 18

I have lost my post, and eternal avocation has kept my Letter back to this moment – but though I have a million of things to tell you, as well as to do, the pressure of my desire to have an answer to what I have already written forces me to remit all till I write again – and to beg you most earnestly to let me have as quick an answer as possible – for This Week decides Alex's return or not to Cambridge – and I will hear and weigh and discuss all at

---

1. And so, my dear friends . . . complete Parisians . . . give me, I beg you, your news. Georgiana Waddington's husband and her daughter Frances had been in France from July to September.
2. Georgiana Waddington had apparently heard of Alexander's mishaps at Cambridge through visits from her husband's nephew James Henry Monk, Regius Professor of Greek, and others.

once – and then – here after – on this theme – forever hold my tongue! various interruptions have brought me to the last moment of the post ere I have a minute to fill my paper – My so amiable namesake will write of France – and even of my poor Alex, if her dearest Mother is unhappily indisposed –

My next Letter shall try to make amends for this merely selfish scrawl – which I am sure you will forgive when you know the conflict of pros and cons that now harrass

your most affectionate

F B d'A.

I beseech you not to let your too ardent friendship disturb you about the Reviews and critics:[3] and I quite supplicate you to leave their authors to their own severities or indulgence. I have ever steadily refused all interference with public opinion, or private criticism. I am told I have been very harshly mangled – but I attribute it not to what alone would affect me, but which I trust I have not excited, personal enmity; I attribute it to the false expectation universally spread that the Book would be a picture of France – as well as to the astonishing *éclat*[4] of a work of 5 Volumes being *all* bespoken before it was published. The Booksellers, erroneously and injudiciously concluding the sale would so go on, fixed the rapacious price of 2 Guineas[5] – which again damped the sale – but why say *damped*, when it is only *their* unreasonable expectations that are disappointed? for they acknowledge that 3600 Copies are positively sold and paid before in the first half year? What must *I* be, if not far more than contented? I have not read, or heard, one of the Criticisms: my mind has been wholly occupied by grief for the loss of my dearest Father, or the inspection of his MSS. and my harrassing situation relative to my own proceedings. Why, then, make myself *black bile* to disturb me further? *No*; I will not look at a word – till my spirits and time are calmed and quiet and I can set about preparing a corrected Edition.[6] I will then carefully read all; and then – the blow to immediate feelings being over, I can examine as well as read, impartially, and with profit, both to my future surveyors and myself.

---

3. Although the initial reviews of *The Wanderer* were highly critical, some later ones were favourable.

4. *Lustre.*

5. The price £2. 2s. was unprecedented for a novel; the maximum for long novels was about £1. 10s. (*Camilla*, in 1796, cost only a guinea.)

6. FB's corrections for a third edition, never published, survive in an interleaved copy of the first edition (Berg Collection).

1814–1815

Waterloo

208. Letter to Princess Elizabeth *pre-15 December 1814*[1]

Madam

The high honour conferred upon me by the so condescindingly writen commission of your Royal Highness[2] would have impelled my immediate and most devoted acknowledgements, had I dared listen to the first impulse of gratitude and delight excited by your Royal highnesses gratious and partial goodness: but I have restrained my intusive wishes till I could give some account of my commission, which, alas! was executed only Yesterday!

A delay so singular, and which unexplained, must appear so unpardonable, forces me to assume courage for entering into a little narrative of the *pourquoi*.[3] And though it must be long and personal, I venture to trust in, the hereditary urbanity, which never judges unheard, of your Royal Highness, to forgive my egotism.

For 10 days after my happiest honours at Windsor, I was confined to my apartment at Richmond by my inveterate cold,[4] which, even then, required a week's slow travelling to bring me to Dover. From thence to Calais, our passage, though short, was so stormy, that it appeared to me an Hurricane, occasioned me such violent and unremitting sufferings, that when arrived, I was unable to walk on shore, and Mr d'Arblay hired me an escort, not a very military one! – of Fishermen, to carry me, by relays, on an arm chair to Dessein's Hotel. In our way, a Gentleman, touched by the almost lifeless state which I appeared to be in, stopt Mr d'Arblay, who walked by my side,

1. Letter Book copy by AA.
2. In a letter of 6 November 1814, the Princess had asked FB to deliver a note to Lady Melville in Toulouse; see *JL*, viii. 1 n. 1.
3. *Why.*
4. After visiting the royal family in November 1814, FB returned to her sister Charlotte's house at Richmond until her departure for France with AA, who had arrived in England in October.

to offer him some cordial medecine for me. Mr d'Arblay turned round to thank him; but while yet speaking, a female voice crying 'Gare!'[5] he hastily turned back, and perceived, but too late to save himself, a man, a monster, I had almost said! standing upright in a cart, which he drove rapidly upon him. Mr d'Arblay was not only renversé, the brancard[6] striking him upon his breast, but flung to some distance by the force of the blow. The wretch, who, no doubt, is one of the still existing Jacobins of the worst of times, had neither cried *Gare*, nor attempted to stop his cart; and neither Mr d'Arblay nor the gentleman whose unfortunate humanity caused this dreadful mischief had heard or heeded its approach. The man could have no personal enmity to Mr d'Arblay whom he had never seen: his action must have been merely the effect of general brutality; and of a nature instinctively at war with whatever appeared less gross and less vile than itself. He was loaded with execrations by the populace; but he escaped his merited punishment, as Mr d'Arblay, who was judged to be fatally wounded! occupied all the attention of the better part. Mr d'Arblay soon, however raised himself, for his head, I praise God! was uninjured; but his breast felt bent double, and he could not stand upright – I, still half dead with convulsive sickness knew nothing of this cruel accident, till sometime after we got to Dessein's, where Mr d'Arblay was put to bed, blooded, and attended by the military surgaon of Calais for several days. We then slowly reached Paris where I had at least the solace to see him under the care of the Prince of Surgeons Dr Larrey.

The commission with which I was honoured, and with which I had been so delighted, I am grieved to say lay all this time dormant. All the inquiries I could make relative to a banker at Toulouse were fruitless, as I had no means to discover the house employed by Lady Melville. I was forced therefore to wait till Mr d'Arblay could see the Viscomte d'Agoult his old intimate and faithful friend now first Equerry to S.A.R. Mme la Duchesse d'Angoulême[7] and high in confidence and favour. The Viscomte immediately sent me an inclosure for the Comte de Ferrand, Post Master General, with an injunction that the letter should be safely delivered into Lady Melville's own hands.

May I, Madam, hope that your Royal Highness will gratiously pardon this long history? May I venture to even lengthen it by adding that Mr d'Arblay is now nearly recovered? But that this succession of retarding

5. 'Watch out!'

6. Knocked over . . . shaft.

7. Antoine-Jean, vicomte d'Agoult, first equerry to Marie-Thérèse-Charlotte, duchesse d'Angoulême. S.A.R. (Son Altesse Royale): 'Her Royal Highness'.

events has brought us into so bad a season, that Dr Larrey is of opinion it is too late for me to travel further; and that therefore, I shall spend this Winter at Paris?[8] I have been and still am, too disordered to dare think, as yet, of my presentation to Mme la Duchesse d'Angoulême, which will, nevertheless take place as soon as I am well enough to equip myself rather less like one of the Witches in Macbeth. I am almost surprised at the courage with which the sweetness and condescension of Your Royal Highness has inspired me; and I am half frightened lest it should appear like presumption. But no. The ties that so long have bound me, with an attachment as ardent as it is dutiful, to my beloved Royal Mistress, and to all your Royal Highnesses, must be my guarantee, that an even fresh devotion is excited by this fresh mark of extream goodness with which your Royal Highness has deigned to distinguish her who has the honour to subscribe herself with the deepest respect

Madame

Your Royal Highnesses

Most faithful, most grateful

and most obedient humble

Servant

Signed FB. d'Arblay

209. Waterloo Journal *27 April and 13 May 1815*[1]

Our last Entertainment here was a Concert, in the great public and very fine Room appropriated for Musick or Dancing. The celebrated Madame Catalani had here a Benefit.[2] The Queen of the Netherlands[3] was present: not, however, in State, though not incognita: and – the King of Warriours, Marshall Lord Wellington, surrounded by his *Etat Major*,[4] and all the officers and first persons here, whether Belgians, Prussians, Hanoverians, or English. I looked at him watchfully all Night, and was charmed with every turn of

---

8. FB had earlier planned, on the advice of AA and Dr Larrey, to spend the winter in the South of France; see *JL*, vii. 473.

1. From a voluminous journal, covering 11 February to July 1815, but written in 1823; see *JL*, viii. 339. With Napoleon approaching Paris after his escape from Elba, FB took flight for Brussels on 19 March. There on 6 April she was joined by AA, on military leave.

2. On 27 April, the Italian opera singer Angelica Catalani gave a concert at the Great Concert Room in Brussels; see *JL*, viii. 149 n. 9.

3. Queen Wilhelmina.

4. *General staff.*

his countenance, with his noble and singular physiognomy, and his Eagle Eye, and Aquiline, forcible Nose. He was gay even to sportiveness all the Evening, conversing with the officers around him on terms of intimacy and pleasantry. He never was seated, not even a moment, though I saw seats vacated to offer to him frequently. Whether this was an etiquette that he thought respectful for the presence of the Queen, to whose courteous inclination of the head he bowed with profound reverence; or whether it was simply from a determination to deny himself every species of personal indulgence, when he knew not how soon he might require an almost supernatural strength to endure the hardships of a Commander in chief during the great impending Battle to which every thing looked forward, I cannot tell. But he seemed enthusiastically charmed with Catalana, ardently applauding whatsoever she sang, – except the Rule Britania:[5] and there, with sagacious reserve, he listened in utter silence. Who ordered it I know not; but he felt it was injudicious, in every country but our own, to give out a Chorus of Rule, Brittania! Britannia, Rule the Waves! – And when an Encore was begun to be Vociferated from his officers, he instantly crushed it, by a commanding air of disapprobation; and thus offered me an opportunity of seeing how magnificently he could quit his convivial familiarity for imperious dominion, when occasion might call for the transformation.

When the full order arrived from Gand,[6] establishing the mission of M. d'Arblay at Luxembourg,[7] he decided upon demanding an audience of the Duke of Wellington, with whom he thought it necessary to concert his measures. The Duke received him without difficulty and they had a conference of some length, the result of which was that his Grace promised to prepare Blucher,[8] the Great Prussian General, then actually at Luxembourg, for aiding the scheme.

M. d'Arblay himself also wrote to Blucher; but before any answer could be returned, a new ordonnance from the Duke de Feltre[9] directed M. d'Arblay to hasten to his post without delay.

13. May, 1815 – My best friend left me, to begin his Campaign; left me, by melancholy chance, upon his Birth Day.[10] What a Day to me! his shattered health, and fading Form for-ever before my Eyes, with the con-

---

5. Patriotic song, written by James Thomson for Arne's masque *Alfred* (1740).
6. Ghent, the provisional court of Louis XVIII.
7. To enlist deserters from Napoleon's army.
8. Field Marshal Gebhard von Blücher, Commander-in-Chief of the Prussian army.
9. The French Minister of War.
10. 13 May was AA's 61st birthday. He had never recovered from the cart accident.

sciousness that a martial sense of duty, and an innately irrepressible bravery, would listen to no prudence, would yield to no pain, would be sensible to no danger, that would try to spare him from any risk, any exertion, or any difficulty, by pointing out his time of life, his enfeebled frame, or his harrassed nerves and Constitution. He would think only, I well knew, of what was Right to be Done, without any sort of reference to his sufferings in its performance. –

I could not that day see a human Being; I could but consecrate it to thoughts of Him who had just left me – yet who from Me never was – never can be mentally absent, – and of our poor Alexander, thus inevitably, yet severely cast upon himself. –

210. From Letter to Alexandre d'Arblay *26 June 1815*

BRUXELLES.

Ce Lundi,

Ce Blessed Lundi[1]

Why have I not a Balloon to be the first to tell you this enchanting news! – or, rather, Wings to fly to you with it myself! Buonaparte has yielded to Lord Wellington! ——[2]

The particulars – how, which way, &c, are told too variously for building upon their correctness – but the Fact seems undoubted – seems, I am compelled to say, for nothing official has been here printed. The sleepiness of this quiet and good, but most drowsy and hum drum people exceeds belief: Especially when I consider que les Francs et les Belges came from one parent stock, i.e., the *Germains*.

O Mon Ami! will not Peace now re-visit us! — My hand shakes – and my spirits are agitated past all description, with an inward fear that all this will not be confirmed. O for an English Gazette! –

The whole City, in spite of its apathy, looked smiling, and even, some few, grinning with contented joy, as I walked out early. I except some others, evidently and gloomily overset. But these last are few. The people of this house, and every shop-keeper had heard the news, though without any positive authority.

1. This Monday, this Blessed Monday.
2. Napoleon had been defeated at the Battle of Waterloo (18 June 1815) and abdicated on 22 June, but he had not 'yielded' to Wellington. He would surrender to the British government at the port of Rochefort on 15 July.

But, about noon, I had a visit from M. de Beaufort[3] – who came, kindly smiling himself, to bring me the first of the news. He had *just* learnt it, at the Commandants' – M. le Colonel Jones.[4] His account was

That Buonaparte had sent to the Duke propositions, by an officer General. *First* To Abdicate, in favour of his Son and a Regency: or *secondly*, in favour of Prince Eugene, the great favourite of the Emperor of Russia; *thirdly*, In favour of the Duke of Orleans![5]

The Duke sent him word he must yield at Discretion, or Fight. He had nothing to do with *Abdicating*, for he was Nothing! He *had* already Abdicated, when he was Emperor.

The Army then sent a deputation, demanding a Truce to prepare a Peace, for sparing the further effusion of human blood.

The Duke answered, Their King might spare it, when reseated on his Throne; but that *for Them*, and *From* Them, the application was now too late.

211. Letter to Alexandre d'Arblay *1 July 1815*

Ah mon ami – qu'êtes vous donc devenu et que n'ai-je de vos nouvelles?[1] Have you quitted Treves?[2] – could not François[3] – if you were too hurried, write one line? – I am a prey to the most terrible uneasiness and so must remain till Monday! for tomorrow there is no Post. I will send this – since you bid me continue writing to Treves – but know not how to add any thing more –

Yet – should you be there, and have no quicker intelligence I ought to tell you That I read last night the King's Proclamation, drawn up by M. Talyrand,[4] which is perfect!

He will pardon *All* but Individuals peculiarly culpable – of those he will select very *few*, and only the *worst*, to banish or bring to Justice.

He declares he has *himself* forbidden *All the Princes of his house* to accompany the Allies into France

3. Jean-Baptiste de Beaufort, old military friend of AA.
4. Leslie Grove Jones, British commandant at Brussels.
5. Napoleon's infant son, the King of Rome; Eugène-Rose de Beauharnais, his stepson; Louis-Philippe, duc d'Orléans.

1. Ah my friend – what has become of you and why have I no news of you?
2. Trèves or Trier, German town near the border with Luxembourg, where AA had been posted.
3. AA's valet.
4. Louis XVIII's Proclamation of 28 June, countersigned by Talleyrand.

And has himself restrained the ardour of all his faithful adherents, who would have fought for him *avec l'Etranger*.[5]

Buonaparte is said to be trying to escape to Havre, or some sea port, with all his surviving officers.[6]

If he succeed, – in 2 years he will again lead us the same dance of death he has so frightfully taught us at this moment. The numbers of dead, whether of Conquerors or Conquered, have not yet been counted! – nor even all the wounded – some are still on the field of Battle, where they are dressed, – their wounds, I mean! – while waiting for carriages, which are constantly on the road!!

Brussels is a Walking Hospital! Maimed and Wounded unhappy men of War are met at every step, either entering, carried in Casts, from the Fields of Battle, or the adjoining Villages, to be placed in Infirmaries, Work houses, Churches, and also at private houses. Every body is ordered to receive all their Dwelling can hold. It is even written on the doors of most houses how many are already refuged in them. The Belgians behave with the utmost humanity to the miserable objects of fallen Ambition, – or contentious struggles on either side. Almost all the Natives prepare to run from the City, in apprehension of some Contagious fever, from the Multitude of Sick! –

O Write! my best beloved! my noble husband! Write – or make Francois write –

At so fearful a time not to have certainty of your health and your position is Agony! nothing less, – mon trop cher Ami![7]

212. Letter to Georgiana Waddington *3 July 1815*

Bruxelles. –

How is it that my dear Mary can thus on one side be fascinated by the very thing that, on the other, revolts her? how be a professed and ardent detester of Tyranny; yet an open and intrepid admirer of a Tyrant? O had you spent, like me, 10 years within the control of his unlimited power, and under the iron rod of its dread, how would you change your language! by a total reverse of sentiment! yet was I, because always innoffensive, never molested: as safe There, *another* would say, as in London; but *you* will not say so; the

---

5. *Against the foreigners.*
6. Napoleon had left Paris for Rochefort on 29 June.
7. My too dear friend!

safety of deliberate prudence, or of retiring timidity, is not such as would satisfy a mind glowing for freedom like yours: it satisfies, indeed, no *mind*, it merely suffices for *bodily* security. It was the choice of my Companion, not of my Taste that drew me to such a residence. Personally, for the reason I have assigned, I was always well treated, and personally I was happy: but you know me, I am sure, better than to suppose me such an Egotist as to be really happy, or contented, where Corporal Liberty could only be preserved by Mental forbearance – i.e. subjection.

The panic impressed upon all the Inhabitants, whether natives or visitors, by the late Invasion, and its consequences, would have cured any one not absolutely incurable of a revolutionary taste; and you have too fair and too liberal propensities ever wilfully to blind yourself against visible facts, or to be deaf against powerful, yet candid conviction. The Belgians have for so many Centuries been accustomed to sanguinary conflicts, and violent, or mercenary, change of masters, that I really thought, from the placid state in which, when seeking here an asylum, I found them, that they were utterly indifferent to the result of the neighbouring struggle, and would just as willingly have fallen again into the hands of Buonaparte as not. They never, of their own accord, opened upon the subject, nor considered nor treated us poor fugitives but as common visitors. I imagined they had gone through too many political changes, to deem one, or two, more or less, an addition worth ruffling their serenity. And Buonaparte, whether from hearing of this passive philosophy, or whether from motives yet unknown, certainly expected not alone that they would not oppose, but that, on the contrary, they would join him. This idea, with respect to the Belgian troops, was indeed, spread, and most alarmingly, here. The Duke of Wellington was warned by several persons not to trust them: and it is generally understood That he determined They should neither be trusted in front, lest they should join the Enemy, nor in the Rear, lest they should run away from their friends. Nevertheless, when the day of the most bloody battle that ever Rival Warriors fought, arrived, I found I had taken the calm of their Natures for indifference to their fate; for when a cry was shouted through the streets That The French were come! That *Buonaparte et les Français étoient à la porte de la Ville!*[1] – the consternation that ensued, the horrour that was depicted on every Countenance, shewed they were alive at least to the evils that menaced themselves – and how few, how very few are really awake to any other! We do not appear to be asleep, because our Eyes are wide open; but dormant

---

1. *Bonaparte and the French were at the City gate!*

lies every feeling that belongs to whatever is not animated, in some or other shape, by Self, except in the very, very few whom Nature has gifted – or condemned – 'to feel for other's woes'.[2] – –

213. Letter to James Burney *10 July 1815*

Bruxelles

Little as I am habituated to the liberality of giving two Letters – (or even, I am afraid! one Letter) – for one, I am indebted to my dear Brother for so much more solid kindness than Epistolary punctuality, that I will not let an opportunity of again thanking him pass gracelessly by. Besides, if Letters are to be considered in their best light, i.e. as marks of Friendship, – how many have you not written me – of late – without holding a Pen? I would not exchange, for Value, your hospitality and kindness to my Alexander, for the best collection of Epistles left by Cicero, Pliny, or even Madame de Sevigné.[1] Nor is even this the only way in which my heart has received, and welcomed, the *Billet doux* which my Eyes have never read: that same Alex had given me a *trait* of your truly brotherly feelings upon the harsh treatment given to my poor Wanderer, in nearly the only Difficulty in which I had not myself involved her,[2] that came home to my bosom, which silently, but warmly, even from this distance, embraced you, my dear James. Nevertheless, sincerely as I am sensible to your animation in favour of this my youngest Child, I am myself gifted, happily, with a most impenetrable apathy upon the subject of its criticisers. I have never read, nor chanced to meet with one word upon the subject. I never expected it would have any immediate favour in the World; and I have not yet shut out from my spying Glass a distant prospect that it may share, in a few years, the partiality shewn to its Elder sisters.[3] Much was against its chances upon its first coming out. There is no such Foe to public success as high Expectation, though there is no such Friend to personal emolument. And Here, Expectation was

---

2. Allusion to Pope's 'Universal Prayer', l. 37: 'Teach me to feel another's Woe'.

1. The Romans Cicero and Pliny and the seventeenth-century Parisian Mme de Sévigné, all famous for the quality of their letters.
2. Alluding to the novel's subtitle, 'Female Difficulties'. Alexander had apparently, in a missing letter, sent FB a copy of James's letter to William Hazlitt of 17 May 1815. Offended by Hazlitt's harsh review of *The Wanderer* in the *Edinburgh Review* for February 1815, James announced 'the termination of our acquaintance' (*JL*, viii. 317 n. 1).
3. *Evelina*, *Cecilia* and *Camilla*.

founded upon Impossibilities, or Improprieties: half the Public expected, from my long residence in France, Political anecdotes, or opinions, and the other half expected, from the title of the Work and my own unsettled life, The History of the Author. The first Volume, nevertheless, was received by the reigning Critical Judges, with almost unbounded applause; – Sir James Macintosh, Lord Holland, Mme de Stael, Sir Samuel Romilly, Lord Byron, Mr Godwin,[4] – and others whose names I do not recollect, sung its panegyric, but Then, the illusion of their own Fancies was not over; one party was not yet quite sure That the Wanderer might not still appear in the Writer: or, rather, the Writer in the Wanderer; and the other, had not yet lost all hope that the scene would change to The Continent, and bring the Reader into the midst of the political bustle. The second volume undeceived both parties: and thence began a Disappointment which, – *I hope*, carried with it a propensity to be displeased through the rest of the Work. Time only can shew the Flattery, or the reality of this idea. If it be true, some future eminent Reader, who, some years hence, shall take it in hand, without any reference, or even knowledge of the circumstances attending its first publication, and who will read, therefore, without prepared prejudice, or partiality, will pronounce '*This is the Genuine* –' Or – '*This is a Spurious* sister of the Young Damsels who were previously honoured with public approbation.'

I ought not, also, to omit another point that has made against any immediate success in Fame – and that is, its immediate success in profit. There can be no doubt that the Bookseller's price did not more widely raise Expectation and Curiosity, than Enmity and Jealousy.

All these concomitant matters, however, will die – and the Book will either Revive, or Expire from the cool and unbiassed Judgement of those who may read it, without thinking of its Critics; or even of its Author, hereafter.

If, at the same time, the First volume had not met with such favour, when seen by *Stealth*, and ere the Plan of the Work, or the Premium of the publishers were known, I should not encourage this notion. But I think nobody, impartially, will pronounce The First Volume to be the Best – Ergo –

But enough; I should not have entered thus largely upon this egoistic subject, had not the interest taken in it by my dear James repeatedly reached me. And, I have been writing so long, and so many Letters upon the state

4. Romilly was a law reformer with an interest in French politics; William Godwin, anarchist and radical philosopher.

of affairs here, that I am not sorry to be called to some other topic; and the less, as a laconic statement up to the moment will save you from reading, or hearing a repetition of all my other Letters.

214. Journal for *22 July 1815*[1]

Arrived at Bonn, the Garde, or directeur, called, I think, le Conducteur, took all the charge of my Passport, according to the promise of my French-Prussian.[2] Bonn is a Fortress, and the residence of the *ci-devant* Prince Bishop of Cologne. The Palace is said to be a quarter of a mile in length. How modest and moderate are the Palaces of England compared with those of even the minor Potentates of the Continent. I saw it not, however; I had not even any desire for the sight, nor for any other. We stopt at the Post office. The house was quite magnificent. But I only entered the Breakfast room, where I had the pain of hearing that we should remain at Bonn two Hours. My fellow travellers, gay and social, ordered a festive repast: I was so fearful of wasting any of my small remaining cash that I only took a Roll and a Dish of Coffee, at a table to which I stood, and then said I would wile away the time by walking in the Garden.

The Garden was of a tolerable size, and really pretty; but some Company from this vast Inn soon broke in upon my solitude, and I therefore stole off, resolving to take a view of the Town –

I went out by a large Iron Gate, but could not venture to ask for a Guide, in a poverty where every shilling became important. The street was entirely without mark or interest, and nearly without any inhabitants that were visible. The late absorbing War made that the case in every town I passed through. I walked strait on, till I came to a large market place. It seemed to me, after the narrow and dim and empty street, very gay, busy, populous and alive. I think it was a sort of Fair. As I saw numerous avenues to it, I stopt at the corner, to fix myself some mark for finding again my way back. And this was not difficult; for I soon observed an 'Unhappy Divinity stuck in a Nich';[3] and one as ludicrous as any mentioned in her passage through

1. From FB's journal, written September 1824–July 1825, recording her hazardous journey to join the wounded AA. She travelled through Liège, Aix-la-Chapelle, Cologne and Bonn, and to Coblenz and to Trèves. Having left Brussels on 19 July 1815, she arrived at Bonn on the 21st.
2. A French police officer employed by the Prussians at Cologne; see *JL*, viii. 493–4. The 'Palace' is a baroque palace, built 1717–30.
3. Anstey, *An Election Ball* (1776), Letter II, l. 31: 'Unhappy Divinity Sticks in a Nitch'.

Germany by Lady Mary Wortley Montagu.[4] It was a short, thick, squabby little personage, whose Wig, Hose, Sandals, Coat, Waistcoat, and trowsers were of all the colours – save those of the Rainbow – for, far from having the bright hues of that 'Radiant token,'[5] the gaudy, but most dingy, muddy and vulgar full Blues, Reds, and yellows of each part of the Dress, and of the figure, seemed struggling with each other for which should be most obstrusively prominent – not graduating off into shades of evanescent softness. The Wig, I think, was blue; the Coat, Red; the Waistcoat, Yellow; the Sandals Green; the Trowsers, purple; and the Hose, pink. I am not certain, at this distance of time, that I give the right colours to their right places; I am only sure that the separate parts of the dress employed, separately, those colours, and that what rendered them almost as prophane as they were risible, were some symbols – either of Golden rays round the Wig, or of a Crucifix at the back, shewed that this hideous little Statue was meant for a young Jesus.[6]

I now strolled about the vast Market-place without fear of being lost. I observed, however, little besides Cattle, Toys, vegetables, crockary ware and cakes. There were Forms innumerable, and almost all covered by seated women, very clean and tidy, with profusion of odd shaped white caps, but not one of them with a hat. At other parts, there might perhaps be other merchandize. The whole was eminently orderly. Nothing like a quarrel, a dispute, or even any grouping for Gossiping. This is not, I imagine, a general picture of a German Market-place; for [nothing] could be general, as nothing was natural. The issue of the War, still to All uncertain, while the Army on the Loire, and the Corps of Grouchy[7] had not submitted, appeared to all the common Inhabitants in the vicinity of France to await but some private project of Buonaparte for ending in his triumph. In all the few places I visited at this period I found this belief predominant, or, rather, Universal; and that alike from the fears of his foes, and the hopes of his Adherents. Constraint, therefore, as well as consternation operated, as if by mute consent, in keeping all things, and all persons, tame, taciturn, and secretly expectant.

---

4. Lady Mary Wortley Montagu's letters, containing accounts of her travels in Germany in 1716, had been published in 1763. A five-volume edition of her *Works*, including letters, appeared in 1803. See Lady Mary Wortley Montagu, *Selected Letters*, ed. Isobel Grundy (1997).

5. Not identified.

6. The statue was apparently not of Christ but a representation of a rainbow; see *JL*, viii. 500 n. 30.

7. Emmanuel de Grouchy, head of the retreating Napoleonic army.

When I had taken a general survey of all that was within sight without venturing from the sides of the houses amongst the people, I looked for my Guide in the Nich, and returned to the Inn. There I heard that, from some Cause I could not comprehend, the Diligence[8] was still to remain two Hours longer. Unable to order any refreshment, I could not bring myself to enter any room for waiting so long a time. Again, therefore, I strolled out; and, having now seen all that led to the Right, I turned to the Left. I walked to the end of the street, without finding any thing to observe but common houses, without novelty, interest, or national peculiarity of any sort, and differing only from ours by having fewer windows, less regularity, and less chearfulness of aspect. In strolling leisurely back, I remarked, at the termination of a sort of lane, or outlet, something that looked like Ruins. I eagerly advanced towards them, and found myself on the skirts of a plain over laid with the devastations of half consumed and still crumbling fortifications. I mounted some old broken steps, protuberating here and there through masses of dust, mortar, and heaped old half-burnt bricks; but the view that presented itself was only terrible, from shewing the havock of War, without including any remains that were noble, elegant, or curious in architecture, or that mixed any emotions of admiration with those of compassion that necessarily are awakened by the sight of dilapidations, whether owing to the hostility of Time or of War.

When I had remained here till I was tired of my own meditations rather than investigation, for there was nothing to investigate, I descended my steps, to return to the Inn. But I then perceived two narrow streets, or lanes, so exactly resembling each other, that I could not discern any difference that might lead me to ascertain by which I had arrived: and I had turned in so many directions while surveying the Ruins, that, not having noticed a second street before I mounted them, I now knew not which way to turn.

Startled, I resolved to hasten down one of them at a venture, and then, if that should fail, to try the other.

This I did, and found myself in a long street, that might well be that which I sought, but I could espie in it no jutting Iron Gate: I therefore hurried back, and made the same experiments down the other lane. This, however, led me on to some other street that I was sure I had not seen.

With yet greater speed I regained my Ruins: but here a new difficulty arose. I saw a third strait passage, which had no more 'mark or likelihood'[9]

8. Public stagecoach.
9. Not identified.

than the two first. It might be, nevertheless, that this which had escaped me, was the Right; and I essayed it directly. The same failure ensued, and I remounted it.

Vainly I looked around me for help – Dirty and ragged little Children, of the lowest class, were playing about, and chattering in German, but, though I attempted to speak to them repeatedly, they could not understand a word I uttered, and ran, some laughing, others frightened, away.

Yet these poor little ones were all I met with in these lanes; which, as they lead only to a barren plain over run with Ruins, were unfrequented.

I was now dreadfully alarmed, lest I should miss the Diligence: and I speeded again to the long street in search of any one who could give me some succour.

I espied a good looking man, who was lame, at some distance. I was with him in an instant, and entreated him to direct me to the Hotel de la Diligence.

He seemed good naturedly sorry for the great perturbation in which I spoke, but shook his head, and shrugged his shoulders, in sign that he could not understand me.

I then saw a poor Woman – and made the same request; but with equal ill success.

Next I saw a Boy – the same story! – Then a Beggar – still the same!

From side to side, strait-forward and retrograding, I ran up to every soul I saw – speaking first in French, next in English, but meeting only with the lowest and most common Germans, who, like all other common Natives know only their vernacular tongue.

I could now only resolve to return to my Ruins, and in making them my rallying point, to start from them, and back again, till I had perambulated every street whatsoever that was in their neighbourhood.

But oh good Heaven! what now was my consternation! I had started up and down in so desultory and precipitate a manner that I could no longer find my way back to the Ruins! I had wandered, I have no knowledge how, from their immediate vicinity, and could not discover any one of the 3 avenues by which I had reached them. Turn which way I would, I met no possible informant; all the Men were in the various Armies; the higher sort of Women were fled from Bonn, or remained in their houses; and the lower sort were all, with the whole of the general population, in the market-place. At least so it was in the streets I patrolled, for nothing did I behold but the maimed, or Beggars, or Children. Most of those above probably would have known a few words of French. And some of these poor souls, when I addressed them, seemed very kindly concerned at my evident distress; yet with a calm, a composure that was wide from even striving to devize means for understanding or aiding me: and their enquiries, in their own dialect, were so insupportably slow and placid, that the moment I found my French not intelligible to them, I flew from their speech as I would have fled from pestilence.

If I should be too late for the Diligence, I too well knew not another would pass for a Week: and even if I could here meet with a separate conveyance, the tales now hourly recounted of marauders, straggling Pillagers, and military Banditti, with the immense Forests, and unknown roads through which I must pass, made me tremble – as I now do, even now, 9 years after – at looking back to my position at this fearful moment.

Oh! this was, indeed, nearly, the most tortured crisis of misery I ever experienced! one only has been yet more terrible! – nay, a thousand and ten thousand – ten million of times more terrible, because – Alas! irretrievable! This, however, was a herald to my affrighted soul of what the other inflicted – To know my Heart's Partner wounded – ill – confined – attended only by strangers; – to know, also, that if here detained, I could receive no news of him; for the Diligence in which I travelled was the Mail: – to know the dread anxiety, and astonishment that would consume his peace, and corrode all means of recovery, when Day succeeding Day neither brought me to his side, nor yet produced any tidings why I was absent – Oh gracious Heaven! in what a distracting state was my Soul! – In a strange Country – without Money, without a Servant – without a Friend – and without Language! Oh never – never shall I forget my almost frantic agony! Neither can I ever lose the remembrance of the sudden transport by which it was succeeded when, in pacing wildy to and fro', I was suddenly struck by the sight I have already described of the Unhappy Divinity stuck in a Niche.

What rapture at that moment took place of anguish little short of Despair! – I now knew my way, and was at the Hotel with a swiftness resembling flight. And There – what a confirmation I received of the timely blessing of my arrival, when I saw that the Coach was just departing! The Horses harnessed, every passenger entered, and the Drivers with their whips in hand extended! – Oh my God! what an escape! and what thankful Joy and Gratitude I experienced!

Now then, at last, my heart became better tuned. A terror so dreadful averted, just when so near its consummation, opened me to feelings akin to happiness. I was now on my right road; no longer travelling Zig Zag, and as I could procure any means to get on, but in the strait road, by Coblentz, to the City which contained the Object of all my best hopes – solicitude – and impatience.

And Now it was that my Eyes opened to the beauties of Nature; now it was that the far famed Rhine found justice in these poor little Eyes, which, hitherto, from mental preoccupation, or from Expectations too high raised, had refused a cordial tribute to its eminent merit; unless, indeed, its Banks, till after Bonn, are of inferiour loveliness. Certain it is, that from this time, till my arrival at Coblentz I thought myself in Regions of enchantment.

The Rhine from hence flows so continually through lofty Mountains, and winds in such endless varieties, that it frequently appears to be terminating in a Lake; and those who sail upon it must often believe themselves inevitably destined to land, as the turnings are so rounded, that no prolongation of the River is apparent. And scarcely is there a Reach that does not exhibit some freshly charming View. Mountains, Towers, Castles, Fortifications half demolished; interspersed with Trees, Hills, valleys, plains, elevations covered with vineyards, thick Woods of Lime Trees, country seats, new plantations, and pictoresque villages. The Houses were highly ornamental to the prospect, being mostly white, covered with blue slate; looking brilliant, however diminutive, because saved from all soil by the purity of the surrounding air.

At first, we had constantly *The Seven Mountains* to form a noble repose for our Eyes as the boundary of the principal prospect: afterwards, we passed through such stupendous mountains on each side, that the Rhine and its Banks, which constituted our Road, made the whole of the valley; while stately Rocks, of striking forms, and hanging woods, of exquisite beauty, invited, on one side, our gaze and admiration; and prospects eternally diversifying varied our delighted attention on the other. Now, mounting some steep ascent, we saw this fine River winding perpendicularly beneath us; now descending again, the Rocks and Woods again seemed to embower us. Almost every eminence was crowned with an ancient Castle or Fortress, whose falling Turrets and scattered fragments, moss grown, and widely spread around, gave as much interest and as great a charm to the scene, as they caused, on the other hand, sorrow, resentment, and even horror to the reflections: for these Ruins were not the indispensable effect of all conquering, irresistible Time, to which we All bow, or, rather, are bowed down, but of wanton, aggressive, invading War, and of insatiable ambition.

215. Letter to Viscountess Keith *20 August 1815*[1]

Treves

In the midst of the almost continual evils or mischiefs that, of late, harass or afflict me, I feel not only a joy but a pride that it is the Partner the noble Partner of my dear and most loyal Lady Keith[2] that gives, and in so lordly a manner gives the word of command to the late tyrant of Nations and Sovereign of Kings you would be pleased to see how Lord Keith is honoured on the continent, for not answering his letter, for declining to discuss his mock objections, and for refusing to accord him a private conference. All here are quite indignant against those who treat him as a royal prisoner, not a perjured usurper. I wish excessively to know wether you saw him and How? Surely when curiosity seemed so universally awakened, you alone Lady of the Lord of the ascendant, have not been, of all Eve's daughters, the sole to disdain hereditary propensities?

I was called hither by a most melancholy accident that befal Mr d'Arblay of a kick of a Horse upon the leg, that for the present, has wholly lamed him. The difficulties with which, and through which I got hither, should I ever be so happy as to be able to relate them to you in the dear tight little Island,[3] will amuse as well as interest you. The surrounding Country was still infested with rambling Buonapartists and the Prussians, our dear Allies have conducted themselves with such imperious presumption upon the rights of conquest that to pass through any town of Belgium or Germany in which they have a military commander, is nearly as difficult for their *bounden friends*, as for their *hostile enemies*; Hostile ennemies sounds a *platitude*; but how happy where it for society, had we as far as Hostile means warlike, no other! Yet though gay *now* to relate, my adventures as they *occured* were even tremendous, and I already look back to them with some surprise that I weathered the storm without more mischief. At one place, Liege, I had omitted to prepare a passport, having in the hurry of fright with which I set out upon my expedition, totally forgotten to sollicit one from Bruselles. Nor will you marvell, when I inform you that the letter[4] which acquainted me

1. Letter Book copy by AA, who mistakenly dated it 'Avril' (April).

2. Queeney Thrale had married Lord Keith, who negotiated the terms of Napoleon's exile to St Helena.

3. The phrase, from a song in Thomas Dibdin's play *The British Raft* (1797), occurs frequently in FB's letters and journals.

4. From AA to FB's friend Mme de Beaufort; see *JL*, viii. 477.

with the accident that had happened to Mr d'Arblay was only delivered to me at about 3 o'clock, and that I set out that very evening, between 6 and 7 and had every thing to prepare, bills to pay, appartments to resign, Banker to demand money of, whom I missed twice and Friends to take leave of, who thought me so mad for undertaking, so circumstanced, and at Such perilous moment, such a journey, that I was obliged to *hide* myself, literaly, to avoid their terrified importunity that I would relinquish my Theme.

1815–1818

Final Years with D'Arblay

216. Letter to Frederica Locke and Amelia Angerstein *18 October 1815*[1]

Dover

Last night, my ever dear Friends, we arrived once more in Old England.[2]

I write this to send the moment I land in London. I cannot boast of our health – our looks – our strength – but I hope we may recover a part of all when our direful fatigues, mental and corporeal, cease to utterly weigh upon and wear us.

We shall winter in Bath. The waters of Plombières[3] have been recommended to my poor *Boiteux*, but he has obtained a *Congé*[4] that allows this change. Besides his present utter incapacity for military service, he is now, unavoidably on the *Retraite* list,[5] and the King of France permits his coming over, not alone without difficulty, but with wishing him a good journey, through the Duc de Luxembourg, his Captain in the *Gardes du Corps*.[6]

Adieu dearest *Both*! Almost I embrace you in dating from Dover. Had you my letter from Treves? I suspect *Not* – for my melancholy new history would have brought me your kind condolence: or, otherwise, *that* missed *me*. Our letters were almost all intercepted by the Prussians while we were there. Not *one answer* arrived to us from Paris, save by private hands –

My kindest love to my dear Lady Martin.[7] I waited a happy moment to write her my congratulations – alas! – I have been persecuted by disaster

1. Copy by Charlotte Barrett.
2. With the lamed AA now retired from the French army, and at the urging of their son, the d'Arblays had determined that their 'future fixed Residence was England' (*JL*, viii. 539).
3. Plombières-les-Bains, French spa.
4. *Lame man . . . leave.*
5. List of *retirees*.
6. *The King's Bodyguard.*
7. Mary Augusta Locke had married Rear-Admiral Sir George Martin the previous May.

almost from the time I left England. – Flights – illness – terrors – and grievous accidents have followed, or met me at every step. –

217. From Letter to Princess Elizabeth *late November 1815*[1]

Madam

Was it a mistake? an airy delusion of self flattery? or did Your Royal Highness indeed deign to indicate a desire that, when settled at Bath, I should again have the Honour of putting forth some sign of life? – Was it also, merely a dream of Fancy that her Royal Highness the Princess Augusta sweetly expressed a similar wish? and is it my imagination alone that has created – or rather, my soothing memory that retains the same gracious indication condescendingly flowing from the lips of Her Majesty?[2] – Wherever there is doubt, our wishes take the lead to bring the balance to their own side. 'Tis therefore I presume to again take up my pen.

Settled nevertheless, we are not yet, for Mrs Bourdois one of my nieces who is a resident at Bath, deceived in her idea of our circumstances by the restoration of Mr d'Arblay to the rank of General, and ignorant of the deranged state of the French finances, which takes off all immediate security, even for half-pay, had engaged expensive appartments for us, in River's Street, that we are now hastening, in prudence to relinquish.[3] We shall not however be *bien à plaindre*[4] in the change for we have found others, that while better suited to our income, are more consonant to our tastes, from being open to one of the surrounding Hills that form the peculiar character of this marvellous City. I have been already 4 times at Bath, and every new visit presents new wonders that gaily invite and richly recompense a new survey. It is at this very time, though near the end of November, in a state of luxurious beauty that would baffle description, and almost surpass even the ideal perfection of a Painter's fancy. Hills rising above Hills, here smiling with verdure, there shadowed by woods, here undulating to catch the Eye to distant prospects, and there striking with noble edifices, terminate almost every street, and spread in broad exilarating views before every Crescent, with a variety of attraction, from local positions or accidents, that are endless

1. Letter Book copy by AA.
2. The d'Arblays arrived in Bath from London on 2 November. Princess Elizabeth had informed FB, in a letter of 28 December 1814, that the Queen approved of their correspondence.
3. The d'Arblays moved to 23 Great Stanhope Street on 29 November.
4. *Much to be pitied.*

in their effects to elevate, or please. Our admiration never tires, though our powers to gratify it, by continually mounting or discending, are by no means equally invulnerable to fatigue.

We have, as yet from a desire, after the turbulent scenes in which we have, per force, been engaged to enjoy complete repose, lived in utter Seclusion, save from one of my nieces,[5] and the *cy-devant* Augusta Lock, eldest daughter of my dearest old Friend, who is here with her husband Sir George Martin. They appear to be perfectly contented with the experiment they have recently made. Sir George seems amiable; sensible, and well bred, and Lady Martin looks gay and happy.

This place, with regard to superfine visitors, fills slowly and the season is expected not only to be late, but thin, of company, from the many families that are rambling abroad. Neither prudence, nor misfortune, apprehension nor expense can cure John Bull of his fidgetty restlessness to see – how the World goes on beyond Seas – though almost always with a disposition to dispise all he may behold, and murmur, nay groan till he return. I speak of old time staunch and Sturdy John Bulls – not of the modern young *Jackys* his spurious offspring – whose prejudices, on the contrary, take a directly opposite turn.

The Waters we have not yet tried, the journey having opened a small wound that is now under the preparatory care of Mr Hay[6] an eminent Bath apotichary, who thinks however that the pump will in a short time be very efficacious. I have the pleasure to learn that several of the old Friends I left here when – an hundred years ago – I spent 3 months at Bath with the *cy-devant* Mrs Thrale, and the present Lady Keith, are still residents of this Town – of which the population from the proofs of its salubrity, encreases annually.

Mr Hay has just informed us that within these last 7 or 8 years, the *Inhabitants* are augmented from 27 to 37000 –! The flux of *visitors* whether for health or pleasure, who only come to go, bears the same proportion of added abundance. When we are fixed in our more permanent abode, I mean to cast off so much of my *sauvagerie*, as may fit me for again hailing the 'Wights of other times!'[7] if their memories have not played me false.

---

5. Sophia Burney, sister of Hannah Maria Bourdois and daughter of Esther.
6. George Edmund Hay.
7. Not identified.

218. Letter to Viscountess Keith *post 16 December 1815*[1]

If I trust, – as How can I do otherwise? to your constant kindness in thus beginning *first* upon my health and next upon my welfare, in that of my Partner, I am sure I should proceed thirdly – vellum like[2] – to speak of Mrs Piozzi.

Already when I was in England, I related I believe the circumstances that brought about again an opening intercourse – i.e. the intimacy that had taken rise between her and my niece Marianne Francis, which occasioned various kind Messages, and finished by a visit *de sa part*[3] to me in Cheyne's Street, made by strange accident, on the only day I was absent from home in attendance at the Queen's house.[4] I returned it the next day . . . but she was already departed, for I believe Bath, or Dr Whalley's. There, all dropt; till I came hither.

Tired and worn, mind and body, I sought no one, nay I flew from everyone, on my arrival and for more than a month after, one of my nieces, who resides here,[5] excepted, and a daughter of my most valued friends Mr and Mrs Lock, who came, soon after me, to pass here a few weeks, for the health of her husband, Sir George Martin. She, of course, found me out – and I could not but recollect a phrase which my dear Lady Keith had repeated to me from one of my old letters, relative to the *goût*[6] which my friends have taken to espousing Admirals[7] – My niece, however, meantime met Mrs Piozzi at the Reverend Mr Thomas's,[8] where my arrival hither was talked of; and *Mrs Piozzi* said to *Mrs Thomas* she should be very glad to see me again. The first day therefore, that I made my first few visits here, to the two Miss Boudlers, Mrs Holroyd,[9] etc. I called upon Mrs Piozzi.[10] I sent up my card, that she might chuse or not to be visible, and to impede any personal mistake, as much we must both be changed since an absence

1. Letter Book copy by AA.
2. Alluding to Vellum, 'the methodical steward in Addison's play, *The Drummer* (1716), in which in early family theatricals she had played the part of Lady Truman' (*JL*, ix. 38 n. 2).
3. *By her.*
4. On 11 May 1813, when FB, staying with her sister Charlotte at Chenies Street, London, was on a visit to the Queen (*JL*, vii. 120–23).
5. Sophia Burney.
6. *Taste.*
7. Sir George Martin and Viscount Keith were admirals.
8. The Revd Josiah Thomas.
9. Frances Bowdler, her sister Henrietta Maria Bowdler and Sarah Martha Holroyd.
10. On 16 December 1815, as recorded in Hester Piozzi's diary.

of so many many years. For I had not once seen her since we met, accidentally, in going to the Royal Chapel at Windsor, when I belonged to the Queen's household.[11] She gave orders for my admittance; and received me in a small back room. She was in mourning, and stood up, stiff, silent, and with an air of petrifying coldness. I was moved, I own, strongly moved at her sight, by the remembrance of all her former fondness, for such only is the word adapted to describe her fervant regard, and the unequalled eagerness with which she sought, struggled rather, to have me incessantly in her sight; but though my first impulse was ready to throw me into her arms, her frigid mein and manner soon chilled every feeling, and restored me to a composure on a par whith her own. A few stammering words and embarrassed attempts at discourse, soon therefore were superseded by conversation on general subjects, tame, common and uninteresting. None of her native spirits broke forth, nothing that bordered upon gaiety, much less upon satyre; not a sally, not a repartee escaped her; she even seemed *consternated*, when I reminded her, incendentally of having called Mrs Whalley (the 1st)[12] the loathly lady, – and said she was *very sorry* she had so done! – with other things to the same effect, as if she were turned rank methodist, and held even playful mirth to be a sin!

Nevertheless I am told she is, by no means, thus solemn with others: it is possible, therefore, she was so with me only from a mixture of awkwardness with regret at her first sight of me since the death of her husband.[13] I stayed a full hour; but there was no brightening up on her side, though I tried that there should be on mine.

I have never seen her since! though she resides not above 20 houses in a strait line from my dwelling.[14] She has called, however, and I have returned her call; but we were both absent from our homes. You were not once mentioned, except *in a lump* with your sisters, in asking if I had not seen you all when I was in England last year.

---

11. In 1790; see selection 127.
12. Eliza Whalley, the first of Thomas Whalley's three wives, a wealthy widow.
13. Gabriel Piozzi had died in March 1809.
14. At 17 New King Street, very close to the d'Arblays' lodgings.

219. From Letter to Charlotte Barrett *16 May 1816*[1]

Great Stanhope Street,
Bath

Your anecdotes of the two B.'s, the two fugitive B.'s, were diverting and new to me. I should not much marvel if they should meet. Where can this trifler with all the Goods of life, with all the endowments of Nature, and all the means of enjoyment, better feed his splenetic speculations than by contemplating a yet greater and madder wilful victim at the violated shrine of long-favouring, but abused, and now exasperated Fortune? – should you not like to see their meeting, and the mingled curiosity and contempt with which they would survey each other. 'Mean fallen Conqueror!' cries one, 'that knows not how to die!'[2] – 'Vain Witling!' cries the other, 'that knows not how to live! –'

220. Letter to Alexander d'Arblay *5 June 1816*

Wednesday.
Stanhope street, Bath.

Are you ill, my dear Alex?
If so, beg your Friend –
    or your Apothecary –
    or your Gip – [1]
to write a line instantly,
and we will be with you immediately.

or

Has any disappointment or mischance annoyed your happiness, and sunk your spirits?
    If so, open your heart at once,

---

1. This paragraph alludes to a lost letter by Charlotte Barrett, containing anecdotes about Lord Byron and Napoleon Bonaparte. Byron had left England permanently on 25 April 1816, but did not meet Napoleon at St Helena.

2. 'In his *Ode to Napoleon Buonaparte*, published 16 Apr. 1814, Byron, disillusioned by the Emperor's abdication (11 April), had denounced his "ignobly brave" choice to "live a slave" instead of dying "as honour dies" ' (*JL*, ix. 136 n. 7).

1. Gyp: a college servant at Cambridge.

comfort and kindness are all that will be offered you: – sympathy, my
Alex, that will sooth and revive you –

But –

If you can have neglected to write,

or only have mislaid a Letter, and not searched for it –

then, indeed. Your own self-reproach –

upon reflection –

will tell you the reproaches you will merit from us: though even then, a
candid and immediate avowal will cancel them.

At all events – If You, or some Proxy – answer not by *return of Post*,
My suspense and uneasiness will make *Me instantly* address Mr Chapman[2]
or Dr Davy.

221. From Letter to Alexandre d'Arblay *28 September 1816*[1]

Rien de si étonnant que ce que vous me dites de Mlle Jarjayes.[2] I have often
heard of simple and natural characters becoming coquettes and des *petites
maitresses*[3] – but of the reverse, never before. What you say of her accomplishments does not at all surprise me; and what you say of her beauty I could
not but expect. I thought in that point, – that captivating point, – she
promised already to be another Mme Recamier,[4] c.a.d. *perfect en son genre.*[5]
But natural! simple? – where was that Nature, where that simplicity concealed when we saw her in 1802?[6] Do you not remember her adjusting her
hair, and then turning round her pretty figure twenty ways, before a high
miroir, to see how she held her train, in a room full of company? and not
from childish ignorance, or thoughtlessness, but – to use your own words,
– *comme une lilliputienne aux airs de princesse?*[7] – Nevertheless, if this early idolatry

---

2. The Revd Benedict Chapman, Alexander's tutor at Gonville and Caius College. FB made
similar threats in several other letters to her son.

1. On 11 August, AA had returned to France on business. In a letter to FB (20 September), he
had proposed a match between Alexander and Augustine de Reynier de Jarjayes. Her father,
the chevalier de Jarjayes, had been a general in the French army.

2. Nothing is so astonishing as what you tell me of Mlle Jarjayes.

3. *Little hussies.*

4. Jeanne-Françoise Récamier, famous Parisian society hostess.

5. That is ('c'est à dire') *perfect of her kind.*

6. Now aged twenty, Augustine was only six when FB and AA saw her in 1802.

7. *Like a Lilliputian with the airs of a princess.*

of her own charms, by whatever means, is cured or curbed, she may have become as exciting and remarkable mentally as externally; for I can easily conceive that her solid principles may be of the first rate, from the high hereditary virtue which ought to run in her veins: But – supposing all to be as complete as her Fortune and Situation are brilliant – Can you – and is it possible – think Alexander *now* fit to propose to her? or that *She, now,* could make Alexander happy? Alas no! Alexander, when his Degree is taken, and his forced studies are at an end, will require to pass Through an *apprenticeship,* chez nous, and avec nous,[8] and his most partial Friends, to call him from his extraordinary and nameless excentricities, and fit him for the enjoyment of *participated* happiness. So early a marriage, though so much youth and beauty might excite an ardent passion, in his juvenile and fervant imagination, would lead soon to a life *faineant,*[9] under which, after a year, or two, at most, he would sink into inertion. He must see the world, and learn to bend his humour from his own exclusive pursuits ere he should become a husband and a Father. He may then be excellent as *both*; and I hope he will! but this young Creature, brought up in the lap of luxury and indulgence, and formed to create admiration where ever she is seen, would soon think herself lost, if not injured, with a sposo[10] who would not one time in twenty know whether or not she was in the room. *Time* must be given him, believe me, to learn that to *be* happy, he must try to *make* happy: and that his darling Mathematics must be his Second, not First consideration, to render felicity mutual in social and domestic life. At present, that he is working Seriously for his Degree, we have nothing to fear for his welfare. He has at this moment a strong predilection for Miss d'Alton,[11] whose dignified modesty and reserve make the smile she sometimes bestows upon him quite bewitching. But from this gentle flame there is No danger, and much good. I have religiously attended to your *motus,*[12] for his Degree would again be lost, were his attention – which he cannot *divide,* – called from it. But, at large, and in *general* discourse, he always declares he never will marry a *French Girl* – for his Father, *who would know how to manage one so much better than him,* always said he never thought of a wife till he came to England. He believes himself, also, *decided* to Live here, from an unalterable persuasion All Men abroad that are not *military,* are insignificant.

8. At our home, and with us.
9. *Idle.*
10. Husband (Italian).
11. Henrietta d'Alton, currently beloved by Alexander.
12. *Edict.*

222. From Letter to Viscountess Keith 7 *November 1816*[1]

Bath

To Lady Keith –

I have something to communicate curious, interesting and wonderful.

A few days after the visit[2] with which you so kindly indulged me, I paid my devoirs in Gay Street. Mrs Piozzi was out or denied – I left word I should have done myself the honour to call sooner, had I known she was returned to Bath. For a visit on my part had been due before her departure. She had been returned, they answered 3 weeks.

Nearly a month passed without *the retort courteous*[3] during which time I heard, from Mrs Holroyd, that the *house warming* had taken place. There were not above 30 persons and the principal attention of the Hostess was bestowed upon her physician (Dr Gibbs.)[4] Mrs Holroid was there and says Mrs Piozzi was all gayety, spirit, and agility, flying from room to room, as if but 15; and doing the honours with a vivacity that charmed every body. There was musick – – – – !! This surprises me greatly, as *she* could so well invite only to a *conversatione* and has done it so many many times, her remembrances and allusions extremely entertaining, and obliging to every body in the highest degree. Mrs Holroyd tells me she calls herself 80 years old? Surely that is impossible. Altered as she is, she does not look more than 70.[5] Her complection, indeed, I except: but her alertness, her voice her spirit, can never belong to an age so advanced.

Above a fortnight ago, a card was brought to me, (*Mrs Piozzi*, Gay Street). And when I made enquiry, I heard she had not asked for me, but merely *whether I lived there*, and then gave in the card and walked away. *This* I concluded was the *retort courteous* for what Alex had done *chez elle*,[6] to procure information whether or not she was in Bath. However, as I had no right to resent the imitation, I returned the call a week after, my card in my hand: but, to my great amazement, I was immediately admitted.

At the sound of my name, she came hastily from her Boudoir, to receive me in the *grand sallon*,[7] I was, as I always am, from a contrariety of conflicting

1. Only part of this letter survives, in a Letter Book copy by AA.
2. In September 1816.
3. Touchstone in Shakespeare, *As You Like It*, V. iv. 71.
4. George Smith Gibbes, fashionable Bath physician.
5. Hester Piozzi was seventy-five.
6. *At her house.*
7. *Drawing room.*

recollection, much removed from being natural, or at any ease: but she was so embarassed so agitated, she could not utter a word, but through the difficulty of respiration that belongs to an asthma. Both spoke and with civility of manner, but nothing was said by either that could be intelligible to the other.

I, however, soon recovered, for nothing had passed on my side to renew this perplexity and disturbance: nor can I guess any motive for it on hers, unless she has heard of our two meetings, and is sore at our unabated intimacy. I had nothing to fear from any examination having fully settled to be frank and explicit, if attacked, and never fail to mark my inviolable attachment for a true and steady friend, because one who so long was so dear to me, knows not how to forgive a sincerity she invited.

Upon enquiring after her health, she gave a very indifferent account of it, but said she had been obliged to leave off the Bath waters, though they had often agreed wonderfully with her. I asked whether her present indisposition was a renewal, or continuation of that which had preceded her Welsh Journey.[8] She had forgotten she had any indisposition at all, at that period! and when I reminded her of some circumstances that called it to her recollection, she answered, in her old manner, i.e. with a sort of gay contempt 'Oh, then? – was I ill then? – Why *that*, I suppose, was from ill humour.'

'If so,' quoth I, gay in my turn, 'take to the Bath waters again, and quaff them till you wash it all away, as speedily as ever you can!'

This, which was rather in *her* style than in mine, ended all embarassment. She took me to her Boudoir, seated me on the soffa, fetched me a hand screen, and entered into a most spirited conversation, with all her old facility, and pleasantry, and singularity. I exerted myself, in my turn, to the utmost, to let her see '*I feared no colours*',[9] and you would have been much amused, so would your dear lively sisters, for we talked, both of us, in Dr Johnson's phrase '*our best*'[10] but entirely as two strangers, who had no sort of knowledge or care for each other, but were willing each to fling and to accept the gauntlet, *pour faire la belle conversation*.[11] She interrogated me concerning France under Bonaparte; I made various enquiries of the state of Italy previous to the Revolution.[12] My anecdotes, which could not help

---

8. In June 1816, before Hester Piozzi left Bath for a stay at her country house, Brynbella, in Wales.

9. I.e. feared no foe: Feste in Shakespeare, *Twelfth Night*, I. v. 6.

10. Boswell's note to the entry for 22 September 1777 in *Life of Johnson*, iii. 193 n. 3.

11. *To make fine conversation.*

12. The Piozzis had travelled in Italy from 1784 to 1786, before the French Revolution.

being new to her, as they were chiefly personnal, seemed to excite all her curiosity; hers, which were recounted in her characteristic and most peculiarly entertaining manner, were to me highly interesting: yet was all far more like a dialogue, in some old Grammar between una Italiana and une françoise,[13] than like the talk of two old friends. A stranger would have supposed we had met for the first time, and without an acquaintance or one remembrance in common, or even that we had ever heard of each other till some accident had thus brought us together.

Nevertheless, I was so well pleased to find again her old gaiety and fertility and originality that I forgot both her dinner and my own, till it grew darkish, and I hastily rose to be gone, involontarily exclaiming:

'Heavens, how late it must be! they'll think me lost at home – but how could I help it! –'

I was flying off; but in a tone changed from all its light merriment, into a sound of affection, she cried:

'Thank you – and God bless you!'

Much surprised, and instantly touched, I turned back, and held out my hand. She gave me hers, and each hand again press the other. 'God bless you!' she again and still more impressively cried, 'and I thank you! –'

Can you wonder – I immediately embraced her; and then hurried away, while she uttered 'I shall wait upon you, and hope soon to see you again.'

223. Letter to Charles Burney *24 May 1817*

Bath

My dearest Carlos,

I beg You will be so good to substitute the word dutiful for filial, in the postscriptum.[1]

Our dear Hetty, and the good Mr Burney,[2] spent the day with us yesterday – or, rather, alas! with *me*, for my poor M. d'Arblay retired from us half the

---

13. An Italian woman and a Frenchwoman.

1. FB had been appointed to write the epitaph for a memorial to CB in Westminster Abbey, the precise wording of which had been much disputed by Charles and other family members. The change of 'Dutiful' for 'Filial' was made. Also in contention was whether all six surviving children should append their initials to the memorial or only the three who had paid the expenses: Charles, Frances and Esther (excluding James, Charlotte and Sarah Harriet). Ultimately, although all did subscribe, it was agreed that none of their names should be listed.

2. Charles Rousseau Burney.

time from pain and restlessness! – But Hetty informed me that Brother James had himself proposed a *general subscription*, though not – of course – an *equal* one, so as to obviate the lasting stigma of the *three* names: and therefore as This was the proposal, jadis;[3] of my dear Charles himself, let us abide by it. And take as *little*, not as *much*, as can content them, for reasons obvious. 'Let them come down with a Guinea each!' you cry, in a former Letter.[4] Hetty and I are most ready to cry 'done!'

———

Here comes your Letter of Yesterday. –

What! My Carlos, take Time to *meditate*, when to be superlative, and to please You are both to be done with so little effort? No! I shall turn my Paper, and comply with your demand incontinently.

And Thus, I hope this Tablet – far from being a source, most unnatural! of Discord, will be a new Bond of union amongst us All, by satisfying every one.

224. Letter to Maria Rishton *May 1817*

Bath

Long as it is since I have either written to or heard from my dear old Friend,[1] I can truly say short has ever been the period, during that time, in which she has been wholly absent from my thoughts – but, frankly, her last Letter had deeply hurt me. I considered it as injurious to the Memory of my beloved, my revered Father, who was actuated by his own ideas of what was Right, without any intentional partiality or prejudice. He had all his Life meant to *portion* his Daughters, and only to *Educate*, and then cast upon their Professions, his Sons.

Whether this were Right in itself, or not, different ways of thinking will always leave questionable. I am well aware I am too much a party concerned to hope that my opinion, should I develop it, could have much weight in what I might urge; yet I think it my *bounden duty* to represent to you, that my dear Father meant not to *disinherit* where he did not deem that there was

---

3. Formerly.
4. A letter to FB of 3 April 1817.

1. Quoting the words 'my dear friend' used by her stepsister in a letter of 21 June 1814, to which this is the draft of a reply. The letter had hurt FB by criticizing CB's treatment of his son James in his will.

any *Inheritance*. All he possessed he had personally acquired; and all he had Acquired had been under disadvantages such as his sons had never felt, and such as he had secured them from feeling. He thought, on the contrary, that he had placed them in a line, and with means, to rise very High in their separate Walks and Rank in Life. That 'political creed' to which you allude, from which my poor Brother suffered so severely – so mercilessly – was also, You cannot doubt, a death-blow to the comfort and approbation of my poor Father.[2] It could not, therefore, be expected that it should urge him to any extra-consideration. Nevertheless, neither that, nor any other circumstance influenced The Will, which he solemnly and scrupulously made according to the early, constant, and unbiassed dictates of his own Judgement upon the relative claims, Male and Female, upon Personal, not Hereditary, property.

225. Letter to Alexandre d'Arblay *18 June 1817*

How has your Letter from Dover afflicted me![1] to have passed such a Night previous to such a Journey – and after such a malady! – alas – – I want words to say how afflicted I feel! – and yet. – Permit me to assert Alex – blamable, horribly blamable as he is in this business, – has NOT an *unfeeling Heart*: – he has simply no *Fore thought*: voilà le vrai.[2] He never thinks of what the next *minute* will produce, much less of what may happen the next *Hour*, or *Day*. I have spoken to him on the subject, in the bitterness of my grief that he had caused you such a Night, and been able to stay away from you at such a period. He looked dismayed, but *stunned*, rather than culpable: but, in result, he owned that Chess had so imperious a power over his whole faculties and Being, that nothing weighed in its scale when once he was engaged in a Game! 'I am sure,' he cried, 'if I were told my Head was to be put upon the Block the very next Hour, – – I should still finish my Game! –

---

2. James's radical political sympathies had effectively ended his naval career. After repeated petitions, however, he would finally be promoted to Rear-Admiral in July 1821, after the death of George III and a few months before his own death.

1. AA had returned to France on business matters. In a missing part of a letter of 14–15 June from London, he had apparently told FB that Alexander had failed to spend the evening with him, as planned, before his departure early the next day for Dover; see *JL*, ix. 436 n. 1. In a heavily obliterated passage at the end of this letter, FB explained that Alexander had become distracted during a lengthy game of chess with his uncle James.

2. That is the truth.

it absorbs me, wholly, literally, and completely, to the utter forgetfulness of All Else during the combat!'

Yet, so *literal* he is, that, as you had given him your hand in parting, he had thought all was over! He was thunderstruck, therefore, when he saw my disturbance, and when I read him such passages as I deemed most likely to make upon him the effect I desired to produce, i.e. to awaken him to his fault and misconduct. I represented to him that, though I had always delighted and consoled myself, through his many irregularities, in thinking that he had not a vice in the World, that This *manie*, This Chess, became a vice if it led him to neglect all his Duties. Confounded, he reflected some time, and I left him to his reflexions: and when I returned, I found he had brought himself to a resolution of offering you the only peace offering and reparation in his power, That of positively renouncing Chess either as a play or a study, till after he has taken his Degree – He said, at first, till he became *more reasonable*; but as that is a term that may admit of dispute, I preferred fixing the positive mark upon the period most important to his welfare.

Accept this offering, my dearest Friend – and try to accept it with comfort. It does not come from an unfeeling heart, for it costs him infinite pain, and yet is voluntary. For the World, however, do not offer him any composition! he would catch at it instantly: and this renunciation, though brought to bear by so melancholy a misdemeanour, may yet go further to promote his proper study for his Degree than any other circumstance could have done. I am sure – and so he acknowledges – it will highly please *Jacob*:[3] for already he had entered into an agreement with one of his young fellow students to play a *parti*[4] *3* times a week at Ilfracomb!!! Yet the time he gives to play is nothing; it might be allowed him for recreation; but the mischief is far wider; for after the Game is over, he is haunted, even in his sleep, with new combinations how he might have moved more scientifically! Sorry as I am for this affair, and shocked by the shock it has given you, it may prove, in its effect, a real blessing to this excentric *Etourdi*,[5] if, as I really trust, he keeps strictly to his promise: for I clearly see, by his *Brochures*,[6] etc., he had meant to allot to this madening Play three times the attention he had intended for his studies!! –

---

3. Edward Jacob, brilliantly successful student at Gonville and Caius College. A year younger than Alexander, he acted as his tutor, and was to bring a study-group of Cambridge pupils, including Alexander accompanied by FB, to Ilfracombe in July.

4. *Game.*

5. *Scatterbrain.*

6. *Notebooks.*

226. Letter to Messrs Longman and Company *30 August 1817*[1]

Madame d'Arblay begs leave to observe to Messrs Longman and Company when an Edition of 3000 Copies, and half an Edition of one of 1000, are disposed of in 3 years, it seems rather premature to decide that because the sale is then at a stand, it is over forever.[2] Mme d'Arblay was too far from the presumption of expecting a quicker circulation to regard This estimate as the Funeral of the Work: Messrs Longman and Company must not, therefore, be surprised that she puts in her claim to retain for herself, and to bequeath to her family, the right of desiring a half Yearly Notice of the future progress, or continued stagnation of this publication.

Mme d'Arblay will be much obliged to Messrs Longman and Company if they will acquaint her whether the 3d Edition is printed, or was stopt? and also, whether Dr Charles Burney misunderstood Mr Straghan that a 5th Edition had been ordered to Press?[3] – as it is the intention of Mme d'Arblay, should this Book ultimately survive the condemnation of Messrs Longman, and Company, to prepare a corrected and revised Copy for some future – though perhaps posthumous Impression.

Ilfracombe

227. Ilfracombe Journal *24 September 1817*[1]

Adventure at Ilfracomb

The latest desire that was pronounced, with respect to the use of my Pen, by Him whose every expressed desire I now execute as a Law, though with pleasure, – nay delight, – was to enjoin my committing to Paper my extraordinary adventure at Ilfracomb, with a view to making it known to

---

1. Annotated by FB: 'Copy of a Letter to Messrs Longman & Co In answer to an account that the Work is at a stand, & utterly hopeless of any renewed sale, *all orders* for it being withdrawn'.
2. A letter from FB to Longman of 1 February 1826 shows that 496 copies of the second edition of *The Wanderer* had been sold by midsummer 1817; see *JL*, xii. 640. Only 35 of these had been sold in 1815–17.
3. See selection 205.

1. FB wrote an account of her escape at Ilfracombe, a resort on the north Devon coast, in French in 1823; this is her English translation.

our invaluable Friend Le Comte Victor de La Tour Maubourg,[2] by my writing it to his dear sister, Madame de Maisonneuve. This I have just done: but, before I part with it, I will run over an English translation of it for my dear Relations and Friends on this side the Channel: not for my Alexander, who was a party too deeply concerned in it to require the recital.

In the year 1817 – the last year of my happiness! – I accompanied my son to Ilfracomb, in Devonshire, whither he went by the kind invitation of his excellent Friend Edward Jacob, to partake of the lessons which that young Tutor, at the Age of Twenty, was giving to 6 or 7 Pupils, preparatory to their taking their degrees at Cambridge on the ensuing January. –

The term for Alexander's studies with Mr Jacob was just finished, and a few days only remained ere the party was to be dispersed, when I determined upon devoting a whole morning to the search of such curiosities as the Coast and Rocks near my habitation produced. Having deposited a Letter for my Then best beloved on Earth, I marched forth, attended only by M. D'Arblay's favourite little Dog, Diane, with an empty large silk Bag, or Ridicule, to see what I could find that I might deem *indigenous*, as a local offering to the collection of my General, who had written me word from Paris, that he was daily increasing his minearological stores, under the skilful direction of his friend, the celebrated Naturalist in that class, M. de Bournon.[3]

Alexander was gone to his Tutor, Mr Jacob, and rarely returned before 3 or 4 o'clock. It was now one. I began my perambulation by visiting the promontory called Capstone; or rather attempting that visit; for after mounting to nearly its height, by taking a circuitous path from the town, by which alone the ascent is possible, the side of the Promontory being a mere precipice overlooking the Ocean, a sudden gust of Wind dashed its force so violently against us, that in the danger of being blown into the sea, I dropt on the turf, at full length, and saw Diane do the same, with her 4 paws spread as widely as possible, to flatten her body more completely to the Ground.

This opening to my expedition thus briefly set aside, I repaired to the Coast, where there are pebbles, at least, in great beauty as well as abundance. The Coast of Ilfracomb is broken by Rocks, large, small, round, pointed, and of all descriptions; which, from their various shapes, bear the evident marks of being fragments of some one immense Rock, which, undermined by the billows, in successive storms, has been cast in all directions, by its own weight, in its fall.

2. Marie-Victor de Latour-Maubourg.
3. Jacques-Louis de Bournon.

My usual walk was to the Sands, to visit the Ocean, and mark its ebb, or flow, and listen to the rustling murmur of the Waves. One Machine only was provided for Bathers, the Limitted smoothness of the sands not extending widely enough to admit another. To stand near this spot occupied much of my time from the peculiarity of the objects which it offered to my Eyes. Springs of the purest Water continually presented themselves, and limpid streams every where intersected the passage from my habitation, to the sea, which was not more than a quarter of a mile; and cascades innumerable, bright, pelucid and refreshing, danced over the points of Rocks that strewed the Ground all about. This spot of which I speak was the common rendezvous of all of Company that assorted to Ilfracomb, whence, after daily viewing the sea, and these details, parties were formed for Walks and adjournments or assemblages elsewhere.

We went down to the edge of the sea, which was clear, smooth, and immoveable as a Lake, the Wind having subsided into a calm so quiet and still, that I could not tell whether the tide were in, or out. Not a creature was in sight, the time for society being earlier or later. But presently a lady descended, with a Book in her hand, and passed on before us to the right, palpably to read alone. Satisfied by this circumstance that the tide was going out, and all was safe, I began my search, and soon accumulated a collection of beautiful pebbles, each of which seemed to merit being set in a Ring. The pleasure they afforded me, from my prospect of their destination, insensibly drew me on to the entrance of the Wildersmouth, – which is the name given to a series of recesses, formed by the Rocks, and semicircular, open at the bottom to the Sea, and only to be entered by the Sands at low tide. I coasted two or three of them, augmenting my spoil as I proceeded, and so pleased with its increase, that on perceiving the lady I have already mentioned seated on a large flat stone, and composedly engaged with her Book, I hurried past, not to disturb her, and I felt urged to profit by this implication of security that all was safe, to visit the last Recess, whither I had never yet ventured. I found it a sort of Chamber, though with no roof but a clear blue sky. The top was a portly Mountain, rough, steep, and barren; the left side was equally Mountainous, but consisting of layers of a sort of slate, intermixed with moss; the right side was the elevated Capston, which here was perpendicular, and at the bottom were the Sands by which I entered it, terminated by the Ocean. The whole was alltogether strikingly picturesque, wild, and original. There was not one trace of Art, or even of any previous entrance into it of Man. Almost, I could imagine myself its first Human Inmate.

My Eye was presently caught by the appearance, near the top, of a Cavern, at the foot of which I perceived something of so brilliant a whiteness, that, in the hope of a splendid treasure for my Bag, I hastened to the spot. What had attracted me proved to be the jaw bone and teeth of some animal. Various rudely curious things, at the Mouth of the Cavern, invited investigation; but I durst not penetrate within it lest some Reptiles should resent my intrusion. Diane, however, brushed forward, and was soon out of sight; but, while I was busily culling, hoarding, or rejecting whatever struck my fancy, she returned, with an air so piteous, and a whine so unusual, that, concluding she pined to return to a little puppy, of a Week or so old, that she was then rearing, I determined to hasten, but still went on with my search, till the excess of her distress leading her to pull me by the Gown, moved me to take her home; but when I descended – for this Recess was upon a slant, – how was I confounded, to find that the Sands at the bottom, opening to the next Recess, whence I had entered this marine Chamber, were covered by the Waves! – though so gentle had been their motion, and so calm was the Sea, that their approach had not caught my Ear. I hastily remounted, hoping to find some outlet at the top, by which I might escape – but there was none. This was not pleasant; but still I was not frightened, not conceiving, or believing that I could be completely enclosed: the less, as I recollected, in my passage to the Cavern, having had a glympse, as I thought, of the lady who was reading in the neighbouring Recess. I hastily scrambled to the spot, to look for her, and entreat her assistance – but – how was I then startled, to find that she was gone – and that her Recess, which was on less elevated ground than mine, was fast filling with Water!

I now rushed down to the Sea, determining to risk a wet Jerkin, by wading through a Wave or two, to secure myself from being shut up in this unfrequented place: – but the time was past! – The Weather suddenly changed, the Lake was Gone – and billows mounted one after the other, as if with enraged pursuit of what they could seize and swallow.

I eagerly ran up and down, from side to side, and examined every nook and corner, every projection and hollow, to find any sort of opening through which I could any way pass. But there was none.

Diane looked scared – she whined – she prowled about; her dismay was evident, and filled me with compassion: but I could not interrupt my affrighted search to console her. Soon after, however, she discovered a hole in the Rock, at the upper part, which seemed to lead to the higher sands. She got through it, and then turned round, to Bark, as if triumphing in her success, and calling upon me to share its fruits. But in vain! the hallow was too small for any passage save of my head – and I could only have remained in it as if standing in the Pillory. I still, therefore, continued my own perambulation, but I made a motion to my poor Diane to go, deeming it cruel to detain her from her little one. Yet I heard her howl, as if reduced to despair, that I would not join her. – Anon, however, she was silent. – I looked after her – but she had disappeared.

This was an alarming moment: – alone – without the smallest aid, or any knowledge how high the Sea might mount, or what was the extent of my danger, – I looked up wistfully at Capstone, and perceived the iron Salmon;[4] but this angle of that Promontory was so steep as to be utterly impracticable for climbing by human feet: and its height was such as nearly to make me giddy in considering it from so close a point of view. I went from it, therefore, to the, much less elevated and less perpendicular, Rock opposite; but There, all that was not slate, which crumbled in my hands, was moss, from which they glided. There was no hold whatsoever for the feet, that did not threaten giving way to the first step, and causing a fall on the hard fragments of Rocks spread every where in this chamber, that must almost inevitably have dashed out my brains.

I ran therefore to the top, where a large Rock, by reaching from the upper part of this slated one to Capstone, formed the Chamber in which I was thus unexpectedly immured. But this was so rough, pointed, sharp, and steep at once, that I could scarcely touch it even with a finger without laceration. The hole through which Diane had crept was at an accidentally thin part, and too small to afford a passage to any thing bigger than her little self.

Two small Rocks, close to the angle of the promontory of Capstone, and probably its Children, torn off from the Mother Rock in some tempest, I next observed, which did not look equally unattainable; but they were so near to the main Ocean, and so high that I feared my head would turn giddy even if I succeeded in scrambling up either of them.

The rising Storm, however, brought forward the billows with seemingly encreased rapidity, and with certainly augmented noise and violence, and, in turning again towards the sea, I perceived by its approach that my wild Asylum lessened every moment.

Now, indeed, I comprehended the fullness of my danger. If a Wave once reached my feet, while coming upon me with the tumultuous vehemence of

4. Weather-vane in the form of a salmon on top of Capstone Hill.

this stormy moment, I had nothing I could hold by to sustain me from becoming its prey; – and must inevitably be carried away into the ocean, and sunk to its bottomless Pit: – and while the prospect of this terrific premature Death struck me with dread, the idea of my poor desolate Alexander – of my many, many affectionate Relations and deeply attached Friends – and – Oh more than all! of the piercing agonies of the tenderest of Husbands – and the dearest –

I flew that thought – and darted about in search of some place of safety, rapidly, and all Eye, till, at length, I espied a small tuft of Grass on the pinnacle of the highest of the small Rocks that were scattered about my Prison – for such now appeared my fearful dwelling place.

This happily pointed out to me a spot that the Waves had never yet attained; for all around was sand, stone, or barrenness which bore marks of their visits. To reach that tuft would be safety, and I made the attempt with eagerness; but the obstacles I encountered were terrible. The roughness of the Rock tore my cloaths; its sharp points cut now my feet, and now my Fingers; and the uncooth distances from each other of the holes by which I could gain any footing for my ascent increased the difficulty. I gained, however, nearly a quarter of the height, but I could climb no further, and then found myself on a ledge where it was possible to sit down, and I have rarely found a little repose more seasonable. But it was not more sweet than short, for, in a few minutes a sudden gust of Wind raised the Waves to a frightful height, whence their foam reached the basis of my place of refuge, and menaced to attain soon the spot to which I had ascended. I now saw a positive necessity to mount yet higher, *coûte qui coûte*;[5] and, little as I had thought it possible, the pressing danger gave me both means and fortitude to accomplish it, – but with so much hardship that I have ever since marvelled at my success. My Hands were wounded, my Knees were bruised, and my feet were cut; for I could only scramble up by clinging to the Rock on *all fours*. Nevertheless, my alarm was such for my Life, that the mischief to my limbs I only became conscious of the following day. Presently, however, a new evil cost me the most mortal apprehension. I could only climb by forcing *my* feet into such nooks or crevices as they could dig for themselves, and by forcing one of them a little too far, I could only draw it back by leaving behind me my Shoe!

Wherever I then tried to place my foot, It was so cut that I was obliged to snatch it away, and my position was so frightful, thus fastened to the

5. *Whatever the cost.*

Rock by one foot, while the other hung in the air, that I have ever since been astonished how I was able to sustain myself while, with the curved top of my Parasol I gently and cautiously regained my imprisoned shoe, and, placing it one step higher, I had the joy to recover its use.

This relief, however, was followed by a New distress: my other shoe, stuck in yet more deeply by having the whole weight of my poor person to support, – remained, like its Brother, in bondage when I dragged out my other foot. But less frightened now, as I had devized a means of redress, I only most thankfully rejoiced that I had preserved my Parasol, which now repeated its good office: but these efforts broke the Ribbon that had fastened the shoe to my ancle, and every fresh step by which I thus slowly ascended forced me to the same operation, for my shoes were become mere slippers, over which I had no command. Unremittingly, however, I continued my toil, which was equally laborious and dangerous, for had I placed one of my feet where it could not rest, I must have fallen.

When I had reached to about two thirds of the height of my Rock, I could climb no further. All above was so sharp, and so perpendicular, that neither hand nor foot could touch it without being acutely wounded. My head, however, was nearly on a level with the tuft of Grass, and my elevation from the sands was very considerable. I hoped, therefore, I was safe from being washed away by the Waves; but I could only hope; I had no means to ascertain my situation; and hope as I might, it was as painful as it was hazardous. The tuft to which I had aimed to rise, and which, had I succeeded, would have been security, was a mere point, as unattainable as it was *unique*, not another blade of Grass being any where discernable. I was rejoiced, however, to have reached a spot where there was sufficient breadth to place one foot, at least, without cutting it, though the other was poised on such unfriendly Ground that it could bear no part in sustaining me. Before me was an immense Slab, chiefly of slate, in layers, resembling a Tomb rather than a Table, for part of it was stone, and all, when not touched, had the appearance of being smooth and plain. But it was too slanting to serve for a seat – and Seat I had none. All the Rock above where I stood was of such rude materials as to have torn my Cloaths to pieces had I leant against it a moment. My only prop, therefore, was holding by the Stony part of the Slab, in fixing myself on a spot where it was of a Convenient height for my hands. This Support, besides affording me a little rest, saved me from becoming giddy, and enabled me from time to time to alternate the toil of my feet.

Glad was I, at least, that my perilous clambering had finished by bringing me to a place where I might remain still, for, with affright, and fatigue, and exertion, I was almost exhausted. Happily for my recruit, the Wind was now abated, and the sea so perfectly calm, that it seemed without motion, and I could not be sure whether the tide was now going out, or still coming in. To ascertain this was deeply necessary for my tranquility, that I might form some idea what would be the length of my torment. I fixed my Eyes, therefore, upon two small but tall Rocks, that stood near the sea entrance into my Recess, almost close to the promontory of Capston, from which they had probably been severed by successive storms. As they were always in the sea, I could easily make my calculation by observing whether they seemed to lengthen or shorten. With my near sighted Glass, hanging to my neck, I watched them – and great was my consternation when, little by little, I lost sight of them. I could then see no term to my captivity, and the desolating solitude, as well as pain of my position, was rendered still more poignant by reflecting on my poor Alexander, and his astonishment and distress when, upon returning from Mr Jacob, he should not find, or know where to seek, or what could have happened to me. The thought of his cruel disturbance, and the fear of some desperate rashness in his researches in a place so filled with Cliffs, precipices and Rocks, made me shudder – turned me sick – and nearly robbed me of all my courage. The open part of the Wildersmouth, where stood the sole machine for Bathing, and where there was breadth of sand for Walking, and looking at the sea, we had often visited together: but the Recesses, to the right or to the left, we had never entered, nor even heard mentioned. Probably they had always been overflowed, as at present, when we had been in their neighbourhood. With my Glass, I now looked wistfully onward to the main Ocean, in the hope of espying some Vessel, or Fishing boat, with intention of spreading and waving my Parasol, in signal of distress, should any one come in sight. But nothing appeared. All was vacant and Vast! – I was wholly alone, wholly isolated; and though without ceasing I rolled about my Eyes, in search of I knew not what, I feared to turn my head, lest I should become giddy, and lose my balance.

In this terrible state, painful, affrighting, dangerous, and more than all, solitary – who could paint the transport of my joy, when suddenly, re-entering by the aperture in the Rock through which she had quitted me, I perceived my dear little Diane! For an instant, I felt as if restored to safety – I no longer seemed abandoned, all my terrours were chaced by the most lively hopes, and with a heartfelt gaiety – such as rarely, alas! I have since experienced, I called upon her to join me, in accents the most carressing, and which evidently convinced her of her even exquisite Welcome. Nevertheless, though her tail wagged responsive pleasure, she hesitated, looking amazed, embarrassed, and frightened to see me perched at such a height, and the sea so near me. She stood still, and, barking gently, and in a tone resembling a cry, seemed to supplicate that I would rather join than await her: but I had no choice; far as I am from being a Giantess, the opening through which Diane had passed could not have admitted me. I repeated, therefore, my invitation, and, at length, she approached. She soon leapt across the flat stones and the sands which separated us, but how great was the difficulty to make her Climb as I had climbed! Twenty times she advanced only to retreat, from the pain inflicted by the sharp points of the Rock, till, ultimately, she picked herself out a passage by help of the slate, and got upon the enormous Table or Tomb-Stone of which the upper part was my support. But the slant was such, that as fast as she ascended she slipt down, and we were both, I believe, almost hopeless of the desired junction, when, catching at a favourable moment that had advanced her poor paws within my reach, I contrived to bend sufficiently forward to hook her Collar by the curved end of my Parasol, and help her forward. This I did with one hand, and as quick as lightening, dragging her over the slab, and dropping her at my feet, whence she soon nestled herself in a sort of Niche of Slate, in a situation much softer than mine, but in a hollow that for me was impracticable. I hastily recovered my hold, – which I marvel now that I had the temerity to let go: but to have at my side my dear little faithful Diane was a comfort, an enlivening comfort, which no one not planted, and for a term that seemed indefinite, in so unknown a solitude can conceive. What cries of joy the poor little thing uttered when thus safely lodged! and with what carressing tenderness I sought to make her sensible of my gratitude for her return. Where she had been I know not; whether prowling about, and seeking Grass and cooling springs, in the upper Meadows; or whether to visit and feed her little one, who was in a Basket in the Garden. I rather think this latter, by the calm with which she now contented herself to abide by me. But she had not been seen, or marked. The Garden was open; and I had not, at that time, been missed.

I was now, compared to all that had preceded, in Paradise – so enchanted did I feel at no longer considering myself as if alone in the World. O well I can conceive the interest excited in the French Prisoner by a Spider, even a Spider![6] Total Vacuity of all of Animation in a place of Confinement,

---

6. Alluding to Byron, *The Prisoner of Chillon* (1816), ll. 381–2: 'With spiders I had friendship made,/ And watch'd them in their sullen trade'.

where its term is unknown, where Volition is set aside, and where the Captivity is the Work of the Elements, casts the Fancy in to a state of solemn awe, of fearful expectation, and of nameless amazement, which I have not words to describe: while the higher mind, mastering, at times, that Fancy seeks resignation from the very sublimity of that terrific Vacuity whence all seems exiled – hidden – dead – but Self – seeks, – and finds it in the almost visible security of the omnipresence of God. –

To see after my kind little companion was an occupation that for a while kept me from seeing after myself, but when I had done what I could towards giving her comfort and assistance, I again looked before me – and saw the Waters at the base of my Rock of refuge, and still, slowly, softly, and gradually rising on, – while both my Rocks of mark were completely swallowed up!

I now earnestly sought to discover how I might grasp, or cling any where in resistance, should the Waves gain my feet – but every attempt I made failed, I could reach nothing that I did not find Steep, or Sharp, or Crumbling.

My next alarm was one that explained that of Diane when she came back so scared from the Cavern; for the Waves, probably from some subterraneous passage, now forced their way through that Cavern, threatening inundation to even the highest part of my Chamber.

This was horrific. I could no longer even speak to Diane – my Eyes seemed transfixt upon this unexpected Gulph, and, in a few short, but dreadful moments, in which the Wind again arose, and drove the sea on with violence, an immense breaker attacked my rock, and, impeded by its height from going strait forward, was dashed in two directions, and foamed onward against each side. –

I did not breathe – I felt faint, – I felt even sea-sick. – On, then, with added violence, came two wide spreading Waves, and, being parted on their arrival, by my Rock, completely encompassed it, meeting each other on the further and upper Ground. Giddy I now felt – in my fear of losing my strength, or self-command, and falling – yet neither my senses nor my faculties played me false, for I gave up my whole soul to prayer – for myself and for my Alexanders – and that I might mercifully be spared this Watry Grave, or be endowed with courage and faith for meeting it with firmness.

The next Waves reached to the Uppermost end of my Chamber, which was now All Sea, save the small Rock upon which I was mounted!

What a situation for a Female Alone – without power to make known her danger – without any resource for escaping its tremendous menace, but by painfully, laboriously, and perillously standing upright, and immoveably on the same spot, till it should be passed – without any human being knowing where to find her, or suspecting where she might be – a Female, and past 60 years of age! –

How I might have been subdued by a situation so awful, at once, and so helpless, if left to its unmixt contemplation, I know not, had I not been still called into active service in sustaining my poor Diane. No sooner were we thus encumpassed, than that poor animal, who had always, from what cause I know not, a peculiar dread of Water, was siezed with a dismay that filled me with pity. She trembled violently, and rising, and looking down at the dreadful sight of Sea, Sea, Sea all around, and Sea still, to the utmost extent of the View beyond, she turned up her face to me, as if appealing for protection; and, when, I spoke to her with kindness, she glided forward to my feet, and no longer heeding the rugged, lacerating surface, there placed herself, and was instantly taken with a shivering fit, so strong and powerful that it seemed to shake the Rock itself.

How was I touched! alas, my faithful little Diane, thought I, wilt thou die? Will thy voluntary return to share my danger, joined to quitting thy little one, cause thy death? – I could neither sit nor kneel to offer her any comfort, but I dropt down as Children do when they play at Hunt the Slipper, – for so only could I lose my hold of the slab without falling, and I then stroaked and carressed her, in as fondling a way as if she had been a Child, and I recovered her from her Ague fit by rubbing her head and back with my shawl, she then looked up at me somewhat composed, though still piteous and forlorn, and licked my Gloves with gratitude. I envellopped her as well as I could in my shawl, wrapping up her head from the Sight of the sea, and she was presently after restored.

Greatly delighted by my success, I cautiously arose, almost crampt to death by my unnatural posture.

While this had passed, the sea had gained considerably in height, and, a few minutes afterwards, all the horrours of a tempest seemed impending. The Wind roared around, me, pushing on the Waves with a frothy velocity that, to a bye-stander, – not to an inmate amidst them! – would have been beautiful. It whistled with shrill and varying tones from the numberless holes and Crevices in the three immense Rocky Mountains by whose semicircular close adhesion I was thus immured; and it burst forth, at times, in squalls reverberating from height to height, or chasm to chasm, as if 'the bigmouthed Thunder'

Were billowing through the vast and boundless Deep.[7]

At times I thought some Miners were at Work in blowing up some distant Rocks: at other moments, I conceived myself on the point of being struck with a thunderbolt, and, fearing the metal of my Parasol, I poized it as distantly from me as I could reach, for a petty Conductor. But so furious were the blasts, that I had nearly equal fear lest they should hurl me from my balance, as that the Waves should mount so high as to wash me into the Ocean. The impression of this suspensive and terrific crisis upon my mind was so strong, so potent, that not an hour passed without its recurring to me, afterwards, till the fatal – all-absorbing 18. of May, 1818[8] – which cast from my thoughts all of my previous feelings to which Earthly Happiness had seemed impended. –

Till that period, my helpless loneliness, the profound silence of all around me save the Elements, and the Destruction that threatened me aloud, thus standing upon a small Rock surrounded by the Sea, without prop, without succour, without the knowledge of any human being where I might be found, or how I might be lost, fastened upon my Imagination with incessant Wonder as well as Gratitude that I escaped falling a Victim to a Death so horrible and so unknown. A Wave, at length, more stupendous in height, in breadth, in foam, and in roaring noise than any which had preceded it, dashed against my Rock as if enraged at an interception of its progress, and rushed on to the extremity of this savage Chamber, with a foaming impetuosity from which I felt myself splashed. This Moment I believed to be my last of Mortality! – but a Moment only it was, for scarcely had I time, with all the rapidity of concentrated thought, to recommend myself – my Husband – the most adored of Husbands – and my poor frantic Alexander, humbly but fervently to the Mercy of the Almighty – when the celestial joy broke in upon me of perceiving that this Wave, which had bounded forward with such fury, was the last of the rising tide! for in its re-bound, it forced back with it, for an instant, the whole body of Water that was lodged on the Ground nearest to the upper extremity of my Recess, and the transporting sight was granted me of an opening to the sands. This sudden recovery of Hope was hailed by a flood of grateful Tears – and Oh! what thanksgiving! – already I felt myself restored to my Husband – my Son – and every dearly loved Friend I possessed in this World.

7. Alluding to Shakespeare, *King John*, V. ii. 173, 'the deep-mouth'd thunder', and Milton, *Paradise Lost* (1667), i. 177: 'To bellow through the vast and boundless deep'.
8. The year of AA's death.

The violence of this re-bound, nevertheless, produced but a momentary view of the sea-hidden sands; they were covered again the next instant, and as no other Breaker of similar Might made a similar Opening, I was still, for a considerable length of time – or what appeared so to me, – exteriorly in the same situation – but internally, Oh, how different! I lost Hope no more. The Tide was turned; it could rise, therefore, no higher; the danger was over of so unheard of an end; of vanishing no one knew how or where – of leaving to my kind, deploring Friends an unremitting uncertainty of my Fate – of my re-appearance, or Dissolution. I now wanted nothing but Time, Patience, and Caution, to effect my deliverance: and the requisite Courage for their use no longer demanded Effort, – it was chearful, it was vigourous, it was even gay.

The threat of the Tempest, also, was over; the air grew as serene as my Mind, the sea far more calm, the sun beautifully tinged the West, and its setting upon the Ocean was resplendant. By Remembrance, however, alone, I speak of its Glory, – not from any pleasure I then experienced in its sight – it told me the waning of the Day; and the anxiety I had now dismissed for myself redoubled for my poor Alexander.

I now turned myself to considering how I might be placed less painfully; for what I had supported while in such iminent danger seemed now insupportable, and when my Eyes, and my whole faculties were no longer monopolized by immediate care of Life, in watching the tide, I was able to devize various contrivances for my better accommodation. I found out crevices for holding my feet so as to allow of my standing Upright, and I discovered a spot of the slab upon which I could occasionally lean one of my Elbows. Not small were these solaces; I felt them to be almost invaluable, so crampt had been my position. But no possible means could I discover for procuring myself a seat: – and this I have since regarded as providential; for, had I been a little more at my ease, the fatigue I had undergone, the profound silence all around me, the heaviness of solitude, and the vast monotony of the view, joined to the relentless necessity of remaining motionless, might have calmed my senses to a species of torpor that must inevitably have invited sleep. I should then have lost my ballance – and my waking start must have plunged me into the Sea. I have reason, therefore, to bless the various torments which saved me from any possibility of drowsiness.

With my bag of Curiosities, I next made a Cushion for Diane, which, however, little luxurious, was softness itself compared with her then resting place. She, also, could take no repose, but from this period I made her tolerably happy, by carresses and continual attentions.

Watch I had none; but the Hour of Repast was announced to us both by pinches of Hunger more certain and more pressing than the loudest Dinner Bell. Diane here was far more to be pitied than myself; and I regretted she could not understand my *lingo*, as else, like the shipwrecked Mariners, I would have sought to wile away the pangs of famine by telling her some story.[9]

But no sooner had every vestige of the dying beams of the sun vanished from the broad Horizon, than a small, gentle Rain began to fall, and not alone the brightness of the Great Luminary of the Universe became invisible, but the light, as well as brightness of the Day became obscured by darkling clouds, wandering in wavering directions in the vast expanse before me, and already lowering at a distance, as if preparing to meet the Waters of the deep.

This greatly alarmed me, in defiance of my joy and my philosophy; for I dreaded being surprised by the Night in this isolated situation. I was supported, however, from a recurrence of my terrours, by perceiving, at length, that the sea was clearly retrograding, and beholding, little by little, the dry Ground across the higher extremity of my Apartment. How did I bless the sight! the sands and clods of sea-mire were more beautiful to my Eyes than the rarest mosaic pavement of Antiquity, and the stones, however unshaped and lumpish, which had been broken from the heights by the Winds, or undermined by the sea, appeared to me more gaily lovely than any precious Gems that could have been shewn me from the East. Nevertheless, the return was so slow, so tardy, so wearisomely gradual that I foresaw I had still many Hours to remain a Prisoner.

And when, after all, the sea should be restored to its Bed, was I sure the sands had not been too deeply and too long immersed to afford me a safe footing? If I sunk into any hole, how could I get out? And if I escaped this transfixture, was I sure I knew my way? I had entered by the broad glare of the sun, and observed, in the adjoining Recesses, Springs, Rivulets, small ponds or standing Waters, which, with fragments of Rock, intercepted, more or less, the whole passage from hence to my habitation: but as I came without fear, and, unhappily, without Wit, I had by no means remarked their placement, and could not, therefore, by twilight, trust to my short-sightedness for not treading into some swamp, or tottering from some ridge or bank, or stony fragments of which I had mistaken, or could not see the form.

9. Not identified.

Nor was this all I had to apprehend; many of the Irish Insurgents who had fled from trial, after the last revolt,[10] were said to have crossed the Bristol Channel, and to have landed on the Northern Coast of Devonshire, which was said to be infested with Banditti that occasionally sought refuge in the caverns and subterraneous hiding places of the Wildersmouth; – the horrour of encountering any of these desperate Men, in the Night, alone, and uncertain even of my way, was a yet more appalling perspective than the other. Darkness now came on by large strides, faster and faster, and the gloom of Night threatened to quickly envellop me: I was no longer, however, out at sea, for the Waves had rolled wholly away from my spiral residence: But the more I deliberated upon the various hazards of wandering by myself in so unsequestred a spot, the less I dared make the experiment; and, finally, I formed the resolution of standing where I was and not venturing to seek my home till the Dawn of the next Day.

This plan once determined upon, I would not permit myself to murmur at its hardships, which I felt to be mere *bagatelles*, compared with the dire End from which I had just escaped. Nevertheless, the nocturnal cold, the occasional pangs of hunger, the solitude, the dead stillness, and the perpetual combats between the Rain and the Wind, for Storm, or for Calm; joined to my ignorance what further evils might be incurred by my position, were sources of inquietude that could not be utterly dismissed, though I sought to keep them down by my true thankfulness. – But that to which I could least reconcile myself, was such a prolongation of the sufferings of Alexander. Yet to risk an eternal Earthly parting from him in so unheard of a manner – could that be truer kindness? no; with my double fears, first of Banditti, and next of losing myself, any experiment that could be avoided would have been madness. One Consolation, however, uniformly solaced me – General d'Arblay was spared any share in this distress.

Thus passed this, to me, most memorable Day. The Night came on – there was no Moon; but the Sea, by its extreme whiteness, afforded some degree of pale light, when, suddenly, I thought I perceived something in the air. Affrighted, I looked around me, but nothing was visible; yet, in another moment, something like a shadow flitted before my Eyes. I tried to fix it, but could not; nor devellop any form: something black was all I could make out; it seemed in quick motion, for I caught and lost it alternately, as if it was a shadow of something that was reflected by the Waters as by a Miroir.

---

10. The most recent was the short-lived rebellion in Dublin, led by Robert Emmet, in July 1803, but FB may have been thinking of the much more violent United Irishmen's rebellion of 1798.

I looked up at Capston; nothing was there, but the now hardly discernable Iron Salmon. I then looked at the opposite side. – Ah, gracious Heaven! what were my sensations to perceive two Human Figures! Small they looked, as in a picture, from their distance, the height of the Rock, and the obscurity of the Night; but not less certainly, from their outline Human Figures. I trembled – I could not breathe – Shall I, I thought, be delivered? or are they but Banditti? This frightful doubt made me precipitately bow down my head; I would have amalgamated myself with my Rock to escape observation, but I did not succeed, for in another minute, I was espied, for a Voice strong, loud, potent, but unknown to my Ears, called out 'Holla! –'

Instantly I felt sure that no Banditti would search thus to proclaim his vicinity, and the exquisite hope as rapidly presented itself that some one saw my deplorable situation with compassion, and might be led to aid me, or to make it known, and therefore I unhesitatingly answered 'I am Safe!'

'Thank God!' was the eager reply, in a Voice hardly articulate, 'Oh thank God!' but not in a Voice unknown – though convulsed with agitation; – it was the Voice of my dear Son! – Oh what a quick transition from every direful apprehension to Joy and delight! yet, knowing his precipitancy and fearing a rash descent to join me, in ignorance of the steepness and dangers of the precipice which parted us, I called out with all the energy in my power to conjure him to wait patiently, as I would myself, the entire going down of the tide.

He readily gave me this promise, though still in sounds almost inarticulate.

I was then indeed in Heaven while upon Earth.

Another Form then appeared, while Alex and the first Companion retired. This Form, from a gleam of light on her dress, I soon saw to be Female. She called out to me that Mr Alexander and his Friend were gone to call for a Boat, to come round for me by Sea.

The very thought made me shudder, acquainted as I now was with the Nature of my Recess, where, though the remaining Sea looked as smooth as the Waters of a Lake, I well knew it was but a surface covering pointed fragments of Rock, against which, except at the height of the tide, a Boat must have been overset, or stranded. Sonorously, therefore, as I could raise my Voice, I called upon my Informant to fly after them, and say I was decided to wait till the tide was down. She replied that she would not leave me alone for the World.

I found, afterwards, she was a very obliging Milliner, who lived near Mr Ramsay.[11]

The Youths, however, soon returned to the top of the Mountain, accompanied by a Mariner, who had dissuaded them from their dangerous enterprize. I chearfully repeated that I was safe, and begged reciprocated patience.

They now wandered about on the heights, one of them always keeping in view.

Meanwhile, I had now the pleasure to descend to the sort of half-way house which I had first hoped would serve for my refuge. The difficulty was by no means so arduous to come down as to mount, especially as, the Waters being no longer so high as my Rock, there was no apprehension of destruction should my footing fail me. I might, however, have been maimed and defaced for life! I therefore used every precaution of care and slowness; but I effected my purpose, and was truly rejoiced to be posted no more on such a pinnacle.

Encouraged by this exploit, Diane contrived to get down entirely to the bottom: but though she found not there the sea, the sands were so wet that her Paws sunk as into a Bog, and she hastily climbed to rejoin me.

Some time after, I descried a Fourth Figure on the summit, bearing a Lanthorn. This greatly rejoiced me, for the twilight now was grown so obscure that I had felt much troubled how I might, at last, grope my way in the dark out of this terrible Wildersmouth.

They All, now, from the distance and the dimness, looked like spectres – such Forms, I mean, as the Drama represents; and as Pictures, and our Ideas represent for Spectres. Had I not known them for Friends, their view and silent motion would have been appalling: for we spoke no more, the effort being extremely fatiguing. I observed, however, with great satisfaction, an encrease of Figures, so that the border of the precipice seemed covered with people. This assurance that if any accident happened there would be succour at hand relieved many a fresh starting anxiety.

Not long after, the sea wholly disappeared: and the Man with the Lanthorn, who was an old sailor, descended the precipice on the further part, by a way known to him, and, placing the Lanthorn where it might give him light, yet allow him the help of both his hands, he was coming to me almost on all fours, when Diane, conceiving him, I suppose, some hostile Stranger or Beggar, leapt to the bottom of the Rock, and began a Barking

---

11. Robert Ramsay, FB's landlord in Ilfracombe.

so loud and violent, that the seaman, fearing she would bite him, stopt short: and I had the utmost difficulty to appease my little Dog, and prevail with her, between threats and cajolements, to suffer his approach.

He then brought me a Coat from my son.

It rained, softly, but incessantly.

'Is it his own?' I cried.

'Yes.'

'Take it then back, and entreat him to put it on. The Wind is abated, and I can hold my Parasol.'

I would take to this no denial, and my Son's Companion, Mr Le Fevre,[12] as I afterwards heard, sent then to the house for another; whence the good Mr Ramsay, my Host, supplied him with the best Coat of his Ward Robe.

For This, however, we waited not; my son no sooner perceived that the seaman had found footing, though all was still too Watry and unstable for me to quit my Rock, than he darted forward by the Way thus pointed out, and clambering, or, rather, leaping up to me, he was presently in my arms — Neither of us could think or care about the surrounding spectators – we seemed restored to each other almost miraculously from Destruction and Death – I pressed him to my Heart – he sobbed upon my shoulder – Neither of us could utter a word — but Both, I doubt not, were equally occupied in returning the most ardent thanks to Heaven.

He could not paint to me – could not try to paint the agonies caused by my disappearance. He concluded I had wandered too far, in my admiration of picturesque Scenery, and that in some lonely spot I had been met by a party of the roving Banditti said to infest the vicinity of Ilfracomb, and had been murdered. This horrific idea nearly deprived him of Reason. His Father was for-ever before his Eyes – that tender Father who for his sake had spared me to remain in England, at a time when more than ever he required his faithful Companion, from the enfeebled state of his health – and the conception of his returning to find me Gone – was indeed a maddening one for a far less effervescent Imagination than that of Alexander. He ran wildly about in every direction – visited Hill, Dale, Cliff, bye paths, and public roads, to make and instigate enquiry – but of the Wildersmouth he thought not, and never, I believe, had heard; and as it was then a mere part of the Sea, from the height of the tide, the notion or remembrance of it occured to no one. Mr Jacob, his cool headed and

---

12. John George Shaw-Lefevre, member of the study-group.

excellent-hearted Friend, was most unfortunately at Barnstaple:[13] and Elizabeth Ramsay,[14] my fondly attached Favourite, was at Barnstaple also, on a visit to a Relation. She, else, as she has since told me, should have thought of the Wildersmouth, which was well known to her from her childhood.

My poor Son had spent some hours in this desperation of misery – during which he never seemed to touch the Ground in his flights, from their frantic speed; though directed no where, and taken at hazardous random – he answered no one, though he interrogated every one; and refused – as the Ramsays told me, – all sustenance, and even a moment's rest, – though once they saw him in tears – which was a great relief to them, as they all – in common with all the little town, thought he had lost his senses – and more than once he was suddenly surprized in some hidden place, on his knees uttering an agonizing prayer – But, he at length thought of Mr John Le Fevre, a young Man who was eminently at the head of the Illfracomb students, and so nearly certain of becoming Senior Wrangler at the ensuing Cambridge examination,[15] that he had resisted going to the Ball at Barnstaple not to lose an Hour of his time. Recollecting this, Alex went to his dwelling, and bursting into his Apartment, called out 'My Mother is missing' –

The generous Youth required no solicitation, and, seeing the dreadful tumult of soul in which he was addressed, shut up his Bureau without a Word, blew out his light, and hurried off with his distressed comrade, to whom he devoted himself wholly – giving up for that generous purpose the precious Time he had refused himself to spare for a moment's recreation.

Nor was Time all he bestowed; he was as laborious in the search – though not as distracted, as Alexander himself; he made enquiry at every house which I had ever entered, sent, or went, to every shop, and every place of mark: hurried one of the Ramsays to the Vicarage; ordered a Boat to sail round the neighbouring Coast – which would have discovered me, but that the violence of the Waves and Wind near Capston prevented the little Vessel from coming so far; – Agnes, the maid of the house, went with her Father 7 miles from the house, in perpetual enquiry and examination – but, at last, – fortunately! providentially! Mr Le Fevre recollected Wildersmouth, and that one of his friends had narrowly escaped destruction by a surprize

13. Town eleven miles from Ilfracombe.
14. One of the Ramsays' three daughters, Elizabeth was devoted to FB and later served as her maid and companion.
15. The highest-placed student in the first class of the mathematical tripos at Cambridge. Jacob had graduated as senior wrangler in January 1816.

there of the Sea. He no sooner Named this, than he and Alexander contrived to climb up the Rock opposite to Capston, whence they looked down upon my recess. At first they could discern nothing, save that one small Rock only was uncovered by the Sea: but at length, as my head moved, Le Fevre saw something like a Shadow. He then called out 'Holla!' etc.

To Mr Le Fevre, therefore, I probably owe my life! for, had I continued in that lone desolation all Night, it is most likely that a fatal Cold would have fastened upon my lungs, even if I had escaped perishing to death, from my painful and dangerous position, in the Midnight Air, and exposed to the inclemency of the Equinoxial Gales on that bleak Northern Coast.

Impatient to aid, to congratulate, or to see me, visitors of all sorts now scrambled to join me; Miss Mary Ramsay the foremost, followed closely by her youngest Sister, Sarah,[16] who jumped over all obstacles, without heeding that her Hat was blown into the sea. All hands offered to assist my descent from my elevated station – but my heart was too full to accept any but from my Son, though his agitated state made him least able to serve me effectually.

I had great difficulty to dismount, for I was no longer insensible, now, to hurts, bruises, scratches, cuts, or torn clothes, or lost shoes; and I was so numbed and stiff that my joints seemed out of play, and I could hardly move – but, with all that, how happy did I then feel! how gay in spirits, how thankful at heart!

The joy of Diane when she saw me descend amounted to extacy; so many hours had passed on that tremendous height, that she had concluded, perhaps, I was rivetted there for life. She barked, fanned her tale with perpetual motion, capered till she was covered with mire, and splashed us all over with the glad shakings of her feathery Coat, and skipt now upon Alex, now upon me, as if felicitating us both, and justly claiming a share in our carresses as well as in our happiness.

We now set out; I took the arm of Alexander, – Mary Ramsay held me by the other side; her Brother[17] carried the Lanthorn; the Seaman was our Guide, for, away from the Sea it was quite dark; and the others followed in procession, while many more continually met and joined us; for the alarm had spread through the town. But what most – and indeed deeply affected me, was finding myself addressed repeatedly, by entire strangers, with an injunction to take care of my Son. 'He must be blooded!' was cried out, and echoed in my Ears from several. 'And why?' I demanded; 'has

16. Elizabeth Ramsay's sisters.
17. Richard Ramsay.

he had a fall?' 'No, Ma'am, no;' was the answer, 'but he has been distract!'

'He has been bereaved, Ma'am!' said another; 'he must be blooded directly!'

My dear Son! – He was now, however, so well, and so completely his own Man again, that he would hear of no such discipline.

Every one enquired how I had been able to support such a situation, so alone and without resource; and many asked how I had escaped Fainting away. Others wondered I had not screamed the whole time.

As the tide had so lately gone down, the pools and mud would have stopt our progress, had we had a Guide less an Adept in the route. I clearly saw I should have been lost had I undertaken such a course alone.

Arrived at our Dwelling, we found the entrance and passage filled with people, the good Mrs Ramsay arranging our Dinner, and her worthy husband making us a fire in the Drawing room – from which he sprang with youthful glee at our approach, and darted forward to shake hands with me almost with convulsive Joy. All the rest of the House had deserted it to join us.

Mr Le Fevre, with a delicacy that equalled the feeling and the judgement of his generous exertions, had retired in Silence. It was not till the next day that I knew my obligations to him. Alexander could relate nothing coherently. He was, besides, almost famished. It was between 10 and 11 o'clock, and he had tasted no food since his very early breakfast.

Our bit of Roast Beef was almost burnt to a Cinder – No one having stayed to attend to it: but Alex and myself agreed we had never tasted food so exquisitely flavoured.

The next day I had the pleasure of Mr Le Fevre's Company to tea, to talk over my Adventure. Mr Jacob was still at Barnstaple, I believe.

2 Days after I visited the spot of my captivity – but it had entirely changed its appearance. A Storm of equinoctial violence had broken off its pyramidal height, and the Drift of Sand and Gravel and fragments of Rocks had given a new face to the whole Recess. I sent for the Seaman to ascertain the very spot: this he did, but told me that a similar change took place commonly twice a year; and added, very calmly, that 2 Days later I could not have been saved from the Waves.

All Ilfracomb, I was told, went afterwards to visit this place. And the impression made by the frantic agony of Alexander is still alive, this 6th year after the adventure; for it is now 1823. And Lady Keith and her Daughter, Miss Elphinstone,[18] the other day demanded of me the truth of

18. Georgiana Elphinstone, granddaughter of Hester Piozzi, aged fourteen in 1823.

the reports of his dreadful distress, and my alarming disappearance, for a Lady then resident at Ilfracomb, had related so strange and frightful a history, that Georgina had thought of it continually, and they had both determined upon examining into its authenticity.

228. Letter to Alexander d'Arblay *c. 30 November 1817*[1]

I was carried in a sedan, last week to the Queen's residence here,[2] and just as it stopt at the door saw a group of Gentleman enter the house. All were in deep mourning,[3] and I hurried past them, *sans ceremonie*,[4] concluding them to be Pages etc. – I had just reached the door of the apartment of Mme Beckedorf[5] when a voice from amongst them called out: 'Ah! How do you do Madam?' in a chearful tone, but one not familiar to my ears.

I turned back and looked hard at the Group, to distinguish some former acquaintance, but vainly. The speaker advanced from the rest and said: 'You don't know me?'

Shocked with the idea it was some one much altered, I answered readily 'Oh yes I do – I only – only – I don't recollect your your!' – I stammered, and he stood stupified. I look earnestly at him while I spoke, but vainly sought to find out Who he was.

'So you don't remember me?' he then cried.

'Oh! Yes: I do' I replied; concluding it was Colonel Greville or General Manners[6] or some ancient Friend of my former cotteries. 'I know you very well, but I cannot recollect your name.' He was silent a moment and then repeated: 'So you don't know who I am?'

'Yes I do – I assure you.'

He then solemnly answered: 'No! you do not!'

I now stared, annoyed and embarrassed but how much more so when he added: 'I am the Duke of Clarence'[7] – I was never more confounded. To have said to a Prince of the blood, I don't recollect your name! as much as to say: I don't know whether you are Mr John or Thomas or Mr Smith or

---

1. Letter Book copy by AA.
2. The Royal Family was spending a month at Bath; FB was a daily visitor.
3. Princess Charlotte had died on 6 November, after giving birth to a stillborn son.
4. *Without ceremony.*
5. Charlotte Beckedorff, Keeper of the Robes.
6. Fulke Greville and Robert Manners were both equerries whom FB had known well at Court.
7. The third son of George III and the future King, William IV.

Mr Brown filled me with the utmost confusion, yet made me involuntarily ready to laugh, from the Molière like incongruity of my phraseology with my situation. I clasped my hands and said. 'I beg Your Royal Highness a thousand pardons!' but felt extreamly disconcerted. He saw this and putting aside something he had experienced of mortification for my forgetfulness, he seemed to attribute to his personal alteration and something of surprise at my easy manner of examining him for an old friend, he came up to me, and taking my hand in the most gracious way possible, said: 'I am very glad to see you!' There was a real sweetness of Good nature in this action that I could not at all expect, and that has won my sincere gratitude. You are aware my dear Alex, a tale like this has but to be spread to be turned a subject for Peter Pindar.[8] Therefore smile at it only *under the rose*.

229. Letter to Charles Parr Burney *26 February 1818*[1]

Your letters,[2] my dear Charles, have caused me to think[3] disturbance. How little can you know my situation to think of thus demanding from me, and upon such a subject an answer without delay etc. –

You have heard, then from no one that I am now merely a Nurse? That General d'Arblay for some weeks past has been so much worse that I have not quitted his side Night or day? and that we have been obliged to call in new medical aid, after being in the hands of the best medical man, according to Mrs Lock and Mrs Angerstein – of Bath for more than a year? Mr Hay, of whose skill your friend the Archdeacon[4] also has the highest opinion – But we have now – alas – had recourse to a more professed Surgeon the first of this City Mr Tudor:[5] and the sufferings of his Patient though he (Mr Tudor) gives me every hope of ultimate recovery are such, as wholly to absorb me.

Nevertheless, if I could believe that the Reputation of my dear departed Brother required 'your Protection' I would rob my eyes of sleep ere I would

---

8. The pseudonym of John Wolcot, author of witty satirical verse.

1. Letter Book copy by AA.

2. One of these letters, written on 7 February, is extant. Charles Parr Burney had learned about his father's having stolen books from Cambridge only after Charles Burney's death of a stroke, on 28 December 1817.

3. Apparently an error by the copyist, for a phrase such as 'no little'.

4. The Revd Josiah Thomas.

5. William Tudor.

refuse to aid you to give it. But I am not of that opinion. I hold his Reputation to stand above such partial support. I hold it to hang upon an eminence and an excellence that You and all of us may look up to with Pride and Gratitude not shrink from with tremulous forebodings.

The Public, Charles, has taken charge of his Fame! What can Envy Malignity, narrow Illwill or unforgiving Malice effect against so glorious a Patron?

Leave such little Workers to their own machinations, and They and their machinations will insensibly dwindle into nothingness. To shew Fear is to invite Attack. Be as courageous for your Father as I am for my Brother, and the illiberal darts that may be cast at his shrine will never reach his character, and scarcely touch its drapery.

When, in fact, may survivors be composed, if We are in tribulation? To suppose that any one of Name and celebrity, can pass through life and Finish a bright career, without bequeathing to Censure the power to tarnish any of its parts, in investigating its progress, and summing up its result, is supposing not alone perfection of Excellence in the departed, but of Candour in the Community.

Have you ever Supposed This for Any other?

Certainly not! – Why then blight the prosperity of this loved Memory by aiming to obtain for it pre-eminence to the lot of Man?

True, my dear Charles, There is, – There was Fault – that sometimes must cast down our Eyes, and which should always instill Modesty into our exultation.

Yet this, my dear Charles, was punished – and ought not therefore, to exasperate even an Enemy: – was pardoned and ought not, therefore, to cover any longer with blushes either his Family or his Friends – And – it was Public, therefore you cannot hide it. Cease then to torment yourself to devellop a sad story that you are the last to wish to see published, or renewed. If you mean to be yourself the Biographer,[6] who will not respect your passing by the details of this melancholy transaction? If you only purpose to help some other with materials, let him not, from YOU have particulars you must desire to see buried in oblivion. The Fact can neither be denied nor disguised, but leave it bare; disentangle it from the circumstances that gave it an even agonizing interest, and it will be read like an

---

6. I.e. writing his father's obituary; it was published in the *European Magazine* for March 1819, and reprinted in the *Gentleman's Magazine* for April – and made no mention of the theft; see *JL*, x. 794 n. 3.

obscure old tale without comment, and from not being allied with any subject that might awaken curiosity and attention will speedily be forgotten.

'Rumour' you say asserts 'that scanty allowance was the cause, and if so the excuse.' 'Is this plea', you add, 'justly founded?' – My dear Father's character is yet more sacred to me than my Brother's; Positively therefore I affirm That my Father was blameless of this implied charge. Nevertheless the allowance, as my poor Carlos once – long after the evil, said to me, was scanty; but solely from the fault of his own juvenile timidity of making that known, never from any denial or restriction. Nor even then, could that cause be the Excuse! He was too candid, and had too just notions of probity not to know that if such was an Excuse, it must annihilate all security to Property. But my dear Brother was in nothing so amiable, in nothing so noble minded as in his fair, frank, unpalliating and unsophisticated manner of speaking of that cruel event. – I have many reasons – many! – for believing the origin of the fatal deed to have been a mad rage for possessing a library; and that the subsequent sale[7] only occurred from the fear of discovery. But he never sought extenuation, nor except from you, ever troubled himself much about concealment: all he coveted was This. —

To have his fault considered as Juvenile as Single, and corrected: and as such though he always looked back to it with regret, he held himself entitled to look forward without shame – Imitate, therefore, and adopt his philosophy; leave Anonymous writers to Themselves, and detractors to contempt.

What, indeed, is there to fear for the Memory of a Clergyman, whose own Parishonners desire to raise a monument to him from personal respect? – or for a Professional man, whose own Pupils subscribe to raise a statue to him from affectionate reverence? – or for a Scholar, a renowned and accomplished Scholar, for whom the National Museum will purchase of his son his treasures of learning, to consign them to a library that will bear his erudite and honoured Name to time immemorial?[8]

---

7. He had sold some of the stolen library books to London booksellers, probably in an attempt to cover gambling debts and avoid discovery by his father.
8. Charles Burney's parishioners raised a monument to him in St Paul's Church, Deptford, Kent; his former pupils erected a bust in his memory at Westminster Abbey; and his splendid library was bought by the British Museum for £13,500.

230. Letter to Hester Lynch Piozzi *26 February 1818*[1]

Bath

There is no situation in which a kind remembrance from *You*, my dear Madam, would not awaken me to some pleasure – but my poor Sufferer was so very ill when your note came, that it was not possible for me to answer it. That I think him so '*very bad*,'[2] is that I see him perpetually in pain nearly insupportable: yet I am assured it is local, and unattended with danger while followed up with constant care and caution. – This supports my spirits – which bear *me*, and enable me to help *him* through a malady of anguish and difficulty. It is a year this very month since he has been in the hands of Mr Hay as a regular Patient: he had already, on our first arrival at Bath, whither we came, originally, for the Waters, been called in to attend him for a wound in his leg, from the Kick of a Horse. Mr Hay was recommended to us by Mrs Lock and Mrs Angerstein, whom he serves as *physician* from their high opinion of his skill and discernment. But alas – all has failed here! – and we have called in Mr Tudor, as the case terminates in being one that demands a *surgeon*. Mr Tudor gives me every comfort in prospect – but prepares me for long suffering, and slow – slow recovery.

Shall I apologise for this wordy explanation? – No: – you will see by it with what readiness I am happy to believe that our interest in each other must ever be reciprocal. –

Believe me, Dear Madam, with unalterable affection

Your ever obliged

and obedient

F. d'Arblay.

I hope you were a little glad that my Son has been amongst the High Wranglers?

1. A copy of this letter by AA is annotated by FB: 'As my beloved & much honoured Patient, who always took peculiar delight in reading my Letters & their answers, amused himself with copying my Reply to this very kind Letter from my once dearest Friend: scarcely more than 2 months before his Departure – so exquisite to the last was his generous interest – his congenial Joy in all that gave pleasure to his adoring Wife – And this renewal was a great – true – & most sensible Satisfaction to me'. This text, in the hand of FB, contains some lines in the hand of Charlotte Barrett, replacing a segment Charlotte removed from the letter. AA, suffering from jaundice and an obstruction of the bowels, would die on 3 May.

2. Quoting Hester Piozzi's note to which this is a reply; see *JL*, x. 799 n. 2.

231. Letter to Alexander d'Arblay *22 April 1818*

Wednesday Morning – Oh my Alex – my poor Alex — I fear you will arrive too late – but he yet lives – set off therefore immediately – no one has prepared me for what I now prepare you – though I have seen hopelessness of *recovery* some time – but now! – Heaven must prepare us both — I see my approaching misery – I did not till yesterday Evening – He sees it all – He calls out to me continually Take care of your health – keep it for Alex – poor Alex! — poor Alex – Be Both to him – and let Him be as Both to you — Live for Him! –

Leave every thing to come instantly – I have just sent to Mr Hay – and he thinks the effort worth making – God Almighty Grant it be not too late! God grant it! God grant it –

There is still muscular strength – and the Head is in all its best powers – and the Heart! – Oh never was Heart more perfect! — Till yesterday at night I saw not the dreadful blow impending over us – To you I write even now – I can neither write or speak to any one else – but you, my Alex – my poor Alex – I feel for as for myself

Mr Tudor is just come – he will yet make an attempt to a little soften his sufferings – to cure them is – he says, impossible! – Oh God! – Hasten – hasten – for Me, at least, you cannot come in vain –

your Letter is arrived –

But the sacrament must be deferred[1] – or you may lose what is irretrievable – another embrace from the tenderest of Parents — what are all considerations compared to that? — even to *trying* for that ——

4 o'clock

God Grant you may be on the road ere this arrives —[2]

To every one but You I still speak of nothing but Hope – as I feel that I expire if I hear any other word from any mouth but the awful one of Heaven — But to *you* I dare not spare myself – lest you miss a Blessing that ——

---

1. Alexander, who had finished tenth in the list of wranglers at Cambridge in January, had been elected Fellow of Christ's College on 6 March, as a condition of which he had to present a certificate showing that he had received the sacrament in a parish church; see *JL*, x. 829–30 n. 10.

2. He arrived the next day, in response to FB's letter of 19 April.

Oh my dear Alex
come – and perhaps
even yet – I must keep

off *utter* Despair or sink –
   But Come – lest the anguish of an abortive journey should —

– come instantly –
coute qui coute – [3]

If he sees you again I may yet have the divine feeling after which I fear to aspire —

Come —

I have a stupour upon me inconceivable – I am Numbed – insensible – I don't shed a tear –

232. Journal *2–3 May 1818*[1]

Narrative of the Last Illness and Death of General d'Arblay

On Saturday – my last Day but one of possible Earthly felicity, – my dearest Patient, awake with all his faculties and all his feelings to his Alex, occupied himself with energy relative to the Communion he was to receive officially on account of his fellowship.[2] Well might he say, as so often he did, 'Je meurs plein de vie!'[3] for all his energies were in their fullest force, his faculties were all brightly perfect; he seemed refined in his sentiments, and invigorated in his intellects: while in Character and Disposition he appeared to grow more and more noble, at once, and more soft and sweet every moment – yet, through-out, with a spirit the most manly, joined to the most unaffected piety.

Over night, Mr Tudor, however, came again, as well as the next morning. This removed, in some measure, the so strong idea of being abandonned as incurable. But when, in the course of the day, something broke from me of

---

3. Whatever the cost –.

1. This is the conclusion of FB's 150-page journal recording AA's final months; it was written in 1820.
2. See selection 231 and note 1.
3. 'I am dying full of life!'

my reverence at his heavenly resignation – and to see him so resigned – 'Resigné?' he repeated, with a melancholy half smile; 'mais – comme ça! – ' and then, in a voice of tenderness the most touching, he added 'Te quitter! – '[4]

I dare not – even yet – hang upon my soul's emotions at those words!

When his pains a little abated, he felt that he could sleep; but, well aware it was to Opium he owed the alleviation, he feared – most judiciously to sleep – he felt that he might wake no more! He commissioned us to make the enquiry on this point of the physicians – but it was a question I had no courage to risk! When Mr Tudor, however, came, on Saturday Night, he, my Beloved, precipitated the demand; 'Le sommeil?' he called out.

Mr Tudor, no adept in French, did not understand him. He then said, firmly and calmly, – prepared for any answer, 'Je crains le sommeil.'[5]

We were forced to translate this. Mr Tudor laughed; – I conclude, now, from embarrassment, but replied with chearfulness, 'O, – you must sleep, Sir! – you must not fear to sleep!' And from that time he began to take some repose, but still not heavily, not alarmingly; – and, I was a Dupe – a willing Dupe to Mr Tudor's chearful manner! happily! – but I believe it was assumed to avoid giving a fatal shock.

The Night passed in tolerable tranquility, and without any symptom of alarm – his pulse still always equal and good, though smaller. Alexander went to Bed, late, but pretty easy. Payne[6] sat up with me. The generous solicitude of my Beloved that I should never remain alone with him will never be effaced from my grateful memory. For Me, I wanted no one. I saw not the hasty strides of my impending misery! – I required only Alexander, for Alexander contributed to the comfort and happiness of my Beloved, and participated in my assiduities with gentleness, sympathy, and true filial feelings, equally awakened for us both. He was, indeed, all I could wish, and to see him by the side of his Mother was evident and smiling peace of Mind to his fond Father.

On Sunday Morning — fatal – fatal – to me for-ever wretched Sunday 3d May, 1818! — my Patient was still chearful, and frequently took saline Draughts, always prepared by our dear Alex; after which, he composed himself tranquilly to rest, and, now, slept often, but not long. This circumstance was delicious to my observation, and kept off alarm – or the least

4. 'Resigned? . . . but – like that! – . . . To leave you! –'
5. 'Sleep? . . . I fear sleep.'
6. Probably Mary Anne Payne, Bath nurse.

suspicion my misery could be so near! We had many difficulties of late in procuring a Night Nurse, when Payne went to Bed: there was one, Mrs Sole,[7] whom I much liked, and had sent for – but Payne came to acquaint me she was ill. While we were talking this softly over, and discussing to whom to apply, my dearest Friend called me to his side: he then whispered me to promise Three Guineas to Payne to engage her to sit up again this Night.

This readiness of hearing, and openness of attention to all that was passing, still sustained my blessed illusion! – yet, the offer of Three Guineas for one Night, to my own Maid, could not be heard without marking to me how critical he thought his situation! – I readily complied, without comment, assuring him she should sleep well in the day.

I immediately made the proposal, to which she aceded with complacency. I knew not then the dire view of a change which she had seen on the Friday! – Alas! She never earned those 3 Guineas – but He had named them, and therefore they were hers. –

I hurried away Alexander to Church, to take the communion that was to have the testimony of the Curate and Church Wardens, for his Cambridge fellowship; my dear sister Esther, with Sophy,[8] assisted as Witnesses.

My Pen lingers now! – reluctant – nay laborious it becomes to finish the brief little that remains – and that deprives me, thence forward, of the precious, though heart-piercing occupation of inscribing these too dear recollections! Yet, the brief little that remains is wholly sweet and consolatory – and recurs ever as the best and most sacred of balms to my poor, wounded, festered heart.

About Noon, gently awakening from a slumber, he called to me for some beverage; but was weaker than usual, and could not hold the Cup. I moistened his poor lips with a spoon several times. He looked at me with sweetness inexpressible, and pathetically said: 'Qui . . . ?'[9] He stopt; but I saw he meant *who shall return this for You*? I instantly answered to his obvious and most touching meaning by a chearful exclamation of '*You*! my dearest Ami! *You* Yourself! – You shall recover – and take your revenge! – ' He softly smiled, but shut his Eyes in silence.

Thus, ever awake was his tender solicitude for me! – and, in the midst of all his sufferings, his intellects had a clearness, nay, a brightness, that seemed as if already they were refined from the dross of worldly imperfection.

---

7. Probably Frances Sole; see *JL*, x. 905 n. 118.

8. Sophia Elizabeth Burney.

9. 'Who . . . ?'

After this, nevertheless, his muscular strength returned, for during the last visit of Mr Tudor – who still came twice a day, – he called for Cocoa, and helped himself to take the Cup as usual. Again – once again! – I glided down after Mr Tudor, and supplicated him to yet make some attempt – he looked sorrowful, but answered he would send to Mr Hay to meet him the next morning, and endeavour to suggest some operation.

This was all I could obtain; and I endeavoured to hail as a good omen that he did not, like Mr Hay, seem to abandon all effort.

I come now to relate the blessed Words through which, by the Mercy of God, I have been supported from that deadly Day to this Moment March 9th 1820. –

I know not the Hour – but about – No, I cannot recollect the hour – but I think about the middle of the Day, he bent forward, as he was supported, nearly upright, by pillows, in his Bed – he bent forward, and taking my hand, and holding it between both his own hands, with a smile celestial, a look composed, serene, benign – even radiant, he impressively said: 'Je ne sais si ce sera le dernier mot – mais, ce sera la derniere pensée – Notre Reunion! – '[10]

Oh Words the most heavenly that ever the tenderest of Husbands left for balm to the lacerated heart of a surviving Wife! – I fastened my lips on his loved hands – but spoke not – it was not Then that those Words were my blessing! – they awed – they thrilled – more than, Then, they enchanted and illumined me.

Very nearly, indeed, were they his *derniers mots*, for once more only did his voice address me! and that, incidentally. – In the Evening, awaking sweetly from a sweet sleep – he found his pillows too low. Payne was gone to Bed; I told him so, but Alex got up behind the Bolster, and lifted him up higher, while I arranged his linen, etc. etc.

'Bien!' he cried, in a cheering tone, evidently meant to be encouraging; 'Vous le faites — presque — aussi bien qu'elle!'[11]

These — his last Words! – he uttered with a smile I thought already angelic, – though, at the word presque, his mouth took a playful expression that seemed even comically marking that his praise was not quite unqualified.

Cheared by his approbation, and exhilarated by his archness, I answered, in a sprightly tone –

10. 'I do not know if this will be the last word – but, this will be the last thought – Our Reunion! –'
11. 'Good! . . . You [Alexander and FB] do it — almost — as well as she [Payne] does!'

'Oh oui! – Je l'espere! – il ne nous manque que la pratique!'[12]

How little knew I, then, that I should speak to him no more!

I sat, watching, in my assigned arm chair; and Alex remained constantly with me. The sleep was so calm, that an hour passed, in which I indulged the softest – though the least tranquil hope, that a favourable crisis was arriving – that a turn would take place, by which his vital powers would be restored, so as to enable him to endure some operation by which his dreadful malady might be overcome – but – when the hour was succeeded by another hour – when I saw a universal stillness in the whole frame such as seemed to stagnate – if I so can be understood – all around – I began to be strangely moved – 'Alex!' I whispered, 'this sleep is critical! – a crisis arrives! – Pray God – Almighty God! that it be p –'

I could not proceed. He looked aghast – but firm – I sent him to call Payne. I intimated to her my opinion that this sleep was important but kept a composure astonishing – for when no one would give me encouragment, I compelled myself to appear not to want it, to deter them from giving me despair.

Another Hour passed – the concentrated feelings, the breathless dread in which I existed – Yet – compared with All since, the Happiness – the Felicity – I experienced –

His Face had still its unruffled serenity – but methought the hands were turning cold – I covered them with new flannel – In this interval, Payne disappeared – I enquired for her – Alex said she had whispered him she would go and take her tea! — I sent him to fetch her again – I watched over the head of my Beloved – I took new flannel to roll over his feet – the stillness grew more awful – the skin became colder –

Alex, my dear Alex – proposed calling in Mr Tudor – and ran off for him –

I leant over him, now, with sal volatile to his Temple, his Forehead, the palms of his hands – but I had no courage to feel his pulse – to touch his lips –

Mr Tudor came – he put his hand upon the Heart – the Noblest of Hearts – and pronounced that all was over!

How I bore this is still marvellous to me! – I had always believed such a sentence would at once have killed me – but his Sight! – the Sight of his stillness kept me from Distraction! – Sacred he appeared – and his stillness I thought should be mine – and be inviolable. –

12. 'Oh yes! – I hope so! – we only need practice!'

I had certainly a partial derangement – for I cannot to this moment recollect any thing that now succeeded with Truth or Consistency; my Memory paints things that were necessarily real, joined to others that could not possibly have happened, yet amalgamates the whole so together, as to render it impossible for me to separate Truth from indefinable, unaccountable Fiction. Even to this instant, I always see the Room itself changed into an Octagon, with a medley of silent and strange figures grouped against the Wall just opposite to me. Mr Tudor, methought, was come to drag me by force away; and, in this persuasion, which was false, I remember supplicating him, with fervent humility, to grant me but one hour, telling him I had solemnly engaged myself to pass it by his side.

By that loved side I stayed two hours. Four times I visited his last remains – his faded fleeting form —

But why go back to my Grief? – even yet, at times, it seems as fresh as ever! And at *all* times weighs down my torn bosom with a loaded feeling that seems stagnating the springs of life. But for Alexander – *our* Alexander! I think I had hardly survived! his tender sympathy during the first baneful Fortnight, with his Claims to my fostering care, and the solemn injunctions given *me* to preserve for him, and devote to him, my remnant life, sustained me at a period which else must have cut off every other.

Heaven, with its best blessings, daily encrease his resemblance to his noble Father!

To Morrow – and fearfully – yet eagerly – I will read, at length the ode *À L'Inevitable*![13] – not more dreading – than delighting – that something still is to come that will be New to me – under his own adored hand. – 9th March. 1820.

13. A solemn address to Death, 'the Inevitable', probably AA's final poem; see *JL*, x. 909 n. 121.

1818–1839

Widowhood

233. Letter to Alexander d'Arblay *14 November 1818*

Unreflecting Alex!

Does then no 'Still small voice'[1] within, ever whisper, '*Have I a Mother?*
What is her health?
What are her spirits?
What are her Occupations?
How does she support her altered life? –
How, my Silence? my Absence? my Neglect?
  Does she grieve at them? –
  or Cease, at length, to care for them or for Me –
  What are her plans?
  What does she know of mine?
Of all these things, what do I know? What have I Enquired?

———

  of None!
I have never thought about the matter. Neither from any sense of filial
Duty,
Nor from any tender pity for her lonely sadness, and lost peace and
happiness. – '
  Unreflecting –
  for still I forbear to *say*, to *think*, unfeeling
Alex! –

1. I Kings 19: 12.

234. Letter to William Wilberforce *25 January 1820*[1]

Nearly on the commencement of the dread visitation which on the 3d of May, 1818, tore up by the root my Earthly happiness, Mr Wilberforce, ever watchfully alive to promote the Calls of Religion, and soothe himself in soothing others, had the kindness to send me a pious tract, as tender as it is energetic, to aid me to support a blow the weight of which he is amongst the very few that I believe capable of even conceiving; for my bereavement can only be fairly judged by such as have some criterion by which to know what is (human) excellence. No insensibility to your kindness occasioned my silence; on the contrary, it was balsamic to me; but I — had no spirit to tell you so! I could not urge myself to write: and afterwards, when better able, I was distressed how to make my tardy apology.

Is it not Now more tardy still? you will ask. Yes; but Extremes are so ever prone to meet, that your Felicity at this moment seems offering its hand to my Sorrow: and I cannot recollect how you felt for my Affliction, without experiencing a kindred feeling for what, I hope, is your Joy.[2] Forgive then, I entreat, both my long taciturnity and its abrupt cessation, and accept my cordial wishes that this young lady may merit the high distinction of being brought under Such a paternal roof – et *c'est tout dire*[3] – and believe me, Dear Sir, with the truest sentiments of esteem

your &c

F d A.

235. Letter to Frederica Locke *17 February 1820*[1]

To Mrs Lock. Elliot Vale

No one, my dearest Friend, can live – and breathe – and think; and dare lament that the so good, so pious, so amiable, and so exemplary *George the*

---

1. Annotated by FB: 'Answer to Lettr 2d. Not written till afterwards, upon occasion of the Marriage of Yg Wilberforce'. Wilberforce had written a note of condolence on 20 May 1818 and sent a tract by Richard Cecil, *A Friendly Visit to the House of Mourning* (1792).

2. Wilberforce's eldest son, William, had been married on 19 January, to Mary Frances Owen.

3. And *that is to say everything*.

1. Copy by Charlotte Barrett.

Third should be gone to his great reward[2] — should be relieved from those trammels of Earthly machinery that were no longer informed by the faculties that for so many years guided him to all that was Right – should have his soul liberated from the malady of his Brain and freed to enjoy the salubrity of those Regions for which it was fitted, – – nevertheless, no one could have known him as I have known him, in all the private excellencies of his domestic benevolences, – and have shared as well as witnessed them – without feelings of depression and sadness that such a Man is now no more! – I do not therefore marvel at myself that I have been extremely affected by his death — and I grieve for my sweet Princesses! they will feel it most sensibly, however religiously; – and not a little lament that all hope is now extinct that the filial piety with which they have hovered in his vicinity – abided in the gloomy Castle to which he was consigned and never once *All* for a single night quitted its precincts will ever reach his mortal Ear, or draw forth from his benign lips the approbation that would have paid them, by one smile, the exertions and the privations of years. The so unexpected and quick death of the Duke of Kent[3] had been a very severe shock to them all, – and the succeeding real and dangerous illness of the new King[4] has filled them with alarm. – Of course, there has been no *correspondence* at such a period – but I have had a few lines from Lady Charlotte Wynn Belasye,[5] written by the kind commands of the Duchess of Gloucester, to remove my *expressed* apprehensions for His Royal Highness's precious health.

Mr George Locke[6] will I hope indulge Alex and me with the reading his Sermon upon my ever dear and honoured King. Alex means to request it. Mr Matthews gave one that was excellent on the first Sunday, and Mr Repton another yesterday.[7] I was disappointed, nevertheless, not to hear my favourite Dr Andrews,[8] but I conclude he was at his Deanery.

. . .

2. George III had died on 29 January, aged 81; he had lived in seclusion in Windsor Castle for some years.
3. He died on 23 January, aged fifty-two.
4. George IV, Prince Regent since 1811, was too ill to attend his father's funeral.
5. Lady-in-waiting to the Duchess of Gloucester.
6. Mrs Locke's son George, rector in Kent.
7. Possibly George Mathew, Greenwich vicar, and Edward Repton, London curate, son of Humphry Repton.
8. The Revd Gerrard Andrewes.

How dreadful this assassination of the Duke de Berry![9] Alex just now enters with the news, which he has heard from Mr John Angerstein! –

What Monsters are these that prowl about the Earth! – poor Kotzebue scarcely yet cold! – and Mr Perceval still in every one's Memory![10]

236. From Letter to Esther Burney *25 November 1820*

But let me now, that I may send a double Letter, perform my promise of detail with respect to the manuscripts of our dear Father.

I am, and have been for some months past, as I told you, elaborately engaged with them: but not in *writing myself*, far from it. – It is in *reading*, in decyfering. The enormous load of Letters, Memoirs, documents, Mss: Collections, Copies of his own Letters, scraps of authorship, old pocket Bookes filled with personal and business memorandums, and fragments relative to the History of Musick, are countless, fathomless! I shall difficultly come to the conclusion. I entirely think with you that I have lost the time for *pecuniary* publication; – but I lost it from circumstances as unavoidable as they were melancholy. I had scarcely been put in possession of these papers by poor Charles, who had wholly to himself the first over-looking and regulating of them all, and through whose hands alone they any of them came into mine, ere my own embarrassments and distresses, and subsequent accidents, Flights, illnesses, or *nursings* in illnesses ten thousand times more terrible to me, absorbed all my faculties – and, with but short intermissions, have nearly continued so to do till within the last few months, that I am – faintly – endeavouring to recover some use of my mind and intellects. Nevertheless, I could not think myself authorized to transfer the business, as I have very long known that my Father *designed* and *wished* and *bespoke* me for his Editor. From the time of the death of my Mother-in-Law,[1] he put the Key of his Bureau of private Letters and papers into my hand, and began employing me to examine, read, preserve, or destroy his long accumulation. This was our constant occupation, *I* reading, and he listening, during the fortnight or 3 weeks I spent with Him at that time: and when I left him for dear – dear Westhumble, he told me I should renew it every

9. He had been stabbed by an assassin at the Paris Opera House on 13 February 1820.
10. The German dramatist August von Kotzebue had been stabbed to death in Mannheim on 23 March 1819, and the former Prime Minister Spencer Perceval shot dead in the House of Commons on 11 May 1812.

1. I.e. stepmother: Elizabeth Burney.

visit I made; – and so I did, in the few intervals in which we were tête à tête from that period before my departure for France. But they were rare, and our joint rummage did not extend, I think, beyond his early Letters: – and he never, I have reason to believe, went on with the investigation himself, further than with his Correspondence with my Mother in Law, and all her Letters and papers, and those of Bengal Richard;[2] of all of which I never found a single vestige. All else, he amused himself in sorting and arranging, but destroyed not a line; not even an invitation to dinner. During my absence on the Continent, he had decided, in case I had not returned, to put Charles into my post, conceiving him, next to myself, most acquainted with his literary habits, intentions, and wishes. Charles, however, gave up *that* with a very good grace, upon my re-appearance, considering the very erroneous ideas he had formed and nourished of the *value* of that post; I mean the *pecuniary* value: for he had concluded the *Memoirs* were such as they would have been if written at the time and in the style of the Italian and German Tours;[3] and had judged of the *Letters* from the high Names of many of the Writers, without knowing their Contents. I, also, at that time, thought the same, and therefore was induced, and with true sisterly satisfaction, to engage to my dear Esther to share with Her, as joint Residuary Legatee, when the expences of Copyists, paper, etc. were deducted, the profits of the Publication. I had an affectionate pleasure in this *perspective*, as the labour would be all my own; but I also thought it just, as this trust was not mentioned in the Will – an omission that has often astonished me, considering the unexamined state of his private memorandums, and the various papers that could not have been spread, even in a general Family review, without causing pain, or Confusion, or mischief. – – When I again was at Chelsea, on my first return from Paris, he again put his Key into my hands, and pointed to the Pigeon holes in which were the packets he bid me read to him. We went through the Letters of Mr Greville, from the commencement of that early intercourse, – all of which were clever, but many disputative, quarrelsome, and highly disagreeable. He did not preserve above 3 or 4. What else we revised, my recollection does not, at this moment, call to mind. The chief of our private time was given to his poetry, and to bits and scraps of his Memoirs, pointed out by himself – and which, taken separately, and selected, and apropos to some current subject,

<hr>

2. Richard Thomas Burney had died in Bengal in 1808, having been banished by his father in 1786.
3. CB's *The Present State of Music in France and Italy* (1771) and *The Present State of Music in Germany* (1773).

or person, read agreeably, – when read by Himself, and consequently intermixt with anecdotes and recollections that rendered them interesting – as was every thing he ever related. – He meant I should go through his whole stores, *to* him, and *with* him; *I* meant and wished it also, most sincerely; but he had no sleeping room for me at the College; our Evenings, therefore, were necessarily very short, – and I lived more at Charles's and with Charlotte than at the College; and my own work, promised to the publick, by Longman, at a stated period, without my consent,[4] – through some mistake – entangled my time so dreadfully that the progress of our manuscript researches was slow and scarcely perceptible. It was at this epoch he told me he had promised all the Letters of Mr Twining to Charles, who had asked them of him. Consequently, all that Charles had not found, and rightfully taken possession of in his own immediate rummage, I collected afterwards, and left for him at Richmond, in a sealed packet, with Charlotte.

At the moment we lost our dear Father, I was in too much affliction for any authorship faculties or calculations; but my internal opinion and expectation were That I had nothing to do but to revise and somewhat abridge his own Memoirs, which I thought would contain 3 Volumes in Octavo; and to select his Correspondence to the amount of 3 more, which would rapidly sell the whole, in chusing them from the Names of Garrick, Diderot, Rousseau, Dr Warton, Dr Johnson, Mr Mason, Horace Walpole. Lord Mornington, Mr Crisp, Mr Greville, Mrs Greville Lady Crewe, Mr Bewley, Mr Griffith, Mr Cutler, Mrs Le Noir Lord Macartney, Lord Lonsdale. Duke of Portland, Mr Canning. Mr Windham. Mr Wesley. Mr La Trobe. Mr Walker. – Mr Burke. Mr Malone.[5] Sir J. Reynolds. Mr Seward. Kit Smart. Mrs Piozzi.

Can any one read such names, and not conclude that the Press would cover them with Gold? – It was not till I came to Ilfracomb that I was completely undeceived, for it was not till then that I had been able to go seriously to work at my always melancholy task – – though Then how *bright* to what any has been since! – Doubts, and strong ones, had, indeed, occurred, from my occasional view of the state of the Repository, in hunting for some secret Letters and papers of Mr Broome, which Charlotte most earnestly claimed from me, and helped me to seek: but it was at Illfracomb, in 1817 that my definitive disappointment took place. In reading the Memoirs

4. *The Wanderer*, which the publisher wished to hasten into print.
5. William Bewley, Samuel Cutler, Elizabeth Anne Lenoir, George Canning, Charles Wesley, Jr, Christian La Trobe, Joseph Walker, Edmund Burke, Edmond Malone.

de suite,[6] with a red pencil in my hand, for little erasures and curtailings, I soon, unhappily, discovered that they really were so unlike all that their honoured writer had ever produced to the Publick, that not only they would not have kept up his Credit and fair Name in the literary World, if brought to light, but would certainly have left a cloud upon its parting ray – attended by a storm of disapprobation, if not invective, upon the Editor who, – for a fortnight's quick profit from his earlier established Celebrity, had exhibited her faded Father's faded talents. – A fortnight, I say; because, the first curiosity satisfied, the Memoirs would have sunk to Waste, and have been heard of no more.

All the juvenile Voluminous Mss. are filled with *literal* Nurse's tales, – such as, narrated by himself, were truly amusing, as his vivacity and quickness and ready Wit rendered every thing that passed his lips: but on paper, and *read*, not *recited*, they were trivial to poverty, and dull to sleepiness. What respected his family, mean while, was utterly unpleasant – and quite useless to be kept alive. The dissipated facility and negligence of his Witty and accomplished, but careless Father; the niggardly unfeelingness of his nearly unnatural Mother; the parsimonious authority and exactions of his Eldest half Brother; the lordly tyranny of his elder own Brother; the selfish assumingness of his Eldest sister, – and the unaffectionate and Worldly total indifference of every other branch of the numerous race to even the existence of each other, – poor good Aunt Rebecca excepted[7] – all these furnish matter of detail long, tedious, unnecessary, – and opening to the publick view a species of Family degradation to which the Name of Burney Now gives no similitude.

In coming to the epoch of Manhood, I had hoped to find some interesting details, and descriptions, relative to our dear and lovely own Mother: but – from whatsoever Cause, he is here laconic almost to silence. 3 or 4 lines include all the history of his admiration and its effects. Whether these were recollections too melancholy for his Nerves, or whether the intensity with which he had once felt on this subject had blunted his remnant sensibility, I cannot determine – but he gives his whole paper at this time to enormous long paragraphs and endless folio pages, upon the City electioneering for organs and Concerts, and Stanley's rivalry, and Frasi,[8] and local interests of the day, now sunk from every memory, and containing Nothing

---

6. *Consecutively.*

7. The actor James MacBurney and his wife Ann Cooper, CB's parents; Thomas, his eldest half-brother; Richard, his eldest brother; and Ann and Rebecca, his sisters.

8. John Stanley, organist, and Giulia Frasi, soprano.

that could either benefit or amuse a single Reader by remaining on record.

Then follow various Cahiers on Norfolk and Lynn, with some more agreeable style of Writing, – but still upon people not generally known, nor even described with circumstances that may create a running interest for them. All is detached, vague, and unknit into any consistence.

At last comes London; and Then all the great Names I have mentioned to you begin to occur: and here I had the full expectation of detail, anecdote, description, and conversation, such as to manifest these characters in the brilliant light of their own Fame, and to shew our dear Father the Carressed, sought, honoured and admired Friend of such a constellation: for such he was, and as much loved and esteemed as if he had been the Universal Patron of them all. –

But alas, what a falling off ensues! – He contents himself with *Naming* all these people, saying where they met, mentioning the first day he made acquaintance with them; where they dined together – the Day, the Week – the Month, the Year – and then stops short, to go to some other date for some other such encounter. There is little more than Copying the minutes of engagements from his Pocket Books, made at the time his Memory was full and gay, and when he purposed dilating upon every Name and circumstance in his Memoirs, as he did, on the moment, in his discourse to his family or friends.

This is the General History of the Memoirs, 12 Volumes in number, through which I have been Wading, painfully, labouriously wading; – for the hand is small sometimes to illegibility, and the Abbreviations are continual, and sometimes very obscure. Some of the Volumes I have read over 4 times, from different Copies, now of his own, and now of some Copyist. When the latter has been *Sarah*, the *writing* is flowing and easy. But – most elaborately, the dear indefatigable author wrote frequently the whole of every Cahier 3 times over him self: and my fear of missing any thing that might be recorded in one, and not in another, and my desire to ascertain whether there were any difference in the narrations, and any choice to be taken, induced me to hold it right not to destroy a line unexamined.

There are, you will be sure, many exceptions to this general *anathema*, but they are partial, and of so little Volume, compared with what is hopeless, that I have not stopt to enumerate, though I shall carefully preserve them.

So much for the Memoirs, which I have now perused through-out, with the most sedulous attention, and have gone over a second time, in marking and separating every leaf, or passage, that may be usefully, or ornamentally, Biographical. While all that I thought utterly irrelevant, or any way mischievous, I have committed to the Flames. Whatever admits of any doubt, or demands any Enquiry, I have set apart.

Thus, you see, my dear Esther, I have, at length, made a great advance – though to produce, I fear, but little purpose. However, it is not nothing to *me*, in the present state of my health, spirits, and life, to have dissected this multifarious Work, and to have removed all that appeared to me peccant parts, that might have bred fevers, caused infectious ill-will, or have excited morbid criticism or ridicule.

My Mind has been considerably easier since I have attained thus far, because, in doing it, I have seen how much evil might have accrued from its falling into other hands, less aware of various allusions, etc. than myself.

Besides, I am firmly persuaded my dear Father would have made all these omissions himself, had he written these memoirs while still living in the World. – And Then – he would have given to what remained the Zest of observation, Conversation, and Anecdote.

I am now occupied, in like manner, in going through the Correspondence – which is fatiguing, in general, past all description, for my dear Father has kept, unaccountably, All his Letters, however uninteresting, ceremonious, momentary, or unmeaning. The Few I find that are not fit to light Candles, even from the greatest Names, is nearly incredible. They are Chiefly invitations, or arrangements of *rendez-vous*. I speak of the Letters of the Great in Rank; those of *Friends* I have not yet begun. Those of great Authors, are concise, and upon some accidental occasion. Letters upon Literary subjects, such as our dear Father was so qualified to write with excellence, very rarely occur, as his time was swallowed up by business or his musical researches. Upon this last subject, I find innumerable Epistles; but the pith of them has been woven into the History of Musick.

I hope you will have selected me something sprightly and entertaining from the very original Mr Cutler?[9] Yet, with all their *agrémens*,[10] and all their excentricities, you will be able *a little* to judge of the toil of reading through Bag after Bag of Collection made without choice thus, by Wholesail.

However, speed the Plough! my Eyes are better, though still cruelly weakened – Who can Wonder? – but I go on as industriously as they will permit me; and, I conclude by surmizing that about 3 years hard reading, for myself, will finally produce about 3 quarter's of an hour's reading to my Lecturers.[11] Such, however, as the poor little Book may one Day be, should

9. Banker and amateur musician – and among the most obscure in FB's list.
10. *Charm*.
11. I.e. readers: a Gallicism.

I live, at last, to edit[12] it, its Net profit shall most scrupulously be shared between the Residuary Legatees. But – if it were not, as it is, a business of Conscience, there is no advantage I would not gladly relinquish to get rid of so toilsome, perplexing, unweildy and harrassing an occupation. It has long hung upon me, heavily and uncomfortably – Yet I ought never to regret that the whole is not Now in the hands of Charles Parr – on whom, had I returned home a little later, it would by this time have devolved. It is not that I doubt either his honour or his delicacy; but he *could* not have found time, and *would* not have found patience, for such a revisal as would have kept to his own breast the innumerable memorandums, etc. that might most grotesquly, from one secretary or amanuensis to another, have got dancing about in the World.

This is quite a pamphlet, my dear Esther, – but I know you are anxious upon the subject, and I know you have no common right to be informed exactly how it is stated. I fear I may have been wearisome, but I wished to make you completely *au fait*; and though I am very sorry to think how disheartening you will find this estimate, no good could have been gained by a longer suspence, and you seem to have had the judgement to prepare yourself for considering the time to be gone by for any emolument. The fact is, I think there was *never* wherewithal to obtain emolument in materials so diffuse and, in general, so uninteresting. For You, I am sorry, and for Alex; – as to myself, my feelings on these matters, – authorship and emolument – are at this moment very obtuse! – blunted, utterly, into a sort of sad Apathy, rather than philosophy.[13]

237. From Letter to Hester Lynch Piozzi *6 February 1821*[1]

11 Bolton Street
Berkeley Square

You would be re-paid, Dear Madam, if I still, as I believe, know You, for the great kindness of your prompt answer, had you witnessed the satisfaction with which it was received; even at a time of New – and dreadful solicitude; for my son returned from Cambridge unwell, and, in a few days after his

---

12. 'Edit' is written over 'write', a telling alteration.
13. FB would abandon her plan to publish CB's correspondence in February 1828, when she discovered that she did not have the copyright for letters to her father; see *JL*, xii. 701. She also gave up editing his memoirs, finally publishing her own of him.

1. Part of a final exchange of letters between the former friends. Hester Piozzi would die on 2 May.

arrival at home was seized with a feverish Cold which threatened to fasten upon the whole system of his existence – not with immediate danger, but with a perspective to leave but small openings to any future view of Health, strength, or longevity. I will not dwell upon this period but to say, it seems passed over. He is now, I thank Heaven, Daily reviving, and from looking like – not a walking, but a creeping spectre, – he is gaining force, spirit, and flesh visibly, and almost hour by hour. Still, however, he requires the utmost attention, and the more from the extreme *insouciance*, from being always absorbed in some mental combinations, with which he utterly neglects himself. I am therefore wholly devoted to watching him, and to the care of his Nutriment; upon which his recovery depends; as Mr Chilver, successor to Sir Walter Farquar,[2] the medical man I have consulted, and trusted, – from personal experience of his sagacity, – assures me to be the case, the seat of his complaints being the stomach. This accords, also, with the nearly general system of Sir George Gibbes.[3] I was glad to find that tribute of honour had been paid to the worthy Doctor. I live so out of the World that I only heard it from your Letter, in which it was one of many things that gave me pleasure. – I am quite vexed not to find the right October.[4] However, I do not yet despair, for in the multitude of MSS. that have fallen to my mournfully surviving lot to select, or destroy, etc., *Chaos seems come again*; and though I have worked at them during the last year so as to obtain a little light, it is scarcely more than *Darkness visible*.[5] To all the vast mass left to my direction by my dear Father, who burnt nothing, – not even an invitation to dinner; are added not merely those that devolved to me by fatal necessity in 1818, but also all the papers, possessed from her Childhood to her decease, of that sister you so well, Dear Madam, know to have been my Heart's earliest darling – and with whose Hair you so kindly wove your own for me in a Locket that travels with me whithersoever I go. When on this pile are heaped the countless hoards which my own now long life has gathered together, of my personal property, such as it is, and the correspondence of my Family and my Friends, and innumerable incidental Windfalls, the Whole forms a body that might make a Bonfire to illuminate

---

2. Samuel Chilver, pupil of Sir Walter Farquhar, who had been CB's physician.

3. George Smith Gibbes, knighted on 10 May 1820.

4. Referring to Hester Piozzi's request in a letter (October 1818) for CB's verses on the month of October, presumably to be transcribed in her 'New Common Place Book'. In her letter of 18 January 1821, Hester Piozzi also refers to verses by CB on June; these survive in manuscript at the John Rylands Library, Manchester.

5. Shakespeare, *Othello*, III. iii. 93: 'Chaos is come again'; Milton, *Paradise Lost*, i. 63.

me nearly from hence to Penzance.[6] And such a Bonfire might perhaps be not only the shortest, but the wisest way to dispose of such materials. This enormous accumulation has been chiefly owing to a long unsettled home, joined to a mind too deeply occupied by immediate affairs and feelings to have the intellect at liberty for retrospective investigations.

What a long detail! – I know not what has urged me to write it – yet I feel as if you would take in it some interest; and an instinct of that flattering sort is always pleasant, though far from always infallible. And, in truth, in This case, Bolton Street offers not much more choice of subject than Penzance; for if You have Nobody to see, I see Nobody, which amounts to the same thing. It is not that my intentions are changed from those I mentioned in my last, of seeking revival, in some measure, to social life for the remaining Acts of my Worldly Drama; my quick acceptance of the assistance to that purpose for which I called from Penzance, and which has been accorded me with such generous vivacity, may shew my steadiness, as well as my Gratitude: but I had not taken into my self-Bargain this illness of my son. However, as he gets better, I shall do better.

238. From Letter to Esther Burney *3 September 1821*[1]

– Just after my return from Twickenham Meadows,[2] I was setting out, (prepared so to do, I mean,) for the Honour of a royal visit to Kensington Palace, when a counter-command arrived from Her Royal Highness the Princess Sophia to change my day: at the same instant a Letter came by the post, returned to me after some delay, from Richmond, whither it had been sent by mistake, to Charlotte's: what was my surprize to read a Summons from Messrs Clayton Scott and Clayton, to attend in person at Lincoln's Inn, to receive Mr Devayne's Legacy, before 2.o'clock, on forfeiture of the same! – It was now one! – I had not a moment to ponder, or ask advice; I thought of Charles Parr – and I knew your disaffection to Law and all its chicaneries: these Messrs also, had written me positive word that the demise

---

6. Hester Piozzi had moved to Penzance, on the coast of Cornwall, in July 1820.

1. Part of a lengthy account of FB's appearance at the Court of Chancery to collect a legacy to CB, made in the will of John Devaynes who had died in 1801. FB and Esther, as CB's residuary legatees, were entitled to divide the 5 guineas.

2. George Owen Cambridge's home.

of the acting Executer without a Will rendered the legacy null.[3] What could this change mean? – *Brief*, I was fortunately equipped, and determined to assume courage to enquire ere I relinquished. I made Ramsay bedizen hastily for my companion; I took Diane for my Esquire;[4] and ordering a King's Chariot, I bid the postilion gallop with all speed to the Court of Chancery. I resolved, as I drove on, to ask frankly for the costs, and, should I find them such as Charles Parr represented, to withdraw, formally, our claim.[5] I am sure of your approveance for this prudence. And I set myself above the ridicule of not being conducted, as is usual, by a Lawyer, and made Ramsay, who had been there before, lead the way to Messrs Clayton. We alighted in Lincoln's Inn, and had to parade sundry courts, avenues, passages, arch-ways, and squares, most of them formed of stone structures of awful and gloomy grandeur, and wearing the desolate appearance of being nearly uninhabited, except by sundry busy clerks, and here and there some perambulating Advocates or Attorneys, with Briefs, parchments, Vellums, and written Documents, hanging over their arms. But – as if all this was not enough to impress me, Ramsay presently called out 'O look, ma'am! there's the Lord Chancellor!'[6] and, crossing a small court to gain an open Corridor, the Lord Chancellor, in his Robes and enormous wig, was just before us. –

We then traversed various passages and stair cases, till I met with a Clerk, who pointed to me the door of Messrs Clayton Scott and Clayton's Chambers. No one asked my Name, nor offered to conduct me. I felt a little queer, but would not be discouraged. My greatest difficulty was how I should make known who I was; and that, all at once shewed me the propriety of a client's being accompanied by a Lawyer. However, this occured too late for any change, all my alarm being lest the Clock should strike 2 ere I was in presence. This fear helped me to exertion; and leaving Ramsay and Diane in the anti room, when I found no one came forth to receive or announce or introduce me, I entered the inner and larger room, of which the door was open, and determined *to behave like a man* – being my first appearance in that Character. A Gentleman in Black was looking over papers at a Desk, standing, and with an Air of arranging them for being gone; and a Clerk was Writing at another Desk in a corner. He had very

---

3. Devaynes's brother William, his executor, had died in 1809.
4. Elizabeth Ramsay and FB's dog Diane.
5. Charles Parr Burney had warned her of the dangers of a Chancery case, in which 'the costs would treble the Legacy' (*JL*, xi. 267).
6. John Scott.

much the air of a Gentleman, though he was so intently occupied, that he neither looked towards me, nor seemed to perceive that any one had appeared. This was rather awkward. I stood still a minute or two, and then, not willing to risk interrupting some calculation, yet not thoroughly satisfied with this mode of waiting his leisure, I quietly looked for the handsomest Chair in the room, and composedly took possession of it. Upon this, he raised his Eyes. I then presented him my Letter, saying 'Mr Clayton, I suppose?' – He Bowed, took it, offered me another seat, proposed shutting the Window if I feared the air and gave me the pleasure of finding that I retain, what my dear Father often loved to call it, *An Honest Face*; for he made no sort of enquiry, demanded no manner of identification, but went to his Documents, my Letter in his hand, with as firm a conviction that *I* was *I*, as if he had known me all his life, and all my Parentage and Kin. Gaining courage by this, I now began to conn over in my mind a little discreet interrogatory as to Fees and Expences. But while waiting till he should no longer seem too busy for interruption without impertinence, all on the sudden he darted to me, with a pen ready dipt in Jet, in his hand, and placing a paper on a Table before me, with a manner and look gravely polite, but in a voice that spoke him accustomed to dispence with any reply, he gave me the Pen, and pointed to a spot on which he desired me to write my Name. Put off my guard by the suddenness and authority of this proceeding – Would you believe it? I actually signed my Name incontinently! But recovering, as soon as it was done, my recollection, though I could not my signature, I determined at least not to act for *you* till I knew better what I was about, and in *your* name, as absent, to enquire about the Fees, before I would take upon me the double responsibility. However, those who think they may do what they list, and say what they wist, to a money'd Man of Business in a Court of Law, have had less experience than *I* have, Now – *or*, a great deal more; for the haste of Motion, and the brevity of Words, are such, that an unpracticed Client has not the smallest chance to catch a moment for any thing but surprized submission to orders: for just as I thought, while he took up my signature to throw some sand over it, that I had formed a phrase with sufficient Laconism to catch his attention without importunity, – before my lips could possibly part to utter it, my soliciter, clapping my paper into a small port folio, which he grasped in his left hand, and clapping abruptly his Hat upon his head, uttered these alarming words 'Please to go with me, Now, ma'am, to the Accomptant General.' –

The Accomptant General? thought I; what kind of a *Badinage* is this for a *modicum* of only 5 Guineas, without the partition? and then, Taxes – Deductions – Fees!!! – Then I reflected upon the prognostics of Charles Parr – Then, upon the sick feelings of my Esther already on the very opening of this business; – and I became so much discomposed, that I hesitated whether I should comply; – but he led the way, quitting the room with a quick pace even while speaking. – If I go not, however, thought I, I may be fined for Contempt of Court! – This suggestion forced me forward. The moment I reached the stair case, which my Lawyer was already descending, out rushed Diane, bursting from the vainly controlling hands of Ramsay, who had in charge to keep her out of the way. Delighted to find me safe, in a strange place, where she had been, Ramsay says, in deep dismay at the separation, she now would not quit me. I therefore told Ramsay to come also, and down we all three followed Master Soliciter. – At the foot of the stair case, he had the courtesie to stop for me, and from thence to walk by my side, my rustic Damsel and my Canine Esquire obsequiously keeping behind – except that the latter, when not called to order by the Damsel, chose to Caper friskily round his mistress, or Bark furiously round her Soliciter. – I now hoped I should obtain an opportunity for my long intended harangue, by his entering into some conversation: but his politeness extended no further than in adopting my pace; for mouth opened he not. This was as new to me as all the rest, having never, that I remember, in my life, begun an attack; – having Always myself been addressed, or remained silent: but I was Now upon Ground where, probably, a word and a Fee are one! I did not, however, think of that till this moment; but soon finding I had nothing to gain by my taciturnity but its reciprocity, I resolved to put an end to it. Which I did, by begging leave to enquire who was the Accomptant General? 'Sir John Campbell;' he answered. 'O – I have not the pleasure to know him,' quoth I. But not a syllable further uttered my Guide. This won't do! thought I; I must come to the point more plumply. 'Give me leave, Sir,' I cried, 'to ask, whether my signature will be accepted, or hold good, for my absent sister, Mrs Burney, who resides at Bath, and could not, for such a trifle be brought to Town?' – 'Perfectly, ma'am' – he replied. 'But I have written only for myself, sir, without naming her; and she is joint residuary Legatee.' – 'Your signature is all that is requisite, ma'am.' – Is This a hoax? thought I; or what does it mean? Total silence, however, ensued; till, seeing, by numerous persons passing and re-passing into a handsome stone building, that we were approaching our place of destination, I again assailed him, and more pointedly; growing really anxious to know whether there were not some errour in the whole matter. 'I have been seldom, sir,' I said, 'more surprized than by your Letter, for I had received one, many Months ago,

to tell me that the Executor having died intestate, the legacy became null.'
– 'And such, Madam,' he now replied, 'is the legal fact. The Legacy is lapsed: but as it is for so small a sum, no advantage has been taken of that accident, and I am directed to pay it You.' – I now became a little comforted; but I was dying to ask *by whom* directed; as there appeared, in the all together of the affair, something mysterious. I had no sooner, however, answered eagerly 'That is very generous, – and I feel very much obliged, – and who ever complains of the Law, and of Lawyers, *I* must stand forth to praise and laud them, –' than he quite unbent his Chancery Brow, and said, with a smile – 'Ma'am, your Legacy will now amount to nine pounds Eleven shillings, as interest upon interest has very nearly doubled it.' A greater surprise I think never came upon me than this speech produced: and if it had not been for my suspence as to costs and Fees and deductions, – I should have mocked Charles Par's prognostics, and have thought I had a very good cordial for my dear Esther's sick feelings. However, we entered – mounted the stairs, – and saw there the Accomptant General, seated at an immense Table, with Clerks and Writer under his command in great abundance, and several clients in waiting, and new ones entering every moment: yet all so silent, so orderly, so awfully under subjection, that the accomptant's voice alone was heard in the vast chamber, every reply being made in humble whispering. Mr Clayton went up to him; what passed no one could hear but the Accomptant: Mr Clayton, however, soon made me a motion to approach; I advanced: a paper again was placed before me to sign: After which, the Accomptant put into my hand a Draft on the East India House for £9.11.0. – Mr Clayton asked me whether I had 4 shillings and sixpence? I said yes. 'Give it me, then, ma'am, and I will save you the trouble to call again to pay your costs. They amount to 4s. and 6d. –' I stared – really not believing my Ears: but Mr Clayton abruptly disappeared. I looked at the Draft, and could not forbear ejaculating 'I am very much surprised, indeed – and very much obliged – though I do not know to whom!' The Accomptant turned quick round to look at me, with a pleased laugh; all the rest smiled – and Ramsay, Diane and I *gracefully* retired. Thus, my dear Esther, I have incurred you a Debt of 2s. and 3d. which I shall, meanly, deduct from your £4. 15s. and 6d. in paying only £4.13.3. to your steward, Edward.

239. From Letter to Charlotte Barrett *c. 16 August 1824*[1]

I shall be vexed to the heart if this should not reach you, first, on account of my request to dear Hetty, next from my earnestness to thank you for the truly welcome Letter which cheated me – so pleasingly – of Julia's, – and lastly, that there should be any further retard in your acquaintance with the consecrating dignity of Camden Chapel's Opening.[2] Alex went early, to be *dizened* in his Canonicals for the reception of the Bishop of London. Mrs Moore, the lady of the Patron of the Chapel,[3] from whom Alex had the honour of his Nomination, invited me to her pew, which of course, being that of the Vicar, is preferable to Alexander's. She is a pleasing, well bred, and still pretty Woman. The Ayles were kept entirely clear for the Ceremony, and as soon as the Mitred Carriage approached, the large folding doors were thrown open, and the Bishop was met in the Portico by Dr Moore, at the head of a body of the Clergy, – among whom I only knew our excellent Friend the Archdeacon,[4] – by the 12 Parliamentary Trustees, the Chancellor (not the *Lord* Chancellor!)[5] the Church Wardens, Clerks, and Beadles and Vergers, and Mr Sam. Wesley, the Organist.[6] – Who mounted instantly after to give his Lordship a welcome of sweet Harmony. The Bishop went into a new robing room, prepared for the purpose and his Lawn sleeves gave no small grace to the ensuing Procession, in which he read, in a sonorous and impressive, but not agreeable Voice, a portion of some of the psalms, – that were followed by responses, utterly inaudible, – owing, I imagine, to a lowly reverence in the *un*mitred accompaniers: so that it seemed as if the Bishop only uttered Verses to the response of silent pauses. Alex, who began now to feel he was going to perform, for the first time, a Discourse – of which he had never heard any precedent, nor seen any example, had a look and air somewhat *drooping*, that pained me considerably as he passed by me in the suite. Imagine, therefore, whether I felt at my ease, when, after this Consecration was finished, and the Bishop had taken

---

1. Charlotte Barrett was in Boulogne with her husband and daughters, Julia and Henrietta ('Hetty'). FB's 'request' was that Hetty should let her know when the family returned to England.
2. Alexander had been appointed Curate at the new Camden Town Chapel. FB had moved into lodgings there for the summer.
3. William Howley, Bishop of London, had recommended Alexander to Dr James Moore, vicar of St Pancras, who appointed Alexander to the new curacy. His wife was Agnes Moore.
4. George Owen Cambridge, Archdeacon of Middlesex.
5. The Chancellor of the Exchequer, Nicholas Vansittart.
6. Samuel Wesley, son of Charles Wesley and a famous organist.

his seat at the Altar, and the Mourning Service, which was beautifully read by Dr Moore himself, was over, and The Two first Verses out of the 3 ordered to precede the Sermon, were sung – when Then no Alex appeared to mount to the Pulpit. The 3d Verse began – and went on – and still no Alex! – the pulpit door was opened – but still no Alex! I grew so terrified that I could with difficulty forbear going forth, in the belief some accident had happened. Mrs Moore looked at me expressively – I felt myself tremble all over – The Archdeacon, who had entered the Vicar's pew, and was seated at my other side, quite *shook*, himself, with apprehension, – he thought Alex had lost his Sermon – or had suddenly conceived a new end for it! – and Mrs Moore believed he was siezed with affright, and could not conquer it – Finally – the last verse finished – and no Alex! Mr Wesley ran and re-ran over the Keys, with *fugish* perseverance – and I was all *but* fainting – when, at length, – the New Camdenite appeared. I was never more relieved.[7] My alarm had been so uncontrollable, that I afterwards heard it had excited a general surmize of whom I might be – the Bishop himself whom, though distantly, I faced, enquired of the Archdeacon if the lady next him was not Mme d'Arblay? – Alex delivered the prayer in a voice hardly audible, and the incomparable one of our Lord, little louder: but, whether feeling his Voice, or recovering from some tremor, I know not, all his pulmonary powers were restored as he gave out the text, which was pronounced with a fullness of tone that carried it, I should suppose, nearly to Hampstead! Imagine my delighted surprize. He sustained this sonorous quality through the whole Discourse. The instant all was over, the kind Archdeacon gave me his hand, with a cordial shake, saying 'I give you Joy! – ' The Committee of Trustees, etc. surrounded the other side of our pew, speaking with Mrs Moore, who, when they dispersed, said 'I hope you have been gratified, Mme d'Arblay, for every body else has. – ' When Alex entered the Vestry room, to make his Bow to the Bishop, his Lordship said 'I am very much obliged to you, Mr d'Arblay, for a most excellent discourse. – ' Dr Moore then came in and said, dauntlessly without waiting to be informed first of the Bishop's opinion, 'My lord, I hope you have been gratified?' 'I have been highly gratified,' he answered; 'and it is the Second time Mr d'Arblay has given me gratification.[8] I think the feeling has been general.'

I have not room – nor occasion to mention more after this. I have filled

---

7. 'The delay had been the fault of the Verger' (FB's note).

8. The Bishop had apparently heard Alexander preach at St Paul's Cathedral on 29 June 1823; see *JL*, xi. 430 n. 9.

my Paper with my long promise; and few are there to whom I could with equal pleasure dilate thus minutely on such a subject. But I know my dear Charlotte's sincere and fervant interest in my Alex.

240. From Letter to Charlotte Broome and
Charlotte Barrett *25 October 1828*

3 days ago I ended my rigid starvation, which had reduced me to a gnawing state of Famine, by a fair breast of Pheasant, bereft of skin and fat, and excluded from all colouring of Gravy, – and I had so happily timed the dismission of bread pudding, Turnips and Potatoes hitherto admitted exclusively to visit the vulgar precincts of existence, that I passed the best nocturnal hours I have arrived at since my seizure.[1] – And, This grand point gained, a most gracious invitation to a visit of condolence happened to ensue for the next day,[2] that, finding it irresistible at such a melancholy period, I cut short at once my strict confinement to the house, and, only making a piteous statement that begged permission for appearing a Fright, – I received not only consent, but command to come forth in that Form where it had never before made its *entrée*, and Mobbled, and Muffled, and Hooded, and *Bas Chapeaued*,[3] I presented myself at Kensington Palace – to the no small wonder, no doubt, – and probably Horror, of the Heralds preceding my ushering into Presence, – who, having received orders to take care I caught no cold, came forward as the royal vehicle drove up to the Gates, Two pages with a large umbrella in front, and two footmen to each touch an elbow in the rear, – and two underlings spreading a long carpet from the Coach steps onward to the Hall, – and all, no doubt, inwardly, sniggering when they saw it was for such a Figure of Fun!

However, I am always so well pleased when I can be beguiled into a little simper myself, that I am ever ready to rejoice when I can produce a sly smile, or an honest Grin, or an unguarded Horselaugh in any of my neighbours.

---

1. FB had been suffering from a 'terrible Cold' and 'palpitations' for over two weeks (*JL*, xii. 720).
2. On 21 October, for an evening with Princess Sophia, whose eldest sister Charlotte had died on 6 October; see *JL*, xii. 722 n. 3.
3. *Hat in hand*.

241. Letter to Alexander d'Arblay *May 1835*[1]

Where could be my Heart – my dearest Alex – if I could read the emphatic request that ends so seriously your entertaining Letter,[2] and hesitate to join in Your Amen! Amen! to your call for my Prayers that you may make '*the sweet and innocent*' object of your choice '*As happy as she deserves to be*!' These, my dear Alex, are phrases far more attractive to me than the brightest eulogiums of her Beauty – which, for a serious engagement, is almost always as hazardous as it can be alluring. Nevertheless, if sweetness and innocence be joined to it – I cannot deny *que cela ne gâte rien*.[3] So I won't make a point of her catching the small pox to get rid of it!

My Prayers, indeed, for You, in this most important moment of your life – and now, for Her, also – since, contracted now in Honour, I look upon you already as one – are fervent in the extreme – though, from my utter ignorance of all accounts but *Yours* – a Lover and a Poet! – they are entangled in a thousand – a million, indeed, – of nameless anxieties. They are not from Doubts of any sort that can offend or vex either of you; but from the precipitancy with which you have hurried into so solemn an engagement without the smallest knowledge, on either side, of each other's principles, Temper, or Modes of Life.

It is true, not only *She*, but *You* are yet young enough, should you form a lasting and solid attachment for each other, to approximate in characters and assimilate in humours: – for a charm there is in reciprocated tenderness that resolves all discordant difficulties into harmony: – Two points only – as far as *I* have seen of life, – oppose this general observation; Religion and Politics: Difference of Opinion there is Mortal! for we must Hope against each other, both for the next World and for This. If, therefore, she be either a *decided* Dissenter, or Republican – O my dear Alex, closely, honourably, and openly consult, and discuss with her, your feelings and your Situation ere your ties become indissoluble.[4]

I will write no more till I have an answer upon these important points,

---

1. Alexander had apparently become engaged to Mary Ann Smith, both in their early forties, within a few weeks of having met her. No marriage took place, but after his sudden death she lived with FB as a companion.
2. This letter is missing.
3. *That it does not spoil anything.*
4. There is no evidence to suggest that she was either.

which in your tremulously hurried return I had no time to mention – nor even to think of. You filled me with emotions so strong and various, I could only promise to withhold all interference that might compromize your Honour.

Assure her, meanwhile, of my highest wishes for her personal happiness, and my highest persuasion of her personal desert. Her apprehension of disappointing *you* – and its modest avowal – has a dignity of candour extremely touching to me. Let *your* fears but take the same turn, my dear Alex, and then your mutual struggles to please will send Disappointment far afield from Both.

God bless you, my dearest Alex! Bless – direct – and prosper you!

242. From Letter to Charlotte Broome and
Charlotte Barrett *20 April 1838*

First let me tell you, I never more wished the very instant I had finished a Letter to acknowledge it, than I did your last – so gay, so good humoured, so putting apart all your right of complaint, and all my *apparent* negligence, without even a hint of a reproach. – Dear, dear *Sister* what true sister in heart and affection! but, in the midst of my tender feelings, I was surprized into a most unexpected burst of laughter – at the sudden appearance of the famous little old woman who did me the honnour to be sure I should be her voucher.[1]

And now I have – happily – had a laugh, I am almost ready – like the poor little woman, to begin to cry – in owning that – for some time past, I have been in a state of dejection that heavily weighs me down – and is beyond my conquest – and it is all owing to the abundance of business I have to transact that has all reference, constant reference, to all that is most dear – and most melancholy! – Were *they* disposed of – those myriads of hoards of MSS. I might enjoy a more tranquil resignation. I might think of my Alex without that perturbation that makes the *thought* of Him so tragic![2] because it is with abrupt recollection, that brings him with some affecting incident to my sight – And – from his living with me his whole life, every paper – every chattel I possess speaks of him. I would fain make him my

---

1. In a letter to FB (8 April), Charlotte Broome depicts the two sisters as old women in a nursery rhyme; see *JL*, xii. 953 n. 1.
2. Alexander d'Arblay had died from influenza on 19 January 1837, aged forty-two.

theme – yet without this agony. Make it with a serenity that should only brighten remnant life by its cheerful prospect – not its inflexible regret –! –

My dear Charlottes both – think for me, with the rest of the kind thinkers, what I had best do with the killing mass of constant recurrence to my calamity. – Shall I Burn them? – at once – or shall I, and can I, so modify a division as to spare for future times various collections that may be amusing and even instructive –[3]

Certainly were I younger and could here wait for the examination – but that is not the case. My Eyes will work at them no more! They are to night very good – but for a fortnight past all has been obscurity! – with *what* pleasure do I think of your arrival, my dearest.

I finished last night – but interruptions this whole morning have been incessant and so here goes the Letter to-morrow!

May it find you well, my dearest dears – and may I hear the same with your wonted lenity!

243. Letter to Charlotte Barrett *30 July 1839*[1]

I will not ask what my dearest Charlott*a* has thought of my long silence; I see by her continued writing, that she generously as well as truly *understands* it. My health is never the same for 2 days together, nor are my Eyes for 2 hours. But I will Harp upon that theme no more; especially as there are many exceptions of most favourable inexactitude. And indeed, were there *not*, in all mortal evils, how would our poor fragile frames bear their redundance?

I think, too, I explained to my dear Richard[2] how different was the fatigue of receiving Letters from that of writing them. And I begged him to assure you how truly and *thankfully* all your Letters were welcomed, by the double mark of kindness in coming unearned. He has not I see forgotten me and indeed, he did not look as if he intended to *try* to forget his protegee.

I entirely concur with you about the Queen; I am convinced she has been betrayed into a wrong measure from being deluded into a wrong opinion, and therefore, though not blameless, is extremely to be pitied; for her hasty

3. Although FB would destroy some of these manuscripts before her death (see *JL*, xii. 954 n. 2) she left the majority to Charlotte Barrett. Her father's correspondence was left to Charles Parr Burney; see *JL*, xii. 980.

1. This is FB's last surviving letter. She died on 6 January 1840.

2. Richard Barrett, Charlotte's son and FB's godson and heir.

order of exile from her presence was a mere unweighed impulse of *Virtue*. How could she disbelieve a medical man? How credit him, without the deepest indignation at such a disgrace to her virgin Court?[3] The matter cannot stop here; the *origin* of the Reports must be detected, and must be punished. There is some mystery in the terrible calumny, to which the poor young innocent and inexperienced Queen is doubtless a Dupe. But this is all from conjecture; I know nothing, for I *have* not been able to seek – or accept any royal intercourse this long long time. I am well enough many days as they *come*, but never with that feel of recovery that gives me courage to promise a *to-morrow* so that I dare make no appointment.

You enquire of Mrs Angerstein – Ah sore is my disappointment there! – save *en passant*, she will come to town no more! – her town house is – or is to be – disposed of! – But I will fly this bitter subject in pity to *You*, my Charlotta, who have given me one to acknowledge so much more *Rose-Coloured*.

I wish I could call up a *spirt* of my ancient spirits to express my satisfaction at the liberal and good humoured approbation of Dr Jones[4] for I am determined to believe him *sincere*! though he writes to the Grand daughter and Niece of the Hero of his praise. There is an open frankness and a running ease in his perfectly natural style that scoffs away any sort of doubt of the urbanity, not Flattery that has instigated his giving you such a pleasure; of which I honestly confess I take my full share. For though I had lost all thought of my extreme vexation at the *Defamation* of Mr Croker,[5] it rises again in perusing the genuine warmth of the Letter of Dr Jones. I can use no softer term than Defamation for the least attack upon my veracity. And now, once more awakened to my original feeling, I poignantly regret that I did not at once answer it – or let my dearest Alex – who could not even Name my wanton calumniator but with trembling emotion. That I may have made a *mistake* in 3 such large Volumes, I readily allow, and would readily repair – but certainly not a wilful – and far – far less a malevolent one. He has started doubts upon matters the most trivial, and then tried to give them the consequence of a solemn refutation. Did I ever shew you my

---

3. Queen Victoria had succeeded William IV in June 1837. One of her ladies-in-waiting Lady Flora Hastings had been falsely rumoured to be pregnant, and was required to leave the Court. The Queen's doctor, Sir James Clark, had examined Lady Flora but failed to diagnose her condition. She died on 5 July, and an autopsy showed her to have been suffering from a liver complaint; see *JL*, xii. 967 n. 2.
4. Possibly the Revd John Jones, who had apparently written to Charlotte Barrett in praise of FB's *Memoirs of Doctor Burney* (1832); see *JL*, xii. 968 n. 4.
5. Croker's vituperative notice in the *Quarterly Review* (April 1833) had caused FB great distress.

revered Bishop of Limeric's[6] Letter upon the Memoirs? If not, I think I must, for My Honour, and for Your Pride, that such a Letter should be written to *your Aunt*, and after that, what motive shall we invent for shewing it to Dr Jones; Alas, the wisest of men has stopt all research on that point, vanity! all is Vanity[7] – and that is rather pitiful, I confess – However, 'tis Honest – so I must console myself – and you, too, if you please, with remembering that that is the first attribute of the noblest work of God.[8] – I have hardly left room for God bless You!

6. John Jebb, an acquaintance of the d'Arblays; his letter of 12 December 1832 in praise of FB's *Memoirs of Doctor Burney* is printed in *DL*, vi. 411–12.

7. Ecclesiastes 1: 2 and 12: 8.

8. Pope's *Essay on Man* (1733–4), iv. 248: 'An honest Man's the noblest work of God'.

Index

READ MORE IN PENGUIN

In every corner of the world, on every subject under the sun, Penguin represents quality and variety – the very best in publishing today.

For complete information about books available from Penguin – including Puffins, Penguin Classics and Arkana – and how to order them, write to us at the appropriate address below. Please note that for copyright reasons the selection of books varies from country to country.

In the United Kingdom: Please write to *Dept. EP, Penguin Books Ltd, Bath Road, Harmondsworth, West Drayton, Middlesex UB7 0DA*

In the United States: Please write to *Consumer Sales, Penguin Putnam Inc., P.O. Box 12289 Dept. B, Newark, New Jersey 07101-5289.* VISA and MasterCard holders call 1-800-788-6262 to order Penguin titles

In Canada: Please write to *Penguin Books Canada Ltd, 10 Alcorn Avenue, Suite 300, Toronto, Ontario M4V 3B2*

In Australia: Please write to *Penguin Books Australia Ltd, P.O. Box 257, Ringwood, Victoria 3134*

In New Zealand: Please write to *Penguin Books (NZ) Ltd, Private Bag 102902, North Shore Mail Centre, Auckland 10*

In India: Please write to *Penguin Books India Pvt Ltd, 11 Community Centre, Panchsheel Park, New Delhi 110017*

In the Netherlands: Please write to *Penguin Books Netherlands bv, Postbus 3507, NL-1001 AH Amsterdam*

In Germany: Please write to *Penguin Books Deutschland GmbH, Metzlerstrasse 26, 60594 Frankfurt am Main*

In Spain: Please write to *Penguin Books S. A., Bravo Murillo 19, 1° B, 28015 Madrid*

In Italy: Please write to *Penguin Italia s.r.l., Via Benedetto Croce 2, 20094 Corsico, Milano*

In France: Please write to *Penguin France, Le Carré Wilson, 62 rue Benjamin Baillaud, 31500 Toulouse*

In Japan: Please write to *Penguin Books Japan Ltd, Kaneko Building, 2-3-25 Koraku, Bunkyo-Ku, Tokyo 112*

In South Africa: Please write to *Penguin Books South Africa (Pty) Ltd, Private Bag X14, Parkview, 2122 Johannesburg*

READ MORE IN PENGUIN

A CHOICE OF CLASSICS

Francis Bacon	**The Essays**
Aphra Behn	**Love-Letters between a Nobleman and His Sister**
	Oroonoko, The Rover and Other Works
George Berkeley	**Principles of Human Knowledge/Three Dialogues between Hylas and Philonous**
James Boswell	**The Life of Samuel Johnson**
Sir Thomas Browne	**The Major Works**
John Bunyan	**Grace Abounding to The Chief of Sinners**
	The Pilgrim's Progress
Edmund Burke	**A Philosophical Enquiry into the Origin of our Ideas of the Sublime and Beautiful**
	Reflections on the Revolution in France
Frances Burney	**Evelina**
Margaret Cavendish	**The Blazing World and Other Writings**
William Cobbett	**Rural Rides**
William Congreve	**Comedies**
Cowley/Waller/Oldham	**Selected Poems**
Thomas de Quincey	**Confessions of an English Opium Eater**
	Recollections of the Lakes
Daniel Defoe	**A Journal of the Plague Year**
	Moll Flanders
	Robinson Crusoe
	Roxana
	A Tour Through the Whole Island of Great Britain
	The True-Born Englishman
John Donne	**Complete English Poems**
	Selected Prose
Henry Fielding	**Amelia**
	Jonathan Wild
	Joseph Andrews
	The Journal of a Voyage to Lisbon
	Tom Jones
George Fox	**The Journal**
John Gay	**The Beggar's Opera**